MW01125688

To my best friend, first love, and cherished wife, Natalina. You are my sunshine.

Acknowledgements

Although this book has one author's name on the cover, Musical U has never been about a single "guru", and this book is no exception. It's been my pleasure and honour to author it, but the ideas, methods and frameworks you'll find inside have been the product of a whole host of contributors to our approach over the last 15 years, and I have drawn extensively on prior material developed by the Musical U team.

First and foremost my eternal gratitude to our Head Educator, Andrew Bishko, whose experience and wisdom have helped shape Musical U into something I never would have expected or hoped for it to be. There's a lot of Andrew throughout everything we do, including this book—and it's all far better for it!

Our team has been blessed with truly incredible, heart-led musicians and music educators over the years. In roughly chronological order, my thanks to team members Stewart Hilton, Adam Liette, Anastasia Voitinskaia, Zac Bailey, Anne Mileski, Ben Marcoux, John Conroy, Hannah Cain, Donald Herndon, Steve Lee, Arias Flory, Thomas Infante, Andy Portas, Camilo Suárez, Mohammed Wael, Mark Hanna, Nicholas Price, Charm Cajurao, and Almut Spaeth.

We've been fortunate to have had the opportunity to collaborate on course creation with Sabrina Peña Young, Gregg Goodhart, Anne Mileski, and Fini Bearman, stretching our curriculum in new and exciting directions each time.

Our Resident Pros have each contributed significant instrumental insight: Sara Campbell and Ruth Power (Piano), Dylan Welsh (Guitar), Clare Wheeler (Singing), and Steve Lawson (Bass).

... and that's not to mention all our Masterclass presenters, Guest Experts, Musicality Now podcast interviewees, and all the other educators I've had the joy of consulting with over the years. It pains me not to name every name!

And last but certainly not least, our incredible member community at Musical U. As early as the launch of the membership site in 2015, it was clear that we could learn as much from our members as they could from us. I'm deeply proud and thankful for our unbelievable community, from those students who just take a single course with us, through our devoted ongoing members, and our remarkable *Next Level* coaching clients. You have made Musical U into the wonderful place it be read in any order[2]. So you may like to read the book from start to finish, but you are also welcome to jump straight to the chapters which interest you most in a "choose your own adventure" way. There are lots of cross-references—but you generally won't be held back if you haven't yet read about something that's mentioned.

There is a lot packed into this book! You would probably be well-served to scan through the whole text lightly to begin with, and then circle back to the sections you really want to go deep in.

About This Book

Before we continue, let me share a little bit of behind-the-scenes info with you...

When we first started the project to write this book, it moved incredibly slowly. The team was putting in the hours, and working hard to gather the material. But something just wasn't flowing. And it took me longer than I'd like to admit to realise why!

It didn't help that I tend to have extremely high standards for what we do at Musical U (while always trying to curb perfectionism... more on that in a later chapter!), but on top of that, what was emerging was clearly lacking a certain something. Even though the potential impact of the material itself was exciting, it all felt a bit dull and lifeless to me.

Then, one day, I was walking home from dropping my kids to school and listening to a recorded lecture by the legendary personal development pioneer Napoleon Hill. As I heard him speak on this old 1950s recording, it was the first time I'd heard his actual voice, despite having read many of his written works. As he spoke, his wit, sense of humour and personality shone through—and something suddenly clicked in my mind.

We had been treating the project like we were trying to write a textbook.

And while the goal *was* to provide extensive in-depth information, and fill in the gaps left by the standard music methods and theory books, something important finally dawned on me. Musical U has

---

[2] Notably: in Part II, the three pitch-focused chapters build on what's covered in *Chapter Eight: Relative Pitch*, and the Rhythm chapter builds on The Beat. With all of those, you'll benefit from having read the opening chapter of Part II (*Chapter Seven: Ear Training*) first. The chapters in Part III are designed to leverage everything covered earlier in the book, but can also be used directly, depending on your prior musical experience and knowledge.

levels. The good news is that the promise and power of musicality training also applies equally across all those varied musical worlds. The "inner skills" of musicality are as universal as music itself.

My hope is that this book will open up some new possibilities for you in your musical life. We'll provide clear, concrete information you can use to start exploring those possibilities and unlocking new levels of musicality for yourself.

This isn't a "method book" or a set of exercises to follow. By its nature, musicality training should be focused on musical activities and music itself, and the details must adapt to the uniqueness of the musician. Our aim is to set you up for success in your journey of musicality training, by filling in the missing pieces that have held you back from your true potential.

And of course, should you want further help as you continue that exciting journey, we would be honoured to assist you more fully at Musical U, where we can provide audio, video, interactive exercises, and personal human support throughout. You'll find information about what we offer at the back of the book. We have also prepared a set of free resources, including additional information and assets to help you put the book's material into practice. Information on this can be found in *Additional Resources*.

Overview

In Part I of the book, we'll cover some fundamental topics which are the foundation for all successful musical development, including setting your own personal vision for the kind of musician you wish to become, and introducing a set of foundational skills which will benefit you throughout your musical life.

In Part II, we'll explore a range of building blocks and "mental models" for understanding pitch and rhythm instinctively, and the ear training activities which can help you master them.

Then, in Part III, we'll look at applications of these new abilities to enable you to improvise, play by ear, write music, play expressively, and perform confidently.

For the most part, chapters are independent of one another and can

which fully embraces the development of holistic musicality we'll be exploring in this book.

INTRODUCTION

The book you are holding was written based on 15 years spent helping tens of thousands of adult music learners online to unlock their true musical potential through musicality training. That in turn was based on countless decades of prior experience in the Musical U team, and principles and methodologies for musicality training which date back over 100 years.

The book was inspired by a simple idea: to distil all the most powerful and effective material we've gathered over the years into a single volume. Something which would be useful both to those who are actively training with us inside Musical U membership or our *Next Level* coaching program, and to those for whom this would be their very first foray into the wild and wonderful world of musicality training.

To put it another way: I wanted us to write the book I wish I had been handed on "day one" of learning music.

Why?

Because, as you'll discover as you read on, so many of the skills and abilities which inspire musicians to pick up an instrument (or open their mouth to sing) in the first place simply aren't taught in mainstream music education. I've found that the average musician may have spent months, years, or even decades "learning music" and still have no idea of what's truly possible for them.

This holds true across all instruments, all styles[1], all ages, all ability

---

[1] I should acknowledge that some styles do explain some aspects of musicality more than others. For example the classical music world does somewhat encourage "composing music", gospel musicians do tend to focus more on playing by ear, the jazz tradition does feature improvising as standard, etc. However there is no single style

Get Additional Resources, Free!

We've prepared an extensive set of Additional Resources for you, to support the material inside this book.

This includes extra explanations and tutorials, quick reference sheets, reading lists and references, as well as audio and video materials to help you succeed.

Get access to the full set of Additional Resources for free:

https://musicalitybook.com/resources

MUSICALITY

How you too can learn music like a gifted prodigy,
unlock your musical instinct,
and unleash your inner natural.

Christopher Sutton

ISBN-13: 978-1-0685109-0-8 (hardcover)
ISBN-13: 978-1-0685109-1-5 (ebook)

First Edition (v1.0.3) published worldwide in 2024 by Easy Ear Training Ltd. (dba "Musical U"), London, United Kingdom.

https://www.musical-u.com/

Illustrations include use of TrueType font SingASign©2011. Owned and distributed by MacMusic Fonts. Website: macmusicfonts.com Unauthorized commercial use of the font is punishable by law. Used here with permission # SWSASCOMLIC240928.

The following terms are trademarks of Easy Ear Training Ltd. (dba "Musical U"): Integrated Ear Training™, Expansive Creativity™, The Play-By-Ear Process™, Listen-Engage-Express (LNX)™, Your Musical Core™, Big Picture Vision™, Supernatural Performance™, Foundations of a Musical Mind™, Performance Free-Flow™, Living Music™, 4-Dimensional Active Listening™.

While every effort has been made to ensure the material presented here is correct and accurate, no book survives publication without the odd typo or small mistake. If you notice any errors or have other feedback to share, we would very much appreciate hearing from you. Simply email hello@musicalitybook.com

TABLE OF CONTENTS

has become. Our approach, as presented in this book, would be a shadow of what it is, without your constant engagement, feedback, and sharing of your own musical journeys in the community.

Finally, a few thank yous on the personal side. Firstly, to all the coaches, mentors and mastermind buddies who have helped me on the business side of building Musical U with such expertise and generosity. In particular, my phenomenal coach Mandy Keene, whose compassionate wisdom has kept me going, even in the darkest times.

And none of this would have been possible for me without the love, support and encouragement of my family throughout. In particular, my parents, Jean and John Sutton, who nurtured an early interest in music, provided the best possible education, and have inspired and encouraged me on my entrepreneurial journey. My daughters, Alice and Laura, who lift me up and remind me not to be too serious. And my wife Natalina, to whom this book is dedicated.

always been about the *human connection,* and being able to make the material personal to each musician who comes to us. This is one of the reasons we've been so successful, and one of the main ways we're able to deliver such consistent breakthrough results for our members and coaching clients—by actually going beyond the information and methods themselves.

In the context of this book, the implication was instantly clear: we couldn't let this be yet another dry, abstract textbook! A written book may not allow for the back-and-forth interaction we take such pride and joy in inside Musical U, but that doesn't mean we can't still let some humanity seep into it.

So although I would never want this to become a "Chicken Soup for the Musician's Soul", prioritising stories over substance, I hope you will allow me to share some opinions and personal experience along the way. And that you'll accept (maybe even enjoy) the conversational style of writing, where I might manage to ignore my meticulous inner editor and allow myself to begin a sentence with "and", end it on a preposition, or throw in the occasional emoticon ;) I won't go as far as emoji though—don't let's be silly.

You'll find that, as a Brit, I tend to use British spellings, except where I've beaten it out of myself over the years, such as in the case of "practice" vs. "practise". We will be capitalising certain key concepts, such as Audiation and Active Listening. You can blame my high school German studies for that, as I found I really liked the capitalising of nouns in that language. And, as you'll discover, these are skills which really deserve a capital letter ;) More seriously though, it will help us to distinguish these specific skills from more casual uses or other meanings of the same words. We'll generally capitalise when referring to the concept or topic as a whole, but not in more specific uses of the same word. For example, capitalising in *"your current ability with Intervals"* but not in *"learn these three intervals next."*

You'll also get to hear from other members of the team as they share their own insights, as well as some of the world-class musicians and music educators we've had the pleasure to work with over the years. I believe this will help to imbue the book with some of the spirit of "Better Together", which you'll be learning more about in the next chapter.

I hope you will find this all makes the book more readable and helps to bring things to life. After all, music is an art, not a science. And even though the proven methods and information we'll be sharing in these pages are, in a sense, "fact" (by virtue of having been demonstrated to work successfully for musicians of all kinds), there's plenty which is still up for debate and subject to opinion. So to write the book in a more personal, subjective way, is true to the fact that it is all ultimately based on practical experience of humans, with humans, occupied in the human art of music-making.

So with that being said, in case we haven't met before, I should probably take a moment to introduce myself and share a little of my own musical backstory.

Hi, I'm Christopher

… and the very first thing you should know about me is that I am not a "natural" musician.

In fact, when I was about five years old, the organiser of a singing group I was in told my mum that she thought I might have a hearing problem! I'm thankful that my mum didn't share that with me until 20+ years later, so I kept singing away happily (and a hearing test confirmed that my hearing was actually fine). There were, however, plenty of other incidents in my childhood which could easily have put me off music entirely.

Such as having one of my best friends in childhood be an apparent "prodigy", able to easily play by ear, compose and perform professionally from a young age. It seemed like he could effortlessly do anything he set his mind to in music (while I could do none of it).

Or how despite being a devoted singer in multiple choirs and barbershop groups for more than ten years, I was never the one chosen to take solos in choral performances.

And then there was the "aural skills" part of the instrument exams I'd take each year, where my teacher would do a special session a week or two before the exam, to run through the tests that would be included. I would fail almost every single one. I think I could reliably clap back a rhythm. That was about it. Interval recognition, sight-singing, improvising a melody—all an epic fail, every time, year after year.

Still, I persisted. My love of music burned strong, and even if I had fully taken on the identity of being a "rubbish musician", I continued to throw myself into it with a passion. So much so that as I lumbered into school each day, lugging some combination of cello, electric guitar, saxophone and clarinet (on top of my school bag and sports kit—and did I mention I was a short and weedy kid, to be trying to manage all that?) I actually earned a reputation among the non-musicians in my year as "the musical one". That only amplified the pain and shame, because I knew that I was possibly the *least* musical kid around—and surely anyone else who did music at the school must know that truth too.

So how the heck did I wind up running the world's leading organisation for providing musicality training, surrounded by a wide variety of online institutions which pride themselves on having the most famous rockstars and virtuosos amongst their staff?

Well, I suppose one way to put it is that if I could crack it for myself —surely there would be nobody I couldn't help!

Over the years my music hobby continued, and I added jazz piano, bass guitar, and blues harmonica to the mix. I read up on music theory. I dabbled in writing my own (embarrassing teenage) songs.

I still carried that identity of "painfully untalented" with me throughout... until in my early 20s I stumbled upon something that changed everything for me.

At the time I was working as an R&D engineer at a small audio technology startup just outside of Cambridge, UK, where I'd studied for my degree. As part of my work, I needed to perform "critical listening" tests, to see if our equipment was harming the quality of the audio passed through it.

My boss Pete told me to study up on "Golden Ears", and fortunately a colleague, Nick, was a BBC-trained sound engineer who was able to give me a nudge in the right direction. As I went through the leading "Golden Ears" training course, I learned to distinguish subtle changes in sound. I started to be able to tell a +3dB boost in the 10kHz band from a +6dB boost in the 12kHz band, or that there was a slight chorus effect being added, or that there was an odd disparity in the stereo field.

It was all fascinating stuff, and "woke up" my ears in an exciting new way. I listened again to music I thought I knew inside-out, and could suddenly appreciate whole new levels of detail.

But that wasn't actually the most exciting part. What was most exciting was the discovery of one simple phrase, "ear training", which set me on a path that would change my life forever.

Now this was back around 2007, when the internet and Google were not what they are today, so finding out more about this topic was easier said than done!

There were two big discoveries though, almost immediately:

1. There was a process called "ear training" which could actually improve my ears and increase my default natural ability to hear things. This was a learnable skill!

2. Alongside the "audio" ear training I'd been doing, focusing on things like frequencies and audio effects, there was a whole adjacent area of ear training for music itself! I found people talking about doing ear training for intervals and chords, and hints that this could actually unlock the kinds of abilities I'd always thought were magical.

As I dove head-first into the world of musical ear training it was like lightbulb after lightbulb were finally coming on. I set aside the "talent myth" (more on that later) and began to see clearly the practically-unlimited musical potential which I, and every other music learner, had actually been born with.

I could now see that the reason I had always failed the "aural skills" tests wasn't because I was naturally deficient or limited. I had just never been taught those skills.

And, as I started to shed my old identity of "painfully untalented", I could see other explanations hidden in plain sight.

Like how it was no coincidence that my childhood friend who was the "prodigy" was actually the son of two professional conductors—and he had been immersed in instrument lessons, theory, and ear training from pretty much the day he was born.

Or that the reason I'd never been selected for solos had little to do with my singing, and everything to do with the fact that I couldn't pronounce my "s" sounds cleanly (a.k.a. had a lisp—which also turned out to be another fixable problem, with the right training.)

The more ear training I did, the more I found I *could* play by ear, improvise, write music, transcribe what I heard, and do everything else that had once felt fundamentally beyond my reach.

Being a geek, I started making iPhone apps to help me with my own ear training. The first one was selected by Apple to be featured on the front page of the App Store. And, to make a long (and very bumpy!) story short, I ended up quitting my day job to go full-time, starting "Easy Ear Training" in 2009 to share with others what I had discovered about musical ear training, and how to make it easy, fun and effective.

I had never intended to start a company, and I tried repeatedly to put the project aside. Somehow, I was never able to.

I knew just how much I had struggled to find good information or resources for ear training. I found myself constantly asking *"How is it possible that there is no go-to company or website to help musicians develop their ear?"* And so, despite being massively under-qualified, and perhaps the least likely person in the world to do it, I found myself taking on the mission of doing something to put that bizarrely-missing piece in place.

From the very beginning I had the good sense to recruit other people more expert than myself to write material and create products with me. And over the years, as we worked with dozens, then hundreds, then thousands of musicians of all kinds, it gradually became clear that "ear training" was only a part of what we were really doing.

In 2015 we rebranded the company and launched a new membership program as "Musical U", devoted not just to musical ear training, but the much broader topic of musicality training. You'll be hearing much more about that in the next section, so for now I'll just say that like ear training, this seemed to be a bizarrely-neglected area.

I found myself asking once again, *"How could something SO important and SO powerful be so utterly missing from most music education?"*

For nearly a decade now we've worked towards a single clear vision at Musical U: *"A world of natural musicians."*

How can we spread the message, create the very best resources, and collaborate with other music educators to have one specific impact: to put musicality at the heart of what it means to "learn music", where it always should have been.

I've been fortunate to have the chance to work with some of the most passionate, experienced and insightful music educators on the planet, and it's been my great honour to serve tens of thousands of musicians inside Musical U, and reach several million more through our public material. That still kind of blows my mind. Yet I know it still only represents the beginning of our journey, if we're to have the impact Musical U was created for.

This book is our latest, and in many ways our greatest, effort towards that mission. So before we dive in, I want to thank you for picking this book up, for reading it, and for anything and everything you do to increase your own musicality from this day on. You are helping to create a more naturally musical world, and that is truly a blessing to us all.

Who This Book Is For

This book is written for any and every person who is passionate about music and devoted to their pursuit of their own musical potential.

If you're like many of those who find their way to us at Musical U, you might not currently identify as "a musician". You might think of yourself as "a hobbyist" or "someone who just messes about with music", while reserving that title "musician" for those who've attained a high level of skill, or make music their profession.

It's our firm belief at Musical U that anybody who makes music is, by definition, "a musician".

As you read through this book, try out some of the suggestions, and start discovering all that is truly possible for you in music, I hope you will naturally begin to take on that identity of "being a musician" more and more.

For now, just know that any time we use the word "musician" in this book... we're talking about you :)

This book has been written with the adult learner in mind. Our rule of thumb at Musical U is "16 years and older[3]". Everything we cover can certainly be used successfully with children, but will need thoughtful adaptation.

If you happen to be a music teacher, I hope that the material will prove interesting and useful for your teaching, and perhaps your own musical growth too. Please know that although I will make various critique of the status quo in music education, and the way things are "normally" done, I would never want that to be seen as criticism of any individual teacher. I have nothing but enormous respect, admiration, and deep appreciation for anybody who devotes their life to music education. Any gripes I might have are purely about the limiting traditions which have been passed down. I also recognise (and am very thankful for) the large number of teachers who *do* make musicality an integral part of their teaching, some of whom you'll find mentioned by name in the chapters which follow.

---

[3] And note that "older" reaches up to 90+ years old among our members! Age is *not* the limiting factor which many assume it must be—more on this in *Chapter Two: Mindset*.

I would also like to acknowledge up front that this book has been written with a focus on Western music traditions, originating in Europe and the Americas. The notation, theory, and examples we'll refer to are common in countries such as the United States and U.K., but of course things do differ country-to-country, and there are vast and wonderful music traditions which exist independently of those. If, for example, you are more focused on Chinese or Indian music traditions, you may find that plenty of the material presented here is still interesting, relevant and applicable for you—but in publishing a book globally, I think it's important to make clear that any words like "normally", "the average musician", "most styles", etc. all take this focus for granted.

Tak Courag

When I was growing up, we would occasionally pass a particular building in London. On its large wall were the remains of what was once a big, painted advertising slogan.

Over the years, time or industry had worn away the last letters of its two words, and it now read:

TAK COURAG

It always caught my attention as we passed in the car, and somehow my young brain still knew what the words must once have been. Each time we'd drive past it, I would feel a little uplifted and encouraged. *"Yes,"* I would think to myself, *"I must tak courag."*

This nonsense phrase has been with me ever since, and I still hear it in my head when something causes me anxiety, or I am faced with a daunting situation.

As we continue in this book, you will be faced with many topics and invited to try activities which may provoke slight anxiety, or feel daunting to you. It will be all too easy to let that turn you into a skim-reader, or let go of your original intention to follow through, and actually *do* the things taught in these pages.

It is going to take courage to succeed with this book.

Not because developing your musicality is anything to be scared of —but because, as Marianne Williamson put it so well in her book *A Return To Love*:

"Our greatest fear is not that we are inadequate.
Our deepest fear is that we are powerful beyond measure."

And so I offer this phrase to you as an odd, but perhaps memorable, mantra. As you read this book and put new musicality practices in place, any time you feel resistance, get nervous, or your "inner critic" tries to make you play small and stay small: Tak Courag.

What This Book Can Do For You

Finally, a word about what you can expect from reading this book. On the front cover, under the title *Musicality*, you'll find the tagline:

How you too can learn music like a gifted prodigy,
Unlock your musical instinct,
And unleash your inner natural.

When I wrote those words, I could almost hear the backlash from critics and cynics. Those are bold claims to make! If those things were even possible for the average musician to achieve, how could a book possibly make it happen?

Rather than dilute down the promise of the book, I decided to stand firm. Because these claims aren't wild speculation. They are the results we've seen, across thousands and thousands of average, everyday music-learners of all kinds here at Musical U.

So while I can't promise that by the time you reach the end of this book you will be a prodigy, feel your musical instinct, or seem to others like a "natural", what I can promise is this: in the pages which follow, you will find all the information, explanations, methods, and guidance you need, to achieve all of those things in your musical life.

If you give this book your full attention, and you put its methods into practice, you will be astounded at what becomes possible for you in music.

And while right now that will make you the rare exception among musicians, who appears to others to have been blessed with magical, mysterious, natural "talent", it is our deepest hope here at Musical U that one day soon, everything we cover here will be a normal part of what "learning music" involves. And that these outcomes, which right now sound too-good-to-be-true, are the norm rather than the exception.

You can be a part of making that change happen, simply by developing your own musicality. This book will show you how.

I'm glad you're here.

Let's begin.

PART ONE

CHAPTER ONE:
MUSICALITY

In the Introduction, I mentioned that this is the book I wish I had been handed on day one of learning music.

Its original working title was "The Missing Manual", and when I mentioned the project to people, some would ask:

"The missing manual for what?"

"Musicality!" I'd cheerfully reply.

And, more often than I liked, what I heard next would be: *"Oh... What's that?"*

Well, ultimately the book's title became simply *"Musicality"*. So clearly I didn't let that point of confusion get in the way! And you have chosen to read it, so clearly you have some grasp of what we mean by the word, and how it could relate to your musical life.

Still, it highlights something important: even if most musicians would have *some* idea of what "musicality" means, it turns out that those ideas vary wildly.

We know it when we see it... Whether that's in musicians who seem to simply *ooze* musicality, like Bobby McFerrin, Victor Wooten, or Jacob Collier—or in those moments (maybe far rarer than we hope) when we feel deeply musical ourselves.

But what *is* "musicality"? And, if this book is to be the manual for it, what would it actually mean to improve, increase, or unlock your musicality?

Before we go any further, let's see if we can clear things up a bit.

What Is Musicality?

Musicality is an informal word. It's not quite slang, but it's certainly less formal than the equivalent word in the classical music tradition: "musicianship".

Musicianship encompasses a range of skills. Dictionary.com defines it as *"knowledge, skill, and artistic sensitivity in performing music."* The Cambridge Dictionary says musicianship is *"a person's skill in playing a musical instrument or singing."*

So essentially: musicianship means "being a musician"? Well, that's pretty vague.

The Associated Board of the Royal Schools of Music gets a bit more specific, connecting musicianship to Audiation (the ability to hear music in your head, which we'll dive into in *Chapter Three: Audiation*):

"Musicianship is a broad concept that covers a complex range of musical abilities… it is loosely defined as the ability to 'think in sound'. This occurs when a musician is able to produce music which they perceive internally and in the imagination, whether through playing by ear, singing, reading from notation, or through improvisation."

In his article "What is Musicianship" Michael Kaulkin (on the Musicianship and Composition faculty of the San Francisco Conservatory) agrees that "inner hearing" is key, writing *"Musicianship is about training the student not just to be a player of an instrument, but to be a Musician. The best way to do that is to take the instrument away."*

That's starting to sound a bit more meaningful. What about the word "musicality" then? Is it different from "musicianship"?

At the time of writing, Wikipedia has a slightly flimsy page, drawing on the Merriam-Webster definition: *"Musicality is 'sensitivity to, knowledge of, or talent for music' or 'the quality or state of being musical'."*

The Oxford Dictionary gets a bit mystical, saying musicality is *"Musical talent or sensitivity"* giving examples of it in use: *"her beautiful,* rich tone and innate musicality" and "his compositions reveal an exceptional degree of innate musicality".

Well, the last thing the world needs is more reinforcement of the talent myth,[1] so let's go ahead and skip definitions of musicality which imply it's a "gift" or something innate rather than learnable.

However, there is something valuable in those talent-based definitions. They capture the ineffable quality of musicality, the fact that it isn't a simple yes/no quality, nor something you can fully define in a single sentence.

So what *is* musicality?

That's a simple question, but one with no single, simple answer! That's why we're going to approach this topic in a few different ways.

Overview

First we'll look at how a broad range of people have described what "musicality" means to them, to get a sense of what it's all about, and why it matters.

Then we'll zoom in and take a very down-to-earth look at the specific skills and abilities that people tend to associate with musicality or "being naturally musical". You can use this to start getting an idea of your own current musicality, as well as what might be possible in future.

Next, I'll share a simple way we like to think about the idea of "reaching your true, fullest musical potential" at Musical U, and the most fundamental framework we use throughout our musicality training. This framework connects all these various ideas, concepts, and skills, enabling you to continually assess your own musicality and identify the best next opportunities for your own improvement.

Then in the next chapter you'll discover a quick and easy exercise you can do to set your "North Star" in music learning in a way that draws all of this together.

What Does "Musicality" Mean To You?

After interviewing over 100 expert musicians and music educators for the *Musicality Now* podcast, as well as members of Musical U, I gradually found that this was my absolute favourite question to ask:

---

[1] More on this in the next chapter.

"What does 'musicality' mean to you?"

The answers were as varied as the musicians themselves, and I wanted to share a number of them here, to help inspire your own interpretation of the word and set the scene for everything we'll be covering in the chapters which follow.

So what is "musicality"?

Musical U members have described it as...

"All of the pieces one needs to be a musician. It is hearing, processing, creating and performing music. It is our ability to take in music on a more refined level and to turn that inner understanding into making music. It can be broken down into many aspects that rely on the ear, mind, emotions and skills we develop."

"Understanding the language of music, its grammar, punctuation, its clarity and most of all its delivery."

"That 'thing' that makes music human, creative, emotional and unique. It's what attracts a listener to some kinds of music more than other forms of music. It's the way the performer makes a piece of music uniquely his/her own. It's more than technical and mechanical ability but something over and above physical capacity to make music."

"Musicality means being able to express your thoughts/feelings through music."

"Musicality is being in the flow of the music instead of struggling with the notes which are written down or how to get them from my instrument."

"It means feeling the music as you play it and conveying that to the audience. The instrument becomes an extension of yourself. It is communication of an emotion, idea or concept through song. It's the expression of your soul."

"The rich blend of playing, listening to, appreciating, interpreting and sharing music. Engaging with it as a whole language in all its diverse forms of reading, writing and speaking; unlimited by idiomatic variations and improvisations."

"Musicality means I am using my ears more than my eyes to play music on my instrument. It means a musician can listen actively to pieces of music,

play it by ear on his/her instrument, jam with other musicians, and create his/ her own music."

"Ability to flow with the music, feel the music like a fish feels the water and a bird feels the air."

I've also had the honour of interviewing many leading musicians and music educators, whose answers have also been fascinating and inspiring. Here are some highlights[2]:

"Musicality to me is being able to play or express any musical idea that you have in your head. To not feel like you're bound by limitations. That you're able to play the music that you're hearing in your head and express it to others.

And how do you achieve that? How, really, do you develop musicality? Well, you have to follow what gives you energy, the energy that is driving us to make us put in all that hard work to actually develop those skills."
— Brent Vaartstra, Learn Jazz Standards

"For me, musicality is the ability of interaction with other musicians when you're performing and when you're making music. So it's the conversation that happens between musicians in an ensemble and how they can create different stories and different conversations within the music."
— Inês Loubet, Singer-Songwriter

"Musicality to me is totally integrated with being human. It's just humanity. And people talk about 'having musicality', but I think about it more in terms of our ability to access our innate musicality.

It's there, you know, it's there the way nature is there. And we could choose to enjoy nature and let it infuse us with its beauty.

When someone says to me, 'I'm not creative' or 'I'm not musical'. I'm like, 'well, maybe you just haven't found the right window or door to open for you to access that, your ability to enjoy it or sense it within yourself.'"
— Melissa Mulligan, Music Career Mastermind

"Musicality: I think about it like my connection to music, how close I feel to

---

[2] These were excerpted from longer answers, given on-the-spot during interviews. So please take them in that spirit, rather than considering them that person's official, full, "Gospel truth" on the subject!

music. I know that I can connect to music through listening. I can connect to music through creating. I can connect to music through understanding. And the more that I practice those three areas of my music learning, the closer I feel to music, the more I feel I understand music. That's how I would define it. It's your connection with music and the desire to continue to get closer to it."

— Tony Parlapiano, popMATICS

"Ah, musicality. I think that is when you start getting beyond the mechanical, maybe beyond the printed page. Musicality is when you get to put some 'you' into it.

What traditional music has us do in the process of learning from books, it's very easy to fall into being mechanical about things and saying, 'there's no wiggle room, it has to be exactly this way, no other way.' And it kind of squeezes out you, or what you might bring to it.

Musicality to me would be when you have a little more freedom to make the best piece you can of any piece of music.

And that could be with notation, without notation, but make something that has some heart in it, that has some heart and soul and breathes a little bit, lets you breathe musically. And really be the way music is supposed to be, which is enjoying the process of making music."

— Jeffrey Agrell, author of the "Improv Games for Classical Musicians" books

"Musicality is when you embrace all aspects of music, whether you're learning to play by ear, whether you're learning to read music. A part of that is, of course, music theory and understanding the universal language and how we can implement that into our musicality."

— Glory St. Germaine, Ultimate Music Theory

"The most important point that I would like to propose about musicality is that it's something that we can choose. It's not something that you have to be born with, or that's only available to people who are musically talented or genetically gifted.

We've certainly all had experiences playing where we're not feeling particularly musical. And hopefully we've had some moments in our lives in which we have felt very musical. So those moments can serve as kind of a treasure map back to that feeling. We just have to ask ourselves, 'What was that moment about? What made that possible?'

I think that one of the ingredients is just playing music that isn't too difficult for you. Sometimes musicians want to play the hardest music they *can. But there is a hidden magic in simplicity. If the music is easy, and if you're relaxed and having a great time, this allows you to access this thing that we call musicality, where you're really grooving with the music, playing in a way that's relaxed and natural.*

I think that musicality is available to all of us all the time. Sometimes we just have to make a conscious choice to play from that place of simplicity and enjoyment."

— David Reed, Improvise For Real

I hope you're starting to get a feel for everything that this single word can encapsulate! I expect some of the descriptions above hit a deep nerve with you, while others may not have resonated at all. That's absolutely normal, and part of the beauty of this single all-encompassing word.

Now that we have the lay of the land, let's get a bit more concrete. What exactly do we mean when we talk about a person's "musicality"?

What Exactly Constitutes "Musicality"?

From the earliest days of Musical U, I was eager to try to bring this amorphous concept down to earth—because if we were going to help musicians to increase and expand their musicality, at some stage all the grand ideas described above were going to need to be translated into concrete, tangible, measurable abilities.

We came up with a list of 15 specific musical skills. These are things which someone who "is musical" tends to be able to do and, contrariwise, which tend to make someone feel unmusical (or "untalented") if they can't do them.

Some musicians will draw from all 15 of these skills to express their musicality, while others achieve a deep connection with their music without having developed all of them. Which skills you choose to develop will depend on your own musical desires, something we'll explore more fully in the next chapter.

As you read through the list below, please keep in mind these two important points:

- These all represent ways to tap into, nurture and express an innate musicality you already have inside you.

- Every time you read the word "musician" in this book, we

mean you.

Even if you're like many who consider themselves only a "music learner" or "hobbyist" and would shy away from calling themselves "a musician", please know that for our purposes, every person on the planet is already "a musician". Everything else is just a matter of degree.

We'll talk more about that principle of "Universal Potential" in the next chapter. For now, just be open to these being possibilities for you, even if right now they seem beyond reach based on your past experiences.

So here (in no particular order) are some of the skills we believe are important parts of musicality.

Talking music

Have you ever listened in to a group of musicians talking and been completely baffled? However experienced you might be in music, if you go outside your chosen genre or your normal musical environment, it's easy to quickly get lost in a jungle of terms and phrases which are new and confusing for you.

Learning the "jargon" or "slang" used by musicians is an important aspect of musicality, as it allows you to easily understand and communicate with other musicians. Although it's possible to collaborate musically without spoken words, it's a lot easier if you are speaking the same language!

An extra benefit is that learning new vocabulary almost always means learning new concepts too, so making the effort to study up on new music jargon extends and improves your musicality by broadening your overall understanding of what's going on in the music you hear and play.

We'll introduce musical terms as they arise throughout the book, and *Chapter Five: Active Listening* will show you how to start expanding your musical vocabulary in an exciting way that's directly connected to the music you hear and play.

Singing in tune

Being able to sing in tune is an important skill for any musician, not just those who consider themselves "a singer". It might not seem like a prominent part of musicality, but just think about the opposite: can you imagine yourself thinking someone is really musical if they always sing out of tune?

You don't need to have a phenomenal voice to be an excellent musician, but you do need to master the basics, specifically two skills called "matching pitch" and "vocal control". This allows you to use your voice as a tool to train your ears and to communicate with other musicians.

Your voice is your natural first instrument, and it's the instrument you always have with you. So once you learn to sing in tune it's an easy and natural way to express yourself in music and show your musicality.

Chapter Four: Singing will provide everything you need to start singing confidently, reliably, accurately in tune—even if right now you think you're "tone deaf".

Having good rhythm

Like singing in tune, having a good sense of rhythm is something musicians often take for granted—but you really notice when it's missing!

There is a basic level of rhythmic ability which all performing musicians must have, and which is normally taught as part of instrument lessons. This includes the true fundamentals like finding the beat and clapping in time (more on that below) but it can also extend to true rhythmic mastery and fine-grained accuracy.

This is actually a large part of what sets a "good" musician apart from a "great" one. When we're shocked by the high degree of musicality displayed by a performer on stage, it's often the rhythm, whether we realise it or not, that has caused us to be impressed.

To reach a basic level of musicality you need to master rhythm fundamentals, and to truly refine your musicality to a pro level you need to upgrade your sense of rhythm even further.

We'll be learning about developing your sense of rhythm in *Chapter Thirteen: Rhythm*.

Keeping the beat

There's one specific rhythm skill that stands out as vital for good musicality: can you find the beat? Can you clap along with it and keep in time?

You only need to go along to a rock concert to see this one in action. If you see 20 people clapping along in time with the band, and one person who seems to be in a world of their own with mis-timed claps all over the place, which one are you going to judge as having limited musicality?

The surprising fact is that even quite experienced musicians occasionally have difficulty with clapping in time. They may be great at playing back complex rhythmic patterns on their instrument, and they may even have mastered rhythm notation, but ask them to clap along with a pop song, or to keep time while someone nearby is clapping out of time, and they may well struggle!

That can be embarrassing for someone who considers themselves to be musical, which only proves its vital importance. So it's worth paying attention to this simple but fundamental aspect of musicality. We'll lay a firm foundation for this in *Chapter Twelve: The Beat*.

Understanding Music Theory

Music theory may not be a favourite topic among musicians, but it's a vital one! Although the "talent" definition of musicality might lead you to believe you can be truly musical even with zero understanding of theory, that's not actually true.

Even the greatest self-taught musicians who claim to know no music theory actually do know a great deal. They may not know the traditional terminology or have taken any formal theory lessons, but through sheer experience and exposure they have actually trained themselves in all the core concepts covered by the term "music theory".

My favourite example of this is the Beatles, who are often cited as a demonstration that "you don't need to learn theory". After I interviewed several professional experts on the Beatles, I found their conclusion was unanimous: the "Fab Four" knew music theory inside-out. They simply learned it through experience rather than from a textbook. The words they used might not have been the official, "correct" terminology or the traditional ways of explaining theory concepts, but they had a deep, hard-earned, learned-intuitive understanding of "how music works".

Studying music theory directly helps us more quickly gain that deep, intuitive understanding of how music works.

Although it's traditionally taught in a dry and boring way, music theory does not need to be dull. In fact, by combining it with listening skills like we do at Musical U, or teaching it in an interesting and engaging way like some modern educators do, it's possible to make the learning of music theory just as enjoyable as music itself.

So don't shy away from it, even if you've had bad experiences in the past. Brushing up on music theory can be a fast, fun and impactful way to improve your musicality.

You'll find that the way musicality is presented throughout this book naturally develops your understanding of music theory along the way.

Reading notation

If you want instant access to a vast library of the music which has moved the world for decades and centuries, there's nothing which compares to traditional "score" notation.

Or is there? If you've mastered playing by ear, you might think that reading from score notation is redundant.

In fact, reading notation is a valuable complement to play-by-ear skills. For example, it allows you to quickly and directly play new repertoire, even without having ever heard it. This is common in the world of jazz where musicians often have to "sit in" and play directly from a lead sheet (see also "lead sheets" and "jamming" below). It's also very valuable for singers, who may need to sight-sing from written notation in a choir.

Learning to read music also allows you to practice Audiation (imagining music in your head) which unlocks extra practice time in your day. You can't play your trumpet on the train to work, but I've often seen musicians on the London Underground reading through sheet music, and I'm sure using the "mental play" technique covered later in the book to practice their technique and work out performance choices.

There's a reason that score notation is still being used throughout the music world today despite dating back hundreds of years. It's simple, versatile, and endlessly useful. That makes it a vital skill for modern musicality, just as it was in the age of Beethoven and Bach.

Chapter Three: Audiation and Part II of this book will help you make the connection between written notation and the corresponding musical sounds.

There are two special cases of reading notation worth mentioning:

Sight-reading music

Most musicians read music notation slowly and carefully, as they learn to play simple pieces on their instrument. In most situations this is fine. You can gradually take the time to work out the notation, note by note, and then play it on your instrument.

However, there is a higher level of reading notation, which is being able to "sight-read" it. This means that you directly play the music from the score, with little or no preparation.

It's normal to find sight-reading challenging, and generally a musician will only be able to sight-read music which is a few notches simpler than the music they play in their learned repertoire.

However, by making sight-reading part of your musical training you can develop this very useful ability: to pick up a new piece of music and play it immediately, even if you've never heard it before. That's a pretty impressive demonstration of musicality!

Playing from a lead sheet

A "lead sheet" is a simplified form of written notation, typically providing just the score for the melody, lyrics (if any), and the chord symbols for the harmony. It can allow a whole song to fit on a single page or two.

Lead sheets are most commonly used in jazz music but are frequently found in pop and rock too, since they allow for literally hundreds of songs to be included in the same printed book.

To play directly from a lead sheet requires a combination of musicality skills, including improvisation, music theory understanding and (if performing in a group) jamming.

If you can read score notation and you have a basic understanding of music theory then the literal act of reading a lead sheet won't be too challenging. But you might find that trying to create a compelling performance as you read the lead sheet actually stretches you in new and interesting ways. It's also a great tool to add to your toolkit, increasing the range of musical opportunities you are prepared to participate in confidently.

Writing music

Once upon a time, composing music went hand-in-hand with being a musician. In the Baroque era, any serious performing musician was expected to be fully trained as an improviser, arranger and composer too. Over the years we've lost this association, and now divide the world of musicians into those who are "composers/songwriters", and those who only perform what others have written.

To feel truly free and confident in music though, it's vital to be creating your own musical ideas.

One way is through improvisation, conjuring up new music in the moment. The less high-pressure way is to sit down and try to compose your own musical creations, whether that's a simple melody, a whole song, or a fully-fledged orchestral arrangement.

Learning to write music pushes your musicality to new levels in a number of areas and (like jamming) it can be a great showcase of what you can do in music.

We'll explore songwriting and composing in *Chapter Sixteen: Songwriting*.

Writing notation

Once you've started creating music, where does it go? In the modern age, it's so easy to record ourselves performing music, or to grab an interactive app which lets us jot down musical ideas in a simplified visual representation such as guitar tab or a "piano roll" display.

However, there is still great value in learning to write traditional "score" notation. It gives you a deeper understanding for reading music notation (as covered above) and it's the most universal written form of Western music. This makes it an important part of musicality, for your understanding of theory and ability to communicate musical ideas.

Don't be intimidated! Although musical notation can become complex (which is actually one of its strengths) it can also be very simple. Once you've learned a few basics you'll soon be ready to start jotting down your own musical ideas in score notation.

In Part II of this book you'll discover the mental models which make it easy to translate from sound to symbol and vice-versa.

Improvising

Another important part of creating your own music is Improvisation, where you express your own musical ideas without prior planning. Of course that doesn't mean to say you haven't prepared!

Improvisation is a learned skill, and you can train your ears and learn creative frameworks which make it easy to conjure up your own ideas reliably. With that preparation done, each improvisation can be original and unique, created in the moment.

Of all musical skills, Improvisation is perhaps the most intimidating before you start to learn it. Fortunately, learning to improvise doesn't have to be challenging. The Expansive Creativity framework you'll learn in *Chapter Fifteen: Improvisation* provides a "safe space" to continually extend and improve your abilities.

Once you start getting the hang of it, Improvisation becomes a fun and powerful way to regularly push the boundaries of your musicality and it's a particularly effective way to increase your musical confidence.

Playing by ear

This is perhaps the most prominent skill people associate with musicality. When you see a musician who can easily pick up their instrument and play any song or piece of music they've just heard (possibly for the first time), without the need for sheet music, a chord chart, or any kind of practice time to learn the piece—now *that's* musicality! Right?

This skill can be so impressive that it is one of the primary causes of people believing that musicality must be an innate "gift".

If you don't understand how Playing By Ear works, then it can seem like you would need a mysterious "talent" to do it. Fortunately, once you learn how to play melodies or chords by ear the mystery dissolves and you realise that (like all other aspects of musicality) this is something you can learn for yourself.

We'll be showing you how to learn this skill in *Chapter Fourteen: Playing By Ear*.

Jamming

From the outside, a musical jam session can look like the pinnacle of "being a natural". A bunch of musicians, each with their own instrument, all sit down together without preparation, and produce coherent, great-sounding music on-the-fly. How do they do it?

Jamming is actually a combination of several other skills, including Active Listening, having good Rhythm, Playing By Ear, Improvisation, and talking music. It's a great representation of the versatile skills covered by "musicality" and joining a jam session can be an effective way to put your own musicality to the test and help you to reach new heights. Not to mention being a lot of fun!

Especially if you've been struggling in the classical world of endlessly trying to perfect repertoire, or slaving away privately in your bedroom for years, learning to jam can bring a new freedom to your music-making that you never knew was missing.

Performing live

It may or may not be one of your musical goals to ever get up on stage and wow a crowd, but it can't be denied that performing music live (whether to a stadium audience or just to your cat) is a key part of being musical.

It might be playing a new pop song by ear, improvising a rock guitar solo, or carefully performing a piece you've practiced a thousand times. However you choose to express yourself musically, learning to do it in a live situation for an audience, where it is framed as a one-off performance to please the listener, rather than a loose play-through for your own enjoyment, is an important skill to develop.

It can be scary, especially when performing something new or when the opportunity is big or exciting. You'll have to draw on all aspects of your musicality to ensure a great performance.

Fortunately there are concrete ways to gradually improve your Performance skills and make performing a joyful, natural part of your music-making. We'll share a powerful framework for this in *Chapter Eighteen: Performance*.

Knowing your instrument inside and out

Learning to play an instrument is perhaps the most obvious defining characteristic of "being a musician", and it's a common trap to consider this the only thing you need to do. Of course, as we've been exploring, there is much more to musicality than just instrument technique.

Supposing you've already got the hang of playing an instrument. Is that all there is to it? Actually, when it comes to musicality, you need to take it a step further.

Speak to someone who is clearly "very musical" and they won't just have mastered playing advanced pieces of music on their instrument. They will be able to take advantage of every playing technique the instrument offers, so that they can most fully express their own musical interpretation in each performance. They will likely be able to tell you about the history of the instrument and the different models available and their pros and cons. In fact, they will probably talk your ear off once they get started!

This passion for your instrument is a hallmark of devoted and accomplished musicians, and knowing your instrument inside and out is an important part of musicality.

Tuning your instrument by ear

Another skill which is easy to overlook in the modern technology-assisted age, tuning your own instrument by ear is still a valuable skill for a musician. Again, consider the opposite: would you think someone was highly musical if they were completely unable to get their instrument in tune when their digital tuner ran out of batteries or went missing?

This is really a proxy for "having precise pitching", which also features even more prominently as part of singing in tune.

You don't want to be wholly reliant on technology for your music-making and it can be a painful experience to inadvertently be playing out of tune. So taking the time to learn how to tune up by ear is a great way to hone your pitch sensitivity and that improves your tuning throughout your musical performance, not just while you're literally tuning up.[3]

Playing more than one instrument

We've already said that musicality means much more than just learning to play an instrument. This is demonstrated clearly by how we associate multi-instrumentalism with musicality.

If we hear that someone plays three instruments, we don't just think they've done three times as much music practice as someone who just plays one. We start to imagine that they have some inner ability in music which allows them to learn instruments more easily than other people.

This is because there are certain aspects of learning to be a musician which carry across from one instrument to another. Specifically, it's all the "inner skills", which constitute musicality.

All of your listening skills (including those which enable playing by ear, improvising and creating your own music), all of your performance skills (including playing from a lead sheet, jamming, and musical confidence), and all of your knowledge and understanding (including knowing how to "talk music" and understanding the theory) can be transferred from one instrument to the next.

This means that although the physical movements for a new

---

[3] We can probably let pianists off the hook on this one, given the far deeper skill involved in piano tuning!

instrument may all be new to you, learning a second and then a third will come much faster than the first. In fact, the more you've developed your musicality, the easier it will all be.

Learning multiple instruments isn't just about impressing people with how musical you are. It's a great way to:

- Learn theory in a more versatile way

- Develop more robust and reliable listening skills

- Be able to collaborate in more varied situations

- Explore new genres and traditions of music

- Improve your musicality more fully and faster

You might worry that taking up a second (or third, or fourth!) instrument will slow down your progress on your main instrument, but many musicians find the opposite is true. Because it stretches you in new ways while honing your inner musicality, it will likely help you to become a more proficient and expressive musician on your main instrument as well.

How Did We Get Here?

As you were reading through this list, you might have been struck by how few of these skills are typically included in "learning music" today. Why not?

Tim Topham of TopMusic Co explains it well:[4]

"Music lessons weren't always like they are now. In the early 1700s, if you couldn't improvise, you couldn't work as a musician [...] Once sheet music publishing became popular in the early to mid-1800s, it had a huge effect on the world of music.

Musicians were encouraged to reproduce the written music as authentically as possible. This meant that the central focus of teaching turned towards converting students into performers, not creators. This is why, when you compare music to any of the other creative arts of the time—sculpture, painting and writing—music stands alone. Musicians are rarely (even to this day) encouraged to create music in the same way a painter would be encouraged to paint a new picture. Where an artist reproducing a painting by another painter would be considered a forger, this is not the case in music.

The advent of method books only sought to reinforce the idea that learning to play music was about learning to read and perform other people's music, which goes a long way to explaining the situation we find ourselves in today, with such a focus on music reading."

So what does "musicality" mean to *you?*

Using a catch-all word like "musicality" is helpful because it's simple and captures the spirit of what we're all pursuing as musicians.

There is another advantage too: its broad generality also makes it adaptable.

This means that your musicality can be different from somebody else's. As all the examples above prove, there is a huge variety of ways to "be musical" and each musician has a different combination of

---

[4] Excerpt from "No Book Beginners", wording adjusted slightly to broaden from piano pedagogy specifically.

current strengths and weaknesses.

Each apparent "weakness" is really a new learning opportunity. So your present musicality and the future of your musicality training are both 100% personal to you.

The 15 skills of musicality listed above can serve as a kind of "checklist" for you. Along with the H4 Model and Big Picture Vision which you'll be learning about next, having these in mind can help you continually refine, extend and improve your own musicality.

As you were reading through the list, some probably stood out to you and made you think *"Wow, I'd love to be able to do that"*. You can!

Everything we've mentioned above is a learnable skill, and as you'll be discovering in the rest of this book, many of them are much easier to learn than you might have expected.

Whatever your next steps might turn out to be, I hope you are now seeing musicality in a new light: as a collection of exciting musical skills, all of which are available to you to learn, and which can be combined in your own unique way to define your own musicality.

The "Complete Musician"

Since musicality is not one single thing, it's never going to be measurable by a simple number or a set of "levels" or "grades", nor a final "destination" that everyone can agree on[5].

Still, after seeing tens of thousands of musicians go through the Big Picture Vision exercise you'll be learning about in the next chapter, we have come up with a simple shorthand which we've found tends to resonate strongly with the majority of musicians:

The "Complete Musician" is one who can step into any musical situation with confidence, and play something that sounds—and feels—great.

It doesn't cover all the bases (for example, maybe you want to substitute "play" for "sing", or perhaps you only ever want to sit alone and compose music without ever stepping outside your own home) so please understand we're not suggesting that this definition should necessarily be your exact goal.

---

[5] In fact, one of our Pillar Beliefs here at Musical U involves the fact that learning music is an *endless* journey. More on that in the next chapter.

Nevertheless, it's proven to be a handy concept for many. In fact, this is the official overall goal of our *Next Level* coaching program. Every musician who comes in is different, with their own distinct musicality and their own unique "Big Picture Vision" for their musical life—but the freedom, versatility, and musical mastery that's implied by this concept of the "Complete Musician" is one that almost always resonates strongly, stokes their inspiration, and increases their clarity.

All of this begs the question then: what would it take to become that kind of "Complete Musician"?

The H4 Model Of Complete Musicality

Back when Musical U was still "Easy Ear Training", and our focus was on making ear training easy, fun and effective, we developed something we called the "trifecta".

This was a way of thinking about "what it takes to be a great musician" by breaking it down into three components:

- Instrument Skills

- Music Theory

- Ear Training

And showing them as a triangle with each one connected to the other two:

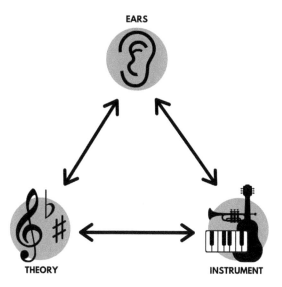

This was a helpful clarifier for many musicians who came to us, and served as the basis for the Integrated Ear Training approach you'll learn about later in the book. All three areas are familiar to most who've been learning music for a while, but few musicians are giving all three their due attention, or thinking about the connections between them.

Over time, as we watched musicians have varying degrees of success with Integrated Ear Training, we discovered that there was a fourth vital component to consider: Mindset.

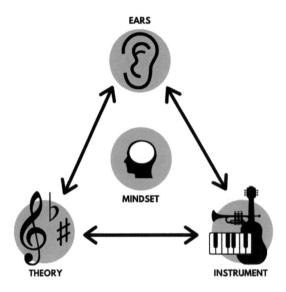

Mindset can make the difference between a musician who has enormous success, and one who struggles, despite having exactly the same "natural abilities" and exactly the same learning material. We'll be devoting a whole chapter to the topic, so I won't go into more detail about it here, except to say that in due course we realised that "Mindset" was an over-simplification. Really, we needed some broader representation of everything that's going on emotionally as well as psychologically in the musical journey.

The result was what we now call the H4 Model of Complete Musicality. It's what our transformational musicality program *Living Music* was built on, and it's the basis of our *Next Level* personal coaching, where we work one-to-one with a musician over the course of a year to help them break through to their personal "next level" in music.

Now I want to give it to you too.

Don't let its simplicity fool you! Adopting this H4 Model as how you think about your musicality can have a huge impact throughout your musical life, forever.

We said that the "Complete Musician" is someone who can step into any musical situation they want to with confidence and play something that sounds—and feels—great. These, then, are the four areas which produce that "complete musicality":

Head, Hands, Hearing and Heart

Head

Your conceptual understanding and the internalised sense of "how things work" in music.

In traditional music education, Head would be called "music theory" and typically taught in a dry, abstract way, full of rules and facts. In my experience, most musicians dislike it, and even those who do like it find it hard to really get much benefit from it beyond the basics of being able to read score notation.

That kind of "music theory" certainly isn't bad as such, but the way it tends to be utterly divorced from real music and real musical activities is a big problem.

What does all the theory actually sound like? How do you *do* something with it when you're sitting with your instrument?

Even students who master theory "by the book" tend to find they still don't really understand music instinctively. That's why we've always taken a very different attitude to music theory here at Musical U and would encourage you to do the same:

Make sure that it's always connected with real music and the musical activities you're actually doing.

There are two parts to this:

1. Flip It

When I had the chance to interview YouTube music theory sensation Adam Neely, he finally put words to what I'd been instinctively feeling, and trying to achieve inside Musical U.

Traditional theory is "prescriptive", meaning it tells you facts and rules about how music is "allowed" to work. It implies that music is a certain way because the theory says that's how it goes.

However, you can instead treat theory as (merely) "descriptive", meaning it serves to describe how music does work.

When we treat theory as descriptive we don't discard all the "rules and facts", but we're able to see them for what they are: an attempt to clarify what music and musicians naturally do. It is a set of helpful ideas, terminology and rules of thumb which can help empower a musician.

Simply flipping our understanding of what theory is from "prescriptive" to "descriptive", it liberates rather than constrains, inspires rather than intimidates, and excites rather than discourages.

2. Integrate It

Even a "descriptive" approach to theory is fundamentally flawed if it exists in abstract isolation from real music.

The solution is to integrate it with the other three H's below. So for example, you don't just memorise the notes in an F♯ Minor chord.

You play it on your instrument, hear how it sounds, learn to recognise the intervals inside it and the overall sound of a minor chord, and so on.

This can go in the other direction too, guiding your exploration of theory concepts to support what you're working on for your Hands, Hearing and Heart.

Where traditional "by the book" music theory is very much a strict "right or wrong" mentality, a descriptive and integrated approach to theory brings it much more in line with the nature of music as a human art. Rather than the goal being to pass a theory test, our goal becomes developing an intuitive grasp of how music works and the musical choices available to us in any given situation.

Hands

How you interact with your instrument(s) to express yourself musically.

It's not an exaggeration to say that 90% or more of music education is focused solely on this one of the four H's. That should already be setting off alarm bells in your head!

Generations of music learners have been taught to focus purely on instrument technique. They concern themselves only with how to play notes and chords, and get it "right". They learn pieces or songs note-by-note from sheet music, chord charts, guitar tab or other notation, or from video tutorials. Step by step, instruction by instruction.

To be clear, there's nothing inherently wrong with that. But it's no wonder so many musicians lose motivation, or feel disappointed about the level they've reached, when only a single one of four vital components of their musicality has been taught!

The entire experience of learning music is transformed into just "avoiding making mistakes". The best you can hope to achieve with that approach is to become a very good "note-reproducing robot".

Well, what about musical self-expression? Creativity? Fulfilment and enjoyment? What about connecting with other musicians and feeling confident, versatile and free in any musical situation you're eager to step into?

Like with "Head", there are two big changes we suggest:

1. Learn Faster

The "Hands" component is absolutely vital, but the other big issue with standard approaches is that they are essentially a "brute-force" approach.

Endlessly repeating the same thing, and hoping it will eventually click. Making the same mistakes again and again, and getting discouraged when the mistakes don't go away after the 99th repetition. Spending endless hours practicing, only to plateau, often at a beginner-intermediate level of instrument technique and repertoire.

Over the last twenty years or so, scientific research has proven there are dramatically better ways to spend your practice time, and that you can literally learn up to 10 times faster—by no longer wasting 90% of your practice time.

We'll cover this in depth in *Chapter Six: Superlearning*. For now, just know that even if your primary (or even sole) focus was the "Hands" component, there is a much better way to go about it.

2. Integrate It

Again, this one of the four components is typically done in isolation. A student is asked to learn a new piece from notation without ever having heard it, without any idea how it should sound, without being able to sing it or even clap the rhythms. That might be okay if your goal is to be a "note-reproducing robot"—but not if your goal is to be a musician.

When you start actively building the connections from your Hands to your Head, Hearing and Heart, it totally transforms the music you play as well as the experience of learning to play it. You're also freed up from relying on notation or tutorials to tell your Hands what notes to play, and start being able to instead bring the music out from inside you.

Hearing

How you interpret, understand and relate to the musical sounds you hear and play.

One big learning point from the "Easy Ear Training" days was that almost every musician we encountered had either never tried ear training, or had tried it and had a poor experience. Even graduates of top music schools and conservatories would tell us they had flunked their ear training semester, or in some cases that they had passed the quizzes but still felt terrible that they couldn't play by ear or improvise, despite having acquired the ear skills "on paper".

Traditional Ear Training consists of endless tedious repetition of abstract exercises and quizzes. It's slightly more engaging in the age of apps (and full disclosure: our very first product was an ear training app which was only slightly better than the traditional drills and exercises!)

Those methods aren't terrible. But they are highly inefficient, and often produce little in the way of practical skills beyond the ability to pass ear training quizzes. It's understandable why musicians either don't do it, or do it but hate it.

Later in the book you'll learn about the "Integrated Ear Training" approach, where we incorporate real music, and real musical activities like Playing By Ear, Songwriting and Improvisation. That way, the connections are naturally formed to your Head and your Hands. As a result you improve faster, and every bit of progress means real-life "new things you can do in music".

Heart

 How you feel inside and how you connect emotionally with music, with your instrument, with other musicians, with the audience.

In a way, I feel silly that it took us so long to explicitly recognise this fourth vital component of musicality. But then I look around and see it still missing from even the very best music education out there. I hope that after reading about it here and in the chapters which follow, you'll likewise come to feel it's a bit insane that this topic isn't actively taught to musicians as standard.

Let me put it this way: Have you ever felt emotions while learning or playing music? Have you ever experienced a negative "voice of self-doubt" inside your head, or heard your "inner critic" giving you a hard time during practice or a performance? Do you always feel truly, deeply connected to all the music you play and the other people around you in music—or do you still wonder if hopefully, some day, that connection might emerge?

If those questions made you feel a bit sheepish or self-conscious, you're not alone. Even with the very best teachers and learning materials, musicians are left struggling with emotional hangups, psychological baggage, limiting beliefs and mental blocks, with no idea what it actually means to "connect" with music or their audience (even though that's what they want most).

The "Heart" component is about recognising that there is deep emotion and a psychological journey involved in learning music and being a musician.

You don't need to feel helpless in the face of it all, or like that stuff should all be shoved to one side and hope that one day, eventually, when you "master your instrument" it will all just disappear.

Instead, you can actively learn mindset principles which can remove lifelong limiting beliefs and unlock new levels of musical ability, as well as to develop performance skills which demystify what it takes to perform in an engaging, compelling, emotionally-moving way, and feel a deep connection to music with every note you hear and play.

Don't Be A Chair With Just One (or Two) Legs!

If you look at any great musician—across instruments and genres, and throughout the ages—every single one of them is strong in all four of these areas.

Head, Hands, Hearing, Heart.

When all four of these parts are developed and connected, it's transformational. You develop your inner musician. You get in touch with your own true musical nature. You connect with—and harness— your innate instinct for music. And instead of the music always being "out there", and your Hands needing to be trained to reproduce it robotically, the music starts coming from inside you.

So I'd invite you to ask yourself now: how well do you think you're doing in each of these four areas? How much time and energy have you put into learning each?

If you're like most non-professional musicians, over 80% of your time has been spent on the Hands, learning technique and new pieces. Maybe 10-15% has been spent on your Head, learning bits of music theory. And perhaps 5% on Hearing, doing a little "ear training". If you're a professional, you may have diligently put a bit more effort into the Head and Hearing—or maybe not.

Can you see now how lopsided that leaves you as a musician?

Imagine trying to sit on a chair which had three of its four legs far too short—or even missing entirely! Or imagine if you had a chair with four good matching legs—but each one stood alone, with nothing connecting them.

Can you see now why you might always have felt a bit unstable and uncertain in music, and why you have been bashing up against barriers which no amount of technique improvement was ever going to conquer?

Those are not inherent barriers. You just haven't yet honed the required areas of your musicality.

Once you see this, you can't un-see it. You'll realise that almost every website, course, and even in-person teacher is just addressing a single one of these areas.

For example, almost every "instrument lessons" website out there just teaches "Hands", as do most in-person instrument teachers.

Endless ear training apps just teach "Hearing". Centuries of music theory textbooks and courses have just taught "Head". And typically only high-level performance coaches will touch on "Heart".

The result is generation after generation of "lopsided" musicians, not realising that they feel so limited only because they've put all of their music-learning effort into just one of four essential areas.

So not only is it important to have the very best methods and frameworks for each area, you will also want to make sure you are developing your musicality in all four.

Connection, Connection, Connection

One of the most crucial and powerful aspects of the H4 Model is that not only are you made conscious that all four of these components are essential, but that they are not isolated skills.

For you to reach your true musical potential each of the four must be connected to each of the others.

When you take a holistic, integrated, approach, you are making sure that each skill is widely usable in real musical situations, enhancing your musical life with every step forwards you take.

As a bonus, this integrated approach means that each step of progress in one area has a positive knock-on effect on all of them, developing your musicality much faster than if you just work on each in isolation.

Using the H4 Model

When you develop each of these four areas—Head, Hands, Hearing, and Heart—as well as the connections between them, that's what produces that incredible "complete musicality" for you.

You can use this model to:

1. Assess where you're at right now. Where there are strengths and opportunities?

2. Look at where you want to get to (your Big Picture Vision, see next chapter), and really get clear on that in terms of the H4 Model. What does that version of you look like, in terms of each of the four H's?

3. Figure out how you can achieve that vision most effectively, designing your learning all along the way.

Keep this model in mind throughout the rest of this book—and the rest of your musical life!

Conclusion

Now that we've explored the spirit of "musicality", unpacked the various skills and abilities that contribute to it, shared this concept of the "Complete Musician", as well as the H4 Model for understanding that kind of complete musicality, it's time to lay the groundwork for you to increase your own musicality in the way you're hopefully feeling inspired to.

I expect you're itching to dive into some of the exciting skills we've been talking about. However, we've found that if you are to actually succeed in developing those skills, it is absolutely essential to first cover a topic which is typically neglected entirely.

Without this, your progress with any musicality training will be significantly impaired—possibly even sabotaged entirely.

With it, you are primed to succeed with anything you set your mind to in music, and do so with ease and with joy.

So don't be tempted to skip over the next chapter or skim-read it... It is quite possibly the most important chapter in this entire book.

CHAPTER TWO:
MINDSET

"Mindset" is probably *not* the topic which would spring to mind first, when thinking about musicality or "becoming more naturally musical." And yet I expect you would agree that as an adult musician, your own mind can be your greatest ally—or your worst nemesis.

In the previous chapter we highlighted the considerable importance of addressing the Heart component of all our music learning and music-making: everything emotional and psychological which goes into learning music and being a musician. "Mindset" is a large part of that. By intentionally and carefully *choosing* our beliefs, attitudes, and mental habits, we can have a significant positive effect on our outcomes.

To be clear, I'm not talking about Polyanna-like rose-tinted spectacles, simplistic "positive thinking", or old maxims like Napoleon Hill's *"Whatever the mind can conceive and believe, it can achieve."* or Henry Ford's *"Whether you believe you can do a thing or not, you are right."*

Those all have their place, and they do have value. But "Mindset" is much bigger, more complex, and ultimately far more rewarding than anything which can be summed up in a sentence or two.

Depending on your background, you may love personal development, introspection, and this kind of "meta" game of learning music. Or you might be itching to skip ahead, thinking this is fluffy nonsense you can do without!

Either way, let me just say that of everything we help musicians with at Musical U, mindset is almost certainly the most important. Why? Because it's the "big domino". With the right mindset, everything else becomes easier or unnecessary. Without it, you will inevitably struggle and suffer more than you need to, and achieve far less than you could.

In this chapter we'll introduce some overarching concepts and principles, as well as one powerful exercise, which can all have an outsized effect on the results you get with everything else in the book.

So if the word "mindset" seems fluffy or impractical to you right now (as it once did to me) I want to strongly encourage you not to skip over this chapter. It might prove to be the most important one you read.

Overview

We'll begin with the single highest-impact activity I've come across, for shaping a musician's musical journey and their success along the way: the Big Picture Vision. We'll explain the exercise and guide you through doing it, and then offer several tips to help make it as effective as possible.

Then we'll look at your musical identity, through a framework we call "Your Musical Core" which can help you to understand more deeply who you are as a musician, and who you wish to become.

Next we'll introduce four "Pillar Beliefs" that can liberate and empower you in music. We'll then turn our attention to a series of mindset choices you can make, to open yourself up to maximum success with everything which follows in the rest of the book, and your musical life as a whole.

Your Big Picture Vision

There's a scene I've always loved in Lewis Carroll's *Alice in Wonderland*. Alice is lost in the Tulgey Wood and encounters the Cheshire Cat.

She asks:

> *"Would you tell me, please, which way I ought to go from here?"*

To which the cat replies:

> *"That depends a good deal on where you want to get to."*

Alice begins to answer:

> *"I don't much care where–"*

And the Cheshire Cat interrupts her to say:

"Then it doesn't much matter which way you go."

Have you found yourself sometimes feeling like you're going nowhere in music? Or perhaps you're not progressing as fast as you hoped? Maybe you keep changing direction, leaping from project to project, idea to idea, trying to move forwards but somehow never quite getting anywhere?

In just a few minutes, you can change the trajectory of your entire musical future.

Using a powerful exercise I'm about to share, you can permanently gain greater clarity, confidence, and success in your musical life. What we're going to do is to set your "Big Picture Vision".

Before we go any further though, I know some readers may hear the word "vision" and immediately start to tune out! I get it. I'm a scientist by background, highly analytical, very pragmatic. It was only through a gradual process over the years and putting these things to the test myself that I realised that something as seemingly airy-fairy as "setting a vision" could have highly practical outcomes.

As Dr. Stephen Covey once famously put it, you need to "begin with the end in mind".

So this exercise is all about getting clear, getting detailed, and getting excited about exactly where it is you want to go in music.

Another disclaimer: This is not about career success. Or maybe for you, it is. But this is something for every musician, whether you're just starting out, or deep into your journey, whether you play music as a hobby, you're trying to make it a career, or you're already a seasoned pro.

Every single musician has a unique Big Picture Vision. This is 100% about you and the things you truly care about.

The Big Picture Vision is one of the first things we have all new members at Musical U do, and if you're a member yourself then you will almost certainly have done this before. Whether you've done this exercise or something like it before, I want to encourage you to take the time as you read this chapter now to do it afresh. Because this isn't a one-time thing, it's worth doing regularly to keep your musical life on the best path forward.

You'll find that your Big Picture Vision is amazing for staying motivated. Especially if music isn't your career, it's likely you find that your motivation and passion for learning music can wax and wane. Even with all the best intentions, sometimes you wake up and you're just not in the mood for practising your instrument today!

But the one thing which never really wavers is your Big Picture Vision, because that literally encapsulates what it is you're most passionate about. Once you have it clearly defined, it can be a touchstone you can keep coming back to any time you're not motivated to practice. You can read through your Big Picture Vision and remind yourself *"Oh yeah! This is what I want and this is why I'm putting in the effort. This is what's going to be possible for me and where I want to get to."*

It's an incredible way to just kickstart your motivation again and again. Whatever might be going on this day, this week, this month, that Big Picture Vision statement can continually re-spark that passion for you.

Another powerful thing about your Big Picture Vision is that it can act as a kind of shield for you. We live in the golden age of YouTube, and while that is an incredible boon, it's also the source of endless "shiny object syndrome" and "squirrels to chase."

It's so easy to let what is a really good thing (our passion) turn into scatterbrained enthusiasm in any and every direction. Those shiny objects and squirrels can become the biggest barrier preventing us from actually making real progress.

So I love the Big Picture Vision for providing a shield against those kinds of distractions, by acting as a filter. You can simply ask yourself *"is this actually aligned with where I want to go? Am I chasing down a rabbit hole just because I'm kind of addicted to the YouTube roulette? Or is this genuinely helping lead me down the path I want to be following?"*

Once you're clear on that "North Star", it becomes a lot easier to stay focused, and rule out things that are going to be a distraction, or pure entertainment which won't actually move you forwards.

Can you see how impactful this could be for you? I encourage you to actually take a few minutes and do the exercise now, as you read on.

The Big Picture Vision Exercise

The Big Picture Vision exercise begins with a simple question:

Imagine yourself 5 years from now.

And for a moment we're just going to suspend all disbelief,
and imagine that everything has gone perfectly in your musical life.

No barriers, no struggles, no failures, no frustrations.

Everything has just magically clicked into place for you.

What does that musical life look like?

Now you might immediately have answers and ideas popping into your head, or you might not.

Maybe you just have a few words or one particular goal you've been thinking about.

I want you to try to stay in that space of *"anything's possible, and everything's gone perfectly."* Because your brain is going to want to immediately jump to *"How would I do that? Could I really accomplish that? I'm not sure I have what it takes"*, and so on.

We want to totally sidestep that analytical brain and any "voice of self-doubt", and capture the truest, ideal future vision. *After* that we can worry about all the practicalities of maximising your odds of actually getting there. For now, let's just get 100% clear on the dream destination.

I'd also encourage you to shrug off any concerns about commitment. I know that for myself, I immediately flinch away from the idea of committing to one particular thing I'm aiming for, especially on a 5-year timescale. So don't worry that this is set in stone. It can and likely will change along the way. But you're going to find that taking the time to set a clear destination does wonders for your progress, even if it gets adjusted and updated periodically. In fact I'd encourage you to repeat this exercise at least once a year, if not once a quarter.

Grab a pen and paper or something you can type on now, and start writing down anything that comes to mind.

Zac Says...

Go with what truly excites you. Don't hold back. If you did have an idea immediately pop into your head, go with that one."

Then, once you have an initial answer to that first question, let's add richness and depth to your vision.

You can explore the various skills of musicality we covered in the previous chapter:

- Do you want to play melodies by ear? Or chords?

- Do you want to improvise?

- How about transcribing music you hear?

- Do you want to be writing songs or composing music yourself?

- Are there particular pitch or rhythm skills you want to hone?

- Are there other ways of expressing yourself that you've dreamed of mastering?

- How about instrument skills? Are there things you want to be able to do on your current primary instrument? Have you wanted to take up a second, or even a third instrument? Is singing something you want to develop and add to your skillset?

- How about theory? Are there areas of music theory that you know you'd love to understand inside-out? Or maybe the whole area of theory is currently a mystery to you but you're keen to peek under the hood? Maybe you've studied the theory already but in future you want to start applying it to great effect in your musical activities?

Speaking of activities…

- What will you be doing with all these new skills and understanding? Do you want to be performing regularly? And if so, what kinds of gigs?

- Is collaboration something you're excited about? Maybe with a partner, or a group, or joining a band, orchestra or choir?

- Is it important to you to make money or build a career around music?

- Are there particular creative projects you've always hoped to one day pursue in music?

- How is music appreciation part of your musical life? How are you discovering new music? Are there genres or types of music you're eager to explore more? Is there one you're keen to go deep on and specialise in?

- Are you listening to music live, on recordings, or in other contexts?

Finally, let's step back a bit...

- What overall kind of musicality do you dream of having?

- What does your daily and weekly musical life look like?

- How is it going to feel when those things become real? Is there a sense of joy? Of excitement? Are you feeling empowered and enjoying a new confidence?

- Has your identity as a musician changed? Has the way you think about your musical abilities shifted?

- Do you have a different relationship with music? Is there a sense of triumph, of satisfaction, of pride—and of ongoing wonder and curiosity about what you're capable of?

Okay, let me check in :) How are you getting on? Is your Big Picture Vision starting to take shape? Are you starting to feel excited?

Depending on your personality and how much of this kind of thing you've done before, you might love this and find it comes easily—or it might feel like hard work!

Be patient with yourself and give yourself the opportunity to daydream a little. Remember we're capturing the ideal. We're not judging ourselves or the ideas or trying to assess how realistic they are. That's not the exercise. So let those kinds of thoughts just drift away, and focus on the dreaming, the imagining, the idealised future.

Once you've thought through all of these questions, you've hopefully written something that's at least a few lines, possibly a few paragraphs, or even a few pages.

I'm hoping that as you went through this you were able to shake off that voice of self doubt, or any self-conscious hesitation, and you wrote down what truly excites and motivates you.

Reading back through your Big Picture Vision, you'll know you did this right if it makes you smile. If you start to feel excitement welling up inside. If it helps put you immediately back into that mental space of "anything's possible" and "my future musical life could be *amazing*".

Next Steps

So what now?

There are two next steps I recommend.

The first is that you want to review this regularly. Reading through it should make you feel good and reignite your enthusiasm and passion—and the value of that is not to be underestimated, because motivation is an essential factor in any musical progress.

Reading through your Big Picture Vision will also help keep you on track towards actually accomplishing it, because as soon as you have this clear in your mind, a lot of the decision-making and uncertainty that can crop up in your musical journey becomes dramatically simpler. Things which before seemed hard to figure out will suddenly be crystal clear to you—because they either align with your Big Picture Vision or they don't. Don't just shove this in a drawer and forget about it. Make it a habit to review it, whether that's once a week or at the start of every music practice session.

After all, once Alice knew where she wanted to go, the Cheshire Cat could point her in the right direction.

The second thing to do next is to start taking action to move yourself towards your Big Picture Vision.

There's value in the vision itself, but clearly it's going to have even more impact if you actually use it as the basis of goal-setting and planning. We have a unique framework for this inside Musical U, to help you set truly effective goals and the step-by-step plans that will get you there—because it's easy to do goal-setting and planning wrong and cause yourself a lot of strife! You'll find this provided in the *Additional Resources*. Having a proven system can make it much more likely you'll actually get to that Big Picture Vision.

Whatever goal-setting and planning process you choose to use, be sure that your Big Picture Vision now serves as your "North Star" that guides it all.

Do that, and you will find a greater sense of clarity, purpose and confidence in your musical life, and you'll start to see the tangible benefits and results that come from being 100% clear on your Big Picture Vision—and where exactly you're going in music.

8 Tips For Big Picture Vision Success

The Big Picture Vision exercise has been a core part of the Musical U membership program since 2015, so we've had the chance to learn a lot about what makes it work well, or not.

There are eight tips I'd like to share with you. These can be used to make your first Big Picture Vision even more effective, or to "turbo-boost" an existing Big Picture Vision if you've done the exercise before.

Tip 1: Written is best.

It's likely that just reading through the exercise description above started to spark ideas for you, and hopefully you took the additional step of actually grabbing a pen or keyboard and starting to write.

One great way to do it, especially if you have some resistance to writing, is to do "stream of consciousness" writing—meaning you try to fully shut off your "inner editor", you don't worry about grammar or punctuation or re-wording things, you just write whatever comes to mind and keep going.

You can always come back later and edit it to perfection. For now just try to capture as much as possible of what you're inspired about.

It's powerful to make it as vivid and descriptive as possible, and to frame it positively in the present tense. So for example, rather than *"I don't want to be nervous when performing"* you could write something more like *"I'm performing regularly at the coffee shop down the road, seeing all the smiling faces in the audience, feeling enthusiasm and confidence as I share the music I love with new people who are excited to hear it."*

In whatever way you'd like to, write it down. As long as it's only in your head, it will always be a bit fuzzy and far less effective. As soon as you start writing it down it will become both clearer and more real to you, starting to stoke your belief that it could all be possible for you.

Tip 2: Emotional and analytical

In working with members and *Next Level* coaching clients on their Big Picture Vision it's become clear that people tend to fall into one of two categories:

1.   Primarily analytical
2.   Primarily emotional

Specifically, some people will produce a very emotional, romantic, inspiring description of the kind of musician they want to be, while others will produce something more like a checklist of skills and abilities.

Neither is better or worse. They are both vital components of a powerful Big Picture Vision.

The tip is that whichever you tend to do by default, make a conscious effort to fill in the other side. It may be a bit uncomfortable, but hopefully you can see that if your Big Picture Vision is only one side or the other, you'll be missing out on a lot of its power and potential for you.

Tip 3: Make it a living document

Doing the exercise for the first time is a huge leap forwards for most musicians, but your Big Picture Vision isn't a "one and done" kind of thing. It's something to keep coming back to and keep front of mind.

I would encourage you to feel free to edit it as often as you want. It probably will stay mostly the same because it's meant to capture your true yearning, that true destination you've always known inside you were aiming for. But at the same time, we're constantly learning and it is a journey. Things are going to change, priorities are going to shift, and you're going to make progress towards that vision.

So just like an aeroplane on autopilot has a fixed destination but is constantly making small adjustments (or sometimes large ones!) along the way, it's perfectly okay to update your Big Picture Vision, and even rethink things if something big shifts for you. Let it be a living document.

Tip 4: Keep it front of mind

As mentioned above, if you write this and then shove it in a drawer and never think about it again, it won't do you a great deal of good.

Instead, find a way to keep it continually front-of-mind.

Many Musical U members have their Big Picture Vision printed out and stuck on the wall in their music practice area. Inside the members website we show your Big Picture Vision right there on your dashboard.

Figure out where you can put it that means you'll often spot it and be reminded of what it's all about for you. That way you will regularly get an automatic motivation boost (as well as a reminder to revisit it and re-evaluate when appropriate).

Tip 5: Shoot for the moon

One of my favourite quotes is from the godfather of positive thinking, Norman Vincent Peale:

"Shoot for the moon. Even if you miss, you'll land among the stars."

There's a lot that can be said about goal-setting, but it's important to understand that the Big Picture Vision exercise is not about setting goals! It's about defining your *vision*, which will motivate, inspire, and guide you (with plenty of realistic goals to be set and achieved along the way).

There's a time and a place for "SMART" goals and being realistic, and of course the last thing we want to do is set ourselves up for disappointment. But if you allow your Big Picture Vision to be more about the spirit of your musical ambition than about "goal-setting and planning" you will have far more success in your musical life.

So set your ambitions high. Shoot for the moon. That will drive you forwards more effectively, it will motivate you more effectively, and it will help make sure that you reach your fullest potential.

Tip 6: Don't be afraid to share it

There are varying opinions on whether you should tell people about ambitious goals or not, and I'm very conscious that not every musician has supportive, encouraging peers around them like musicians inside Musical U do.

So I can understand that you might feel very hesitant to share your newly-written Big Picture Vision with anybody.

But again, remember that this isn't about setting a goal and telling everybody you're going to accomplish it by a certain date. It's about getting crystal-clear about why you do music, and the kind of musician you dream of becoming.

So if you do have a "safe space" where no-one will tear you down, criticise or discourage you, like we've cultivated among our membership community, I would strongly encourage you to be brave and share your Big Picture Vision.

You might be surprised at the support and encouragement you receive, and that will only help you stay focused and motivated in pursuing that vision over time.

Tip 7: Be ruthless

This may sound funny—but I would advise you to be as ruthless as you can about pursuing your Big Picture Vision.

It comes back to that "shiny object syndrome" danger. Once you're clear on that "North Star", really trust it and be ruthless about what does not fit it.

A lot of us come to music learning with a lot of baggage as to what we "should" do, and how music learning is "meant" to go, and what practice "should" look like.

You can use your Big Picture Vision as a filter and just be very ruthless about it. *"Nope, that's not for me. That seems interesting but I'm not going to go in that direction, because it's not aligned with where I'm trying to get to."*

This applies both to external "distractions" and external "shoulds". In *Chapter Six: Superlearning* we'll be going deeper on this idea of truly taking ownership and responsibility for designing your own practice, and your own learning journey as a whole.

Again, the key point is that it's really empowering to have your concrete definition of your ideal destination in mind. That way you always know what matters to you, and that all the other stuff can safely wait (or be ignored entirely).

Tip 8: Ask for help

If there's one secret to our success at Musical U it's that we've always put a huge emphasis on providing personal support and guidance.

So whether you're pursuing your Big Picture Vision with our help or not, I would be remiss if I didn't throw in this last tip, which is to encourage you to (please!) ask for help when you need it.

If you're struggling to define a good, clear, motivating Big Picture Vision, get together with a musical friend and talk about it with them. If you're having trouble figuring out what resources or approaches are aligned with your vision and which aren't, get a second opinion. If you find your motivation waning and your Big Picture Vision doesn't seem to be re-stoking your fire the way it's meant to, get some help digging into what might be missing.

Our team and community particularly love helping with this kind of thing, but even outside of Musical U, please don't be shy about asking for help when you need it!

Your Musical Core

Who are you, as a musician?

In the previous chapter we laid out a long list of skills which contribute to a person's musicality. I expect that some of these skills you could relate to and identify with, while others currently felt irrelevant or out of reach. We also introduced the H4 Model of Complete Musicality (Head, Hands, Hearing and Heart) and I invited you to reflect on how much attention you've been giving each of these H's, and how you could develop them all in a more holistic and integrated way in future. And I shared the idea of "The Complete Musician", as one who *can step into any musical situation with confidence and play something that sounds—and feels—great."*

Now that you've spent a bit of time pondering your Big Picture Vision (and hopefully even writing it out, in some detail), you likely have a new perspective on the musician you want to become.

Perhaps you realised that as exciting as that long list of skills was, and as amazing as it might be to become that "Complete Musician", actually your own Big Picture Vision had a certain focus to it.

This might have stemmed from limiting beliefs about what's possible for you—and as we continue in this chapter I'm going to share some beliefs and mindsets which can help you break open a whole new level of aspiration and possibility in your musical life.

But it will also have reflected your own unique musical identity.

At Musical U we hope to nurture every member, and especially our *Next Level* coaching clients, towards becoming that "Complete Musician"—because it represents someone who *can* do anything they wish to in music. But that doesn't mean you have any obligation to!

The flip side of this point is really important: even if you do aspire to one day be the Complete Musician, it does not mean that you need to do "all of the things, all of the time".

Something we've discovered over the years at Musical U is that even though every musician is different, and even if they *did* all aspire to one day be "The Complete Musician", in fact there are three clear archetypes we see. Each one has their own direction and focus for their musical passion. We refer to these as the three "Musical Cores".

I'd like to share these with you now, because our members have been finding it extremely helpful and clarifying. Just like personality profiles such as DISC or Myers-Briggs, they are imperfect and incomplete as representations of "who you are"—but just like personality profiles, they can still provide deeper self-understanding and clearer self-identity. These three archetypes can help you to understand who you are as a musician, and what kind of musician you most want to become.

As you read through the descriptions, I invite you to see which of them resonates most with you—both in terms of your musical journey so far, and the musician you described in your Big Picture Vision.

The "Performer" Core

The "Performer" loves playing music they've prepared in advance.

They focus on gradually building up a repertoire of pieces or songs they can perform well, and improving the reliability, accuracy, and musical expression of their performances.

The "Jammer" Core

The "Jammer" loves to just dive in and figure it out.

They focus on developing their in-the-moment instinctive ability to express music that fits, and would probably rather try something new than refine something they've learned already.

The "Creative" Core

The "Creative" loves to conjure up their own musical ideas.

They focus on expressing their own, personal creativity, whether that's on-the-fly with improvisation, or through activities like songwriting, composing or arranging.

Your Unique Core

Which of the three Cores resonated most with you? We've found that in most cases there is a single one which stands out for a musician —but if you found yourself thinking *"well, I'm a bit of this, a bit of that"* or *"I love all three of those"* you're certainly not alone either!

Note that all three Cores can involve sharing your music with others, or not. So don't assume that a musician with a Performer Core is necessarily out there on stages, the Jammer is always joining in live with others, or that the Creative has yet shared their musical creations with anybody just yet! We see that activity of sharing your music as a step on the path of these three Cores. It's something we'd encourage as early as possible, but by no means a pre-requisite for you to identify as one of them.

You may find that a single one of these brought immediate clarity for you. One of the most common reactions we hear is a great sense of *relief*. You may suddenly understand why you've been drawn to certain aspects of learning music but repelled by others, and the knowledge that these three archetypes exist, and no one of them is any "better" or "worse" than the others, can bring a sudden and welcome sense of self-acceptance.

Here's the thing. Although these three archetypes provide a helpful perspective, and you *might* identify strongly with one and not the others, the reality is that *your musical core is unique.*

In fact, you might find it helpful to sketch a little pie chart of how your own Musical Core feels to you:

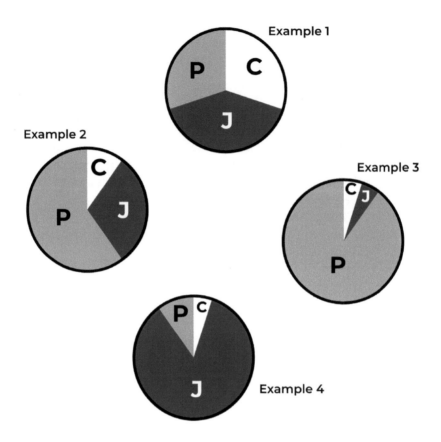

You could do this twice: once to reflect "you now", and one to reflect the version of you which you imagined in your Big Picture Vision.

This can help guide you throughout your musical training. We'll provide some light pointers in the rest of the book, as to which skills and activities are most suited to each Core—but you can probably already see that for yourself. If you cast your eye down the table of contents for this book, with your own unique Musical Core in mind, I suspect you will immediately know which will be most valuable and impactful for you.

Achieving Your Musical Potential

I hope that the Big Picture Vision exercise and this idea of Your Musical Core have been enlightening and inspiring for you.

And yet... if experience has taught me anything, it's that you might immediately also be feeling blocked from that inspiration and aspiration. Perhaps you heard a nagging voice saying *"well, that sounds nice... but I'd never actually get there."*

So I want to share with you a set of Pillar Beliefs and Mindsets which can help to quiet that nagging voice, shift some false (and limiting) beliefs about your musical potential, and free you up to proceed through the rest of this book in a way that lets you move at full speed in developing your Core and achieving that Big Picture Vision.

Pillar Beliefs

Everything we do at Musical U is built on four "pillar" beliefs. These emerged over the years not as something hypothetical which we wanted to believe—but as a way to encapsulate what we in the team clearly did believe, and how we do everything we do.

I'd like to offer you these four beliefs, which you can choose to adopt for yourself. You'll find they can be inspiring, encouraging, supportive, reassuring, comforting—but most of all, empowering.

As you read through these, they may or may not ring true. If any seem fanciful or overly romantic to you now, I'd invite you to return to this chapter again after reading more of the book. You might find, as we have, that these begin to seem less like "beliefs" and more like simple, self-evident truths.

Musical Inside and Out

Every person has a natural connection to music.

By developing the "inner skills" of musicality, anybody can learn to understand music instinctively, find their musical voice, and feel free, confident and creative in music.

At Musical U we have a vision of every person on the planet feeling empowered to reach their highest potential in music. We have a firm belief that everyone is already innately musical and has the fundamental capacity to achieve whatever they want to in music.

For historical reasons we've ended up with mainstream music education focusing almost exclusively on the "outer" skills of music-making, specifically "how to play an instrument". The "inner" skills are expected to just magically be there, or somehow automatically develop over time.

While the outer skills are, of course, important, there are three major reasons to really focus on becoming "musical inside and out":

1. When all you can do is play the notes you're told to, either from dots on a page or rote-learning, you never feel true ownership of the music. It's easy to fall into feeling like a music-reproducing robot, and continually reinforce the idea that you're "not naturally musical".

2. The inner skills are what create musical freedom for you. Whether that's playing a song you just heard or remember (without needing to run off and find the sheet music), conjuring up your own musical ideas on-the-fly in improvisation or composing, or just knowing you've "got music inside you" and will have something of value to contribute when joining in with other musicians—until you feel like you're bringing the music out from inside you, you'll never feel truly free in music.

3. It's aligned with the natural spirit of music. Throughout the ages, music has been a natural part of what it means to be human, and the deep biological connection to music-making is very much an "inside and out" phenomenon.

This is a vital belief to adopt because without it, you'll be prone to the biggest danger to your musical success: losing hope.

The "inner skills" being missing from almost all mainstream music education is no small part of why a heart-breakingly high proportion of people who start learning an instrument give up within their first 18 months.

The sad state of things in almost every country around the world is that most people consider themselves not musically gifted or not naturally musical. And even those who have devoted hours, weeks, months, years, in some cases even decades of their life to learning music, still feel predominantly *un*-natural with it.

The reason? They've only been shown how to be musical "on the outside", not how to bring the music out from inside themselves.

The more we can empower you to be *Musical Inside And Out*, the more fulfilled you will be and the higher potential you will be able to reach in music.

(Side note: the word "voice" in the definition above wasn't an accident. We also believe that singing is your natural first instrument, and every musician should be a singer too. But more on that in a later chapter...)

Andrew Says...

Musical Inside And Out is the idea of connecting with the musicality that we have within, having faith that we have that within us, and then being able to bring it out and manifest it.

Because so many people have such a powerful connection with music, they can hear it in their minds, and they're wondering "why can't I make this happen?"

We help people make that connection with the music that's inside them and be able to bring it out to their own personal and musical satisfaction.

Musical Inside And Out is about connecting with the innermost parts of oneself and bringing them forth and expressing them through music. It's about who I am inside, and my expression, and who I am in the world, and how I'm relating to other people through music, or giving to people through music, or to myself... There are no obstacles there.

Universal Potential

Every music learner is different – but all have the potential to become a highly capable musician and feel fulfilled in reaching their own true potential in music.

Adults and children each have their own advantages in learning and age is no barrier to fast, enjoyable music learning.

The vision we have is one in which everyone takes for granted that they can learn all of the amazing musical skills of musicality we discussed in the last chapter.

Nice idea. But is it really possible?

Improvising, playing by ear, jamming, performing with confidence, writing music, singing, having great rhythm, collaborating easily with other musicians…

If you took a random 100 people on the street, I bet 95 of them would say:

"You've got to have a gift to do that"
"You've got to be talented to do that."
"I can't do that. I'm not naturally musical."

With our members inside Musical U, we see clear proof every day that these things are all learnable, and by anyone. We have seen so many examples of breakthroughs and transformations and of those identity shifts from *"I am learning music"* or *"I'm just a hobbyist"* to *"I've got that instinct, I've got that intuition for how to play. I can pick up my instrument, and the music comes from inside me, out through my instrument."*

Sadly that's just not the case in the vast majority of music education (online or offline). If you look around, most everyone is still learning from notation, they're learning by rote memorisation or from a step-by-step video tutorial. They're feeling like they can only play the notes somebody else has told them to play. And that is a huge part of why most end up feeling disillusioned and very low in musical self-esteem.

The *Universal Potential* belief says that every music learner is different, but *all* have the potential to become a highly capable musician and feel fulfilled in reaching their own true potential in music.

Everyone's musical journey is uniquely their own. The fact that everyone can do this does not mean everyone is exactly the same in music, or that a single "method" can magically work perfectly for everyone. It just means everyone is capable of the highest heights.

It's also important to know that adults and children each have their own advantages in learning. We find a lot of people start out thinking *"kids can learn music quickly but it's harder for adults."* And there's a grain of truth to that. As a parent myself, I can attest that kids certainly can be "like a sponge" for new learning!

But adults have more discipline and persistence. They have clearer motivation (especially if armed with a well-defined Big Picture Vision!). They can more easily plan and structure their practice. They can comprehend more advanced concepts more quickly. They have a lifetime of absorbed musical knowledge in their subconscious that they can draw on, a stronger instinctive sense of "how music works". And, as you're demonstrating right now by reading this book, they have an unlimited capacity to continue learning and striving to reach their fullest potential.

I'd also like to mention in passing that the scientific research on brain plasticity, coupled with the accelerated learning and rapid memorisation techniques you'll be learning about later in this book, mean that it's entirely realistic to expect yourself to learn as fast, if not much faster, as an adult than you would have as a kid.

So this belief is, in a way, a rejection of two false beliefs many adult musicians are burdened by:

- The talent myth ("those people can do it, but I can't, because I'm not naturally good enough")— more on that below when we talk about Growth Mindset.

- The age myth ("it's too late for me. I wish I'd started learning music as a kid, or kept it up instead of letting it fall aside over time. Now it's unrealistic for me to still reach my musical dreams")

The *Universal Potential* belief flips both of those on their head, and empowers you to achieve everything you've been dreaming of.

So when we talk about our vision of "a world of natural musicians" we're really talking about a world where anyone, from age 5 up to age 105, knows with certainty: *"I can learn whatever I want to in music. Those amazing musicians I admire, I could be like them."*

Instead of generation after generation being trained as musical robots, we aim to put musicality back at the heart of music education, the way it genuinely was centuries ago when these things were taken for granted as an inherent part of what it meant to "be a musician".

Stewart Says...

We've had many people who have come in with that baggage of feeling like they're tone deaf, they can't do music, they can't keep a beat. It's not that they just can't do it, it's that they've never had the chance to learn it.

We're seeing people who come in totally shy, they only want to play at home. And they learn their musicality, they get into it, and now they're performing for everyone on our live calls.

Zac Says...

We can do anything. We are, at our innate selves, creative and musical. Universal Potential means I can expand my creative mind into the universe, and then just constantly be attracting new worlds. Everyone has that power inside them to create new worlds.

Better Together

Learning happens faster when it's done among like-minded friends and with direct access to personal help from experts who genuinely care about your success.

We are committed to a spirit of collaboration, not competition, and always excited to work with other music educators for the benefit of music learners.

Confession time: I nearly didn't include any community features in Musical U when we launched it in 2015.

As a firm introvert myself, who is perfectly happy going for days on end without speaking to another living soul, as well as being a scientifically-minded person who's generally focused on methods and exercises and practical solutions, the idea of adding "social chit-chat" to our training website didn't strike me as a particularly helpful thing to do. In fact, I was worried it would dilute the effectiveness of everyone's musicality training, by providing constant distraction like social media.

Fortunately I listened to wiser, more experienced online educators. And the results soon blew me away.

From the very beginning the power of community became clear.

We saw members learning tips and tricks from each other as much as from the material we provided. We were able to continually improve the material based on their shared experiences. And what surprised me most was the clear power of community to inspire and motivate our members, and keep them in continual momentum with their training.

On top of that, having access to personal help from a human expert was an absolute game-changer for our members. It really is a night-and-day difference.

We saw that the members who thrived and had the biggest breakthroughs were those who engaged most with the community and support on offer, while those who kept quiet and just used the material in isolation had good, but much lesser results. There was, and still is, a clear correlation between community engagement and results.

Community acts as an amplifier for everything you do. When you're sharing that journey with other people, it expands and accelerates what you do, and everyone gets better together.

That's true inside Musical U, but it is true universally. Whatever musical community you can assemble around you can have the same effect.

I'll be honest—there's a small part of me that wishes this wasn't true!

Like with anything involving human beings, it makes everything more complicated. Part of me still wishes we could just create good material, hand it over, and be done with it! But with almost a decade of experience running the membership, I know it would be a crime against the people who come to us for musicality training to do that.

A book like this is, by nature, something you go through alone. But like I mentioned in the introduction, I knew it couldn't just be "a textbook". And I knew we had to make sure we really emphasised this Pillar Belief for you.

Don't make the mistake of trying to "go it alone" in music.

The second part of this belief is about collaboration not competition, and I'd suggest thinking about that in two ways:

Firstly, if you're encountering musicians who are competitive, and elitist, and exclusionary—please run in the other direction, fast.

There is still a lot of that going on in certain musical communities. It's a painful byproduct of the "talent myth", everyone trying to prove that they are special. We're *all* special. Surround yourself with musicians who believe that too, and who will build you up, not tear you down.

The other way to think about this is when choosing who to learn from in music. I'm happy to say that across all the online music educators I've had the pleasure to connect with over the past 15 years or so, the majority do share this spirit of collaboration. Like us, they're happy to recommend another provider or resource than their own if it will better serve the student. It's why we have a prominent "Friends" page on our public website, why we're regularly recommending other resources to our members, and why we're vocal about the vision and mission we're pursuing—because we'll get there much faster if we're all working together.

> ## Hannah Says...
>
> *As a community we can support each other, we can share our musicality, and we can learn from each other. Not just from our teachers, but from the people that are alongside us. And generally, the more we share, the more we can learn.*
>
> *Music is about sharing and collaborating together. It's about communication. I've seen how much our members spark off each other, how much they rely on that shared experience. Hearing other people sharing 'I found this difficult too, but now I've got it' and taking encouragement and inspiration from that.*

Enjoying the Journey

Learning music is a lifelong journey with endless new horizons to explore.

With a flexible approach which nurtures creativity from the start and makes use of the latest breakthroughs in the science of effective learning, this journey can be one of ease, joy and continual improvement.

We've touched on this one in various ways already, so hopefully you've already gathered that our goal with this book (and everything we do at Musical U) is absolutely to help you achieve real concrete results—but with a spirit of ease and joy. Not the painful drudgery, beating yourself up, and brute-force approach which is unfortunately the default in status quo music education.

Your musical journey can be just as rich, varied, and limitless as music itself.

There is, of course, enormous value in setting clear goals, being diligent and consistent about pursuing them, practicing carefully, and "putting in the work".

But the surprising truth is that "fun" is not the opposite of "learning".

As you'll be discovering later in the book, adding more creativity, exploration, experimentation, and a spirit of play to your music learning actually makes it more effective, not less.

We see so many musicians who've fallen into the trap of thinking if they want better results, they have to work harder. If they're enjoying themselves too much, they must be doing it wrong. Gradually all the life and enthusiasm gets sucked out of their music-making.

This is another common reason for people to give up completely. Even worse, they walk away from music blaming themselves, thinking they "didn't have what it takes" or "didn't have enough discipline".

The truth is they just forgot about *Enjoying The Journey*.

As adult learners we tend to be particularly prone to this. A lifetime of "should"s, a factory-style education system, and endless rote-learning have drilled into most of us that learning is "hard work" and if you don't struggle and suffer, you won't get results. The saying "no pain, no gain" is perhaps the clearest description of that attitude. In Chapter Six: Superlearning we'll unpack this in more detail, because there is a grain of truth to it. Overall though, it will tend to lead you in exactly the wrong direction in music learning, and threaten the very passion that keeps you moving forwards.

You'll find that this book is packed with ways to develop your musicality while keeping your passion for music burning bright. Just remember that enjoying yourself can actually be a sign you're doing it *right*.

Adam Says...

There are constantly new things that we can explore. Music is a never-ending gift, where once you think you've made it, you discover a new genre or a new instrument... we encourage just being creative. The journey is just as important as the destination.

Stewart Says...

I knew a guitar teacher who, when a student first started, the first lesson, no matter what their goals were, was to have them memorize scales and modes.

This was their whole first month of learning the guitar. Doesn't that sound fun?

Andrew Says...

Enjoyment is a choice. We can actually choose to enjoy ourselves. We can put joy into what we are doing. There is no way to happiness, happiness is the way. Look for the opportunity to make things easy and joyful, while still getting the work done. If you can just stop and relax and remind yourself that 'ease and joy' is the quickest path forwards, there's almost always a nearby solution that can help you find that.

The "Talent Myth"

"I think [what holds musicians back] is being concerned with what other people think, and a feeling that the people who make great things are somehow special, and that they [themselves] are not special.

And that's just not true. Everyone has the capability to make great things—and none of us are special."
                    — Legendary music producer Rick Rubin

Most musicians today are burdened by society's ideas about "talent" in music. We've already touched on this several times so far. And I wanted to begin this short section with that Rick Rubin quote because it captures the slight subtlety we need to be aware of when confronting this issue.

At this stage, science has conclusively proven that there is no such thing as a magical "talent" you need to be born with to accomplish great things in music, and that every impressive high-level musical skill is learnable.

I won't go into all the scientific research and proof here. That would literally take a book in itself! If you'd like to know more, I highly recommend picking up one of the several pop science books such as "Talent is Over-rated" by Geoff Colvin, "Peak" (by Professor Anders Ericsson, who carried out much of the most significant original research on the topic), or others you'll find in the Reading List in the *Additional Resources*. If you're a podcast listener you might also enjoy my interview with Professor Ericsson where we discussed the truth about "talent", also linked in the Additional Resources.

For our purposes here, it's enough to take it as a given that the idea of a magical, mysterious "talent" or having a "gift" for music is simply untrue. If you find yourself skeptical about this, I encourage you to dive into this topic and learn just how clear-cut the research findings are. Or, you can simply "take it for testing" as one of my mentors likes to say, and discover for yourself the truth about your own "talent", as you start to apply what you'll learn in this book.

So the science is clear: "talent" is a myth. And yet most people today still believe whole-heartedly in that myth!

It's easy to see why. The Talent Myth is constantly reinforced by our celebrity culture and media. We put the "greats" up on a pedestal and tacitly imply that those people are a breed apart. The regular person in the street should admire them, but it would be unrealistic to aspire to that level of ability themselves.

It's also a romantic notion, which appeals to a certain part of our psychology. And that's where the slight subtlety mentioned above comes in...

When we choose to recognise the scientific reality, and acknowledge that behind every apparent child prodigy or overnight success actually lay an extensive amount of very specific learning and practice, our intention is not in any way to diminish the accomplishments of those "greats". On the contrary, it's to fully respect all the effort and expert skill development which let them accomplish their great feats. If anything, it actually makes them even more impressive.

It may be romantic to imagine these heaven-blessed aliens who can do things in music no mere mortal could ever hope to—but I would propose that it's equally romantic in its own way to imagine all the diligent, devoted, heartfelt toil that went in to turning themselves into the kinds of musicians who seem so other-worldly.

Here's a suggestion, to help you start ingraining this new mindset, that talent is no more than a myth:

When we see an incredible musician, our default response, ingrained in us by society, may well be to feel intimidated. *"Gosh,"* we think, *"I wish I'd been born with that kind of talent!"*. When we accept that talent is just a myth, we can choose instead to feel inspired. *"Wow,"* we can think, *"I can't wait until I can play like that!"*

This simple shift, from "intimidation" to "inspiration", is a small one. But it will make a profound difference in your musical life.

Growth Mindset

Once you escape the false constraints of the Talent Myth, the world is your oyster! To some, that's immediately exciting. To others, overwhelming.

That's why it's vital to also adopt a "Growth Mindset". And whether you've been aware of it before now or not, the chances are high you currently operate under what's called a "Fixed Mindset" in your musical life. This may only affect certain areas or skills, or it may be happening across all your music learning. Either way, if you want to reach your true musical potential, it's important to really understand this concept and become aware of how it's affecting your musical journey.

A behavioural psychologist named Carol Dweck found that people with what she came to call a "Fixed Mindset" believe that they have a certain set of innate capabilities—and all they can ever hope for is to struggle their way towards those built-in limitations. There are things they're naturally good at or bad at, and the sensible thing is to steer clear of things they're bad at and try to get better at things they're good at.

That sounds perfectly reasonable—and certainly in line with what society tells us is true. Except that the research shows it's pretty much nonsense.

In fact, there's a different mindset which demonstrates this clearly. And simply by choosing to adopt this alternative mindset, the very same person can quickly become "good" at things they were previously "bad" at.

"Growth" Mindset is the belief that anything is learnable for you. And that struggling or making mistakes is actually a good thing because it shows you where you can improve.

Here's a comparison:

A Fixed Mindset says...	A Growth Mindset says...
Your abilities are limited to what you were born with.	Your abilities come from work and can be improved.
Challenges are to be avoided.	Challenges are to be embraced as an opportunity to grow.
Making an effort just means you're not naturally good enough.	Effort is an essential ingredient of mastery.
Feedback is something to be taken personally.	Feedback is useful.
Setbacks are discouraging.	Setbacks help, by revealing to you what to do next.

People with a Growth Mindset accomplish more than those with a Fixed Mindset by pretty much any measure, and enjoy the process more.

Here's the kicker: it's a choice. This isn't "Fixed *trait*" vs. "Growth *trait*". It's not a genetic thing, it's a mindset which you can simply choose to adopt.

Choosing a Growth Mindset is probably the #1 most important thing you can do for your success in learning music—or life in general!

Now, I'm not going to pretend it's easy to shake off the shackles of perhaps decades of Fixed Mindset thinking. But you can do it, and step increasingly into that Growth Mindset. As you do, you'll find yourself more and more able to learn new skills, improve quickly, and reach levels of ability you might have always assumed were beyond you.

In fact the only thing that can truly limit you is the belief that you're limited.

Commit now to cultivating your Growth Mindset, and I promise you a double payoff.

First, you'll find that whole new levels of possibility and opportunity open up for you. And second, you'll be able to relax and enjoy the process a lot more too (a.k.a. *Enjoying The Journey*).

In particular I would really encourage you to take a different view on struggle than you may have in the past. When you try something and it's hard, or you feel like you're just not "getting it", or you start having those thoughts of *"I don't have what it takes"*, I would invite you to remember Growth Mindset. See those moments not as a negative sign that you should give up—but on the contrary, a sign that you have found the opportunity to improve, and you are in exactly the right spot to gain the skills you set out to.

Be on the lookout for that inner voice which resists learning when things get tough, or starts to scupper your momentum with discouragement or self-doubt. You're going to replace it by choosing to think instead *"these challenges are awesome, this is where I'm going to learn"* and *"I'm having trouble right now. Cool, that means I'm pushing myself into new learning and exciting new abilities are on their way."*

Having a Growth Mindset makes an enormous difference to how much and how fast you can learn. And of course Growth Mindset is itself a learnable skill! So don't worry if that "Fixed Mindset" list sounded more like you right now.

If you can cultivate that kind of positive, encouraging self-talk, all based on the idea that everything is absolutely learnable for you, I think you will be amazed at the difference it makes.

Beginner's Mind

> *"I can't understand why people are frightened of new ideas. I'm frightened of the old ones."*
>
> — John Cage

Beginner's Mind is a concept from Zen Buddhism, and the idea is simply that you try to see the world with fresh eyes and treat every experience like you are a beginner going through it for the first time. Whatever your background, whatever your experience, whatever your past beliefs and preconceptions, you show up as if you're a beginner, and you look to see what there might be to learn.

Why? Because if we don't, we are cheating ourselves out of a substantial amount of the potential learning available to us.

However smart and experienced we might be, we never learn it all the first time through. There are always some gold nuggets just waiting for you if you return to the same topic again. On top of that, when you return to the same fundamentals, you often find new depths and layers to propel you even further forwards. But you can only spot those opportunities if you come in open-minded. With a "Beginner's Mind".

This is why the best sports coaches have their team constantly focused on fundamentals. Like the legendary basketball coach John Wooden taking considerable time on the first day of practice each year to teach his players how to properly tie their shoes. Or american football coach Vince Lombardi bringing his players right back to the basics by starting out the season with *"Gentlemen, this is a football"*.

It's why many of the most successful investors have the simplest investment strategies. And it's why even at a very high level in music, wind players are constantly doing "long tones" practice.

It's often the things we might write off as "beginner-level stuff" that actually has the highest potential impact for us.

There is a lot that could be unpacked on this topic, and how it relates to things like mindfulness and humility and mastery. It's a powerful and wide-ranging principle.

The most impactful point is that Beginner's Mind lets you shed all your preconceptions, your emotional and psychological baggage, and any limiting beliefs and unhelpful assumptions that might have accumulated in the past. It lets you really be open to absorbing something new.

At Musical U we've seen so clearly and consistently how absolutely vital it is that you be willing to take a Beginner's Mind.

If you come into musicality training, or even this book specifically, ready to say *"yep, I know that"* or *"skip the easy stuff!"* or *"I'll do it differently because I know better"*, you're going to be cheating yourself out of the results you came for.

The solution to that is very simple: remind yourself to see things as if you are a beginner.

If you make that simple mindset shift, you'll be amazed at the riches and discoveries that are waiting for you.

You don't need to just take my word for it though. Here are three specific reasons to take this seriously:

1. **In every field, the top experts extol the virtues of "focusing on fundamentals".** Remember that often the seemingly-simple things are the most critical for true mastery.

2. **As adult learners we can really get in our own way.** It's awkward and painful for an adult to admit we don't know something, or to allow for the idea that we might still have something to learn when it comes to the basics. We often miss out on learning because we've decided in advance that we know it all—or at least want to appear (to others or just to ourselves) that we know it all already.
   Even when we are well informed, we have blind spots. We "don't know what we don't know". That's why it's so valuable to stay open to the possibility that there's more yet to be discovered in familiar topics.

3. **Music is an art, not a science.** It's easy to think that understanding something intellectually is all there is. We forget what children know instinctively to be true: that learning means *doing,* and just because you know how something is supposed to work it doesn't mean it's not worth testing and experimenting and exploring deeply.

I won't pretend this has been easy for me! I know from personal experience how hard it is sometimes to put yourself back in the beginner's shoes. But it is one of *the* most powerful mindset shifts you can make.

Any time you find yourself thinking *"I know this already!"* or *"this is too easy!"* or you're feeling resistance because you feel something's not a fit for you, remember that child-like curiosity, and openness to discovering something new. Remind yourself that it's always valuable to firm up fundamentals, and there's often treasure waiting for those who bother to come around again.

If you can approach your learning always willing to be open to the possibility that something that seems familiar or something that "you already know" actually might be well worth exploring afresh, I guarantee that is going to pay massive dividends for you.

So I invite you to adopt that mindset now and try to keep reminding yourself of it.

You can ask questions like these to help:

- "What would a beginner hear, see, or experience here?

- "How is this different to what I've heard before?"

- "How does this apply to me, my instrument, my music?"

- "Am I doing this fully already—or are there some new opportunities here?"

You might be approaching a musical term, a concept, a skill, a track or genre. Really, anything you encounter in your musical journey. Open yourself up to experiencing it in a fresh new way, allowing for the possibility that something you thought you just "knew" or was "obvious" actually might yet have a lot to be revealed to you.

When you take a Beginner's Mind, not only do you avoid the big trap of thinking *"I know this already"* and skimming over (or even skipping entirely) some lessons that still have plenty to teach you, you're also able to glean much more from going through that material, because at every moment, you're actually *allowing* learning to take place at a much higher level. You're priming the brain to be on the lookout for new ideas and new understanding, rather than going in with a slightly disengaged attitude that will only notice the biggest, most glaring learning points.

It's like switching your brain from a hardened piece of clay that really requires work to change shape at all, back into soft putty that can be shaped and moulded with ease. Or like taking a sponge that's already saturated and can't absorb any more, into a fresh new sponge that's just itching to soak up something new.

The challenge is to set your ego aside, quiet that voice that says *"I know this already"* or *"this is a waste of time"*, and be humble—be proud even—to be a beginner. And feel excited that perhaps even some seemingly very basic things might yet have secrets in store.

Trial and Improvement

You know that Baz Luhrmann song? The one that starts: *"If I could offer you one tip for the future... sunscreen would be it."*

Well, sunscreen is great. But if I could offer you one credo or motto to live by, "Trial and Improvement" would be it.

I remember first hearing this phrase back in school during a maths lesson. We were doing some problem-solving that involved gradually finding the right answer through trial and error. The teacher told us to use the phrase "trial and improvement" instead, because it more accurately captured how we were gradually moving towards the right answer.

That has always stuck in my head, because we're so indoctrinated to think "errors" are bad and something to feel ashamed of—whereas "improvement" is something to be proud of and aspire to. Just changing that wording somehow really altered the emotional experience of doing those exercises, and our success with them.

A lot of the musicality skills we'll be exploring in this book can seem like "all or nothing" skills. Something you can either do, or you can't. In fact, each of the skills of musicality exists on a spectrum—just like any musical skill.

For many musicality skills, musicians tend to think they belong right at the "zero" end of the spectrum. And so it's vitally important to understand that the way to learn these skills is not to instantly, magically jump to the other end of the spectrum. It's to travel along that spectrum from one end to the other, step-by-step. Just like with any skill we learn.

In this book you'll discover the frameworks, techniques, and building blocks which let you move along the spectrum of each skill much more quickly. But you cannot jump to the other end of the spectrum where you have mastery of the skill in one leap. The only way to get there is being willing to travel along the spectrum, step-by-step.

That means tolerating making "mistakes" along the way. And none of it works if you get stuck in nervousness, embarrassment or self-doubt. Because mistakes are part of the process, and mastering skills is a process of trying, testing, experimenting. Just like in those maths exercises when I was a kid, it's "trial and improvement" that will get you to the right answer.

As you travel along the spectrum, you are always going to be pushing your comfort zone, and trying increasingly challenging things. That means you're always going to need to tolerate mistakes and your own current limitations, as part of the learning process.

Remember: Tak Courag.

Each time you practice, you are taking a concrete step forwards. All you need to do is show up, and keep courageously taking steps forwards, and not letting limiting beliefs around mistakes or errors hold you back.

Here's a critical thing to keep in mind: it works this way for everyone.

This isn't a cop-out method you use if you're not "gifted". Again, every skill we think might be a "talent" or a "gift" is actually learnable, and has been learned by those who can do it.

Even if you encounter a musician who has a great ability to play by ear, for example, I guarantee they didn't get every note right the first time they tried it! What distinguishes them from all the musicians who can't play by ear is only their trial-and-improvement process, and whether they had the courage to persist or not.

It's a really exciting and empowering feeling as a musician when you take another clear step along the spectrum, knowing that you've earned your progress.

If you can adopt this "trial and improvement" mindset as you apply everything you learn in this book to accelerate your journey, then I guarantee you'll be delighted by the exciting progress you make along the spectrum of whichever skills of musicality contribute to your own Big Picture Vision.

Convergent Learning

Have you ever felt like you were just bashing your head against a brick wall in music learning? It's an all-too-common experience, and you probably know already that the solution is rarely to just "keep bashing" or "bash harder".

Convergent Learning is a kind of "meta tool", meaning a principle for using all the other tools, frameworks and techniques you'll learn. It can also be considered a mindset, since it is very much about how you think about your learning journey and the choices you make along the way.

The principle is simple: approaching the same thing from multiple directions or perspectives delivers better, faster results.

I'll share a few examples below, because I know it might seem odd at first.

In most education contexts we're told that there is a single straight-line "best" path you should follow. When you read a textbook or you go through a typical training course, that's generally the approach. You're shown one particular method, sequence or system, and taught to follow exactly that from A to Z, with the expectation that you will get to the end and achieve the intended results.

I'm confident that you've experienced for yourself just how rarely that actually happens!

It's extremely uncommon for a straight-line course like that to work very well for the majority of students. In some subjects, like learning history, it is a reasonable idea because you're mostly learning facts. In many subjects it fails because (unless there's a high degree of really good personal support) students will get stuck and struggle in various places, often resulting in them losing momentum, giving up, and never reaching the end, let alone accomplishing all the results they came for.

In some subjects, including music, it's simply not a realistic idea to string things together "from step 1 to step 100" in a single, linear path. That's one reason we've always emphasised flexibility and personalisation inside Musical U's training system, and why we focus so much on personal support. To help make sure members can keep moving forwards and succeed in their learning.

It's also why this meta principle of Convergent Learning and approaching the same thing from different angles is so powerful.

When you have multiple ways to approach the same topic, three big things happen:

1. A large group of diverse students can each find their own best approach within the material provided. The same training can cater to a wide variety of backgrounds, learning styles and aspirations, because there's a degree of mix-and-match possible, while still leading to the same overall outcome.

2. Each individual student can approach the same topic in multiple ways, not only finding the ones which work best, but being able to zig and zag, to keep moving forwards if any one way becomes challenging.

3. If it's done right, you end up with something that's greater than the sum of its parts. Meaning not only do you get the benefit of each individual approach, there's a kind of synergy and multiplication that happens, so that it actually ends up being much more effective than any single one of them would

have been.

This is really important to understand—because it's quite different from the norm in most education, including in music.

It would be easy to make the mistake of thinking there would be wasteful repetition, or that if you've already come across one approach to a topic you don't need the others. When you understand the power in Convergent Learning you're able to get the fullest benefit and make fastest progress.

Let's look at three concrete examples to help make that clear.

Example 1: Ear Training

This is a topic we'll cover in depth later in the book, but it will be instructive to take a quick peek now at how we'll approach it.

Traditional Ear Training is done as dry, abstract, isolated exercises. Endless drills for skills like interval recognition. And there is real value in those kinds of exercises, but these alone rarely get the job done.

Alternatively, some people get caught up in all the corresponding theory, memorising interval spellings and going deep on jazz harmony rules, but neglect their ears and never manage to actually do much on their instrument.

Still others focus purely on the playing. They either just work on instrument technique forever and hope that the ear skills will naturally develop automatically over time (which they do, but *incredibly* slowly), or they actively practice playing by ear or improvising. But without having done any dedicated exercises, this is a really painful and frustrating process where it always just feels like you're guessing and hoping.

If you're seeing a one-legged chair in your mind right now, you've got the right idea ;)

The solution is to let yourself draw on the benefits of all three of those. That's what we do with our "Learn, Practice, Apply" *Integrated Ear Training* approach, where you learn the theory, practice the drills, then apply it on your instrument right away. It combines Head, Hands, Hearing and Heart.

Not only do you benefit from each of the three components, you're also developing all the connections between them, and the result is much greater than the sum of its parts.

Example 2: Improvising

Again, we'll be going in depth on this topic in a dedicated chapter later on, but let's see how Convergent Learning is at play.

We teach Improvisation with the *Expansive Creativity* framework. One component of that framework is "Play-Listen/Listen-Play", where again, we take two things which are typically seen as either/or and instead combine them.

Instead of just playing and hoping the right notes come out and making improvements as you go ("Play-Listen"), and instead of trying hard to imagine the perfect music in your head and bringing it out through your instrument correctly ("Listen-Play"), we combine both of those in a loop. This allows us to both express from the inside-out and to learn from what we hear ourselves play.

Again, we end up with something that's greater than the sum of its parts. Without an understanding of this Convergent Learning approach we might make the mistake of thinking they were different approaches and we ought to simply choose one or the other to focus on.

Example 3: Multi-Modal Learning

In Part II you'll be introduced to some powerful mental models for understanding pitch and rhythm instinctively. These are so fundamental and versatile they end up letting you make the connections between notes you hear, imagine, sing, play, read and write.

One reason these approaches work so well is that you don't just start from *"let's learn to read notes, and then bolt on how to audiate or sing those notes, and then learn how to play those notes"* and so on. It's not that kind of straight-line path. Instead, you're able to continually approach the same material in multiple ways, or in multiple "modalities":

- You're hearing it.

- You're singing it.

- You're writing it down by ear.

- You're composing and improvising with it.

Again, not only does it mean the approach works for a wide variety of students, and not only does it let you do a bit of mix-and-matching and focus more on the bits which help you most, it also produces this "bigger and better" effect than any one of those methods or each of them done in isolation would deliver for you.

Convergent Learning for Musicality

So those are three examples of this principle of Convergent Learning in action. It's a really powerful idea to keep in mind as you move through this book and through all your music learning.

Don't assume that picking one approach and really going deep on it will be the most efficient route forwards. Look for these opportunities to come at the same thing from multiple directions, and you'll find it actually helps avoid a lot of sticking points and keep you moving forwards as quickly and enjoyably as possible.

Often the fastest way to learn something is not a straight line "from A to Z" or from "step 1 to step 100". It's to approach the same topic from multiple complementary angles, giving the brain multiple ways to "get a handle" on the thing it's trying to learn.

This is especially effective for musicality training, where we're trying to develop both your conscious understanding of what's going on, and your instinctive recognition and playing skills, and we want to develop all four H's (Head, Hands, Hearing, Heart) and forge connections between them.

Take a "Loose Grip" Mindset

The Convergent Learning process will work best if you do not try to "dot every i and cross every t". Try not to fixate on pinning down every detail of understanding every step along the way. Like in many other musical contexts, that kind of perfectionism is actually your enemy here.

Part of the advantage of this approach is that it can flex and mould itself around you, personally, but that can only happen if you take a slightly loose grip with it. We call this a "Loose Grip" Mindset.

As you continue through this book and along the journey of developing your musicality, you're going to find some things come easily, others not so much. Some things are obviously connected to each other, others don't quite seem to link up.

Be aware that some of the most magical breakthroughs for you are going to come only if you let things stew and simmer a bit along the way. The human brain and musical ear really are phenomenal in what they can accomplish, and how much of it can happen instinctively and subconsciously.

So try to take a "Loose Grip" Mindset and allow that growth to happen. Let go of the need to take 100% responsibility with your conscious mind for every single step along the way.

Take a Loose Grip Mindset, let these ingredients all mix together naturally... and you're going to love how it all ends up converging into something truly incredible.

Conclusion

In this chapter we've covered some of the components which can provide you with an empowering and resilient musical mindset.

Armed with a Big Picture Vision and a sense of your Musical Core, you'll have new clarity and confidence about where you're trying to reach in your musical journey.

Adopting our four Pillar Beliefs can defend you against the negative messages and myths that society otherwise tends to burden us with.

Choosing a Growth Mindset continually keeps you open to reaching your fullest potential, and Beginner's Mind lets you find exciting new opportunities even with familiar musical material.

Setting the expectation that you will develop your skills towards mastery through Trial and Improvement produces fast, consistent progress and keeps you moving forwards step by step, and taking a Loose Grip Mindset allows for Convergent Learning to occur, so that you can benefit fully from the synergistic effects of a range of concepts, methods and practices.

Since starting to teach these Mindset principles inside Musical U it's been striking to see the impact they have on musicians' results. Even more striking is that those who enjoy the most success are those who regularly revisit this material and give their mindset a regular "tune up".

That's why before we dive into the subsequent chapters, which are all more practical and skills-oriented, it's so important to have taken the time to introduce these mindset principles—and why this may well be the chapter you'll want to plan on revisiting the most.

CHAPTER THREE:
AUDIATION

Whether you've ever heard of it or not, Audiation is a core skill which permeates the entirety of your musicality.

It's a skill which many overlook, and most don't think to actively develop. Yet the more you improve this skill, the easier and more effective all your music learning and music-making will become.

Simply put, Audiation is the ability to hear music in your head. It's sometimes called "inner hearing" or "hearing in your mind's ear" (analogous to "seeing in your mind's eye").

It's the aural equivalent of visualisation, and just like visualisation there is a whole spectrum of ability levels, from being able to conjure up only very basic imagined sounds, through to a full, rich "playback" in your mind.

With visualisation, we can imagine either a static, fixed image—or a video-like scene which evolves over time. Music is always expressed with a time component (even a single note you hear or play has a beginning, middle, and end), and so there is a time component to Audiation too. As we'll be exploring below, one aspect of your audiation skills is the length of a musical phrase or excerpt which you can comfortably conjure up. This is closely related to your "musical memory".

Another useful way to describe Audiation is "thinking in sound" or "thinking in music". Just like with spoken language, there is an imagined equivalent (hearing words and sentences in your head as you think), we can develop the ability to "think" in music by hearing it in our mind on demand.

It's worth noting that the word "audiation" was originally coined by the music education pioneer Edwin Gordon, as part of his "Music Learning Theory" approach, and that within that system it has a precise technical meaning. However, it has also come to be used in the more informal way described above, meaning simply "to imagine hearing music in your head". At Musical U we use this more informal definition because it provides a useful catchall for this broad and versatile skill.

Below we'll look at the benefits of Audiation and how it connects to various other musical skills and activities, with a particular highlight on singing. Then we'll explore some ways you can assess and then actively develop your audiation abilities.

Audiation is a powerful skill to develop, but it's important to know: this isn't a new skill to learn from scratch. In fact, you already audiate frequently! Any time you get a song stuck in your head, or you remember a song in your mind, or if I ask you to imagine how "Happy Birthday" goes, as soon as you "hear" music in your head, you are audiating. So although we'll be covering lots of ways to improve your ability to audiate, don't feel intimidated or overwhelmed at all. It's an ability you already have, we're just looking to refine and extend it.

Developing your Audiation has a positive effect on a wide range of musicality skills, and it can significantly increase your overall enjoyment and appreciation of music. Although we'll be making plenty of concrete suggestions for incorporating audiating into your musicality training (for example, as part of our "Listen-Engage-Express" framework for Playing By Ear), it's valuable to keep in mind that Audiation is so fundamental a part of your musicality, that it can and should be part of almost every musical activity you do!

That's why we're featuring this chapter so early in the book. The more you become aware of the role of Audiation and the more you develop your audiation abilities, the more you'll see it is relevant and involved throughout everything you do in music. So although we'll cover some specifics below, please keep in mind that there are no fixed and firm boundaries to Audiation!

Overview

In this chapter we'll begin by looking at the benefits of intentionally improving your audiation abilities and the connections to other areas of musicality. We'll then introduce three levels of Audiation which can be helpful to assess and improve your audiating, and exercises you can do to practice with each level.

Benefits and Connections

It's quite shocking how little Audiation is discussed in mainstream music education, given how widely impactful it can be on so many areas of a person's musicality. Let's look at some of the specific ways that improving and extending your Audiation will benefit you in your musical life.

Musical Memory

An easy way to start thinking about and developing your Audiation skills is with musical memory. Think of a piece of music you're learning to play, or just your favourite song. Stop reading for a moment and see if you can conjure up that music in your mind. Can you hear how it goes? How much of it can you remember? How vividly do you hear it? For example, is it just the rough shape of the melody, or a full, detailed musical arrangement?

When you're just starting out, don't be discouraged if you find your musical memory is surprisingly lacking! It can be a shock to realise that a piece of music you thought you knew well is actually quite difficult to "play back" in your mind, without looking at the notation or having heard a recording of it recently.

On the other hand, you may find that there are certain songs or pieces that you have a clear mental imprint of, and you can "press play" in your mind and hear it almost as vividly as if you were listening on headphones.

Musicians often worry about having a "bad musical memory". We'll be covering memorisation in detail in *Chapter Six: Superlearning*, but for now it's helpful to note that memorising how to play music is distinct from remembering the sound of the music.

Improving your Audiation and improving your musical memory go hand-in-hand, and even if your focus is on remembering how to play the music, you'll find that having a clear, detailed, reliable "mental representation" of the sound of that music is actually a huge component of being able to remember how to play it. More on this in the section on "Mental Play" below.

Musical Imagination

Your ability to conjure up great-sounding music in the world depends entirely on your ability to conjure up great-sounding music in your head[1].

Audiation can be used purely to "play back" existing music you've heard or played. However, it can also be usefully combined with creativity frameworks, providing you with a kind of "musical playground" in your mind, where you can experiment with new musical ideas.

Again, the language analogy is helpful here. Sometimes we do speak without thinking first, but can you imagine being able to speak a language without the ability to form sentences or think of words in your mind? Even if we're not preparing sentences and hearing them in our head before speaking them, it's clear that the ability to conjure up original sentences on-the-fly is directly dependent on our brain's ability to imagine language and think in words.

Similarly, if you want to be able to express original musical ideas out loud, you'll want to develop the ability to create original musical ideas in your mind first.

Relative Pitch

This connection between being able to remember music and being able to audiate it easily and vividly also has implications for skills like playing by ear and improvising. To put it simply, it's hard to play a

---

[1] That goes double for improvising, if you're following an improvisation approach which focuses on bringing the music out from inside you, like the Expansive Creativity framework you'll learn about in *Chapter Fifteen: Improvisation*. There are other improv methods which rely on memorised "vocabulary" and strict "patterns" and can operate with zero Audiation. However, for that very reason, these approaches tend to produce limited, robotic, generic and same-y sounding improvisation. More on that in the Improvisation chapter.

song by ear if you can't actually remember how it goes!

When we talk about "improving your ability to audiate", one major focus is the accuracy of your sense of pitch in your mind. This is a topic we'll cover in depth later in the book, but for now just be aware that your ability to judge the pitch distances between notes in music (called "Relative Pitch") is crucial, and it all starts in your mind. The more accurately you can "hear" the notes and their relationships in your mind, the easier it will be to process and recognise them when you hear them in the real world. Audiation is a really powerful tool in Relative Pitch Ear Training, because when your ear is trying to figure out the distances between notes, a lot of what you end up doing is mental gymnastics and imagining e.g. *"Oh, is it this interval or that interval?"*

Another example of the connection between Audiation and Relative Pitch is how a lot of musicians think they "can't sing" because when they try, the pitches don't come out correctly. Often it turns out that their ability to match pitch and their vocal control (see next chapter for details) are actually fine—but they don't have a clear mental representation of the pitches they intend to sing i.e. they can't audiate the melody. This is a bit like trying to hit a bullseye without having a clue where the dartboard is! You can have the best aim in the world, but if you don't actually know where the target is, of course you're going to struggle.

Which leads us to…

Audiation and Singing

Even if you don't consider yourself "a singer", there is nothing that compares with how directly singing is tied to your sense of music and your ability to express yourself musically. That's why we'll be devoting a whole chapter to the topic.

When it comes to Audiation, Singing has particular significance.

Singing and Audiation are really two sides of the same coin— Audiation can be considered as "singing in your head" and singing can be considered as "audiating out loud".

Just like Audiation, Singing can become a kind of "universal mastertool" which you can apply in a wide variety of musical activities to help you better learn, improve and perform.

We'll be exploring the connection between Singing and Audiation more in *Chapter Fourteen: Playing By Ear* and looking at how exactly you can use the two together. In short, you can think of both as stepping stones between the music you have inside, and the music you express outside.

So even if right now you have no desire to sing in front of anybody, the combination of Audiation and Singing is a "dynamic duo" which lets you better process, understand and express music—something you'll soon wonder how you ever did without!

Audiation Bridges Ear and Instrument

For a musician who has been focused exclusively on the "Hands" part of their H4 musicality, one huge step forwards is to start making connections to their "Hearing".

This can mean learning to play by ear or improvise, but it can also be as simple as starting to make sure you actually really learn the sound of each piece you play, not just the instructions for which buttons to press when, on your instrument.

There are a couple of simple exercises shared below to help you get started with this. You'll find it makes a remarkable difference to have a vivid mental representation of the music you're playing (i.e. the ability to audiate it well). Suddenly it becomes easier to memorise, easier to play, easier to be expressive with. You're actually getting "inside" the music rather than just reproducing notes robotically. It all starts with Audiation.

Audiation Bridges Sound and Notation

When you develop your Audiation in tandem with the Pitch and Rhythm ear skills covered later in the book, you develop the ability to look at written notation and immediately hear in your head how it should sound.

This is particularly exciting for singers, who can begin to "sight sing" music they've never heard before, just by looking at the sheet music. It's also exciting for instrumentalists, since you no longer need to play through a piece dot-by-dot to find out how it sounds—you can simply look at the page, hear it in your mind, and know exactly what you're aiming for when you pick up your instrument.

This connection works the other way around, too. When you develop both your Audiation and your "mental models" for Pitch and Rhythm, you'll be able to hear music in your mind (whether remembering something you heard, or conjuring up something new) and write it down in notation, without needing to "hunt and peck" for notes on an instrument first.

Audiation Boosts Enjoyment and Creativity

As with so much of musicality, ultimately it all comes back to enjoyment. Improving your Audiation to the point of having a really vivid musical imagination allows you to hear beloved pieces almost as if they're playing back in your mind. This brings music to life and enhances your listening experience.

We'll be exploring the skill of "active listening" in *Chapter Five: Active Listening*, and it's another skill which is intimately tied to Audiation. The more vividly you can imagine music in your mind, the more alert you'll be to details in music you hear and play. Likewise, the more sophisticated and detailed your appreciation of music you hear and play, the easier it will become to hear those same depths and details in your musical imagination. You'll find that Audiation becomes a really great way to assess your Active Listening abilities and vice-versa, simply by checking: *"Can I 'play back' in my head everything I think I heard?"*

This also has a clear knock-on effect to your musical creativity. The more restricted your musical imagination, the simpler your creative output will be. The more sophisticated your musical imagination becomes, the easier it will be to create rich, varied, and interesting music yourself.

Levels of Audiation Ability

As noted above, Audiation is a broad and varied skill which has connections and involvement throughout your musicality. It's not an easy thing to measure or evaluate[2].

Here's a simple 3-level system you can keep in mind, to help you understand different degrees of Audiation:

1. The first level is just being able to remember in your short-term memory, roughly how a brief passage of music went.
2. The second level is being able to vividly recreate a *melody* in

---

[2] Edwin Gordon's Music Learning Theory does define a detailed classification system for different types and stages of Audiation. However this covers not only the "musical imagination" but also extensive musical understanding, incorporating abilities we will cover later in this book as belonging to Relative Pitch and Rhythm skills.

your mind's ear, from long-term memory or by looking at sheet music.

3. And the third level is recreating in rich, vivid detail, the entirety of a musical recording or arrangement.

Progressing through these levels will push your pitch, rhythm and harmony skills, as well as your awareness of instrumentation, audio production, form, and all the other facets of music we'll explore in *Chapter Five: Active Listening*. It extends you in all directions at once.

As beautiful and varied as music is, that's how beautiful and varied your audiation skill becomes. It's a great way to continually stretch yourself as a musician.

These levels can be used to self-assess your overall audiation abilities. They can also (more usefully) be used to approach audiating any new piece of music. You can start out just seeing what you can audiate back immediately after hearing or playing it, then progress to a "Level 2" audiation of it after some time has passed, then combine it with some Active Listening practice to start really fleshing out your mental playback for Level 3.

Let's look in more detail at each of the three levels, and then some exercises you can use to start developing each.

Level 1: Short-Term Musical Memory

Your auditory memory is, in some ways, already really strong. Can you remember the "Happy Birthday" song? Or "Twinkle Twinkle, Little Star"? Can you remember any TV commercials or TV show theme songs from when you were a kid?

The auditory memory is one of our strongest types of memory. And yet, when it comes to using it for concrete musical tasks, we can find ourselves struggling much sooner than expected.

I remember back in my school days, the one of the few parts of the "aural skills" section of my instrument exams which I could easily pass was "clap back this rhythm."

I've found that most people who've been learning an instrument for a year or two can clap back a basic rhythm fairly well, if it's a measure or two long (think 5-8 seconds). Once it's longer than that, they will often struggle, even if the rhythm is still quite basic. This indicates they are reaching the limits of their short-term musical memory.

Typically singing or humming back a short melody is a little harder than purely-rhythmic patterns—but again, the limiting factor tends to be the length of the melody more than its complexity. There's plenty of work that can be done to improve your sense of Relative Pitch and ability to audiate melodies accurately, but it's likely that the first limiting factor for your Audiation will, in fact, be the length of your short-term musical memory.

In Level 1, we're just practicing audiation with very short sections of music which we've just heard, so that our short-term musical memory can assist us in recreating the sounds in our mind.

Level 2: Audiating Melodies

The next level we define is audiating melodies, meaning hearing one note at a time in your mind's ear. Just a single note-by-note melody, nothing more complex than that, but working with longer passages than in Level 1, so that we're going beyond our immediate short-term musical memory.

We're not worrying about what instrument it is, the chords underneath, or the details of the recording. We're really just thinking about *"what is the sequence of notes in that melody?"*

Stop reading for a moment, and see if you can hear the melody of "Happy Birthday" or "Twinkle, Twinkle, Little Star" in your head. Then try something a little less familiar, maybe a piece you're working on playing, or some other song you listened to in the past few days.

You might find that you can hear the melody vividly—or that certain parts are a little fuzzy. You might well find that you can hear the words in your mind, but actually you're not really hearing the different pitches clearly (or vice-versa!)

Many of our members at Musical U have found it disconcerting to realise that they actually can't "play back" the music they're working on in their mind's ear. However (remember Growth Mindset!) this immediately provides a wonderful opportunity, as it proves to have been the hidden limiter for their playing from memory, playing by ear, playing expressively, and more. Applying focused effort on developing this ability suddenly frees them up to new levels of ability in several other areas.

This is really the crux of Audiation for most musicians. If you can nail this, you're winning.

Level 3: Audiating Full Musical Passages

Once you can easily audiate melodies, the natural next step is to expand to harmonies and full arrangements.

This is a big change, and it is closely related to Active Listening, where one important skill to develop is what we might call "vertical listening", where you're able to be aware of multiple musical parts happening simultaneously.

At first you can start trying to hear the tonality (major vs. minor) of the harmony which goes along with the melody. Then perhaps adding the bassline movement, or the details of the chord voicing.

Personally, a gateway for me here was barbershop, close harmony singing, and 4-part choral harmony. At first I could only remember and audiate my own vocal part, but over time and with practice, I was able to become aware of all the other parts while listening, and then start being able to "play them back" in my mind too. To this day, putting on a Quebe Sisters track and simply paying careful attention to each of the three vocal parts at once—or doing the same purely in my mind's ear—is a musical activity which brings me inexplicable levels of joy.

The other direction here is in terms of the audio production. For example, not just hearing the notes of a guitar solo, but really hearing vividly the tone and timbre of the guitar, the effects used, and so on. Or the stereo mix, to actually hear in your mind's ear that there's a guitar over *here* and the hi-hat over *there* and so on.

Taken to its fullest, imagine for example if you wanted to compose or conduct an orchestral arrangement. Without strong Audiation skills, you would need to play around and experiment in your arrangement software or DAW, or rely on the full orchestral score to orient yourself while conducting. With strong "Level 3" Audiation you would be able to conjure up the full, vivid music in your mind, and bring it out into the world from there directly.

Exercises to Develop Audiation

Compared to most other skills of musicality, Audiation is more about simply making it a habit than following a step-by-step process or curriculum. So here we will suggest a number of easy ideas you can start incorporating into your music learning and have in mind as you progress through the rest of this book.

Level 1 (Short-Term Musical Memory) Exercises

Here are four contexts where you can start developing your short-term musical memory:

1.   When you're learning a new piece of music. With each
       measure or phrase you tackle, take a moment to try hearing it
       back in your mind's ear before the next time you play (or sing)
       it.

TIP:

   One fun way to do this is to select certain
measures as "inner hearing only", and when you
reach that measure stop playing/singing and
instead hear it in your mind's ear before continuing
on as normal. Gradually increase the number of
measures you do this with.

If you're playing with a backing track, try muting
the track for a measure or two and imagine in your
mind's ear what you would play during those
measures. When you unmute the backing, are you
still in time? This is a great way to dial in your
"inner metronome" and time-keeping accuracy.

---

2.   When listening to music you enjoy, hit "pause" and see if you
       can recreate in your mind's ear the passage you just heard.

3.   When practicing Playing By Ear or Improvisation, each time
       you do an exercise, take a moment to try hearing what you
       intend to play in your mind's ear first. As you'll be hearing
       about in the dedicated chapters on those skills, this "bridge"
       has an enormously positive effect on your results, as well as
       continuing to build that core Audiation ability itself.

4.   When memorising new music, make sure you are memorising

not just how to play it, but also the *sound* of it, through audiating.

The more opportunities you find to take a moment and listen back in your mind to the music you just heard, the faster your musical memory will improve.

With each of these, remember you can gradually increase the challenge by:

A. Starting with rhythm only, then adding pitch (or vice-versa)

B. Increasing the complexity of the melody (the range of notes used, the sophistication of the scale, the rhythmic complexity, etc.)

C. Extending the length of passage. Start with just a few notes, extend to a whole phrase, then a whole section, etc.

Zac Says...

Memorising songs can be challenging, and would sometimes trip up members inside Living Music where we're using songs to develop Solfa skills.

I developed a fun method called The "Audiation Sandwich" which members have found really helps them to memorize new songs quickly.

Here it is...

EXERCISE: The "Audiation Sandwich"

This is a three-step process. Start by choosing two songs you are having trouble memorising. We'll call them Song 1 and Song 2, and assume you have an example "source" recording of each.

1. The Source Sandwich: Audiate yourself singing Song 1, then

listen to your source recording of it, then audiate yourself singing it again. Repeat the sandwich with Song 2.

2. The Recording Sandwich: Audiate yourself singing Song 1, then record yourself singing it, then audiate yourself singing it again. Repeat the sandwich with Song 2.

3. The Listening Sandwich: Audiate yourself singing Song 1, then listen to the recording of yourself singing it. After listening, audiate yourself singing it again. Repeat the sandwich with Song 2.

(cont.)

The great thing about this method is you don't even need to get the songs right for it to help.

Don't worry about perfection. Perfection is the enemy of a sandwich. Sometimes when you make a sandwich it's really sloppy, but it's delicious.

When we work on improving our memory in this way, we will make a lot of mistakes at first. This is a good thing!

On your very first Audiation sandwich you might not be able to audiate the song at all. That's expected: you don't have it memorized yet. Just do your best. After listening to the source recording, it will be easier to audiate.

As you enjoy more Audiation sandwiches you'll naturally start correcting mistakes and audiating easier.

This is a memory exercise. It's not a test of your musicality or how good you are at singing or playing. The goal here is simply to help you to memorize the songs.

Trust in the process. Don't try and perfect the song. Just enjoy each sandwich, one bite at a time.

For short songs like in Living Music or those you'll find in Chapter Nine: Solfa, each sandwich takes about 1 minute. With two songs, the whole 3-step process won't take more than 10-15 minutes. Do this once a day with the same two songs, and within just a few days you will have the songs memorized really well.

Level 2 (Melody Audiation) Exercises

Level 2 is about audiating melodies which you *haven't* just heard a moment before. This might be when sight-reading from sheet music, audiating each melody before playing or singing it aloud, or it might be recalling a melody that's familiar (but haven't just heard).

This is a great one to practice with your existing repertoire. Any time you're pulling out a song you know well, pick sections to audiate before (or instead of) playing them out loud.

Try to be precise with rhythm and pitch. Vividly imagine each note in turn. The more you do this, the easier Audiation becomes.

Level 2 Audiation sets you up with a "mental gym" for doing Ear Training exercises. It's one thing to practice recognising Intervals, Solfa or Chords which you've just heard. It's another to generate those examples in your mind's ear and perform the same recognition tasks!

Audiation can also provide an extremely useful "middle step" for all Ear Training, giving you the chance to "check your answers" in your mind's ear. For example, I remember when I was struggling to distinguish between the Intervals called Perfect Fourths and Perfect Fifths. If I simply listened, then guessed, I really had a hard time with it. When I started to take a moment to imagine in my mind's ear what a Perfect Fourth and a Perfect Fifth would sound like, it was suddenly easy to check which of the two I had just heard, and get the answer right. More on this in *Chapter Fourteen: Playing By Ear*.

Level 2 is also where we can start connecting Audiation with creativity. As you discover the creative frameworks later in the book, keep in mind that they can all be practiced in your mind's ear.

This is why we sometimes refer to Audiation as the "secret music practice skill". With Audiation you can be improving your musical ear and your improvisation chops while standing in line waiting for a bus! You can even take it one stage further with…

Mental Play

If you want to turbo-boost your Audiation practice, try Mental Play. I came across this idea for the first time in Chuan C. Chang's wonderful book *The Fundamentals Of Piano Practice*.

The idea is simple: while you play back the music in your mind's ear, also visualise yourself playing it.

Just like Audiation itself, this is something that sounds easy, but might shock you with its difficulty at first! It really reveals how much you might be relying on autopilot and "muscle memory", or on the notation to tell you which notes to play, rather than having formed a firm "mental model" of the music.

To be able to really *feel* yourself playing the part, while you imagine the musical sounds it creates, also has a profound effect on how free and confident your actual playing will be.

So there are three huge benefits to this simple exercise:

Firstly, it makes sure your "mental representation" of how to play the piece really is dialed in. Just like Audiation itself, you'll probably start finding that sections you thought you knew are actually quite fuzzy when you try to conjure them up in your imagination. For example, you're able to play a certain passage, but when you try Mental Play you realise you don't consciously know the fingering pattern. This reveals that when you're actually playing it, your brain is still guessing to some extent, opening you up to making mistakes at that point in the music. More on this in *Chapter Six: Superlearning*.

Secondly, it gives you the same kind of "mental gym" for instrument playing as mentioned above for ear skills. You can actually try out different fingerings, or really slow down a section and make sure you've got it dialed-in. If there's a passage that's troubling you, try doing Mental Play on it a few times between your regular instrument practice sessions. I guarantee you'll be pleasantly surprised how much easier it is to actually play it when you next set fingers to instrument!

This goes for Singing too. Again, that deep biological connection with your singing voice means it's the epitome of really *feeling* what it's like to perform it, even without making a single sound out loud.

Research has proven that this kind of imagined practicing has a clear tangible effect on your progress[3]. And you can probably imagine how valuable it is to be able to practice "that tricky bit" 50 or 100 times while waiting in line at a shop or walking down the street!

Coming back to when I first learned about this technique in the book for piano, at the time I was really struggling with integrating the right- and left-hand parts. The book revealed that going slowly and very gradually combining the two was the key to success, but it also added this idea of Mental Play. I found that trying to imagine what both hands were playing, note by note, slow enough to get it all right, was shockingly effective compared to just "brute forcing" trying to play the two parts at once.

Finally, the third huge benefit is that it develops your instrument skills and Audiation skills in tandem. That's why has become one of my top tips for any instrument player to use Mental Play as a way to

---

[3] See, for example, "Mental practice promotes motor anticipation: evidence from skilled music performance" by Bernardi et al., Frontiers in human neuroscience, 2013 which presents a relevant study as well as citing various other studies which demonstrate the impact of Mental Play.

find extra practice time. It works really well, and it's a double win, because you're practicing your instrument and repertoire—but of course you're also practicing up your Audiation skills. So, the more you use Mental Play in your learning, the better you'll get, and that impact will increase over time.

Level 3 (Full Music Audiation) Exercises

Level 3 is about "full music"—in the sense of a full arrangement rather than "the full piece" (though that's also interesting to aim for!). Here we're looking to fill in the harmony, the rhythm section, each and every instrument, the distinct timbres and/or audio production being used, etc. The goal is that your imagined version of the music is as close as possible to a full recorded or performed version.

In its simplest form this would mean taking a solo instrumental piece, for example an unaccompanied flute or saxophone melody, but starting to really vividly hear the sound of that instrument in your mind, not just having a sense of the note pitches. Naturally most of the music around us each day features multiple instruments and all kinds of detail, so you'll want to extend this ability towards those fuller, more complex tracks too.

The key exercise here is to combine Audiation and Active Listening. We'll be going in depth on that skill in *Chapter Five: Active Listening*. For now you just need to know the overall idea, which is to listen to music while zeroing in your attention on a particular aspect of it. That could be a certain instrument, a certain part, the rhythms, audio effects, or any other component of the music. You'll be learning the 4-D Active Listening framework and a particular approach to help with this.

When it comes to Level 3 Audiation, the trick is simply to alternate Active Listening with Audiation.

So each time you listen through to a track practicing Active Listening and really paying attention to one particular aspect of the music, you then take a moment afterwards to try to re-create either that particular aspect in your mind's ear, or the full track with that aspect more vividly filled in.

For example, supposing you're working on Michael Jackson's classic track "Thriller". You might start out with only Level 1 Audiation ability, able to hear back the vocal part in your short-term memory (and perhaps even that would require some repeats, to get the lyrics down and be confident in the pitches you're hearing). Next you might work on Level 2 for the vocal melody, being able to recall the vocal part in your mind's ear even if you haven't heard the track recently. Level 3 would then be about starting to fill in some of the instrumental parts, perhaps the drums, bassline, horns, and so on.

Again, a word of warning: don't be discouraged if this is hard at first! To be consciously aware of multiple parts at once is a real challenge for most musicians in Active Listening to begin with, and carrying that across to Audiation even more so! Like most musical challenges though, the benefits are proportional to the initial difficulty, so take your time and be patient with yourself.

> **TIP:**
>
> Our Active Listening and Audiation skills tend to be stronger for instruments we ourselves play, so those can be good ones to focus on first.

Remember the old adage *"What's the best way to eat an elephant?"* Don't expect yourself to hit "play" on your mental Walkman and instantly hear the full, rich detail of a track from beginning to end. Start with small sections, start with one or two aspects at a time, and gradually build it up. You might like to start with simpler arrangements, for example an acoustic performance by a singer-songwriter with just vocals and guitar rather than a Beach Boys or Pink Floyd extravaganza ;)

The important thing to know is that although it may take time to do this for a single track, the process will accelerate the more you practice it. Eventually, you'll find that your default level of Audiation is a solid Level 3, and you're able to easily and quickly conjure up rich and vivid representations of music in your mind's ear.

Conclusion

Audiation is a fundamental skill which both supports most other skills of musicality and connects them to each other.

Your Audiation ability will naturally improve over time through any musicality training you do, but giving it concerted direct effort will greatly accelerate the process.

Audiation is itself a valuable and useful skill, as we've seen in the various examples above, but it also "raises the baseline" for other aspects of your musicality, making it easier and faster to succeed with them.

Be on the lookout for opportunities to insert an Audiation step in any musical activities you do, and you'll find your skills improve quickly. We'll include plenty of reminders and specific guidance for this throughout the rest of the book.

Before you know it, you'll have a powerful and versatile ability to "think in music".

CHAPTER FOUR:
SINGING

"The only thing better than singing is more singing."
— Ella Fitzgerald

Our singing voice is every human being's natural "first instrument". Yet even among those who devote countless hours to musical development, many still shy away from singing.

In fact, I've found that the majority of instrumentalists are reluctant to sing, generally because they think they "can't sing" or sound "bad" when they try. Yet your singing voice is the most direct way to bring music out from inside you, and it has an unparalleled power for developing your musicality.

You deserve to have this unique tool in your musical toolkit.

The goal of this chapter is not to turn you into a stage singer who grabs the mic and fronts a rock band, joins a choir, or auditions for the next "Pop Idol" contest. It is far more modest, but at the same time far more important: to get you feeling comfortable and confident using your singing voice as a tool for musicality training.

If you are already a comfortable, confident singer, then awesome! This chapter will provide some guidance and suggestions for how to leverage that ability to accelerate your musicality training and further your musical growth.

On the other hand, if you would currently classify yourself in that group of musicians who "can't sing", here are two big lessons I want to share with you, which come from working with tens of thousands of musicians of all kinds at Musical U:

1.   Any past experiences which have given you the idea that you can't sing or don't have a good voice can be safely ignored.
      A lot of people have heard negative or critical comments about their singing from teachers, friends, family members or other musicians, and I know it can be hard to shake those off. However, as we'll be discussing more below, those are not actually any indication of whether you can sing or not.
      I won't pretend those comments were just nonsense, or tell you that you actually do sound amazing right now when you sing. But I am going to tell you it's 100% possible for you to learn the singing skills you need to start sounding good. So begin right now by changing that *"I can't sing"* to *"I can't sing… yet."*

2.   Once you put a couple of simple skills in place (which can be done quickly) you'll likely be surprised how much you start to enjoy singing, and how indispensable it becomes in your music learning, and especially your musicality training.
      Two frequent comments we hear from members going through our singing material are that A. They actually really enjoy singing now, and B. They wish they had learned this skill much sooner.

We won't go in-depth teaching you singing in this chapter. Singing is an instrument in its own right, and although we have extensive training for it inside Musical U, this book is not the place to try teaching you an instrument through words alone!

What we are going to do is show you how to get started using your singing voice confidently, accurately and reliably to express yourself musically and develop your musicality. If you find that you enjoy singing enough to want to explore it further as an instrument, that's a wonderful bonus, and you'll find some pointers in this chapter for how to take the next steps.

Overview

In this chapter we'll begin by looking at what specifically holds musicians back from singing, and establish a clear aim (which may well be different from what you would expect).

We'll discuss "Singing as a Tool" and the myriad ways singing can accelerate your musical development once you learn to use your voice in this way.

After briefly covering essentials of posture and breathing, we'll tackle the two core skills which let you since confidently, accurately and reliably in tune: matching pitch, and vocal control. Through a series of simple exercises we'll help you get comfortable singing, no matter what level you're starting at. We'll wrap up by discussing how to continue practicing your singing skills and integrate it with the rest of your musicality training.

Why Do You Think You Can't Sing?

If you think you can't sing, there are probably four contributing factors in play. Not coincidentally, these map to the 4 H's of musicality:

1.   You don't understand how singing actually works or what it takes to "sing well". (Head)

2.   You have difficulty judging pitch, so can't reliably hear when a sung note is too high or low. (Hearing)

3.   You have poor vocal pitch control, so can't adjust your sung note quickly and easily to reach the target note. (Hands— though the instrument technique is not literally in your "hands" in this case!)

4.   You have emotional or psychological hangups about singing, so you don't sing, or do so timidly which makes it harder to control your pitch and sound good. (Heart)

The balance of these will vary for each person, but it's always some combination of them which causes a person to believe they can't sing.

For #1 (Head), not understanding how singing works: in this chapter we'll help you to understand the mechanics of singing in tune, known as "Matching Pitch".

For #2 (Hearing), difficulty judging pitch: if you've been learning music for a while then this is probably not your limiting factor, though there may yet be some work to be done to improve and refine your pitch discernment. This will be covered in this chapter as part of learning the two core skills of Matching Pitch and Vocal Control.

For #3 (Hands), poor vocal control: the cause is simply that you have not yet learned this skill. It's the unfortunate flip-side of singing being everyone's natural first instrument. We assume "you've got it or you don't", and so if your pitching is all over the place when you sing, it must be because you have a "bad voice". But that's nonsense—we don't expect ourselves to be able to operate a motor vehicle, or a computer keyboard, or a guitar or piano for that matter without spending time learning the physical motions. Why should our singing voice be any different? In this chapter you'll learn the basics of Vocal Control.

For #4 (Heart), emotional or psychological hangups: This often the biggest blocker to people learning to sing. Sadly, for many it started young. If you are otherwise a good musician, this barrier can be particularly powerful, as you may feel guilty for not being as good as you feel you "should be". As a result many musicians simply refuse to sing so they can avoid confronting this painful issue.

Rather than try to undo that past conditioning directly, the most effective solution is to simply prove to yourself, in a safe and unintimidating way, that you actually can sing. By following the suggestions in this chapter, you'll be able to see those past experiences in a whole new light. They will gently fade away and no longer be a blocker or an anchor holding you down.

So the good news is that you already have everything you need to sing well. If you're reading this book then it's safe to assume you love music, and that means your ears work. If you can speak, then we know your voice works. So the Hearing and Hands components are ready for development, and as you go through this chapter we'll address the Head and the Heart components too.

A quick word about "tone deafness"

Have you ever been called, or called yourself "tone deaf"? This is a serious blocker for a lot of musicians when it comes to singing.

Culturally, there is a strange blurring together of that term "tone deaf" and the skill of singing, when they are actually two completely separate things.

Around 2014 I got a real bee in my bonnet about this. I kept talking to musicians who were using our Ear Training materials, and when I'd suggest using singing to help them improve their ears, all too often they'd make a comment about being "tone deaf".

Tone deafness is a real phenomenon. The precise scientific term for it is amusia. It's extremely rare. It means you literally can't distinguish higher notes from lower ones at all.

I knew that the musicians using our resources were not tone deaf. How could I know? Because if they truly suffered from amusia, they would not enjoy listening to music! Can you imagine how bizarre or boring music would sound to you, if all note pitches sounded the same?

If you want to be certain about it, I actually ended up creating a simple test you can take at ToneDeafTest.com, based on the scientific measures of amusia, which will tell you in 5 minutes or so whether you are actually "tone deaf" or not.

Our findings from over 2.3 million people taking that test over the past nine years confirm the scientific estimates: we've found that less than 1.5% of people are truly "tone deaf". It's likely even less than that, since we know that some who take the test will just answer randomly on purpose.

For every single one of the 98.5% who passed the test (and almost certainly you too) it is absolutely possible to learn to sing in tune, sound good, and benefit from singing in your musical development.

Our Aim

Before we begin, let's first define what our aim for this chapter. We are not expecting you to develop an incredible, versatile, knock-your-socks-off ability to sing. We are not expecting you to declare yourself "a singer", volunteer to front a band, join a choir, or even sing at the next karaoke night[1].

Our aim is simply to reach the point where if you want to sing a certain note or sequence of notes, they come out clearly and accurately on the intended pitches.

If you've never sung, or have been told that you can't sing, or you feel too nervous to even try, then the best thing I can do is to encourage you to step back from that intimidating idea of "being a singer".

It might even help you to pretend, at least for now, that there are actually two types of singing.

There's the impressive, professional, up-on-stage, artistic-mastery kind of singing. And then there's the everyday kind. Like when you hum a tune to yourself, sing your kids a lullaby, sing to yourself in the shower, or maybe even take part in the occasional alcohol-assisted night out at the karaoke bar.

You can also think of it as the difference between becoming a public speaker or Hollywood actor—versus just learning how to talk. Or the difference between being an Olympic-medal-winning speed cyclist—versus just being able to ride your bike down to the shops. Or the difference between becoming a famous portrait painter—versus just being able to paint the living room walls.

In all those examples, we understand that there's a kind of basic competence that we can reasonably expect to achieve. And the fact that some people make it an art or build a career around it doesn't hold the rest of us back from learning to do the useful, everyday level of that same skill.

Think "functional." "Serviceable." "Fit for purpose." "Gets the job done." That's what we're looking for. You feel comfortable using your voice, and you can basically sing the notes you mean to.

Now don't get me wrong—as always I do want you to aim high and dream big! And I hope you will connect with your voice and want to cultivate that part of your musicality further, and make "being a singer" part of your musical identity.

But if right now you're in that spot of thinking you can't (or don't want to) sing, then start with just aiming for the basics. That good enough, basically-works level of singing.

---

[1] Though past experience has shown you may well find those opportunities starting to appeal to you, once you start down this path!

That alone is enough to make singing a powerful tool for you. And it doesn't need to take long. To give you some idea, with the way we teach it at Musical U that you'll learn in this chapter, you're looking at maybe a few weeks of practice to get to that level.

The 16 Keys to a "Good Voice"

If you find yourself starting to enjoy singing, and are interested in developing your voice further, we've identified 16 aspects of your voice that contribute to whether it sounds "good" or not.

You can learn about all 16, as well as common mistakes and easy ways to fix them in the *Additional Resources*.

Singing as a Tool

So what's the value of getting to that basic level of singing ability if you're not looking to perform as a singer?

Singing is a foundational musical skill like Audiation, Active Listening, and Superlearning, which will have positive effects throughout your musical life.

Perhaps the simplest way to put it though is that singing is a way to bring musical ideas from your head out into the world directly, without the added complication of searching for the notes you want on an instrument.

If you don't have singing as a tool then it can feel like there's a big gulf between hearing something or imagining it in your mind's ear, and then playing it on your instrument. When you have a basic level of singing ability, you're able to bridge that gap or even remove the need for the instrument step entirely, depending on the task.

Let's go through some specific benefits and applications of singing as a tool.

Improved sense of pitch

Learning to sing in tune is one of the best ways to train your sense of pitch. Singing in tune requires two major components: not just controlling your vocal pitch, but also being able to very clearly and accurately hear and imagine the pitch you're aiming for.

So as you learn to sing in tune you'll be training your ears to hear better whether notes are sharp, flat or perfectly on-pitch. This is something that you might never have had to do before, depending on the instrument you play, and it's a fundamental skill which you absolutely do not want to overlook.

Improved Audiation

As well as this "real world" pitch training, you'll also be training your mind's ear: your ability to audiate (i.e. imagine music) with accurate pitch.

Just as Active Listening practice helps increase the richness and detail of your Audiation, learning to sing in tune develops the accuracy with which you can pitch notes in your mind.

Easy Ear Training[2]

Singing is also an enormous help for Ear Training. This is something we really emphasise at Musical U. When you use your voice as part of Ear Training exercises, you can progress a lot faster.

You'll learn more about this in Part II, but as a preview here are some specific ways it helps:

- Learning to sing also helps you sing "in your mind", so when you're trying to do Ear Training exercises and recognise notes, chords, etc. you have a more powerful musical imagination to bring to the task.

- Singing gives you a way to experiment out loud during Ear Training. For example if you're trying to recognise an interval, you might sing the start of a reference song to see if it matches up. If you're trying to recognise a chord progression, you might sing along with the root notes of the chords or the bassline, to see how those pitches could reveal the chords being used.

  You can also do some nifty vocal acrobatics. For example, if you're trying to identify a harmonic interval (meaning two

---

[2] Tee hee

notes played at once) being able to sing those two notes back individually transforms it into an ascending or descending interval that you might find it easier to recognise.

As you improve over time, you'll do these things in your head or skip them entirely as they become subconscious instincts. Until then, it's really helpful to be able to experiment out loud by singing.

- Singing lets you test whether you heard what you think you heard. In fact we might even say that if you can't sing back what you heard, then you haven't really heard it.

  One example would be recognising a chord as major or minor. You can listen for the overall sound of the chord, but that's prone to mistakes, especially in a rich musical context. It also gets harder as you try more ambitious chords like seventh or extended chords. If you're able to sing back each note of the chord, that both tests that you truly heard what was going on, and gives you a clear set of notes to explore and evaluate to identify the chord type (for example identifying the Solfa name of each note or the Intervals between them).

  If you find yourself struggling with a pitch-related Ear Training task, it's likely that you aren't actually hearing clearly enough yet to be able to sing back each of the notes. Once you practice that and use Singing as a tool in this way, the actual task tends to become much easier.

- In Chapter Nine: Solfa you'll learn the "Solfa" approach (also known as *solfege* or the do-re-mi system) for recognising pitches by ear. We've found this is by far the easiest and fastest way to start recognising notes to play by ear, improvise, transcribe music and more. It's a sung system, meaning you learn it most effectively by singing notes with their solfa names. The basic level of singing ability we've been talking about so far is plenty sufficient to enable full-speed Solfa success. In fact, many Musical U members inside the *Living Music* program find learning Solfa to be a really great way to gradually develop a confident and reliable ability to sing, even if they had previously thought they couldn't sing.

Easier and Freer Experimentation

Singing enables easier and freer experimentation and creativity in music. Yes, you can sit with an instrument and noodle around with scales or patterns and try to create something. But that's both more complicated and more limiting than doing it with your voice.

Your singing voice is the most direct path to bring musical ideas you imagine into the world. You have total freedom of pitch so you're not trapped in memorised patterns, or strict rules, or limited by your level of instrument technique. You can immediately express what you want to, and then analyse it (during or after) to transfer it onto an instrument or write it down.

You may have noticed legendary improvisers like Keith Jarrett or Oscar Peterson sing along as they improvise, for this very reason. The musical ideas are born inside, and simultaneously expressed directly with their voice and their instrument.

Singing is the most natural and direct form of musical expression available to us. It may seem intimidating at the outset but once you break past that little barrier it's enormously natural and liberating to be able to create music directly with your voice. Singing (especially with Solfa) allows us to practice and explore music anywhere at any time.

Easier Communication

Being able to express musical ideas with your voice isn't just helpful for creating privately by yourself. It also makes a huge difference when collaborating with other musicians.

If you don't feel able to express your ideas with your voice it can be very frustrating in a band or other group to have to try to translate what you're thinking onto your instrument to communicate it. If instead you can just quickly and easily sing the idea you have in mind, you skip all the instrument specifics and complications, and can bounce ideas back and forth immediately and directly.

Going Beyond Singing As A Tool

I must end this section with a slightly more romantic take on Singing. I'll keep it short, because I could wax lyrical about the emotional and spiritual and psychological benefits of singing all day long. Not to mention the scientifically-proven social and physical benefits, especially when you do it as part of a group with others.

Instead I will just share my personal experience: there is nothing as emotionally cathartic, deeply healing, and spiritually moving as singing yourself the music which is most meaningful to you.

We opened this chapter with the statement that the singing voice is every human's "first instrument", and so even if our focus is to develop that basic, functional, everyday form of "singing as a tool", I'd be remiss if I didn't at least mention to you how deeply rewarding it can be to really adopt singing as an instrument and explore all the rich wonders it can bring to your musical life.

So I hope that your first steps in this chapter may well lead to walking… running… and taking flight. And that Singing may one day prove as meaningful and rewarding to you as it has to me.

Give It A Try!

At this point I know from extensive experience how personal and sensitive a topic singing can be among musicians, so I'm not going to ask you to commit to making Singing a part of your musical toolkit. However, I am going to ask you to commit to giving it a try.

Again, you needn't see it as "becoming a singer" or taking on some big new challenge. Just play along with us for this chapter, and see how you get on. Start trying to use Singing as you go through the material in other chapters of the book.

It might feel weird. You might experience some negative emotions or emotional resistance. You might feel extremely self-conscious, even if there's nobody else around to hear you.

Do your best to Tak Courag. Nobody is going to judge you or ask you to sing in front of a crowd. This is 100% about you, and equipping yourself with a powerful tool to unlock your musicality. Even if you never sing a note in front of anybody else in your life, I guarantee you this will be well worth it, and you will be very glad that you added this powerful tool to your toolkit.

There is nothing like your own singing voice for expressing yourself in music—and I think you will be surprised and delighted about what you can achieve.

The Story of Your Voice

When we invited renowned improvisational singing instructor Davin Youngs to teach a two-week singing training inside the creativity-themed "Summer" Season of our *Living Music* program, he kicked things off with a simple but powerful exercise which I'd now like to share with you.

It's called "the story of your voice"—and it's not any more complicated than the name suggests!

EXERCISE: The Story Of Your Voice

Take a few minutes and simply write the story of your voice.

This is a way to learn more about the experiences and ideas you're starting with, when exploring singing.

It is intentionally an open-ended exercise. Your "story" could be a poem, an actual story, freeform text, even a song! However you would like to explore the topic, write for yourself the "story of your voice" and see what comes up.

Many of our members have found this an enlightening and empowering exercise. For some it's a particularly emotional one. This is a really powerful way to start developing a new relationship with your natural first instrument.

TIP:

As you go through the exercises in this chapter, it can be helpful to have recordings of sung notes to refer to. We have prepared a page in the *Additional Resources* with note examples, as well as demonstrations of the sung exercises.

Preparation

We won't go into great depth on Singing technique here, as our goal is solely to master the fundamentals of singing in tune. So we won't be covering the details of your throat and lungs anatomy, or exercises to "upgrade" your vocal instrument, etc.

However, your singing voice is a physical part of your body, so it's important to cover some basics of posture, breathing and how to warm up. This will both set you up for easiest results, and help to prevent any possible negative effects such as over-straining your voice.

There are many schools of thought when it comes to teaching Singing technique, but all agree on one thing, which I want to put front-and-center as the most important rule of thumb to keep in mind:

Singing should never feel physically strained or painful.

You may be pushing yourself emotionally, you might run out of breath sometimes, you might need to work a little harder at the far ends of your note range. Some occasional light discomfort is normal, but you should never keep pushing through discomfort or a sense of straining.

Since we're not aiming here to sing for extended periods of time or at great volume, the only real "danger zone" is trying to sing outside your natural range.

If you're working on the exercises below and it feels like you're really having to push hard or strain your voice to reach the note, you may be trying to sing in the wrong octave/register, or too far outside your comfortable range. There is no need to force it.

We'll talk more about range below, but for now just know that to use Singing as a tool for musicality, you almost certainly have a wide enough comfortable range already to hit any note you need in some comfortable octave. No straining required.

Note: If you're not yet comfortable singing at all, feel free to wait until the "Matching Pitch" section below to start actually trying out the suggestions below. That will get you singing your first notes, and you can then start incorporating the information below about posture, breathing and warming up as you continue.

Posture

If you choose to go further with singing, posture can be a huge topic. For our purposes, there are just a few basic things to keep in mind:

- Overall, try to minimise tension in your body. Your back, shoulders, neck, and facial muscles should all be relaxed.

- Whether standing or sitting, you want your back to be straight (not slouched).
- Your neck should be straight and aligned with your head and your back. Don't have your head leaned forwards or pulled backwards.

Breathing

Singing is powered by your breath. To be able to reliably and easily produce strong, clear, well-pitched notes, it is essential that your body is providing enough air to the voice, and in the right way. The speed and concentration of how air is released through the mouth and nose is called the "breath support" for your voice.

Breathing is another huge topic in Singing, but again, for our purposes we only need some basic principles under our belt.

Aspects of Breath Support

Here are some key aspects of breath support, and a couple of simple exercises that will help you become aware of them naturally and easily.

1. Posture

Allowing more air to go through your throat at a slower rate is key to vocal control. To help open your throat, make sure your neck and shoulders are relaxed, and that your head is in a natural position in line with your spine, with your back held comfortably straight. If you're standing, your weight should be on your heels, not the balls of your feet.

You can also use the "artificial yawning" trick to open the throat: as you breathe in, pull your tongue back. You should feel a cold sensation on the back of your throat which is identical to what it feels like before you yawn!

2. Inbreath

Breathe deeply, and fairly slowly, so that you'll have a good oxygen supply each time you sing a series of notes. The more air you have in your lungs, the stronger a foundation you have for a good sound. Over time and with practice, you will learn how to breathe more deeply at a quicker rate in a useful way.

3. Outbreath

If you think of a sneeze, you tend to breathe in quite slowly (*"aaaaaaaah"*), but then the nose and mouth constrict and cause the air to come out extremely quickly (*"choo!"*). For Singing, it's better to have more air passing your throat at a slower, more consistent rate than less air passing through faster and more abruptly.

Your lungs, diaphragm, nose and mouth all respond differently to different speeds of air flow, and when singing you want to make sure you don't force the sound out through your nose and mouth too quickly.

A big secret is that singing quietly requires just as much air as singing loudly. Singing quietly is also a lot harder to sustain than singing loudly, because for loud sounds you can use projection techniques to make your voice carry. For our purposes you'll generally want to be singing at about the same volume you would speak at when talking to a friend sitting nearby.

EXERCISE: Breath and Dynamics

Practice singing wordless notes, going firstly from soft to loud. Choose a vowel sound such as "ah" or "oooh". Try to grow the sound as slowly and consistently as possible.

Then do it again but the other way around, loud to soft. Try to get as quiet as possible without losing the sound.

Do it in different parts of your vocal range (higher and lower in pitch), as some will be stronger and more comfortable than others.

---

4. Efficiency

If you want to sing louder, you breathe out more quickly, sending more air through your throat more quickly. You already understand instinctively how to do this—it's the same way you raise your voice when speaking, to talk louder or even shout.

You can get control over that airflow pressure in many ways. Your breathing mechanism acts like a balloon and where you push it increases the pressure.

According to the research, some version of "belly-in" breathing is the most mechanically efficient way to increase your pressure. That just means pulling your belly in gently as you're singing.

EXERCISE: Finding Your Breath Support Muscles

Let go of any abdominal tension and breathe in, freely and easily.

Place your hands around your waist, in between your ribs and your hips, and give a gentle cough. You'll probably feel something pop out a little bit, become a little firmer bit under your hands. Those are the muscles you can use to increase the air pressure while singing.

Don't Overthink It!

How are you going to focus on delivering a beautiful song when you're worrying about your lining up your head and back, opening up your throat, how fast or slow your air is moving, whether it's time to add more breath support or…?

The answer is, you don't need to worry about it. All we want is to be able to breathe in freely and easily, and then tailor our air use to what we're going to sing. For example, if you're singing just a few notes to use Singing as a tool, you don't need to take a huge breath in each time.

You'll only need to increase pressure actively if you're singing loudly or at the end of a long phrase and your breath supply is running low. In most cases if you just get the musical intention right, and your vocal control is on track in your throat, the breathing will probably take care of itself.

Warming Up

You probably wouldn't think of Singing as particularly physically demanding, compared to something like sports. You don't move around that much, you only use a handful of muscles, you needn't get out of breath or work up much of a sweat.

And yet, Singing is surprisingly similar to a sport, and as with sports, it's important to warm up the body beforehand.

Since this chapter is focused on using Singing as a tool, doing dedicated warmups is probably overkill. However, if you find yourself starting to sing a lot during practice, or if you want to really develop your singing voice, then it will be well worth learning some simple warmup exercises you can do to best prepare your voice for the task at hand. We have included a guide with beginner, intermediate and advanced warmups, with accompanying audio demonstrations in the *Additional Resources*.

One simple tip worth mentioning here is to make sure you're well hydrated. Drinking some water before or periodically during singing practice can help to ensure your vocal muscles will perform at their best.

Core Skill 1: Matching Pitch

There are many aspects to having a "good" or "nice-sounding" singing voice, but without a doubt, the first thing to figure out is whether you have problems with pitch and tuning.

As discussed above in the section on tone deafness, we know your ears can fundamentally judge pitch because you enjoy listening to music. This means you can use your ears to evaluate and train your own voice. Ultimately this is how you'll sing in tune: by relying on your ears (including your inner hearing i.e. Audiation) to keep your voice on target.

In time this will become automatic and subconscious for you, and you will easily sing in tune naturally. At first, though, you will need a helping hand and to pay careful attention.

In this section we're going to:

- Find "Your Note": a single note you'll know you can sing well.

- Explore to find "Your Range": the highest and lowest notes you can comfortably sing.

- Learn a simple process for practicing matching pitch.

- Get tips on keeping your pitch steady when you sing.

Find "Your Note"

I once interviewed a fascinating chap for the Musicality Now podcast, George Bevan, who was head of music at Monkton school in the U.K. He had started a choir in the school specifically for students who thought they couldn't sing. It was named, aptly enough, "The choir who can't sing"! And, through his diligent efforts to help them match pitch and learn vocal control, it emerged that actually, they could sing pretty darn well :)

The exercise you're about to try is one I learned from him. This was one of the things he did to help people who think they can't sing to take their first steps towards becoming a capable and confident singer. If you've ever worried that you can't sing at all, this exercise will be particularly useful for you.

It is simple but powerful. How do I know? In the past few years, almost half a million people have used a similar exercise in our SingTrue app to find their note and take their first step to singing, not to mention countless members inside Musical U where we have a training module which walks you through it interactively.

The idea is this: the first step to matching pitch is to sing and sustain one single note. And if you find a note which is particularly comfortable for you, that will be a whole lot easier.

Most people who try singing jump ahead several steps without even realising it. They immediately try to sing a song, maybe in the car or at karaoke night—and then they're surprised and disappointed when all the pitches don't come out right!

That's kind of crazy when you think about it.

When we learn to write we don't begin by trying to copy out a whole section of a book. Instead we begin with just writing a single letter and getting the shape correct, clear and consistent. From there we can build up to words, sentences, and eventually whole passages.

It's the same with singing: first you need to be able to sing one note. Then you can learn how to sing other notes and control your voice well as you move between them. Then you can start thinking about verses, choruses and lyrics and everything else.

The "Find Your Note" exercise is built on a key insight: we actually all have some degree of vocal control already, whether we know it or not.

As you listen to people talk, their voices go up and down in pitch as part of how they convey meaning with their words. Their voices move through part of their vocal range, producing the different pitches that the brain intends.

So clearly we all do have a foundation for singing – otherwise, we would all talk in a monotone like robots.

Flipping the Dreaded Singing Test

Unfortunately, too many of us have experienced the sort of "singing test" where a music teacher, perhaps during your childhood, played a note on the piano, and you were asked to sing it back. That seems simple and reasonable enough, but even that is actually skipping a couple of steps!

Let's flip it around. Instead of hearing a specific note and trying to sing it, we'll start with you singing—and then discover what that note is.

Find "Your Note"

The goal of this exercise is to find just one pitch that you can comfortably sing. We're going to call this "Your Note", and you'll know that whatever happens, singing Your Note will always feel easy and comfortable.

For this exercise you will need an electronic tuner, like you use to tune a guitar or wind instrument, which shows the name of the note it detects using a microphone. You can also use a web-based tuner (you can do a web search for "online instrument tuner") or any tuner app on a mobile device. Choose one which shows a dial, not just each individual note. That way you can see exactly where your current pitch falls, even when it's between notes.

EXERCISE: Find Your Note

Start by singing *"ahhhh"*—on whatever pitch comes out. We know you can do it because you can speak! It's just like being at the dentist when they tell you *"say ahh"*.

Just relax. Take a breath. And sing a pitch, whatever comes out.

If even that feels a bit intimidating, you can instead try talking in a monotone voice (like a stereotypical "robot voice") and say *"Hi, my name is Jeff"* (or whatever your name is) but hold the last word: *"HI MY NAME IS JEEEEEEF"*. That last sound you made was a note![3]

---

[3] The "My name is..." approach is also useful because it helps avoid one of the common beginner mistakes, which is to assume your singing voice is "up there" somewhere, when in fact (not coincidentally) the pitches you normally speak at tend to fall nicely

Now turn on your tuner and again sing "Your Note" on *"aaahh"* (or do the robot sentence with your name).

What's Your Note? Jot down what the tuner shows.

_____

Your note has both a letter name, such as "C" or "F♯", and an octave number, such as "3" or "5". Most tuners will show both. If you aren't familiar with the idea of an "octave" you can think of it as being an indication of the overall pitch range the note is in. For example there are several "C" notes on a piano keyboard, from a very low "C" up to a very high "C". So a male person with a low voice might do this exercise and get a "C3" note while a female person could do it and get a "C5" note.

That's it, you've found your note!

What's next?

From there, you can try singing another note, a bit higher or lower. And then you can start to build on that, developing your ability to match pitch and have vocal control.

As we go through other exercises below, you'll have the opportunity to practice, beginning with Your Note and extending to other note pitches.

You might wonder *"Will my note be the same every day?"* and sometimes people get a bit hung up on this, so to clarify: "Your Note" isn't set in stone! We name it like that to encourage your confidence that you can confidently and reliably sing a note, but it's entirely possible that if you do the exercise again tomorrow you'll get a slightly different note.

For example today it might be "C3" and tomorrow you find it's "D3", just a little bit higher. But it's unlikely to suddenly jump to "C4" which would be a whole octave higher in pitch.

So this idea of "Your Note" is useful because we have now put a pin in the range of all possible pitches and found that yes, you can sing a note that's around this pitch. It's not a defining characteristic of you

_____

within your comfortable singing range. So trying to sing at around the pitch you'd automatically speak at is a great place to start.

forever more! Just a helpful starting point to remember.

You have sung one note—so there's no reason you can't sing many more, all in tune.

As you proceed with practicing singing, you will build on this, to produce a clear and steady pitch. Then you can begin to match the pitch that you sing to a specific pitch that you hear or aim for.

From here it's a matter of building up your ability step-by-step. Remember that singing isn't all-or-nothing! Just because you can't yet sing a whole song totally in tune it doesn't mean you can't sing.

If you've just gone through this "Find Your Note" exercise, then you know you can sing one note. And many more can follow!

Find Your Range

Now that you've found "Your Note", let's expand out to see what other notes will be easy for you to sing. This is important because one of the biggest causes of beginner singers singing out of tune is that they're trying to sing outside their comfortable vocal range.

Your vocal range

Every singer has a range of notes their voice is physically capable of producing. Generally, the middle of this range feels "easy" and you can sing well there. We might call it your "sweet spot".

There are advanced techniques and long-term training which can extend both your full range and your "easy" range, but as a beginner, you want to make sure you stay comfortably within your "easy" range. As soon as you start stretching your voice too high or too low your pitching will suffer. I'll remind you that singing need never feel like you're physically straining—that can be an indicator that you're pushing yourself too far beyond your comfortable range.

EXERCISE: Determining Your Vocal Range

We know that "Your Note" is inside your comfortable singing range, so you can treat it as an "anchor note": a starting point to explore your range.

Step 1: Explore the limits

Warm up by singing Your Note (whatever comes out) and then

from this note, try slowly sweeping up and down in pitch with your voice, like a siren.

Practice extending your up-sweeps and down-sweeps gradually and see how far you can go before your voice starts to feel strained.

Step 2: Determine Your Range

Knowing the precise notes that are at the upper and lower limits of your comfortable range will be very useful for making sure that your voice is at its best as you continue practicing, and later for choosing the best songs and keys to fit your voice.

Turn on your tuner and do an up-sweep from "Your Note". When you arrive at the upper note, hold it out for a moment or two and notice the note name shown. Then sweep down to the lowest note in your comfortable range and notice the note name shown there too.

You might like to jot down the notes that define your range, like this:

My Note: F3

My sweet spot: E3 - B3

My approximate range: C3 - F4

Keep in mind that technology is not fool-proof, so a bit of common sense will be needed here! Most singers have a comfortable range of half an octave up to 1.5 or 2 octaves in their "normal" singing voice.

Male singers may be able to find extra high notes with "falsetto" (think of a man doing an impression of a woman and using an artificially-high speaking voice) which stretch them beyond that. But if you are a beginner singer sweeping up and down from "Your Note" you can expect to find your "sweet spot" in this exercise is about an octave, and your full range a bit beyond that. For example "C3 to C4" is one octave, "C3 to E4" is a bit more than an octave.

Now you have one big aid to singing in tune: as you do exercises and start singing songs, try to stay in this range. You'll save yourself a lot of pain and frustration and find that singing (and accurate pitching) comes much more easily.

Practice Matching Pitch

So far we've been taking important steps to get acquainted with how our voices produce pitch. The next phase in learning to sing in tune is learning to *match pitch*.

Matching pitch means simply that you hear a note and then you can sing that note.

We will practice with exercises in which you literally hear the target note, but in the future, you will internalise this skill so that the note you "hear" is actually just imagined in your head. So "matching pitch" can also mean "you know what note you want to sing and then you can sing it".

It doesn't matter for now if you have a nice tone or strong-sounding voice, all we're interested in is: can you sing back a note you hear?

We're going to look at the basic process of how to match pitch and then three exercises you can use to practice.

How to match pitch

Matching pitch is easy to practice. The process is to:

1.   Listen to a note.

2.   Try to sing it.

3.   Judge whether you got it right (i.e. were you "in tune") or not.

4.   Try again, either with the same note or a different note.

These look like simple steps, but it's worth breaking them down a little further:

1. Listen to the note

Play a note from your range using an instrument or single-note sound clips such as those in the *Additional Resources*.

Rather than jump into singing right away, really give yourself some time to listen to the note and take it in. When I interviewed Nashville hit songwriter, singer, and vocal coach Judy Rodman she suggested that before singing, you "mime" the note while you are listening. Pretend that you are singing it yourself, on the syllable "yaaaa" or "laaa". When you do this, your imagination prepares the vocal mechanism for a much greater accuracy.

If you are an instrumentalist then another idea from Jeremy Fisher (co-founder of Vocal Process, one of the most impressive and useful singing websites) recommends that you "air-play" the note on your instrument for much the same reason: all your experience playing that instrument will engage your imagination (i.e. Audiation) and prepare your body to sing that note's pitch.

Even without doing either of those things, taking a moment to Audiate (hear in your head) the note you're about to sing before you open your mouth will make an enormous difference to your chance of hitting the note dead-on right away.

Over time you won't need to actually take a moment to do this, it will happen implicitly and naturally, but at first give yourself that chance to "take aim" before you "fire".

2. Try to sing it

As you start trying to match pitch (and especially if you're watching a digital tuner) you may notice that you're constantly making little corrections to slide back onto pitch. If your first attempt is way off, or if your voice seems to "stick" a bit too low or high, loosen up by sliding into the note from below and above, as we did in the warmup exercises earlier in the chapter. Then mime the note, as described above, and aim to hit it right on.

3. Judge whether you were "in tune" or not

Using your digital tuner is one way to do this. The tuner's accuracy and visual real-time feedback are extremely valuable. One risk with the tuner though is that it's possible to be so focused on the visual display that you stop listening to yourself, and don't feel what's going on with your voice. So when using the tuner, remember not to "turn your ears off". Keep listening, keep feeling, so that you can produce the results without visual feedback.

You can also grab an instrument and check against that, or you can record yourself and listen back.

You will make fastest progress and develop a robust and versatile ability if you alternate your practice among these different methods.

4. Try again, either with the same note or a different note

To practice hitting notes right away without audibly sliding, think of your exercise as "target practice": "ready, mime, fire!" at your target note. You can make a real game out of it by recording your accuracy (for example, a tuner may show how many cents[4] flat or sharp you were). You may find that certain notes, or certain areas in your range are easier or harder, so you can see what to focus on in practice.

This exercise should be a daily habit until you are confident in your ability to match pitch across your range.

Remember that watching a digital tuner is just one way to "calibrate" your voice. Include the other methods mentioned above in your practice too for best results.

Keep it Steady

One problem you might encounter as you start to practice matching pitch is that your singing pitch wobbles or slides when you try to sing a note. This can be frustrating when you're trying to hear whether you have the note right or not.

Producing a steady pitch is an important part of being an able singer, so if you are able to match pitch with your voice but find it hard to hold a steady note here are a few tips which can help:

1. Check Your Range

Go through the steps above to find your range and then make sure you're not singing outside those limits. Start with using notes from your "sweet spot" easy range.

2. Adjust Your Volume

The volume you sing with can greatly affect how easily you can keep a steady tone. If you're singing quietly, you may find that singing louder makes it easier to hold a steady pitch. On the other hand, if you're pushing your voice to be too loud, that can put strain on it. If you sing a bit quieter you may find the pitch control easier.

Remember that breath support is vital to comfortable singing, so be sure you're taking a decent breath in before singing.

Experiment with a range of volumes to find the level that's easiest to hold a note steady with. For most people this will be around their normal speaking volume.

3. Listen Carefully

Make sure you are listening and paying attention as you sing. It's easy to "turn off" your ears when you start to sing and this makes it

---

[4] A "cent" is 1% of a Half Step. Each Half Step has 100 cents.

harder to auto-adjust your pitch.

TIP:

Forgetting to listen as you sing is one of the biggest mistakes untrained singers make which makes them sound bad to other people! Until you are practiced, singing without thinking or listening puts you at risk of singing very out-of-tune without even realising it.

Make it a habit to listen to yourself as you sing and you can easily avoid this mistake.

For practicing, try putting aside the tuner if you're using one. Then try just singing some long notes and listening as you sing. Try to judge for yourself whether the pitch is steady. This increased awareness should help you improve pitch consistency and in time it will become a subconscious process, happening automatically every time you sing.

Try each of these three suggestions and you should be able to pinpoint the source of your singing pitch problem and fix it.

You are now equipped to learn to match pitch easily, accurately and reliably!

Remember that this skill is not something you'll master instantly. The exercises described above should be done daily and it will typically take a week or two of practice before you feel like you can reliably match pitch without needing to slide around too much.

However, put in that practice and soon you'll find you have equipped yourself with a skill for life—and one that will serve you very well throughout your musical journey!

Core Skill 2: Vocal Control

Once you have a basic ability to match pitch, one note at a time, the next step is to practice moving between notes accurately. Once you put this second core skill in place you have everything you need to sing simple melodies easily and reliably, which is sufficient to get all the benefits of singing described at the beginning of this chapter.

Listening to Yourself

The most important part of improving vocal control is learning to listen to yourself as you sing, and to adjust your voice when you notice you could make a better sound. Listening to ourselves provides the feedback loop, where we can learn what we like, what we don't like, and where to deploy the various aspects of vocal control we'll cover in the rest of this section.

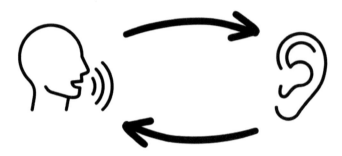

We touched on this already above: the source of many singing problems is that we have "turned off" our perception of our own voice. This happens easily when we're singing along with a recording, at a concert, or with others. With that sea of sound surrounding us, it's easy to lose track of our own voice. But it even happens when singing solo, when we focus so intensely on the sound we're imagining that we lose track of what's really coming out.

Once you simply shift your attention, this becomes easy to fix, and in time will even become second nature for you.

There are three ways we can listen to our own voices. When we make use of all three, we can form a more complete picture of our vocal sound, and therefore have more of an idea what to change in our vocal control to produce the sound we desire.

1. Internal

Normally, we hear our own voices mostly through bone conduction —the way the sound waves travel within our bodies. These waves are further dampened and modified by a very sophisticated system of muscles which keep us from blasting out our own ears and overwhelming other sounds around us.

2. External

Recording yourself and listening back will be a tremendous aid in developing vocal control. Recording picks up the sound of your voice as it travels through the air, so you will be able to hear yourself as others hear you.

There's an important warning I need to give you though! Because you're used to hearing your speaking and singing voice via bone conduction, when you first hear yourself on a recording, your voice is likely to sound downright weird to you! This makes it a very uncomfortable experience for most people at first.

However once you're aware of this phenomenon it's easier to be gentle with yourself, knowing that just because your voice sounds weird to you, that doesn't mean that it sounds weird to other people.

The solution is simply to keep recording yourself and listening back. The more you become accustomed to hearing your recorded voice, the more you'll be able to judge more objectively what you really need (and don't need) to fix.

Singing in a resonant room (for example a tiled bathroom) can be a good halfway measure combining both internal and external hearing, as you can hear your own voice reflected back to you as you sing.

3. Audiation

We've already seen how helpful audiation can be for matching pitch, to "take aim" before we sing a note. Audiation can also be a very useful tool for vocal control, when coupled with "reality checks" from internal and external listening.

EXERCISE: Listen to Yourself Sing

Sing a short, simple melody, such as a folk song or nursery rhyme you know from memory (e.g. "Mary Had a Little Lamb", "Happy Birthday", "Jingle Bells") and pay close attention to the sound you're hearing internally. Then audiate the same melody, miming as you do.

Jot down any differences or other observations you have when comparing your sung and audiated versions.

Now, record yourself singing the same melody. When you listen back, compare (as objectively as you can!) the recorded, audiated, and internally-heard versions. Jot down what you notice.

We're not trying to "fix" anything in this exercise. Just take a little time to sensitise yourself to these three ways of listening, their advantages and limitations, and how you can start combining them to have a clearer picture of your voice. As you continue to learn more vocal control exercises, you'll have a much better idea of how to improve.

Free Up Your Voice

When people start learning to sing, a common problem is not knowing how to use their muscles to produce different notes. It can feel like your voice is "all over the place" and it's natural to think that what you need is to restrict it to the right notes.

It's slightly counter-intuitive, but if we want to move accurately from note to note, hitting each one right on target, it's actually helpful to free up our voice and really get fluid across our vocal range.

The two exercises below will help you start to free up your voice across your range. Each should be practiced daily to begin with, and the benefit you get will be dramatically amplified if you record yourself and listen back as we covered above.

EXERCISE: Sighing Through Your Range

Breathe in, and then as you breathe out, do so with a vocalised sigh. You'll notice this sounds like a pitch sweeping downwards like we practiced earlier in the chapter, but it will probably feel more natural.

Take a good breath beforehand and try to make your sigh as vocalised as possible so it's closer to actually singing.

Repeat this, starting from different places in your range.

By doing these sighs, you're allowing your vocal anatomy to get used to working the muscles used to change pitch.

As you get comfortable moving through different parts of your range, you will probably find you open up your voice to singing more notes than before i.e. expanding your range. Then we have the opportunity to start being more intentional about where in our range we move our pitch when we sing.

The next exercise is similar to the previous one and to the "siren" part of the "Determining Your Vocal Range" exercise earlier in the chapter, but this time it's more controlled and with a specific start and target end note in mind:

EXERCISE: Pitch Sweeps

Pick a specific note from the range you can comfortably sing.

Then try sliding down to the same note one octave lower.

If this is too far for your range, choose a note a Perfect Fifth lower instead (count down 7 half steps).

The slide should be really slow and exaggerated. The key to this exercise is to keep it slow and pay attention to how far you are moving down in pitch.

You can also try this exercise starting on the low note and sliding upwards in pitch to the high note.

To refine your sense of pitch further you can also use an instrument to play each Half Step up the scale so you get an idea of the notes you are passing as you sweep your pitch. Make sure you keep your sung slide smooth though!

Hone Your Sense of Pitch

Now we'll start to refine our sense of pitch and precision of vocal control. These exercises are also useful to practice daily, including recording yourself and listening back.

The first exercise is similar to "Pitch Sweeps", but turning our smooth slide into a series of steps.

EXERCISE: Sing Half Steps And Whole Steps

Sing through an octave in your range, but instead of a smooth sweep, this time adjust your pitch in steps.

You can use either Half Steps (a.k.a. "semitones" or "minor seconds") or Whole Steps (a.k.a. "tones" or "major seconds"). So if you're covering a full octave that will mean singing 13 Half Steps or 7 Steps.

Half Steps will be easier for most people because you are only rising in very small amounts. Again you can use an instrument or a digital tuner to help you pitch each note at first. Singing Whole Steps across a whole octave is a lot harder and may sound quite strange at first, as scales using only Whole Steps are not very common in music.

> **TIP:**
>
> If you are familiar with scales you might like to know that the Half Steps option means singing a chromatic scale, while the Whole Steps option is singing a whole tone scale—not a major scale, which would involve mixing both Whole and Half Steps!
>
> Once you've practiced with Half and Whole Steps, then if you're familiar with the pentatonic or major scales you might like to practice Vocal Control with those too.

Practice singing Half Steps and Whole Steps, first along with the audio or an instrument, then without. If needed, shift up or down an octave, or find a starting pitch more suitable to your range, usually somewhere in the lower part of your "sweet spot".

Sing Intervals and Solfa

Although Half Steps and Whole Steps are the smallest "building blocks" of pitch, songs will normally also include larger leaps in pitch, i.e. bigger *intervals*. As a singer, it is therefore important to practice controlling your voice as it transitions between pitches which are further apart.

We'll give some basic information on Intervals and Solfa below, enough to let you practice with these exercises, before we cover them fully in Part II.

Solfa is a naming system for each note of the scale, and an interval is simply the distance between two pitches.

If we choose the note C as our tonic or "home note" (i.e. we're in the key of C Major, and using the C Major scale) then the Solfa names, note names and Intervals are:

- do-re (C-D) = Major 2nd

- do-mi (C-E) = Major 3rd

- do-fa (C-F) = Perfect 4th

- do-so (C-G) = Perfect 5th

- do-la (C-A) = Major 6th

- do-ti (C-B) = Major 7th

- do-do (C-C) = Perfect Octave

One of the best ways to practice both Ear Training and vocal control is to sing pairs of notes with the Solfa syllables, and then name the corresponding Intervals:

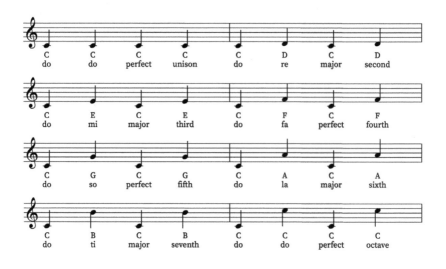

EXERCISE: Singing Solfa Intervals

Practice singing these "solfa intervals", first along with the audio from the *Additional Resources* or an instrument, then without.

Again, if needed you can shift up or down an octave, or find a starting pitch more suitable to your range, usually somewhere in the lower part of your "sweet spot".

Apply all of the vocal control techniques we've covered so far. Keep careful awareness of breath support. Warm up your voice with sighs and sweeps. Audiate before each note to "set your aim". Listen attentively, and record your practice so you can observe where there's room for improvement.

This is an especially useful exercise because while you're improving your pitching accuracy you'll also be internalising Intervals and Solfa recognition which can start to enable Playing By Ear and sight-singing from written notation. More on all this in Part II!

Start Your Daily Practice

This chapter has been full of information and exercises—you might be feeling a bit overwhelmed! The most important contributor to your improvement will be daily practice.

When you're learning to sing, you're training sensitive muscles, and it's crucial that you don't overdo it. Short, regular practice sessions are far better than occasional long sessions. You will make more progress with 5 or 10 minutes daily than 30 or 60 minutes a few times a week. Be gentle, learn your limits, and have patience.

Here is a summary of the exercises we covered which can be useful to practice regularly.

Breath Support:

*   Breath and Dynamics: Practice singing different wordless notes in your range, going firstly from loud to soft. Then loud to soft.

*   Find Your Breath Support Muscles: Inhale, letting go of any abdominal tension. Place your hands around your waist, in between your ribs and your hips, and give a gentle cough.

Matching Pitch:

*   Practice Matching Pitch: Listen to a note, sing it, assess your pitch accuracy (with an electronic tuner, your own ears while singing, or recording), try again.

*   Listen to Yourself Sing: Choose a short, simple melody you know well. Sing it. Audiate yourself singing it. Record yourself singing it. In each case, pay attention to the pitching.

Vocal Control:

*   Sighing Through Your Range: Take a good breath and then breathe out with a vocalised sigh. Repeat this, starting from different places in your range.

*   Pitch Sweeps: Pick a note from your range and slide down to the same note one octave lower. If this is too far for your range, choose a note a fifth lower instead.

*   Sing Half Steps and Whole Steps: Sing through chromatic and whole tone scales.

- Singing Solfa Intervals: Practice singing "solfa intervals", first along with the audio or an instrument, then without.

None of these exercises need to take very long, and they can be memorised quickly to use as part of your warm-up routine at the start of each music practice session. Depending on what your focus is and the opportunities you're seeing to improve, some exercises will naturally become ones you want to practice regularly, while others will no longer be so useful for you.

You will also discover plenty of other opportunities to use your singing voice in Parts II and III of this book which can all serve as further Singing practice too.

Conclusion

In this chapter we introduced Singing as a powerful tool for your musicality and showed you some easy first steps towards confident, reliable and accurate singing.

For many people Singing can seem intimidating, uncomfortable or even scary. But this only demonstrates the deep, biological and psychological connection we all have to our natural first instrument.

When you add Singing to your musical toolkit, you'll find endless opportunities to use your voice to learn faster and express yourself more easily in music. It doesn't take long to get to that "basic, everyday" level of Singing which proves so valuable, so I would encourage you to put in a little time over the next couple of weeks to practice the exercises in this chapter, and start using Singing as you continue through the book, both where it's specifically suggested, and any time you feel the urge to sing something you're hearing, playing or imagining.

As you gain confidence in your Singing skills, you will probably find yourself automatically starting to hum or sing tunes to yourself during the day, for example when hearing a song you love. Don't shy away from that! Allow yourself to gradually accept that identity of being "a singer" if it's naturally starting to emerge, and cultivate it where you can.

Singing can be one of the most rewarding, satisfying and fulfilling musical activities, so learning to sing is a great gift to give yourself, and will pay off throughout your musical life for years to come.

So dive in! Drink some water, be aware of your body, listen as you sing, and enjoy the journey into Singing.

CHAPTER FIVE:
ACTIVE LISTENING

"A lot of people are hearing, but not many are listening."
– Jeremy Burns, Music Student 101

Thinking about all the music that's passed through your life in the last few days, did you just hear it? Or were you actively *listening* to it?

When musicians think about developing their brain and ear for music they often make the mistake of jumping straight to music theory and ear training, thinking that what they need is all about specific concrete skills like recognising intervals, understanding the rules of harmony, or learning to adjust EQ bands on a mixer by ear.

But there's one big-picture skill that's possibly more important than all of those, as well as providing a great opportunity to put those other skills to use: Active Listening.

Active Listening simply means your mind is truly engaged in the activity of listening.

This is closely related to the idea of "music appreciation". If you take a traditional class on music appreciation it helps you start learning this skill of Active Listening, and equips you with some key concepts to put into action as you do it. But it only scratches the surface, and few musicians have actually studied even that basic form of Active Listening.

As a result, many of us wander in music for years, not realising just how much we're constantly missing out on in the music we hear and play.

Through intentionally cultivating our Active Listening skills, we can become more aware of all the rich detail in music, as well as understanding more about how it all fits together, and why.

If you've ever been frustrated, knowing that there's much more going on in the music you love than you seem to be able to pin down or explain—or if you've felt overwhelmed or intimidated hearing other people describe music with a level of vocabulary, conceptual understanding, and detail that just seems way beyond what you could manage yourself—then you're going to love this chapter.

Overview

In this chapter we'll begin by looking at the benefits of Active Listening, and all the ways it can permeate and enhance your musical life.

We'll explain how Active Listening works, and introduce the one core technique we recommend for practicing Active Listening: to listen "with a question in mind."

As Tony Robbins says, *"The quality of your life is a direct reflection of the quality of the questions you are asking,"* and so we'll provide guidance on the types of question we want to be asking, as well as providing lists of example questions you can use, throughout the chapter.

Next we'll introduce the 4-Dimensional Active Listening framework, which lets you deconstruct any music you hear or imagine in a methodical and flexible way. We'll go one-by-one through the four Dimensions: Timbre, Pitch, Rhythm and Dynamics, covering the basic concepts, terminology and theory of each, as well as how to start listening for them.

The music we hear and play exists in the real world, whether live or in a recording. It's therefore illuminating to explore what we can consider a fifth Dimension: the *audio* side of music, including Audio Frequencies and Audio Effects.

Finally we'll look at the bigger picture of how music is arranged in time, through Form and Texture, and how to listen for each.

We'll round off the chapter with a 7-Day Practice Plan which you can use to start putting Active Listening into action, using any music you choose.

Benefits of Active Listening

Active Listening will add immensely to your own enjoyment of music, and your ability to share that enjoyment with others, not to mention doing wonders for your own musicality. Let's explore some of the specific benefits you can expect when you learn this exciting skill.

Active Listening increases your musical understanding

When you listen actively, you begin to understand how different parts of the music fit together, how different sounds and instruments combine together, how a piece of music is organised into verses, choruses, and different musical sections. You can listen to pieces of music from different genres and eras, recognising all the different elements and how they come together. Naturally this is invaluable in creating and expressing your own music too.

Music critics will often make remarks like *"It sounds like a cross between The Beatles and Nirvana, with just a touch of '80s synth pop, sprinkled with a few droplets of 'Yes'."*

It can sound impressive, and clearly they are hearing music in a deeper, richer way than the average person on the street. But unless you want to write reviews yourself, when it comes to sitting down with your instrument and actually playing the music you want to play, what does all that talk of *"It sounds a little like this, a little like that, somewhat like this… "* get you?

Does it tell you what notes or chords to play and how to play them? How to organise them into a cohesive, whole piece of music? How to make it sound more like this and less like that?

Sadly not. So how do you gain that ability, to translate from these loose wordy descriptions into clear, precise, practical implications? Active Listening is the answer.

Active Listening "wakes up" your ears

Everything you're learning in music—Head, Hands, Hearing and Heart—all of the related skills can be applied to, and will benefit from,

Active Listening.

With Active Listening, every time you hear a song, you have an opportunity to both put your musical skills to use and also improve those skills.

Whenever Musical U members are looking for more time for music practice amid a busy life, Active Listening is high on our list of recommendations—because there aren't many of us who don't have opportunities during the day for at least listening to music.

You might be walking the dog, washing the dishes, driving a commute—all those times when music is normally just in the background can become valuable opportunities to level up your musicality through Active Listening.

Active Listening and Musical Memory

When you listen actively, you are also training your musical memory. To be able to mentally analyse what you heard, in the way that Active Listening involves, your musical mind needs to hold it in place for a moment. It starts forming a mental model of what's going on, and that kind of modelling and mental structure is exactly what you need to more easily remember longer sections of music you hear and play.

Active Listening and Audiation

As you're probably realising if you read *Chapter Three: Audiation*, Active Listening is closely connected to the skill of Audiation. When you practice Active Listening, you're teaching your brain to conjure up vivid mental representations of music, and that's something you can then apply to music you're creating in your mind yourself as well as the music you've heard.

In the chapter on Audiation, we shared one powerful exercise for combining your practice of both skills: after practicing Active Listening (like you'll learn about in this chapter), pause the recording or just take a moment after it ends, and try to recreate the song in your mind in as much detail as possible. This simple practice will develop your Active Listening, your Audiation, and your musical memory all at once.

The more you've explored a song or piece in detail with Active Listening, the easier you're going to find it to remember, and reconstruct it in rich, accurate detail in your mind.

The Gift of Active Listening

If you can say exactly what is going on in a piece of music, if you can talk precisely about the bassline, about the drum part, the guitar part, the rhythm, the different sections, the content of the lyrics, and so on, then you're going to be far more able to grab your own instrument or voice to make your own great music happen.

Now you're thinking, talking, and behaving like a musician.

Active Listening is a wonderful practice. It's a "gift that keeps on giving" for your whole life, as you learn to have deeper enjoyment of all the music you hear and bring a deeper knowledge and understanding of music to your own musical expression, whatever form that takes.

How Active Listening Works

At this point you're probably wondering: *"Alright, but what exactly are you doing when you're 'practicing active listening'?"*

Active Listening is not a new invention. As noted above, the idea of music appreciation or "critical listening" has been around for a long time.

For example when I was younger, I took a number of "music appreciation" classes. We would listen to a track and then discuss it, with the teacher generally providing most of the "right answers". Honestly, I loved it, because it was like a series of musical adventures, exploring music I never would normally have listened to. And I certainly did pick up some musical knowledge along the way.

More than anything else though, it just made me aware of how much I *didn't* know! I could tell you all about the tracks we had covered in class, but barely felt any more able to describe or understand other music I heard or played.

As we built Musical U, we found that most material on this topic follows a similar approach. It provides lots of descriptions of music, and expects the student to somehow turn that into the ability to produce those kinds of descriptions themselves. This can serve to wake up your ears a bit, but nobody seemed to be really teaching a method for doing it yourself.

That's why we developed our *4-Dimensional Active Listening* framework, which all centers around a single, simple method for practicing active listening.

Listening With A Question In Mind

One way to think about Active Listening is that you're thinking while listening. You are not just letting your thoughts wander, or being distracted by some other activity. You are focusing your full attention on the music you're hearing.

Easier said than done!

We've found that the easiest and best way to do this is by using a *question* to focus your mind.

Instead of just trying to generally "pay attention to the music", you ask yourself one or more specific questions about the music, and then use your ears to try to answer them.

If you took just one idea away from this entire chapter it should be this:

Listen With A Question In Mind!

You can begin with the overall question *"If you had to describe this song to someone, what could you tell them?"*

TIP:

You might like to choose a favourite track and take a moment right now to jot down how you would describe it to a friend. Then as you go through this chapter, try applying what you learn to that track. At the end, write a new description based on everything you've discovered.

To answer that overall question, you can then ask yourself a variety of follow up questions. For example:

- What instruments are present? It might be a rock band of guitar, bass, drums, keys and vocals, it might be a string quartet, it might be a full classical orchestra, etc.

- Can you hear each of the instruments present if it's a small group, or each of the sections if it's an orchestra? Of course this can change during the course of a song or piece, so this alone can be a great question to pay attention to throughout. Try to follow one or more of the instruments by ear and stay conscious of whether it's present and what part it's playing in the arrangement.

- What's the overall structure of the song or piece? Which parts repeat and in what sequence? This lets you form a big-picture mental model of the song, and a lot of the other questions we'll cover can slot into that structure once you figure it out. If you know the proper terminology or theory by all means use it, but a simple labelling system like "section A", "section B" and so on will work fine too.

- How many measures are in each section? Count it out if you can, e.g. "1, 2, 3, 4 / 2, 2, 3, 4 / 3, 2, 3, 4 / 4, 2, 3, 4, etc."

- What types of rhythm are being used? Is the beat straight or swung? Are syncopated rhythms being used? Is it the downbeat or the upbeat being emphasised?

- Is the song in a major or a minor key?

- What's going on in the harmony? You can try to hear which chords are major or minor, or if there are more complex types of chords being used. If you've studied Chords and Progressions in your Ear Training, you can try to hear the actual progressions, I-IV-V-I, etc.

- If you've been learning Solfa or Intervals, can you figure out the melody notes by ear? It can be handy to have an instrument or a keyboard app on your phone to check if you got it right. This starts to bridge into Ear Training (more on that connection later).

- What production techniques or audio effects are being used? For example, have real instruments been recorded in a simple way, or is it a full-blown electronic creation?

Now as you read through that list, even without a particular track in mind, no doubt some of those questions struck you as *"Oh, sure, I could do that"* while others had you thinking *"Wait, what?! There's no way I could answer that just by listening."*

Remember the famous principle from *The Hitchhikers Guide To The Galaxy:*

Don't panic!

In this chapter we're going to equip you with all the concepts and terminology you need to start answering these kinds of questions. And, as you'll discover below, Active Listening is not a quiz or a test, where you are striving to get every answer "correct".

The list above is intended only to paint a picture of what will be possible for you in the future, and what well-developed Active Listening skills can deliver you, in terms of musical understanding.

So the core activity of learning and practicing Active Listening is simply to listen to a piece of music, once or multiple times, actively asking yourself specific questions as you listen, and trying to answer them in your head.

Convergent and divergent questions

As part of the *Living Music* program we were fortunate to have leading educator Victoria Boler present a workshop on the topic of "Creative Listening", and one valuable distinction she introduced was that musical questions can be either *convergent* or *divergent*.

Convergent questions generally have one "correct" answer. For example *"what instrument is playing the melody?"*

Divergent questions have many possible answers. For example *"why do I love this melody so much?"*

By incorporating both convergent and divergent questions into your Active Listening practice, you expand your awareness even further and start transforming your listening into a creative practice. We'll come back to this below, when we talk about "Creative Listening".

How To Practice Active Listening

If you start practicing Active Listening like you'll learn about in this chapter then when someone mentions a new track, instead of you saying something like:

"Oh yeah, I heard that. It's a pop song, right?"

You might be able to say something more like:

"Oh yeah, I know that song. It's got kind of a country shuffle beat to it,

simple trio of guitar, bass and drumkit with the vocalist on top. Just follows a basic I-V-vi-IV progression in the verses, with a I-IV-V chorus. Starts out with an intro then it's just verse chorus verse chorus bridge chorus. In that bridge the bassist gets a solo and throws in these great syncopated rhythms to spice things up. The melody pretty much sticks to the major pentatonic in the verses but has these phrases lingering on the 7th note, the "ti" in the chorus which match up well with the lyrics about yearning. I love the barebones sound, just has a little bit of reverb but it's otherwise totally clean."

Now you're not just sounding like a music fan – you're sounding like a musician![1]

Imagine having this kind of awareness of every song you hear, and the impact this would have on learning new songs or collaborating with other musicians in a band, as well as the impact on your ability to play by ear or write your own music.

Active Listening is the key to developing a truly aware musical ear.

We might even call it a "mindful" ear. One that doesn't just drift through its experiences unaware, but is fully present to all the rich detail and structure in all the music you hear, so that you're able to hear, appreciate, understand and remember it all in a powerful way.

Does that sound like a lot of work?

Well, it's true that at first Active Listening does take a lot of conscious thought. But in time, although your attention will be focused on the music you hear, you'll find you don't need to think through all those questions so much. You will have awakened your ear to everything it can appreciate and be aware of in the music. Most of the question-and-answer process will happen automatically and subconsciously.

On top of that, possibly the best thing about Active Listening is how easy it is to get started. You could literally start practicing right now, using only what you've already learned so far in this chapter. Everything that follows will only make it faster and easier to improve.

There are many ways to include Active Listening practice in your musical life. Like Audiation, it's a skill that you'll find starts showing up everywhere for you, once you open the door.

You can base your practice entirely on what you're currently working on in your other musicality training. Or simply begin with your own music collection and the information in this chapter, and start exploring.

---

[1] We trust you to use this skill with good judgement—don't be "that person"! :D

You can start out with the basics, like listening for the instruments present and trying to tune in to a particular one throughout the song. Then, with every new concept or skill you learn in music, bring that to the task and ask yourself what this song is doing in relation to that concept or skill, such as tonality, harmony, rhythm, and so on.

You'll also find a 7-Day Practice Plan at the end of this chapter which suggests an easy step-by-step way to start putting it all into practice.

Active Listening and Ear Training

In some of the examples and descriptions above you might have found yourself thinking *"This sounds like ear training"* or *"How could I possibly recognise that by ear without doing tons of practice exercises?"*

The answer is that Active Listening and Ear Training are companion skills.

Either can be done independently, but both benefit hugely from the other.

If you are doing Ear Training exercises, that's going to give you some powerful skills to add specific detail to the questions and answers you use in Active Listening. And if you practice Active Listening, it's going to give you extra and interesting opportunities to actually apply all the new skills you've developed with Ear Training.

So for example, with only Active Listening and no Ear Training you might describe a melody simply as *"It's an ascending pattern of notes with a long-short-short, long-short-short rhythm"*. With some Ear Training that could become *"It's a do-re-mi melody, so if we're in C Major that's the notes C, D and E, and that rhythm pattern of quarter note with two eighth notes is played twice"*. Or for Chord Progressions with no Ear Training under your belt you would still be able to practice Active Listening and say *"It sounds like that classic 50s "rock and roll" progression in the chorus"* — whereas with Ear Training you could say something like *"The chorus is a I-IV-V-IV progression"*. And so on.

This means you don't need to feel obliged to do Ear Training, and you don't need to worry if you haven't already developed those kinds of skills. They are a wonderful optional addition to your Active Listening practice.

If you are doing Ear Training then since Active Listening is something you can do each and every time you hear a piece of music, it's an amazing way to fit in a huge amount of additional useful Ear Training practice in a very practical, applied way.

4-Dimensional Active Listening

The technique introduced above, "Listening with a question in mind", is the process we recommend for practicing Active Listening.

By itself though, this can leave musicians feeling a little overwhelmed and lost!

That's why we also developed a framework for classifying the different "dimensions" of music, to help you know the directions you can explore with your ears, and what kinds of questions belong with each.

Later in this chapter you'll be introduced to those four dimensions and how to start listening for each.

How do you know if you're getting it "right"?

One big way in which Active Listening differs from Ear Training is in the end goal. As soon as we start talking in terms of "questions and answers", your mind may have automatically assumed our goal was to get "all the answers right, all the time".

And naturally, it is generally better to be "right" than "wrong"! :)

But here's the crucial thing to know: Active Listening is an internal activity which is done as much for the sake of your own experience as for any external results it produces.

We can break down Active Listening's "question-and-answer" process into two parts:

A. Are you hearing what you need to hear?

B. Do you know the correct "name" for that thing?

This applies throughout. For example, it is entirely possible to be 100% aware of the Form of a piece, with an elegant mental visualisation of how it all fits together—without having a clue which bit should be called the "chorus" or whether it is a classical "rondo" structure. It's entirely possible to be hearing and analysing the instrumental makeup of a piece accurately—even if you have no idea whether one particular instrument you're hearing is a clarinet or an oboe.

The point here is that yes, it's great to know the correct terminology wherever possible, and understanding the theory and names for things can actually help you hear and understand more precisely. However: the heart of Active Listening is in the listening, not the naming.

If you took yourself off to live like a hermit in a cave with nothing but your music collection, it would still be entirely possible to become an expert active listener, even with no theory books or teachers or reference material to tell you the "correct" names for all the things you were beginning to hear.

So learning the theory and terminology is helpful for improving your skills more quickly and it's helpful for communicating the new things you're beginning to hear. But don't be intimidated by not knowing that side of things (yet). It is all learnable, and it is not the most important part of learning or practicing Active Listening.

With all that being said: how do you know if you're getting it "right"?

If it's just you alone in a room with the music, then the most useful tool you have is self-consistency.

Take the example of musical Form. You might be mixing up the assignment of "verse" and "chorus" when you try labelling the sections of a song. But what matters more is the underlying "ABABABB" or "1, 2, 1, 2, 1, 2, 2" structure you're hearing. So as long as you're being consistent about which section of the music you're calling the "verse" and which the "chorus", that's the main thing.

Or similarly, suppose you're mixed up about which audio effect is called "reverb" and which is "distortion". You might practice Active Listening for a week noticing all sorts of uses of what you think is "reverb". Does it matter that the correct name is actually "distortion"? For the purposes of training your ear and your mind, no.

Now I realise it might seem strange for an educational book to tell you it's okay to be wrong! But the valuable work in Active Listening is the time you spend listening and analysing in your mind. These mistakes of terminology can be very quickly corrected.

When someone points out to you that the crunchy sound is actually called "distortion", not "reverb"—or explains that a "chorus" is the bit that's always the same words and the words of the "verse" change each time—in an instant, you're corrected. All the time you spent listening for those things isn't invalidated. In fact it's just as valuable as before, you simply make the small tweak to use the right terminology.

So the main thing is to keep putting in the practice, and check yourself for self-consistency.

Now, with that being said, most of us don't live like a hermit, completely in isolation. So you do actually have a range of options available for "checking your answers".

Here are a few suggestions:

- **You can ask a musical friend.** Their knowledge and their ears will be different to yours, so they may both hear things you didn't yet hear, and they may know more about how to describe those things in the common vernacular. You might soon be surprised to discover how much more you are hearing than most of your musical friends, once you start practicing Active Listening.

  Tip: If you're focusing your active listening or you have a particular doubt about a certain thing, such as an instrument or genre of music, it's great to seek out a musician who specialises in that. Even if they haven't spent time on Active Listening they may have passively accumulated the ear skills and knowledge required to help you, just through their regular musical activities.

- **You can ask a teacher.** An instrument teacher, particularly one who studied music at a college level or above, will generally have strong ear skills and knowledge that can help check what you think you're hearing.

- **You can "ask the internet".** Often a Google search will turn up blog posts or discussions about a particular music track or an aspect of music. For example you might search for: "classical music forms", "distortion guitar effects", "timbre of different instruments" and so on. Or you might search for "Joni Mitchell voice characteristics" or "chord progression analysis Beatles Let It Be".

- **You can "ask your instrument".** Although Active Listening itself is an internal activity in your mind, when it comes to "checking your answers" in some cases it's helpful to experiment in the real world. For example you could try playing back a melody by ear to see if you were identifying the notes correctly or you could use composing software to enter a rhythmic pattern and see if you were hearing the pattern of notes you thought you were.

- **You can ask a community.** Whether in person or online, communities of musicians can be a great place to ask any Active Listening questions you have. There's no quicker way to get a discussion going than ask a probing question about the music people love! And compared with seeking out a particular friend or teacher, this way you'll get a variety of answers that may be more useful than any one expert.

  There aren't many communities that specialise in these "inner skills" of music, but Active Listening questions would be welcome in most online musician communities, and it is a particular focus at Musical U where we love to discuss this stuff, and have experts on hand, as well as many musicians of varying backgrounds and levels of experience.

So as you can see, there are a variety of ways you can "check your answers"—and each of these will typically lead to enlightening conversations and discoveries which advance your Active Listening far beyond the specific question you were seeking an answer to!

Always remember that *getting* it right is far less important than *doing* it right. As long as you are paying attention to the music, asking yourself specific, interesting questions, and carefully analysing the music in your mind to try to answer those questions, then you are doing it right.

Creative Listening

With all that talk of "right" answers, and before we dive into the nitty-gritty of the four dimensions of music, now is a good time to return to the idea of "convergent and divergent questions" and how Active Listening could actually become a creative activity for you.

We tend to assume that listening to music is a passive act. With our technique of "listening with a question in mind" you're hopefully already beginning to see that it can become quite active indeed! More than that, it can become not just an act of consuming or experiencing, but actively *creating* too.

It's like that old chestnut *"If a tree falls in a forest and no one is around to hear it, does it make a sound?"*

In a sense, unless somebody is listening, music does not exist. Sound waves might be moving in the air, but it is not until a person hears it that it becomes music. By listening, we are already creating the experience of music, completing the loop that started when a musician performed, or otherwise conjured up the music in the first place.

Whenever we listen to music, we are constantly making choices about what to pay attention to, and generating judgements and reactions based on what we hear. That goes double if you engage in an Active Listening approach.

We can take this creative role further, with the idea of *Creative Listening*.

When we take a Creative Listening approach we might:

A. Bring creative activities to our music listening,

B. Bring Active Listening activities to our music-making,

In practice, these two will quickly merge for you, as you start to recognise where both creating and listening are happening whenever we're engaged with music.

You can start bringing more creativity to your music listening by exploring Active Listening questions and activities like the following, which were suggested by Victoria Boler in her workshop on the topic, inside the *Living Music* program:

- Can you move to the music?

- What do you naturally notice most about the music?

- If this music accompanied a story, what would the story be about?

- Can you improvise along with the music? (clapping, singing, with your instrument)

- Can you draw a picture of this music?

- Can you draw a map of what someone else could listen for?

- What's your favourite thing about this piece?

- What would be a good title for this music?

- What do you think the creator was feeling or thinking?

Try a few of these out! You might feel self-conscious at first. That's normal with any creative act, something we'll be exploring more in *Chapter Fifteen: Improvisation* and *Chapter Eighteen: Performance*. For now, just try to suspend any judgement of what you create, and focus on enjoying the creative act itself.

You can start bringing more Active Listening to your creative activities by:

- First, just try to bring very engaged attention to listening as you play. Whether you're performing pre-written music, playing something by ear, or improvising, try to really build up the habit of listening while you play.

- Next, you can start using exactly the same kinds of questions you'll be learning about in this chapter, but applying them to the music you're playing, not just music played by others.

As you practice bringing more creativity to your listening, and more listening to your creative music-making, you'll find that Creative Listening becomes a natural and automatic part of how you experience all your musical activities.

Tips For Active Listening Success

Before we continue into more detailed instructions, here are a few general tips we've found can help you succeed with Active Listening:

- **You don't have to know it all.** In fact, you don't have to know anything! You may be presented with terminology that seems new or strange at first. It is not important that you master it all. Just allow it to wash over you and see what sticks, what seems the most accessible. Remember that concept of a "Loose Grip" Mindset and Convergent Learning. All you have to do is listen with a question in mind. And your question can (and should) be simple, and building on what you know.

- **Wear good headphones where possible.** They will help you access more details in the music. In the past I used to provide people with guidance on what constitutes "good" headphones. These days, to be honest, even freebie headphones tend to be pretty good quality. As a rule of thumb, if you paid money for your headphones or earphones, or they were made in the past five or ten years, they are probably well up to the task. So the main thing to know is "listen on headphones or earphones" rather than relying on speakers. The immersion and isolation makes a huge difference. I should also mention that higher quality headphones or earphones, such as those you would typically pay $50 and above for, can often reveal a greater depth of detail and make some listening tasks easier for you.

- **Checking is not cheating!** Remember the options above for "checking your answers" and keep in mind the Growth Mindset that says every mistake does you a favour by revealing the learning opportunity. So check the answers, listen again, and see how those answers raise your listening awareness.

- **If you're a member of Musical U, participate in the community discussions.** It's particularly helpful for developing the skill of Active Listening to learn from what other people are hearing and describing. I'm proud to say we have the most helpful, supportive, and interesting community of musicians anywhere, and our team is also there in the discussion boards every day, ready to help.

- **Keep moving forwards.** Keep it light and fun and don't get stuck on any one question or task. Your Active Listening skills will grow simply by going through these exercises. You do not have to master everything in order to get amazing results. And you can always come back and review again and again for deeper learning.

- **Start today.** Active Listening is as much a habit, or a way of life for a musician as it is an "exercise" you do or a skill to dedicate practice time to. As noted above, you now know enough already to start practicing Active Listening, even before reading the rest of this chapter. There's also the 7-Day Practice Plan at the end of the chapter to give you a structured way to get into momentum with Active Listening.

Recap

We've looked at what Active Listening is, and some of its many benefits. You've learned one simple method for practicing it: Listening with a question in mind. And we've shared some guidance for getting up and running with Active Listening.

Now it's time to introduce the 4-D Active Listening framework which you can use to continually explore further and deeper in all the music you listen to and play.

We will look at each of the four dimensions in turn, and then the "bigger picture" of Form (the different sections of a piece of music) and Texture (how different musical layers work together).

The 4 Dimensions Of Music

"Writing about music is like dancing about architecture."

— Frank Zappa

There are probably as many ways to classify and categorise different parts of music as there are musical genres[2]. A songwriter might think in terms of "lyrics, melody and harmony". A classical composer may think in terms of the different orchestra sections, and classical forms such as sonata, rondo, theme and variations, and so on. An electronic music producer may think in terms of their Digital Audio Workstation (DAW) interface with its layers of tracks and piano roll representations.

Ultimately, no formal system of describing music can ever be perfect or complete, since music is by nature an ever-evolving art constrained only by the limits of human imagination.

The framework you're about to learn is therefore not intended to be a "correct" or even canonical way of describing music. However we have found it to be highly versatile and extremely useful, especially when it comes to Active Listening.

This is a framework you can have in mind for any musical activity, not just listening. Musical U members have found it highly useful in creative activities such as improvising and writing music too. You'll find that it makes an excellent companion for the "Constraints and Dimensions" of Expansive Creativity presented in *Chapter Fifteen:*

---

[2] And, as we'll be exploring in this chapter, genres are a highly debatable construct!

Improvisation and learning the musical "language of emotion" in *Chapter Seventeen: Expression*.

So this is very much a framework for thinking about, describing and exploring any music, and going as far and as deep as you like with your thoughts, descriptions and explorations.

Let's start simple though, and begin with the smallest musical element: one single note.

As rich and complex as music can be, it all starts with a note, which simply means "a sound used to make music".

A note has four dimensions:

- Pitch

- Rhythm

- Timbre

- Dynamics

Pitch is the perceived highness or lowness of a sound. That's one thing we're going to be asking ourselves a lot: *"Where on the whole continuum of high sounds to low sounds does this particular pitch in the music fall?"*. Not all notes have a single well-defined pitch, but almost all musical sounds can be described in terms of where they exist on this dimension of pitch.

Musical notes also exist for a certain length of time. The musical term "**Rhythm**" describes the pattern of the longness and shortness of notes and the silences in between.

Timbre is a word borrowed from the French and pronounced like the first part of the word "tambourine". An English term with similar meaning is "tone colour". It refers to the properties of a sound that can make one note sound different than another, even if they're playing the same pitch.

For example if you listen to a flute playing the pitch we call "A440" (the A above middle C in standard tuning) and you listen to a piano playing that same "A440" pitch, you can immediately tell the difference between the piano and the flute by their timbres.

Sounds carry varying degrees of energy. When it's a small amount of energy, the sound is what we call a "soft" or "quiet" sound. Sounds with a large amount of energy are called "loud". We refer to this as softness, loudness, or "volume". Changes in volume over time in music are called **Dynamics**.

These are the four dimensions of a single musical note: Pitch,

Rhythm, Timbre and Dynamics. These dimensions then combine in infinite variations to create more structures in the music for us to listen to.

Right now, even with nothing but your new awareness of these dimensions, you could start listening to music and asking yourself:

- *"What different timbres can I hear? Can I figure out what instruments there are?"*

- *"How is the pitch of the different notes, the highness and lowness of sounds, used in this piece?"*

- *"What's going on with the rhythms here—overall and for a particular instrument?"*

- *"What are the dynamics? Is the music loud or soft overall? Do the dynamics change at any time?"*

Next we will look more deeply into each of these dimensions, the structure of music, and how you can employ these understandings to more deeply appreciate and understand all the music in your life.

A Quick Word About Genre

In what follows, we'll be making various references to musical genres. The idea of a "genre" in music can be highly contentious, and often the genre of a given track can be debatable. At last count Spotify recognised over 6,000 "genres"! And that's up from about 1,500 in 2016[3].

Musical "genre" labels are a human construct, and admittedly a highly imperfect one. However the concept is still extremely useful, by providing us with shorthands for a whole collection of musical traits—which you can then describe more specifically and in more detail with your newfound Active Listening skills.

So when we make statements below about musical genres or styles, keep in mind the "descriptive" approach to music theory we discussed in *Chapter One: Musicality*. Any "rule" in music should only be seen as a guideline or a musical tendency. So being aware of the norms for a given genre isn't about making sure you get it "right"—but rather about giving you the conscious choice of whether to match the

---

[3] You'll find a link to a fascinating analysis of this in the *Additional Resources*.

conventions, or defy them in your own creative way.

1. Timbre

We'll begin with this dimension because listening for Timbre (and particularly different instruments) is the easiest way to start your Active Listening practice. Each instrument immediately distinguishes itself from others by its unique timbre, sound, or "tone colour".

Scientifically, Timbre is the complex recipe of sound waves that makes up each instrument's characteristic sound. It can also vary individually, from one performer or model of instrument to another.

When it comes to electronic instruments, this whole dimension becomes exponentially more varied, as different keyboard and synth players devise crazy new timbres, or as instruments such as the electric guitar—a veritable timbre-generating machine—is processed through all different kinds of pedals, amps and various other electronics.

There are lots of descriptive words that we use to describe Timbre.

For example, "twang". We can say *"Shania Twain sings with a twang."* With a singer that means they have a more nasal timbre. An instrument can be "twangy" too. For example, we can say a banjo typically sounds more "twangy" than a guitar.

We can also talk in terms of the complexity of a timbre, with words like "simple" or "rich". For example, an electric guitar that isn't plugged into an amplifier has a very simple timbre. It sounds like a metal wire being plucked, which is one of the simplest musical sounds we can create. Similarly, the triangle in an orchestra produces a very simple sound when it's played.

On the other end of the spectrum, when you hear a cello play even a single note slowly, and with feeling, there is great richness and complexity to the sound which hits your ears. The human voice can have such a rich timbre that it connects deeply and emotionally with us—even without using words or having any complexity to the pitch or rhythms used.

Timbre is something to listen for in itself, along with how it contributes to the overall structures and textures in musical Form (which we'll discuss more, later in the chapter).

Instrumental Timbre

Music uses Timbre in a variety of ways. Often, the contrasting timbres of instruments play off each other, but even individual instruments can use contrasting timbres in their performance.

For example the guitar—even a single acoustic guitar—can produce many different timbres, depending on how it's played: close to the bridge, over the sound hole, close to the neck, with metal or plastic plectrums, fingernails or fingers.

Different individual instrument models, styles, woods, and techniques all contribute to the timbre. As you actively listen to different guitars and guitarists, for example, you'll develop a deep appreciation for all the ways that Timbre can be used musically, and clarify what choices you will make in your own musical development and expression. The same goes for most instruments. They can produce a wide range of timbres, depending on the pitch range. Whether it's a high or low note, for example, might yield a different kind of a timbre that you could be looking out for in your Active Listening. Or with a saxophone, for example, you may find you want to be adjusting your embouchure or the reed that you're using to produce a certain timbre you've heard.

Listening for Timbre can therefore give you a clue as to what you might do with your instrument, or a particular sound that you might want to re-create, or be inspired by. This is a perfect example of how your Active Listening practice can inspire and fuel your own musical creativity.

This is one reason that if you play an instrument yourself, listening out for that instrument can be a great starting point in your Active Listening. You will have a headstart, because your ear and mind are already attuned to that instrument's specific nature. And you will see a greater payoff faster, because your new listening discoveries can provide such direct application in your musical life.

Timbre and Genre

Timbre also can help you to listen for the genre of a piece of music. So for example, if you hear someone playing a saxophone with a round, deep sound which is called "sub-toning" then you might know to identify that with the jazz ballad genre.

If you hear the saxophone being played with a very wide, open kind of nasal tone, you might associate that instead with modal jazz from the 1960s. Or if you hear it being played with growling sounds (produced by singing and playing at the same time) you may associate that with rock'n'roll.

Learning these connections between Timbre and genre can also help you when you're playing music, by revealing how to play appropriately for that genre.

You probably wouldn't want to be playing a big growly saxophone sound on an old jazz standard ballad! Similarly, a guitarist would choose certain guitar sounds because these vary by the genre. The guitar sound that you would use for metal won't be the same as the one you'd use for jazz.

As well as these individual instrument timbre considerations, there are different ways that instruments combine their timbres together ("ensembles") that can also tell you about what kind of music it is.

For example, if you hear a banjo, a mandolin, a fiddle, and a bass, and a guitar, you're likely listening to bluegrass or some kind of Americana music.

If you're hearing a string quartet, often it will be classical music. Or, if you're hearing sections of saxophones, trumpets, trombones, along with bass guitar and a piano, you might be listening to big band jazz.

So different instrumentations are associated with different genres of music, and listening for Timbre is your gateway to identifying those instrumentations—and by extension, the likely genre.

Again, remember that these are guidelines and not strict rules! In fact, the musical effect is often enriched when genres cross paths. For example, bringing a banjo into a rock'n'roll band evokes a taste of a different genre, adding richness to the music.

How to Start Listening for Instruments and Timbre

As you start actively listening for timbres and different instruments, one exercise that can get you quite far is to simply pick one instrument, "tune in" to it in the mix, and follow it throughout the song.

By default, we as music listeners tend to be focused on the most prominent instrument (the "lead" instrument) at any given time. In certain songs, there might be an instrument that's always in the lead, but more often it varies over time. The challenge for you as an active listener is to follow a particular instrument whether it is the "lead" or not!

For example, you might practice listening to the electric guitar in a certain rock song, but most of the time the guitarist won't actually be leading through the whole song. There might be a vocalist coming in, and when they sing the guitar will be playing counter-melodies, or backing riffs. Or the guitar may switch between lead and rhythm playing, becoming more prominent when playing a solo as lead and less prominent when playing the rhythm guitar part in the background. Can you follow that same guitar even as its role and prominence changes?

If you listen out for that timbre, and follow the guitar through the song, you're going to learn a lot about what things you'll need to learn to play or write that kind of music yourself, as well as deepening your appreciation of how that kind of music works, purely as a music listener.

Listening for Layers of Musical Texture

To give another example for the exercise above, you might choose to follow the bass guitar through the whole song. Rarely does the bass take the lead in mainstream popular music, but it's a very important element and you can normally follow it throughout the song and hear how it's interacting with everything else that's going on.

At that point you may even find yourself wanting to follow the exact pitches the bass is playing, and to learn to identify them by ear, or understand how they relate to the Chord Progressions. We'll get to the Pitch dimension shortly, but the point for now is this: following one instrument throughout the song can really open up your ears to how all the layers of music are put together.

Similarly, you may even follow the drum set, or even just one drum. What is the snare doing in this song? What is the kick drum doing? What are the cymbals doing? Often, we take the percussion part for granted even though it has a huge impact on our experience of the music as a listener! Tuning in to the percussion, even dissecting it into its component parts, can quickly transform your appreciation of how important that layer of the music is.

Listening for Similarity and Contrast

Another important aspect of listening for Timbre is to think about the similarity and contrast of timbres present.

If you're listening to classical music, you may be trying to follow the individual parts of the brass instruments, or the string instruments. In some cases that can be quite difficult, because the timbres blend together so well! For example, a viola and a violin have such similar timbre that it may be difficult to distinguish them except by listening in terms of pitch instead. So listening for one of those instruments can be quite a challenging exercise (in a good way!)

In other cases, the timbres are quite different. For example, a French horn versus the string section. If you're following the French horn part you're unlikely to accidentally tune in to what the strings are doing.

This same principles hold across all different kinds of music, including electronic music (by which we mean music produced by an electronic synthesiser, or a computer). Even though in that case all the music might technically be produced by one "instrument", each synthesised sound in electronic music can be considered a different instrument with its own timbre, and so you can listen for and follow that timbre.

Listening for Roles

Electronic music is a useful genre for illustrating how listening for Timbre can help us understand musical roles.

Often in electronic music, the synthesised instruments mimic the roles of traditional acoustic instruments. So even though everything may physically be played on an electronic keyboard, you'll likely still have a "bass part", a part playing harmonies and chords, and a part playing melodies. You can often find these different roles through listening for the different timbres, and listening for how they work together from there.

Developing Your Ensemble Skills (Even Before You Have a Band)

One major side benefit of this kind of Timbre-based Active Listening is how much it enhances your appreciation of other instruments and how ensembles work together.

Musicians have a tendency to get laser-focused on their own instrument, particularly when we hear music—it's our own instrument that tends to draw our attention by default.

If you've taken up a second, or third instrument, you'll know what I mean! I remember vividly how within the first week or two of starting to play bass guitar, suddenly it felt like the bass parts in the music I listened to day-to-day were leaping out at me. They had always been there... but now my ears were alert to that instrument, and curious about what it was up to. The music opened up for me in a whole new way. Likewise when I started to play drums—I suddenly realised how blurry and subdued my awareness of the drum part in songs had always been before!

You can gain much the same heightened awareness simply by consciously focusing in on a certain instrument. You might like to set the intention to listen out to one instrument or role for a period (e.g. *"This week I'm going to really listen out for backing vocals"*) or you might like to work on increasing your awareness of all the instruments/roles at play.

By practicing Active Listening and paying attention on each instrument present and how they work together, you broaden your appreciation and understanding of the ensemble and the music as a whole. This will make you a far more capable musical collaborator in musical groups in the future. We'll revisit this topic in Chapter Eighteen: Performance when we discuss listening actively to other musicians when you perform together.

Questions in Mind

Here are some questions you can use to explore Instruments and Timbre.

Keep in mind that almost all questions can be asked for the whole piece of music overall, as well as for a particular instrument, a particular section, etc.

- *How many different instruments can I hear?*

- *What instruments am I hearing? (this can be broad e.g. "strings, brass, woodwind" or specific "two violins, a viola and a cello")*

- *Are there any clear groupings of the instruments, by timbre or instrument family, or by the role they're playing in the music?*

- *What is the timbre of this particular instrument like? How does that compare to what's "normal" for that instrument, is there anything distinctive about this particular timbre?*

- *How are the various timbres present similar to each other? How are they different?*

- *Is the instrumentation or the mix of timbres changing over the course of the piece? If so, how is it changing? From one section to the next section, and during each section?*

- *What's the impact of instrumentation and timbre on the mood of the music? How is it being used artistically, for effect on the listener?*

What would this piece sound like with a particularly different instrumentation/timbre?

- *What other music do I know that sounds like this, in terms of timbre? (Bonus points if you can cross genres!)*

- *What are the musical roles I can hear? (e.g. lead melody, rhythm section, backing harmony, countermelody, etc.) How do they correspond (or not) to the different timbres present?*

2. Pitch

Our next dimension is Pitch. When we're thinking about pitches in music, we can think about how they move forward on the horizontal time axis, which is the *melody*.

Or how the pitches are all stacked up vertically on top of each other at any given moment, which is *harmony*.

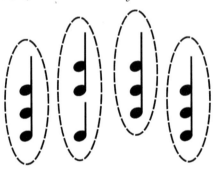

Let's explore each of these two in turn.

Listening for Melody

When you take a series of notes with Pitch and Rhythm, you have a melody.

As a starting point, listening for when the pitch rises and falls can tell you a lot about the music. We call this the *Pitch Contour* of a melody.

From note to note, the pitches in the melody can progress in one of three ways:

- Up

- Down

- Stay the same

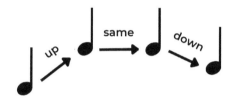

This Pitch Contour is critical in how musical phrases are shaped and how the overall message and emotion of the music moves forwards.

NOTES:

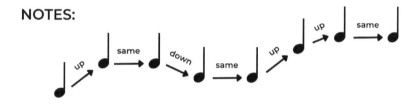

PITCH CONTOUR:

We can get more specific in our Active Listening for pitches, especially if we've done some Ear Training.

The notes of a melody are generally taken from a particular scale, meaning a collection of note pitches. When pitches from outside the scale are used, these typically stick out a bit to our ears. Most melodies tend to move around using mostly (or exclusively) the pitches of the scale.

Sometimes the pitches are close together, moving in *steps:* up and down the scale without making any jumps or skipping any pitches. This is called "stepwise motion".

Or you might find there are jumps in pitch where a note from the scale is skipped over. We call these *skips*.

So a great starting point when listening for melody is to try to identify the Pitch Contour (you can draw it on a piece of paper as a line moving up and down, as in the diagram above) and perhaps also whether it's mostly using steps or skips.

With Ear Training, you can also learn to identify the specific notes being used. There are two main approaches to this: Intervals and Solfa. The Intervals approach involves judging the pitch distance between any two notes (for example, one note of a melody to the next). The Solfa approach involves judging the distance of pitches from the scale's base note or *tonic*, so you are essentially identifying which note of the scale it is.

We'll be covering this note recognition skill in detail in Part II, and mention it here just to explain how it relates to Active Listening. Most musicians, including those who are very good at Active Listening, will not be able to name the specific notes being used in every melody they hear—so don't worry if this seems beyond you for now!

Listening for Harmony

Harmony is created when multiple different pitches are played at once. The term "harmony" also refers to how the pitches resonate and combine with each other to create an overall musical sound.

There are many different levels of harmony. Some music doesn't use harmony at all: there's only one voice, one instrument, with no harmonic backdrop behind it.

One level beyond that would be a simple form of harmony that's used in various forms of world music: a *drone*-based harmony, where there are just one (or two notes) which establish the harmonic context, and they are played constantly throughout the music. This is common, for example, in classical Indian music, Hindustani or Carnatic raga.

In most mainstream Western music there is a much greater degree of harmony used, often expressed in terms of *Chords*. A Chord is a combination of three or more note pitches, and there are various ways to classify and identify chords, which we'll explore in detail in *Chapter Eleven: Chords and Progressions.*

Different genres tend to use different numbers of chords. For example in most styles of popular music, often the songs may use only three or four chords, but in jazz you might find 10 or 20 different chords used in a single piece.

It can be helpful to think about how the harmony is being produced. Specifically, how does the number of instruments relate to the number of pitches you're hearing? The chord we call "C Major" always consists of the notes C, E and G—but it sounds quite different when there is a guitar strumming those three defining notes across six strings than when there is a four-part choir of one hundred people singing those same three chord notes, or when a pianist plays an eight or even ten-note version ("voicing") of the same chord spanning several octaves.

Listening for Harmonic Rhythm

Chords generally change during a piece, so there's also a horizontal time-based dimension to harmony, known as *harmonic rhythm*. A chord can change every measure, or every half measure, or every beat, even[4]. You will hear some crazily-fast chord changes in some jazz music! Or in ambient music genres you might have a chord that stays the same over several measures or even minutes.

Listen for when there's a change in harmonic rhythm: you may have a chord that's going for a long time and then all of a sudden there's a lot more chords that come at a more rapid rate. That can indicate a change in the *Form*, meaning a different section has begun. We'll cover Form in more detail later in the chapter, and the harmonic rhythm can be one of the easiest ways to tune in to what's happening in the Form.

Pitch and Timbre

With different pitches come different timbral qualities in an instrument. When you're playing high squealing sounds in a guitar solo (e.g. Eric Clapton's opening riff on Derek & the Dominoes' Layla), or low deep sounds (like the opening riff and ongoing fingerstyle-guitar backing part in Johnny Cash's classic song "I Walk The Line") there are very different timbres to the instrument, and much of this can stem from the pitch range as much as any other timbral effects being used.

The same thing goes for the human singing voice. Often, when we're singing pitches that are high in our range, there's a sense of

---

[4] We'll define "measure" and "beat" later in the chapter. If you're not familiar with the terms, for now just know that a measure is typically less than ten seconds long and a beat is typically half a second to a second long.

urgency or intensity, and when we're singing low in our range, it's more mellow-sounding. Higher pitch in vocal lines often indicates a higher emotional content in the lyrics, so this is another thing to start listening for.

Questions in Mind

Here are some questions you can use to explore Pitch.

Keep in mind that almost all questions can be asked for the whole piece of music overall, as well as for a particular instrument, a particular section, etc.

- *Are the pitches I'm hearing relatively high or low? How does that differ by instrument? How does it compare from section to section of the form?*

- *What's the Pitch Contour of the melody (or whatever instrument I'm tuning in to)? With each phrase is it ascending, descending, tracing an arc up and then back down, something else?*

- *Are there leaps in pitch or is it simple stepwise motion? If there are leaps are they large jumps or just small skips?*

- *With vocal melodies: When do the pitches go up? What emotional qualities does this lend to the sound? When does the singer have to work harder to produce the pitch?*

- *If you've been developing your sense of Relative Pitch with Ear Training: Can I identify the specific intervals or scale degrees (solfa) being used?*

- *Can I hear multiple instruments playing in unison (the same pitches)? How many different pitches can I hear at once?*

- *Does the arrangement follow the normal configuration of melody being the highest pitches, harmony beneath that and bassline at the bottom?*

- *What kind of harmony is being used? e.g. no harmony, a simple drone, chords. Does that change over time?*

- *What's the harmonic rhythm: how often and with what pattern are the chords changing?*

- *What's the overall pacing of changes, are they frequent (e.g. multiple chords per measure) or relatively slow (one or more measure per chord)—and does that change from section to section?*

- *How is the timbre being affected by changes in pitch?*

3. Rhythm

Our next dimension is Rhythm. Note that as with Pitch, we will devote whole chapters to the details of this dimension in Part II of the book, and you'll find a lot more guidance there on how to tune your ear in. Here, we will provide some simple explanations to help you start incorporating Rhythm questions into your Active Listening.

There are several different inter-related aspects of Rhythm that you can be listening for, together and separately. The first thing to listen for is the *pulse*.

The pulse is made up of a steady series of *beats*, like a heartbeat. The word "beat" can be used in different ways in music. For example the whole percussion and backing section is often called the "beat" in rap or hip-hop music. We'll be using the word to refer to the steady ticking of the pulse, in the sense of *"there are four beats per measure"* or *"this note lasts for two beats"*.

Pulse

The pulse is steady, and underlies everything. You can think of it like a yardstick that measures out the music. This is the first thing to listen for with the dimension of Rhythm, because when you can hear the pulse, you can use it to measure the other rhythmic qualities.

One great way to find the pulse is to clap along with the music. Clap along with music which has a stable, consistent beat (most music does, most of the time) and see if you can find that steady pulse with the music in your body.

Once you've found the pulse, you'll have a baseline for measuring all the other rhythmic aspects.

Difficulties with the Pulse

As we noted in *Chapter One: Musicality* when discussing the various skills that contribute to your musicality, this ability to find the beat and clap along sounds like it should be easy and basic—but it's not always so! Often rhythms can be accented or notes can fall at times not matching up with the pulse which can throw you off. This is called "syncopation" and we'll talk a little bit more about it later in the chapter.

In certain kinds of music the pulse is less obvious. If you can imagine a slow classical piece, in which there's a beautiful melody, you might not readily determine the pulse, because it's not being played explicitly by any specific instrument. But it's still there.

The pulse is underneath everything, and it's what helps musicians to be able to know how long or short to play their notes.

In other kinds of music, the pulse is actually being played beat-by-beat by an instrument such as a drum or other percussion instrument, so you can more easily hear the pulse clearly, throughout the piece.

Meter

In most musical styles the pulse has a regular pattern of "accented" (meaning louder) and "unaccented" (meaning softer) beats. This is referred to as the *meter*.

A tremendous percentage of popular music uses a "quadruple" (meaning four-beat) meter, where there is a strong accent on the first beat of those four beats: 1, 2, 3, 4. Often the third beat also has a softer accent:

1, 2, 3, 4, 1, 2, 3, 4, 1, 2, 3, 4, 1, 2, 3, 4...

Even sticking with a four-beat meter the beats can be accented in different ways though. For example, in some blues styles and early rock-and-roll, and popular styles, you might hear an accent on the second beat and the fourth beat, rather than the first and the third beats which are the stronger accents in classical music.

1, 2, 3, 4, 1, 2, 3, 4, 1, 2, 3, 4, 1, 2, 3, 4...

This turns things around a little bit, and plays up against the melodies, which are likely still accenting on the first beats.

Measuring Music with Our Ears

Hearing the meter helps us to measure the music in time. The meter divides the beat into regular groupings called "bars" or "measures". You can actually count the number of measures of a piece of music while you're listening, and then you'll know how long each section is.

A common practice to help you keep track is to replace the first "one" of each measure with the number of the measure. For example let's say you were counting a piece of music in quadruple time, instead of counting "1, 2, 3, 4 / 1, 2, 3, 4 / 1, 2, 3, 4 / 1, 2, 3, 4" and trying to separately count the measures too, you would count "1, 2, 3, 4 / 2, 2, 3, 4 / 3, 2, 3, 4 / 4, 2, 3, 4" and so on. In this way, you are able to easily keep track of the measures while also counting how long a particular section of the music is.

More Meters

There are, of course, many other metrical possibilities besides the one described above. Another very common one in western music is "triple meter" which organises the pulse in groups of three (or six). It's not nearly as common as quadruple meter in popular music, but it is very common in classical, older styles of dance music, and folk music.

Triple meter is counted:

1, 2, 3, 1, 2, 3, 1, 2, 3, 1, 2, 3

Many times, we think of this as a waltz rhythm. This brings up something else interesting about music and rhythm: a lot of music is intended to be danced to, or is brought from that kind of dance music into other genres. So rhythmic patterns often have origins in the way we like to move our bodies.

If there are heavy pulses which make the music easy to dance to, that's another thing that we can be looking for in the Rhythm of the music that we're listening to.

How to Start Listening for Meter

The easiest way to listen for meter is to find the pulse (e.g. by clapping along or tapping your foot in time with the music) and then count either "1, 2, 3" or "1, 2, 3, 4" along with the music. One of them is going to fit better and feel more comfortable and natural to you, indicating whether the meter is triple or quadruple.

You can go further than this, into subdivision of beats and compound meters, which we'll explore more in Part II. But simply tuning in to the beat and identifying the type of meter is a great start.

Rhythm

Beat and meter are both aspects that form a background structure for the Rhythm itself.

Remember that "rhythm" refers to how long and short the notes are, and the spaces between them. So the rhythm of the notes is played against the beat and meter established. When you're listening, is the rhythm going right along with that steady beat or are there a lot of rapid notes squeezed into a certain time period, or slower notes, longer notes, shorter notes? What about the silences in between them?

One thing to listen for is how the rhythms change from one section to another. So, for example, if you are listening to popular music in "song form", then during the verse you may have more rapid shorter notes. Then, when it comes to the chorus, you may have longer notes. Very typically, in effective songwriting, the rhythm of each section contrasts with the other sections. There's also a place for having mixed long and short rhythms, which gives its own effect.

The notes themselves may fall right on the beat, or they may fall off of the beat—often on what is called the "and"s of the beat (because we count a beat subdivided in two like this: *1 and 2 and 3 and 4 and*").

When notes fall "off the beat" and they are accented, we have what's called *syncopation*. In some forms and styles syncopation is typical, while in others syncopation is something unusual.

For example, in ragtime music you have very frequent syncopation throughout the piece. It's very clearly demonstrated in ragtime piano pieces, because the left hand plays a straight-ahead march rhythm, while the right hand plays off-beat rhythms.

In ragtime, syncopation is expected, so when the rhythm does go "straight" (falling on the beat) it's a sharp contrast. On the other hand in classical music, syncopation is saved for special moments, so when it happens it's more of a surprise.

So listening to whether the beats are falling "on the beat" or "off the beat" is another clue as to the genre and how the particular piece follows or defies the expectations of that genre.

Tempo

One final aspect of rhythm to consider is how fast or slow the beat is moving. This is called the *tempo*.

When we talk about music being fast or slow, we're typically talking about the tempo: how fast the underlying beat is moving. Tempo can stay constant throughout a piece or it can change over time.

In classical music, changes in tempo are widely used for expressive effects, to mark a passage coming to its end.

In most popular music, the tempos are very steady throughout. If they do change, they typically change all of a sudden. For example in indie rock music, it's common to start with somebody strumming on acoustic guitar, then all of a sudden the full band comes in at double the tempo.

When there is a change in tempo in popular music, it's usually halved or doubled in some way, in a direct ratio to the previous tempo. In classical music and some other styles, more gradual or nuanced changes in tempo are more common. In certain genres of Greek music, for example, you find a very slow and steady increase in tempo, called "accelerando". If you can imagine dancing to this and you're dancing in a circle with other people, this can be very exciting as it gets faster, and faster. Again we see that connection between musical rhythm and the corresponding dance activities for which it was originally written.

Questions in Mind

Here are some questions you can use to explore Rhythm.

Keep in mind that almost all questions can be asked for the whole piece of music overall, as well as for a particular instrument, a particular section, etc.

- *How fast is the music overall? Does that change over time? If so, are those changes sudden or gradual?*

- *Can I clap or tap along the beat (even just in your head) and divide it into measures? Can I hear which beats in each measure are accented, for example just each "1", or is it every "2" and "4"?*

- *Are one or more instruments clearly expressing that steady beat?*

- *Does each beat subdivide in half or into three? Can I identify the meter e.g. 4/4 or 3/4?*

- *How does the rhythm sit on top of that beat? Is it simple and tightly-bound, mostly placing notes right on the beat or evenly in between beats? Or is there more unusual and unpredictable note timing?*

- *Is the beat straight (steady and consistent) or swung (a pattern of long-short, long-short)?*

- *How does the tempo and rhythm compare to what's normal for this style of music?*

- *How does the use of rhythm differ across instruments or musical roles?*

- *How important is rhythm to the musical impact of this piece? How creative and innovative has the song-writer or composer been? Is rhythm a distinctive part of this piece—or is it tackled simply in order to showcase other aspects e.g. the melody or lyrics.*

4. Dynamics

Dynamics refers to the changing of how loud or how soft musical notes are. In classical music, dynamics are used to create highly expressive effects. There's a wide range, from very, very soft sounds to very, very loud sounds. You can learn a lot about a piece's structure by listening carefully for that.

In much popular music, the overall dynamics are pretty steady throughout. Sometimes there will be sudden jumps in volume in a song, but usually the jumps that feel like dynamics are really a jump in texture (more on this later). Partly due to the commercial pressures of making songs stand out when played on the radio or streaming, there's actually quite a narrow range of dynamics used in most popular music today.

The use of dynamics can change over the course of a piece. Sometimes this change is very gradual and sometimes it's very sudden. Often sudden dynamic shifts can indicate a change in section of a piece, for example starting off with a soft section and then suddenly becoming loud. Other times changes in dynamics are used for effect within a section.

Micro-Dynamics

The large-scale dynamics that are written into a piece of music or performed are one thing to listen for. But there's another level of dynamics which we can call *micro-dynamics*.

Small, quickly-changing dynamics are typically used in melodies to shape a phrase (a short series of notes that are grouped together in the music). They can even be used to shape one single note, for example starting soft and then getting louder and then soft again. This could all happen in less than a second! These kinds of micro-dynamics are used to great effect in all forms of music.

It's something that singers do quite naturally, as these shifts are embedded in pronunciation and suggested by the meaning of the words they are singing. In spoken language, we wouldn't speak the words of a sentence at a completely flat volume. We would naturally vary the emphasis of different syllables and parts of the sentence. Similarly, singers bring this same kind of enunciation to how they shape their sung phrases. Instrumentalists often learn a lot about how to effectively shape a phrase by listening to singers, for this very reason.

These small gradations of dynamics to use to shape a phrase and shape a melody are something to listen carefully for in your Active Listening. Appreciating them will help you to learn these techniques for yourself and make your own music more expressive. We'll explore this more in *Chapter Seventeen: Expression*.

Articulation

One other more subtle shaping technique that can bring a melody to life is *articulation*. This refers to how notes begin and how they end.

You may be familiar with playing "staccato" (each note sharply detached from the ones before and after) and "legato" (each note connected in a flowing way to the notes before and after).

Different instruments each have their own techniques and possibilities for varying the articulation of a note. For example wind players have a range of mouth techniques which can be used to shape the start and end of a note, just as string players have different bowing techniques, and guitarists have different finger-picking or plectrum techniques.

When we listen to our musical heros, we will find there is actually an infinite range of expressive articulations, which we can enjoy, and then emulate in our own playing.

One way to tune your ear in to articulation is to focus on the dynamics of a single note. Does it start suddenly and loudly and taper off? Or does it have a soft, smooth start but a sudden ending? These effects are often produced by the articulation techniques of the instrument. You can usefully practice Active Listening with your own instrument, exploring these possibilities. We'll be diving into this idea further both when we learn the Expansive Creativity framework in *Chapter Fifteen: Improvisation* and the musical language of emotion in *Chapter Seventeen: Expression*.

Questions in Mind

Here are some questions you can use to explore Dynamics and Articulation.

Keep in mind that almost all questions can be asked for the whole piece of music overall, as well as for a particular instrument, a particular section, etc.

- *How are dynamics being used overall in this piece? Are there sudden or gradual changes? How does this contribute to the musical impact of the piece?*

- *What is the relative volume of each section? (simple labels like "really quiet", "the loudest", etc. are fine, or you may like to use precise terminology like "mezzo-forte", "fortissimo", etc. if you know it.)*

- *How do the volume levels of different instruments compare? Does that change from section to section or at particular moments (perhaps when musical roles change)?*

- *What can I hear in terms of microdynamics: how is each note or phrase shaped using changing volume?*

- *Can I hear any particular articulations being used, such as staccato or legato playing, or any instrument-specific articulation techniques?*

- *How important are dynamics in this piece of music? If every note or every section stayed at a steady volume how much would that detract from the piece's expressiveness?*

5. Audio

Up to this point, everything we've discussed has been about music in the abstract. The pure "music" of music.

We defined the four previous dimensions as "the dimensions of the music". So why are we adding a fifth?

In reality we generally experience music through some kind of real-world rendition. Although it is possible to look at a piece of sheet music and use Audiation to hear in your mind how it would sound, the music you'll generally be practicing Active Listening with will be either:

- A live performance, or

- A recording of a live or studio performance which we are playing back.

In these cases there is a whole other world of listening to consider, relating to the real-world characteristics of the sounds being produced.

This can loosely be referred to as the "Audio" side of music. We're talking about the equipment, the speakers, the room environment, the electronic processing that might be happening. All the factors that affect the way the sound is produced or perceived, beyond the fundamental musical intentions we've discussed so far.

You could take the same piece of music, played with the same instruments, pitches, rhythms, form, and so on, but play it:

- Live in a huge, empty concert hall.

- Live in cramped basement bar full of people.

- Live in a professional recording studio.

- From a CD on a nice home stereo system.

- From a low-quality MP3 on cheap in-ear earphones.

Can you imagine how different the music might sound in each case? Now imagine being able to hear, understand and explain in great detail how and why each of these scenarios sounds different. That's what the Audio side of Active Listening can empower you to do.

The practice of Audio Active Listening is no different than that of the "musical" side: we are listening with a question in mind. In the case of Audio, these questions can roughly be divided into two groups:

A. Questions about audio *frequencies*

B. Questions about audio *effects*

Although the process is the same, these Audio questions wake up quite a different part of your brain and ears, so even a little practice in these areas can open up a whole new level of music appreciation for you.

As you heard about in the Introduction chapter, audio Ear Training and what I called "critical listening" back then (but would call Active Listening these days) was the gateway to all my exploration of musicality. It showed me how much my own awareness, appreciation and enjoyment could be increased, with even a small amount of training. Even today, I would credit the Audio Ear Training and Active Listening I did back then as a huge part of what lets me hear and play the way I do.

Now I realise that for many musicians, many of these audio concepts will be totally new. Don't be put off. You don't need to understand these things fully to start listening for them and building up your awareness and appreciation of what's going on in the Audio side of the music you hear. And I think you'll thoroughly enjoy peeking your head through this door, just like I did.

We'll tackle each of the two types of Audio question in turn: audio frequencies, and then audio effects.

Audio Frequencies

We aren't going to go deep into the science of sound here—and fortunately we don't need to! Here are the two things you need to understand to make sense of audio frequencies:

1. Every sound we hear exists as a pressure wave in the air which reaches our ear.

The air molecules are becoming more densely packed and less densely packed over time, in a gradual wave back and forth. Our ear detects that changing pressure and that's what our brain interprets as sound.

This change in pressure can happen at different speeds. We call this the *frequency* of the wave.

The pressure could be changing very quickly, which we call a "high frequency", or very slowly, which we call a "low frequency". We measure frequency in a unit called Hertz (abbreviated "Hz"). A low frequency sound might be at "20 Hertz" while a high frequency sound could be as high as 20,000 Hertz.[5] This is the human hearing range for frequency: from 20 Hertz right up to one thousand times that: 20,000 Hertz.

---

[5] One thousand Hertz is called one "kilohertz", so you might also hear that referred to as as "twenty kilohertz" or written 20kHz.

2. Every sound actually consists of a combination of multiple frequencies.

It is possible to generate a single-frequency sound (called a "sinusoid" or "sine wave"), but in nature and with musical instruments there will always be a number of frequencies present. The exact mix of frequencies determines both the perceived pitch of the sound and a large part of the timbre of the instrument.

For example, the note an orchestra tunes to, called "A440", is the note A, in the octave (or "register") where that A is at 440 Hertz. Every instrument in the orchestra will produce a sound where the most prominent frequency is 440 Hertz and that's the pitch we will perceive the note as.

In reality though, every instrument will also be producing a number of other frequencies, most notably *harmonics* which are multiples of that "fundamental" frequency. The balance of these other frequencies is a big part of what makes each instrument in the orchestra sound different i.e. have a different timbre.

So clearly pitch and frequency are related: both describe how high or low a sound is. We can think of "pitch" as meaning "the single measure of how high or low we *perceive* a note to be" while "frequency" is all the rich detail which both determines that single perceived pitch and has a great influence on timbre.

So why would we be interested in listening for frequency, if pitch already tells us about the highness or lowness of a note?

Well, there are some highly practical purposes of developing your ear to appreciate frequencies. For example, live sound engineers and studio engineers will learn to recognise the balance of frequencies in great detail which allows them to adjust dials on their mixing desk to improve the overall blend of the sound, a process called "equalisation" or "EQ". This is a crucial part of what lets a musical group produce a clear and coherent sound together with a sound system when performing live, or on a recording.

However, for our purposes as active listeners, the major benefit is that it opens up a completely different window for us to listen to the same music. We learn to hear what's happening in the various frequency ranges of music.

This is a very different question to that of pitch. With pitch we might ask *"Which instruments are playing high notes right now?"* but thinking in terms of frequency we would ask *"Which instruments have a presence in the high frequency range?"*. And these two questions would produce different answers!

For example it might only be the singer who is actually singing high notes at a given moment—but actually you realise that up in that high frequency range you're also hearing the drummer's hi-hat cymbal, some of the echo-y reverb of the guitar player's riff from a moment before, and even the top part of the timbre of the bass guitar, even though the notes it's playing are way down low.

How to Start Listening for Audio Frequencies

Learning to recognise different frequency bands in detail is a long process of Ear Training. Studio engineers begin by learning to divide sound into 10 different frequency ranges (often called "frequency bands") and then might extend to roughly 30 bands, which means that each band is about a third of an octave—just four notes, quite precise!

However you certainly don't need to go that far to get the benefit of audio active listening, and tuning your ear in to this way of listening is actually very fast.

A great starting point is to develop your internal "3-Band EQ": just dividing sound into bass, mid-range, and high frequencies. You've probably seen stereo equipment that provides exactly these three dials. In some cases there are just two dials, "bass" and "treble", but this normally still provides the same three-band control (since cranking both the bass and treble right down will leave you with just the "mid" left over).

This is actually the best way to start tuning your ear in: play around with EQ settings on your music device.

Listen to the same section of the same track with the dials set to extremes. Adjust the dials for "all bass", "all mid", "all treble", and listen to the effect on what you hear.

Which instruments do you hear in each band? How is their timbre affected?

This is an interesting exercise in itself, but here's what's really cool: after playing around like this on a variety of tracks and paying attention to how the sound is affected by tweaking those dials you will begin to hear these separate bands even when listening to the full, normal, sound. That is, you can ask your ears *"What is happening in the bass range right now?"* and mentally it will be like you just tweaked those dials to isolate the bass. Your ear will zone in on just that frequency range and pay attention to what's going on there.

Naturally this skill is particularly useful if you're involved in live sound, recording or mixing music. But it also gives you a deeper awareness and appreciation of everything that's happening in those processes to produce the nice (or not-so-nice!) sound you hear at live gigs or on a recording. It's a whole new window onto all the music you hear.

Audio Effects

The other major area of audio Active Listening is called *audio effects*. This encapsulates all the other things which can be affecting a sound apart from its component frequencies.[6]

You will already be familiar with many common audio effects by name or by sound.

One prominent example would be "reverb", meaning how much a sound echoes in an environment. We all know from our natural real-world experiences that if we were to sing in a tiny empty room it would sound quite different than if we were singing on a stage in a grand concert hall. Or that we can tell just by listening to a recording whether the microphone was right next to the speaker's mouth or across the room from them, even if the overall volume is the same.

We'll use reverb as our example here and then cover a few other common audio effects below to help you start listening for them.

The description of reverb above should help you see right away that audio effects occur naturally, even though the term is most commonly associated with artificial electronic processes that are applied to sound. So an audio effect can be a natural phenomenon, or it can be an artificial process applied to a sound (live or on a recording).

In the case of reverb, for example, there is a staggering range of guitar pedals, software plugins and other electronic devices to artificially add various kinds of reverb to an instrument or overall musical mix. This can be done to simulate a different environment (e.g. so the listener believes the notes were produced in a vast concert hall

---

[6] It is important to know that this idea of "effects" is just a helpful abstraction. In literal terms, a sound is defined completely by the mix of frequencies it contains over time. There is nothing "more" to it than that.

So any audio "effect" we discuss will, in some way or another, be some kind of modification of that sound's frequencies. But for the sake of simplicity it's useful to think about a sound's "frequencies" as being all about pitch and EQ (as presented in the last section), and group the more complicated frequency behaviours under this idea of "effects".

versus a cramped recording studio) or for artistic effect (e.g. just a small amount of reverb applied so as to "thicken" the sound and help the mix sound nicely-blended into a coherent whole).

So what is the benefit of Active Listening for audio effects?

Well, the first thing to say is that there is a strong connection between audio effects and Timbre. So all the benefits of appreciating timbre already discussed apply here too.

One way to think about it is that "timbre" defines "how an instrument sounds" and then "audio effects" describes "how an instrument's sound is modified from its default natural timbre". So the timbre of an electric guitar is, depending on where you draw the line, a very simple and thin-sounding one. If you have heard an electric guitar string played without the guitar being plugged into an amplifier, or indeed plugged into an amplifier with no kind of effects applied, you will know: it sounds like a simple metal wire being twanged! However, the sound of an electric guitar can become wildly different and complex in all kinds of ways once audio effects are introduced. It can sound big, heavy and angry, it can sound pure, sweet and elegant, it can sound remarkably like a human voice, it can sound electronic and robotic—almost anything is possible through effects!

These days an instrument can even become simply a controller for completely synthesised sounds, where the resulting sound is completely independent of the natural timbre of the instrument. So in a way we're talking about a spectrum, with natural timbre on one end, completely synthetic timbre on the other end, and in between there is a realm of audio effects where the natural timbre is adjusted more and more in artificial ways.

As well as the general "Timbre understanding" that Active Listening for audio effects provides, there is a practical angle: understanding audio effects lets you know what's possible. This can be useful for your own performing and recording, but it also makes your mental model of the music you hear more vivid.

For example, when you listen to certain recordings you probably instinctively have a feel for the environment the musicians were playing in. An intimate recording of a singer-songwriter can make you feel like you're right there with them, alone in a small room. A live recording of a packed stadium rock show can make you feel like you're there in the crowd, surrounded by thousands of other fans, experiencing it in an exciting way.

This mental image of the music you are hearing and the powerful visceral impact it can have on your experience and enjoyment of the music is given greater richness and sophistication as you become more and more aware of the audio effects involved.

That's not to say that you would literally be thinking through *"Oh, I can hear a long-delay reverb therefore I must be in a stadium, and there is some distortion on the guitar therefore I know it's an electric guitar plugged into an amp"* etc.! But once you wake up your ear to all those factors you will instinctively and automatically conjure up more accurate and more powerful mental experiences as you listen to music.

We've mentioned reverb as one example. Let's now look at a few other audio effects you might like to explore. Keep in mind that each audio effect can be applied to the overall sound, to individual instruments, or both.

Chorus

If we think purely in musical terms, there is no difference between a solo voice singing a melody and a choir of 20 people singing that same melody in unison. It might literally be a single word on the sheet music that indicates which of the two it should be! But of course the two sound completely different to us. Why is that?

The answer is that no two humans can perform the same music exactly the same, simultaneously. Even the same human in a recording studio trying to repeat exactly the same thing will end up producing something slightly different.

The obvious differences will be in the Rhythm. Notes will start and end at slightly different times, even if they are all played with the "correct" rhythms. And the Timbre may be different, especially in the case of human voices, where everyone's voice is unique. It's possible that the Pitch will differ too, especially with singing, even if they are technically playing or singing "the right notes".

All these minute differences combine to create an effect called "chorus". This happens in the real world when multiple musicians or singers perform together in unison, so you can think of it as "the choir effect". This is where it gets its name from, in the sense of a choir being called a "chorus" (not from the "verse and chorus" sense of the word).

In its simplest synthetic form a chorus effect will create multiple copies of the same sound, starting at slightly different delays from the original. This creates a slightly artificial-sounding effect so must be used in moderation (or in its extreme, for intentional artistic effect). It adds a really distinctive colouring to the sound. It's hard to put into words, but some people describe it as turning a single colour into a rainbow.

More sophisticated artificial choruses will vary the delay of each copy over time or adjust the EQ of each to better simulate actually having multiple performances.

Chorus effects can also be created artificially but manually, by recording multiple takes of the same section and laying them on top of each other in the studio. This is done a lot in rap music where a line or just a few key words will be recorded multiple times and laid on top of each other, so as to emphasise that line or word, as if multiple versions of the same rapper are saying it together. This has an interesting artistic effect on us as a listener: we perceive it as multiple voices but somehow we also understand that it is still just one person, so it doesn't change our interpretation of it being one person communicating with us.

Distortion

Alongside reverb, distortion is probably the most commonly-used and most familiar audio effect in the modern age. The evolution of the electric guitar's role in music would be very different without its close companion, distortion effects!

As you might guess from the name, distortion originates with an unwanted effect: when we crank the volume too high on audio equipment we overload the speakers, and the sound gets distorted from what it's meant to be. It begins to sound "noisy" or "crunchy". When distortion happens to the whole of a musical track featuring multiple instruments, it sounds pretty terrible.

Apart from this overall "crunchiness", another way distortion manifests by accident is with *feedback*. When a microphone or an instrument's pickup is placed close to its own speaker, the sound goes in a loop from mic to speaker, round and round, gathering volume each time and modifying its frequency mix, resulting in a loud high-pitched whine. You've no doubt heard this once or twice if you've ever been to a live rock gig or heard a sound-check before a performance.

However, used in certain ways and for only particular instruments in the mix, distortion becomes a powerful and flexible audio effect. Even feedback can be used intentionally, as in the case of rock guitarists intentionally approaching their amp on stage to produce feedback in a controlled way.

Applied intentionally, distortion can produce a surprising range of timbres. Sticking with the example of electric guitar (though distortion can be applied to any instrument), distortion can be created via the amplifier and/or dedicated effects pedals and can produce a really beautiful sweet sound, such as Carlos Santana's signature guitar tone on "Smooth" or "Maria Maria", a noisier tone, such as the classic opening riffs to Nirvana's "Smells Like Teen Spirit" or Deep Purple's "Smoke on the Water", or a harsh, heavy, crunchy tone such as Black Sabbath's "Iron Man".

Auto-Tune

A prominent audio effect in recent years has been "auto-tune". This was originally created as a tool to help studio engineers neaten-up the pitching of notes on recorded tracks. By nudging pitches closer to the "correct" pitch of each note, slightly sloppy performances could be transformed into clean, accurate renditions.

However, like many audio effects, it emerged that taking the effect to its extreme could have artistic potential, and so auto-tune became an audio effect used to dramatically change the perceived timbre of human voices, even to the extent of being used for comedic effect!

This is a good example of a general principle: when used in a tasteful way, audio effects are normally intended to be unnoticeable to the listener. They are used to enhance and adjust the sound, or to create new timbres which our ears happily accept as an instrument sound.

Auto-tune is a rare case where the average music listener is often consciously aware that a particular audio effect has been used. However, you as an Active Listener will soon have this awareness of all audio effects being applied—not just those being taken to an extreme!

Questions in Mind

Here are some questions you can use to explore Audio Frequencies and Effects.

Keep in mind that almost all questions can be asked for the whole piece of music overall, as well as for a particular instrument, a particular section, etc.

- *What's the overall frequency presence of this track e.g. does it sound broad and bassy or light and airy?*

- *What can I hear is present in the low-, mid-, and high-frequency bands?*

- *How does the frequency presence of each instrument combine to make a balanced overall sound? Are there any instruments which would normally occupy the same range and might have been adjusted with EQ to fit together better? e.g. sometimes a bass guitar will have its mids and highs reduced to keep it in its own space at the bottom of the mix, other times it might be trimmed to just the highs, to keep the overall track sounding light and airy.*

- *Can I discover anything new about how the music is put together by listening to just one particular frequency band?*

- *What audio effects can I hear? What does the overall environment sound like? e.g. does it sound like a pristine studio recording or a live concert hall performance.*

- *Is there a noticeable reverb? If so, does it sound like a small or large space?*

- *Are there noticeable effects on any particular instruments? e.g. distortion on a guitar*

- *Have any instruments' timbres been transformed into something noticeably unnatural?*

- *Why have these effects been used? Is it to a subtle degree to create a certain musical atmosphere or is it to a greater extent to produce particular noticeably-different sounds?*

- *What influence does the audio frequency balance and the use of audio effects (if any) have on the artistic impact of this piece? How different would it be if those things were changed dramatically?*

The Bigger Picture: Form and Texture

When artists paint a picture they mix their paints to create a range of different colours. All they really need are three colours (red, blue, and yellow) with black and white to create any possible colour. Those source elements are brushed on the canvas in specific forms and structures to represent the picture that the artist wants to paint.

In music, we can look at the source elements as being the four dimensions of music covered above (Timbre, Pitch, Rhythm, Dynamics). Those are like the three coloured paints with black and white. They aren't the artwork in themselves, but they're used to create a range of material for the music to be built from. The musician then arranges these into forms and structures to create the music. The musician's "canvas" is the span of time from the beginning to the end of the piece of music.

Horizontal and Vertical

When you're scanning a painting from left to right, you're looking at its horizontal axis. And if you look at it from top to bottom, you're looking at its vertical axis. This creates, in the case of a painting, a two-dimensional picture.

Music also has a horizontal and vertical axis. At any given moment, there can be a whole bunch of things going on. You could have maybe a guitar, a keyboard, and a bass playing at a certain moment, playing certain pitches that form a certain chord. That is the vertical axis. The horizontal axis is then how the music moves forward through time.

These two axes—what's going on in the moment and then how music is moving and changing through time—are ways for us to look at music when we're Actively Listening to it: *"What just happened in that moment, and then how did it change as it moved through time?"* What happens in the moment is the vertical axis. How it changes over time is the horizontal axis.

How things change over time and the resulting structure of different sections is called "Form". For example, you may have the chorus for 20 seconds. And then you have a verse for 20 seconds. Then another chorus. These are sections that proceed one after another, that follow each other through a span of time.

Sections are defined by how the musical elements are arranged within them, and the musical Form is created when these musical elements change from one section to the next. For example, the verse may be characterised by a low, rhythmic vocal line, a particular chord progression, played on acoustic guitar, sparse bassline and drums played with bundle sticks. Then the chorus arrives and the layers change, bringing in a new chord progression played on electric guitar, with a driving bassline and heavier drums.

All these different layers of what's happening in any given moment is called the "Texture" of the music.

In the example illustration below, the top pitch contours might represent an oboe melody, the larger ones beneath the woodwind section and the strings, with the dotted lines beneath showing the double bass. Notice the repeated patterns along the horizontal axis— these are the sections of the Form. How the different sets of lines stack up within a section is the Texture.

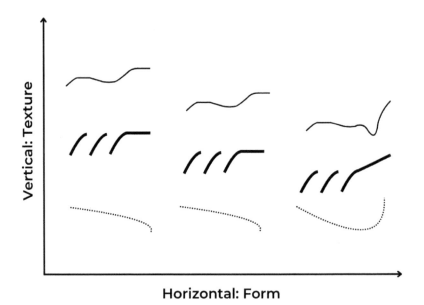

Horizontal: Form

Texture

Texture can be a revelation when you begin actively listening to music. When you ask your ear questions about Texture, you start to become aware of all the different elements that are stacked up in a piece of music.

People often use descriptive terms such as "dense", "thick", "sparse" or "ambient" to describe Texture. But these terms don't help us much in translating what we hear into our own musical expression. While the texture of any musical moment can be as unique and individual as a fingerprint, learning about some broad categories of musical textures can assist you greatly when you want to "go deep" into your active listening—and in your own music creation.

Monophonic Texture

The word *monophonic* comes from Greek roots meaning "one voice". We use the word "voice" here to include the voices of instruments as well as the human voice. So "a voice" could be one human voice singing *a capella*, or one Native American flute playing in a canyon. You only hear one thing going on at that particular moment. One note, one rhythm, one melody. One pitch on one instrument means one voice.

There's no accompaniment or backing music. There's just one musical line, moving through time.

Traditional Gregorian chant is another example of monophonic texture. This is an old form of church music and although you may have several people singing it together, they're all singing the same pitches in the same rhythm at the same time. There's no other accompaniment, traditionally, so that's still considered "one voice" and a monophonic texture. Another example of monophonic texture would be group of instrumental musicians all playing the same melody together, such as a class of children with recorders, all playing "Oh When The Saints".

Polyphonic Texture

Polyphonic texture means having multiple voices. Most of the music we listen to can be called "polyphonic" because usually there's more than just one voice present. In a typical band, you may have the bass playing one line. One guitar playing chords in a certain rhythm, with a second guitar playing lead lines. The drum set itself playing a whole combination of different patterns that are layered on top of each other. And then a lead vocalist over the top of it. We can call that a polyphonic texture. But let's narrow it down a bit.

In a more strict sense, polyphonic texture refers to two or more melodies happening at once, where both of these melodies are of roughly equal importance.

A simple round, like "Row, Row, Row Your Boat" is a good example. Multiple people sing the same melody but starting at different times, and it produces an overall piece which is polyphonic.

Polyphonic textures can be found frequently in classical music, especially from the middle ages up to the mid-1700s. For example, a Bach "two-part invention" has two melodies, one played by the right hand, one played by the left hand on piano. They're both of equal importance, musically.

Sometimes you can find three, four, five, or even six melodies that weave together where one doesn't necessarily pop out as the main melody. This is not nearly as common in our popular music today, although you can sometimes find examples of pop polyphony used for distinctive musical effect.

Homophonic Texture

What's much more common in popular music is a particular kind of polyphonic music where there's lots of things going on, but a melody which pops out as being the main voice. When one melody or one voice stands out as being the lead, in an otherwise-polyphonic texture, we call it *homophonic* music. This is the texture that most of us are most used to hearing in Western popular music.

Almost all popular music and most classical that we listen to in the Western world has one melody that is clearly sounds on top or in front, usually sung by the lead vocalist, or when there's an instrument like a lead guitar or a lead synth which takes the main melody.

There can be all kinds of other things going on. All kinds of layers of sound, of synths, and drums, and guitars, and basses. But if there is one melody that pops out on top as the main, lead melody, we call that a homophonic texture.

Listening for Texture

Musical texture is extremely important and useful for Active Listening, because it takes you from hearing one big wash of sound to paying attention to all the layers that are in the music.

Most of the time, we have our greatest attention on the lead. The lead vocals, the lead instrument, the melody. We keep most of our attention there. But our Active Listening can be deepened considerably if we start to listen to the other layers in the texture.

As we touched on already in the section on Timbre above, one fun, easy, and extremely useful Active Listening technique is to choose a layer (or an instrument, since instruments are often assigned to a layer and stick to it) and to follow it with your ears throughout the song. Let's say you choose the bass part and you follow that bass part with your ears. Or you choose the rhythm guitar part and you follow that.

"Going deep" in your listening is that easy! You will learn so much about music through this simple exercise, and build a much greater understanding of what to do when you're playing—whether you're jamming some cover tunes, rehearsing with your string quartet, or composing your next EDM masterpiece.

You can also start trying to stay aware of multiple voices at once. We might call this "listening vertically". You may remember me mentioning in *Chapter Three: Audiation* that trying to follow all three voices at once in Quebe Sisters recordings (whether the three vocal parts or three fiddle parts) is still one of my favourite activities.

This kind of vertical listening "stretches" your ears and musical awareness in a particularly satisfying way, as you become aware of multiple voices in the texture simultaneously.

Form

As soon as you have two notes, one after another, you have a kind of musical Form. We can talk about musical Form from very small units like that, through to very large units such as the verse and chorus sections of a song, and everything in between. Here's some vocabulary that will help you discern musical Form in your Active Listening:

- **Motif:** A small unit of melody, often less than half a dozen notes. Motifs can be repeated, varied, extended and generally remixed to build very large forms. Indeed, Ludwig van Beethoven spun out his entire Fifth Symphony from one simple motif: three short repeated notes and one long lower note.

- **Phrase:** Sometimes called a "musical sentence". Phases are sections of melody with a discernible beginning and end.

- **Section:** Musical sections can widely vary depending on the genre and type of musical piece. They are often marked by a decisive change in any combination of the musical dimensions and textures we've touched on so far. Sometimes these sections are labeled simply by numbers or letters, like "Section A", "Section B", etc. Other times they have specific names according to the genre. So in pop song form we talk about the "verse", "chorus", and "bridge", for example. Rap often has a section called the "hook". Classical sonata form has the "exposition", "development", "recapitulation", and "coda".

- **Larger forms:** in classical music you often find larger forms (such as Concertos and Symphonies) that include several *movements*. Each movement is a self-contained piece of music with a form of its own. Inspired by classical, some progressive rock bands have followed suit by extending into longer songs and even whole concept albums where the sequence of songs creates an inter-related structure.

Listening for Musical Form

Form is defined by repetition and change. This applies to any musical dimension or Texture.

For example, in standard pop song form you have three different sections: verse, chorus, and bridge. To these sections can be added a pre-chorus, intro and outro. When you're listening to most popular music (including pop, country, R&B, a lot of hip-hop, rock and more) you'll be able to tell these sections apart by comparing the melody and lyrics: the verses each have the same melody but different lyrics, each chorus has the same melody and lyrics (which are different to any of the verses).

Song form consists of a series of these different section types, such as:

Verse, Chorus, Verse, Chorus, Bridge, Chorus

Or a more varied form, still following the basic alternation of verses and choruses, such as:

Intro, Verse, Verse, Pre-chorus, Chorus, Verse, Pre-chorus, Chorus,
Bridge, Chorus, Chorus

Even without knowing the details of these different types of song section, or the right terminology to use, you could begin to listen for (and even write down) the overall form of a song, just by noticing what changes and what stays the same in different parts of the song as you listen.

We'll explore song form more in *Chapter Sixteen: Songwriting*, including details on the commonly-used types of section and what you can listen for to identify the form of a song.

This kind of song form has been used for literally hundreds of thousands of songs since the middle of the 20th Century, and it's built from folk music forms that have been around for thousands of years. Our ears have come to expect it, so when there's a departure from it, it's quite noticeable.

How Musical Elements Define Form in Different Genres

In the case of the song form above, we looked at just the melody and lyrics. But any musical element can be used to define sections in music. Any of these elements can then combine to form musical textures that change from one section to another. The changes in melody and lyrics described above are often accentuated by producers, songwriters, and artists by changes in chord progression, instrumentation, and texture.

Here are a few examples of other genres and how they create Form:

- **Classical:** Changes in key, rhythm, melody, harmony, texture, and even tempo are used to clearly define the sections of purely-instrumental pieces.

- **Jazz:** Performances frequently begin with playing the melody of a song, known as the "head", followed by each musician improvising new melodies over the same chord progression. Each round of the chord progression is called the "chorus". The performance typically concludes with a repeat of the head.

- **Electronic Dance Music (EDM):** In dubstep and dance music you typically have a section called the *drop*. This is where there's a sudden deepening in the bass and a change in the rhythm that contrasts from the music that came before. Here you have a change in pitch and a change in the timbre of the instruments. A drop section is usually also instruments-only, so you're typically moving from a vocal section to an instrumental section.

The Benefits of Listening for Form

Active Listening for musical Form helps us greatly with memorisation. If you know, for example, that a certain part is coming up, and it's going to be the same chord progression as the previous section and then it's going to repeat, or it's going to do this or that differently than the time before, it's far easier to assemble your mental model of the whole piece.

Active Listening for Form also helps in Playing By Ear. For example, if you understand that the same chorus is going to keep coming around, then you don't have to figure out the chords each time they're coming up because you already know them. The part you play during a verse might also be the same each time, or close to it. Suddenly there's a lot less to work out!

Form is also hugely important for composers and songwriters. One common pitfall musicians face when they try to write music is that they try writing a song from beginning to end. They start with a great inspiration, but then they get stuck and can't finish the song. Many simply don't realise that their favourite songs have just two or three repeated sections. So if you simply repeat a section of music and then change the lyrics for the verses, keep the same lyrics each time for the choruses and you lay out these repeated sections in a predictable fashion, suddenly your song has practically written itself. All because you use a predetermined form.

Note this doesn't mean you're not being creative! In fact, it helps your creativity because you're freed up to focus on what matters and you don't have to create the form from scratch. Through Active Listening you can learn more and more about the nature of each section, and all the varied ways in which your favourite artists solve this musical problem.

Good musical forms are used again and again, and the listener doesn't mind at all. The composer or songwriter can still be successful and tremendously creative, even while using only standard forms. For example in classical music, there is a form called "sonata form" which endured for centuries and is still used in composition today.

When we learn about, listen for, and understand musical Form, it both increases our appreciation for the music and the creative way in which that form is being used, and gives us tools to build our own musical compositions and better understand the music we're playing.

Questions in Mind

Here are some questions you can use to explore Texture and Form.

Keep in mind that almost all questions can be asked for the whole piece of music overall, as well as for a particular instrument, a particular section, etc.

- *What type of texture is it: monophonic (single voice), polyphonic (multiple independent voices), or homophonic (single "lead" voice supported by other voices)?*

- *What layers can I hear in the music, in terms of the melodic lines and harmony or in terms of the instrumentation?*

- *What is the form of this piece? How many different types of section can I identify and how do they repeat in a sequence? Are there standard labels I could apply to them?*

- *What changes (in any and all of the musical dimensions of Pitch, Rhythm, Timbre and Dynamics, as well as Texture) as the music moves from one phrase/section to another? What stays the same?*

- *How does this form compare to what's expected in this genre? Is there anything unusual happening in terms of Form?*

- *Within a section, what's the structure over time? e.g. how many lines in each verse, is there a pattern of call-and-response phrases, etc.*

- *How are repetition and change being used to define the form? What aspects of the music (e.g. Pitch, Rhythm, instrumentation, lyrics, etc.) are changing, and which are repeating within a section and across different sections?*

- *Can I identify any repeating motifs or melodic fragments? Are there musical patterns which multiple instruments/roles are playing at the same time, or one after another?*

- *What other music can I think of which has the same form as this and defines its form using the same kinds of repetition and change? (Bonus points for crossing genres!)*

7-Day Practice Plan

With everything covered in this chapter you might be feeling a bit overwhelmed by all the possibilities!

Here is a simple plan you can follow for your first seven days practicing Active Listening, to get you into the habit and open up some avenues to explore further.

We'll use writing things down as a way to help you keep track of what you're discovering, but keep in mind that this is optional and just to help you learn as you get started. It's the time spent during the listening itself which constitutes the actual Active Listening.

Day 1
Choose three music tracks from your collection, ideally from a variety of styles and genres, and a mix of tracks you feel you know well and ones you are familiar with but don't know so well.

Listen to each track twice and think about the Form.

Try to write down the overall structure of the track, and use the other example questions in the section above on Form to add as much detail as you can.

You can start to cross-compare the three tracks and see what is similar and what is different.

Day 2
Using the same three tracks, listen again to each one two or three times, now thinking about instrumentation and Timbre.

Try to add to your notes about the form with what you can hear about the instruments and timbres present. Again, use the example questions to prompt you on what to explore, and once you're done try comparing across the three tracks to see if that reveals any other interesting points.

Start writing down any other interesting questions or angles that occur to you to explore with Active Listening.

Day 3
Next explore Dynamics. Listen again to the three tracks in turn, now paying attention to the volume. The overall level and how it changes over time, and also carrying this analysis to particular instruments or groups of instruments.

How do the dynamics relate to the form? Is that different or the same for each of your three tracks?

Again, jot down any observations and points of interest!

Day 4
Moving on to the slightly more challenging musical aspects to analyse by ear, this time listen to your three tracks thinking about the Pitch.

What's the overall pitch range? How does it vary by instrument?

What Pitch Contours are used in the phrases of the main melody, and of other parts?

Write down your notes in whatever level of detail you're able to discern.

Day 5

Next up, it's Rhythm. Building on all your observations so far, how does Rhythm fit into the picture for each of your three tracks and each of their sections?

This is a good time to start thinking in terms of genre, too. Do the rhythms used help convey the genre of these three tracks? What about the other aspects you've been listening for—as far as you know, are they in keeping with what's normal in that genre?

Day 6

The final aspect to listen for is Audio Frequencies and Effects. For many musicians this will be the least familiar so remember to start simple.

You can begin by just asking yourself *"how bassy or treble-y is the overall sound?"* and then carry that a bit further, asking what instruments are prominent in the low frequency range and which are prominent in the high frequency range. Remember that you can learn a lot by playing around with the EQ dials on your playback device or software!

On the effects side you can begin with the broad questions about the apparent musical environment, such as the size of the room it sounds like the musicians are playing in. Are there any really obvious effects like a strong distortion on one instrument, or auto-tune on the vocals?

Always keep in mind it's fine to recognise things even if you don't know the "official" name for them. So as you write notes on the three tracks feel free to use whatever words and descriptive phrases are meaningful to you. The most important thing is the listening and mental analysis. Correct terminology can come later.

Day 7

Having explored these three tracks in such detail it's nice to do two activities to wrap things up:

- The first is to try writing a description of the track. You should have plenty of raw material now to draw from, so see if you can turn it into a coherent description of what's most distinctive and interesting about the track. This might be a few lines, or it might be a few pages!

•   Then, as a final step, simply listen one more time, now *not* consciously asking a question. See how your ears and your brain respond to the music now—and just take a moment to recognise how your appreciation of the track has been transformed.

That's just the beginning!

This is a simple 7-day plan designed to get you up and running with Active Listening. If you enjoy it, by all means you can continue in just this way with new tracks and new explorations.

Normally though, Active Listening will be done more loosely than this. You might find a particular track interesting and so listen to it several times, digging into it in various ways. Or you might choose to pay attention to just one aspect of every song you hear for a few days, to really hone your awareness of, say, Rhythm, or to skill up on the Audio side of things.

Active Listening can and should be a flexible and ongoing part of your musical life, so find the ways to practice it which best suit you— and enjoy!

Conclusion

In this chapter we introduced the skill of Active Listening as a way to open up your ears and mind to all the rich depths and detail in music, and how it all fits together. The core technique is to "listen with a question in mind."

We covered the four dimensions of music: Pitch, Rhythm, Dynamics and Timbre, as well as the fifth dimension of Audio. In each case we covered the basic concepts you need to start listening for those aspects of the music, and suggested example questions you could use in your Active Listening practice.

We discussed the "vertical" and "horizontal" axes of music, and how the different ("vertical") layers of musical sounds create Texture, and how the way things change or stay the same over time ("horizontal") define musical Form.

I hope that you tried out some of the suggested exercises along the way, and had fun with the example questions. If you're like most of our members inside the *Living Music* program (where we include Active Listening training and exercises throughout), you will have been astonished at just how much more there is to hear, even in music you thought you knew well—and how easy it is to start waking your ears up in this way, just by "listening with a question in mind."

If you followed the suggestion in the Tip box at the start of the chapter, to write a description of a music track you like, then now is a great time to return to that same track, listen once or more, and write a new description based on everything your ears have now been woken up to.

Aside from all the practical benefits, and the emotional satisfaction which Active Listening delivers, perhaps the best thing about it is how light and easy it can be to put into practice.

Simply by reading through this chapter, you are now fully-equipped to start listening in a new way, and taking your musical ears and mind on exciting new adventures—in any music you listen to or play—from this day forwards, and for the rest of your life!

Want Step-By-Step Guidance?

When we teach Active Listening inside Musical U, there are plenty of listening examples and guided exercises along the way.

If you'd like to learn more, and get access to a full set of "Listening Guides" which walk you through practicing Active Listening step-by-step with specific music tracks, please visit:

https://musicalitybook.com/activelistening

CHAPTER SIX:
SUPERLEARNING

Have you been feeling stuck or frustrated in your music learning? Have you ever found yourself working on the same piece or section of a piece for weeks on end, without any real progress? Maybe you've hit an overall plateau, like you've reached an intermediate level but can never seem to go beyond that. Do you find it hard to memorise music, or to build up a range of material you can reliably play from memory? Perhaps it's been hard to keep up your motivation to practice, because some days it just feels like *"What's the point?"*

These problems are familiar to almost every music learner I've ever met. And when they experience them, most musicians make two big assumptions:

1. These kinds of struggles are inevitable. I've just got to put up with it.

2. If I was more "talented" I would improve faster and struggle

less (i.e. *"it's my own fault"*)

It might shock you to hear that neither of those things are true. In fact, every one of those issues mentioned above is actually just a symptom of using an outdated, ineffective, and needlessly-frustrating approach to music practice.

In this chapter we'll introduce an alternative which, if you choose to adopt it, can dramatically change the speed and joy with which you learn music going forwards.

The traditional approach to music practice is based on what the scientific literature calls "massed repetitions". That means brute-force repeating of the same thing, and hoping your skills will automatically improve through sheer repetition. If that sounds familiar, it should. It's what almost every musician has been taught to do during "practice time" for literally hundreds of years.

But you might have heard also the saying *"Practice doesn't make perfect—practice makes permanent."* Which means if you're playing the same mistakes again and again, you are, at least to some extent, actually learning to make those mistakes more reliably! What's more, if your goal is solely to "play each note exactly correct", even a "successful" outcome would have you being a mere note-reproducing robot.

So there are two major problems with the traditional model of music practice:

- Firstly, the methods used are incredibly inefficient. This wastes up to 90% of your practice time on activities that don't actually trigger the brain's "learning mode" and improve your skills.

- Secondly, the focus is generally only on "getting the notes right", rather than producing beautiful music which you find deeply fulfilling and satisfying.

In terms of our H4 Model we might say it's a Hands-only approach —and a highly inefficient one, at that.

It completely neglects:

- Head: Do you understand what you're playing, and why it's those notes rather than other ones?

- Hearing: Do you have a vivid mental model of how you want it to sound? Are you listening as you play? Can you play that kind of music by ear, or improvise with it?

- Heart: Do you feel truly connected to your instrument, to the music, to other musicians you play with, to your listeners? Are you able to put your own expression into every note you play?

So What's The Alternative?

In this chapter we'll invite you to reconsider what "music practice" means, and what it should look like. Heads up, this is going to involve a lot of words and terms being put in quotation marks, as we try to really re-examine our intentions, expectations and assumptions around practice!

We'll introduce the most powerful concepts from the scientific research on accelerated learning and rapid memorisation, including the "Superlearning" techniques which have been proven to allow any average person to learn and memorise music up to 10 times faster than normal. And we'll explore a variety of ways to bring musicality into your practice, connecting your Hands to your Head, Hearing and Heart.

We'll mostly be focused on "music practice" in the sense of "sitting down with your instrument to practice playing particular pieces of music you want to be able to play". However, as you'll discover, the principles and concepts we'll cover can actually be applied to any music-learning activity you do, including all the musicality training covered in the rest of this book.

We're at an exciting moment in history. After centuries of music learners being handed the same-old practice methods that waste most of their time and cheat them of the results they could potentially enjoy, finally things are starting to shift. Now the same methods that apparently-gifted "prodigies" and "virtuosos" had been using to learn music dramatically faster than everyone else, are getting into the hands of average, everyday music learners.

Some of the concepts around the science of accelerated learning are gradually becoming more mainstream, with pioneers such as Gregg Goodhart (The Learning Coach), Dr. Josh Turknett (Brainjo), Jason Haaheim (The Deliberate Practice Bootcamp), Michael Compitello, Dr. Molly Gebrian (author of Learn Faster, Perform Better), Sarah Niblack (SPARK Practice), and Mark Morley-Fletcher (Play In The Zone) teaching classes and courses on Deliberate Practice and more. Other concepts, especially those combining Superlearning and musicality, are things we've been creating, developing, and proving out with our own members inside Musical U.

Overview

In this chapter we'll begin by re-imagining what "practicing" music means, and look at ways you can effectively practice, even without touching your instrument. We'll look at how the brain learns—and how it doesn't—and the implications for learning efficiently. We'll introduce two tools, recording and the metronome, which can both make all your practicing more honest and more effective.

Then we'll get into the nitty-gritty of Superlearning techniques, with Deliberate Practice, Desirable Difficulty, and Contextual Interference. One of the biggest learning points for us at Musical U has been the vital importance of combining Superlearning with musicality, in the spirit of the H4 Model, and so we'll cover specific ways you can benefit from doing both together.

Next we'll tackle memorisation. Remembering how to play a piece is a skill in its own right, whether your aim is to play from notation or get "off book". We'll cover the specific techniques which can let you memorise dramatically faster, and retain a wide repertoire with a fraction of the usual time.

Finally, we'll look at how to structure each practice session, and how the dynamic decision-making of Deliberate Practice can be put into action in several ways to maximise your use of time. And we'll wrap things up with an example illustration of what a Superlearning-based practice session might look like.

We are going to cover a *lot!* But as soon as you start using even a small number of the ideas and techniques shared in this chapter, you'll find that the results you get from your regular music practice rapidly (and in some cases instantly) transform, helping you move faster and faster towards that Big Picture Vision of the musician you want to become. I'm excited to share this with you. Let's dive in.

1. The Art and Science of Music Practice

The traditional view of music practice is as a means to an end. Practicing means *"I'll work hard now, so that some day I can play the music I want to."*

What if practicing music was its own reward? What if "making music" wasn't the eventual payoff of all our practice... but instead the practice itself was a musical—even creative—act?

You may remember from *Chapter Two: Mindset*, when we mentioned (in the context of *Enjoying The Journey*) that "fun is not the opposite of learning". The surprising truth is that when we make our practice activities more enjoyable and more musical, it's not a distraction or a dilution—we can actually learn *faster*.

For example, with an approach we call "Creative Superlearning", we can combine the nuts-and-bolts learn-faster methodology of Superlearning which you'll be learning about in this chapter with our creative frameworks such as Expansive Creativity (see *Chapter Fifteen: Improvisation*). The result is a learning process that is both faster and develops versatile musical creativity along the way.

This is a case where you really can "have your cake and eat it too". You just need to be open to truly re-thinking what music practice is, and how you'll spend your practice time in future.

So how can we transform our regular practice into a creative and self-rewarding musical experience? Well, we must begin with the key question:

What is "Practicing"?

Have you ever stopped to really ask yourself that question? For the average music hobbyist, they've taken some instrument lessons with a teacher, or gone through some online tutorial videos, and then they're told:

"Okay, now go and practice."

What exactly does that mean? How do you practice? What do you practice? What exactly *is* "practicing" anyway?

Generally those questions don't really get asked (though they might have nagged at the back of your mind) and the answer is assumed:

Practicing means "playing it over and over until it gets better".

For a student to be "good at practicing" normally means they have some habits they stick to, such as:

- Regular timed practice e.g. a 30 minute session each day.

- Starting each practice session with "warm-ups".

- Playing scales and other technical exercises.

- Playing through each piece or song you're working on.

- When you make a mistake, stop and try to play it properly, then move on.

- Start at the beginning of the piece/song, and play to the end.

- Practice only pre-written music, written by people the world has deemed to be "good" songwriters or composers.

I don't think it's an exaggeration to say that probably 99% of hobbyist musicians would agree that's how you "should" do music practice.

Let's come back to the observation made at the beginning of this chapter though. Nowhere in the list above is there anything from the science of accelerated learning, which goes back over 30 years and proves conclusively that some strange and counter-intuitive methods can help you learn up to 10x faster. Nowhere there is there anything about creativity. Nor Head, Hearing or Heart... or making the connections between those and your Hands.

In fact, even though the list above might have seemed to you to be a good, diligent plan for music practice, it's almost the exact opposite of how we would recommend practicing, if you ever want to reach your true musical potential or become more of that "Complete Musician" we talked about in *Chapter One: Musicality*.

Before we continue into the details of what effective and musical practice involves, there's an important distinction we should make. Or rather, un-make...

Practicing vs. Performing

Traditionally we distinguish between "practicing music" and "performing music". We do our daily practice routine, trying to get the music "good enough", and then when we're ready we schedule a "performance" where we play our music for other people and try to nail it.

This introduces a whole host of problems when it comes to performing, which we'll tackle in *Chapter Eighteen: Performance*. But it's also responsible for many of the problems with practicing.

The solution on both fronts is to allow that strict distinction to dissolve.

In that later chapter, we'll look at how *performance practice* can help ease many of the challenges around "the big performance". In this chapter, we'll concern ourselves with how allowing our practicing of music to be more like a performance can both accelerate results and enhance our musicality.

This isn't to say your practice time becomes "performing the piece/ song again and again". That would just be a different form of brute-force "massed repetition". Without any dedicated, focused work to learn to play the notes you intend, it would be a recipe for even more frustration and lack of results.

Playing Music

To a large extent, what we're talking about is allowing both practicing and performing to blend back towards simply "playing music".

How often during your practice time do you currently feel like you're really "playing music", rather than "practicing music" or "learning music" or "playing through sections of music"?

As you read about the various techniques covered in the rest of this chapter, you'll find that some seem like "exercises for you to practice" while others seem more like "playing around with music". Throughout them all, I encourage you to think less in terms of "practicing" or "performing", and more simply "playing music" or "making music".

This in itself will help to integrate Hearing and Heart, and help to frame all of the various activities you're doing as simply enjoying spending time in music-making.

2. Practicing Without Your Instrument

One of the first changes to make to our "music practice" is to get away from having "practice" mean strictly "doing things with my hands on an instrument"[1]. Certainly that can still be a big part of how we spend our dedicated session of practice time, and we will be looking at ways to improve that. But we need to expand our idea of where and when "learning music" happens, and how musicality training can spread beyond just "Hands".

Hopefully by this stage you're convinced of the power and potential of developing your musicality, not just your instrument skills. But

---

[1] If you're a singer rather than an instrumentalist, the equivalent is to get away from it meaning strictly "I spend time singing the exercises and pieces I'm working on".

allow me to illustrate with a story…

I'm generally a pretty easy-going guy, I don't get worked up easily. But once in a while, something will really infuriate me. It happened recently, in the context of helping one of my daughters learn to play the piano.

A friend of hers had been learning keyboard with an app. I won't name names, but it's one of the two or three piano apps that have become popular in recent years. My daughter was keen to try it too, so we downloaded the app, started it up, and I sat with her while she followed the instructions.

Within minutes I was flabbergasted. And utterly enraged.

It was the epitome of "turn someone into a note-reproducing robot". Notation and a keyboard were shown on screen, with no explanation, and then the student was instructed to play the keys which light up, when they light up.

"Okay," I thought, *"maybe this is just for the first few minutes, to get them going, and then it will start actually teaching them some music."*

But no. We actually spent a couple of weeks with this app, to give it a fair shot. And it never progressed beyond "do what the light-up notes tell you to do".

The student had no idea what the music should sound like. They weren't helped to feel the rhythm. They couldn't have clapped along, let along sung along. They would have no inner sense of what music they were trying to create, only the outer experience of what happens if they press the buttons somebody (or something) else tells them to press.

It was the ultimate Hands-only experience. And it drove me crazy. Because I know that even students who "succeed" with the app will wind up feeling frustrated, unmusical, and disappointed in themselves, within a few months (if not weeks, or even days).

In truth, the app was little more than a videogame—and to present itself as a way of "learning music" is, if you ask me, unforgiveable.

Even without going as far as the kinds of musicality skills we'll be covering in Parts II and III of this book, if the app had included even a *little* of any one of the three off-instrument practice activities below, it could have cultivated the student's musicality, their autonomy, their musical connection, and set them up for success and joy in music.

Let's make sure you don't miss that opportunity yourself, in your music practice.

If you're reading through this book in order, these three activities will already be familiar to you, and hopefully you've even started practicing them yourself. Now let's make the connection between them and what you've probably thought of as your "music practice" on your instrument up until now. Each of these activities can be done both during your regular practice session (i.e. when sat with your instrument) and at other times in the day, making them a wonderful way to find endless extra time for "learning music" even when you can't sit for a full session with your instrument.

A. Active Listening

We define "Active Listening" as listening with careful attention, as opposed to "just hearing". There's also a particular method we recommend, of "listening with a question in mind".

You can apply this in a wide variety of ways to support your instrument learning. The two main opportunities are:

1.   Listen to recordings of the music you're learning, either by artists you admire, or recordings of yourself playing it.

2.   Practicing Active Listening during your instrument practice i.e. really truly listening as you play.

The benefits of the first should be clear. The more vivid your mental representation of the music you're learning to play, the more empowered you are to craft a compelling rendition yourself. More on this when talking about Audiation, below.

The second one ties in closely with the principle of Deliberate Practice which we'll cover later in the chapter. The more alert attention you can bring to the results of each thing you attempt to play during practice time, the more you'll be able to adjust your approach and continually refine and improve your playing.

In both cases, if you're learning music from notation (e.g. sheet music, chord charts, tablature) then practicing Active Listening while looking at that notation can be a valuable approach, helping you to bring life to the dots on the page and develop your instinct for how symbols and sounds relate.

As well as these two opportunities, there is also the broader Active Listening practice you may be doing, which helps build up your understanding of music. Even if it's not with the specific pieces you're learning to play, this time spent in listening actively will help you better understand, appreciate, and ultimately perform that music too.

For example, one of the major benefits of Active Listening is how it helps you understand the Form of a piece of music, and how each layer of the Texture is contributing during each section. That alone can do wonders for how you approach playing your own part.

We had one notable example of that inside *Next Level* coaching recently. One of our violin-playing clients had always struggled with overwhelm when trying to play her own part in orchestra rehearsals and performances. She could play her parts when alone in the practice room, but would make mistakes or struggle to keep up when surrounded by the full orchestra.

She was amazed at how quickly some off-instrument practice eliminated this problem for her. Simply working on her Active Listening skills and better understanding "the big picture" of the piece she was playing (including how all the orchestra sections' parts fit together) helped her to be at ease and play her own part far more freely. What she'd thought was a limitation of her Hands turned out to be far more in the Head and Hearing, and so was most effectively addressed with a bit of direct work on those.

B. Singing

The idea here is simple: whatever you're trying to play on your instrument, sing it. In *Chapter Four: Singing*, when discussing ear training, I asked the provocative question *"if you can't sing it back, are you really hearing it?"* This is a big opportunity when it comes to instrument practice too.

Remember that app I mentioned above, which simply ordered the student when to play each note, without the student having any clue how the music would come out sounding?

Using Singing for off-instrument practice is the opposite of that. If you are able to sing the music you're learning to play on your instrument, that proves you know inside how the notes should sound.

What's remarkable is how powerful this is for identifying the source of issues in our playing. If you keep fumbling the same section of a piece, or you keep playing the same wrong note, making sure you can actually sing through that section of the music is a great way to distinguish *"is this mistake in my head or my hands?"* Often fixing the issue in your sung version will immediately correct it in your instrument playing too.

In a roundtable Masterclass with the Musical U team, our Instructional Curriculum Designer Anne Mileski shared a wonderful anecdote illustrating this point. When she was working on a recital piece at college, she always struggled with a certain fast passage. Her teacher asked her to sing it... and even slowly, she found she couldn't! Once she worked on slowly singing through that sequence of notes, she was able to pick her trumpet back up and nail it. The problem wasn't in her Hands after all.

Singing also lets you explore many of the expressive possibilities available to you, to make the music your own when you play it. We'll explore this more in *Chapter Seventeen: Expression*.

C. Audiation

If you think of some of the pieces you've been learning to play on an instrument or sing, could you hear them in your head, from beginning to end, with each note clear and precise in your mind's ear?

If not, this may well be a major source of difficulties and struggles you've faced in learning to play it. While it's true that written notation can "tell you what notes to play when", until you have an internal representation of how the music should sound, everything will be harder.

That's why proactively working on your ability to audiate the music will hugely help your success in learning to play it on your instrument.

If you also incorporate the "mental play" technique we covered in *Chapter Three: Audiation*, where you visualise yourself playing it on your instrument as you hear it in your mind, you can also directly tackle technical challenges and physical problem-spots in your playing.

For example, if there's a run of notes you often fumble, practicing Audiation and Mental Play can let you very slowly run through it note-by-note, without ever touching your instrument in reality. And the somewhat magical thing is, once you iron out the kinks in your imagined playing, more often than not they disappear from your actual playing too.

As mentioned in that previous chapter, I first tried this technique while learning piano. I'd been struggling to get my right and left hand to play their parts together, even though each one could handle its own part fine. I was shocked to find that going through the music with

Mental Play, really giving my brain a chance to understand how the two parts fit together, suddenly allowed my hands to work in perfect collaboration.

Remember to start audiating with very short sections at first, because your musical memory is a limiting factor. One helpful exercise to try is to make it a habit that before you play through a piece for the first time in a practice session, look through the notation and try to hear inside, measure by measure or phrase by phrase, how the music will sound.

You may well have seen professional musicians doing exactly this on a bus or a train. They'll be sat there with their instrument in a case beside them but sheet music in hand, reading through the music with their eyes and imagining in their mind how it would sound and how they would be playing it. You might never have guessed that a trombonist could practice on a train without all the other passengers complaining! But clearly they know the very practical power of this "secret music practice skill".

Developing Your Vivid Mental Representation

Each of these three activities—Active Listening, Singing, Audiation —will not only increase your musicality, which can then be expressed through your instrument, they can each also help directly with the tasks you're focusing on during hands-on-instrument practice time. They can be combined with each other and with your instrument practice in an endless variety of ways, to suit what you enjoy and find to be most effective for you, personally.

All three of them can be seen as ways to help you develop a crystal-clear and vivid mental representation of the music you're learning to play.

That's why you'll find that actively listening to, singing, audiating, and mentally playing the music you're learning, even when away from your instrument, has a major impact on how fluidly and quickly you can play it when back at your instrument.

This vivid mental representation is also what lets you escape "muscial roboticism" and start bringing the music out from inside you each time you play.

When we expand our practicing off-instrument, mindfully cultivating a sense of joy and fascination with the music itself, we tend to find that when we return to instrument practice, many of our musical "problems" have already been solved.

3. The Learning Brain

Our exploration into Superlearning here at Musical U really took off when we started collaborating with "The Learning Coach" Gregg Goodhart, and one saying of his that I often come back to is this:

"The brain doesn't learn the way we think it learns."

— Gregg Goodhart

This is really the central insight for everything relating to Superlearning: that so many of the ideas and methods we've inherited for music practice are based on fundamental misunderstandings and wrong assumptions about how to get our brain to learn new information and skills.

Fortunately, the scientific research which revealed that has also identified how the brain *does* learn most effectively, and specific techniques you can use to keep your brain in its optimal learning mode.

How The Brain *Doesn't* Learn

The human brain requires a tremendous amount of energy to run. Up to 20% of the whole body's energy use, in fact! So it has evolved to conserve energy whenever possible.

One upshot of this is that when our brain decides that our currently activity doesn't require much thought or attention, parts of the brain literally shut down.

For example, if we choose a task that is not challenging enough, our brain may well decide to withdraw energy from the parts which don't seem necessary to produce the desired result. To go through the motions for a task "on autopilot" requires far less energy than when we try a new task for the first time.

You're probably already seeing the big implication here for music practice.

Most of us have been taught to repeatedly play the same piece of music over and over again, and call that "practicing". At the end of a practice session with a great number of these "massed repetitions", we may even see some improvement and think we've succeeded in our learning efforts. Then the next day comes and our skill level has dropped back down, and we wonder why yesterday's improvement didn't "stick".

Research has shown that our brains essentially become bored with this kind of "massed repetition" and shut down the deep learning processes. This means that we might be spending 90% of our practice time carrying out repetitions which don't trigger any further learning in the brain at all!

On the other hand, novel or challenging activities stimulate a much higher level of brain activity, and thus a higher level of learning. Almost all of the musical Superlearning techniques you'll discover in this chapter can be seen as ways to keep our brains awake, excited, and fully engaged—and that's what enables learning to occur most rapidly and effectively.

The Power of "Not Finishing"

Here's one simple example of how the brain doesn't learn the way we think it does. Most of us have been taught that it's good to complete the tasks we take on during a practice session. For example, if you're working on playing a certain section of a piece, try to get it to the point of being able to play through it correctly by the end of the session.

One counter-intuitive truth from the world of Superlearning is that actually it can be more efficient to *not* finish the task at hand.

When we don't finish something, it creates a kind of "open loop" in our brains. A problem which has not been solved. This causes our brain to keep working on the task in the background, even when we're not consciously aware, trying to solve that problem and close that loop.

So we are quite literally recruiting more parts of our brains into the learning process over a longer period, even after our official practice time has come to an end.

This is amplified even further when we factor in the significance of sleep on learning. During sleep the brain performs various house-keeping tasks including consolidating memories and processing the events of the day into new neural pathways for the future. When we go to sleep with an "open loop" or two (for example, the muscle movements required to finger a certain passage of notes), our brain can actually make progress on those tasks during the night.

"The primary purpose of practice is to tell our brains what to do when we're sleeping."
— Dr. Josh Turknett, neuroscientist-turned-banjo-instructor.

You can give this a try yourself, by simply choosing to stop working on something during practice when you feel you've got it about 80% correct rather than 100% correct. It may help to remind yourself of this task (e.g. by listening to, audiating, or mentally playing the section of music) right before going to bed. See if the next time you sit down to practice you're still at that 80% correct level or lower... or if, in fact, your brain has managed to bring about some improvement in between. I think you'll be pleasantly surprised!

4. Courageous Music Practice

It's time to introduce the most powerful principle in Superlearning. But before we do, I need to give a little warning.

See, when we first taught the techniques you're about to learn, in the *Musical Superlearning* course we created with Gregg Goodhart, we faced an unusual problem.

Up until then, our courses had generally been very positively received by the students going through them. They enjoyed the process, they had a good time learning, and they were generally delighted with the results.

This time it was different. For the first week or two of the course, there was actually a lot of griping and complaining! The musicians going through it were really *not* enjoying the experience. That came as a bit of a painful surprise to us on the team. But when we looked at what exactly was causing the negative emotions, it all became clear.

In the years since, we've refined and expanded our approach to Superlearning, and the way you'll be exploring it in this chapter is designed to help you keep *Enjoying the Journey* :) Most notably, by integrating musicality training and combining all four H's, rather than it being a strictly Head-and-Hands experience.

But there is still one point of potential frustration which I need to alert you to in advance.

When you first start practicing music the way you're about to discover, it can be very uncomfortable. It can feel like you're actually getting a lot more things "wrong" than you were before. On top of that, recruiting the whole brain for the task at hand is (by definition) more tiring than when the brain is just coasting along.

This can make the whole thing a challenge in the "Heart" sense, as you experience thoughts and emotions that could discourage and derail you.

The good news is threefold: you will experience greater progress and results than ever before. You will find new ways to enhance your musicality while learning new repertoire and instrument skills. And, just like regulars at the gym come to enjoy the burning sensation in their muscles that means they're making progress, you will come to genuinely enjoy what Gregg Goodhart calls "the blearn": the "burn of learning".

Now that you know to expect this experience to be somewhat uncomfortable at first, it needn't discourage or derail you. But this is why we've titled this section "Courageous Music Practice"—because ultimately it will take some courage on your part to try doing things such a different way, and persist long enough to see the big payoff. For some people that will be instant, as one of these techniques may let you finally crack something you've been struggling with for ages. For others, it may take a week or two before things click and you start to see your results transform.

Remember Growth Mindset, Beginner's Mind, and Trial and Improvement mindset. Tak Courag, and stick with it!

Deliberate Practice: Plan, Play, Reflect

Probably the single biggest discovery in the scientific field of accelerated learning comes from the great Professor Anders Ericsson, whom I had the honour of interviewing before he passed away.

He conducted the pioneering research into the question of where "talent" comes from. Was it genetic? Inexplicable magic? Or were the "talented" individuals in various fields, from sports, to literature, to art and music, actually doing something differently to everybody else.

As we covered in *Chapter Two: Mindset*, the research revealed clearly that "talent" was essentially a myth. All the accomplishments and abilities of so-called "talented" musicians, artists, sportspeople, and other experts had been gained through a vast amount of a particular kind of learning activity.

"I've been reviewing this now for about 30-40 years, trying to find something which seems to be necessary for you to be successful at some domain, that really can't be influenced by training.

Once you start looking and finding that those individuals who have certain types of abilities, once you look back and see what they were doing there in the first five or eight years of their life... you find that they were engaged in [particular] activities and that actually seems to be related now to their ability here.

[...]

It's really the training that is critical.

I'm not saying that we will never find genes that actually will give you a sort of a head's-up on your success. But what I would say is that basically so far I'm not seeing any compelling evidence.

People have now been mapping out the DNA for hundreds of thousands of people, trying to actually see how [for example] the best long-distance runners might have different genes from those who are far less successful. And so far, as far as I know (and this is based on other people who are actually doing the research) we actually have not found even a single gene that actually would be of useful value to help you know whether you're going to be successful in long-distance running, or sprinting, or whatever."

— Professor Anders Ericsson, Musicality Now interview

Ericsson named this different kind of learning, which all the seemingly-talented experts have been doing, "Deliberate Practice".

The defining trait which distinguishes it from the blind brute-force "massed repetitions" approach, is introducing a "reflection" step, where you analyse how things went and what you might try differently next time.

In the music context we can see Deliberate Practice as having three parts which operate in a repeated cycle:

1. Plan

2. Play

3. Reflect

The traditional "massed repetition" approach is to simply Plan then Play. We pick what we're going to run through, then we play it. Repeat. Hope it gets better. (And be disappointed when it generally doesn't.)

In fact, if we're honest, often even the "Plan" step is skipped. We show up for a practice session and somewhat mindlessly run through our routine. We feel like we did our duty because we did the "Play" step. But we aren't even making thoughtful plans about what to play, or how to play it differently each time through.

With Deliberate Practice, we introduce a "Reflect" step, where we pay careful attention to what just happened, and we use what we observe to influence our next "Plan".

For example, you might be working on a certain two-measure phrase, which you just can't seem to play at the target tempo. It's fine when you play it slowly, but you make several errors when trying to to play it faster.

You might Reflect that you're always late playing the third note—so you Plan to try moving your finger a little earlier to hit that one. Or you might Reflect and notice that actually your finger is landing a little off-target which is why half the time you play the wrong note in that spot—so you Plan to be more intentional about that finger placement at that moment. Or you might Reflect and realise you're obeying the "instructions" on the page, but actually your mental representation of that passage is a bit of a blurry jumble of notes—so you Plan to slowly play it through note-by-note and then audiate it after, to build a better mental representation of what you're trying to play.

Andrew Says...

In much music learning both the Plan and Reflect steps are given over to the teacher, so the student is only responsible for the Play.

I had these young students once that were brought up in a culture that highly valued blind obedience. They would practice their piano music according to what they thought the page was telling them to do, even when it sounded awful. At the lesson, the first question I would ask was "How does that sound to you? Does that sound good to you?"

They would look at me in terror before sheepishly responding "No." I would then walk them through the steps of solving the problems themselves.

It just flabbergasted me that they would spend all week sounding terrible without questioning. But this is actually quite common and occurs with young students and adults alike.

There are various ways to explain why introducing this "Reflect" step is so effective.

One is that this kind of intentional reflection "wakes up" the brain more fully, activating its learning processes. It also allows us to thoughtfully troubleshoot and problem-solve, which greatly shortcuts the learning process by helping us jump more quickly to an effective way to do the task at hand.

You can also think in terms of conscious and subconscious mind. The traditional "massed repetition" approach is relying on our subconscious mind to somehow automatically make us better at the task through sheer repetition. And while the subconscious mind is incredibly powerful, we need to set it up for success by giving it something to work with. The "Reflect" step is using our conscious mind to feed some new experiments and experiences to our subconscious mind, which can then figure out the new neural pathways needed for success.

And finally, I like to think of it as a way to become your own best teacher. By conducting a new little "experiment" each time around the Plan-Play-Reflect cycle, you discover for yourself the most effective ways to move your muscles and play the notes you intend to, a skill which itself becomes better and better over time. You become both student and teacher, as you continually optimise your own learning process.

One reason I like this "becoming your own best teacher" framing so much is that it sets the scene for integrating the various musicality aspects we'll explore below. You are empowered to choose the "experiment" to run next at any given time, and use it not just to "get the notes right" but to move you along the path to your own Big Picture Vision, developing exactly the kind of musicality you care most about.

Recording and Honesty

Remember those frustrated students I mentioned going through our original course on Superlearning? As you start using Deliberate Practice, it's common to find that things seem to be getting worse instead of better.

While part of that comes from the "Desirable Difficulty" technique you'll read about in the next section, part may also be due to the fading away of what is known as the Dunning-Kruger Effect (named after the researchers who first described it).

They discovered that people learning a new subject or skill area are prone to over-estimating their own expertise. In music that means we believe that we are playing better than we really are.

For example, imagine that you've listened to that one particular David Gilmore solo hundreds of times. You may now have such a strong and emotionally meaningful mental representation of that remembered version that when you go to play it you're actually hearing David Gilmore rather than yourself!

When we start leveraging Deliberate Practice, our perceptions and reflections sharpen, and we begin to see more clearly what's really going on and what we want to improve.

If you're feeling truly courageous, you'll want to start using recording as a regular part of your music practice. Audio (or even video) recording is a great way to keep ourselves honest about our playing.

You can use any physical or software audio recording device, including a recorder app on your phone or tablet. Generally the audio quality of any modern device will be sufficient to enable an effective "Reflect" step, so don't let concerns about microphones, audio gear or room acoustics hold you back from starting to record yourself.

I recommend starting today. This may be painful at first, but "the truth will set you free".

Once you know the actual problems and limitations you are dealing with, you can use the Plan-Play-Reflect process of Deliberate Practice (as well as the more specific techniques we'll cover in the rest of the chapter) to do something about them. It will take much less time, and produce much greater success than if you rely solely on listening in the moment as you play.

TIP:

If you're feeling truly courageous then remember the Pillar Belief of *Better Together*, and consider sharing a recording with a friend or a musician you know. You'll find that their "Reflection" on your playing may well bring to light both positive and constructively critical observations that you might not have spotted yourself.

Metronome in Mind

Along with recording, one powerful (yet intimidating!) tool at our disposal is the good old metronome. When a musician says they "can't play something" or that they "always make mistakes", generally the reality is that they can play the music if they play through it very slowly, thinking carefully about each note in turn—but they can't play it at the target tempo without playing wrong notes or making other mistakes.

So tempo is always a factor in music practice, and many of the Superlearning techniques introduced in the rest of this chapter need to be done as part of varying our playing speed to gradually work towards a successful play-through at the target tempo.

When it comes to "getting a piece up to speed", the traditional brute-force "massed repetition" solution is to keep trying, again and again, gradually increasing the tempo bit by bit, and hoping our fingers somehow figure out how to play it correctly at each new faster speed. We treat it like lifting weights at the gym, where we want to add a little bit of weight each time we do the exercise, and let the muscle grow stronger each time.

That does work, to some extent. But the limiting factor is almost never how fast our fingers can physically move. Coming back to the H4 Model, we need to make sure none of the "legs of our chair" are too short—and often the Head and Hearing (i.e. your brain's mental representation of how to play it correctly) are actually the weak points, rather than your Hands.

So taking that traditional approach of simply increasing metronome speed bit-by-bit is actually painfully inefficient, compared to more intentionally helping the brain to form that "ideal mental representation" of how to play the piece correctly. The Contextual Interference techniques you'll learn about below do exactly that. But to use them most effectively, you'll need to form a new friendship with your metronome.

For many musicians, the metronome is synonymous with feeling pressured. It's always ticking, seemingly faster and faster, as we struggle to make our speed goals. That way of using the metronome only creates more tension, and tension is the greatest enemy of speed and fluency in our musical expression.

Let's also call out the elephant in the room. Many musicians don't even use a metronome in the practice room, except perhaps momentarily, to get a sense of the tempo they should be practicing a piece at.

Just like recording ourselves, playing along with a metronome forces a brutal honesty during practice, and it's easy to just shy away from that, and wing it during practice instead.

Here's the thing though. Most of our discomfort and disagreement with the metronome arises from misunderstanding as to what it is for and how it can even become a powerful friend in our quest for musical Superlearning.

The Metronome and Mental Representations

We've been talking about trying to form the "ideal" mental representation in the brain. If we imagine ourselves able to successfully perform a piece at the target tempo, that ability exists in the brain as a set of neural pathways which enable our body to carry out the actions required to pull it off.

The metronome can help us by creating a type of sonic "grid" in our brain that helps us to organise where all our notes go relative to the beat. This happens at both a conscious and subconscious level.

This function can be completely separated from the idea of speed. Instead, we focus on lining everything up with the beat until our brains have a crystal-clear idea of the placement of each musical event. In other words, we can use the metronome to tidy up the rhythm of our mental representation of the music, which actually produces greater confidence and relaxation.

Once this is done, changing tempo (faster or slower) becomes a separate task, and is much easier and more enjoyable!

Again, many of the problems and mistakes which crop up when we try playing a piece faster don't come from some physical limitation of our bodies. They come from our brain's mental representation of the music being too fuzzy. A large part of that fuzziness tends to be the rhythms and how they relate to the "grid" of the beat.

Re-introducing Metronome: Your Practice Buddy and Jam Partner

It's understandable why many musicians see the metronome as a tyrant and an enemy. But the metronome is there to teach us about the beautiful dance between beat and rhythm. While it may seem to be just a machine, the metronome helpfully shows us where the beat is, which is the thing that all our rhythms relate to.

So celebrate this relationship and shift your attitude to the metronome. Pay attention to the sound and timbre of the click, and jam with it as if it were your best musical friend sitting in the room with you. In your mind, make that click a part of the musical experience, and engage fully in your musical conversation with the metronome.

You'll enjoy yourself more, and internalise your own inner sense of the beat on a profound level, which will accelerate all your rhythm learning.

A great way to get started with this is as follows:

EXERCISE: Refine Your Tempo Grid

1. Take a section of music you're learning from notation and mark very carefully in the music where each beat falls. If you

are working by ear, then sing your part and clap the beat, or play the music and tap your foot to the beat.

2.   Make special notice of when the note falls:

   • On the beat

   • In between beats

   • Sustained over multiple beats

3.   Now play through your segment at a comfortable, stress-free tempo with the metronome. Try to listen for the interplay of beat and rhythm.

TIP:

   If the second step is challenging for you, it just means that you have to do some work on understanding the relationship of the rhythm to the beat. This understanding is fundamentally important to being able to use a metronome at all! So either choose a segment with simpler, more straightforward rhythms, or dedicate some time to learning more about Beat and Rhythm in Part II of this book.

Notice that these kinds of exercises do not require clicking up faster and faster! Yet the more you do this kind of exercise, the more you improve your sense of the interplay between beat and rhythm, and the easier you'll find it to play music at faster tempos. In other words, even without leveraging the various Superlearning techniques introduced below, simply practicing more mindfully with the metronome will help you achieve more success faster in learning new music.

It's also worth noting that often the difference between a good-sounding musician and a great-sounding musician comes down largely to their rhythmic precision. As listeners, we tend to appreciate the difference subconsciously, but just imagine a player who always places each and every note in *exactly* the right place in time to perfectly synchronise with the other musicians and convey just the right groove or most impactful phrasing. That's what spending time "jamming" mindfully with your metronome can unlock for you.

Click Up, Click Down

When we separate the tasks of rhythmic precision and speed, our brains seem to breath a sigh of relief! We are saying to our brains that no matter how fast or slow the metronome goes, everything is still locked in place.

The traditional way of using the metronome to increase speed is to keep clicking it up, faster and faster. This creates tension, as each faster speed is expected to be "harder"—and tension is just the opposite of what we need to play quickly and joyfully.

Here's a simple but magical exercise which reinforces the message that rhythmic precision is the same at any tempo, and does marvels to keep us from tensing up at faster speeds:

EXERCISE: Click Up, Click Down

1. Choose a starting tempo that is totally comfortable for you. Let's say you've decided on 84 BPM (Beats Per Minute) for a piece you hope to eventually play well at 105 BPM. Play through the passage once at that speed.

2. Now click up to a random faster tempo, say 92, and play through again.

3. Then go slower than you started, maybe 80, play through at that speed.

4. Then a faster tempo, like 87.

5. Continue "wiggling" randomly, for example: 83, 94, 90, 68, 97, 94, 102.

We have found it to be surprisingly effective if you don't make huge leaps, but instead wiggle around in "close quarters". For example, 102, 103, 101, 105, 107, 104 etc.

Don't worry if your repetitions are not perfect! Just play through once at each tempo and move on. If you find yourself tensing up, you may want to wiggle the speed downwards. If not, try wiggling upwards until you are at your target speed (and faster).

It's also quite possible that slower speeds will be *more* difficult. What this tells you is that you still haven't locked in the separation between the speed of the beat and the precision of where the rhythms fall inside it. If this is your experience, you'll be surprised how much good wiggling around at slow tempos does for your high-speed playing.

One final comment on the topic of metronomes and tempo. We'll be exploring this further in *Chapter Eighteen: Performance*, but it's valuable to know now that if you want to be able to reliably perform a piece at a certain tempo, you'll actually want to aim for 10-20% above that tempo during practice. This adds further resilience to your playing abilities, since if you can comfortably and reliably play a 100 BPM piece at 120 BPM during practice, to play it at "just" 100 BPM will feel far more relaxed than if you've only ever got it up to 100 BPM during practice. In other words, it adds a buffer which can help shield you against a variety of performance-time challenges.

It takes courage to truly engage with the metronome like this, and examine precisely how well you are playing at different speeds. As you start to play around with the metronome in this more exploratory and creative way, you will find your relationship with it changing, as it helps you to uncover hidden problem spots and resolve them effectively.

Believe in Yourself

The Dunning-Kruger Effect (over-estimating your own expertise) seems to have grim implications, but it has a powerful upside potential too.

In Greek mythology, the sculptor Pygmalion carves a statue so beautiful that he falls in love with his creation, beyond all realistic hopes. The Goddess Aphrodite sees his plight and brings the statue to life so it can return his love.

Psychologists have noted that those who have high, even unrealistic expectations, tend to achieve greatly improved performance—often beyond what an outside observer may have thought possible. They call this the "Pygmalion Effect".

So how do we reconcile the "emperor has no clothes" aspect of Dunning-Kruger with the limitless potential of Pygmalion?

Simply believing in yourself can be more powerful than either one.

If you chose to pick up this book and read this far, you must believe in yourself enough to think that you might be capable of the wild-sounding promises of dramatically faster music learning and becoming something like the "Complete Musician" we described in *Chapter One: Musicality*.

So when the going gets tough, remind yourself of the belief that first set you on this new journey: that there is, in fact, a better way to learn music and achieve your musical dreams, and that you can and will find that better way for yourself.

Plan-Play-Reflect All The Things, All The Time

The most common interpretation and application of Deliberate Practice is for small-scale, minute-to-minute practicing during a practice session. And it is indeed a tremendous process for that. Using it in that way alone will transform the effectiveness of every minute you spend practicing.

However, as you start to tune in to the Deliberate Practice way of thinking, you'll soon realise that this Plan-Play-Reflect process can exist on all timescales and at all levels of your musical life.

For example, when you have a big recital or performance coming up, naturally you'll Plan for it, and then you'll Play (i.e. do the performance itself). But how often do you bother to really Reflect afterwards? You could make it a habit to take even a few minutes after each performance to self-assess, or possibly even listen back to a recording, and make the observations that can feed into preparing to make your next performance even better (i.e. your next "Plan").

Another example would be in organising your musicality training. Guided by the "North Star" of your Big Picture Vision, you should have a clear sense of the direction you want to go. Reading through this book will arm you with a whole array of options for exploring in that direction. Next you'll need to Plan what you're actually going to put into action. You'll need to follow through on that (i.e. Play, in both the musical and the playground sense of the word!) And then you'll want to periodically Reflect, perhaps each day, week, month or quarter, to assess how the Plan is working out and what adjustments might be helpful.

So you see, this Plan-Play-Reflect cycle of Deliberate Practice is more than just a practice room routine. It's really an iterative optimisation process that can be applied throughout your musical journey, to help you have more success faster in every area.

I'll mention the key point one more time: most of us already Plan and Play by default. It's adding that intentional "Reflect" step and feeding the observations back into a revised Plan which makes all the difference in the results you'll enjoy.

5. Desirable Difficulty

If Deliberate Practice is the most important over-arching process in Superlearning, then Desirable Difficulty[2] is where the rubber meets the road. As you read a moment ago about adding a "Reflect" step, you might have felt a bit uncertain: how do you actually know what "experiment" to try next, to address whatever problem has come to light? Or what if you're coasting along and can't really spot any obvious issues to "fix" during the Reflect step?

The concept of Desirable Difficulty is a simple one: everything we could try in the practice room exists on a spectrum from "so easy you won't learn anything" through to "so hard you don't have a chance". Somewhere on that spectrum is a "just right" zone, which we might call the "Goldilocks Zone", where you're pushing your brain just enough to maximise its learning potential.

And here's the clever bit. Instead of simply playing everything "by the book" and stumbling around among the mistakes we happen to make, we can intentionally introduce additional challenges (*Desirable Difficulty*) which both engage the brain more fully, and uncover hidden problem-spots which might otherwise have been hard to recognise.

This lets us go from a semi-passive learning experience, where we're just hoping problems come to light and we can come up with ideas to fix them, to a learning experience you get to actively drive forwards yourself, introducing just the right challenges to essentially force your brain to fully learn what you want it to, as rapidly as possible.

---

[2] As presented in the research paper "Making things hard on yourself, but in a good way: Creating desirable difficulties to enhance learning" by Bjork, E. L. and Bjork, R. A. (2011) Psychology and the real world: Essays illustrating fundamental contributions to society.

As well as a set of specific techniques you'll learn about below, Desirable Difficulty can be seen as a shift in attitude from *"I hope everything will be okay when I play this"* to *"let's go seek out all the possible problems and fix them."*

Mistakes As Friends

Imagine having a friend that will always be there to support you in being the best you can be. Believe it or not, that's what mistakes can be for your music practice.

You may have been raised to think mistakes in music are something to be embarrassed about. It might even be combined in your head with the talent myth i.e. *"If I was naturally good at music I wouldn't make so many mistakes."*

This mindset has two major negative ramifications:

1. We get discouraged, letting mistakes sap our musical enthusiasm, which harms our momentum and scuppers our consistency with practicing.
2. We tend to want to gloss over mistakes, and just rush on and play something we're more capable with. This cheats us of the learning and progress which that mistake was offering us.

For now, at least inside our practice room, it's time to flip our relationship with mistakes on its head.

Mistakes tell us where we need to focus our attention. They are an infallible guidance system as we Plan-Play-Reflect our way through our practice journey.

They also tell us a lot about our emotional reactions, and teach us where we can shore up and build a true Growth Mindset to accelerate our Superlearning.

Our best and most immersive learning experiences come when we're making mistakes—even if during live performances, mistakes are not nearly as desirable!

The good news is that the more we embrace and even enjoy our mistakes while practicing, and the more we dissolve the strict distinction between the two (more on that in Chapter Eighteen: Performance), the fewer mistakes we'll make when performing. What's more, if we do make a mistake in performance, we'll be much better equipped to handle it with poise and grace.

When you start seeing mistakes as opportunities and you have a set of tools for tackling them effectively, you'll find that you start almost looking forward to the next mistake you make, knowing it's your next step forwards towards success.

When we change our relationship with mistakes, practice looks more like this:

EXERCISE: Make the Mistake on Purpose

- Plan: Choose a segment where you have a particularly troublesome spot, like one where you keep making the same mistake over and over. That might be getting a note wrong, bodging a rhythm, fumbling a sequence of notes, making a strange noise, or anything else your Inner Critic tells you is "a mistake".

- Play: Play through the segment, and be very intentional about playing your familiar mistake on purpose! Repeat this two or three more times.

- Reflect: How did that feel? Did your fingers flow with the mistake, or did they "fight" it? What do you notice in your thoughts and feelings that may be leading you to the make that mistake? What could you do differently to play it correctly?

- Plan: Let's gain further clarity on the difference between the mistake and the correct version.

- Play: Slowly and carefully, alternate playing through with the mistake and with the correct version. Try increasing the tempo.

- Reflect: What happened? When? Remember to pay careful attention to your thoughts and emotions as well as the mechanics of playing.

As you start approaching mistakes this way, with Deliberate Practice, you'll find yourself appreciating how mistakes really are your friends. Our end goal may well be to perform without any mistakes, but finding mistakes and addressing them head-on in the practice room is exactly how to achieve that goal most quickly and effectively.

The Goldilocks Zone of Learning

Our brains love a challenge! That's why we can learn more when we make things harder on ourselves. On the other hand, being overwhelmed sends us into fight-or-flight mode which shuts down the learning process.

So the key for Superlearning is to find that "Goldilocks Zone" of Desirable Difficulty.

As mentioned above, Desirable Difficulty is a general principle and can be leveraged in many ways. Anything you do to keep yourself in that sweet spot, where you're generating enough "grist for the mill" to make the Reflect step of Deliberate Practice valuable will be effective.

However, there is one particular technique called Contextual Interference, which is like a powertool for generating Desirable Difficulty on-demand.

To understand what "interfering" with "context" might mean, we need to first become more aware of our context when practicing music.

Context

Our goal when practicing a musical task is to get our brains to form the new neural pathways which enable us to succeed with that task. If we're learning to play a new piece of music, you can think of this as your brain's "mental representation" of how to play that piece successfully.

Any time we make a mistake or struggle to play the piece correctly, that's an indicator that something is not yet as it should be in our mental representation of how to play the piece.

Here's the rub: when we're practicing music, we aren't operating in a pristine laboratory environment where we get to just feed in perfect data to a perfect system and produce the perfect mental representation right away.

In fact, the process is utterly drenched in what we might call *context*. We can distinguish between *outer* and *inner* context:

- **Outer context** means everything that's going on around us as we practice. This includes our bodies, our instruments, our chair, the sheet music or devices that we're looking at for notation, the wall that we face, the pictures on that wall, the room where we sit, how we sit or stand, sounds from the next room or the street, time of day, etc. Believe it or not, all of these will have some effect on how well the brain manages to "encode" the information we're trying to pass into it, as well as creating "cues" that it relies on to help bring the required memories forth.

- **Inner context** is about what's going on inside us. Thoughts, emotions, focus, reactions, distractions, enjoyment (or lack of it), audiation, judgements, etc. Again, all these things will influence the speed and accuracy with which the brain turns our experiences of playing music into new neural pathways.

How the brain learns is a deep, complex process, which any neuroscience researcher would admit we still only partially understand. However, the influence of context is clear, and the research has revealed a fascinating opportunity…

One might think that the fastest route to get the brain to form the ideal mental representation would be to make our input as pristine as possible, to reduce or eliminate context, or at least make it so consistent that it shouldn't bias the information we're feeding into the brain.

But here's the big counter-intuitive finding from the research: if we intentionally manipulate our context, and feed the brain a wider variety of experiences, this actually helps the brain to form that ideal mental representation faster.

You can think of this as how carrying out a variety of experiments can be more instructive than just doing the same experiment repeatedly. Or how if the human body is never exposed to cold, germs, or physical strain, it actually makes your health very fragile and prone to illnesses—whereas introducing those "challenges" help the body to become strong and robust against dangers and harm.

Intentionally manipulating our context for the sake of faster, more successful learning is called *Contextual Interference.*

Contextual Interference

We'll explore three forms of Contextual Interference you can start using to accelerate your music learning: Inner and Outer Context, Musical Context, and Creative Contextual Interference.

A. Inner and Outer Context

Above we shared various examples of Inner Context and Outer Context. All of these influence how your brain learns, and so manipulating any of these can provide helpful new stimulation.

Here's a wonderfully easy way to try it out. I picked this up from Mars Gelfo, creator of the popular Modacity practice-tracking app. We were discussing Contextual Interference, and he said one of the easiest and most basic ways to experience its effects is to simply change where you practice.

If you can, move to a different room. Or simply face a different direction to normal. You could also sit if you usually stand, or stand if you usually sit.

If you play piano or a similar non-movable instrument, you can instead do something to change the visual context around you. For example, if you usually play with the lid down you can open it up. Or you can change the picture hanging above the piano. Or drape an interesting piece of fabric over the top, or add a row of small stuffed animals… Have fun and use your imagination!

Carry out your practice session as normal. You'll probably notice your brain is just a little bit more alert and engaged. It might feel a bit distracting. There might be strange changes to the tone or sound of your instrument. You might notice some thoughts or emotions coming up which don't usually arise for you. You may make some odd mistakes you don't usually make—hooray, more grist for the mill!

Remember that this is a subset of the principle of Deliberate Practice, so you want to try the experiment above in a cycle of Plan-Play-Reflect. Once you complete your practice session in the new location, be sure to reflect on how it went, and anything you learned or might want to do differently next time. For example, did this generate a desirable level of difficulty? If it was too challenging, maybe next time you don't change room, you just face a different direction. If it was too easy and there wasn't much effect, maybe next time you try standing on one leg, change location every five minutes, or have some background music playing that doesn't match what you're trying to practice.

I love this exercise both for how simple and easy it is to do, and because of how much it reveals about the difficulties we have with musical performance.

We'll explore this more fully in Chapter Eighteen: Performance, but for now I just wanted to bring your attention to it. If you find yourself having odd thoughts, or making new mistakes after simply moving to a different location, you can probably see why practicing at home and then performing up on a stage somewhere can be so challenging, and why it can be so hard to perform the music as well on stage as we did in the practice room.

Hopefully you're also starting to see the great value in this kind of intentional contextual interference, for building a more robust ability to play the music as you intended.

You can be very methodical with how you vary Inner and Outer Context, or you can simply make it a habit to introduce a small degree of chaos to your music practice!

It often reminds me of that famous Frank Sinatra line, which I think sums it up well:

> "If I can make it there, I'll make it anywhere."
> — "Theme from New York, New York", lyrics by Fred Ebb

If you can play a piece reliably well, even after you've just run up a flight of stairs, sat down with an instrument you've just been loaned, in a room full of strangers, and found one page of the sheet music missing, you'll know you're ready for anything!

B. Musical Context

As well as the inner and outer contexts explored above, we can also make effective changes in the context of the music itself.

This is perhaps the strangest and most counter-intuitive part of Superlearning. Even if our goal is to play the music exactly as written, we can actually get there dramatically faster by practicing playing it in a variety of other ways. We intentionally change the music itself, and practice playing those altered versions—and nevertheless, it feeds the same learning process in the brain which will ultimately converge on the "ideal" mental representation that lets us play it successfully as written.

A very simple example would be to try playing a piece starting from a randomly-chosen measure, rather than always from start to finish. You might be surprised how challenging this can be! If our mental representation has always relied on that flow from measure to following measure, forcing our brain to start in the middle can really throw a spanner in the works. Playing a single measure at a time, jumping around the piece, can seem like a nonsensical exercise—but by interfering with the musical context in this way you actually develop a far more deep and robust mental representation of the whole piece.

Another commonly-used method is to change the rhythms of a passage. You're still playing all the same note pitches as before, so your fingering sequence on the instrument stays the same—but you're playing around with the timing of each note. This forces the brain to really focus on the notes and finger movements with fresh attention.

For example, supposing our goal was to play a straight C Major scale:

We might try alternating longer (marked "L") and shorter (marked "S") notes:

And then shorter and longer:

These kinds of rhythms are known as "dotted rhythms" after way the notation which describes them uses dots to show the note durations being extended.

The "reverse dotted rhythms" (where the shorter note comes first in each pair) is a particular favourite of Gregg Goodhart, who has found it's one of the most reliable types of Contextual Interference, to get a musician directly into what we call the Goldilocks Zone of Desirable Difficulty

The scale example above started from a series of notes all with equal duration, but this can be applied to any music.

EXERCISE: Dotted Rhythms for Contextual Interference

- Choose a passage you struggle to play correctly, or which you can play slowly but not at target tempo.

- Begin by evening out the rhythm, turning whatever sequence of notes you're aiming to play into one where every note has the same duration. That in itself may well produce some desirable difficulty!

- Then play them with the Long-Short or the Short-Long pattern introduced above.

There are a couple of interesting things that you'll notice when you try this. Firstly, it often brings to light some underlying issues. The "new" mistakes you make typically aren't random ones that only belong to this altered version of the music. Often they are actually present in the normal version too. So bringing out those mistakes gives you the chance to correct them.

The second thing you'll notice is that even if you don't consciously apply Deliberate Practice to "new mistakes" in the altered version, simply practicing that altered version and then returning to playing the music normally (i.e. as written) tends to produce progress.

Keep in mind our earlier principle of "Not Finishing". When you're playing these variations, you don't need to practice them until you can play them perfectly. In fact, it's better not to! Aim for about 80% correct, and then return to playing it as written.

The Many Faces of Contextual Interference

Contextual Interference is only effective when it produces Desirable Difficulty. For example, if you always do dotted rhythms, and you get really good at them, they stop working. That's why it's helpful to develop a wide toolkit of Contextual Interference techniques.

Almost any variation you come up with to alter the music slightly can be an effective form of Musical Contextual Interference, and as we'll be exploring below, that can become a great creative practice in itself.

Here are some specific suggestions for ways you can try playing a tricky passage you're working on:

- Backwards (yes, really!)

- Upside down (if playing from sheet music you can literally turn it upside-down)

- With different articulations or playing techniques (specific to your instrument)

- Exploring even more rhythmic patterns (use arbitrary patterns, or swap rhythm and pitches across pieces)

- Changing the dynamics (loud to soft, etc.)

- Changing instruments (different models of your instrument or even a whole different instrument)

- Combined with various outer contexts such as changed body position and location

- Combined with various inner contexts such as intentional thoughts and emotions (even "negative" ones like frustration or anger, to produce more difficulty)

These may seem crazy to consider, and sound crazy to your ears. And it will seem weird at first to go through all that effort to make the music sound so different from the way you want it to sound in the end.

But each time we make one of these changes, especially if it produces the right level of Desirable Difficulty, we are also allowing our brains to explore the music in different ways, with different focus of attention. And though it seems counter-intuitive, this actually results in more efficient and robust encoding of the music in our brains, enabling that end goal of successfully playing the music at tempo, as written.

C. Creative Contextual Interference

As the list above demonstrates, there is no limit to the number of creative Contextual Interference variations and combinations you can come up with! You might find it helpful to keep in mind the 4-Dimensional Active Listening framework from *Chapter Five: Active Listening,* and any insights or ideas you glean from your Active Listening practice to find new ideas for Contextual Interference.

It can be liberating to bridge from the nuts-and-bolts of Contextual Interference as described above, to the more creative and expressive musicality exercises we'll explore in the next section, by thinking in terms of "Creative Contextual Interference".

Once you know that anything which produces Desirable Difficulty will actually help your brain to learn faster, it's much easier to allow time and space for creative experimentation in the practice room. Creativity no longer needs to feel like a distraction, or some additional thing you're trying to practice. Creative exploration can be integrated directly into working on tricky sections in pieces you're trying to master.

So I would recommend treating Contextual Interference as a creative process, not just a practice exercise. That means listening as you play, and forming your own aesthetic judgements about what sounds "good" or what you like. You might just surprise yourself!

When you incorporate your creativity in this way, it's a double win: your Superlearning becomes more enjoyable, almost a game, and the resulting progress in learning is boosted even further.

6. The Power of Musicality

"Make an art of your practice."
— Steve Lawson, Resident Pro for Bass at Musical U

Before we continue, I'd like to share a little behind-the-scenes info with you about Superlearning and musicality... because I think you might find that our experience at Musical U actually mirrors your own personal journey.

In 2020 we created our first training on musical superlearning, the course referred to earlier, which was called just that: *Musical Superlearning.* As far as I know, it was the world's first online training dedicated to applying the principles of accelerated learning to music specifically.

But we almost didn't make it.

The opportunity was clear. We knew these techniques worked

extremely well, both from the scientific research and the team's own experience using them. Not to mention the extensive experience of Gregg Goodhart, with whom we would be creating the course. So we knew we could offer something really valuable and impactful.

But I was torn.

Up until that point, we had been focused for over a decade purely on "musicality training". I was worried this would confuse what Musical U stood for, or distract us from our mission.

What gradually dawned on me was that in fact, Superlearning was perfectly aligned with our mission. It was simply a different way of enabling musicians to debunk the "talent myth" and step into their own true musical potential. The focus was instrument skills and repertoire rather than the "inner skills of musicality"—but it certainly still fit the mission.

That satisfied me enough to go ahead and create the course, which proved to be a smash hit with our existing community of members.

But honestly, there was still something nagging at me for the following year or two. It felt like we now had two areas of special expertise: musicality and superlearning. They both helped the same kinds of growth-oriented musicians, so that worked out okay. But it always felt a little awkward to have essentially two separate training paths on offer.

It wasn't until we launched the *Next Level* coaching program in 2022, and had a new opportunity to work one-to-one with passionate musicians who were eager to pursue both musicality and superlearning, that things finally clicked. We were able to formulate what we now call *Creative Superlearning*, neatly marrying the two worlds, and showing that the whole could be greater than the sum of its parts. Musicality training benefitted from Superlearning techniques, and Superlearning for instrument skills and repertoire benefitted from musicality-themed enhancements.

This was also finally the solution to that frustration which the original course had produced. Some of that was necessary and inevitable, because Deliberate Practice is more challenging than just coasting through a practice routine. But looking back, and comparing it with how we now teach Superlearning, it's clear that a big part of the problem was the lack of musicality and the imbalance of the 4 H's.

Even though the course did effectively accelerate learning, it still followed the traditional flawed practice model by focusing exclusively on Head and Hands. Incorporating musicality into our Superlearning practice fixes that.

We've already begun to touch on this in the previous section, with the idea of Creative Contextual Interference, as well as highlighting the danger of letting "music practice" be a dry, strictly right-or-wrong experience, where the outcome can only be music-reproducing robots.

In this section we'll explore a number of ways you can enhance your music practice with musicality training, to both accelerate your learning of instrument skills and repertoire, and increase your musicality naturally along the way. I hope that as you experiment with some of these ideas, you'll come to see Superlearning and musicality the way we now do: not as two separate areas, but as a wonderful pairing, with endless possible interplay between the two.

We'll be giving several specific examples of musicality-enhancing (or musicality-enhanced) practice, but the main goal of this section is to further revise and broaden your concept of what "practice" can be.

The two major themes are enjoyment and creativity. The more ways you can find to make your practice more enjoyable and more creative, the more success you will enjoy.

- Enjoyment, because "fun is not the opposite of learning". Making practice fun not only keeps your passion for learning music burning bright, boosting consistency and typically increasing how much time we dedicate to practice—it also helps keep us in a Growth Mindset and fully engaged with the learning process.

- Creativity, because nothing engages our brains quite so completely as being creative! When we approach practice with a creative mindset, we engage our imagination in a way that goes beyond simply repeating exercises and drills. Instead, we actively shape and transform the music we are learning.

One easy way to boost both enjoyment and creativity to any music practice is to focus on the expression, bringing out the emotions that you feel in the music.

Expression

Some of our definitions of "musicality" at the start of this book were really focused on playing expressively. The idea of making the notes you're playing sound truly *musical*.

We'll be going deep on this topic in *Chapter Seventeen: Expression*, exploring what exactly it means, and what specifically you can do to bring a greater level of expressiveness to your playing by learning the "musical language of emotion."

The challenge for a lot of musicians is that they have a sense of what they're reaching for, in terms of playing expressively—but they haven't been given any tools for getting from here to there.

Fortunately, even before arming you with the specifics of that dedicated chapter, which will help you find more success faster, you already have everything you need, right now.

If you can tell the difference between a beautiful, moving musical performance, and a robotic, artificial, basic MIDI-generated reproduction of a piece of music—then between Active Listening, Audiation, Singing and Deliberate Practice, you are more than capable of finding your way there yourself.

We just need to remove one big barrier for you.

That barrier is the idea that we have to learn the piece before we can be expressive with it. Musicians slave away in the practice room trying to get each note correct. And then finally, eventually, if time allows before the big performance, they try to "add more expressiveness."

That's how it's often taught. And it's another case where that's okay —it sort of works, sometimes—but it's far from ideal. Not least because many of us lose momentum or motivation with a piece before ever getting to that stage of "making it sound musical."

Aiming to play the notes expressively can start on day one of learning a new piece. It can be part of every note you play, even during scales and technical exercises.

Your goal is to "find the music in the music". Don't let the dots on the page, or the recording you're learning from, be just a set of instructions on what buttons to press when. Instead, always remember that our goal is to create beautiful, fulfilling, satisfying music.

Personally, I would prefer to hear "Hot Cross Buns" played slowly, elegantly and beautifully, than a lightning-fast rendition of a Van Halen solo which hit every note "correctly" but was devoid of any emotion. How about you?

When you really bring your attention to "finding the music in the music", it's a powerful form of Contextual Interference. To illustrate that, just imagine for a moment how much concentration and brainpower it would take for you to transform something super-simple like "Hot Cross Buns" or "Happy Birthday" into something which could touch a listener emotionally. Think about all the exploration you would have to do, and how much more deeply you would come to know those seemingly-simple pieces. Now think about how your inner instinct for playing expressively would automatically be increased by doing so.

In our Summer Series workshop on Superlearning, our Head Educator Andrew shared a beautiful example of this. He had spent a long time playing Klezmer music, where there's a lot of expression and rhythmic elasticity. He then went back to playing Bach, and was stunned by all the musical depth and playing opportunities he'd been oblivious to before. His appreciation and instinct for expressive playing had levelled up, and he was able to feel the music in a whole new way.

There's so much more "music in the music" than we're typically aware of when solely focused on "getting the notes right". When you start proactively looking for it, you're going to feel that. Your audiences are going to feel it. And it becomes a wonderful tool for both increasing the beauty of your playing, and for accelerating your learning by serving as a new kind of Contextual Interference for you in your practice.

Andrew says...

One of my favorite exercises when I have fast technical pieces is to take segments and really slow them down. Play them super rubato, play everything like it's Chopin, or opera or something like that. With all kinds of fermatas, and this and that, and really expressive tone, and just over-the-top emphasis.

Really milking the expression for all I can. Even on the most technical things, stuff with lots of scales and flurries of notes and things like that.

It helps me to get in touch with the meaning of each note. And that shows up when I then start playing it fast.

Improvise to Learn

If the word "improvise" in that heading just struck fear in your heart, don't skip ahead just yet! Many musicians believe that they'll need to master a whole lot of music theory and technique before they could learn to improvise. But the truth is that we can begin to improvise from the moment we begin to sing or play an instrument, and Improvisation can be an invaluable tool for Superlearning.

We'll dedicate *Chapter Fifteen: Improvisation* to this topic, and equip you with a powerful framework for gradually learning to improvise in a free and creative way that sounds truly your own.

For now, the key concept you need to know is that the assumption above—that you need to study a lot before you can improvise—can actually be flipped on its head.

Rather than "learn to improvise", we can "improvise to learn".

We've found this to be a staggeringly effective approach for our members at Musical U. Another way we put it is that *"creativity is the vehicle, not the destination."*

When Improvisation is seen as an isolated skill to learn, it's easy to get caught up immediately in worrying about which notes to choose, and how to make sure it sounds "good".

But think about it instead in the context of Contextual Interference, as we've been exploring in this chapter.

When you're learning a piece of music, try challenging yourself to improvise new and different notes for a measure or two. You don't need to start from scratch and play something completely different, you can try just varying a note or two, here and there.

This immediately brings a wide range of benefits. For example:

- It helps you better understand which notes "fit" at that moment, and why.

- It reveals hidden insights into the music which can unlock greater expressiveness or fluency.

- It helps your fingers become more comfortable and versatile in the key (assuming you choose to stick to the notes of the key!)

- It helps you make your playing of the measures before and after that section more resilient (because you're forcing your mental representation of those to stand alone, rather than relying on the measures in between—similar to starting playing a piece from a random measure rather than always start-to-finish, as covered earlier in the chapter).

• It increases how engaged and activated your brain is.

And on top of all that, you also get the chance to improve your improv skills. If you combine this practice technique with what you'll learn in *Chapter Fifteen: Improvisation*, you'll really begin to appreciate the power of Creative Superlearning.

What If?

Improvising an alternative version of a measure or two is one example of a broader creative technique: asking *"What If?"*

With Deliberate Practice we've already got away from the traditional predetermined "practice routine", and with Contextual Interference we've seen the power of playing something other than what's written on the page.

What if we loosened things up even further?

What if we started each Deliberate Practice cycle with a creative "What if?" question?

What if that proved to be the key to truly exploring a piece of music deeply, while also learning it more swiftly than ever?

Hopefully you see the open-ended power of "what if" questions :)

Here's a short list of example what-if's which can help get you started:

• What if I played it as fast as possible?

• What if I slowed it down to a crawl?

• What if I danced while I played it?

• What if I only played every second note?

• What if I played it in another octave (register)?

• What if I transposed it to a minor key?

• What if I played it like a conversation between a dog and a cat?

• What if I sang or hummed it instead of playing?

• What if I kept all the rhythms and changed all the notes? (or vice-versa)

- What if I sang it like Frank Sinatra?

- What if I reharmonised it with minor 7th chords?

- What if I called my auntie and played it for her?

Remember, as with everything suggested in this chapter, you'll get greatest benefit if you do it as part of an overall Plan-Play-Reflect process of Deliberate Practice. So don't just blitz through a bunch of what-if's. Take the time to Reflect after each one, and let that inform the next *"What if…?"* you ask and explore.

Direct Practice

A running theme in this chapter is to question the "should"s of music practice, and instead empower ourselves to design and direct our practicing. This can be daunting, but the rewards are tremendous.

What about the biggest question of all, though: *"What should I practice?"*

We already have part of the answer. Instead of a fixed practice "routine", we should be thinking of a practice session as *"I should spend time doing the Deliberate Practice cycle, focusing on what most needs improvement"*. But even that statement included a "should" which you might, quite rightly, push back against at this point!

Direct Practice means to practice the thing that you really want to do. Even if that means focusing less time and attention on the things you "should" do. Whether that's what our instrument teacher told us to work on, or the exercises included in a course we're following, or even the practice recommendations made in this very chapter. To temporarily set aside what we "should" do, and instead allow ourselves to play what we *want* to is itself a valuable and powerful practice technique.

Beyond indicating what we should practice, Direct Practice would also have you practicing it in a way that was as close as possible to the actual experience you want.

For example, let's say that your dream is to play a solo singer-songwriter gig, but you're spending most of your time practicing instrument technique and cover songs. It might be better to do Direct Practice by focusing on your own songs, and even trying to duplicate the experience of performing in the venue in your practice space.

Maybe get just the right stool, set up mics (or even just empty mic stands for now), turn down the lights, make a set list and play through it, complete with banter addressed to a picture of an audience you've tacked up on the wall, or even for a cat, friend, or family member.

The concept of Direct Practice doesn't have to go this far to be highly effective as a guiding principle. Sometimes we hold ourselves back unnecessarily from playing the music we really want to because we think we aren't "ready", when in reality we could make great strides by diving in and giving it a good try.

Musical Dreams

"Don't dream it. Be it."

— Tim Curry as Dr. Frank-N-Furter,
The Rocky Horror Picture Show

What are your pie-in-the-sky musical dreams? A certain piece of music? Being a music creator? Jamming with friends? Playing shows? Composing a movie soundtrack?

If you followed the Big Picture Vision exercise in *Chapter Two: Mindset*, you should have a detailed, vivid and inspiring snapshot of the musical life you yearn for.

In the spirit of our *"What If...?"* exercise, what if you started trying to be that version of yourself now?

This may be an uncomfortable question for you to face! You may have even found yourself reluctant to write down your true musical dreams. Notice how this indicates the presence of Fixed Mindset, and possibly a complete lack of Direct Practice up until now...

You don't need to go as far as we did in the singer-songwriter example above to start practicing being the dream version of yourself.

Something we often do inside *Next Level* coaching (which our clients are initially very suspicious about!) is to take a "dream piece" or a certain skill they hope to be good enough to tackle in a year or two, and instead have them start working on it right away. With the kinds of techniques you're learning about in this chapter, even without personal one-to-one coaching from an expert, you can make far more progress than you've probably thought possible.

EXERCISE: Play Your Dream Song... Now.

- Plan: Choose a "dream song" or "dream piece" you'd love to perform some day, and select just a short section—perhaps a couple of measures, or the most memorable passage.

- Play: Spend some time practicing it. You can leverage all the Superlearning techniques covered in the chapter so far, using further Plan-Play-Reflect loops.

- Reflect: How did you get on?

What's interesting about this exercise is that it may genuinely be beyond you to master the entire dream song or piece right now, at least in any reasonable timeframe—but try this out, and you might be surprised how quickly you can get a short section of it under your belt, and how deeply rewarding and exciting that will feel. Don't underestimate how valuable that is for your musical development!

We Could Be Heroes

Deliberate Practice teaches us to focus on minute details with greater and greater awareness of what we are doing. We may begin to notice the most nuanced micro-movements of our fingers or our breath.

Through increased contextual awareness, we may begin to also notice the shape and movement of our emotions and how they sync up with or hinder our musical Expression. We have also begun to be aware of the vast unknown reaches of our brains and what they are capable of accomplishing—even when we are sleeping!

Reinventing our music practice is as much a change in mindset as a change in habits. When we begin to fully adopt a Growth Mindset, and we get a taste of Superlearning success, we might even entertain the possibility that we are so much more powerful than we know...

Building on the "dream song" exercise above, try another what-if: *What if you played it like your musical hero?*

EXERCISE: Play It Like Your Hero

- Start your recorder going, and play through a piece you can play comfortably, just as you usually would. A video recording is particularly useful for this particular exercise.

- Who's the first person who comes to mind as "your musical hero"? Yo-Yo Ma? Steve Vai? Miles Davis? Pink? Joni Mitchell? Jacob Collier? Pick one.

- Take a few moments to visualise and audiate your hero of choice playing the piece. How might they play it? We tend to automatically observe our heroes particularly closely. They way they move, sound, their facial expressions.

- Now press "record" again, and this time play it like a hero! Let your imagination run wild. Try and imitate all the mannerisms of your chosen musical hero.

- Don't skip the "Reflect" step. Listen back or watch the two recordings. Compare them. What was the same, and what changed? What does that reveal about your own default way of playing—and what opportunities does it bring to light?

Just Play

"First you learn the instrument, then you learn the music, then you forget all that s*** and just play."

— Charlie Parker[3]

Consistency is important to our musical forward motion. Hopefully you're starting to see that with the great variety of concepts and practice strategies in this chapter (along with the endless possibilities that open up when you can use these principles creatively and enjoyably in your practice) consistent music practice no longer needs

---

[3] There are a few variants of this quote which are popularly attributed to Charlie Parker, though a definitive trustworthy source is hard to find! I decided to include it in spite of that, because it's just such a great line.

to rely on a superhuman level of "self-discipline".

As much fun as all this reinvented music practice is though, it's important to remember that point about letting "practicing music" and "performing music" both blur back towards simply "playing music", and to regularly give ourselves the opportunity to "just play".

I love this anecdote from Victor Wooten's book "The Music Lesson":

"What instrument do you play?" I asked.

He turned and took a seat in the chair across from me. Laying his skateboard in his lap, he tucked his hair behind his right ear and took a breath before responding. "I play Music, not instruments."

"What do you mean by that?" I asked, losing my imagined control of the conversation.

"I am a musician!" he answered. He placed his hand on his chest to emphasize his point before gesturing at me. "You are just a bass player. That means you play the bass guitar. A true musician, like me, plays Music and uses particular instruments as tools to do so. I know that Music is inside me and not inside the instrument. This understanding allows me to use any instrument, or no instrument at all, to play my Music. I am a true musician, and one day, you too shall be."

Much of what we get hung up on in our practicing has to do with the technique of playing our instruments. The initial thing that attracted us to picking up the instrument in the first place—the music—fades, as our goals become more and more technical than musical.

We've all seen musicians who had lots of technical fireworks, but forgettable musicality. While there are others where the technique seems to melt away and we lose ourselves in their musical expression.

The Gateway

Technique is important because it helps us take the music we have inside and produce the sounds we want to hear and share on our instruments. But it's only the *gateway* to the music. Too many aspiring musicians get stuck milling about at the gate and never truly make it through into the lush garden of the music itself.

That's why this chapter so emphasises reflection and consideration of the creative and expressive aspects of music-making—whether we call it "practicing", "performing", or just "playing".

It's worth regularly dedicating either a whole practice session or part of every practice session to "just playing".

Draw on the ideas presented here on Expression, Improvise To Learn, What If, Direct Practice, the Playin like your hero—or just go completely freeform, following your heart.

Simply play whatever you feel like playing, in the most enjoyable way you can imagine.

You might find you love the compare-and-contrast learning of recording a "normal" version and then your *"really playing it!"* version. Or you might like to remove even that expectation of yourself, and focus purely on being in-the-moment as you play. Either way, a "Reflect" step afterwards is essential to get the fullest benefit.

This is a perfect case of "fun is not the opposite of learning". You'll find that some of your greatest discoveries and breakthroughs may happen during the time spent "just playing".

Andrew Says...

It's really important to make your music fun. It's not irresponsible. A lot of times in the culture that we grow up in, we think that having fun means being irresponsible.

And it's actually quite the other way around. It's our responsibility to have fun.

It's music. We're not like solving world hunger or anything like that. We're playing music, right? So it should be fun.

---

7. Encoding and Retrieval

What does it mean to have learned a piece of music? Is it being able to play through it, start to finish, at tempo, without mistakes? If so, what does it mean if you try again a few days later and make a bunch of mistakes—have you un-learned it?

Musicians often struggle to build up and then maintain a repertoire of pieces or songs they can play. Doubly-so if we're talking about playing them "off book", without notation. It can feel like every time you put something new in, something old gets forgotten.

Another common complaint is that the more music you have in your repertoire, the more time you need to spend keeping it all at a playable level. Soon your entire practice time is taken up just "refreshing" the music you know you should be able to play, and there's no time (or brain capacity!) left for adding anything new in.

We once had a *Next Level* client, for example, who was spending 2-3 hours per day on piano practice—but after scales and warmups, all that time was spent just playing through learned pieces. Why? Because otherwise she found she would "lose them" and have to pour endless hours into learning to play them all over again. As a result she had really struggled to add any new pieces or increase her skills. It took all the time and energy she had just to stay in the same spot[4].

All these problems stem from a misunderstanding of the learning process and how the brain's memory system works.

When it comes to music practice, we tend to use the words "learn" and "memorise" loosely, and to mean two different things. For most musicians, to "learn" a piece means practicing it to the point where they can reliably play it mistake-free, at tempo. To "memorise" it means they can do the same thing, without the visual context of sheet music or other notation in front of them.

What's fascinating is that from a brain science perspective, all of that is, in a sense, "memorisation". Even if we're relying on notation, and even if we can still only half-play the piece correctly, our brain is going through a process of forming new memories and recalling them. In fact, the "mental representation" we've been referring to in this chapter, which lets your brain instruct your body on what movements to make when, is in reality a "memory" in the brain.

What is "Memorising"?

Just like scientific researchers have studied how so-called "superlearners" (a.k.a. "prodigies", "the gifted", "talented people") can learn new skills ultra-fast, they have also studied how the top memory champions can do what they do.

The people who can memorise the order of a pack of playing cards in under 60 seconds, or memorise hundreds of random words or numbers in a matter of minutes (such as in the World Memory

---

[4] This is one common cause of the dreaded "plateau", where your ability level seems to stall out at a certain point and it's hard to make any further progress. Another common cause is lacking the other Superlearning tools in this chapter, so that sticking points and challenging music seem insurmountable—because no amount of massed repetitions ever moves the needle for you. Fortunately that won't be a problem for you any more!

Championships) use a range of practical techniques to accomplish these seemingly-magical feats. We'll cover the most relevant one for musicians below.

Aside from specific techniques though, there is one massive lesson for us from the world of memorisation research. Like all things Superlearning, it seems odd at first, but makes a lot of sense once you understand it.

If the central concept of Superlearning is Deliberate Practice, with Contextual Interference as a powerful toolkit to support it, then the second most important concept is to distinguish between *Encoding* and *Retrieval*.

The average musician thinks of "memorising music" as something you do to get off-book and be able to play without notation, and the method used is usually massed repetitions i.e. just try to keep cramming it in there, and hope it sticks.

There are two problems with that. Firstly, as noted above, memorisation is happening throughout the music-learning process, not just when we want to get away from the visual cues which notation provides. And secondly, massed repetition is once again the least efficient way to achieve our aim.

The research reveals that there are actually two distinct processes involved in memorisation:

1.   *Encoding* is the process of building up the brain's "mental representation" of the music we're trying to learn to play i.e. "getting the music in there"

2.   *Retrieval* is the act of accessing that stored representation, to play the music i.e. "bringing the music out again"

And here's the key: both of these require dedicated practice effort! So one way to look at the traditional way of trying to memorise music is that we're using a very inefficient Encoding process... and then not actually practicing Retrieval at all. We just try to brute-force the Encoding, and when it comes time to perform, we hope the Retrieval goes well. If it doesn't, we assume that means we haven't practiced enough, and need to spend more time "getting it in there". In fact, we simply needed to spend more time practicing "bringing it out again".

So the opportunity here is to recognise these are two distinct processes, and be intentional about when we are focused on Encoding new music, and when we have completed that stage and are ready to move on to practice Retrieving it.

We've already covered how to Encode new music more efficiently: Deliberate Practice, Contextual Interference, and most everything we've covered in the chapter so far has been about that process of "learning to play the music". Now it's time to examine what "Retrieval practice" might be, and how to make it as efficient and effective as possible.

Getting "Off Book"

We have just broadened our definition of "memorising the music" to encompass the whole process of learning to play it, whether with the visual cue of notation or without. It's worth clarifying then that what we'll cover in this section can be applied in both cases.

Even if you only ever perform the music with notation in front of you, the same distinction between Encoding and Retrieval applies, and the same technique of Retrieval Practice (presented below) can be used.

If you do want to get "off book", and reliably and successfully bring the music out again without the visual cue of notation in front of you, that will most often be done as an additional phase of learning the music. Once you have successfully Encoded "how to play it", and can reliably Retrieve "how to play it", you can work on Encoding "how to play it without the notation" and practice Retrieving "how to play it without the notation".

With that being said, some musicians prefer to incorporate getting "off book" from the outset, as part of the initial Encoding phase, and we recommend this. Or if you're learning a piece by ear rather than from notation, that's actually your only option.

Again, all the same principles apply. It's just a choice of whether "getting off book" is part of what you include in the initial Encoding phase, or leave it as a later separate task of Encoding and Retrieval Practice.

Retrieval Practice

If our goal is to intentionally add a Retrieval Practice stage to our learning of a piece of music, the first step is to discern when the music has been successfully Encoded and is ready for retrieval. This isn't a black-and-white question and it's not always obvious. But roughly speaking, once you've ironed out the kinks and any sticking points, and you can play through a piece successfully, the piece is probably ready for you to begin Retrieval Practice with it. One good indicator is when mistakes occur more randomly, rather than it always being the same "problem spots" which trip you up.

In reality, it's not a strict "A then B" process. There can be some back-and-forth between the Encoding and Retrieval stages, as Retrieval Practice reveals problem spots that actually need a bit more Deliberate Practice to firm up that mental representation. Or, contrariwise, going through Retrieval Practice may actually resolve some issues you thought would require a lot more Deliberate Practice in the Encoding stage. However, for the most part, our overall process is to get a new piece through Encoding and then into Retrieval Practice.

Note that pieces do not necessarily have to be up to target tempo to begin Retrieval Practice. We've found that pushing something into Retrieval Practice sooner than you think you should can, in fact, be quite powerful.

Retrieval Practice isn't a complicated or mysterious process. We are literally talking about simply practicing "bringing the music out again".

If you take just one idea away from this section, let it be this: when you return to a piece of music and struggle to play it, that may not mean you haven't learned it well enough. It probably just means you need to practice that act of retrieving what you previously learned.

The Power of Forgetting

Let's come back again to the traditional method of learning or memorising music. We spend all our time "cramming it in there". Then some time passes, and then we try to "bring it out again".

What happens in the middle? There is some level of forgetting. We think this is a bad thing, so if we want to "learn it better" or "memorise it better" we generally try to do more "cramming it in there".

In reality, just like mistakes can be our friends once we understand Deliberate Practice, that forgetting stage can be our friend, once we understand Retrieval Practice.

The reason we struggle to bring the music out again is that we aren't giving ourselves enough opportunities to practice that middle step: time passing, before we try playing it again. Doing more "cramming it in there" only makes that worse!

Retrieval Practice is about turning forgetting to our advantage. Similar to how Contextual Interference deliberately introduces additional challenges so that we can learn to overcome them, Spaced Repetition is the idea of deliberately allowing ourselves to "forget" a little, so that we can learn to overcome that.

Spaced Repetitions

Spaced Repetition means we intentionally design how much time passes between our attempts to Retrieve a memory. The goal is to wait just long enough that it's a bit of a struggle to bring that "mental representation" up again. If we play the music again too soon, we aren't practicing Retrieval. If we wait too long, the mental representation (i.e. the memory) will really fade, and we'll need to go back to Encoding it again.

It's important to note another similarity with Contextual Interference: this can be brutal! We are intentionally setting ourselves up to struggle. As long as you know that, you can be prepared and not let it discourage you. Don't be surprised if you find yourself making a lot of mistakes and feeling like "things are getting worse" when you first try using Spaced Repetitions. Have faith that the music is well encoded, and that forgetting will lead you to remembering.

Spaced Repetitions are the bread-and-butter of Retrieval Practice. We play the piece once and only once, with no "do-overs" or corrections. Then we wait for a certain interval of time before repeating that.

We leverage the way the brain gradually forgets by increasing the interval each time. For example, you may begin by interleaving your repetitions in between 10 or 15 minutes worth of other practice, maybe three times in a day. Then perhaps we reduce it to once a day, then once every two days, and so on.

Just like in Interleaved Practice (covered below) and the "80% correct" guideline for Contextual Interference, Retrieval Practice recruits more of our brain to the task, by introducing an open loop e.g. *"I retrieved that piece and it was awful. While I'm sleeping, brain please go ahead and figure out what needs to be adjusted or reinforced in my mental representation to bring this out when and how I want it."*

Spaced Repetitions take time to work their "magic". When embarking on a course of Retrieval Practice, it's good to give yourself 4-7 days before you evaluate the results. After that time, you can go through the music several times at different metronome speeds and see what happens. If needed, you'll have plenty of other Superlearning tools to then make any other improvements necessary.

Here's an example schedule for Encoding and doing Retrieval Practice on a new piece of music, or most likely a particular segment of a piece:

Example Plan For Encoding And Retrieval Practice

Stage 1: Encoding Off Instrument (1-3 days)

Before bringing in the instrument, it's a good idea to get to know the music as much as possible.

Goal: to gain as much mental and emotional familiarity with the music as possible before beginning with instrument.

You can use any or all of the following:
- Active Listening to a recording (if available)
- Active Listening with notation (if available)
- Singing
- Audiating

Stage 2: Encoding On Instrument (1-3 days)

Step 1:

Goal: full comprehension of the rhythms and pitches at a playable tempos.
- Sight-reading (and/or Playing By Ear)
- Slow playing with Deliberate Practice

Step 2:

Goal: music playable all the way through, at ~50% or more of target tempo.

Add various Contextual Interference techniques, metronome techniques, and Deliberate Practice to be able to play the whole thing at a certain tempo (no matter how slow) with about 80-90% accuracy.

Optional: if your intent is to get "off book" (i.e. play without notation in front of you), this stage is the best time to start! It may take a little longer, but it will be easier in the long run than if you wait until after your first round of Retrieval Practice.

Decision point:
Listen to the message of your mistakes. Are you making identifiable mistakes consistently in certain places more than 50% of the time? If so, return to Step 1 for those segments.

Are your mistakes more random? If so, move on to Stage 3: Retrieval Practice.

Stage 3: Retrieval Practice

Remember, no matter what happens, you will only play the piece once per retrieval. No stopping, and no "going over" anything. Contrary to Master Yoda's wisdom, trying *does* count!

- Day 1: Interleave 3 retrievals with other things you're practicing, with at least 10 minutes between retrievals.

- Day 2: Retrieve twice, with 30 minutes to several hours between retrievals.

- Days 3-6: Retrieve just once per day.

- Day 7: Retrieve once, reflect, then play through several times at different tempos (faster and slower). Reflect and do some Deliberate Practice for any opportunities which came up. Then play through again.

- Day 8: Decision point: Listen to the message of your mistakes.

Are you playing at a satisfactory tempo with very few mistakes? Hooray! Put the piece into longer cycles of Retrieval to keep it in your repertoire. Alternately, you may want to return to Deliberate Practice targeting certain aspects of expression, emotion, etc.

Are you still making random mistakes? Continue Retrieval Practice, perhaps lengthening the time between retrievals to two days or more.

Are there certain sections that are still troublesome? Cycle them through Stage 1 and Stage 2.

Notice that once a piece moves into Retrieval Practice, the total number of retrievals (i.e. play-throughs) is actually very small, compared with the traditional "massed repetition" approach, where you might try playing it 3-5 times a day, every day, for weeks before a big performance. This is where the huge efficiency gains come from.

Remember at the beginning of this section, when we talked about the struggle of building up your repertoire, because so much time needs to be spent just keeping it all "fresh"? Spaced Repetitions provide the solution. As you can see, it's possible to keep far more music in the later stages of Retrieval Practice, and continually "fresh", because so many fewer repetitions are required when they are spaced efficiently.

And that coaching client I mentioned, who'd been spending 2-3 hours a day just keeping her repertoire playable? Once she switched to this approach, she found she could easily keep everything "fresh" with just a fraction of the practice time each day.

Now clearly this is a very different way to approach "learning new music". Don't let that overwhelm you!

As a starting point, try taking an inventory of the various music you've learned to play so far, and categorise which are currently in the "Encoding" phase, which could be moved to "Retrieval" phase, and which you can reliably Retrieve. Then you can start designing your practice to include the right kind of practice on the right items, and get more and more of them to the point where you can successfully play them any time you like, at the drop of a hat.

Remember to stay agile. With everything mentioned above, Creative Superlearning is ultimately about developing the art of practicing, through the experience and wisdom gained through a Deliberate Practice mindset. Trying things, seeing what they do, making adjustments, and so on, taking full ownership of and responsibility for your learning journey.

First Retrieval

There's one final important thing to be aware of when doing Spaced Repetitions, and Retrieval Practice in general. We mentioned above that we expect play-throughs to be a bit rocky each time you practice retrieving the music from memory. That's to be expected, and exactly what is necessary to gradually firm up that mental representation.

However, this can also happen when you "dust off" an old piece for the first time in a long time... and that doesn't mean you've forgotten it!

For example, suppose you've gone through the Retrieval Practice process described above and you think you've got a piece locked in tight. A few weeks pass, and you decide to play it again. You find yourself stumbling, hesitating, playing wrong notes.

At this point it's easy to think you haven't successfully Encoded it, or haven't done enough Retrieval Practice.

But that so-called "first retrieval" is a special case. You have to re-awaken the parts of the brain that were storing that mental representation, or "dust off the cobwebs" so to speak. The first play-through will do that for you, but your playing may not come out perfectly.

The good news is that once that "first retrieval" has been done, subsequent play-throughs immediately after should go far more smoothly. (If they don't, then you may indeed need to put the piece back into the "Retrieval Practice" phase, or possibly even back to further Encoding.)

If you're preparing for a big performance, simply playing through the music in the hour or two before showtime will serve as that "first retrieval" and make sure the memories are fresh enough to enable a successful play-through when the time comes.

As you start making use of the Retrieval Practice process described above, this is just something to be aware of: the first retrieval isn't generally representative of how well you've learned the music. So don't be discouraged if you thought you'd really learned something well and then find yourself stumbling again when you return to it. Most likely you have learned it well, and just need to allow that "First Retrieval" to refresh the mental representation you had successfully stored.

8. Practice Time Management

> "With great power comes great responsibility."
> — Uncle Ben, in the classic Spiderman comics

In this chapter so far we've explored a number of paradigm-shifting ideas about music practice, and for all their power and potential, they do come with a catch: the risk of overwhelm. The traditional model of having a "music practice routine" may be deeply flawed in terms of its effectiveness and how quickly it allows you to learn… but it does at least mean you can sit down each day feeling confident that you know how you'll spend your practice time.

In this section we'll explore a handful of ways to approach the question of *"How can I design my music practice to best leverage Superlearning techniques?"*

The reason there's a risk of overwhelm when diving into Superlearning isn't just that there are lots of options, nor that we're removing that pre-determined "Play X for Y minutes" routine. It's also that the entire topic involves a shift in responsibility. Rather than relying on a teacher, or a course, or some blog article to tell you how to spend your practice time, Superlearning empowers you to make all those choices yourself.

At first, that responsibility may be unnerving. Recognise the Heart challenge of stepping into that role, and really owning that your activities and results are entirely up to you. You may find it useful to jot down the thoughts and emotions it stirs up, and reflect on them.

Throughout the ages, writers, painters, musicians and all those involved in creative pursuits have faced the challenge of the "blank page" and its unlimited possibilities.

Let's equip you with some options and ways of thinking about how to start sketching structure onto that "blank page" of the practice session. I encourage you to experiment with each for a week or two, to discover which are most useful as your regular approach, and which may be useful just occasionally.

Organisation

Before we look at ways to approach or structure things within each practice session, we must first consider the overall organisation of your music learning.

If you're like most musicians, then up until now you've probably relied on outside sources to direct your music learning. That might be a teacher, a course, a website, a book, a series of grade exams, or perhaps a musician friend who mentors you.

Just like the Pillar Belief of *Musical Inside And Out* is about empowering you to bring music out from inside you rather than always relying on other people to tell you which notes to play when, Superlearning brings with it the opportunity to design your own music learning journey in a way that's truly aligned with you, your background, and your own musical aspirations.

Skills

Hopefully you went through the Big Picture Vision exercise in *Chapter Two: Mindset* and so you have that clear "North Star" to guide you. That chapter (and the entirety of this book) is intended to provide you with a comprehensive map of all that's possible for you, to turn that vision into reality. The H4 Model can serve as a useful way to self-evaluate. As noted in that earlier section, we use this to help musicians create a "snapshot" of their abilities each quarter inside the *Next Level* program, which then guides their focus in the following quarter.

The idea here isn't to throw out all those external sources of plans and "routes". There's still huge value in them. But remember another of the Pillar Beliefs, *Universal Potential*, which says not just that we are all capable of achieving great things in music, but also that each individual musician's path will be different. This is why all our training programs at Musical U are always designed to be highly flexible and personalisable, and why your learning journey must be too.

So you don't need to design your own music-learning curriculum from scratch. Instead, it's simply about that shift in responsibility and authority, empowering you to use the Plan-Play-Reflect cycle to adapt and pivot and refine your path as you go. As long as you're drawing on good, proven resources or instruction for the Plan phase, and taking the time to really Reflect, you can avoid the plateaus, sticking points, and loss of momentum that typically happen when you blindly follow an A-Z one-size-fits-all path or course.

Repertoire

When it comes to learning new pieces or songs, the traditional approach tends to look something like this:

- Choose a piece or song that's at your current playing level or slightly beyond it.

- Spend a few weeks or months learning and practicing it each day with a "massed repetitions" approach, perhaps leading up to some planned performance.

- Have a few pieces or songs you're currently working on, along with some scales or other technical exercises that help you improve your playing technique, hopefully aligned with the music you're learning (e.g. scales corresponding to the keys of the music you're focused on).

- During practice you follow a set routine (e.g. start by warming up with scales and exercises, then work on Piece A for 10 minutes, then Piece B for 10 minutes, then Piece C for 10 minutes).

- Once you feel you've got the hang of those, move on to some new ones. Maybe go back to older pieces once in a while.

A typical Superlearning approach would be different in a number of key ways:

- We needn't restrict ourselves as much when choosing new music to work on, since Deliberate Practice and Contextual Interference allow us to tackle more challenging passages more reliably and quickly.

- We'll consciously organise our practice of pieces based on whether they are in the Encoding or the Retrieval Practice phase of being learned. You'll want to keep a written list of which pieces are currently in which phase, and update that as needed after each practice session as part of an end-of-session Reflect step.

- We'll be systematic about scheduling and rotating pieces which are in the Retrieval Practice phase so as to make most efficient use of our practice time and keep a far larger repertoire at a "reliably playable" level.

- If our goal is to get the music "off book", we'll be designing for that—either as an integrated process from the start, or a secondary process of Encoding and Retrieval Practice.

- Practice time can be sequenced in a variety of ways (examples below) but always following the Plan-Play-Reflect loop of

Deliberate Practice.

- During practice we are particularly strict about limiting distractions (e.g. turn phone notifications off!) since we'll need our full brainpower at all times. We will be especially present and mindful of what's happening, each time around our Plan-Play-Reflect loop. We'll make use of a metronome and audio/ video recording to maximise our results.

- We'll blur the lines between "practicing" and "performing" back towards simply "playing" and incorporate musicality-enhancing exercises like those in the previous section, so that our "learning repertoire" is not separate from our "musicality training".

Now that we have a sense of how to organise our practice overall, let's look at some good ways to think about how to spend time during each practice session.

Two things to remember:

1. The most important principle is simply to apply Deliberate Practice. If you made no changes to the traditional practice routine described above, but you spent the time continually going around the Plan-Play-Reflect loop during each activity, you would already see dramatically better results! Everything else we're discussing is just further optimisation of that fundamental change.

2. The suggestions below about how to allocate time are all aimed at Encoding. Retrieval Practice defines its own best timing, so you'll want to factor that in, but not necessarily apply the ideas below directly to pieces in the Retrieval Practice stage. For example, you can use the Interleaving method we're about to cover by including the single play-through of a piece from your Retrieval Practice list, but you wouldn't keep interleaving multiple play-throughs of that piece because that wouldn't be Retrieval Practice.

Example Superlearning Session

Let's begin with an illustration of what a practice session could look like, leveraging various Superlearning principles and techniques.

You've chosen what to practice and separated your choices into categories. Rather than having one huge "project" piece, you'll have a range of repertoire in the "pipeline".

You've chosen seven musical pieces/segments, 1, 2, 3, 4, 5, 6, and 7, and defined five categories:

- A. New pieces needing slow and careful Deliberate Practice

- B. Somewhat-encoded pieces, ready for more Contextual Interference

- C. Short retrieval (one or two retrievals per day)

- D. Long retrieval (one retrieval every 2-3 days)

- E. Maintenance retrieval (one retrieval every week or two)

Thinking about the 7 pieces, you have categorised them like this:

Category	Pieces
A: Just Starting	1, 3
B: Contextual Interference	2, 7
C: Short Retrieval	6
D: Long Retrieval	5
E: Maintenance Retrieval	4

Then, during each practice session you alternate between the different categories to keep your brain fully engaged (see Interleaving below). For example:

1. Let's say you begin with piece 1. You're just starting with this piece, but have been listening to it a lot. So your first task may be to read through the notation slowly, reflecting and marking out the measures which you believe will be more challenging.

2. Then perhaps you switch gears to one of your "short retrieval" pieces, let's say piece 6. You play it straight through without

stopping, and make a mental note of what you'd like your brain to work on remembering, reflecting that you want to take some time later to audiate that rough spot in the pre-chorus.

3. You switch to some Contextual Interference using dotted rhythms on those rapid sixteenth notes in measures 42-47 in piece 7, noting your starting and ending top speeds.

4. Then you pick a long retrieval, piece 5, playing through once and reflecting on the progress you've made.

5. You then move back to piece 3, where perhaps you're learning the melody by ear. You focus on listening and singing, again making notes on where you might want to come back later and dig deeper.

6. At this point, you come back to piece 7, but focusing this time on the expression and tone in measures 31-37.

… and so on. Always allowing your Plan-Play-Reflect cycle to determine the path of your practice.

This "jumping around" during a practice session might initially seem strange and scatter-brained to you, but in fact there's good reason to allocate practice time like this…

Interleaving

One of the first ideas from the research into accelerated learning which started to gain mainstream awareness among music learners was *Interleaving*.

Remember the description of a traditional practice session above, where we spent 10 minutes on Piece A, then 10 minutes on Piece B, and then 10 minutes on Piece C? With Interleaved Practice you might still spend the same total amount of time on each piece, but instead of practicing each in turn, you interleave them. For example, you might spend 3 minutes on Piece A, 3 minutes on Piece B, 3 minutes on Piece C, and then return to Piece A for another 3 minutes, and so on.

Like so many things in Superlearning, this is somewhat counter-intuitive, given everything we know about the power of focus, and the importance of "not jumping around from thing to thing". But in fact, interleaving has been shown to be much more efficient overall[5].

You can see Interleaving as a kind of Contextual Interference: by switching task, we prevent the brain from starting to tune out or go on "autopilot", recruiting its full attention once more for the new task.

We're also leveraging "The Power of Not Finishing", allowing our subconscious mind to be churning away on the previous task even while we consciously engage with the new task.

There are also opportunities for Convergent Learning, in which we can (consciously or subconsciously) transfer what we are learning from one piece or activity to another.

The result: we make a lot more progress with each of the tasks by interleaving our time spent on each.

Interleaving can be planned out in advance, or be more "improvised" based on Deliberate Practice decisions. Simply having a clock or timer in sight when you practice can help you stay mindful of everything you want to cover and avoid practicing something for longer than is optimal.

As a starting point, you can try interleaving five-minute time segments, though anything from one or two minutes up to ten minutes can be effective, depending on what you're working on and the particular practice strategy being used during that time.

Task vs. Time

Many of us have been taught, often as children, that we should practice for a certain amount of time each day. We watch the clock tick. 27 minutes... 28... 29... Done! We might even have had checklists that we turned in to our teacher each week, showing that we had "done our 30 minutes a day".

You probably know all too well from experience though that merely "putting in the time" does not guarantee progress. And as we've been uncovering in this chapter, most of the methods which *do* guarantee progress don't involve any pre-set timing at all.

In most areas of our lives, we think in terms of task, not time. For example, when we wash the dishes, we start when they are dirty and finish when they are clean. If we wash them in 10 minutes rather than

---

[5] .See the Reading List in the *Additional Resources* if you're interested to know more about the relevant studies.

20, we don't chide ourselves that we didn't spend enough time washing dishes!

When we practice music by task rather than time, as we have been learning to throughout this chapter, we can be much more efficient, focused, and attentive, rather that just filling up the time with less productive practice activities. When we do use timed practice, we can use time as a limit to keep our brains alert, rather than something empty that we have to somehow fill.

The idea here is simple. It may still be helpful to set aside say 30 minutes each day for "music practice", but that's purely for the sake of scheduling our lives. When it comes to the practice session itself, all you need is a list of practice activities you want to include (e.g. the exercises, the pieces, musicality training) and trust the Deliberate Practice loop to tell you when to move on.

For example, in the past you might have set aside 10 minutes to play through older repertoire to keep it "fresh". Now, armed with your list of pieces in Retrieval Practice, you know exactly the tasks you need to include, and playing through them more than once would defeat the point. Or you might previously have allocated 10 minutes for a new piece you're working on. Now you might decide your goal is to really iron out the kinks in bars 36-40 and use Deliberate Practice and Contextual Interference to get it playable at 90 BPM. You don't need to spend endless time on it until you crack it, nor berate yourself if you don't—because you know the power of not finishing, Convergent Learning, and sleep for forming that mental representation you're aiming for.

It is often helpful to have an overall plan in mind before the practice session. You can start by allocating 5 minutes each to your Deliberate Practice segments and the length of each song/piece for your Retrieval Practice segments. Remember, you can do more than one 5-minute segment on a task during a practice session, as long as it's interleaved with something else.

Once you become more familiar with the art of practice, your Deliberate Practice reflections may guide you to use different segment lengths, say from 1 to 10 minutes.

Composed vs. Improvised Practice

In thinking about our practice as a musical experience, we can "compose" our experience in much the same way as a composer composes music. Rather than the traditional fixed "practice routine" or the "blank page" of deciding everything on-the-fly, we can apply Plan-Play-Reflect to each practice session.

As you shift to thinking in terms of Deliberate Practice, and separating Encoding from Retrieval Practice, you'll naturally start to see what to work on next. There will probably be many things you know need attention!

There won't be a strict hierarchy of priorities and there is no one "right answer" to what to work on next. Let that be liberating and exciting rather than intimidating. The wonderful thing here is that if you trust yourself and stay true to Deliberate Practice, you can feel confident that your practice time will always be well used.

Composed Practice is where we intentionally plan the practice session in advance. You might write it down, or it may be simple enough that you don't need to. Either way, you begin the session knowing clearly the tasks you want to tackle, and perhaps also how long to spend on each (for example when using Interleaving).

This is a great fit when we're wanting to build up our repertoire, since there can be so many pieces in the Encoding and Retrieval Practice stages, we need to be organised and intentional about which to include in each practice session.

The alternative is *Improvised* Practice, where we embrace the "blank page" opportunity of each practice session. From the traditional viewpoint this could be seen as disorganised, irresponsible, or even messy. But again, Deliberate Practice is the silver bullet!

You can, quite reasonably, show up to each practice session without having made a plan in advance, armed only with your sense of which things you're interested to work on, and use Deliberate Practice to continually decide where to spend your next minutes.

This can be a particularly great fit if you're eager to explore Creative Contextual Interference and incorporating musicality training into repertoire work, because when you're feeling inspired and in the flow (more on that below), the last thing you want is a timer to dictate that you move on to something completely different.

Ideas like "What if?" practice, "improvise to learn", "just play" and the other creative concepts introduced in this chapter will ensure that you can find your way out of any box and keep your Superlearning vibrant, fresh, and successful.

It's worth noting that even our most carefully planned Composed Practice can never be 100% predictable, since Plan-Play-Reflect will always reveal new opportunities and guide us to new decisions that we couldn't—and should not try to—predict.

Remember also that Contextual Interference requires Desirable Difficulty to work. So even if you believe you've got your Composed Practice "dialed in", it's crucial to always be open to shaking things up as well!

Finding Flow

We often use the term "flow" in a loose, colloquial sense when talking about music, to mean "things are flowing nicely". We also use it to refer to that experience of "being lost in the flow", which for many musicians is the ultimate goal, because of how deeply moving and satisfying it can be. Some people call it "getting in the zone" and one of my favourite sites devoted to optimised music learning is even called "Play In The Zone".

In some ways this is the epitome of musical experience for us as musicians, especially when coupled with a connection to our audience like we'll be exploring in *Chapter Eighteen: Performance*.

Although we use the term colloquially like this, researcher Mihaly Csikszentmihalyi has actually analysed and defined this "Flow state" precisely, and one of the most exciting things about Superlearning is how much of what we've been learning to do in this chapter can actually help us tap into that Flow state.

When we achieve Flow, we often feel a sense of exuberance and confidence. And despite what we might assume, this does not happen by playing the easiest material we can[6]!

One of the key hallmarks of the Flow state is striking the right balance between challenge and ease. We've encountered this same idea in the form of Desirable Difficulty. So it's no coincidence that research has shown that our ability to learn new information and develop new skills becomes extremely efficient in the Flow state.

Some people mistakenly associate the Flow state with more dreamy

---

[6] Side note: Really getting absorbed in the experience of playing music can happen without it being the technical "Flow" state we're discussing here, and in fact David Reed's answer to "What Is Musicality?" in *Chapter One: Musicality* highlighted how actually playing quite simple music can be the easiest way to really connect with your musicality. So we're not discounting the value, pleasure and fulfilment that playing simple music can bring—merely distinguishing this particular kind of "flow" in the scientific sense. We'll explore this more in *Chapter Eighteen: Performance*.

states of consciousness. And while it's true that we often feel a sense of altered consciousness in Flow, this feeling is more due to our increased awareness, focus, and conscious attentiveness to the task at hand.

Paradoxically, the attention to minute musical details that we've been cultivating through Planning, Playing, and Reflecting (i.e. Deliberate Practice) and our Contextual Interference can be instrumental in producing a Flow experience, both while practicing and performing music. And since we as humans tend to find great joy in experiencing that Flow state, this is yet another way in which "fun is not the opposite of learning."

One of the simplest and fastest ways to find Flow in your music practice is to continually aim for that "Goldilocks Zone" of learning, where you're tackling tasks in new and interesting ways that keeps your brain fully engaged and alert. We'll explore this more in *Chapter Eighteen: Performance.*

As a starting point, you might like to start adding Flow awareness to your new practice habits by making a note about how "in flow" you felt during each practice session. You could score or grade each activity, or the session as a whole.

Conclusion

The learning revolution that is unfolding before us is changing the way we understand and approach music practice. By incorporating contributions from other fields of knowledge, such as neuroscience and psychology, we can enhance our practice habits and make them more efficient, accessible, and creatively engaging.

By this time, you've had the opportunity to build a rich resource of new ways of thinking about and doing your music practice, that will lead you to much faster, more satisfying, and more musical results.

Feel free to return to this chapter as many times as you like and use it as a template for your expanding practice skills.

Remember, that even though the core principles we've discussed in this chapter stem from scientific research into accelerated learning, music is an art—and your playing during "practice time" can be just as much of an art as the music itself.

Like any art, skill and creativity must combine to produce unique individual expressions. You can be using the same concepts and exercises as someone else, and yet your practice sessions may look and feel very different from each other, and still both produce amazing results.

Bringing It All Together

To help bring everything together, here is an example illustration of a Superlearning-enhanced practice session. This would likely include jotting some things down, but most of what's written below would actually be inner dialogue.

- **Plan**: What am I going to practice today?

I'm going to work on:
  A. Improv for Summertime
  B. Retrieval for Chopin Nocturne
  C. ii-V-I chord voicings around the Circle of Fifths
  D. Start learning "Clean Slate" by the Mountain Goats for a YouTube cover
  E. Retrieval for Piano Man

- Gather my metronome, sheet music, iPad, voice(!), Circle of Fifths reference for ii-V-I, timer for interleaving.

- **Reflect**: I'm excited about how my new practice skills are helping me do so much more! Understanding Encoding and Retrieval, and using Interleaving really help.

- **Plan**: I'll schedule out the session.

- Create interleaving schedule: A: 3 mins, B: 5 mins, C: 3 mins, then D, E, A, B

- **Reflect**: Looks like a good plan. I'm doing two Chopin retrievals because I've just started Retrieval Practice for that one. This whole schedule won't take long, so I'll do another cycle through it (after Reflecting).

- **Plan**: A: Narrow down Summertime to go deeper on the phrasing

- **Play**: 3 mins on Summertime first 4 bars, variations on the melody, call and response with voice and piano

- **Reflect**: Doing that long on just the first 4 bars really forced me to get creative!

- **Plan**: B. Retrieval Chopin Nocturne

- **Play**: Play through once, no stopping.

- **Reflect**: Well, that first retrieval had a lot of mistakes, but I know that's to be expected as part of the Retrieval Practice process. It took some willpower not to repeat it!

- **Plan**: C. Evaluate what needs more work with ii-V-I

- **Play**: 5 minutes playing ii-V-I around the Circle, begining in first inversion.

- **Reflect**: That only took a minute. I'm making more mistakes with the keys of B, F♯, D♭, and A♭. I think I need to focus on those.

- **Plan**: Keep working on this till the timer runs out, set the metronome to a slower tempo.

- **Play**: Go very slowly with the less familiar keys. Repeat at different slow tempos until the timer goes off.

- **Reflect**: They improved when I went slower. The fingerings are really the same—I just have to think a bit more about the notes until they're more familiar.

- **Plan**: D: Let's start the new song with Active Listening

- **Play**: 5 minutes listening to "Clean Slate" while looking at the lyrics, finding the verse and chorus, and noting anything else about the form.

- **Reflect**: There are repeating sections, but the section I might call the chorus has different lyrics each time. There's an easy piano riff I can incorporate on my cover. Since there are so many lyrics and not much repetition, it's going to take some memorisation effort.

- **Plan**: E: Retrieve "Piano Man"

- **Play**: Piano Man

- **Reflect**: Well that's a little better than yesterday. Maybe this Retrieval Practice is working after all...

- **Plan**: B: Retrieve Chopin Nocturne

- **Play**: Chopin Nocturne

- **Reflect**: That's also a little better. I'm going to leave it here and see how it goes tomorrow.

So far this session hasn't taken long and I've accomplished quite a bit! I'm up for another round :)

- **Plan**: Do another round without the Retrieval segments, and make some modifications based on my initial reflections from the first round.

   ...

By definition, every Superlearning-based practice session will be different to the last, but hopefully this illustration gives you a good sense of how varied and adaptable it can be, as well as how many opportunities there are to improve on the traditional "massed repetition" approach, keeping your brain fully-engaged and your learning at full throttle.

The Definition Of Insanity

They say the definition of insanity is doing the same thing over and over again, and expecting a different result. And nowhere is that more true than music practice.

Clearly, this applies to the traditional "massed repetition" approach. Just playing through a piece again and again, hoping your mistakes will automatically disappear, is perhaps the least efficient practice method possible.

Before we wrap up though, I wanted to take a moment to emphasise that this principle also applies to your practice methodology as a whole. Meaning if you read through this chapter but then continue practicing the same way... that would be insane :)

Your practice habits may be deeply ingrained after years or even decades of learning. Don't expect yourself to change them completely, overnight.

Another popular saying I like is:

> "The best time to plant a tree is 20 years ago.
>
> The second-best time is now."

Take even a single one of the practice-changing concepts from this chapter, and start using it today.

We've packed a lot into this chapter. Don't let that distract you from the fact that even if all you did was implement the Deliberate Practice cycle... or start using Contextual Interference whenever you hit a sticking point during practice... or start regularly using a metronome and/or audio recorder during music practice... you'll be amazed at the difference.

Keep coming back to this chapter and adding new Superlearning tools and techniques to your practice toolkit, and you'll be able to continually accelerate your learning speed. Soon that Big Picture Vision won't seem so far away at all.

PART TWO

CHAPTER SEVEN:
EAR TRAINING

Building on the foundational skills covered in Part I, In Part II of this book we'll focus on *Ear Training*, as a way to open up new possibilities in our musicality.

This is a topic particularly near and dear to my heart. Perhaps not surprising, given that I originally founded Musical U as "Easy Ear Training"! If you read my backstory in the Introduction chapter, you'll understand the impact that discovering and exploring ear training had on my own musical journey.

I have to admit though, it was a shock to me when I found that almost every musician I mentioned Ear Training to had one of these two reactions:

1.   "Ear training? What's that?"

Or

2.   "Bah! Ear training... I hate ear training."

In this chapter we'll briefly dig into why these were (and still are) the two most common reactions to the mention of "ear training", as well as introducing the approach we now use at Musical U, called *Integrated Ear Training*.

We've found that this unique approach avoids the most painful aspects of traditional ear training, and serves as an enjoyable and effective way for any musician to unlock all of the ear-based skills mentioned in *Chapter One: Musicality*. Equipped with this approach and the "building blocks" introduced in the chapters which follow, you'll be well prepared to dive into the specific applications in Part III, such as Playing By Ear, Improvisation, and Songwriting (including composing).

So whether you've never heard of "ear training" before, you've tried it and struggled, or you're an Ear Training aficionado looking for some new ways to improve even faster and with more joy, I think you're going to be excited by the new possibilities that this part of the book opens up for you.

Overview

In this chapter we'll begin by defining what "Ear Training" is, and the two distinct skills all Ear Training consists of. We'll then cover the two most common approaches (Passive Ear Training and Traditional Ear Training), their limitations, and the root causes of the frustration and limited results most musicians have experienced when trying ear training before.

We'll then share how our approach at Musical U developed over the years, into what we now call Integrated Ear Training, and how this relates to the H4 Model introduced in *Chapter One: Musicality*. We'll discuss the experience and results you can expect when adopting this new approach, and then give a brief overview of the chapters which follow in Part II.

Let's begin with the most basic question…

What Is "Ear Training"?

Given the strong reactions some people have to the term "ear training", as well as the wide variety of activities people refer to with that term, it's worth starting with a clear definition.

Back in 2009, the very first article we published on our public website (then EasyEarTraining.com, now Musical-U.com) asked and answered this very question. I was already aware of some of the confusion and frustration surrounding this topic, so I intentionally began with a very broad definition:

"'Ear training' is, most simply, anything somebody does to improve the way they hear."

The article included one of my favourite illustrations we've ever commissioned, included here because it still makes me chuckle:

The article introduced the idea that ear training consists of developing two distinct skills:

1. Learn the different types of a musical element
   e.g. different notes, different types of chord, different types of instrument, etc.

2. Learn what to call each type
   e.g. "C,D,E,F, …", "major, minor, diminished, …", "oboe, flute, clarinet, …"

Sometimes the first part is easy. For example, most musicians can easily hear the difference between a major and minor chord without practice. Once they've been told that the "happy-sounding" chord type is called "major" and the "gloomy, sad" one is called "minor", they have the second part too.

Using descriptive words like this is an over-simplification, but a helpful one when you're just starting out. We'll explore this more in subsequent chapters.

You might think that only the first step matters. After all, if you can always hear what category something fits into, why does it matter what label you put on it?

Well, if you read *Chapter Five: Active Listening*, you'll know already that there are two good reasons for learning the labels:

1. Having clear, well-defined labels for the types of thing you hear greatly speeds up learning to reliably classify them, by giving the brain something concrete to attach to the sounds you hear.

2. Using the commonly-accepted terms helps you collaborate and play better together with other musicians, and learn from them, as well as other educational resources.

Almost everything we do in the process of Ear Training can be seen as developing both of these abilities together. However I've found it's helpful to be aware of these two distinct skills, because it helps us get away from a strict "right or wrong" mentality and appreciate that our ear skills exist on a spectrum. Rather than thinking *"I always get perfect fourths and perfect fifths wrong"*, for example, we can become aware of how much we hear the difference, or how reliably we hear the difference, or what aspects of each type we can consistently tune in to.

It also helps us stay focused on the sounds, preventing Ear Training from becoming a purely intellectual quiz-passing exercise. In other words, we stay aware that recognising musical elements is a combination of Hearing and Head (and to some extent Heart if we're using emotion-related descriptive words in the process). More on this when we explore different approaches to Ear Training below.

So Ear Training, then, is the process of improving our ears for music, and one way to measure that is by how reliably and accurately we can put suitable labels on the various musical elements we hear.

This immediately begs the question: What are we going to *do* with that ability to label the things we hear? Or, to put it another way, what about the Hands and the Heart?

Well, it should come as no surprise that the Integrated Ear Training approach we'll be building up to below is one which incorporates all four H's: Head, Hearing, Hands and Heart.

To better understand this approach, let's first cover some of the other ways musicians have traditionally approached ear training.

1. Passive Ear Training

The first thing to say is that some musicians develop their musical ears without ever consciously "doing ear training".

If you remember the example of the Beatles back in *Chapter One: Musicality* when we talked about music theory, one beautiful thing about music is that it's entirely possible to master the craft without ever doing dedicated "drills", "exercises", or "studying".

Just like the Beatles mastered music theory without ever cracking open a theory book, some musicians develop the ability to play by ear, improvise, or write wonderful music without ever "doing ear training".

For example, the jazz musician who spends years "woodshedding" their improv skills may well develop a free, creative, versatile ability to improvise purely on instinct. The blues guitarist who is constantly gigging and participating in blues jams may well find after a decade or two that they can generally "figure stuff out by ear" without thinking much about it.

This can actually perpetuate the Talent Myth, by adding further examples of musicians who can "just do it". They can't quite explain how they can do what they do, and even though it's taken them years rather than being an ingrained "gift" since childhood, it adds to the mystery which commonly surrounds the skills of musicality.

However, just like in the case of theory, if we spend some time actively, intentionally practicing our ear skills, through the process of Ear Training, we not only improve dramatically faster, we also gain a conscious understanding of how we do what we do.

When I speak to musicians who've inadvertently gone the route of passive Ear Training, often they're a little sensitive about their abilities. They know they can do it. Well at least, normally they can... most of the time...! But they're never quite certain they'll be able to pull it off. On the other hand, *active* Ear Training, while it doesn't necessarily make your skills any more "perfect", does generally produce a greater confidence in your abilities—because you have conscious understanding of how you're doing it.

While we would never recommend passive Ear Training as the approach to follow (because of how painfully slow it is to produce real, usable levels of ability), it is valuable for making us aware of just how powerful the brain is when it comes to music.

We make this concrete with the idea of Convergent Learning

(introduced in *Chapter Two: Mindset* and covered more specifically in the rest of Part II to follow). Although our active Ear Training will involve dedicated drills and exercises, it's amazing how good our musical brain is at "joining the dots" beneath the surface.

Passive Ear Training also plays into the "Apply" part of the Learn-Practice-Apply process introduced below. In a way, those "woodshedding" musicians are doing solely the "Apply" step, and missing out on the power of what we'd call "Learn" and "Practice". Or in terms of the H4 Model, we could say they're doing mostly "Hands" with a bit of "Hearing".

So it's not that passive Ear Training is bad. It's simply incomplete, just like the traditional approach to Ear Training we'll cover next.

2. Traditional Ear Training

When I first encountered the idea of "ear training", it was through a book-and-CD set which consisted of a series of exercises. I had one for "Golden Ears" audio training on frequencies and effects, and later another for Relative Pitch, and even Perfect Pitch.

At the time, this was a godsend. I had been flunking the "aural skills" section of my instrument exams for years, and so any process to actually improve those skills was a blessing!

It took me a number of years to realise the significant limitations of this kind of approach.

The traditional Ear Training method looks something like this:

1. Pick something you want to learn to recognise, for example Intervals, Solfa (i.e. notes of the scale), or Chord Progressions.

2. Limit yourself to a subset of the "types" of that thing, for example Major Thirds and Minor Thirds in interval recognition.

3. Do some kind of exercise, drill or quiz where you hear an example of that thing, try to name what it was, find out if you got it right or wrong.

4. Repeat step 3 until you master it (or go insane).

I'm only half joking with that last point! In reality most musicians get bored or frustrated, and simply give up. But remember that common definition of insanity: "doing the same thing again and again, and expecting a different result."

This is another case of the "massed repetitions" approach to music practice (see *Chapter Six: Superlearning*). It does work, but it's far slower and more frustrating than it needs to be.

For the first few years at Easy Ear Training our focus was on improving this process. Looking back, it feels like a clear case of "putting lipstick on a pig".

It was helpful to gamify the exercises with an interactive mobile app. We were able to break things down in a useful way, help the student to track their progress, provide a clear progression, with a bit of flexibility to reduce the risk of getting entirely stuck at any point.

But the overall process was still a "brute force" one. And, most crucially, I found for myself and our students that it was actually entirely possible to ace every Ear Training quiz—and yet have little or nothing to show for it in your actual musical life. Everything was done in the abstract, divorced from real music or real musical activities.

This is why I would hear so frequently from musicians who had attended conservatory or done a music degree, struggled and eventually passed their Ear Training requirement there… but would sheepishly admit they still couldn't play anything by ear, improvise, transcribe, or do any of the real musical tasks they thought Ear Training would enable them to.

The good news is that if you have spent some time already on traditional Ear Training, you'll find that your past efforts pay off in a new way when you adopt Integrated Ear Training. Not only will Ear Training be easier and more enjoyable for you going forwards, you'll be able to "connect the dots" in a new way, which may well that reveal your ears had actually developed much more than you thought, and you are finally able to start benefitting from those past efforts in the ways you had hoped to.

3. Learn-Practice-Apply

Learning from these experiences with traditional Ear Training, we developed a better approach when we launched the Musical U membership site in 2015.

Recognising that the drills and exercises alone could leave the student still confused and unable to actually benefit from their new quiz-passing prowess, we developed three distinct kinds of Ear

Training modules:

- "Learn" modules introduced the concepts, the theory, and the terminology, as well as providing hints, tips and techniques to help recognise each type of musical element.

- "Practice" modules provided interactive versions of the recognition drills, sequenced in a way we knew would be effective, and providing flexibility for the student along the way.

- "Apply" modules showed step-by-step how to take those core recognition skills to real musical tasks, including hearing those elements in real music tracks, and using them to play by ear and improvise.

All of this happened in a community environment where members could track their progress, learn from their peers, as well as get direct help from an expert team.

This corresponded to the "Trifecta" of theory, ear training, and instrument skills, which you may remember from *Chapter One: Musicality*. The "Learn" modules would provide the theory, the "Practice" modules would develop your ear, the "Apply" modules would help you bring it to instruments.

Once you see this approach, it's clear that traditional Ear Training is actually providing learners with only "Practice"—the middle step of a 3-step process!

TIP:

One simple but highly-effective piece of advice which we've taught from the outset but is often missing from traditional Ear Training material is this:

When it comes to developing ear skills, "a little and often" is best.

That means you will be far better off spending 5-10 minutes a day, every day, than grinding away for 30-60 minutes, once in a while.

This can be explained in a number of ways:

1. The ears fatigue quickly, especially when you're first starting out. You can easily get to the point where you actually start getting worse during an Ear Training session, rather than better.

2. The brain needs time to digest and process the input you've fed it during practice. We unpack this more in Chapter Six: Superlearning.

3. There is a lot of "under the hood" learning happening when we do dedicated Ear Training exercises, and the principle of Convergent Learning (see Chapter Two: Mindset) means we will do better if we allow space for that to happen, rather than trying to force it as quickly as possible.

The idea of "guerilla practice", where you try to sneak in a few minutes here and there, throughout the day, can be particularly effective with Ear Training. Not least because it can be done without access to your instrument!

So even if you're used to the idea of setting aside a dedicated 30-minute block for "music practice", and you really want to focus on Ear Training, we wouldn't recommend working away at the same thing for 30 minutes. At the very least, tackle a wide variety of exercises, with no more than 5-10 minutes spent on any single one. All of the principles of designing your practice time from Chapter Six: Superlearning can be usefully applied here too.

Learn-Practice-Apply was a big leap forwards, and it felt like we'd cracked it. Our members were getting better results in their Ear Training than any previous traditional methods had allowed them to.

But there was still something missing.

Yes, it made a big difference to cover the intellectual understanding, and provide specific tips to help the student with identifying each type of musical element. Yes, the way we implemented the drills and exercises was effective, drawing on everything we'd learned prior from thousands of students. And yes, having direct personal support from an expert team also helped reduce frustration and accelerate results.

I have to give a big tip-of-the-hat to our Head Educator Andrew Bishko for helping us see the missed opportunity. He actually called it out early on in his work with us at Musical U, but at first I wasn't convinced. In retrospect, the way I had learned ear skills myself really biased me about how it "should" be.

Thankfully he persisted, and we began adapting the way we did things…

4. Integrated Ear Training

The big observation from Andrew was that it didn't make sense to separate those three activities so much. His own ear skills had developed more through on-instrument activities (like those mentioned when talking about passive Ear Training above), and so to him, it was odd to spend days or weeks mastering the core recognition skills, and only then pick up your instrument and do some things with it.

As we explored more in this direction, we found that our members both enjoyed it more and improved faster, when we really *integrated* the whole process.

This came to dovetail neatly with the development of the H4 Model of Complete Musicality, so that Integrated Ear Training is a process of developing your Head, Hearing, Hands, and Heart—not as individual separate activities, but as four parts of an integrated whole.

We still leverage the power of each type of activity from the Learn-Practice-Apply model, because it's still the case that "just studying", "just woodshedding" or "just doing drills" is incomplete. But it's done in a much, much shorter loop. Every single practice session includes a mixture of all of them: Head, Hearing, Hands, and an awareness of the Heart.

In this way, every step forward you take in training your musical ear has direct and immediate payoff for you, with real musical activities like playing by ear, improvising, transcribing, and writing music.

This is the approach we'll be guiding you through in the chapters which follow.

 You'll learn (Head) the concepts and terms you need to know.

 You'll practice (Hearing) the core recognition skills.

 You'll apply (Hands) those recognition skills using your instrument.

 You'll feel (Heart) a deep connection to and through the music.

These will be done together, in an integrated way, which not only develops all four H's but also the connections between them. The result is something which looks very different to passive Ear Training or traditional Ear Training, and delivers vastly better, faster results.

This is an approach which naturally involves many of the powerful methods of Superlearning (see *Chapter Six: Superlearning*) such as Deliberate Practice, the power of not finishing, Contextual Interference, and creativity. So you don't necessarily need to think or plan for how to add Superlearning to your Ear Training, though there certainly are plenty of opportunities to do so if you like (for example, using Spaced Repetitions to determine what you focus on when).

What to Expect

When you adopt the Integrated Ear Training approach, the journey of developing your musical ear instantly becomes a far richer and more rewarding one.

Unlike passive Ear Training, which takes years and can feel like "a hope and a prayer" even once you seem to have got the hang of it, and unlike traditional Ear Training, which puts ear skills in a box off to one side, divorced from the real music and real musical activities you're excited about, the Integrated Ear Training approach is the embodiment of *Enjoying The Journey*.

You get to design each Ear Training practice session in a way which perfectly matches your own Big Picture Vision, working towards the musicality skills you're most passionate about, and providing clear, concrete payoff all along the way.

When we first taught this approach, the students were able to start playing by ear, improvising, and writing music literally from day one. In the chapters which follow, you'll discover how that's possible, and how to enjoy the same results yourself.

Overview of Part II

In the following chapters we'll be covering the "building blocks" of pitch and rhythm which empower you to relate instinctively to all the music you hear and play.

We'll be following the Integrated Ear Training approach, so you will learn the concepts, practice the core skills, apply them to real musical tasks, and develop your intuitive connection to the music.

We will begin with pitch, introducing the topic of Relative Pitch, and how it's distinct and preferable to an Absolute Pitch (or "Perfect Pitch") approach. We'll look at the Solfa system for naming the different notes of the scale, and the Intervals system for naming the distances between musical pitches. We'll use these to explore melody (one note at a time) and then look at harmony through Chords and Progressions, formed when we stack multiple pitches and they vary over time.

Then we'll shift tack and look at Rhythm. We'll first look at ways to hear and connect with the Beat, and then the rhythms that are created on top of it. We'll learn a particular "rhythm syllables" approach which is a powerful addition to the traditional "count chant" method for understanding the timing of notes.

It's important to mention that although we'll cover pitch and rhythm in sequence, that's no indication that you should learn them sequentially! In fact, our most effective training for learning these skills, in the Spring Season of *Living Music*, elegantly weaves the two together module-to-module. Music is itself a combination of pitch and rhythm together, and your Ear Training can be too.

These chapters are not intended to be a comprehensive course on any of the topics covered, but they should be plenty sufficient to get you up and running, and enjoying real, tangible benefits from the Ear Training you do.

More importantly, the Integrated Ear Training process you'll learn, along with the frameworks for Playing By Ear, Improvisation, and Song Writing you'll find in Part III, will equip you to continue designing your own successful Ear Training journey, up to any level of skill your heart desires.

CHAPTER EIGHT:
RELATIVE PITCH

Many of the abilities mentioned in the answers to *"what is musicality?"*, and featured in the list of 15 skills in *Chapter One: Musicality* rely on an ability to recognise pitches by ear.

That could be identifying the notes of a melody so that you can play it on your instrument without needing to look up the notation or learn it in advance. It might be improvising on-the-fly without relying on strict rules, patterns, or guessing to tell you which pitches to play. Perhaps for you the focus is transcribing the music you love, or composing your own, whether on paper or with software. In each of these cases, being able to recognise note pitches by ear is central.

In *Chapter Five: Active Listening* we defined four "dimensions" of music: Pitch, Rhythm, Timbre and Dynamics.

It is possible, but generally not necessary, to do dedicated Ear Training exercises for Timbre or Dynamics—Active Listening alone will serve you well there.

Rhythm skills do certainly benefit from Ear Training, and we'll be covering those in *Chapter Twelve: The Beat* and *Chapter Thirteen: Rhythm*.

This is particularly true for making the connection between sound and symbol, so that you can write down rhythms you hear in notation, or sight-read new rhythmic notation and produce the corresponding timing accurately. We'll also see how it can open up more rhythmically-precise playing, and rhythmic creativity. However, when it comes to Playing By Ear, Improvisation, and Songwriting, we've found that for the vast majority of musicians, the Rhythm side actually comes relatively easily.

That's why we'll begin this part of the book by focusing on Pitch recognition skills, which tend to be the biggest barrier between the average music learner and being able to play by ear, improvise, write music, jam, and more.

Naturally, this is most relevant to those who identify primarily with having a Creative or Jammer Musical Core, but if you're firmly in the Performer camp, don't tune out. You'll find that developing your ear for Pitch has wide-reaching positive effects on all the music you learn, play and perform.

When you develop your ear using the "building blocks" of Pitch you'll discover in *Chapter Nine: Solfa*, *Chapter Ten: Intervals* and *Chapter Eleven: Chords and Progressions*, a whole new world of musical abilities will quickly open up for you.

Overview

In this chapter we'll introduce Relative Pitch and the three types of "building blocks" you can take advantage of to develop your own sense of Relative Pitch. We'll introduce a process for identifying the key of a piece of music by ear, which will allow you to "translate" from Relative Pitch into the corresponding letter names. Finally, we'll talk briefly about some applications and benefits of Relative Pitch, which will be covered more fully in Part III of the book.

As with many other topics in Musicality, if we are to truly understand what does work, we must first get clear on our definitions, and address any common-but-faulty approaches which might otherwise lead us in the wrong direction.

When it comes to Pitch, the first and most important thing to discuss is our choice of *Relative* Pitch as the approach to take. In particular, distinguishing Relative Pitch from "Absolute" or "Perfect" Pitch.

Absolute (or "Perfect") Pitch

Often when a musician sets out to try learning to recognise notes by ear, they start from the sheet music world of note names and key signatures—and so assume they would need "Perfect Pitch": the ability to hear a note and automatically know the corresponding letter name. Or, to give it a more accurate name, "Absolute Pitch". That's "absolute" in the sense of *"being independent from anything else"*.

As a result, they may do a web search for something like "learn perfect pitch". What they'll find is a confusing quagmire of myths and misleading information, along with some sensible-sounding (but unhelpful) methods for learning the skill.

Let's clear it all up.

Absolute Pitch, colloquially known as "Perfect Pitch", is the ability to name a note you hear without any reference to a known note.

So for example, if you haven't heard any other music and someone plays a single note on a piano, and you can name that note just by hearing it (for example, *"That was an E flat"*) that is using a sense of "Absolute" or "Perfect" Pitch.

The name "Perfect Pitch" is confusing, since it also implies an infallible ability to name notes with ultimate precision. For example, knowing that a pitch isn't just "an A" but is "A432" (i.e. 432 Hertz) rather than "A440" (i.e. 440 Hertz). If the term "Hertz" is unfamiliar to you, don't worry. We cover it in *Chapter Five: Active Listening* when talking about audio frequencies, but the point here is just that the term "Perfect Pitch" only makes naming notes by ear seem like even more of a magical and mysterious "gift".

The term "Perfect Pitch" also gets used in the context of Singing, to mean that a singer always hits notes dead-on. If you've read *Chapter Four: Singing* then you'll know that being able to judge pitches precisely with your ears is an important part of hitting notes accurately, but there's also the Vocal Control side of things. In any case, that sensitivity to precise pitch differences is a distinct skill from the Absolute Pitch (being able to name notes by ear) which we're discussing here.

For those reasons, although the term "Perfect Pitch" is more commonly used, we'll stick with calling it "Absolute Pitch" going forwards.

When we talked about the Talent Myth in *Chapter Two: Mindset*, I mentioned that there are certain physical traits which can give you an advantage and which you do need to be born with. For example, a basketball player's height.

In music, having Absolute Pitch is perhaps the one and only such trait. Estimates vary, but roughly speaking we're talking about less than 1% of the general population. Perhaps as low as one in ten thousand (0.01%)[1]. That's comparable to the proportion who have *amusia* and are truly "tone deaf". So it's a very rare trait.

It certainly can seem magical. I once knew a musician with Absolute Pitch who used to have fun by announcing the notes of car horns and other random beeping sounds when we were out and about. That was pretty funny, and it is a beautiful demonstration of how music can be such a core part of somebody that even random sounds have a musical meaning.

It's not just a party trick, though. Absolute Pitch is genuinely useful. By enabling you to recognise note pitches by ear, it directly unlocks the various pitch-related skills of musicality mentioned at the start of this chapter. So when you meet a musician with Absolute Pitch who has essentially been able to do all those things from an early age, without needing Ear Training, it's impressive—and it can be particularly hard for the average musician to see it as inspiring rather than intimidating!

Can you learn Absolute Pitch?

It's natural to start wondering, then: if Absolute Pitch is such a cool shortcut, and so useful to the musicians who have it, can you learn it yourself?

The answer is "yes"... but only barely.

The scientific research on the subject shows that in general you need to be born with Absolute Pitch, or at least have it from a very young age[2]. It's not understood what causes it, though there is a higher prevalence in countries where the spoken language is tonal, for example Mandarin.

It's also not clear how much it's nature versus nurture. Anecdotal evidence suggests both have a role. For example, that musician I

---

[1] 2. D. J. Levitin and S. E. Rogers, "Absolute Pitch: Perception, Coding, and Controversies," Trends in Cognitive Sciences 9, no. 1 (2005)

[2] I highly recommend the fascinating book *The Evolving Animal Orchestra: In Search Of What Makes Us Musical* by Prof. Henkjan Honing (MIT Press) which explores the biological roots of musicality across various species of animal, including a discussion of Absolute Pitch.

mentioned before was born of two parents with Absolute Pitch—but also (not coincidentally) grew up in a highly musical household, making it hard to piece apart genetics and upbringing.

Based on that, you might think *"Okay, fine, well I wasn't born with it, so never mind"*. But unfortunately it's not quite that simple... and this is where musicians get misled.

It is possible to develop some degree of Absolute Pitch as an adult.

The way I like to explain it is that actually we are all biologically capable of Absolute Pitch—it's just that our brains didn't think it mattered, so now we don't interpret sound in that way. But there are clear examples that you can re-train your brain to care about Absolute Pitch.

One example is in the world of audio. In *Chapter Five: Active Listening* we talked about it being normal for audio engineers to do Ear Training to let them recognise different frequency bands. For example, so they can adjust the EQ on a recording or live sound equipment, and fix problems, or enhance the overall mix. That is using a form of Absolute Pitch, where they need to hone in directly on a certain frequency band by ear.

Experienced engineers can spot things down to a band that's a third of an octave wide, meaning four semitones, corresponding to just a few notes. So they're not getting as precise as one specific note name, the way we usually think of Absolute Pitch as working—but they're getting pretty close! And that third-octave band skill level is quite common among professional engineers.

A second example is that if you ask someone to sing a song they know well, often they will actually sing it in the correct key. This is known as the *Levitin effect* after the author of the scientific paper first introducing the phenomenon[3]. Their highly-reinforced memory for that piece of music has stored the absolute pitches, and they are exhibiting a kind of Absolute Pitch when they sing the right notes.

That leads on to a third example, which is the one form of Absolute Pitch ear training which I do recommend as worthwhile, and that's to memorise a single "reference pitch".

Some musicians choose the A440 note that orchestras tune to, guitarists sometimes choose the low E string, pianists often middle C. The idea is just to pick one pitch and regularly practice trying to

---

[3] "Absolute memory for musical pitch: Evidence from the production of learned melodies", Daniel J. Levitin, Attention, Perception & Psychophysics, July 1994

remember it and sing it, then check your answer. This can gradually reinforce your memory of this pitch and give you a simple way to do Absolute Pitch-like tasks. More on this later when we discuss finding the key of a piece of music by ear.

Should you try to learn Absolute Pitch?

So clearly there is evidence that our adult brains are capable of learning Absolute Pitch, but here's the catch: to get to the level of instantly recognising any note, and to do it even when there are multiple notes played at once like in an actual piece of music, is incredibly hard and slow-going. Perhaps so difficult as to be, for all intents and purposes, impossible.

I've been studying and working extensively in the area of Ear Training for almost 15 years now, and I have yet to meet or hear from a single person who has reached that level of Absolute Pitch as an adult.

What I have heard from is hundreds of musicians who have spent months or even years chasing this goal, and getting to only a rudimentary level, where they can recognise a handful of notes, reasonably reliably, when played in isolation. They generally still can't apply that to more than the most basic musical tasks.

There are a few commonly-discussed methods for learning Absolute Pitch:

1.   One is the simple "guess and check on a regular basis" mentioned above when discussing learning a single "reference pitch". You gradually try to do this with more and more pitches, working up to all 12 and making it reliable across octaves and timbres.

2.   A second is to really listen deeply and try to hear the "pitch colour" characteristic of each note. This was popularised by a very well-known book-and-CD course about 20 years ago. I don't want to be sued, so I won't name names! :) With this approach you are essentially trying to develop a light form of *synesthesia*, where your brain interprets one sense with another —in this case feeling/seeing colours when you hear sounds.

3.   The third method is analogous to the "reference songs" way of

learning interval recognition, which we'll cover in a subsequent chapter. You try to memorise the sound of certain melodies, choosing 12 different reference melodies, each one starting from a different note. Then you rely on your musical brain's desire to "autocomplete", to let you recognise a note you hear based on which melody it sounds like it's starting.

I could go into depth about each of these. I diligently tried all three myself in my twenties, and I've had students try them. I think all that's worth saying is that they all sound reasonable, and they do all deliver some encouraging early results after a week or two, which might make you think it's worth persisting. However, as I said before, I have yet to meet a single person who has developed anything close to full Absolute Pitch who didn't have it from childhood[4].

Do you need to learn Absolute Pitch?

"As far as we know, perfect pitch has little to do with musicality. Generally speaking, people who have perfect pitch are no more musical than those who do not have it. In fact, the vast majority of professional musicians in the West do not have perfect pitch."
— Henkjan Honing, *The Evolving Animal Orchestra: In Search*

---

[4] A brief case in point: recently a new blog post started appearing at the top of Google search results for "learn perfect pitch", with a title along the lines of "I Learned Perfect Pitch in 30 Days". While there was a lot to commend about the author's learning process and how they documented and shared it, on examination it turned out that:

A. They were actually using the "reference pitch plus relative pitch" process mentioned in this chapter, rather than true (meaning direct) Absolute Pitch.

B. They succeeded in passing a note identification quiz, which was their original objective, but there was no evidence it actually allowed them to do anything practical. They acknowledged that things fell apart if they didn't have a second or two to process each note in turn.

To their credit, they fully acknowledged the shortcomings, and that what they'd developed was only a lightweight step towards "genuine" Absolute Pitch. In fact, in spite of the clickbait-y title, it was actually a very good exploration of the opportunities and limitations of trying to learn this skill as an adult, as well as a great example of how much time one can easily spend chasing this "magic bullet" without having much in the way of useful results to show for it, even when you apparently "succeed".

of What Makes Us Musical

If you found it discouraging to hear that learning Absolute Pitch is essentially impossible as an adult, please don't. The good news is that of all the skills which Absolute Pitch enables, such as:

- Playing melodies by ear

- Recognising chord progressions

- Composing music

- Transcribing music

- Improvising

- Party tricks

… there is just one of those where Absolute Pitch is the only way to do it. Can you guess which?

Yes, it's the party tricks, like declaring that a car horn or alarm bell is *"a B-flat!"* And actually even those are within reach if you use the "reference pitch" method and the alternative approach to pitch we're about to cover.

It's also worth knowing that (as any musician with Absolute Pitch will tell you) it also comes with limitations. For example, if someone relies on their sense of Absolute Pitch to let them play by ear, it can be quite confusing and challenging if they need to switch into a different key. Or when a band is in tune with each other but not with the "correct" A440 tuning, it can sound unbearably awkward to the musician with Absolute Pitch, even while the band and the rest of the audience thinks it sounds perfectly fine! On top of that, many musicians with Absolute Pitch find that it somehow fades as they get older, which can be truly frustrating and challenging after a lifetime relying on it.

With the alternative approach we recommend, it doesn't matter what musical abilities you were born with. It doesn't matter if you're young, middle-aged or retired. It's easy to maintain, throughout your life. It can be adapted to suit any instrument and it can be used for any pitch-related tasks in your real musical life. With an Integrated Ear Training approach (as introduced in the previous chapter), you can start freely and confidently playing by ear, improvising, and more, right from the outset. And it can absolutely (pun intended) get you to the level where other people see what you can do and assume that you must have been born with "perfect pitch".

So what is this alternative to Absolute Pitch? It's a well-developed sense of *Relative* Pitch.

Relative Pitch

As a musician, you're probably aware that it's possible to play a given melody starting from any note.

If you ask a random passer-by on the street to sing "Mary Had A Little Lamb" for you, then (assuming they have a decent grasp on the two core skills of singing covered in *Chapter Four: Singing!*) they will sing a series of notes which are recognisably that melody.

They didn't need to run off to a piano keyboard to find the correct starting note. They just picked a starting note[5], and went from there.

If you then asked three more people to sing the same tune, they might each choose a different starting note—and yet each rendition would be recognisably the same melody. That's true even though in a sense, every single note they sung was different from the person before. If you replicated what each person sang on an instrument, or you wrote it down in traditional notation, literally every note would have had a different pitch. If you're familiar with the idea of a musical "key", each performance was in a different key, and so the particular notes used were completely different as a result.

And yet... it still sounded like the same melody!

To understand why, we need to shift the way we think about notes in music. Again, for most people, "learning music" means "learning to play an instrument", and when that's your starting point, the way you think about notes typically immediately becomes a world of letter names, sharps and flats, and having dots in a particular place in written notation.

When it comes to Ear Training and developing an instinctive ability to recognise notes by ear, we need to focus first and foremost on how the music *sounds* above all else. And so it makes sense that we need a different way to think about notes, and in particular about note pitches.

---

[5] Quite possibly "Their Note"! See *Chapter Four: Singing*.

The Relative Pitch Solution

There's one big insight which musicians who go down the Absolute Pitch rabbithole are missing: as much as we humans love to think of music in a scientific, analytical way where everything is written down very specifically… that's not actually where music comes from.

Music has emerged from the way our brain and ear biologically interpret pitches. And we were doing that long before anybody gave notes letter names or wrote down a key signature, and without needing to be the "one in ten thousand" with Absolute Pitch.

As the hypothetical "Mary Had A Little Lamb" example just demonstrated for us above, our ears really don't hear in terms of a specific key, letter names, or sharps and flats.

Our body and brain actually understand music based on *relative* pitch.

Relative Pitch is about interpreting the notes you hear based on their relationship to other notes. Specifically, based on their *pitch distance* from other notes. When you listen to music, your ear and brain are constantly measuring all these distances and using them to interpret each of the notes, *relative* to the other notes.

That's why if someone plays or sings a melody in a random key, or the DJ on the radio pitch-shifts a song, you can still recognise it without a hitch. Your ear is automatically tuning in to the relative pitch distances, regardless of the specific key it's in.

In other words, if you shift everything up or down together (which is what it means to "change key"), it makes very little difference to the music itself.

Here's where this can become a superpower for you: if we focus on the relationships between the notes, we can leverage what our ears have *already* spent a lifetime doing!

Believe it or not, you already have highly-trained musical ears that are, in a sense, identifying all the notes you hear. It's just not happening at a conscious level, which makes it hard to do anything like naming the notes with it.

At first your conscious mind can only judge *"this is a big gap"* or *"those two notes are quite close together"*. But as you practice, you make that "internal pitch ruler" more and more precise, and more and more reliable, to the point where you can easily "measure" all kinds of things you hear, and so identify the notes. That can include how to "translate" it into any key you choose, letting you play it on an instrument or write it down in notation.

So even though Relative Pitch may be a new way of thinking about pitch for you, we don't need to try to persuade our ears to hear in a completely different way. All we need to do is to refine that "pitch ruler" we have in our mind, and practice putting labels on the different distances we measure with it. That's what Relative Pitch Ear Training is all about.

In some cases you will consciously be thinking about "distances" and even the "pitch ruler", while in other cases it will just be at work under the hood as a refined ability to judge relative pitches.

In the following chapters we'll focus on developing your sense of Relative Pitch, using three types of "building block". Each is a different way of refining and using that internal "pitch ruler":

- Intervals are all about measuring the distance from one note to the next note.

- Solfa is all about measuring the distance from one note to the "home note" or "tonic" note of a piece.

- Chords and Progressions are about measuring both the distances among a set of notes played simultaneously, and the distance of all those notes from the "home note" or "tonic".

You'll be learning much more about each of these as we continue. For now, all you need to do is to let go of the idea that "pitch" must mean keys, letter names, and fingerings on your instrument. Of course those things are a part of the practical skills we're looking to unlock, and we will be tackling those "translations" back to Absolute Pitch along the way. But you want to be thinking primarily in terms of Relative Pitch.

If you do, you'll soon discover that there's an enormous wealth of information you can pick up in the music you hear, long before ever getting to the point of pinning it down to a specific key and note names or buttons on your instrument.

Start here: Pitch Contour

When the average musician decides to "try ear training", more often than not they dive head-first into trying to recognise Intervals. That happens due to the historic prevalence of Ear Training materials focusing on that topic, rather than because it's necessarily a great place to start.

In fact, before we start practicing with Intervals and the other "building blocks" we'll be covering, there is a much simpler Relative Pitch skill to put in place.

In *Chapter Five: Active Listening* we introduced the idea of a "Pitch Contour": in any given series of notes (for example, a melody) the pitch can go up, go down, or stay the same. This creates a *contour*, the overall shape of the pitch movement over time:

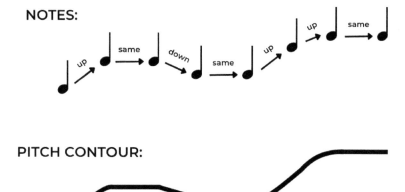

When the series of notes happens to be a melody, we can also call this the "Melodic Contour". Since we'll also be applying this concept to basslines, chord root notes, and other cases, we'll use the broader term "Pitch Contour".

This is an extremely simple idea, but it proves to also be extremely useful. In fact, it's turned out to be one of the biggest *"Why did no-one ever teach me this?!"* concepts we teach at Musical U. Our members often remark on how astonished they are that something so simple was never explained to them, even though it's relevant and useful across a wide range of musical tasks.

The Pitch Contour is useful because it provides the "broad brushstrokes" sketch of a melody (or bassline, or other series of notes), without requiring any prior training. We've found that almost every musician who comes to us with at least a few months of music learning under their belt has little trouble immediately starting to sketch out Pitch Contours for the music they're hearing or working on.

In other words, this is a starting point for Relative Pitch which doesn't require any Ear Training at all!

Above, we introduced the idea that you have a kind of "mental pitch ruler" which allows you to judge the distances between pitches in music, and that Ear Training can help you increase the granularity and reliability of those judgements. Think of the Pitch Contour as your starting point. It's not very precise—we're only judging direction, not necessarily even trying to judge the size of distances up or down. But you'll probably find that it is quite reliable for you, even before you begin practicing with it.

You may never have tried doing this before, but when you listen to a melody (for example the vocal part in a song you love), can you hear when the notes are going up, down or staying the same?

When you stop and think about it, this must surely be a precursor to do anything more sophisticated like recognising the notes—and yet almost every musician who comes to us having tried to learn Intervals or Solfa has been skipping this step!

Showing the Pitch Contour

There are two main ways you can "show" the Pitch Contour:

1.   Draw the Pitch Contour. Just like in the diagram above, when you listen to a melody, or even when you're reading one from notation, it's instructive to literally grab a pen or pencil and a sheet of paper, and sketch out the shape of the pitch movement.

    Don't worry too much about the distances or scale of it all for now. If you can tell, for example, that the note it ends on is higher than the note it started from, then great, and by all means try to represent that in your sketch. But our goal is to simply capture the up/down/same movements between notes.

2.   Demonstrate the Pitch Contour with your hand. As you listen to or sing the notes, hold one hand out in front of you (you might like to point with a finger) and move your hand up and down to match the movement of the notes.

    We'll be exploring the "Hand Signs" method more when we

cover Solfa, and this is a great stepping stone towards that. You'll get some of the same benefit already, in terms of making a visceral connection to the pitches in music through your physical movement.

Start with simple melodies. You could, for example, sing or hum a nursery rhyme like "Mary Had A Little Lamb", or listen to a piece of music with a clear and relatively slow-moving melody line. Try both methods and see which feels more natural, interesting or useful to you.

Practicing with Pitch Contours

As we continue, you'll see various opportunities to use the Pitch Contour as your first step in a musical task. For example, if you're trying to figure out the Solfa for a melody, make sure you first have a rough sense of the Pitch Contour. Or if you're trying to transcribe music in traditional notation, make sure you know the Pitch Contour first. We also already saw in *Chapter Five: Active Listening* that the Pitch Contour is a great thing to listen for as part of your Active Listening habit. We'll be making some specific suggestions for using it along the way, but this is a highly versatile concept which you'll find becomes a frequently useful "first step" for you across many musical activities.

Like everything in Active Listening and Ear Training, at first figuring out the Pitch Contour will be a very conscious, step-by-step explicit process for you, but over time it will become instinctive and you won't need to literally draw or demonstrate it physically. You'll just automatically have an awareness of the Pitch Contour as part of your mental representation of the music.

So the rule of thumb is to "do it… until you don't need to."

Even once you're skilled with the more precise forms of Relative Pitch judgement (using Solfa and Intervals), it can still be useful at times to literally sketch the melodic contour. For example, in the Play-By-Ear Process described in *Playing by Ear*, a good starting point is to sketch out the Form of the music (see *Chapter Five: Active Listening*) as well as the Pitch Contour of the melody or any other parts you intend to figure out by ear.

The Pitch Contour can also be highly useful in creative tasks like Improvising and Songwriting, by serving as a *constraint*. We'll cover this in *Chapter Fifteen: Improvisation* when we explore Expansive Creativity, but the basic idea is that you would decide on the overall

Pitch Contour of the melody you're creating, and then fill in the details of exactly which notes are used. By setting the constraint of following an overall Pitch Contour, you limit the possible note pitches, while still leaving plenty of creative freedom within that.

Introducing Our "Building Blocks"

Once we have the Pitch Contour clear, how do we get more fine-grained? How do we figure out not just the direction but the *distance* from note to note? How do we make that "mental pitch ruler" more precise?

Remember that recognising notes with Relative Pitch is all about the *relationships* between pitches. Although theoretically any pitch distance is possible, and the exact pitches can vary around a note's defining pitch (such as when sliding between notes, or applying *vibrato* to a note), in practice there are certain pre-defined *steps* in musical pitch. That means there are also set distances between pitches which we can expect.

With our "mental pitch ruler" analogy, it's like if you knew that any distance you wanted to measure would be an exact number of centimetres, so you would only need your ruler to have centimetre markings.

The upshot of this is that (like with all Ear Training) developing our Relative Pitch involves recognising the different "types" or "classes" of distance, and learning the right label to put on each.

So even though it can seem overwhelming to think about all the possible relationships between all the possible pitches in music, in fact it all comes down to a limited number of "types" of distance. We can consider these our "building blocks" for pitch.

There are three types of building blocks we've found useful. Together they let you tackle any melody or harmony you might encounter. They are each a different way to think about the pitch relationships in music, and so each represents a distinct "mental model" or way of thinking about how Relative Pitch works.

Here we'll briefly introduce each of the three to give you an overview, before they're covered more fully in the dedicated chapters which follow.

Introduction to Solfa

The Solfa system is all based on the *key* of the music. If you're not familiar with that concept, we'll be covering it in detail later in the chapter, but here's a simplified explanation for now: a given piece of music (or section of a piece) will have a particular set of notes it uses, called the "key", and one of those notes is called the *tonic* or "home note" of the key. When we put the other notes in a sequence of ascending pitches with the tonic at the bottom, that creates the key's *scale*.

With Solfa, we give each note in the scale a name. Not just any name, but a single-syllable, singable name, which is distinctive (i.e. we don't use it for any other musical purpose—it always means "this particular note of the scale"). For example "do", "re" or "mi".

Why would we want to do that? Well, remember earlier, when we said that Relative Pitch lets us leverage how our ears and brain *already* understand musical pitch? In fact, more than anything else, we understand it based on how everything relates to the tonic of the current key.

By naming each note of the scale, we can begin to familiarise ourselves with the characteristic sound of each note in the scale, allowing us to start recognising them when we hear them.

Coming back to our Pitch Contour, the Solfa approach would allow us to spot where in that contour the home note featured, as well as identifying the specific other notes being used, just by the way they sound. Once we identify the key of the song (e.g. "C Major"), which we'll cover below, we can also translate those Solfa names into the corresponding note letter names, to be able to write them down or play them on an instrument.

Introduction to Intervals

The Intervals approach is still all about the relationships between note pitches, but instead of relating everything to the tonic like we do with Solfa, with Intervals we can examine the distance from any note to any other note. For a melody, that would generally be from each note to the one before or after it. For harmony, that would be between the various notes which are happening at the same time, as well as between the "root" note of each chord compared with the root note of the next.

This is very much about making our "mental pitch ruler" more precise, learning to judge different distances with accuracy. However, as mentioned above, there are certain specific distances which are used in music, due to there being just 12 notes in an octave and typically only seven or fewer being used in a particular key or scale.

Here's the clever bit about recognising Intervals: even though our end goal is to "measure" the distance, in fact we find that the various distances have characteristic sounds. So just like how Solfa lets us learn the characteristic sound of each note in the scale, Interval Ear Training lets us learn the characteristic sound of the various distances between pitches.

The names we use may seem a bit weird at first (for example "Minor Third", "Perfect Fifth", "Tri-Tone", etc.) but these names are meaningful, not arbitrary, and just a little bit of theory will make sense of them for you.

In terms of the Pitch Contour, gaining Interval recognition skills will allow you to precisely determine the distances from each note to the next. And once you know the letter name of any single note in the sequence (which might be the tonic, but doesn't need to be) you can determine all the other letter names too.

So by recognising each type of Interval, you can figure out precisely each note of a melody or of a chord.

Introduction to Chords and Progressions

Once you can identify individual notes heard one at a time, what about the combination? How do we handle harmony?

There are two components to this:

1.   Recognising different types of Chords e.g. major, minor, dominant seventh, etc.

2.   Recognising how these chords change over time, called "Chord Progressions" e.g. I-V-vi-IV or C Major, G Major, A Minor, F Major

Many styles of music (e.g. typically rock, pop, jazz) actually define harmony in terms of chords and progressions, but even those which don't can generally still be handled using them.

We can learn to recognise the various types of chords based on their notes, using Solfa, Intervals, or a combination. For example you might hear "do", "mi" and "so", or you might hear *There's a Major Third and a Perfect Fifth*—either one will reveal it's a type of chord called a "major triad" that you're hearing.

We can learn to recognise Chord Progressions by listening for the relationship of each chord to the tonic using Solfa, or identifying the distances between the root note of each chord using Intervals. In both cases we might have already sketched out the Pitch Contour of the chord movement as a starting point, and will be using our Chords skills to identify the quality (major, minor, etc.) of each chord in the progression.

Again, the system we'll use is a Relative Pitch one, so depending on the task there may be an additional step of "translating" what we've heard into a particular key, to determine the notes' letter names.

Convergent Learning

For a long time at Musical U (too long!) we taught Solfa and Intervals as two alternative approaches. Both can allow you to identify individual notes by ear, and they each have advantages and disadvantages.

Through helping many thousands of members to learn these skills, and continually exploring new ways to teach them, we made two crucial discoveries:

A. For the vast majority of musicians, Solfa is easier to get results with, and lets you more rapidly start applying your skills to real musical tasks such as Playing By Ear and Improvisation.

B. If approached in the right way, the two systems aren't "either/or" alternatives. There is a "both/and" combination which is more powerful and effective than either one alone.

On top of that, Chord Progression recognition is best approached with a sense of Relative Pitch developed through Solfa and/or Intervals[6].

In *Chapter Two: Mindset* we introduced the idea of "Convergent Learning": that often in music, the best approach is not a single, focused straight-line—but rather some kind of smörgåsbord of activities, designed in a way which lets it all "add up to more than the sum of its parts".

This is perhaps nowhere more true than with Relative Pitch Ear Training. As we continue, we'll share the connections between these

---

[6] It *can* technically be learned in isolation—if you insist!

three types of building blocks, to help your conscious mind make sense of it all. But please *don't* allow yourself to be a "completionist". You do not need to cover every inch of each topic or skill before moving on.

Explore all three together, allow some space for the stew to simmer, and you'll be surprised at the faster progress you'll enjoy.

In the Autumn Season of *Living Music*, where we first really embraced this Convergent Learning approach for the three building blocks of Relative Pitch, our students saw greater results than the "isolated" approaches had ever allowed, and we saw a constant stream of surprise and delight, as working on one of the three somehow "unlocked" greater abilities in one of the others. The happy result was a strong, versatile, instinctive sense of Relative Pitch.

The 80% Rule

In everything that follows, there can be a great risk of perfectionism. Especially when Ear Training exercises are presented as some form of "quiz", it can be hard for some people to settle for less than 100% before moving on.

Just like Convergent Learning can be the antidote to completionism, by revealing that the fastest route to your goal is actually to allow yourself some flexibility to move between topics rather than focusing on a single one for too long, there is also an antidote to perfectionism.

Naturally we do want to "get the answers right", and it is important to make progress with one thing before moving on. But does that need to mean "100% correct"?

We've all been the victim of diminishing returns in our music practice, where you keep working away and working away at something, and it just feels like your improvement is getting slower and slower. Naturally the techniques of *Chapter Six: Superlearning* are a solution in many cases, especially relating to technique and repertoire. Ear Training is, by nature, a "fuzzier" skill, and particularly prone to a maddening speed of diminishing returns. So knowing when to "move on" is especially important here, if we are to stay motivated and enjoying fast progress.

In all our experience at Easy Ear Training and Musical U, we've discovered that there is a "sweet spot". A level of competence which indicates you have mastered a certain skill or ability enough to move on successfully.

Going beyond this level is, in a sense, wasting your time—since further perfection can be gained faster by moving on to the next challenge, rather than spending more time on the same task. Moving on before hitting this level of ability may also waste your time— because you're rushing ahead and trying to build on top of too weak a foundation.

We've found that "80% correct" is a very reliable rule of thumb for this sweet spot.

That could mean getting 80% of the answers right in a quiz. It could also mean *"I'm not 100% reliable with it, but I can almost always do it."*

So for all the exercises and learning sequences suggested in the following chapters, steer yourself away from perfectionism and remember that once you've got something about 80% mastered, you'll probably be better served by moving on than by trying to nail that final 20%.

If you prefer using 90% rather than 80%, I'm not going to argue with you :) And if you want to lean heavier into Convergent Learning, and jump around a bit more with "70% correct" as your rule of thumb, that's fine too. Just make sure you're allowing yourself that leeway to find your own personal "sweet spot".

This duo of Convergent Learning and the 80% Rule are a powerful combo. For example, if you're working on something and find that even getting to 80% correct is a real struggle and you just feel stuck, you *could* relax your target and move on to the next thing… or you could trust in Convergent Learning and jump to another Relative Pitch skill area for a while. Either one will release that "stuckness" and let you keep moving forwards with ease and joy.

The Basic Drill

Remember our original definition of Ear Training, from the previous chapter? To:

1.   Learn to distinguish the different types of a musical element, and

2.   Learn what to call each type.

With Solfa, our goal is to hear one or more notes and be able to put the corresponding syllable name on each, based on their scale degree. For example, to hear a note and recognise *"that's do"* or *"that's fa"*.

With Intervals our goal is to hear two notes (simultaneously or one after the other) and name the interval, for example *"that's a major second"* or *"that's a perfect fifth"*.

With Chords our goal is to hear three or more notes together and name the type of chord created, for example *"that's a major triad"* or *"that's a dominant seventh chord"*. With Progressions it's to hear a series of chords and recognise *"that's a I-IV-V-I progression"* or *"that goes ii-V7-I"*.

This means the most basic practice exercise we could design would be:

1.   Hear an example

2.   Try to identify it

3.   Find out if you got it right or not

This is where traditional Ear Training methods often leave it. Many quizzes, apps, and courses consist solely of a set of exercises, each of which plays you various examples to try to identify.

But if that's where we leave things, it means that in step 2, you're really just guessing—and hoping that by sheer brute-force repetition, you'll improve over time. That can work. But it's far harder and slower than it needs to be.

For us, with an Integrated Ear Training approach, this "Basic Drill" is just our starting point.

In the chapters which follow we'll equip you with a number of ways to recognise the different types, and a range of other exercises and activities you can do to improve your skills.

We introduce this exercise here as our "Basic Drill" not because it's what you should spend most of your time doing (it isn't!) but because it's a very simple structure for an exercise which you can then extend and improve using all the other methods we'll cover.

You can use this Basic Drill as a simple way to both:

•   Assess your current skills. For example, it's a clear way to pinpoint which types you tend to mix up or struggle to recognise.

•   Improve your skills, in conjunction with all the other exercises and specific guidance covered in the subsequent chapters.

The examples you listen to in step 1 can come from one of four sources:

A. Pre-Made Audio Tracks

You can find pre-made audio tracks (e.g. MP3s) which play a series of examples, and may also announce the "answer" for each one after a short pause. You'll find a range of these provided in the *Additional Resources*.

B. Interactive Apps

You can use interactive apps or quizzes which play an example and then invite you to press a button to give your answer. You'll find suggestions for these provided in the *Additional Resources*.

C. Play It Yourself

You can play your own examples on an instrument. This has some limitations, but also huge advantages.

The main limitation is that you will normally need to "know the answer" in order to play an example. In most cases it's hard to produce suitable examples by playing notes at random!

However, a considerable advantage is that you're hands-on with your instrument, helping to forge that Hearing-to-Hands connection. It also gives you full, flexible control to explore and experiment e.g. playing the example again, adjusting the way you play it, comparing and contrasting with other examples to hear the differences, and so on.

For these reasons, this is something to consider doing alongside A or B rather than having it be your only source of practice examples.

There is one exception to that though: a powerful modification to the Basic Drill is to record yourself doing it. You can then use the recording as your own home-made practice audio track!

You can also choose to leave a pause before announcing the "answer" each time. In this way you can combine some time spent playing through examples and already knowing the "answers", and time spent listening back to the recording and seeing if you can correctly guess each one.

This gives you full flexbility and develops your H4 musicality beautifully. So even if options A and B seem easier or more convenient, I would encourage you to try practicing this way too!

D. Trade Examples With A Friend

If you're fortunate enough to have a musical buddy you can get together with who is also interested in Ear Training, getting together and exchanging examples is a fun and rewarding way to practice.

Simply take turns playing a series of examples for the other to guess, then swap roles. In this way, you get practice with both producing examples on your own instrument, and training and testing your ears. It will likely also naturally open up interesting other avenues for creativity and collaboration!

Using the Basic Drill

So to recap, our Basic Drill exercise is simply:

1.   Hear an example

2.   Try to identify it

3.   Find out if you got it right or not

You can use various sources of examples as outlined above, and leverage tips like recording yourself and the specific guidance in subsequent chapters, to enhance and extend the exercise. As we continue and explore each of our three sets of Pitch building blocks in turn, we'll keep returning to this Basic Drill in a variety of forms, offering more detailed instructions and suggestions for how to use it for those building blocks, specifically.

Remember always that we want to follow an Integrated Ear Training approach—so however much you're using some form of the Basic Drill, be sure to also make use of the "Applied Activities" recommended in each chapter too.

Also, keep in mind that even a "drill" exercise like this need not be dry and robotic! We want to bring our Head, Hands, Hearing and Heart to all our music-making. Most notably here, remembering to sing or play expressively. We aren't just "giving answers", we are making music with each and every note. And, not coincidentally, that will help you get the answers right more easily too.

How To Use The Chapters Which Follow

In our training modules inside Musical U, we tend to structure things as a series of lessons, each of which moves through Learn, Practice, Apply for a particular focus. For example a lesson might focus on certain Solfa syllables, or certain types of Intervals, or certain Chord Progressions. This provides a clear yet flexible path for musicians to follow, from A to Z, doing a short loop of Learn-Practice-Apply each day.

Our aim in this book is a little different. In the chapters which follow, you will still find a clear, flexible sequence to follow, but to prevent each chapter being vast, and to make sure the book can serve as a reference for you throughout your learning journey, we won't be spelling out the L-P-A loop for each and every step of a particular fixed sequence.

Instead, the structure of each of the pitch building blocks chapters (*Chapter Nine: Solfa, Chapter Ten: Intervals, Chapter Eleven: Chords and Progressions*) is as follows:

1. In the "How It Works" section, you'll be introduced to all the essential terms and concepts for the topic.

2. In the "Getting Started" section, you'll begin exploring the sounds of the musical elements you've just been learning about.

3. Then, in the "Start With Aiming For" section we'll suggest a particular target you can aim for, and a sequence to follow to reach it. These are chosen based on our experience of what represents a "solid, usable level of skill" for each topic.

4. In the "Going Further" section we'll introduce any more sophisticated, complex or niche areas of the topic, which you may wish to explore later.

5. Finally, the "Additional Exercises And Activities" section presents additional "Practice" exercises and "Apply" activities which you can use at any stage, to provide a rich variety of activities you can tailor to suit your own musicality while developing your skills.

So you can see, each chapter is "front-loaded" with a focus on

Learn, but from there it's a blend of Learn, Practice and Apply, so that you can develop your Head, Hands, Hearing, and Heart as you move through the chapter.

This structure provides you with a clear map of everything relating to that topic, a suggested path towards the most meaningful substantial milestone to aim for, and a range of ways to get there. This not only allows for a clear, flexible path forwards, but will also equip you with the knowledge, understanding and familiarity required with each topic to continue to develop your skills to any level you should wish to.

You may wish to read through each chapter in full the first time, perhaps pausing to try some of the "Getting Started" exercises. Then you can return to that section and the "Start With Aiming For" section as you begin regularly practicing the topic, introducing additional activities from the "Further Exercises" section along the way.

While this level of freedom in "what should I do when?" may seem overwhelming at first, remember the principle of Convergent Learning: your activities don't need to be perfectly logically sequenced in order for your musical brain to learn effectively. In fact, as we saw in *Chapter Six: Superlearning,* more variety and randomness can actually do you a lot of good!

All of this means that you can have faith that diligently putting in time practicing with the various exercises and activities included in these chapters, and roughly following the sequences suggested in a way that suits you, will prove to be an effective way to develop your skills in all three areas.

Before we move on to our three building blocks in detail, there's one bigger-picture topic we must address…

An Ear For Keys

When you start thinking in terms of Relative Pitch, rather than specific keys, scales or letter names of notes, it's liberating. You start to realise how much your ear is already understanding intuitively about how music is put together, and with some dedicated Ear Training you begin to be able to identify the specific pitches of notes.

Then… there's a sticking point. Because there's no "do" key on a piano keyboard, nor standard fingering for a "Major Third" on clarinet! If you want to actually play what you heard, if you want to bring an imagined (audiated) melody out into the world for others to hear, if you want to jot down your compositional ideas in traditional notation… suddenly you need to plunge back into that world of letter names, sharps, flats, and key signatures.

Depending on the circumstances, you may know the key, or it may be easy for you to find it out. That is perfectly fine, especially when you're first starting out with Ear Training. You can have great fun developing your ear with the building blocks and exploring Playing By Ear, Improvisation, Songwriting and more, without ever learning to recognise the key by ear.

For that reason, you may wish to skip what follows, and dive straight into those other chapters. You can rely on "finding out" the key rather than "figuring out" the key. You have my enthusiastic permission to do so :)

However, if you want ultimate ear-based freedom in music, you will also at some point need to learn to find the key by ear.

Fortunately, that process doesn't need to be laborious. In fact, there's a simple 3-step process you can follow to identify the key of any music by ear, which we'll cover in the remainder of this chapter.

Before we dive into that process, let's cover a bit of background theory on keys, tonics and scales. Not only because these may be unfamiliar terms for you—but because we've found that even if the terms are familiar, often musicians have quite a fuzzy understanding of exactly what is meant by each and how they relate. Here's what you need to know…

Keys, Tonics and Scales

Key is one of those music topics that can really get people in a muddle. Depending on your musical background, you might actually think of key as something quite different to another musician.

If you're like I was for a long time, you might think of key as just meaning "the key signature". At the start of a piece of music in traditional score notation, we have a set of sharps and flats that tell us how to modify the notes in that piece. So in the key of D Major, for example, you always have to remember that each F is F♯ and each C is C♯.

Or if, say, you're a bass guitar player, you might think of key as just being a note. You know your riff starts from a certain note, and that is your "home note". Then if you're going to play a pentatonic solo, you're going to start that pentatonic scale from a certain fret and string corresponding to that note. You know that if you need to shift to another key, you'd have to move that whole pattern on the fretboard, so you might think of "the key" as just being a note.

As another example, supposing you're a jazz musician who plays solos on the sax. You might think of key as being a "set of notes that you're allowed to use". This certain set of notes will sound good when you're picking different notes to play for your solo.

On top of these differing perspectives on key itself, the key is very closely related to two other concepts in music: the *tonic* and the *scale*. These three things are not the same, but they're very closely related. Let's look at each in turn.

The Key

A *key* is a set of notes, with one of them being identified as the "tonic".

When we talk about keys, tonics and scales, we generally don't worry which octave (or "register") a note is in. So we don't mind whether a note is sung down in a baritone range or high up in a soprano range, whether it's played down low on the E string of a bass or way up top at the top of the guitar fretboard, or in which of the seven octaves of the piano keyboard it's played. As long as it's the same letter name, we're going to consider that the same note when discussing the key.

So a key is a collection of note pitches, and one of them is identified as the *tonic*. That is our full definition. But there are certain conventions in western music that mean that we have some useful shorthands for the details. Some things sound "good" or "normal" to our ears, and so songwriters and composers tend to follow those conventions (at least, most of the time!).

You may know that in Western music we have twelve "chromatic" pitches in each octave: C, C♯, D, all the way up to B. These are sometimes referred to as the different "pitch classes", so that all C's on a piano keyboard, or all C's across the guitar's strings and frets belong to a single "pitch class" of C.

We're going to pick a subset of these twelve pitch classes to be in a key. But we don't pick at random!

Conventionally, a musician or composer is going to pick seven of them, and is going to pick a certain pattern of notes that go well together. So even though a key could technically have any number of notes and choose any combination of those twelve chromatic options, in practice, there are conventions that mean it's not any arbitrary set of possible notes, and we don't have to specify every single one of them to define a key.

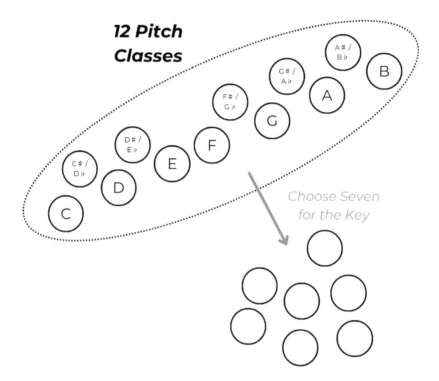

That means when it comes to finding the key by ear, we've already got a big shortcut, because we don't need to figure out each and every one of the notes to know what key we're in. As we'll see as we continue, we need to find the tonic and we need to determine the *tonality*.

The Tonic

We've said that a key is a collection of notes, with one selected as the tonic. So what exactly is that "tonic"?

It just means the note which is the most musically significant of all the notes in our key.

The tonic might be C, it might be F♯, it might be D♭ —any single note from the collection we've chosen for our key. Remember, we're ignoring octaves, so if our tonic is C then any time we play any C we're playing the tonic.

The tonic can also be called the "root note" or the "home note" of the key, because it's the note which everything centers around, musically. With the earlier example of a bass guitar player who thinks about key as just one note, it's the tonic they're thinking about. The tonic is quite often the very first note of the melody and it's almost always the last note, to bring the music "home". The chord built on top of the tonic note is very often the final chord of a piece of music too. These are handy pointers when finding the tonic by ear, as we'll discuss more below!

Let's put it in concrete terms. Supposing the notes you chose for your key were C, D, E, F, G, A and B, and that you chose C as the tonic. That's a choice you have when deciding "what key is this?" That particular case would create the key we call "C Major".

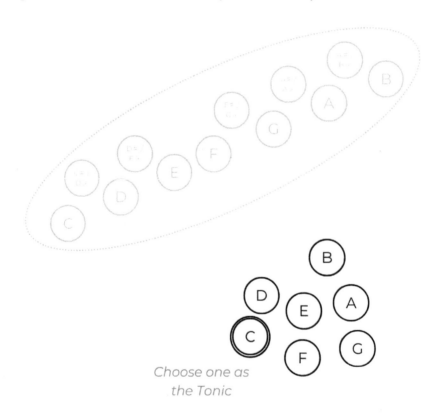

Choose one as
the Tonic

If instead, you took the exact same set of notes, but said that A was the tonic, that would actually define a different key. It would create a different feel in the music if you started using A as the tonic. So the tonic is a crucial part of what defines the key.

The Scale and Tonality

A *scale* is simply a set of notes, in order of pitch (ascending or descending).

If we took our notes from the key and arranged them in order, starting with the tonic at the bottom (and normally repeating it at the top), it would create the corresponding scale:

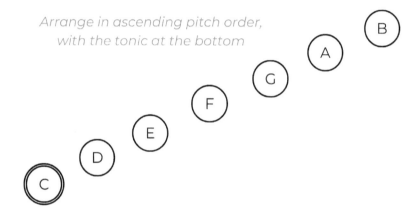

Note that we haven't introduced any new information or choices there. All we've done is taken the decisions we already made about our key (a set of notes, with one chosen as the tonic) and we've arranged them in order.

Now where this gets interesting is that this is where the "shorthand" mentioned before comes in. In Western music, typically the collection of notes a composer or a songwriter will have chosen actually correspond to one of two types of scale: "Major" or "Minor".

Those are just two labels which refer to the pattern of pitch distances between these notes—the "building blocks"used. As we continue in the subsequent chapters, we'll see the details of this pattern in terms of Solfa and in terms of Intervals.

All you need to know for now is that some of the pitch distances between the notes are going to be bigger ("Whole Steps", corresponding to two chromatic steps), and some are going to be smaller ("Half Steps", corresponding to one chromatic step), and the pattern of these bigger and smaller steps creates what we call either a "major scale" pattern or a "minor scale" pattern[7].

When the pattern is "Whole, Whole, Half, Whole, Whole, Whole, Half", that's a major scale. If you play that pattern of steps from any note (i.e. any tonic), it sounds like a major scale. It has a certain sound to it.

This is shown visually below. All twelve chromatic pitches within the octave are shown on a "Pitch Ruler" on the left (repeating the first to complete the octave) and the pattern of Whole and Half Steps for the Major scale on the right.

We'll be unpacking this a lot more in the following chapters, but it may help you to see it visually sooner rather than later!

---

[7] You may be familiar with playing multiple types of minor scale on your instrument: "melodic minor", "harmonic minor" or "natural minor". When we're talking about the scale corresponding to a key, it's specifically the "natural minor". We'll explore this a bit more in *Chapter Nine: Solfa*.

Pitch Ruler   Pitch Ladder

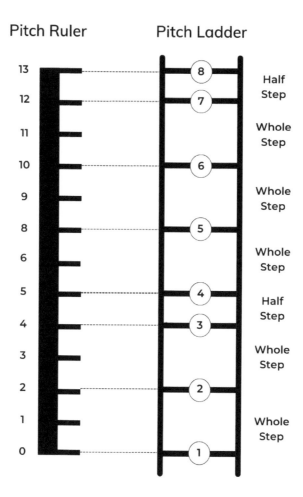

And here's what it would be for our example of choosing the notes C, D, E, F, G, A and B, with C selected as the tonic:

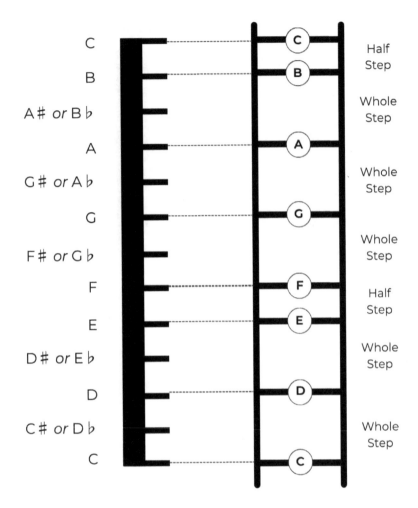

Similarly, there's a pattern for a minor scale: "Whole, Half, Whole, Whole, Half, Whole, Whole". If you start that pattern from any note, it's going to sound like a minor scale with its own distinctive musical character and sound.

Since the set of notes in a key will generally follow one of these two patterns, we can simplify our definition of key by taking advantage of this shorthand. Instead of specifying each and every note in the key, we can simply say it's "Major" or "Minor". We call that the "tonality".

So then we can simplify our definition as "a key is a combination of a tonic note and the tonality".

It might be "C Major", it might be "E♭ Minor", it might be "A Major", and so on. Those are all different possibilities for "tonic plus tonality", which is how we'll define a key.

Using The Key

So why is all of this useful to us? Well, if we want to translate our Relative Pitch understanding of the notes being used in music we hear into specific letter names (to play on an instrument, or write down in notation) we can immediately see why knowing the key is a powerful shortcut.

Instead of needing to try to "translate" each and every note individually from Relative Pitch to its Absolute Pitch equivalent (i.e. the letter name), we can simply find the tonic note, and determine whether the tonality is major or minor. Then we immediately know all the notes which will be featured in the music.[8]

For example, if we've listened to a melody and determined the Solfa names of each note, if we also figure out by ear that the key is "C Major" we can immediately re-label each of the notes with their corresponding letter names, based on the C Major scale.

So now that we're clear on the concepts of key, tonic, scale and tonality, how do we figure out the key by ear?

Finding The Key

Even with rudimentary ear skills, you can quickly find the key by following this 3-step process:

1. **Find the Tonic**

    Before we try to identify which letter name the tonic note is, we need to hone in on it in the music. Our goal is to be able to audiate, sing, or hum the tonic.

2. **Identify the Tonic**

    Once we can sing, hum, or audiate the tonic clearly, we can use a single known note (a "reference note") and our sense of Relative Pitch to identify the tonic's letter name.

3. **Determine the Tonality**

    The final step is to determine whether the tonality is major or minor. Once we know the tonic's letter name plus the tonality,

---

[8] Barring the occasional out-of-key note, something we'll discuss in subsequent chapters.

we know the full set of notes in the key.

We'll also cover below how to "check your answer" once you've found the key by ear.

Step 1: Find the Tonic

Our first step is to try to hone in on the tonic note by ear, so that we can hear it very clearly in our mind's ear and we can hum or sing it back.

It's important to note at the outset that finding the tonic is a slightly "fuzzy" skill. A lot of musicians won't be able to explain how they can find the tonic by ear. It's something that genuinely does develop quite naturally as you learn music. You can accelerate that a lot by doing the specific steps we're covering here, but even then you might feel like your ability isn't rock-solid. Why? Because the tonic itself is a slightly intangible thing!

We have a formal definition in terms of the key, but that's a music theory construct. If we think purely about listening to music, the tonic is not actually a scientifically-defined characteristic of a piece of music. It's not a 100% clear-cut thing and in some cases it can be very debatable!

The more you practice, the more you'll find it easier to identify the tonic, but it's a matter of using "clues", trusting your instinct, and doing a bit of experimenting, rather than there being a foolproof way to always jump to the exact right answer.

So don't worry if at first you get it wrong, you find it tricky, or you're not quite sure what you should be listening for. Trust that this will develop in time as you keep practicing.

You can listen for the tonic in a number of places.

In music with a prominent melody (for example a rock song with a vocal part, or jazz trio where the pianist or guitarist plays the lead), that should usually be your first place to focus. However, we can also find the tonic through the harmony, by listening to the chords or by tuning in to the bassline. Draw on your Active Listening skills to explore the music! Since the tonic is such a core, defining property of the music, it's the same across every instrument. Unless the composer is doing something really wacky, they will all be playing in the same key, and so they'll have the same tonic.

Wherever you choose to focus your listening, there are two main "clues" which can help you find the tonic:

Clue #1: The Tonic Sounds Like "Home"

The tonic also gets called the "home note" of a key or a piece of music because it feels like coming home. It's the note which sounds most at-rest, or most stable.

It's often the most-commonly used note in the music. You'll normally find it coming up a lot in the melody and in the harmony, so it's a very prominent note. It's also very often the note that each section (e.g. verse or chorus) or the whole piece of music will finish on, because it has that sense of completion, resolution, being at rest. So if you take a certain melody, for example, it's going to use all kinds of different pitches, but there's going to be one that, more than any other, makes it sound like that melody is complete. Like if you stopped on that note, it would be okay. Whereas if you stopped on one of the other notes, the listener would be left feeling like, *"oh, it hasn't quite come to the end yet…"*

So that's the main thing to listen for. Once you practice tuning in to that role the tonic plays, you'll find it easy to automatically notice it. This is a special case of what we talked about earlier regarding Solfa, that each note of the scale has its own distinctive character in music, and you learn to spot *"Oh, it's that one!"*

Clue #2: The Tonic Is Always Welcome

The tonic, generally speaking, is going to sound good throughout the music. As always, we have to throw in a caveat that in certain pieces, or certain styles of music, or certain temporary moments in a piece, that may not hold true! But overall, you can think of the tonic as a note which is always welcome, musically. Other notes of the scale will sound good with certain chords, or they'll sound fine momentarily as a passing note in a melody, but the tonic is the most consistently and universally "comfortable" note throughout.

This "clue" actually serves as a really useful way to do a quick check. Supposing you used Clue #1 and had found a note you thought was the tonic. Now try singing or humming that note as you listen to the music.

If it generally sounds comfortable (or "consonant"), that's a good indicator you've found the right note. If you find it's often clashing (or "dissonant") with other notes, that suggests you may have tuned in to a note other than a tonic.

Just hum or sing the tonic for 5–10 seconds and see: does that sound like it's the central note, the "home note"? Does it sound like the resting place that all of the others are built around? If so, you've probably correctly found the tonic.

Step 2: Identify the Tonic

Once we've found our tonic and can sing or hum it, it's time to identify it. What is the letter name of that note?

This is where most musicians struggle, because often they can find the tonic by ear but then it becomes a matter of total guesswork to find that corresponding note on their instrument. They hunt around, playing notes at random, trying to find the one which matches.

Remember from *Chapter Two: Mindset* that we want to aim for "Trial and Improvement" rather than "Trial and Error". So our basic process is similar, using an instrument to check, but we won't guess at random. Instead we'll use a single known "reference note" and our sense of Relative Pitch to go more quickly (and eventually directly) to the correct note.

If right now you don't feel like you have a good sense of Relative Pitch, don't worry. That's exactly what you'll be developing in the subsequent chapters! As you gain skill with Solfa and Intervals, you'll be able to use those to more directly hear the relationship between your known reference note and your found tonic, and so identify the tonic.

For example, you might have a known reference note of "C". You hum or sing the tonic note you found, and can hear it's a Perfect Fourth above the C, so you know the tonic is an F. Or you might use your Solfa skills to recognise that the C sounds like "re" compared to your tonic, so your tonic must be B ♭.

Where do you get the "known reference note" from? There are a few options:

1.   Simply play a note (e.g. middle C) on an instrument, or use a tuning fork

2.   See what other musicians are doing. For example in a band practice you might be able to spot that the bassist is playing an F.

3.   Memorise a single reference pitch, as covered in the section on Absolute Pitch above.

The option you choose will depend on the situation. For example, using a learned reference pitch is great if you've learned one, and there isn't music playing—but if you're joining in a jam session, it may be hard to audiate that reference pitch clearly and reliably, and you'd likely be better off quietly playing one note on your own instrument, or looking to other musicians to spot a note or a chord you can use as your known reference.

Armed with that known reference note, you can use Intervals or Solfa to identify the tonic you found. At first, don't expect yourself to nail it! Remember "Trial and Improvement". Even if using your Relative Pitch skills just gets you close to the correct answer, it can mean you identify the tonic with only two or three guesses, rather than the totally-random hunting-and-pecking that can take several guesses before you finally luck out.

> ### Zac Says...
>
> *Something I like to do is sing the tonic note loudly (inspired by our Resident Pro Ruth Power's idea of the tonic note being the "Queen Bee"), and play a note on an instrument. Then use relative pitch to guess the interval and/or solfa relationship between the note I'm singing loudly and the note I'm playing on my instrument. Then move on my instrument based on my solfa/interval guess to find the tonic note.*
>
> *Surprisingly often, I will even play the tonic note correctly on the instrument the first time. I find that if I relax, and sing loudly, then it's like my finger just knows what note to go to on my instrument.*

Step 3: Determine the Tonality

The final step is to determine whether the key is major or minor. Like with finding the tonic, it's something that musicians often find just comes naturally. You've spent so many years playing major scales and minor scales, or major chords and minor chords, it's very easy to just judge *"is this piece major or minor overall?"* But if you haven't acquired that skill passively, you will need to do a little bit of practice to learn to distinguish major from minor, and again there are various clues we can take advantage of.

Clue #1: Listen for the Third

This is a helpful clue if you've spent enough time playing scales to be able to sing a major scale and a minor scale. One critical difference between major and minor scales is whether the third note of the scale is a "Major Third" Interval from the tonic, or a "Minor Third".

Having found the tonic, try singing up from it as if it's a major scale, and then as if it's a minor scale. That third note will either sound like it belongs neatly with the music (e.g. the notes used in the melody) or it will stick out oddly, revealing whether it's a major or minor scale being used, and therefore whether the tonality of the key is major or minor.

Clue #2: Listen for the Tonality of the Chords

In major keys, typically most (if not all) of the chords used will be major. In minor keys, most (if not all) will be minor. Again, depending on your musical background, you may find it easy to tell a major chord from a minor chord, or not. If not, we'll be covering that in *Chapter Eleven: Chords and Progressions*.

It's not always obvious, or clear-cut. Sometimes the exact harmony of a piece or the sequence of chords in a progression can muddy the waters, so that the simplistic rules of thumb like "major sounds happy and minor sounds dark or mysterious" don't help. A lot of the time though, musicians will have a sense of major versus minor, and applying this to the chords can help you sense the tonality of the music overall.

Assuming you feel like you can tell major chords from minor chords by ear, simply ask *"are most of the chords in this music major or minor?"* and you'll have the tonality of the key.

Clue #3: Listen for the Tonality of the Root Chord

One chord is even more revealing of the tonality than all the others: the root chord, or tonic chord, meaning the one built with the tonic as its root note. Most music will end on that tonic chord, and often start with it too, and (like the tonic itself) it's the one which sounds most "at rest" or most like "home".

So if you can spot the tonic chord by ear, and tell whether it's major or minor, that will tell you the key's tonality too.

How To Check It

So you've listened and tried to hone in on the tonic note, and you think you're singing the right one. You've identified that tonic note using a known reference note and your sense of Relative Pitch, and you think you've got that letter name right. And you've listened for the tonality and determined whether it seems to be major or minor.

Now you'll probably want to check whether the key you've identified is correct or not. Without needing to run off and look up the notation, here are three ways you can self-check:

1. Check the tonic
    As noted above, generally the tonic will sound like the "home" note and it will pretty much always sound welcome or comfortable. So listen again, and simply play the tonic you've identified constantly or repeatedly as you listen (this is called an "ostinato").
    Does it mostly sound fine? Or are there quite a lot of clashes?

2. Check with the tonic chord
    Knowing the tonic and the tonality tells you the tonic chord. For example, in the key of C Major, the tonic chord is a C Major chord. In the key of B Minor, the tonic chord is B Minor. If you play a chordal instrument (e.g. guitar, piano), play the chord throughout the music. If you play a melodic instrument (e.g. saxophone, violin) you can use the broken chord or *arpeggio* (i.e. play each note of the chord in turn).
    Again, does it fit in pretty well with the music throughout? Or does it seem like it's only occasionally comfortable? It won't match everything all the time, since the music is probably moving between various chords. But if you've chosen the wrong tonic, or the wrong tonality, you'll probably find it only rarely sounds "at home" in the music, if at all.

3. Check with the scale
    Knowing the tonic and tonality tells you the scale being used. You can use this to self-check in three ways:
    Firstly, you can simply play the scale up and down, just like we did with the tonic and tonic chord, and see if it "fits".

Secondly, you can use the scale to try playing the melody or
other parts of the music by ear. You should find that almost all,
if not all, the notes you need can be found in the scale you've
identified.

Thirdly, you can try improvising using the notes of the scale.
Again, if it's the right scale (i.e. you've found the right key),
your improvisation should fit in well with the rest of the
music, otherwise it's an indication that you might need to
check the tonic and tonality again.

Remember what was mentioned above, that the key of a piece of
music is very clear and precise in music theory terms, but can be very
fuzzy indeed when it comes to the sound of the music itself! So allow
yourself a lot of grace as you practice finding keys by ear.

Unless you're branching into some forms of modal jazz, post-
modern chromatic music, or similarly specialised genres, you'll
probably find that the music does have a single, clear key throughout,
and it's easy to check your answer using the options above and feel
confident that you've got it.

Of course, the proof is in the pudding, so the real test will come
when you start using the key you've identified to carry out the actual
musical activities you were interested in to begin with! For example, as
you try translating your Solfa-identified melody notes into absolute
pitches to play by ear on your instrument, or you try using the
Intervals you audiated to improvise what you imagined out loud. You
may have made a mistake or two with the Relative Pitch side of things,
but if everything comes out sounding "wrong", that's a good sign you
may need to check the key again!

Key Changes

One last note about keys (no pun intended!). One tool which
songwriters and composers have in their toolkit is to change key
during the piece of music, known as *modulation*. This creates a feeling
of "everything is a bit different now" and often marks a significant
change in section, as discussed in *Chapter Five: Active Listening* when
we looked listening for the Form of the music.

This is good news and bad news for you, as the budding key-by-
ear-finder. The bad news is that you'll need to be aware that there may
actually be more than one key used in the piece of music you're

working on. The good news is that its "everything is a bit different now" nature tends to make it stand out quite prominently. Even if you haven't known about this before, you are almost certainly familiar with what it feels like when a piece of music changes key. With a bit of practice, you'll be able to easily spot when that happens, and simply apply the process above to each key separately[9].

See This In Action

If you'd like to see a step-by-step explanation and demonstration of this process, we've made our training "An Ear For Keys" available for you inside the *Additional Resources*.

Conclusion

Once you get the hang of the Pitch Contour, develop your sense of Relative Pitch using the three building blocks, and practice finding the key and translating from relative to absolute pitches, you will be able to recognise the notes in any music you hear or play, entirely by ear.

This lets you play music by ear, with no need for notation. We'll be covering Rhythm Ear Training too in later chapters, but you'll probably find that mimicking a rhythm you hear is relatively easy—so as long as you know which notes to play, you're all set! This can make jamming with other musicians far easier and less intimidating too, since you know you can always find a way to join in, even if you don't know the music in advance.

It also lets you improvise more freely and creatively because (along with the Expansive Creativity framework you'll learn in Part III) you start to be able to bring out any music you hear in your head (audiate) or sing directly on your instrument, so that your note choices don't

---

[9] There are common conventions in key changes, for example the famous "Truck Driver's Gear Change" where the key is shifted upwards by a half step or whole step, to inject fresh energy for the final chorus of a pop or rock song, modulation to the relative minor key (the key with the same set of notes but a tonic which makes the tonality minor rather than major), or modulation by an interval of a Perfect Fifth up or down. Knowing a bit about these conventions can shortcut your process of identifying the new key, though the self-check steps will still come in handy!

depend on strict rules or memorised patterns, but can be truly free.

Having good Relative Pitch will likewise boost your creative expression in Songwriting and composing by giving you a way to translate from sound to symbol and vice-versa. Again, you needn't rely on patterns or guesswork to find what sounds good—you can simply imagine it, and write it down.

That sound/symbol connection also allows you to sight-sing or audiate from traditional (score) notation. Imagine being able to glance at a new piece of sheet music and know immediately how it would sound! In this case some Rhythm Ear Training will likely be required too, to help you translate from the rhythmic symbols to their corresponding sounds, but for most musicians it's the pitch side that's the biggest blocker. Relative Pitch Ear Training can remove that block for you.

And last but not least, developing your Relative Pitch will improve your Active Listening and your musical memory. The new "mental models" you'll develop for understanding pitch relationships, as well as the more fine-grained "pitch ruler" you'll have for identifying specific notes and chords, will create far more vivid and precise mental representations of the music you listen to and learn, as well as making it much faster to form those mental representations for any new music you tackle.

We'll explore all of these applications more in Part III. For now, let's continue to look at each of our three building blocks for Relative Pitch Ear Training.

CHAPTER NINE:
SOLFA

If I had to choose just one "building block" to empower you to play by ear, improvise, write music, and more, it would be Solfa. Fortunately, we don't need to choose just one! :) But the fact that Solfa is typically overlooked when musicians pursue Ear Training, compared with Intervals, Chords and Progressions, is quite possibly a large part of the reason most musicians struggle to see real, tangible, practical payoff from their Ear Training efforts.

Whatever your background may be, you've almost certainly come across Solfa before. It might have been called "solfege" (an alternative name which we'll discuss and clarify below) or simply "the do-re-mi system". Perhaps the only place you've heard of it was in the classic movie *The Sound Of Music* with its famous song *"Do-Re-Mi"* (popularly known as *"Doe, a Deer"*)—which, despite arguably doing some harm to music education by forever connecting Solfa with children in the minds of the public, did actually do a pretty good job of explaining and demonstrating what Solfa is all about: *"When you know the notes to sing, you can sing most anything"*. Substitute "recognise and identify" for "sing", and you've pretty much got it!

In my own journey, Solfa was a late discovery which I wished someone had clued me into sooner. I'll share a little of that story below. Suffice to say, it was an absolute game-changer for me, just as it has since proven to be for so many of our members over the years.

So whether you're at the start of your own Ear Training journey, or you've been at it for years, I'm excited for you to dive into this chapter and discover everything Solfa can do to unlock your instinctive ability to recognise notes (and everything pitch-related) by ear.

Overview

We will follow the Learn, Practice, Apply approach of Integrated Ear Training. We'll go through these one by one in this chapter, and you will probably want to read through the chapter in order to begin with—but remember that when it comes to actually doing Ear Training, these are best done as a short loop: learn a little (e.g. by re-reading part of the chapter), practice a little (doing an exercise or two from the chapter), try applying it (doing one or more of the applied activities at the end of the chapter).

Learn

In this chapter we'll explain the basic concepts (Head) in "What Is Solfa?" and "How Solfa Works".

Practice

Then in "Getting Started" we'll look at how the Basic Drill can be used for practicing Solfa, and how you can start to recognise each solfa note (Hearing, Heart, Hands (in this case, Singing)).

In the "Start With Aiming For..." section we'll identify one particular scale, a subset of the major scale, which is particularly well-suited to learning Solfa and a meaningful, useful milestone to aim for first. In "Going Further" we'll discuss how Solfa can be used, even beyond the major scale it's normally associated with.

Apply

Finally, in "Additional Exercises and Activities" we'll briefly explore taking our Solfa skills to practical musical tasks (Hands: Singing and instrument), which will be covered further in Part III of the book.

What Is Solfa?

When you first encounter Solfa it can seem a bit strange and arbitrary. Why are we putting some whole other set of names to musical notes? Is it all about singing? Isn't it just for kids? If it works so well, why isn't everyone using it? So it's worth taking a moment to look briefly at its historical origins, before we dive into the practicalities and how it can be useful for you in the modern day.

The earliest known origins of Solfa are in the 11th Century, when an Italian Benedictine monk named Guido d'Arezzo noticed that in the hymn *"Ut Queant Laxis"*, each line began on the next-higher note of the scale—from the first note of the scale up to the sixth—and therefore one could use the first word of each line as a way to refer to each note. He realised that it would be valuable to have a clear way to refer to each degree of the scale, regardless of the specific key of the music. As we learned in *Chapter Eight: Relative Pitch*, this matches the way our ear naturally interprets musical pitches.

This produced the note names *ut, re, mi, fa, sol,* and *la*. This proved a helpful tool for singers to learn new songs by ear and to sight-read from notation, and in time "ut" was replaced with "do" and "ti" was added for the seventh scale degree (after temporarily being "si", still used in some traditions).

This system is known as "moveable *do* solfege" a.k.a. Solfa. Why "moveable *do*", you might wonder? We'll unpack that a bit below.

Another big step forwards came in the 19th Century. An English music teacher Sarah Ann Glover created a system for teaching sight-singing based on this "moveable do" idea and using the same syllable names for the notes. Then another English music educator, John Curwen, developed this further with one significant addition[1]: a way of showing each note visually with different "hand signs":

---

[1] He also introduced a written/spoken way of indicating rhythmic patterns, an early precursor to the approach used by Kodály and which you'll discover in *Chapter Thirteen: Rhythm.*

MENTAL EFFECTS AND MANUAL SIGNS OF TONES IN KEY.

NOTE.—*These diagrams show the hand as seen by pupils sitting on the left-hand side of the teacher. The teacher makes his signs in front of his ribs, chest, face, and head, rising a little as the tones go up, and falling as they go down.*

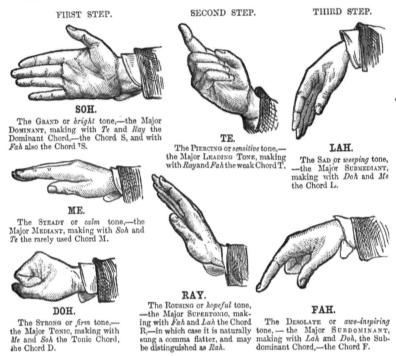

FIRST STEP.   SECOND STEP.   THIRD STEP.

SOH.
The GRAND or *bright* tone,—the Major DOMINANT, making with *Te* and *Ray* the Dominant Chord,—the Chord S, and with *Fah* also the Chord ⁷S.

TE.
The PIERCING or *sensitive* tone,—the Major LEADING TONE, making with *Ray* and *Fah* the weak Chord T.

LAH.
The SAD or *weeping* tone, —the Major SUBMEDIANT, making with *Doh* and *Me* the Chord L.

ME.
The STEADY or *calm* tone,—the Major MEDIANT, making with *Soh* and *Te* the rarely used Chord M.

DOH.
The STRONG or *firm* tone,— the Major TONIC, making with *Me* and *Soh* the Tonic Chord, the Chord D.

RAY.
The ROUSING or *hopeful* tone, —the Major SUPERTONIC, making with *Fah* and *Lah* the Chord R,—in which case it is naturally sung a comma flatter, and may be distinguished as *Rah.*

FAH.
The DESOLATE or *awe-inspiring* tone,— the Major SUBDOMINANT, making with *Lah* and *Doh*, the Subdominant Chord,—the Chord F.

⁎⁎⁎ For *fe* let the teacher point his first finger horizontally to the left. For *ta* ditto to the right. When seen by the class these positions will be reversed, and will correspond with the Modulator. For *se* let the teacher point his forefinger straight towards the class.

(Extract from The Standard Course of the Tonic Sol-Fa Method, John Curwen. 10th edition, 1892)

Curwen popularised this method and it became widely used throughout Britain at the time, with sheet music for singers typically including the solfa syllables below the notes to enable easy sight-singing. As this chapter goes on, you'll understand how singers could simply look at the written solfa syllables and immediately know how the music should sound.

The third significant leap forwards for this methodology was in the 20th Century when the Hungarian classical composer and devoted music education reformer Zoltán Kodály (pronounced like *"cod eye"* with emphasis on "eye") both developed the approach further, and campaigned to popularise it in his home country of Hungary. This dramatically improved the standards of childhood music education, to the extent that the approach spread internationally as people noticed the incredible musicians beginning to emerge from Hungary[2].

Depending on who you speak to, what happened next was either:

A. The Kodály approach continued to thrive, and lives on in vibrant Kodály-based music education traditions around the world. Or

B. For a mixture of historic/political reasons, and the increasing cultural focus on learning to play music from written notation as being the "gold standard" of learning music, the Kodály approach remained a niche methodology.

I would say both are true.

I have enormous appreciation and respect for the lively communities of Kodály music educators around the world, including the professional bodies and associations which support and promote the approach (such as the British Kodály Academy and the Organization of American Kodály Educators) and the individual teachers who study and apply the approach. In certain places, and in certain educational systems, the Kodály approach is alive and continuing to have massive positive impact on young musicians.

At the same time, as someone who spent 25+ years studying music in a range of ways and a range of places in the United Kingdom, and perhaps only heard of Kodály once or twice—and as someone who's devoted their life to *adult* music education—it pains me that the average adult music learner today has likely never even heard of Kodály, let alone benefitted from the approach in the way they could.

The Kodály approach certainly isn't the only place Solfa is used today, but both Kodály and more broadly Solfa have gradually come to be used only in very rare or niche contexts, or exclusively in childhood music education. This, to me, is a tragedy.

When I did discover Kodály myself, it was a revelation. I had already been doing ear training and even running Easy Ear Training / Musical U for several years, but had always focused on Intervals for Relative Pitch. I had a basic understanding of Solfa but hadn't really

---

[2] Let's not overlook the fact that the huge number of "talented" Hungarian musicians were produced not by a sudden genetic trait or mysterious "gift"—but by a revolution in how they learned music.

practiced with it. I had come across the name "Kodály" (alongside some other traditional music education approaches which do put emphasis on musicality, such as Dalcroze, Orff, and Music Learning Theory) but I hadn't really explored it.

Around 2016 I decided to investigate further, and began taking 1-to-1 lessons with one of the top Kodály instructors in the U.K., Cyrilla Rowsell. She was one of the few I could find who was experienced teaching adults Kodály, rather than only children (though even then, generally with a view to training them to teach children rather than primarily for their own musicality).

From my very first lesson, it was mind-blowing! She got me doing things with pitch and rhythm that I'd never been able to do before— and I was hooked.

As I began to see the power of the Solfa system, as well as the Rhythm Syllables system you'll learn about in *Chapter Thirteen: Rhythm*, I realised we needed to bring these into what we did at Musical U.

We collaborated with Anne Mileski, one of the top "teachers of teachers" when it comes to all things Kodály, to create our very first standalone course, *Foundations of a Musical Mind*. The incredible results which that course delivered for students (ranging from complete beginners who'd thought themselves "tone deaf", through to experienced music teachers and professional musicians) meant that we continued to double down on integrating these tools into all of our musicality training.

So although I wouldn't say Musical U follows the Kodály approach (since there are things in that approach which we don't necessarily adhere to, and there's a vast range of topics we cover which go around and beyond Kodály) I have to give enormous credit to Zoltán Kodály and the amazing teachers who've continued his work over the years. A lot of what you'll learn and benefit from in this chapter has strong roots in the traditional Kodály approach.

Zac Says...

Before taking Foundations, I had been obsessively studying music theory for a few years, and drilling scales on the piano. I didn't understand how any of the theory I was studying and the scales I was practicing could be used to make music. Anything I tried to compose or improvise was not satisfying and did not excited me.

I had been making music for years with DJing, sampling, improvising on the keys, and rapping, so I knew I could make music. But when I tried to apply theory and scales to making music it seemed to make my music worse.

In my obsessive pursuit of music theory understanding I did discover ear training apps, and I'm really good at playing games so I would get good scores and advance through the levels. But it didn't help me make music and didn't help me understand the music I heard. I would score well on interval and chord quizzes but when listening to music and trying to figure out the intervals and chords I was just like, "huh?" It was frustrating and confusing.

Foundations totally changed my life. It equipped me with a process of learning theory and training my ear by listening to actual music and creating my own music. The theory and the ear training clicked into place and I could improvise and compose with greater awareness, confidence, and satisfaction. It's been about six years since I first went through Foundations and I'm still discovering new benefits from using the the solfa and rhythm syllables.

Solfa vs. Intervals

Solfa and Intervals are often seen as two alternative approaches to recognising note pitches by ear. As we've already covered when introducing our pitch building blocks in *Chapter Eight: Relative Pitch*, they are in fact a wonderful pairing to use together.

It can be enlightening to compare and contrast the strengths of each and how best to use the two. We'll do so in the following chapter on Intervals, so that if you're reading through the chapters in order, both topics will have been introduced first. If you know a little about Solfa and Intervals already, you have my permission to flip ahead and read that now, if you like :)

How Solfa Works

Solfa is, in its essence, simply a system for naming each note of the scale, relative to the tonic. In the previous chapter, we talked about the prime importance of the *relationships* between note pitches, and how it's the *relative* pitches which give everything in music meaning, rather than the "absolute" pitches or specific letter names.

The entire Solfa system hinges on one powerful observation: if the way our brains and ears interpret musical pitches is all based on the relationships of notes to the tonic, then the way we identify notes should be too.

It's a simple idea, but one with enormous power for us as musicians interested in developing our instinct for pitch, and specifically our sense of Relative Pitch.

In Solfa, we give the root note of the major scale (the tonic) the name "do". When speaking, we tend to pronounce that like "doe" (as in "a female deer"!) but to be accurate when using it in Solfa activities, it should be pronounced more like the very start of the word "Dorothy". This is because we want our Solfa names to be a single syllable, so we should avoid it becoming a two-syllable sound with the diphthong "w" sound at the end of "doe".

No matter what letter name our tonic might be, it is always referred to as *do*. We then give each of the other notes in the major scale their own names too:

Note: As we continue, we'll show some examples on the staff like this. If that notation isn't familiar to you, you can simply focus on the letter names beneath the notes. We will often use C as the tonic of the scale, but this is purely for clarity and consistency. All the patterns and distances could be based on starting with any note as the tonic.

Notice that no matter our starting note, the Solfa names (which we can call "syllables", since they are each a single syllable in length) are always the same. The first note is always *do*, the second is always *re*, and so on.

Here is how to pronounce each of the syllables:[3]

Solfa Syllable	Pronunciation
do	*"doh" (as in "Dorothy", not "doe")*
re	*"reh" (as in "resin", not "ray")*
mi	*"mee" (as in "I am me")*
fa	*"fah" (as in "near or far")*
so	*"soh" (as in "soil", not "sew")*
la	*"lah" (as in "hey la, my boyfriend's back")*
ti	*"tea" (as in "nice cup of tea")*

You might like to try singing up a major scale now, using each of the Solfa syllables.

There are further details of the Solfa system, including how minor scales and chromatic notes can be handled, which we'll cover below. But really, what's explained above is all you need to get started!

What's remarkable is just how far we can go in developing our ears, simply by adopting this different way of naming notes. The specific activities which will help you do that will be our main focus for the rest of this chapter.

The Pitch Ladder

One visual representation which can be helpful is to imagine the

---

[3] You may come across the syllable "sol" used for the fifth scale degree, rather than "so". This was the traditional syllable (and is where Solfa gets its name from: "sol-fa") but over the years "so" has become more standard. This is primarily because it is more easily singable as a single syllable—similar to wanting to avoid the diphthong of "doe" mentioned above.

notes of the scale as existing on a vertical set of steps, which we can call a "Pitch Ladder":

You'll notice that not all the rungs are equally spaced! Here is the Pitch Ladder alongside a "Pitch Ruler" which has all 12 ("chromatic") steps of the octave:

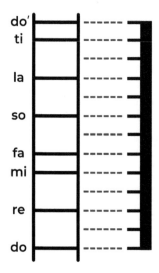

Notice that all our Pitch Ladder steps correspond to steps on the Ruler, with most being two rungs apart (which we call a "Whole Step" or "Major Second") and some being just one rung apart (which we call a

"Half Step" or "Minor Second"). We'll explore this a bit more in the following chapter on Intervals.

For now, you might find the Pitch Ladder a helpful visual aid as you practice moving between Solfa notes.

Fixed vs. Movable Do

We mentioned that Solfa is sometimes called "solfege". The reason we prefer the term "Solfa" is that although the word "solfege" *can* be used to refer to the same thing, it can also refer to a distinct system which uses the same syllable names—but for a very different purpose.

The two solfege systems are called "Fixed Do" and "Movable Do", and both use the syllables *do, re, mi, fa, so, la,* and *ti*.

The approach we introduced above, and what the term *Solfa* is exclusively used to mean, is "Movable Do". This refers to the fact that the name "do" is given to the tonic, no matter what note that is. So the note letter we call "do" moves, depending on the key. In C Major, "do" is C. In D Major, "do" is D. And so on.

With the other system, "Fixed Do", the name "do" is always the note C. This means that it's essentially just a different set of names for the different pitch classes in music. In certain countries, such as France, this is simply how they refer to notes, either instead of (or as well as) using the letter names.

Because Fixed Do solfege does not correspond to the musical relationships of the major scale, it doesn't bring any of the Ear Training advantages that Movable Do does. If you were to try learning to recognise the Fixed Do notes of *do, re, mi* etc. by ear, you would simply be doing Absolute Pitch Ear Training—which, as discussed in the previous chapter, is not a useful route forwards!

So Fixed Do solfege isn't a system for understanding music by ear, the way Movable Do solfege is. It's worth knowing about, since this can cause confusion. For example if you're collaborating with musicians who grew up in a country where "do" always means C.

Fortunately, to save us from having to constantly specify that we're using Movable Do, we can simply avoid the term "solfege" and instead use the term "Solfa", which always refers to Movable Do.

What's In A Name?

Often when musicians first encounter Solfa they wonder *"If Solfa is just a system for identifying scale degrees, why don't we just use numbers?"*

For example, instead of *mi*, why don't we just say "three"? Instead of *ti*, why don't we just say "seven"?

That can seem like a simpler solution, since you don't need to learn which Solfa syllable corresponds to each degree. However, that's something which is quick and easy to learn, and there are some considerable advantages to using names instead of numbers:

1. We avoid confusion with other musical elements we use numbers for. Numbers are everywhere in music! We use them to refer to our place in a piece (e.g. *"measure 37"*, *"verse 3"*, *"movement 2"*), we use them to count time (e.g. *"one, two, three, four, one, two, three, four"*), we use them to number fingering on piano (e.g. right-hand thumb is 1, right-hand index finger is 2, etc.), we use them to identify chords in functional harmony (e.g. 1 or I for the tonic chord, 4 or IV for the subdominant, 5 or V for the dominant), and so on. By using dedicated syllable names for scale degrees—names which aren't used to mean anything else—it helps make immediately clear what we mean when we say them.

2. The names are single syllables, making them more easily singable. If you're trying to sing a melody using scale degree numbers, "seven" can quickly become awkward! All the Solfa syllable names (including the chromatic variants which replace e.g. "flat seven") are just a single syllable. They've also been chosen to have distinctive vowel and consonant sounds.

3. The names are chosen such that their leading consonants are unique. This allows us to write only the first letter of each, as a shorthand (e.g. "mrd" for "mi, re, do"). That's helpful, for example, when quickly jotting down a melody you hear. We can also append a comma to indicate "one octave lower" (e.g. *l, d* would be ascending from the *la* below a *do* rather than moving downwards from the *la* above) and an apostrophe to indicate "one octave higher" (e.g. *s l t d'* would be a sequence running upwards from *so* up to the *do* above)

4. These names are a common language among musicians who

know the system. So while "a rose by any other name would smell as sweet", if you learn to recognise the scale degrees as "Bob", "Jeff", "Danny" or any other names you might quite validly choose, you'll have a harder time communicating effectively with other musicians.

5.   Finally (and in my opinion most importantly), using distinctive names allows us to more easily associate each scale degree with its musical "character" or role. As humans we're hard-wired to attach meaning to names. Just like when you get to know someone called "Diane Jones" you come to associate various traits, behaviours and relationships with that name, you will come to get to know *do, re, mi* and the other Solfa notes quite intimately.

I know that if you've never learned Solfa before, that can be hard to imagine, but musicians who train their ear for Solfa really do start to hear *"oh, there's a re, now we've moved to fa"* etc. simply by virtue of how each of the Solfa notes has its own "personality" through its own distinctive sound and the role it plays, musically.

Hand Signs

Everything we've covered so far would already be enormously useful for you, in developing your Relative Pitch and learning to identify notes by ear. However, there's an additional part of Solfa which massively amplifies its power—as long as you're willing to get a little weird!

Each of the Solfa notes has a corresponding "Hand Sign": a distinctive shape you can make with your hand, to indicate that note. You can combine making that shape with moving your arm up and down to indicate the pitch of the note too, so that you can actually demonstrate a melody, even in total silence.

Remember in the last chapter when we explored the idea of the Pitch Contour, and mentioned you can show pitch by moving your hand or a pointing finger vertically up and down? Hand Signs take this to the next level by giving each scale degree its own hand shape. This lets you indicate precisely which notes of the scale you're moving between as you move your hand up and down.

Note that while this 2D view of the hand signs generally shows them well, for *la* your hand should be facing forwards, not across, so that the backs of your fingers are facing away from you rather than sideways. You can also see these demonstrated in a video in the *Additional Resources*.

The shapes can seem arbitrary—even arcane—when you first see them, but they're actually quite elegant in their design. For example:

- *do* is a firm, closed fist, like a solid rock—just like the firm stability of the tonic note.
- *re* slopes upwards from *do*, reflecting how it sounds like a departure from the tonic.
- *mi* and *so* have a flat hand and flat, horizontal position— showing how they are stable points of the scale, like *do*, and contrasting with the other notes which have curved, sloping, or pointing shapes.

- *fa* has thumb pointing downwards to where *mi* would be, just like the sound of *fa* wants to resolve down to the stable *mi* a Half Step beneath.
- *ti* has index finger pointing upwards to high *do*, just like the sound of *ti* wants to resolve up to the stable *do* a Half Step above.

So why is all this useful? It's because this makes your experience of the note pitches physical in a powerful additional way. Opinions vary about whether the concept of "learning modalities" such as you being primarily a "visual learner" or an "auditory learner" hold weight or not, but one thing's for sure: adding this physical component to Solfa is valuable and effective for any musician.

If you practice Solfa not just with the sung syllables but with the corresponding hand signs too, it develops a visceral instinct for note pitches which the singing alone does not. In other words, you start to instinctively want to make the corresponding hand sign when you hear or sing a particular scale degree, because you've made that association. We've found this greatly accelerates the learning of recognising notes using Solfa, and I would strongly encourage you to give it a try—even if you feel a bit silly doing it, at first!

Getting Started

Later in the chapter we'll suggest a range of ways you can practice Solfa and integrate it into various musical activities. Let's get started with our "Basic Drill" exercise, and look at how to recognise Solfa degrees.

How To Use The Basic Drill

Remember that our Basic Drill is simply "listen to some examples of different types of building blocks, and for each one try to recognise which type it is."

EXERCISE: The Basic Drill For Solfa

With Solfa, the Basic Drill would look like this:

1. Establish the key, or "tonal centre". In a major key, that means knowing the sound of *do*.

2. Hear an example note from the key's scale, or a subset of its

notes that you're currently focused on (e.g. just *do re mi*), often referred to as the "toneset"[4]

3.   Try to recognise which solfa note it was, and name it, ideally singing back the syllable on the same pitch.

4.   Check your answer.

5.   Repeat steps 2-4.

Generally you'll stay in the same key and toneset for a series of examples, allowing you to keep a sense of the tonic and compare the sounds of different scale degrees, before periodically changing the key.

At first in step 1 you'll probably want to play through the whole set of notes you're working with, up and down, to establish that whole toneset in your mind's ear. To challenge yourself more, you can then move on to playing only the tonic, *do*, and relying on your own singing or audiation to find the others.

You can use this Basic Drill as a simple way to assess your current skills (for example, it's a clear way to pinpoint which Solfa degrees you tend to mix up or struggle to recognise) and a process for improving your skills, in conjunction with everything covered below.

So, equipped with that Basic Drill, how do we make sure that recognising the degree you heard is not just a random guess?

How To Recognise Solfa Notes

In the following chapters on Intervals and on Chords and Progressions, we'll equip you with a range of ways to "tune in" to the characteristic sound of each type of those musical elements. We will lead with ear-based recognition, and use singing as an accelerator for developing your skills.

---

[4] The word "tone" has various uses in music, including:
A. "tone meaning overall sound, akin to 'timbre'"",
B. "tone" meaning 'a whole step' or 'interval of a major second'", and
C. "tone meaning 'a note pitch'".
It's worth noting that "toneset" is a phrase meaning "a set of scale degrees" in the context of talking about Solfa i.e. using that third sense of "tone" just meaning "a note pitch". It has nothing to do specifically with timbre or whole steps. To help keep this clear, we will write it as a single word, "toneset", though elsewhere you may find it written as two words, "tone set".

With Solfa, our approach will be a bit different. Why? Because the most powerful way to train your ear to recognise notes with Solfa is through singing. We will focus first on learning to produce each solfa syllable with our singing voice, and allow that to train our ears.

Many musicians are surprised to find that they already have some rudimentary Solfa skills. For example, I once taught a workshop where I played the notes *do, re, mi,* naming each, then played one of the three at random, and asked attendees to name it. Almost without exception, they got it right!

Now, you might say, that's easy enough when it's just three notes and you've just heard all three pitches to compare with. That's true. But it's a small step from there to hearing only the *do,* and singing or audiating the *re* and *mi* yourself before answering.

In a sense, this is what we are trying to do with all our Solfa Ear Training: to establish the solfa scale in our musical mind as a skeleton or template, against which we can compare any notes we hear. And the most effective way to ingrain that template, along with the corresponding solfa syllable names, is to practice singing it, and practice singing melodies using it. Almost all the exercises and activities introduced below can be seen as some form of doing this.

You can start to familiarise yourself with Solfa now by simply singing through the major scale using the solfa syllables and corresponding hand signs:

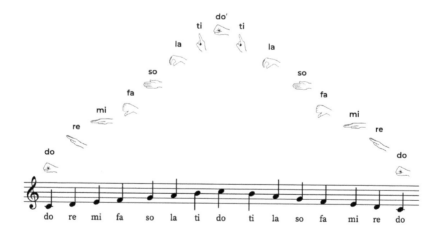

Go up and down the scale, slowly, checking your pronunciation of the syllable and the shape you're making with your hand. You can begin with just the first two or three notes, singing up and down: *do, re, mi, re, do*. Gradually add further notes as you get comfortable.

Be sure to move your hand up and down as you make the signs, to show the rise and fall in note pitch that way too. In subsequent diagrams, for the sake of space we won't necessarily arrange them vertically like in the one above—but hand signs should always involve this vertical movement too.

Andrew Says...

To me, solfa isn't just a scale—it's a matrix of pitches.

Think of a family, a rather large family with seven members. Each one is a distinct individual within the family. We can line them up from oldest to youngest, like a musical scale, but through the day they all interrelate in a matrix of complex patterns, depending on their unique personalities and their role in the family.

Most importantly, each one is always himself or herself.

When one takes center stage—perhaps through a birthday party, meal preparation, or a graduation—the matrix of relationships re-forms around them, establishing a different family "mode" of being. They all keep their names and identities, even if one is in the spotlight.

When we name our pitches with solfa syllables, we access this same natural truth about the family matrix of pitches and their musical relationships.

Seven syllables and signs may seem like a lot to take in at once—but on the other hand, imagine how much music will unlock for you once you master just these seven notes!

You actually don't need to master the entire scale at once though. In fact, what we recommend aiming for first is just five of those seven notes: the ones which form a *major pentatonic* scale.

Start With Aiming For The Pentatonic Scale

There are varying opinions about the best sequencing to gradually familiarise yourself with the seven solfa notes (and beyond). With children, the most widely-used traditional Kodály approach starts with *so* and *mi*, since that combination (an interval of a Minor Third) commonly appears in children's rhymes and has been found to be relatively easy for young children to mimic. From there it's common to add *la*, and then move on to *do, re, mi* and later *fa* and *ti*.

With adults, especially those who have had some musical training, we have found that starting with *do, re* and *mi* is easy and feels natural. If you've spent a lot of time playing major scales, for example, that sound of the start of an ascending major scale (i.e. *do, re, mi*) will be very familiar. It also has the advantage of immediately including the tonic note, something which is left a bit fuzzier for longer in the traditional approach with children. Whether this matters from an aural perspective is debatable, but for the adult learner who intellectually understands the idea of "the tonic", we've found it's more rewarding to start from a set of notes which includes it.

Where to go from there? One option would be to continue up the scale, with *fa* and *so*. However, there's another five-note option which is actually more useful and effective, which is to complete the *pentatonic* scale by adding *so* and *la*.

This major pentatonic scale, corresponding to the first, second, third, fifth and sixth notes of the major scale, is ubiquitous in Western music. Across a startling variety of independently-arising musical cultures around the world, the same pentatonic pattern has emerged, featuring in a wide range of folk music traditions. These have then formed the basis of our modern genres, from Classical through rock, pop, electronic and more.

Both the major and the closely-related *minor* pentatonic are staples among lead guitarists when soloing, and this actually gives us a hint about why the pentatonic is such an apparently-natural feature of music…

If we come back to our Pitch Ladder and Pitch Ruler and compare the notes of the major scale with those of the pentatonic scale, you might notice one significant difference:

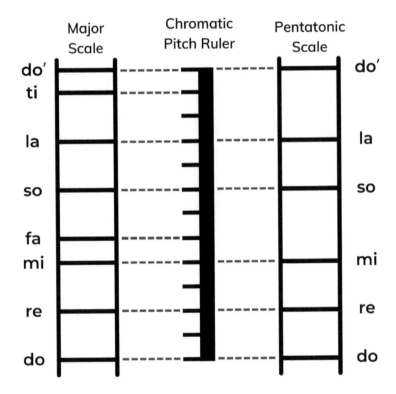

While the notes of the major scale are separated by either one or two chromatic steps, all the notes of the pentatonic are separated by at least two. As we'll discover in the next chapter on Intervals, notes separated by just one chromatic step (the interval of a "Minor Second") have a particularly *dissonant* sound (meaning harsh, clashing, uncomfortable) when played together.

The result is that the pentatonic scale has no dissonant note combinations. Every pair of notes sounds good together, and you can freely wander around a pentatonic scale when improvising, knowing that you'll never hit a note that sounds "bad", "wrong" or uncomfortable.

This combination of features—that it's a "skeleton" inside the full major scale, that a large amount of music only uses the pentatonic scale, and that all the notes "sound good"—make it the ideal choice for learning Solfa. We can draw on a large library of music (both traditional folk tunes and modern songs) which use it. It's easy, fun and feels "safe" to experiment creatively with it. And it isn't a distraction from learning the full major scale—it's a stepping stone towards it.

Once you've got the hang of Solfa with the pentatonic scale, simply adding *fa* and *ti* to your skillset can be done quickly, and with the added benefit that since those are the notes of the major scale which tend to "stick out" most, it's relatively easy to start spotting them and getting the hang of recognising them too.

Step 1: *drm*

As mentioned above, we've found that *do, re,* and *mi* are a good place for adults to get started with Solfa.

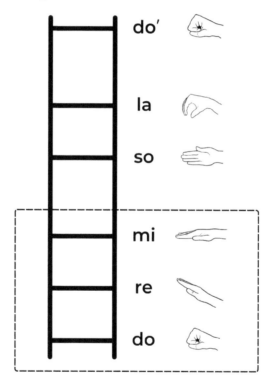

You can begin familiarising yourself with these three scale degrees using the Basic Drill (as outlined above) as well as either or both of the following:

EXERCISE: Sing The Toneset

- Choose a note in your comfortable singing range to be your tonic, do. Play the note, and sing it back as "do".

- Play up and down the scale formed by the toneset. With the drm toneset, these are the first three notes of the major scale, so you may well know immediately how to play them in various keys on your instrument. If not, it's helpful to know that the three notes are each two chromatic steps apart, allowing you to easily figure out what re and mi would be for any given do.

- Sing the corresponding Solfa. With our drm toneset it's a 3-note scale which we would sing up and down as: do re mi re do. Don't forget to use Hand Signs! As you get started, you might like to check your pitching using an instrument, and check your hand signs in a mirror or by video-recording your practice.

- Choose a new note as your tonic and repeat.

- As you progress, you can try skipping step 2—so playing just the do as your prompt, and producing the re and mi entirely by ear.

EXERCISE: Sing Solfa Songs Which Use The Toneset

At this end of this chapter you'll find a set of Starter Songs, grouped by the toneset they use.

1. Select a song from the appropriate toneset group (so for now, the *drm* toneset) and practice singing through it, using the lyrics. You may like to refer to the audio recording provided in the *Additional Resources* to learn the melody to begin with.

2. Now sing the song using its solfa syllables, with Hand Signs.

Use these three—the Basic Drill, singing the toneset, and singing songs in solfa—to begin to familiarise yourself with the characteristic sounds of *do, re* and *mi*. You can also start to make use of all the "Additional Exercises And Activities" covered at the end of the chapter.

The main thing to focus on at first is the feeling of "coming back home" to *do*, and how *re* and *mi* each sound in relation to *do*. Words fail in describing the character and role of each note—it's something you'll find comes more instinctively and subconsciously as you practice. As a suggestion though you can listen for how *re* sounds a bit unstable or unresolved, creating a sense of tension that makes you want to return to *do*, while *mi* is a bit more stable but floats above *do*, recognisably "not home".

As mentioned above in my story about the workshop (where attendees found it surprisingly easy to identify *do* vs. *re* vs. *mi*) when you've just heard the three notes played, you probably won't find it hard to identify each, just relying on your musical memory of which pitches match. As you practice, that "template" for the three scale degrees' pitches will become more internalised and instinctive.

One of the additional exercises introduced below is worth mentioning sooner rather than later, which is to improvise your own melodies. This can flow very naturally from singing up and down the 3-note scale—simply experiment with moving through the notes differently. For example, sing *do re mi re mi re do*, or it could be *do mi re mi do*. You can also repeat notes e.g. *do do re do re re mi*. This is a fun, creative, and highly effective way to really ingrain each of the solfa notes in your musical mind.

One of my favourite things about the *drm* toneset is that it provides one widely-usable bit of "musical vocabulary": a considerable number of songs and pieces will use the sequence *mi, re, do* to finish a phrase or even the whole piece. Spend a few days singing *Hot Cross Buns* as suggested below, and you'll likely start hearing this little sequence jumping out at you all over the place! And suddenly you have a little three-note phrase you can always play by ear, transcribe, or improvise with.

Now is a great time to start singing songs in Solfa! You'll find some recommendations for songs which use only the *drm* toneset at the end of the chapter.

Step 2: Add *so*

Once you have a firm grip on the *drm* toneset, you can introduce *so!*

The good news: *so* is a leap in pitch from *mi*, so tends to stick out as being noticeably higher than the *do, re* and *mi*. The bad news: that can also make it more challenging to produce the right pitch yourself!

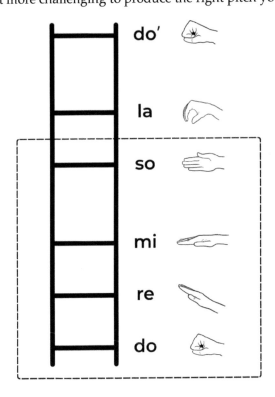

As you practice with Hand Signs, remember that they are intended to show the highness / lowness of the pitch by the height of your hand, as well as indicating its identity with the particular hand shape. So as you move from *mi* to *so*, you'll want to leave more of a "gap" than when you move from *do* to *re* or *re* to *mi*, to reflect the structure on the Pitch Ladder.

One very helpful reference for many musicians will be the arpeggio of the major scale: *do mi so*. You can usefully practice this pattern as well as the whole *drms* toneset, which will get you more comfortable with those "skips", and use it as a mental reference for finding *so*. We'll talk more later in the chapter about the technique of audiating in-between notes, but for now the tip is simply that if you have a sense of your *do* and want to pitch *so*, you can audiate the arpeggio pattern *do mi so* in your head, which may well be easier than trying to leap to *so* in one bound.

You can practice with introducing *so* using the same exercises mentioned above for *drm*, and all the other exercises and activities introduced later in the chapter.

Something interesting about introducing *so* is that we actually have two options: we can introduce the *so* above *do*, or we can instead (or as well) introduce the *so* below *do*, written with a comma after: *so,* Many songs will actually use the *so, do re mi* toneset rather than the *do re mi so* toneset.

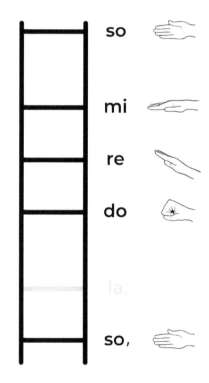

As you'll learn in *Chapter Eleven: Chords and Progressions*, the fifth scale degree *so* plays a pivotal role in both the structure of common chords, and the most commonly-used chords in progressions. With the *drms* toneset you are also getting familiar with two common intervals: the Major 3rd (between *do* and *mi*) and the Minor 3rd (between *mi* and *so*)

which also feature widely in scales, melodies, and chords.

Continue practicing by singing songs in Solfa. You'll find recommendations for songs which use only the *drms* toneset at the end of the chapter.

Step 3: Add l (+ d′)

Once you're comfortable with the *drms* toneset, you can introduce *la*. This is a step above *so*, creating the following structure of three notes together, then a gap, then two notes together:

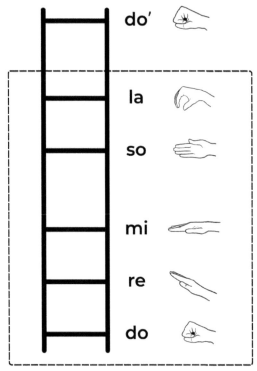

You can use the same practice exercises again: the Basic Drill, Singing The Toneset, and Singing Solfa Songs Which Use the Toneset.

Remember that with the Hand Signs you'll want to move your hand up and down to reflect the smaller gaps between *do, re* and *mi*, and between *so* and *la*, and the larger gap from *mi* to *so*. Spoiler alert: in the future, that's where you'll slot in *fa!*

As with *so*, you can also introduce the "low la", meaning the *la* below *do*, written *la,*

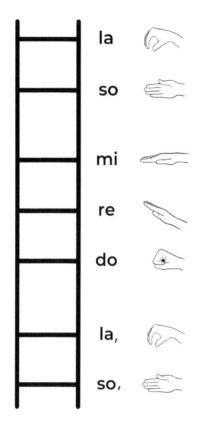

Side Note:

This can be an easy gateway to exploring minor tonality in Solfa: using the toneset *la, do re mi so la* produces the minor pentatonic scale, so simply using the same notes but putting your emphasis on *la*, rather than *do*, you'll start to hear the minor flavour created. Begin by just getting very comfortable moving from *do* to that low *la*,

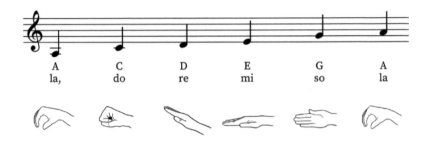

Play around with melodies using *do re* and *mi* and then move down to *la,* and finish phrases on the *la,* rather than the *do* . Listen for how things start to feel and sound darker and more mysterious. More on this below!

Now is also a great time to add the high *do*: *do re mi so la do'*, completing the pentatonic scale!

You now have a wide range of possibilities to explore with improvisation activities, especially when incorporating the low *so* and low *la*, or exploring those minor, *la*-based melodies.

And don't forget to keep singing solfa songs! Once you reach the full pentatonic scale in your Solfa practice, there is a great wealth of songs to choose from. You'll find recommendations for pentatonic songs at the end of the chapter, as well as pointers on where to find even more.

Going Further

The Full Major Scale

As soon as you're comfortable with the major pentatonic, the full major scale is within reach! You've now seen on the Pitch Ladder what we mentioned earlier—that the pentatonic exists within the major scale—and have hopefully also experienced how the notes of the pentatonic all "play nice" together.

If we return to the Pitch Ladder for the full major scale...

... you can see that it's just *fa* and *ti* which you haven't yet become familiar with. These are the two notes which have just a Half Step between them and an adjacent note in the scale, and this means they both tend to "stick out" a bit, compared to the notes of the pentatonic.

As you begin to introduce *fa* and/or *ti* to your Solfa practice, you will likely find them relatively easy to get the hang of. Not only can you add them one at a time to the pentatonic toneset you're now well familiar with, their distinctive sound which "sticks out" from the comfortable pentatonic context you're used to will make them easy to spot and to sing.

You can use the exercises above, as well as those in the "Additional Exercises and Activities" section below, to introduce each of the two notes.

If you have any difficulty, remember Convergent Learning and The 80% Rule. In particular, you can always restrict the toneset further. For example, if adding *fa* to the pentatonic feels like too much to handle, you can spend some time with just *do re mi fa*. Or if adding *ti* is getting you in a muddle, going down to the low *ti* can help you tune your ear in—for example with the *ti, do re mi* toneset. Using various tonesets like this will help you get a feel for the relationships between various combinations of the solfa notes, and building up to the full major scale will become much easier.

Accidentals

A popular misconception about Solfa is that it's only suitable for the major scale, and can't handle music featuring accidentals[5]. As a result it seems suitable for "basic" music such as folk songs, but not appropriate for genres such as jazz where accidentals are common.

In fact, Solfa can handle accidentals quite easily, and in a way which is fully aligned with the overall system. To indicate a note has been raised or lowered from the default scale degree pitch, we simply modify the syllable sung:

---

[5] Meaning: when a note is raised or lowered from the pitch which belongs in the scale. For example if an F♯ appears in a melody in the key of C Major. The "F" note in C Major is F natural, and so the sharp F is an out-of-key note, called an "accidental".

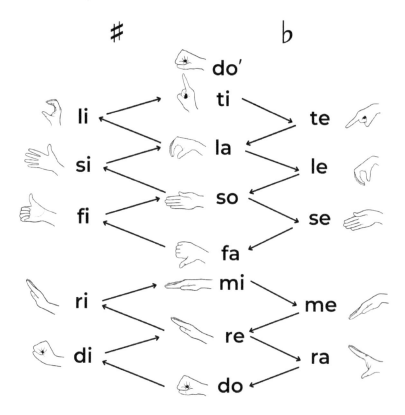

This is elegant because we are still conveying the musical meaning of the note (its place in the scale), and so all of the aural advantages of using Solfa (i.e. the correspondence to our sense of Relative Pitch) still apply.

We won't be focusing on accidentals in this chapter, since for most musicians getting up to speed with the pentatonic or the full major scale will be a huge leap forwards! However it's good to be aware of the system, so that you can draw on it as needed when you bring your Solfa skills to real music. Simply refer to the table above. If you want to get more fluent with them, singing up and down the chromatic scale (perhaps with sharps on the way up, flats on the way down) including hand signs is a great core exercise to work with.

Minor Keys and Scales

If you have some musical experience, you've probably been

wondering already whether Solfa can be used for minor keys as well. There are two approaches which can be used.

The first approach is to simply use the accidentals defined above, to modify the notes as required to make the key's scale minor. Specifically, flattening the third (*mi* becomes *me*), sixth (*la* becomes *le*) and the seventh (*ti* becomes *te*). This works fine and is neat for showing the difference between major and minor, but it's a little cumbersome and there is a different approach which is actually a better fit for the strengths of Solfa.

In the prior chapter we defined a Key as "a set of note pitches, with one chosen as the tonic". The major key and its scale are created when we choose a set of note pitches and a tonic which produce a particular sequence of intervals (W-W-H-W-W-W-H where "W" indicates a Whole Step and "H" a Half Step). These correspond to the *do-re-mi-fa-so-la-ti-do'* sequence we've been using so far.

If we use that same set of notes but select a different one to be the tonic, this is called a *mode* of the major key. There are seven modes in total, since we can start from any one of the seven pitches.

We introduced Solfa above based on the major scale (which is named the *Ionian* mode). In fact, Solfa doesn't have any inherent preference for which note is the tonic.

To use Solfa in a different mode, we needn't rename our notes. We simply choose a different Solfa syllable as our tonic. For example, you might be familiar with the *Dorian* mode based on the second degree of the major scale—we would simply treat *re* as being our tonic.

The huge advantage here is that although some familiarisation is necessary for each mode, the bulk of the work we do in Solfa Ear Training transfers naturally from one mode to the next. In particular the distinctive character of each note (and hence your ability to recognise them by ear) carries across directly.

So what's the significance of all this to minor keys and scales? Well, the minor key and its corresponding scale (the "natural minor" scale) is actually the *Aeolian* mode of the major scale, created by selecting the sixth degree of the major scale as the tonic.

You can therefore sing a natural minor scale in Solfa as:

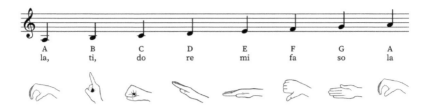

We call this "La-based minor" in Solfa, indicating that we're handling the tonality not by keeping our tonic as *do* and adding accidentals, but instead simply rooting everything on *la*.

Again, the big advantage is that the same Ear Training can power both skill sets. Once you're comfortable singing, say, a major pentatonic (*do re mi so la do'*) it takes very little practice to be able to sing a minor pentatonic (*la do re mi so la'*). And likewise for recognising notes from the minor scale—once you've got the hang of Solfa in major, extending to that different mode tends to come quickly, and in our experience much easier than by sprinkling in accidentals.

The thing to keep in mind is the "Descriptive" mindset for music theory (see *Chapter One: Musicality*). If we took a "Prescriptive" approach, then it seems sensible to add accidentals: *"We make a minor scale from a major scale by lowering these scale degrees by a half step."* However, if we look at how the music actually works, and why people began using the minor key, and what's going on when they write or play music in other modes, under the hood what's happening is the selection of a different tonic note from the same set of note pitches. That's why it makes sense and why it benefits us so much to use a naming approach and Ear Training process which reflects that.

Additional Exercises and Activities

Now that you're familiar with how Solfa works, let's look at some ways you can start practicing with Solfa, and developing your ability to both produce and recognise notes using Solfa.

Solfa Practice

Here are some exercises which we've found particularly effective, for daily development and reinforcement of Solfa skills. With all of these, you can use any toneset you like. Your goal may be the full major scale, but starting out with just *do, re, mi* and gradually extending to the pentatonic and beyond will help ensure you don't get overwhelmed or frustrated unnecessarily.

You can watch a video demonstration of each of these exercises taken from inside *Living Music* in the *Additional Resources*.

EXERCISE: Sing Solfa Scales

As we've already explored in earlier exercises, simply singing up and down the scale with solfa syllables is an important foundation for Solfa Ear Training.

1. Choose a note in your comfortable singing range as your tonic, *do*.

2. (Optionally) Play up and down the scale to demonstrate it for yourself.

3. Sing up and then down the scale using solfa syllables.

This could begin with just the *drm* toneset: *do re mi re do.* Then build to:

- the pentatonic (do re mi so la do la so mi re do) as recommended above
- the minor pentatonic (la, do re mi so la so mi re do la,)
- the pentascale (do re mi fa so fa mi re do)
- the full major scale (do re mi fa so la ti do' ti la so fa mi re do)
- the full natural minor scale (la, ti, do re mi fa so la so fa mi re do ti, la,)

While it may seem like this isn't "testing" your ear in the way other Ear Training exercises do, in fact by requiring yourself to produce the right pitches for each solfa syllable, you are implicitly training your ear to know how they should sound.

This is even more powerful if you add hand signs, or introduce the variations below, which can all usefully be begun by singing up and down the scale you've chosen to use for them.

Once you're comfortable singing up and down a given scale in stepwise motion (i.e. no notes skipped), you can try the following exercise:

EXERCISE: Audiate the In-Between "Stepping Stone" Notes

This is both a useful practical technique and a standalone practice exercise. For a scale you can comfortably sing in Solfa step-by-step, try picking certain notes to omit. When you get to that note, instead of singing it, audiate it (imagine it in your mind's ear—see *Chapter Three: Audiation* for more).

This is a fantastic stepping stone to being able to jump around the scale from any note to any other. It's also a really handy technique when you're using Solfa to play by ear or transcribe, since in the context of a given melody, you might not immediately recognise a note —but if you can sing up in your mind from *do* to that note's pitch, you have an easy way to identify it in two steps.

If you're practicing with hand signs, you can still make the sign for the audiated note—and in fact, this is a great showcase for the power of Hand Signs, as you'll start to find that physical "cue" of making the right hand sign helps you start jumping straight to the note you need.

If you want a great, fun, and creative way to really get intimately familiar with the solfa notes, look no further than the next exercise. This is probably my favourite solfa practice exercise, and the one which had the biggest impact for me as I learned Solfa.

EXERCISE: Improvise Melodies in Solfa

1. Choose a note in your comfortable singing range as your tonic, *do* and start by singing up and down your chosen Solfa scale. For example, the pentatonic: *do, re, mi, so, la, so, mi, re, do.*

2. Now take a walk! Just wander up and down the scale. You've anchored the sound of each note (and hopefully the hand sign too) by establishing the scale. Now practice going up and

down in stepwise motion, changing direction randomly.

3.   As you get comfortable, start leveraging the technique from "Audiate the In-Between 'Stepping Stone' Notes" by audiating some notes so that you can introduce "skips". Soon you'll be able to skip around to your heart's content without needing that Audiation step.

If you enjoy this exercise, here is a more advanced version:

EXERCISE: Sing "One of Everything" Melodies in Solfa

•   Follow exactly the same steps as before... but with the constraint that you must use each note of the toneset once— and only once!

For example, if you're using the minor pentatonic (*la do re mi so la'*) you might improvise any of the following melodies:

la mi re do so la'

la' do so re mi la

mi re do la la' so

As you can imagine, this really puts your skills to the test! But the lovely thing about it is that it's up to you how ambitious to be. You can begin with mostly stepwise motion, and you can take your time to decide each next note (e.g. to audiate the "stepping stone" notes as in the previous exercise).

The next exercise is a trickier one, but very powerful. As you're aware by now, Solfa is all about relating things to the tonic. For most musicians, most of the time, the music will be in a major key and that tonic is going to be *do*. You therefore get a lot of "bang for your buck" by really practicing the relationships of each note to *do*.

EXERCISE: Sing Each Interval From *do*

1.   Choose a note in your comfortable singing range as your tonic,

do.

2.   Now sing up from *do* to each note of the toneset in turn e.g. *do re... do mi... do fa...* and so on.

3.   Then repeat from the top *do'* down to each note: *do' ti... do' la... do' so...* and so on.

Remember that you don't need to start with the full major scale! You might begin practicing this exercise with just *do, re* and *mi*, and including the repeated *do* for completeness: *do do... do re... do mi... do re... do do...*

If you're a comfortable singer then this should be "so simple you cannot fail". If you do find it tricky, use an instrument to play the notes along with your singing for reference and/or use the audiation technique from #2 to help with the skips.

Zac Says...

I like to call this "solfa pivots" and find that it's very powerful to do from all notes in a toneset, and then add more notes to the toneset.

For example:

dd dr dm
rr rd rm
mm mr md

Once that's comfortable, add in so or fa, and do all the "pivots" again.

For bonus points (and to help you start making connections to the Intervals approach we'll cover in the next chapter) you might like to sing the Solfa, then sing the corresponding interval name:

EXERCISE: Sing And Name Each Interval From *do*

1.   Choose a note in your comfortable singing range to be your tonic, *do*.

2.   As before, sing to each note in the toneset from *do* in turn using the solfa syllables, but then follow it up by singing one part of the corresponding interval name on each of the two notes e.g. sing *"major"* on the pitch of *do* and *"second"* on the pitch of *re)*.

3.   Repeat for the intervals coming down from the top, *do'*

_____

For the major pentatonic toneset, going up from *do* you would sing:
do re, major second
do mi, major third
do so, perfect fifth
do la, major sixth
do do', perfect octave

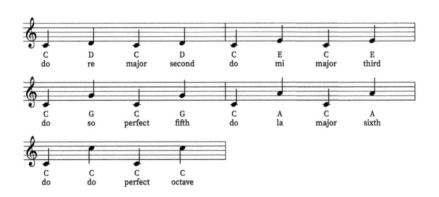

And coming down from *do'* you would sing:
do' la, minor third
do' so, perfect fourth
do' mi, minor sixth
do' re, minor seventh
do' do, perfect octave

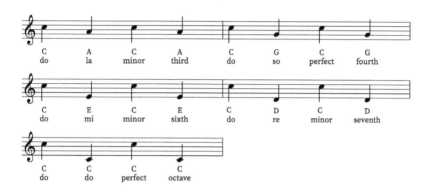

Once you're comfortable going up from *do* and down from high *do'* like that, it can be helpful to mix the two by singing the inversion pairs:

do re, major second, do' re, minor seventh
  do mi, major third, do' mi, minor sixth
  do so, perfect fifth, do' so, perfect fourth
  do la, major sixth, do' la, minor third
  do do', perfect octave, do' do, perfect octave

e.g.

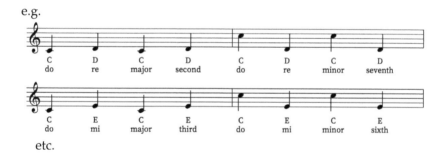

etc.

Naturally you can extend this to the full major scale too:
  do re, major second, do' re, minor seventh
  do mi, major third, do' mi, minor sixth
  do fa, perfect fourth, do' fa, perfect fifth
  do so, perfect fifth, do' so, perfect fourth
  do la, major sixth, do' la, minor third
  do ti, major seventh, do' ti, minor second
  do do', perfect octave, do' do, perfect octave

This can be a real challenge, and you may want an instrument handy to check your pitching to begin with, but it is an extremely effective way to internalise the links between Solfa and Intervals within the scale.

Sing Solfa Songs

One key tenet of the Kodály approach was what we can call "Song-based learning". Although Zoltán Kodály made use of "exercises", even those were carefully composed to be *musical*, not just abstract series of notes. He was also philosophically very determined that all musical learning should be based on music, and specifically the folk music of the student's culture.

I would encourage you to use a range of approaches to develop your Solfa skills, including the applied activities below and dedicated "drills" above, but if you're putting together a practice routine for Solfa, singing a handful of songs with the solfa syllables should almost certainly be a part of it. In fact, if I had to pick just one way for you to practice, it would be singing songs in solfa.

On top of the inherent benefit, if you make this a daily habit, you will quickly find yourself instinctively wanting to figure out and sing the solfa for other melodies you hear or play. It's as much a mindset as it is a habit. Form the habit, and the mindset will follow.

The process is very straight-forward, just an expansion of the earlier exercise "Sing Solfa Songs Which Use The Toneset":

EXERCISE: Sing Solfa Songs

1.   Choose a simple song

2.   Look up or figure out the corresponding solfa

3.   Sing the song, using the solfa syllables instead of the lyrics

That's it! Just doing this regularly, with a handful of songs, will quickly and easily build up your familiarity with the sound of each syllable, and improve your ability to pitch them on-demand.

Almut Says...

It is surprising how natural this can feel after a time. A few days ago I had set myself a timer to remind me of making a phone call. When the timer went off, I was busy doing something else and just hit "stop" and continued with what I was doing.

A bit later I had this solfa melody in my head: do do do do so mi.

I was a bit confused where this came from, sang it out loud and realised that this was my timer ringtone. I then remembered that I was supposed to make the call :)

When it comes to song choice, folk songs are often conveniently diatonic (i.e. the major scale with no accidentals, though they may be in different modes as noted above) and have the advantage of featuring idiomatic patterns, what we might refer to as "musical vocabulary". One can argue for using folk music "on principle", as many Kodály educators would, but from a purely practical perspective, there's a huge advantage in using the music which all modern music has evolved from. You don't just learn to recognise each solfa note in isolation, you get familiar with the "vocabulary" that's commonly used.

You'll find a small collection of suggested "Starter Songs" at the end of this chapter, drawn from the English and American folk heritage.

We already saw one concrete example of this when discussing the *drm* toneset: one very common pattern in music is to finish a melody with the sequence *mi re do*. This gives a satisfying "coming home" feeling, and once you practice singing some folk songs which end in that way (or, in the case of *Hot Cross Buns* or *Mary Had A Little Lamb*, feature it throughout), you'll notice yourself starting to spot it everywhere! Now you have a handy shortcut: you can recognise that "unit" of three notes in one fell swoop, any time it crops up—or indeed use it yourself, as part of Improvisation or Songwriting.

Speaking of which...

Applied Activities

If you remember our Integrated Ear Training approach, the goal is not to just do "ears" practice (Hearing) or even just "singing" practice (Hands), but to develop our instinct for pitch and rhythm through a combination of all four H's (Head, Hands, Hearing and Heart) and in a way that's always connected to real music.

So as well as singing through songs in solfa, you can practice in any or all of the ways below.

In all these cases, we can see that Solfa is useful as a "middle step" between sound and symbol, helping you figure out pitches based on the musical role they play, before then pinning things down to a particular key.

The important thing to remember is to match the activity to your current Solfa skillset, and particularly which solfa syllables you are focused on and experienced with.

Start simple (meaning short passages of music that are melodically and harmonically simple-sounding), and be prepared for "mystery notes" in case accidentals are being used, or you haven't yet familiarised yourself with the full major scale in solfa.

You can use a placeholder syllable where needed. For example, when I introduced my two young kids to Solfa we focused on *do*, *re* and *mi*. When we first tackled a song featuring *so*, we just sang *"Bob"* for that mystery note, until it was time to reveal its true name! That way we could highlight "some other note is being used there", even before we knew its name and its exact place in the scale.

This is the secret to what I mentioned in the previous chapter, that we were able to get musicians playing by ear and improvising from day one with Integrated Ear Training: restrict the note choices to begin with, and you'll be surprised just how easy playing by ear and improvising become for you! And from there it's just a matter of gradually extending the set of solfa notes you're familiar with.

Playing By Ear

Listen to a (simple!) melody line, sketch out the Pitch Contour, and identify the key. Now sing the scale in Solfa, and use that to identify each of the notes. You can use an instrument to help you at first.

Once you've got it, practice singing the melody with the solfa syllables (you might like to add this to your daily "Solfa Songs" practice!).

More on this in *Playing by Ear*, with the Play-By-Ear Process.

Transcribing

Similarly, if your goal is to write down the notes of the music you hear, you can start by identifying the key, and then use the solfa scale as a helpful indicator of which notes are most likely to be used.

Figure out the notes in Solfa first, then (if you choose) translate them to letter names to write them down in traditional notation.

Improvising

Choose a key (perhaps to match a backing track), and play the scale. Then sing it in Solfa. Now use those solfa notes as your options to improvise with.

At first this can be simply picking solfa notes somewhat at random. You might like to restrict yourself to the pentatonic scale, for the reasons discussed earlier in this chapter. You can start with "stepwise motion" meaning only moving up and down the scale note by note but choosing your next direction each time. Then introduce "skips" where you leap from one note to one which is elsewhere in the scale. The Practice exercises covered earlier will help you get comfortable with these leaps in Solfa.

More on improving in *Chapter Fifteen: Improvisation*, when we introduce the Expansive Creativity framework.

Writing Music

Just like with improvising above, you can use the solfa scale as your set of options for choosing melody notes.

This is a great way to get more familiar with the musical role of each note. Which ones sound "resolved" or like they complete a melody? Which ones stick out, or sound unstable? What can you learn about stepwise motion and "skips" by experimenting with the melodies you write?

Even if you don't (yet!) consider yourself a songwriter, composing your own solfa melodies is a fantastic way to extend the activity of "singing solfa songs", allowing you to create your own practice songs for any given toneset or sequence of solfa notes, and hone your skills in exactly the way you need, in a fun way which nurtures both your creativity and Singing skills.

We'll explore Solfa for composing further in *Chapter Sixteen: Songwriting*.

Conclusion

You now have a comprehensive understanding of how Solfa works, and a variety of ways you can begin practicing solfa singing and note recognition, and developing that instinctive sense of how each note of the scale sounds.

Start today, by selecting some of the Starter Songs below, and sing through them once or more each day. Experiment with improvising melodies in Solfa and practice some of the more "drill-like" exercises above too. Include a Solfa perspective on any Playing By Ear, Improvisation, transcribing or Songwriting activities you're doing.

As you do, keep these three tips in mind:

1. Remember, it's all about the tonic. Any time you feel lost or confused, come back to the tonic note.. That's your "home", and the more you practice going to and from that tonic, the easier it will be to handle whatever notes come along.

2. It's not "cheating" to check! Particularly as you start, it's perfectly fine to play through the scale on an instrument to check your pitching and make sure you're not getting names muddled (e.g. singing *re* on a pitch that's actually *mi*)

3. Use Hand Signs! It feels weird at first, and it can feel like "another thing to do". Please trust me when I say that the extra effort will really pay off. Your instinct for hand signs becomes a powerful counterpart to your aural instinct—but that only happens if you develop that instinct by practicing with them!

Start simple, gradually build up the set of solfa notes you're using, and I think you'll quickly find Solfa becoming an indispensable part of your musical life, like it has for so many of our members at Musical U —even those who initially thought it was "just for kids"!

Starter Songs

Here are some example songs you can use as you begin practicing with Solfa.

You'll find songs for each of the tonesets we introduced above as steps towards the pentatonic. Each song is shown with:

- Solfa syllables, and the Stick Notation for rhythm which we'll introduce in *Chapter Twelve: The Beat* and *Chapter Thirteen: Rhythm*

- Lyrics

- Traditional staff notation

Remember that although the staff shows a particular key, these songs can be sung with any note as the tonic, and you should choose one which makes it comfortable to sing within your range (see *Chapter Four: Singing* for more on that if needed).

TIP:

For practical reasons, we can include only a handful of songs for each toneset here, and ideally these would be learned by ear first rather than from written notation.

While a few well-chosen songs can go a long way in learning Solfa, and what's provided here is enough to get started with, I would highly encourage you to also check out the *Additional Resources*.

There you will find example recordings of each of these songs, as well as a larger "songbank" you can draw from for your Solfa practice.

Hot Cross Buns

(trad.)

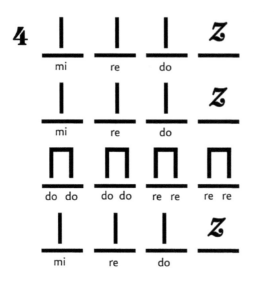

Hot Cross Buns,
Hot Cross Buns,
One-a-penny, Two-a-penny,
Hot Cross Buns.

Mary Had A Little Lamb *(trad.)*

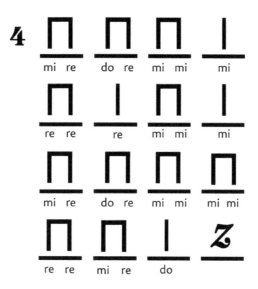

Mary had a little lamb,
little lamb, little lamb,
Mary had a little lamb,
its fleece was white as snow.

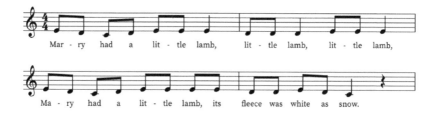

Variant of line 2 melody: *re re re mi so so*

Sailor, Sailor on the Sea   *(folk)*

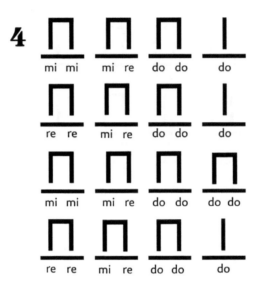

Sailor, sailor on the sea,
Sailor, sailor on the sea,
Sailor, sailor on the sea,
What treasures have you brought to me?

Note: Traditionally performed with a swung beat (see "Rhythm")

Starter Songs for *do re mi so* toneset

Bought Me A Cat

(folk)

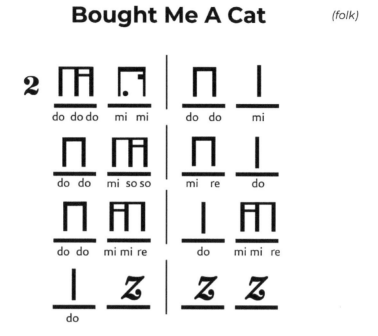

Bought me a cat, the cat pleased me,
fed my cat under yonder tree.
Cat went fiddle-i-fee, fiddle-i-fee.

Hush Little Baby

(folk)

Hush, little baby, don't say a word.
Mama's gonna buy you a mockingbird.

Rain Come Wet Me

(folk)

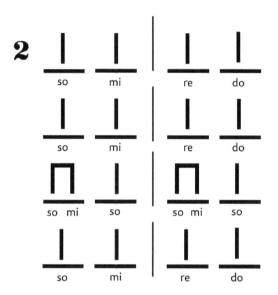

Rain come wet me,
Sun come dry me,
Keep away, pretty girl,
Don't come nigh me!

Starter Songs for *do re mi so la* toneset (major pentatonic)

Chatter With The Angels   *(folk)*

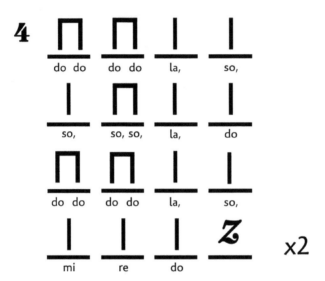

Chatter with the angels,
Soon in the morning.
Chatter with the angels,
in that land.

Chatter with the angels,
Soon in the morning.
Chatter with the angels,
join that band!

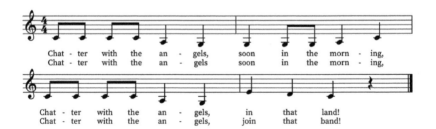

Chat - ter with the an - gels, soon in the morn - ing,
Chat - ter with the an - gels soon in the morn - ing,

Chat - ter with the an - gels, in that land!
Chat - ter with the an - gels, join that band!

Frosty Weather

(folk)

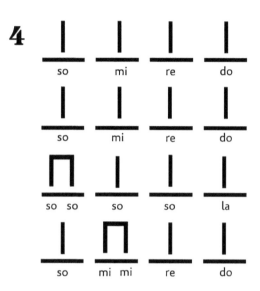

Frosty Weather,
Snowy Weather,
When the wind blows we all go together.

Rocky Mountain *(folk)*

Verse

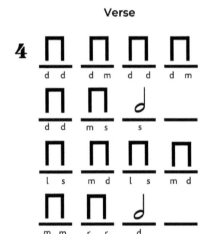

Chorus

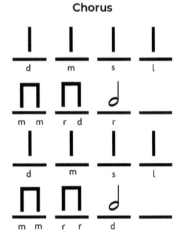

Rocky Mountain, rocky mountain,
Rocky Mountain high,
When you're on that rocky mountain,
Hang your head and cry.

Do do do do,
Do remember me.
Do do do do,
Do remember me.

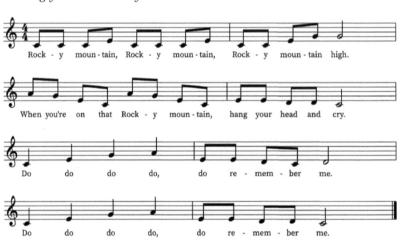

Tideo

(folk)

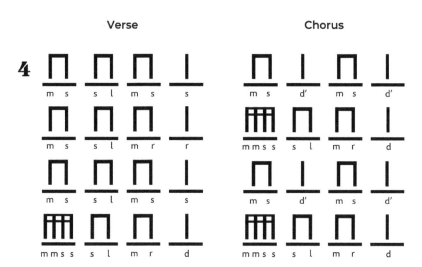

Verse

Pass one window, Tideo,
Pass two windows, Tideo,
Pass three windows, Tideo,
Jingle at the window, Tideo.

Chorus

Tideo, Tideo,
Jingle at the window, Tideo. (x2)

Pass one wind - ow, Ti - de - o, Pass two wind - ows, Ti - de - o,

Pass three wind - ows, Ti - de - o, Jing - le at the wind - ow, Ti - de - o.

Ti - de - o, Ti - de - o, Jing - le at the wind - ow, Ti - de - o.

Weevily Wheat

(folk)

A Section

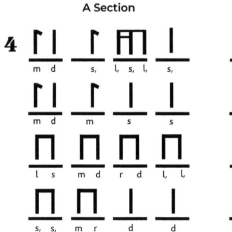

B Section

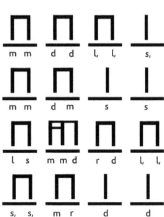

Don't want your weevily wheat,
Don't want your barley,
Take some flour in half an hour,
And bake a cake for Charlie.

Five times five is twenty-five,
Five times six is thirty,
Five times seven is thirty-five,
And five times eight is forty.

CHAPTER TEN:
INTERVALS

Intervals are often where a musician starts, when they discover Ear Training. Unfortunately, in most cases, that's also where they end up stopping! As you'll discover in this chapter, Intervals are an enormously useful building block, and a powerful way to develop your sense of Relative Pitch—but they come with certain properties which can also present major challenges to the uninitiated.

Frankly, it took us quite a while at Musical U to figure out quite where Intervals best fit in, for the average music learner eager to gain the benefits that a strong sense of Relative Pitch offers. In many ways, the approach we've settled on (which has proven to be reliably effective across a wide range of musicians who've studied with us, particularly inside the *Living Music* program) mirrors my own journey with Intervals.

When I first discovered musical Ear Training and started looking for resources to help me, the bulk of what I found focused on Intervals, and predominantly from a music theory perspective. Learning to recognise intervals provided me with a huge leap forwards in my musicality. For the first time I was able to unlock abilities like Playing By Ear and Improvisation which I had always thought beyond me.

The experience of learning interval recognition, however, made it very hard to "enjoy the journey"! Thankfully, I enjoyed the payoff enough to persist, and the early mobile apps I developed (originally created solely to help myself, before I made them available for others) made the process a bit easier and smoother. But both the learning of Intervals and the use of them still always felt like hard work.

Partly this was due to taking a brute-force "massed repetitions" approach, which (as discussed in *Chapter Six: Superlearning*) typically wastes up to 90% of your practice time. Partly, it was because I was taking a purely "Head and Hearing" approach, learning the theory and doing abstract drills and exercises. The lack of Hands (i.e. application) in particular was a big missing piece, as mentioned in *Chapter Seven: Ear Training* when we introduced Integrated Ear Training as the solution. But it was also partly due to not truly understanding the nature of Intervals, and the pros and cons as compared to taking a scale-based approach (such as Solfa).

When I discovered Solfa, I found that my existing interval skills let me progress very quickly, and enjoy the practical benefits of that approach immediately. Suddenly Playing By Ear, Improvisation, and other Relative Pitch tasks like transcribing just flowed in an easy, natural way. In the previous chapter, when I described how mind-blowing my first Kodály lesson was, a big part of what made that possible was the fact that I already had a sense of Relative Pitch which was, in a way, well-developed.

That was my first clue that Intervals and Solfa could be complementary. Up until then, we had taught them as two separate approaches. In fact, due to the heavy bias towards Intervals in all the existing Ear Training material available, we first introduced Solfa simply as a method for learning Intervals!

Over the following years, as we experimented and developed novel approaches at Musical U, we came to better understand the relationship between the two, how each is helpful in its own particular way, and how the two can be effectively combined as complementary "building blocks" you can draw on when working with Relative Pitch.

Overview

We will follow the Learn, Practice, Apply approach of Integrated

Ear Training. We'll go through these roughly in sequence in this chapter, and you will probably want to read through the chapter in order to begin with—but remember that when it comes to actually *doing* Ear Training, these three are best done as a short loop: learn a little (e.g. by re-reading part of the chapter), practice a little (doing an exercise or two from the chapter), try applying it (doing one or more of the applied activities at the end of the chapter).

Learn

In this chapter we'll first introduce you to the theory (Head) of Intervals in the sections "What Are Intervals?" and "How Intervals Work".

Practice

Then in "Getting Started", we'll show you some simple ways you can start to learn the core skill of interval recognition (Hearing and Heart).

Along the way we will also relate Intervals to Solfa, so that you can see how these two sets of building blocks can work together, and the advantages of combining both approaches. If you haven't yet read *Chapter Nine: Solfa* or started learning Solfa, don't worry if some of those bits don't make sense or use unfamiliar terms for now. You might like to circle back in future when you do add Solfa to your musical toolkit.

In the "Start With Aiming For..." section we'll suggest the most useful types of interval to focus on learning first, and introduce each in turn. Using the Basic Drill and the guidance on how to recognise intervals from the "Getting Started" section, you'll be able to start distinguishing between the most common types of interval found in music.

Apply

Finally, in the "Additional Exercises and Activities" section we'll go beyond the Basic Drill with Singing exercises and applied activities (Hands), to help you make real, practical use of your new interval recognition skills.

What Are Intervals?

In *Chapter Eight: Relative Pitch* we said that Relative Pitch is all about recognising the relationships between note pitches in music, letting you understand at a conscious level what your brain and ears already understand subconsciously about how music works.

The Solfa approach focuses on the relationship of any given note to the tonic note of the key.

With Intervals we focus on the relationship between *any* two notes. Coming back to our "Pitch Ruler" analogy[1], learning to recognise Intervals is really about calibrating and connecting with our internal ability to judge pitch distances. By learning to recognise different distances (analogous to the different numbers of centimetres marked on a ruler) we can use those building blocks to identify notes relative to any other note.

This is why my own interval skills let me progress rapidly when I started with Solfa: I already had a good ability to judge pitch distances from the tonic, as a subset of my interval skills. This is also where the advantages and disadvantages of Intervals arise…

Solfa vs. Intervals

If the power of Solfa comes from its focus on relationship to the tonic, mirroring how music itself works, then the power of Intervals comes from being independent of that—but this is a double-edged sword.

At first, intervals might seem like the most fundamental building block of music. After all, if intervals allow us to judge the pitch distance between *any* two notes, surely Solfa is just a subset of that— and we'd be better off always thinking in terms of intervals?

There is an element of truth to that. But when's the last time you listened to music that had just two notes? :) Even the simplest music we listen to every day features melodies and harmonies comprised of many notes, and our brains are always seeking to put the musical sounds that we hear in context. As soon as we hear a note, we're subconsciously and instinctively listening for the notes that come before it, after it, and around it, to construct mental models of our musical experience.

---

[1] See "The Relative Pitch Solution" in *Chapter Ten: Intervals*.

This is why traditional Ear Training for Intervals so quickly becomes challenging and frustrating for musicians, and why it's possible to get very good at recognising intervals during an Ear Training exercise or to ace the quiz in an app, but still struggle to actually do anything useful with that in our musical lives.

If you only focus on Intervals, what you quickly discover is that when faced with a real piece of music, you essentially need to *de-contextualise* a pair of notes in order to recognise them. This takes quite a bit of mental effort, as our brains are naturally seeking for ways to make sense of all the sounds together as a stream of music (i.e. a musical *context*).

To give a concrete example: you might get very proficient at distinguishing the types of interval called a Major Third and a Minor Third, and never confuse them during Ear Training practice. But in a real musical context, a Major Third above the tonic sounds quite different to a Major Third above the second note of the scale! So if you're trying to play a melody by ear, or improvise using those Major and Minor Thirds, you can quickly get confused and struggle.

The result is that a musician who has focused solely on Intervals will often find even simple, slow melodies move too quickly for them to "think through" all the intervals they're hearing. This problem is compounded if they are relying on the popular "reference songs" method for recognising intervals, which we'll discuss below.

It is possible to get to a usable skill level with Intervals, by practicing to the point where you don't need to consciously think through recognising each one, and instead rely on your now-instinctive "Pitch Ruler". But it's a long and slow-going journey to get there.

"Alright," you might be thinking, *"we should just use Solfa then?"* Well, as mentioned above, this independence of Intervals from context isn't just a disadvantage—it can also be an advantage.

Not only can interval Ear Training accelerate your mastery of Solfa (through the power of Convergent Learning), it also provides liberation from the scale. In the previous chapter we discussed chromatic Solfa for handling accidentals, which is one way to handle notes which lie outside the scale. But Intervals provide a powerful way to handle this too.

For example, supposing you're working out a melody by ear and most of the notes are comfortably jumping out to you as their solfa note names, but then there's one which falls between *re* and *mi*. If you've mastered chromatic solfa you might be able to recognise this as *me*, but if you've been learning Intervals you might also easily spot that it's a Minor Second above the *re* you already recognised. In fact, this is typically how a Solfa-focused musician will handle chromatic notes. They may label them with the corresponding solfa name, but rather than learning to recognise all the chromatic scale degrees directly, they'll rely on hearing *"it's a bit above/below that Solfa note I know well, so it must be..."*, essentially recognising the interval of a Minor Second, even if they're not thinking in those terms. A strong ability with Intervals lets you handle all kinds of leaps in pitch which go outside the scale, in a direct way.

Intervals can also unlock greater creativity, as you'll discover in some of the suggested exercises in this chapter. If Solfa is powerful because it matches "the way music normally works" then you can probably see how fascinating it can be to experiment with improvising or writing music using Intervals, which don't necessarily obey those conventions at all!

These two advantages—accelerating your Relative Pitch skill development through Convergent Learning, and providing a versatile way to handle notes beyond the comfortable Solfa framework—make Intervals a valuable addition to your Relative Pitch toolkit.

How Intervals Work

An *interval* is simply the distance in pitch between two notes. Since the pitches we use in music aren't completely arbitrary, there is a finite number of distances we're likely to hear.

A note's pitch might vary, for example if the musician slides up to or down to the note's notional pitch, or applies *vibrato* to waver the pitch up and down around the note's pitch. Even then though, the note has a single specific pitch associated with it. In traditional score notation we'd show this by its vertical position on the staff. In guitar tablature it would be indicated by the string and fret number to be played.

Similarly, one can technically use various tunings other than concert-standard "A440", changing the pitches of all the notes being used—but even then we still identify a finite set of note pitches to be used in the music.

This means that within an octave (from one named note to the same-named note in a higher register, such as from Middle C to the next C above it) there are just 13 note pitches, and 13 possible distances within that range. We measure these in Half Steps, also known as Semitones or Minor Seconds. The diagram below shows those 13 units marked on a vertical line on the right, and the 13 possible distances (from 0 Half Steps through to 12) with brackets on the left:

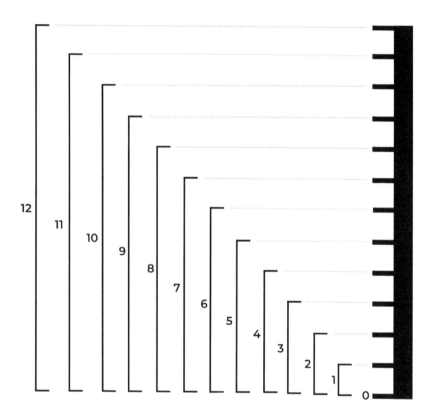

These different distances are our building blocks in the Intervals approach. Naturally it is possible to jump further than an octave in a single leap, but it's relatively rare that you'd need to handle that by recognising that as a single interval. In practice, as we'll see in "Compound Intervals" below, you would use your recognition skills for the same distances shown above, and note that you've also jumped up or down an octave.

Forms of Intervals

Since an interval is a pair of notes, there are three possible *forms* of an interval:

- Ascending (the second note is higher in pitch)

- Descending (the second note is lower in pitch)

- Harmonic (the two notes are played at the same time)

As a shorthand we can refer to both ascending and descending intervals as "melodic". So if we say an interval is *melodic* it means the two notes are sounded one after the other, and if we say it's *harmonic* it means the two notes are sounded together[2].

Whatever the form of the interval, we refer to the lower-pitch note of the pair as the *root* note of the interval.

Types of Intervals

The pitch distances shown in the diagram above above constitutes our set of building blocks, but it proves useful to also give them names.

The names of the different "types" of interval are simply a shorthand for different pitch distances. For reasons relating to the underlying music theory, instead of saying "this note is 1 unit of pitch from that one", "that interval is 3 units of pitch", etc. we actually name intervals according to two characteristics: *degree* and *quality*.

The degree is a simple numbering from one to seven, for the seven distinct notes in a major or minor scale which spans an octave.

The quality of an interval is a word, most commonly "major", "minor" or "perfect", but can also be "augmented" or "diminished".

The combination of these two characteristics results in interval type names like "Major Third", "Perfect Fifth", "Augmented Fourth", "Diminished Seventh", and so on.

---

[2] Note this doesn't necessarily imply a connection to a melody or to harmony, in the broader musical context.

While we will most often use melodic intervals when dealing with melodies, and harmonic intervals when dealing with chords, the terms "melodic" and "harmonic" refer purely to whether the two notes are played together, or successively.

We might, for example, sing melodic intervals when analysing a chord to identify the intervals present. Or we might sing the tonic note while hearing a melody, and use our harmonic interval recognition skills to identify the melody notes based on the harmonic interval we're creating between them and the tonic.

So the terms stem from "melodic intervals create a two-note melody, and harmonic intervals create a two-note harmony" rather than "melodic intervals belong to a melody and harmonic intervals belong to harmonies".

This way of naming intervals brings some of the advantages of relating things to the scale, without tying us to it:

- The quality names are helpful as a way of grouping similar-sounding intervals.

- There is some connection between "major" intervals and "major" keys, scales and chords, and between "minor" intervals and "minor" keys, scales and chords. We'll explore this a bit more as we continue. It's not a direct correspondence, so it's best just to see this as a connection rather than an equivalence, and also a hint that the sounds of intervals with those qualities may be reminiscent of the sounds of the keys, scales and chords with those qualities.

- Strictly speaking, you can think of "major" indicating the larger of the two types of interval for a given degree, and "minor" indicating the smaller (e.g. Minor 2nds are smaller distances than Major 2nds). We'll explore this (as well as "augmented" and "diminished") more below.

- The "Perfect" quality gets its name from the frequency ratios of the pitches, which for Perfect intervals are all neat, exact mathematical ratios. It's not a coincidence that these intervals all have a particularly broad and resonant sound.

On first encounter, the names of different types of Intervals can seem intimidating, overwhelming, and even arbitrary. Remember that *"a rose by any other name would smell as sweet"*, and fundamentally intervals are defined by the distances in pitch. The names are just a shorthand which proves convenient and meaningful in various ways. Also keep in mind our general rule-of-thumb with Ear Training, which is to start small. You needn't learn or memorise all the names, nor learn to recognise the corresponding intervals by ear, all at once! We'll provide specific guidance in this chapter on getting started.

Below is the full list of names for the most common interval types you'll encounter. The number is how many "pitch units" each one represents. These units are known as "semitones", "half steps" or "minor seconds", or as we'll use below "chromatic steps".

Some intervals have different names in different countries or traditions—choose whichever you prefer or is familiar. Some actually have multiple names from a music theory perspective (for example the Tri-Tone can also be referred to as an "Augmented Fourth" or "Diminished Fifth") but for recognition and listening skills you don't need to worry about that.

We'll also list the abbreviation we use for each in brackets after the name.

Here are the most common interval types:

0.   Unison (U)

1.   Minor Second (m2) a.k.a. Semitone (ST) or Half Step (HS)

2.   Major Second (M2) a.k.a. Tone (T) or Whole Step (WS)

3.   Minor Third (m3)

4.   Major Third (M3)

5.   Perfect Fourth (P4)

6.   Tri-Tone (TT) a.k.a. Augmented Fourth (A4) or Diminished Fifth (d5)

7.   Perfect Fifth (P5)

8.   Minor Sixth (m6)

9.   Major Sixth (M6)

10.   Minor Seventh (m7)

11.   Major Seventh (M7)

12.   Perfect Octave (P8)

With Perfect Unison and Perfect Octave it is common practice to omit the word "Perfect" and call them simply "Unison" and "Octave", because it can be safely assumed that Intervals of these degrees have that particular quality only. You'll also find this done with other interval types where either the "Perfect" is implicit because the other forms are so unusual (Fourths and Fifths), or where the Major/Minor quality is unimportant or ambiguous (for example talking about a melody "moving in Thirds", or building chords by "stacking Thirds").

There's a lot of music theory behind intervals. You can go deep into where they come from, how they relate to keys, scales, chords, and progressions, how to invert intervals, how intervals are used in harmony, composing and arranging, and so on.

One common rabbit-hole is worrying about the "spelling" of intervals. For example, trying to memorise that a Perfect Fifth above a C is a G, and a Major Third below a C is an A ♭, how to work out the interval name from a pair of note names etc.

This is a useful skill at times, particularly if you're working a lot with traditional notation (e.g. trying to sight read music in choir, or transcribe based on intervals). However, don't make the mistake of feeling you need to memorise the spelling of every interval in every key to progress with interval recognition.

With the approach we recommend, of working in Relative Pitch and "translating" to/from a particular key, you don't need to learn any further theory to start benefitting from Intervals. For now, just learn the names of each interval type listed above (which you can do gradually as you start practicing with limited numbers of the types).

Interval Spelling

If you do want to dive into the "spelling" of Intervals, you'll find two guides in the *Additional Resources* which will get you up to speed and provide you with several helpful shortcuts.

Intervals and The Pitch Ruler

Up until now, we've used the analogy of a mental "Pitch Ruler" as a way of understanding how our sense of Relative Pitch (and corresponding Ear Training) work. Just like we did when introducing the Pitch Ladder in the previous chapter, it can be helpful to actually turn this idea into a visual aid. This gives us a way to visualise both notes and Intervals in relation to one another.

Each notch on the Pitch Ruler represents one of the 12 defined pitch classes found in the Western music system. The 13th pitch repeats the first to complete a full octave:

In the course of history, Western music evolved to add "extra" pitches to the original seven pitches of the major scale. These pitches were said to add "colour" or "*chroma*" to the music. Eventually, the system evolved into a total of 12 equally-spaced pitches. So the 13-note Pitch Ruler is usually referred to as "The *Chromatic* Scale":

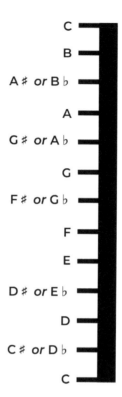

Note: The diagram above starts and ends with the pitch class of C, but there is no "correct" note to start this ruler from. You can begin and end on any one of the 12 chromatic pitches.

The Pitch Ruler and Our Instruments

Most of the commonly-played Western instruments have the ability to play all twelve pitches of the chromatic scale. These are called "chromatic instruments", and include keyboards, guitars, ukuleles, and most of the usual band and orchestra instruments.

There are a few common Western instruments that still reflect the original seven-pitch system. These "diatonic" instruments include the diatonic harmonica, Appalachian dulcimer, some harps, the Celtic whistle, and a variety of diatonic accordions and concertinas.

The design of the piano keyboard, with its mix of white and black keys, reflects both. The 8 white keys in each octave correspond to a C Major diatonic scale, and the black keys add the additional 5 notes of the chromatic scale.

Since so many of our instruments are organised according to the chromatic scale, thinking in terms of the Pitch Ruler can be very convenient for "translating" our musical perception of intervals into notes we actually play on our instruments.

Here's a great way to get familiar with the sound of these chromatic steps (a.k.a. Half Steps), which you may have already practiced in Chapter Four: Singing as part of the "Sing Half Steps And Whole Steps" exercise:

EXERCISE: Play And Sing The Chromatic Scale

1. Select a starting note within your comfortable singing range.

2. Play the note on an instrument which can produce Half Steps, and sing it back.

3. Now play up an octave note-by-note in Half Steps from that starting note, each time playing the note and then singing it back.

4. As you gain confidence, try singing up the Half Steps without the instrument's example to prompt you.

5. Choose another note and repeat.

Regular practice with this exercise will greatly improve your Vocal Control (see Chapter Four: Singing) and make it easier to reliably recognise and produce the various building blocks for Solfa, Intervals and Chords. You are refining both your mental "Pitch Ruler" and your ability to express its various notes with your voice.

Intervals on the Pitch Ruler

Any interval can be represented on the Pitch Ruler, with the distance between the two pitches corresponding to how far apart or close together the pitches are musically.

Let's look at two intervals on our Pitch Ruler, the Major 2nd and the Perfect 5th:

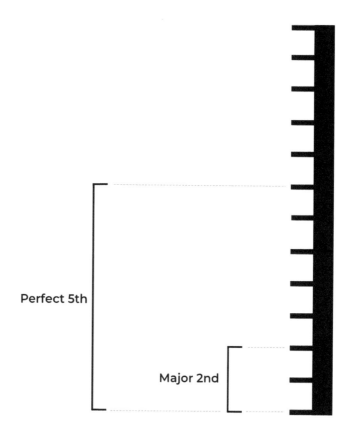

You can see clearly that the two pitches of the Perfect 5th are further apart. You may have noticed that the Major 2nd spans two chromatic steps, and the Perfect 5th spans seven chromatic steps.

How could this knowledge be useful for something like playing by ear? Well, for example, suppose you play a B and you hear that the next pitch you want is a Perfect 5th higher. You can count 7 chromatic steps up on your instrument (for example, seven frets up on your guitar or seven keys to the right on the piano) and find that the note you seek is an F♯:

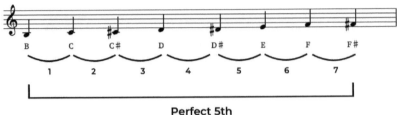

Perfect 5th

We can also see this as a way to make our Pitch Contour more granular, by pinning down the specific chromatic steps the series of notes is moving between:

ORIGINAL PITCH CONTOUR:

REFINED:

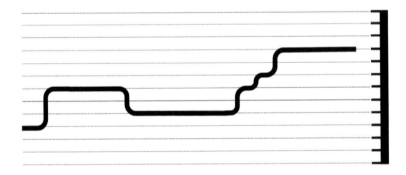

The Pitch Ruler is so clear and systematic with its neat, evenly spaced pitches that you may be wondering, *"Why don't we base all our ear training and music theory on this chromatic scale?"*

Well, it might look good on paper, but the big issue is that we don't hear music in this way. Let's return to the Pitch Ladder introduced in the previous chapter as a way to visualise Solfa, and see how the two relate.

The Pitch Ladder

Although we have 12 pitch classes in our system, it's very rare that a given piece of music will make use of all twelve. For example, as we saw in Chapter Eight: Relative Pitch, much of Western music uses pitches exclusively from the major scale. To represent these pitches, we can use a Pitch Ladder:

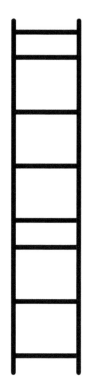

Now, let's compare our Pitch Ladder to the Pitch Ruler:

Pitch Ladder   Pitch Ruler

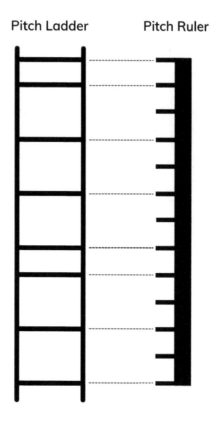

As you can see, all the pitches on the Ladder line up with pitches on the Ruler. In the Pitch Ladder though, not all pitches are spaced equally apart, and some pitches shown on the Ruler are not found on the Ladder. This is because the major scale does not use all 12 pitches, just a select seven (plus the octave) that form the scale, and these seven pitches are not all equal distances apart.

The Pitch Ladder more accurately represents how our brains organise music, and so is more closely related to what we are actually hearing. That's why together, the Pitch Ruler and the Pitch Ladder can be a powerful combination.

We said earlier that the names we use for intervals, in terms of "degree" and "quality", bring certain advantages. The Pitch Ladder is a helpful way to start understanding this.

The "degree" is the number part of the interval's name and refers to the distance between the pitches *on the Pitch Ladder*. When we count the distance, we include both the beginning and the end pitches:

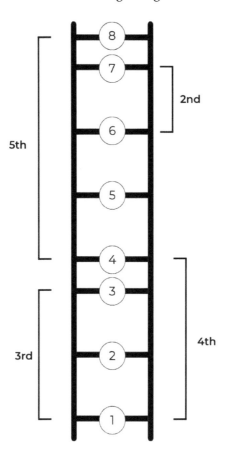

If you measure intervals with the unequal steps of the Pitch Ladder, it is possible to have two intervals with the same number, but which are not the same distance as measured with the Pitch Ruler:

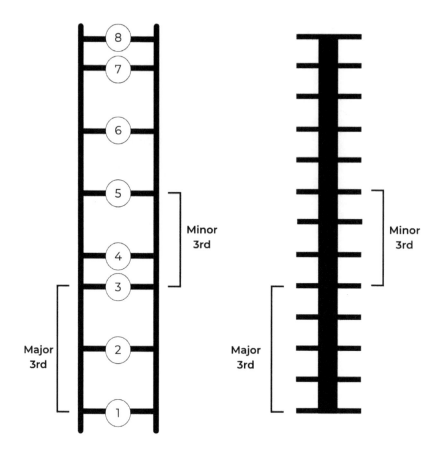

We therefore add the "quality" label to differentiate between the "bigger" and the "smaller" version of each interval. As a reminder, the words used to describe quality are Major, Minor, Perfect, Diminished, and Augmented.

So you can see that although the types of interval are fundamentally defined in a purely numeric way (as the number of chromatic steps apart two pitches are), by naming them in terms of degree and quality, we also glean some useful information about how far apart the notes are in terms of the scale.

We can also make the connection with Solfa names:

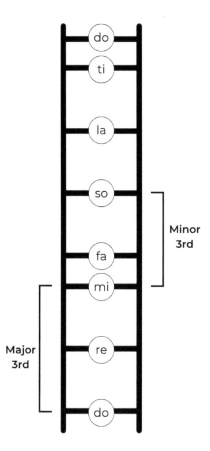

For example, learning that the interval from *do* to *mi* is a Major 3rd, while the interval from *mi* to *so* is a Minor Third. Even though both are a "Third" (because both are three notes apart), the underlying pitch distance is actually different. This gives us a different perspective on the pitch relationships within the scale.

We already met one exercise in the previous chapter which can help you forge the connections between these two approaches: singing up to each Solfa note from *do*, and naming the corresponding interval (e.g. *"do, re, major second, do, mi, major third, etc."*). We'll introduce further exercises below to help you continue to explore this.

Compound Intervals

Compound intervals are intervals larger than an octave. It tends to be jazz musicians who talk about these the most, as they're often thinking in terms of extended chord voicings which use them.

Most musicians don't need to worry about compound intervals. Firstly, because recognising compound intervals doesn't arise all that often, for most musicians in most genres. Secondly, because when it does arise, you can typically use your interval recognition skills for the types listed above to recognise those bigger intervals too (because they sound similar, just in a different octave).

For example, suppose you want to recognise "ninth" chords in jazz standards, which feature not just the root, third, fifth and seventh notes, but also the ninth. Your interval Ear Training has equipped you to recognise what quality of 3rd, 5th and 7th are featured—do you now need to learn to recognise Major and Minor 9ths? The answer is no, not really—because the interval of a Ninth takes us to the second degree of the scale, in the octave above. As a result, you can use your skill with Minor and Major 2nds to distinguish between the two types of ninth chord directly. That's not to say that no practice will be required to distinguish ninth chords—just that you don't need to add another type of interval to your interval Ear Training. You can directly focus on that specific task, drawing on your abilities with the intervals up to an octave.

Recognising Intervals

Now that you're familiar with how Intervals work and the essential theory, let's move on to the Ear Training side of things. Learning to "recognise intervals" means that when you hear a pair of notes in music you know the name of the type of interval between them, which indicates how far apart the notes are in pitch. When people talk about "interval ear training" they are referring to this process of learning to recognise intervals.

There are two ways that your brain learns to recognise different types of interval:

1.   **By hearing the characteristic sound of the interval.**

     For example, "major" intervals tend to sound happier and brighter than "minor" intervals. That's an over-simplification, and something we'll unpack more below! There are also other aspects which can make intervals distinctive, for example some have a clashing, uncomfortable sound, while others sound comfortable and at rest.   The "reference songs" method also falls into this category: you are listening for an inherent, recognisable aspect to the sound of the interval, in this case whether it sounds like the beginning of a particular song's melody or not.

2.   **By directly estimating the distance in pitch.**

   For example, even without training most musicians could tell you that the notes of a Major 6th are further apart than the notes of a Major 2nd.   You can refine this ability to judge pitch distances by practicing interval recognition.

These two approaches work together. At different stages of your training and in different circumstances you'll use one skill more than the other.

For example, the characteristic descriptive words tend to be helpful when first starting out, but mostly for harmonic intervals. Reference songs can be helpful when first starting out, but mostly for melodic intervals. Judging pitch distances can be hard for adjacent types of interval (e.g. Major 3rd vs Minor 3rd) but this skill gets stronger with practice and is ultimately the more useful and instinctive version of the skill.

Most of interval Ear Training focuses on the first approach, since this is a clear, conscious process. The second approach happens automatically along the way. Generally when you consciously try to "use intervals" for a musical task, you'll be drawing on approach #1, and that will be our focus when we talk about learning interval recognition below. However it's worth knowing that approach #2 is happening "under the hood", calibrating your mental Pitch Ruler and helping you to judge pitch distances instinctively.

Using Intervals

Since we'll follow an Integrated Ear Training approach, the exercises recommended below and in the following chapter on Chords and Progressions will include applying your new interval skills to real musical tasks. It's therefore worth briefly covering how Intervals can be used:

- **Chords**: Intervals help you recognise different types of chord (e.g. C Major vs. C Minor vs. C Seven) because you start to hear the pitch relationships between the notes of the chord. Each pair of notes in the chord forms an interval and you can learn the intervals which each type of chord is built from. For example, if you know that a "major triad" chord consists of a Major 3rd with a Perfect 5th, when you hear a 3-note chord and your interval skills let you recognise a Major 3rd and Perfect 5th, this reveals to you that it's a major triad chord.

- **Chord Progressions**: Intervals are also helpful for chord progressions (sequences of chords), because they let you hear the movement of the base ("root") note of the chords. For example, to recognise a C-F-G progression in the key of C you might hear that it sounds a bit like a perfect fourth (C up to F) and then a major second (F up to G). Or that the final chord sounds like a perfect fifth above the first one (C up to G).

- **Improvisation**: Intervals help you to improvise by letting you understand the music you imagine in concrete terms. You know how the second note relates to the first, and the third to the second, so that when you want to actually play those notes, you can. You know how far above or below each note the next one should be. As already discussed, it can be tricky to do this fast enough to be practical, so in practice most musicians would be combining their raw interval skills with knowing the notes of the key and/or Solfa.

- **Playing By Ear**: When you listen to music with interval-trained ears you hear in a much more structured and precise way. This means that you can apply your interval recognition skills to work out the notes you've heard. You can then write them down or play them on your instrument. To play exactly the notes you heard, you generally do need one known note to base all your other relative judgements on. For example, you might identify the key of the song (as covered in Chapter Eight: Relative Pitch), or just dabble on your instrument along with the recording to identify one note to serve as your known reference note. Once that one note is known, all the rest follow from the intervals between them.

- • **Audiation and Musical Memory**: As with all our Relative Pitch building blocks, Intervals help to refine the pitch precision of your Audiation as well as your musical memory. By learning to more accurately and reliably distinguish between different distances in pitch, you are able to form a more detailed and precise mental representation of the sounds of a song or piece. Additionally, you can consciously use your skills to help you remember. For example, knowing that your next entry in a choir piece begins a Major 3rd above the note you last sang helps you to then pitch that note correctly when you sing it.

Getting Started

Later in the chapter we'll suggest what to initially aim for as you start learning Intervals, as well as various activities you can do to develop your skills. First, let's get started with the "Basic Drill" exercise, and how you can recognise intervals.

How to Use The Basic Drill

Remember that our Basic Drill is simply "listen to some examples of different types of building block, and for each one try to recognise which type it is."

As you'll remember from Chapter Eight: Relative Pitch, this Basic Drill is the single exercise most commonly used in traditional ear training.

The most widespread method for learning interval recognition is through some kind of "quiz". That can take the form of a practice audio track which you listen to, an interactive app (mobile or web-based) which plays examples, or a musical friend who's happy to take turns playing examples for each other.

For us, with an Integrated Ear Training approach, this kind of "drill" still has its place, helping us both to assess our abilities and to gradually develop them, in conjunction with various additions, modifications and other activities. Doing the Basic Drill need not be strictly "Head and Hearing", in the traditional way. Use your Heart to tune in to the feeling or emotion of the sounds, and work with your instrument (Hands), not just pre-recorded examples or quizzes.

So how do we use the Basic Drill for Intervals?

EXERCISE: The Basic Drill For Intervals

Select your source of examples (pre-recorded tracks, an app/quiz, or playing on an instrument yourself or with a friend) and then:

1. Choose a set of interval types and forms to include (e.g. "Minor 2nd and Major 2nd, ascending")

2. Hear an example of an interval drawn from those types and forms.

3. Give your answer (e.g. "ascending Major 2nd")

4. Find out if your answer was correct

5. If not, listen again to the example, ideally also with playback of what you guessed, so that you can compare the two.

Repeat steps 2-5 with various examples being given. Over time vary the choices in step 1 to gradually develop your interval skills.

In its simplest form, this process risks quickly becoming dull and leaving you prone to getting stuck. Here are some tips for keeping it interesting and effective:

1. Don't only do this! Make sure to also use the other exercises below.

2. Start simple, by always using the same root note for the examples (e.g. C). This gives you a more direct comparison between subsequent examples, and allows your musical brain to have a sense of a key. In this way we can sidestep the issue mentioned in the introduction to this chapter, that Intervals can be challenging because our brain always wants musical context. Once you can reliably distinguish different types with the same root note, start varying that root note each time.

3. Incorporate your instrument. For example, try playing back each example after giving your answer. If you're using a fixed

root note as mentioned above, you can save the step of finding that note on your instrument each time (though that's a valuable exercise in itself!)

4. Sing back each interval after you hear it. Not only does this connect you more deeply with the sound of each interval, it also develops your Vocal Control and ability to produce each interval when singing. It can also provide a handy stepping stone for harmonic intervals: if you've got the hang of ascending/descending, singing each note of the harmonic form lets you turn it into an ascending/descending interval and recognise that. Over time you can skip the actual singing by audiating instead. Eventually you won't need the stepping stone at all.

5. Vary the instrument sound. Depending on your source of examples, this may be an easy thing to do or not. Many musicians find that their own instrument's sound is the easiest to work with, but it can be enlightening to try with examples on a different instrument. For example, wind instrument timbres can make Perfect intervals particularly challenging because of the way the harmonics of those instruments line up. Sometimes just switching instrument, for example from piano to guitar, reveals different sound characteristics which you can then tune in to and hear across other instruments. This can also be seen as a form of Contextual Interference (see Chapter Six: Superlearning), waking up your brain more fully than if you always use the same timbre for examples. Using a Digital Audio Workstation (DAW) or composing software can be great for easily producing interval examples with a variety of instrument timbres.

Practice Tracks

We've prepared a set of interval training MP3s in the *Additional Resources* which you can use both passively (just listening and tuning in to the sound of different Intervals) and actively (with gaps left for you to give your answer before hearing the answer spoken).

How To Recognise Intervals

Equipped with our Basic Drill, how do we make sure that our "answers" aren't pure guesswork? Let's look in more detail at the two main ways of recognising intervals mentioned above: reference songs and characteristic sounds.

1. Reference Songs

If you asked 100 musicians how interval recognition works, I'd be willing to bet at least 90 would say *"you learn a song for each interval, like 'Here Comes The Bride' for a Perfect Fourth."*

It's part of the unfortunate status quo regarding Intervals and Ear Training that generation after generation has been taught what is essentially a temporary stepping stone, as if it's the full solution. So it's not that this "reference songs" approach is bad, it's just extremely limited. As a result, musicians who think it's the only way to learn intervals, just get frustrated and disappointed even faster.

The basic idea is a simple one: our musical brain is particularly good at remembering melodies, and you've already spent years or more likely decades building up a "mental songbook". So why not leverage that, by learning which interval the first two notes of various familiar melodies correspond to?

For example, since you can probably already recognise the first two notes of the *Star Wars* theme tune, or sing it back on demand, learning that this interval is called a "Perfect Fifth" should let you recognise Perfect Fifths, right? Well, kind of.

The huge and real benefit of the reference songs approach is that it does genuinely get you up and running quickly. Once you assemble your list of songs corresponding to each interval, that can be enough to get you passing some interval quizzes right away.

There are, however, three huge drawbacks:

1. **This method is particularly unusable for real musical tasks.**
   Try using reference songs to identify each interval in turn
   during a melody, or when improvising, and you'll quickly
   realise you simply can't take 2-3 seconds to figure out the
   corresponding reference song each time!

2. **This method is particularly vulnerable to musical context.**
   We've already said that this is a weak point of Intervals
   overall, but while the "characteristic sounds" method covered
   below has some resilience to the context in a melody or
   harmony, the reference songs method is almost completely
   unusable. It's just too hard to audiate "Here Comes The Bride"
   or "Star Wars" while listening to a completely different piece of
   music. On top of that, the reference songs will come with their
   own implied tonic, which may or may not match up with the
   tonic of the music you're listening to.[3]

3. **This method is not directly usable for harmonic intervals
   (both notes together).** You can transform a harmonic interval
   into a melodic one by singing or audiating its two notes in
   turn, and then use your reference songs to identify it—but
   while that might get you through an intervals quiz, it again
   falls apart with most real musical tasks.

There's also the fact that for 12 types of interval (we'll ignore the
Unison since it's generally pretty obvious—just a repeated note!) you
actually need a song for each of the two melodic forms, ascending and
descending. That means coming up with a list and familiarising
yourself with **24 reference songs**, at least!

So while we do encourage making use of this method at Musical U,
I would recommend seeing it as:

A. An easy way to bootstrap your interval recognition skills and

---

[3] This is the same "a Major 3rd sounds different going up from the first note of the scale
than from the second note" problem mentioned earlier.

get started quickly, and

B. A way to prove to yourself, immediately, that you do "have
    what it takes" to recognise intervals.

For these two reasons, it is worthwhile to explore the reference
songs method a bit at first. You may find that certain ones do prove
useful to you long-term.

So what songs should you use? Well, if you do a web search for
"interval songs" or "interval reference songs" you'll turn up plenty of
suggestions. The traditional ones can be a bit dull—lots of Christmas
carols, nursery rhymes, and examples from old music you may never
have heard of. The good news is you certainly don't need to limit
yourself to those standard examples! You are free to use any song
which starts with the interval as your reference song for that interval.
In the *Additional Resources* you'll find an extensive list of modern
options for interval reference songs.

Everybody has different musical tastes, so if you find yourself
lacking songs for certain intervals, try to figure out your own. This is a
great exercise in itself:

EXERCISE: Find Your Own Interval Reference Songs

*   Play an example of the interval on your instrument, and see if
    any song pops into your head. This is leveraging your musical
    mind's desire to "autocomplete" a melody.

*   If not, try another random example of that interval type. It can
    help to play the corresponding major chord first, to give your
    brain a harmonic context. For example, play a C major chord,
    and then the interval starting from C.

*   You can also try adding a random third note after the interval
    to help prompt your brain to fill in the rest of a tune (though
    it'll still be the first two notes of the song which serve as your
    reference, once you find it).

Alternatively, you can start from your 10 favourite songs and figure out what the corresponding interval is for each.

You can also make up your own interval reference songs, which can be a fun creative exercise. For example, the way I finally cracked distinguishing Perfect 4ths from Perfect 5ths was to make up a quick little ditty that went:

(Showing note letter-names, with Solfa beneath, and lyrics at the bottom.)

Now, although that notation may look a little complex, it's really just singing back and forth between a Perfect 4th and a Perfect 5th, from the same root note each time. The brackets on top show the little section which can be repeated, again and again, alternating back and fourth between P4 and P5.

Once I could reliably sing this, any time I heard an interval and wasn't sure which of the two it was, I could just sing my little ditty and listen for which of the two top notes matched the one I'd heard. Clearly that's a slow process—but it worked, and it let me bootstrap my P4 vs. P5 recognition quite effectively.

Another useful source of interval reference songs is anything you're familiar with through your instrument practice. For example, many musicians know the sound of the start of a major scale very well, which can be used as the reference song for a Major Second. They may also be practiced in playing arpeggios (broken chords) which can act as references for Major and Minor Thirds. Guitarists used to tuning their instrument using adjacent strings may find that the sounds of Perfect Fourths and Perfect Fifths are already familiar to them from that. Trumpet players used to pitching notes which are a Perfect Fifth or Perfect Octave apart by changing their embouchure may find that well-ingrained musical memory serves as a reference song for those interval types.

After exploring some online lists and trying some of these exercises you should be able to compile your own personal list of interval reference songs for the ascending and descending form of each of the 12 intervals.

2. Characteristic Sounds

The more resilient method for recognising intervals is to familiarise yourself with their characteristic sounds. Initially this can be done in a conscious way, using descriptive words for their distinctive sounds. Over time this can become a more instinctive, Heart-based ability, tuning in to the indescribable "feel" of each interval. You can also listen for how *consonant* or *dissonant* the interval sounds.

Descriptive Words

An example of using descriptive words is the classic oversimplification used for keys, scales, chords and intervals that *"'major' sounds bright and happy, 'minor' sounds sad, dark, mysterious or gloomy"*.

Here are some common words used to describe different types of interval:

Interval Type	Descriptive words
Minor Second	tense, clashing, awkward, uneasy, scary
Major Second	friendly, comfortable, smooth
Minor Third	sorrowful, dark, somber, mysterious
Major Third	bright, cheerful, uplifting, strong
Perfect Fourth	grand, complete, resonant, stable, triumphant
Tri-Tone	uncertain, scary, uncomfortable, threatening
Perfect Fifth	grand, complete, resonant, majestic
Minor Sixth	dark, somber, mysterious
Major Sixth	airy, light, uplifting, warm
Minor Seventh	jazzy, juxtaposition, prominent, soulful
Major Seventh	tense, leading, yearning, incomplete
Perfect Octave	large, same-y, grand, complete, resonant

It's important to note that this is very subjective! And it can be affected strongly by the musical context, as well as the Form of the interval. So I would always encourage you to discover for yourself which words seem best to describe each type of interval, and which are useful to you.

Consonance and Dissonance

You can also listen for consonance and dissonance. These ideas are extremely important to the way we hear music, both melodically and harmonically.

Consonance describes sounds that have a sense of rest. Parts of music which seem stable and don't leave your ear wanting closure or relief are described as "consonant" sounds.

Dissonant sounds may be best described as "active" ones. They are not bad-sounding (as is sometimes suggested). Rather, they are the sounds that create forward musical motion and harmonic direction.

In Western music, dissonant sounds "resolve" to consonant ones. This is analogous to the rising tension and its eventual release in drama, such as a TV show or movie.

We can hear musical intervals as having varying degrees of consonance or dissonance:

Consonant ← → Dissonant
PU, P8, P5, P4, M3, m3, M6, m6, M7, m7, M2, m2, TT

The most dissonant-sounding intervals are the Minor Seconds (hence its use in the *Jaws* theme!) and the Tri-Tone (once called "The Devil's Interval"). You can hear a "crunchy", "spicy", dissonant, or active nature in these intervals.

The Perfect Intervals have an open and clear sound. The Thirds and Sixths have a "sweeter" sound.

You can combine these traits with your overall sense of the size of the interval to help you narrow it down. For example, hearing a consonant "sweet-sounding" interval you can judge whether it's smaller (so probably a Third) or larger (so probably a Sixth).

Generally these kinds of described properties are easiest to hear with harmonic intervals (both notes together). It can be a bit harder to hear them with the melodic forms.

And, not to keep beating the same drum, but it's important to note that these properties can be easy to hear in the context of an ear training quiz or exercise, where you don't have other musical context bringing its own "mood", and when you can directly compare e.g. Major Thirds with Minor Thirds and only need to distinguish between those two versions.

This can become a fairly usable and robust method though, mostly because of the "under the hood" Pitch Ruler calibration that's occurring as you practice recognising intervals in this way.

3. Resolution

There is one lesser-known but valuable approach to recognising intervals, which we cover extensively in our training on the Circle of Fifths at Musical U, but is rarely taught. This is to consider the *tonicity* of each interval.

We introduced the idea of tension above, that dissonance "wants" to resolve to consonance, musically. This goes hand-in-hand with the idea of the tonic as our "home" note that the music generally wants to return to, giving a sense of completion.

Each interval can be seen as tending to resolve either downwards (like its lower note is the tonic) or upwards (like its top note is the tonic).

If we consider the major scale, we can see that the Major intervals appear going upwards from the low tonic, while the Minor intervals appear going downwards from the high tonic:

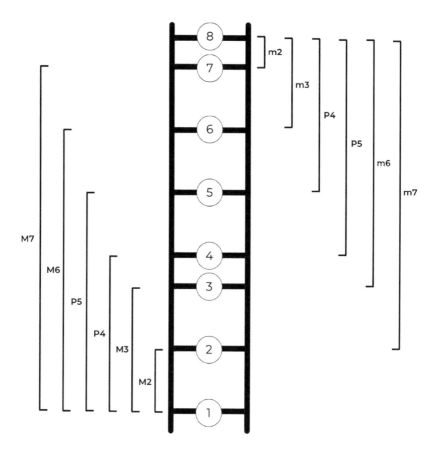

The result is that:

- Ascending Major intervals tend to have an "opening" feeling (like they are beginning a journey away from the low tonic), while descending Major intervals tend to have a "closing" feeling (like they are completing a journey back to the low tonic)

- Ascending Minor intervals tend to have a "closing" feeling (like they are completing a journey back to the high tonic), while descending Minor intervals tend to have an "opening" feeling (like they are beginning a journey away from the high tonic)

- Perfect Intervals tend to have an open, resonant sound

(especially the harmonic versions)[4].

This is quite a different way of listening to intervals, but our members have found it can be enormously helpful for aiding recognition, as well as giving new insight into what's happening musically when we use different kinds of interval.

Zac Says...

Sometimes members find this idea of interval "resolution" challenging to understand. They have found success by being very relaxed, singing the intervals, and focusing on how they "feel" rather than how they sound.

Sing back and forth slowly between the intervals' notes and notice how the "opening" and "closing" feelings show up in the body. Other ways members have described the "opening" feeling is like a "blooming" or "blossoming"—there is a need to continue. The "closing" feels like "settling", "restful".

Start With Aiming For The Pentascale

As you saw in the list above, there are 13 types of interval and they come in three different forms (ascending, descending and harmonic). That's a lot!

So how do you know what to focus on, to begin with? Fortunately, you don't need to worry about mastering them all. In fact, just *half* of those 13 types are the most important.

Here's what we recommend, and why:

- Start by learning Major and Minor 2nds, because they are the steps the other intervals are built from and they're the most common interval used between notes in melodies.

---

[4] They do also have a tonicity, which is where the connection to the Circle Of Fifths (based on Perfect Fourths and Fifths) comes in, but this is less apparent than with the Major and Minor Intervals.

- Learn Major and Minor 3rds because they're important for chords and harmony (and also common in melodies).

- Learn Perfect 4ths and 5ths because they're important for harmony, and especially for chord progressions (as you'll see in the next chapter).

- These intervals can also be combined to help you handle the larger 6ths and 7ths (for details, see the "Interval Tips and Tricks" section below)

The Perfect Octave is important too, but most musicians find that comes fairly easily. It can bring up challenges with singing (e.g. Matching Pitch in a different octave to the note you hear) but in terms of just recognising the interval, its melodic forms have a clear character ("a big leap to a note that sounds kind of the same") and the harmonic form is easy if you've got the hang of Perfect 4ths and 5ths (which are otherwise the most common source of confusion).

Study all three forms: ascending, descending and harmonic. It's normally best to practice with the different forms of one type of interval fairly close together in time. For example, you don't want to ignore all the harmonic forms for weeks until after you've mastered them all in melodic form. It's normally easier if you practice with the harmonic form soon after the melodic forms, or vice-versa.

Naturally, it is helpful to eventually learn every type of interval, but focusing on the types listed above will help you get practical results from your practice as soon as possible.

If these types of interval (m2, M2, m3, M3, P4, P5) are to be our focus, this gives us a natural milestone to aim for, which also helps provide some meaningful context for practicing with those intervals.

We can find our Major and Minor 2nds, Major and Minor 3rds, Perfect 4th, and Perfect 5th intervals contained within the major *pentascale*: the first five notes of the major scale[5].

---

[5] Note that this is different from the *pentatonic* scale we recommend as a milestone for learning Solfa: that is *do, re, mi, so, la* where the pentascale would be *do, re, mi, fa, so.*

While it would be neat to use the same scale as a target milestone in both cases, we've found that the pentatonic is better-suited to the song-based learning in Solfa, and the pentascale best for the set of intervals it features.

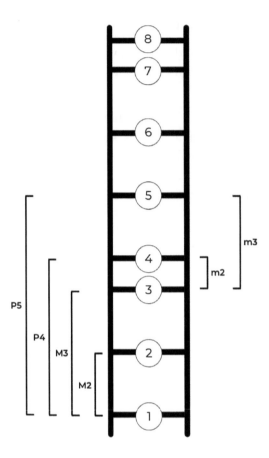

We can take this a step further and find multiple instances of intervals within the pentascale:

On top of that, getting familiar with both scales sets you up for great success tackling the most common Chord Progressions, as we'll see in the next chapter.

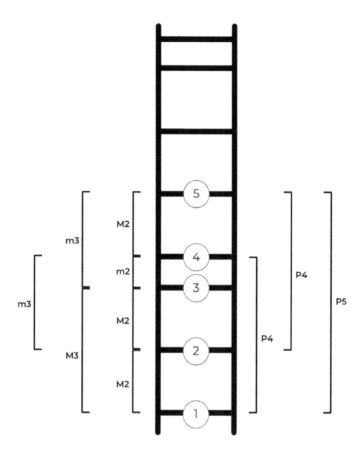

Here's the same thing shown on the staff for the C Major pentascale:

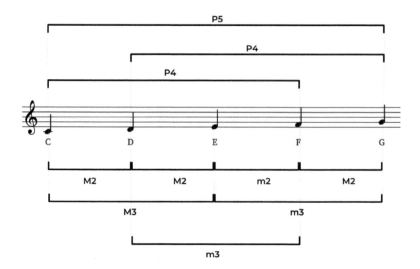

Note: As we continue, we'll show some intervals on the staff like this. If that notation isn't familiar to you, you can simply focus on the letter names beneath the notes. We will use C as the root of each individual interval shown, and the tonic of the pentascale, but this is purely for clarity and consistency. All these patterns and distances could be based on any note.

Having this encapsulating scale will be a great help later on for our applied activities such as improvising, as it provides a Playground (see *Chapter Fifteen: Improvisation* on Expansive Creativity) for experimenting with these types of interval.

How to Practice

Let's start getting to know each of these interval types. As you read through the following sections which introduce each type of interval, you can use the Basic Drill to start familiarising yourself with their sounds, according to the "How to Use the Basic Drill" and "How to Recognise Intervals" sections above.

I would highly recommend having your instrument handy, and starting to play examples of the intervals to listen to. You can count in chromatic steps to find the second note of the interval. For example if you choose C as your starting note for an ascending Major Third, you would count up five chromatic steps to find the second note. You can also use the *Additional Resources* which provides examples for you to listen to.

As we go through each type of interval, listen to various examples (by choosing different starting notes in the Basic Drill) and use the "Listen with a Question in Mind" technique from *Chapter Five: Active Listening* to explore questions like:

- *What words would you use to describe the harmonic form?*

- *Can you hear those same characteristics or different ones in the melodic forms?*

- *More broadly, what do you notice is different between the harmonic, the ascending and the descending forms?*

- *How does the sound compare to the other intervals which have the same quality?* (e.g. Minor 2nds vs. Minor 3rds)

- *How does the sound compare to the intervals which have a different quality?* (e.g. Minor 2nds vs. Major 2nds)

- *Do any of the forms sound more "complete", "closed" or "resolved" than the other forms?* (You might like to revisit the notes above on hearing "resolution" in intervals.)

- *Do the melodic forms remind you of the start of any particular melody?* (you can start assembling your own list of reference songs!)

It's a good idea to jot down your own notes as you go through. This will assemble a great collection of "clues" you can start using to familiarise yourself with each type of interval and spot it in future.

As a sneak peek of the Play-By-Ear Process we'll cover in *Playing by Ear*, I would also recommend using Audiation and Singing throughout. For example, after you play an interval, sing it back. As you start getting familiar, you might like to try audiating or singing the second note of the interval before you play it, which will start to develop your ability to produce intervals as well as recognise them.

Perfect Unison

What is the smallest possible interval in music? From our discussion above about the chromatic scale and Pitch Ruler, you might reasonably say "a Half Step", "Semitone" or "Minor Second". But the smallest possible interval is in fact one which has no pitch distance between the two notes i.e. the same note played twice.

We refer to this as a (Perfect) Unison. We use this same word "unison" more broadly in music to mean "multiple instruments playing the same notes together"—we say they are *"playing (or singing) in unison"*.

Here is the Unison interval played harmonically and melodically with root note C:

Back when I created the original interval ear training app (from which Easy Ear Training and later Musical U were born), I deliberated over whether to even include Unisons. It was so obvious it felt like cheating! I ended up including them, for the same reason we're including them here: there's no harm in having a "gimme" no-brainer included when you're first getting started with interval recognition :)

On a more serious note (pun intended!) there's value in recognising Unison as an interval in its own right, since any time we're listening for movement in pitch (for example in Playing By Ear, Improvisation or Songwriting) it's important to always remember that "staying on the same note" is a valid—and common—musical choice.

Minor 2nd

The Minor 2nd is the smallest minor interval found in Western music, and the smallest possible pitch distance between two different notes: just a single chromatic step. This interval can also be referred to as a "Half Step" or a "Semitone". Many musicians recognise it as the end of an ascending major scale (moving from *ti* to *do'* in Solfa terms).

As we learned above, in isolation it has a very harsh, dissonant sound. The famous tension-inducing *Jaws* movie theme is just alternating between two notes a Minor 2nd apart. However, it also exists naturally in the major scale, between the third and fourth notes (*mi* and *fa* in Solfa) and the seventh and eighth notes (*ti* and *do'* in Solfa).

Example from root note C:

| Ascending Minor 2nd | Descending Minor 2nd | Harmonic Minor 2nd |
| C   Db | Db   C | C,Db |

It's primarily the absence of Minor 2nds (by omitting the fourth and seventh notes, *fa* and *ti*) which gives the pentatonic scale its universal, "safe", comfortable sound, as we discussed in the previous chapter. As soon as we have those Minor 2nds in the mix, a far greater level of musical tension becomes possible.

Try playing a melody you know well, but shift one (or more) of its notes up or down a Minor 2nd. If these happen to be the ones which take you to another note of the scale, it will sound like an alteration, but a fairly "normal-sounding" one. In most cases though, you'll find yourself outside the scale, and things will suddenly sound very tense indeed!

So we can see, there is great power in these dissonant-sounding Minor 2nds, which makes them both fairly easy to spot, and highly useful in our own creative music-making.

Major 2nd

The Major 2nd is the smallest major interval found in music, corresponding to a distance of two chromatic steps. Many musicians recognise its ascending form as the first two notes of the ascending major scale—the *do* and *re* in Solfa terms. This interval can also be referred to as a "Whole Step" or a "Tone".

Example from root note C:

Together, Minor and Major 2nds are the building blocks with which we construct major and minor scales. Our Pitch Ladder, with its uneven rungs, is using either a Minor 2nd or a Major 2nd for each rung. Each of our Solfa notes is either a Minor 2nd or a Major 2nd away from its two neighbours.

TIP:

This fact, that the notes of a scale are all either a Minor 2nd or Major 2nd apart, gives rise to a little musical nugget that musicians often love to discover:

Any time you guess a note (for example when Playing By Ear), you are only ever one Minor 2nd away from a note of the scale. For practical purposes, that means if you guess and it sounds wrong or dissonant, try nudging it up or down a half step, and you'll land on a note that feels "good" or comfortable again. With a bit of flair you can even consider this a creative embellishment, since these "half-step slides" into target notes are frequently used, especially in blues and jazz music!

Compare the Major 2nd with the Minor 2nd in particular. What differences can you hear, in terms of size/distance, consonance and disonance, resolution, descriptive words?

Minor 3rd

If we stack a Major 2nd and a Minor 2nd, corresponding to a distance of 3 chromatic steps in total, we create a Minor 3rd. The Minor 3rd can be found as the interval between the first and third notes of a minor Scale, and as the bottom part of a minor chord[6]. Many musicians recognise its ascending form as the start of a minor arpeggio.

In our pentascale, Minor 3rds occur between the second and fourth notes (*re* and *fa* in Solfa) and the third and fifth notes (*mi* and *so* in Solfa).

---

[6] Specifically a root-position triad i.e. the first, third and fifth notes of the corresponding scale, in ascending pitch order. This is what we might consider the simplest or the "prototypical" form of a minor chord. The term "minor chord" could also refer to inversions (moving notes into different octaves), and chords with more than three notes being played, where the intervals would vary.

Example from root note C:

Major 3rd

The next-biggest major interval found in music is the Major 3rd, corresponding to a distance of 4 chromatic steps in total. That's like stacking two Major 2nds. Many musicians recognise its ascending form as the start of a major arpeggio.

The Major 3rd appears in our pentascale between the first and third notes (*do* and *mi* in Solfa).

Example from root note C:

Compare the Major 3rd with the Minor 3rd in particular. What differences can you hear, in terms of size/distance, consonance and dissonance, resolution, descriptive words?

Perfect 4th

The Perfect 4th corresponds to a distance of 5 chromatic steps. Its Perfect quality puts it in a group with Perfect Unisons, Perfect 5ths and Perfect Octaves.

Perfect 4ths appear in our pentascale between the first and fourth notes (*do* and *fa* in Solfa) and the second and fifth notes (*re* and *so* in Solfa).

Example from root note C:

Compare the Perfect 4th with the two types of Major interval we've covered so far. Then with the two types of Minor interval. What do you notice about the character, mood, or overall sound of each? You might like to focus on the harmonic forms.

Perfect 5th

The Perfect 5th corresponds to a distance of 7 chromatic steps. It's another Perfect interval, like the Unison and Perfect 4th.

The Perfect 5th appears in our pentascale between the first and fifth notes (*do* and *so* in Solfa).

Example from root note C:

Compare the Perfect 5th with the Perfect 4th and Perfect Unison, in harmonic form. Then see how does their sound compare to the Major and Minor Intervals?

Remember to also use other Active Listening questions like those listed above, to now explore and experiment with all seven types of interval you've encountered.

Side Note: Inversion Pairs

The Perfect 4th and Perfect 5th can be tricky to distinguish. Not only do they both have the same quality, they are also quite similar in size. More than that though, they are actually quite closely related! A glance at this diagram will show you how:

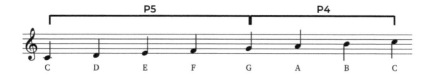

Going up a Perfect 5th from C takes you to G, and going up a Perfect 4th from G takes you back to a C. Similarly, if we instead went up a Perfect 4th from C we'd land on F, and a Perfect 5th up from F would take us right back to a C:

Here's the same thing shown on the Pitch Ladder for both cases:

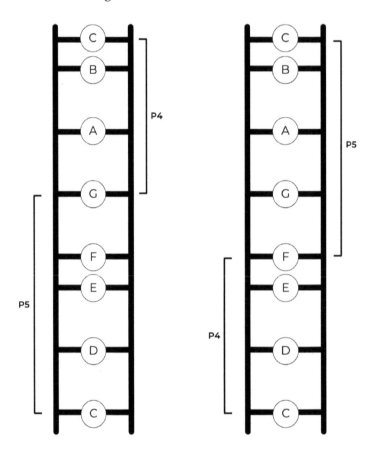

This works, no matter what starting note we choose: stacking a Perfect 4th and a Perfect 5th gives us a Perfect Octave, bringing us back to the same pitch class we started from.

To put that another way: a Perfect 4th up from a given note takes you to the same note as going down a Perfect 5th, and vice-versa (just in a different octave).

This is called an "inversion pair": going upwards by one interval takes you to the same note name as going downwards by the other. So we can see that the Perfect 4th is the inversion of the Perfect 5th and vice-versa.

All Intervals have an inversion pair:

- Perfect Unison / Perfect Octave

- Minor 2nd / Major 7th

- Major 2nd / Minor 7th

- Minor 3rd / Major 6th

- Major 3rd / Minor 6th

- Perfect 4th / Perfect 5th

- Tri-Tone / Tri-Tone(!)

So what does all this mean for our Ear Training?

Since Fourths and Fifths both have that very resonant sound of the Perfect interval quality, are close together in terms of degree (i.e. they're roughly the same pitch distance as each other), and are an inversion pair, they can be particularly tricky to tell apart by ear.

This is one case where the "resolution" approach can be very helpful.

As mentioned when introducing that idea earlier, this way of listening for intervals is not generally taught. It emerged as a significant discovery for us with our members in the Winter Season of *Living Music*, where the Circle of Fifths provided a whole new and exciting gateway into Ear Training. Not only did it illuminate the "tonicity" of Major and Minor intervals for them, the "ingoing vs. outgoing" way of looking at Perfect 4ths and 5ths also had a huge positive effect on their interval recognition skills.

Even without exploring the wonders of the Circle, you can make good use of this different perspective on what characterises interval types. As you practice with the intervals (e.g. P4 vs. P5) simply listen to the sense of *movement*, and whether they seem to ask or answer a question. You might also hear this as "opening" vs. "closing", "resolved" vs. "unresolved" or "complete" vs. "unsettled".

Summary

You have begun to familiarise yourself with the seven most common intervals. As you started listening, playing and singing these types of interval, it's likely you found some things very clear and striking. For example, you might have found the "start of a major scale" touchpoint made melodic Major 2nds immediately familiar to you. Or you might have found the difference in quality (Major vs. Minor vs. Perfect) with harmonic intervals was easy to hear.

At this stage, don't expect yourself to be reliably recognising the different types of interval. As we continue into additional exercises and activities, you'll want to limit the number of types and forms you work on at once. However, this full set corresponding to the pentascale is a great milestone to have in mind, and hopefully you're already getting a sense of how interval recognition will become possible for you.

More Tips And Tricks

Over the years we've gathered quite a variety of tips and tricks to assist with learning interval recognition, covering ways to accelerate and ease the overall process, as well as specific tips for each interval type. You'll find this available to you in the *Additional Resources*.

Additional Exercises And Activities

So far we have covered the theory of Intervals (Learn) and begun to explore their sounds in an isolated way (Practice). Now let's continue with exercises you can use to Practice and Apply your interval skills. In the spirit of Integrated Ear Training, you'll likely also want to refer back to the information above and continue with "Learn" moments as you work to Practice and Apply, developing and connecting your Head, Hands, Hearing and Heart.

With all of the exercises suggested below, start small. Pick just two or three types of interval to include, and one of the three forms. Then add either a different form for the same set of types, switch to a different set of types, or expand the set of types.

For example your sequence might look like this:

- m2 and M2, harmonic

- m2 and M2, ascending

- m2 and M2, descending

- m3 and M3, harmonic

- m3 and M3, ascending

- m3 and M3, descending

- m2, M2, m3, M3, harmonic

- m2, M2, m3, M3, ascending

- m2, M2, m3, M3, descending

- Continue to P4, P5, and various combinations

Or your sequence might look like this:

- m2 and M2, ascending

- m3 and M3, ascending

- P4 and P5, ascending

- U, m2, M2, m3, M3, ascending

- U, m2, M2, m3, M3, P4, P5, ascending

- Then repeat for descending, then harmonic

Naturally, if you find that adding additional types becomes too challenging, you can adjust which ones you include in practicing, to help you pinpoint where you're getting stuck or confused.

The main thing to know is that mastery of each interval type and form is not necessary. It's not necessary before moving on with your training, and it's definitely not necessary to start using intervals in your music-making either.

In fact, allowing yourself to be flexible will typically accelerate your training, by letting you skirt around obstacles and sticking points. When you return to them later you will often find that your improved sense of Relative Pitch has already removed the problem (remember Convergent Learning from *Chapter Two: Mindset* and the 80% Rule from *Chapter Eight: Relative Pitch*).

So don't be afraid to move on before 100% perfect mastery of certain interval types. Aim for 80% or "I normally get it right", then come back later and polish up any problem spots.

Be persistent, because it does take time and repetition to teach the brain new skills. But if you find yourself feeling stuck or getting frustrated, remember that moving on to something else can actually accelerate your overall progress.

Make sure to leverage the foundational skills from Part I of this book (Singing, Audiation, Active Listening and Superlearning) and combine learning Intervals with learning Solfa. You'll find additional tips in the "Tips and Tricks" in the *Additional Resources*.

Singing Exercises

As we learned in *Chapter Four: Singing*, the feedback loop between your ears and your voice is unparalleled. It's therefore a great accelerator to use your singing voice as part of your interval Ear Training.

Even the simplest exercise, a variant of our Basic Drill, is still a very useful one:

EXERCISE: Sing Example Intervals

1. Pick a note on your instrument, and sing back that note

2. Now, for each type of interval you want to practice, try singing that interval ascending or descending from your starting note.

3. Check on your instrument if your pitch was correct. If not, sing the corrected pitch and your guessed pitch, and learn from the difference you hear.

Naturally this is suitable for melodic intervals (unless you've mastered Tuvan throat singing and can sing multiple notes at once!) but you'll find that really getting "inside" the intervals in this way helps unlock the harmonic recognition for you too.

The advantages of singing intervals can't be overstated. You're developing your voice, you're leveraging that feedback loop, you're feeling the sounds of the intervals literally deep inside yourself, you're calibrating your inner Pitch Ruler both for recognition and production of note pitches, and you open up the use of Intervals instinctively as part of creative activities.

Another way to use Singing is comparable to the "Solfa Songs" exercise for Solfa:

EXERCISE: Sing Through Sets Of Intervals

Very simple:

- Prepare certain sequences of intervals you're going to practice singing, and then sing through them regularly each day.

A great starting point for that would be the pentascale: sing up from the tonic to each note in turn (on a neutral sound, like *"ahh"* or *"doo"*) and name the interval each time:

You can also sing the adjacent Intervals, which is a great way to get a feel for Minor 2nds and Major 2nds:

Finally, you can try navigating between notes by choice, to practice with all the interval types in the Pentascale. For example moving from C up to E, up to F, down to C, up to G, it would sound like this:

At first you'll probably want to check yourself against an instrument, to make sure you're singing the notes you intend to. As you get

familiar with the sound of these "melodies" you won't need to keep doing that, and can simply sing through them, starting from various tonic notes. You can also ditch the initial *"doo"*s, and just sing the interval names directly.

Simply singing through each of these sequences daily will go a long way to developing your interval skills, and it's a perfect example of off-instrument practice you can do any time you have a moment or two to spare. If you get strange looks while standing at the bus stop singing intervals, just don't blame me!

Applied Activities

With Integrated Ear Training, the goal is not to just do "ears" practice (Hearing) or even just "singing" practice (Hands), but to develop our instinct for pitch and rhythm through a combination of all four H's (Head, Hands, Hearing and Heart) and in a way that's always connected to real music. Another way to say it is that we want to move from "Practice" exercises more into "Apply" activities.

Instrumental Drills

The Basic Drill for intervals is typically done with recorded or app-generated examples, but can also be done by using your instrument to provide examples yourself. Naturally the "guessing" step won't be necessary (unless you're working with a friend) since you'll already know the type of interval you're playing. However, there is still great benefit in listening actively to a range of examples, comparing and contrasting, singing back, audiating in advance the second note, and so on.

Depending on your instrument this may be straight-forward. For example, the guitar fretboard and piano keyboard are organised into chromatic steps, and so you can directly find the required notes for a given interval type without needing to "spell" the intervals in letter names. For other instruments, you can either count up in chromatic steps, or use the resource mentioned earlier in the chapter for learning about spelling intervals if you'd like to more quickly know the second note to play. As mentioned above, it's a good idea to start out with a fixed "root" note for a whole series of examples, which simplifies things too.

One benefit of doing these Instrumental Drills is that it will naturally lead to you wanting to explore more practical, exploratory and creative activities, like those we'll cover next.

Playing By Ear

Here's a simple exercise to begin playing melodies by ear with Intervals:

EXERCISE: Play By Ear, Using Intervals

1. Listen to a simple melody (for example you can make use of the Starter Songs from *Chapter Nine: Solfa*).

2. Sing back the melody and sketch the Pitch Contour. You might like to mark each of the notes on the line.

3. Go through the melody, note by note, using your Pitch Contour to stay oriented. Sing and listen to each pair of notes in turn and try to identify the interval.

4. Once you've decided your "answers", check them on an instrument by translating your Relative Pitch representation into a particular key. For ease, use the same tonic as the example you listened to in the first place—though it would be instructive to then pick another key to express the same melody in!

As noted earlier in the chapter, most melodies move in stepwise motion (i.e. Minor and Major 2nds) most of the time, and when skips do feature they are often skipping a single note (i.e. moving in Minor or Major 3rds). This means you don't need to have gone very far with your interval recognition skills to have some good success with this. Remember it's fine to leave a blank or write a question mark if you're not sure. Finding out the answer and singing it with the corresponding interval name will help develop your skills further.

That's a simple example of how you can start exploring Playing By Ear using Intervals. We'll cover this more fully in *Playing by Ear* with the Play-By-Ear Process.

Transcribing

You can use the same process to practice transcribing music i.e.

writing down the notes. Use whatever notation is familiar and comfortable for you, whether that's simply writing down the letter names, using traditional staff notation, guitar tablature, or a Pitch Contour with your own system of annotations.

Musicians often think that transcribing is a very advanced skill, but as you can see, a simple step-by-step process combined with developing your Relative Pitch can quickly make it possible to write down any melody you hear. You'll discover in the next chapter how the same can be true of harmony, through Ear Training for Chords and Progressions.

Writing Music

Even if you've never written music before, and you're right at the beginning of your journey with Intervals, you can begin using them to write music and even to improvise.

Here's a simple exercise. You might like to treat it as a "game", as this removes some of the intimidation factor which composing and improvisation can otherwise bring! It will begin as writing a melody, and we can then extend it towards improvising a melody on-the-fly.

Remember our Pitch Ladder and staff diagrams of the intervals in the pentascale:

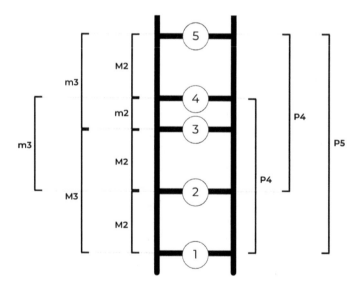

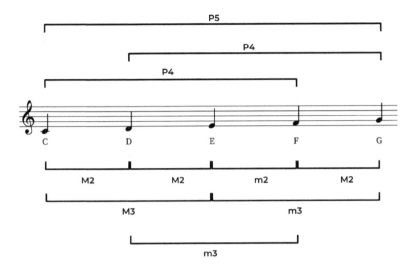

Have one of these two diagrams in front of you (whichever you prefer) as you try the following. Do it in a step-by-step way, taking your time.

EXERCISE: Write Music Using Intervals

1. Make up a sequence of Unisons, Major 2nds, Major 3rds, Perfect 4ths or Perfect 5ths at random (one or two of each is plenty – keep it short!). Do this by starting from the tonic of the pentascale, and choosing intervals ascending or descending to keep you within the notes of the pentascale. The diagrams above show your options from each note.

2. Write down the resulting notes as your melody. You can write in staff notation if that's comfortable for you, but just writing the letter names of the notes is also fine.

3. Play it through a few times, recording yourself, and experiment with the rhythms.

4. Listen back and choose the version you like best.

You just composed a melody! Now let's try another experiment…

1. Again choose a series of Unisons, Major 2nds, Major 3rds,

Perfect 4ths or Perfect 5ths at random, ascending or descending… but this time do not restrict yourself to the pentascale.

2.   Break your series of intervals up into short melodies of 4-6 notes each.

3.   Put note names to each melody—you may want to use the Pitch Ladder and/or Pitch Ruler to help you there.

4.   Play through these melodies. Explore adding rhythm, dynamics, and phrasing (see *Chapter Seventeen: Expression* for more ideas)

How did your melodies sound this time? What happened to them when we lifted the constraint of the major pentascale?

We'll explore writing music more in *Chapter Sixteen: Songwriting*.

Improvisation

Once you've spent some time playing around with writing melodies in this way, try Improvisation. You can follow the exact same process as the Writing Music exercise above, but do it on-the-fly, making your interval choices in the moment. You might be surprised how easy and fun improvisation is once you've first experimented with it in a no-pressure step-by-step way, and you use the same "constraints" as you've become familiar with through the writing exercise.

That's a simple starting point for improvising with intervals, and a great way to start tuning yourself in to the stepwise and skip motion of melodies, as well as the interplay between interval types and scale degrees.

We'll explore improvising and the idea of "constraints" more fully in *Chapter Fifteen: Improvisation* with Expansive Creativity.

Conclusion

In this chapter you learned all the essential theory relating to Intervals and began to familiarise yourself with their sounds. You now know a range of ways to practice interval recognition, and continually increase your skills. You've also seen some of the connections between Intervals and Solfa, and how they can each help the other, either by explicitly being used together, or through the under-the-hood magic of Convergent Learning.

In Part III we'll go deeper on applied skills like Playing By Ear, Improvisation, and Songwriting, showing you the frameworks you can use to learn each, including where Intervals can be leveraged to help you, through your sense of Relative Pitch.

Whether you had previous experience of Intervals, or this was your first time encountering them, I hope you are feeling excited by the potential that these powerful building blocks have to offer you!

CHAPTER ELEVEN:
CHORDS AND PROGRESSIONS

For a long time, I wandered lost in a sea of chords. I had studied harmony in music theory, and I had learned how to play a wide variety of chords on both piano and guitar. But my ears were essentially deaf to how chords worked, why certain chords were chosen, or how I might make any creative use of chords myself.

All I knew was that harmony seemed a lot more complicated than melody! And since I couldn't do anything with melody except learn to play what was written, note-by-note, it frankly didn't even occur to me that I might be able to do anything more than that with harmony. It probably didn't help that I was learning piano, where "harmony" seemed to mean "playing up to eight notes at once across both hands", with no real understanding of *why* it was those notes that were written on the page.

I want to cut right to the chase and share with you the two big epiphanies which broke the world of Chords wide open for me. We'll be leveraging these two ideas in this chapter to help you quickly get comfortable and confident working with Chords in your Ear Training and across all your music-making:

1. Although "harmony" can mean any possible combination of notes played together, in fact the same pitch relationships we explored in *Chapter Eight: Relative Pitch* mean that there is particular musical significance to certain combinations of notes in a given Key.

In all the genres of the Western music tradition we focus on in this book, harmony can be usefully understood in terms of which degrees of the scale are being used, and how that changes over time.

To put that another way: it's not arbitrary! There are certain patterns, combinations, and note choices which are commonly chosen, because of the musical effect they have on the listener. Just like the shorthand of saying "the key is C Major" rather than specifying each and every note we've chosen for our key, there is a shorthand of describing harmony, which will be introduced below and allows us to say things as simple as *"It's a I-IV-V7 progression in C"* even though there might be dozens and dozens of notes involved.

2. A staggering number of songs use just a handful of Chords. Again, there may be many, many notes being played, but only three or four different Chords. Even better: it's actually the same three or four Chords which are so extensively used!

You might have heard of the idea of a "three-chord song" or a "four-chord song". Particularly in pop, rock and country music, but also in classical, electronic, and more varied genres, *the same* three or four Chords are being used. The key may vary, the particular "voicing" of those chords with specific notes may vary, the arrangement across instruments may vary —but once you understand the shorthand of Chords, you'll see (and hear!) that the same three or four Chords are at play, perhaps up to 90% of the time.

In this chapter we'll introduce a particular way of thinking about Chords and developing your ear for them, which allows you to fully leverage the two points above. This will transform "harmony" from something that seems endlessly complex and overwhelming, into something that feels just as simple as the note-by-note movement of a melody.

So far, in the previous chapters, we have covered two types of building blocks:

- **Solfa**, where we recognise one note at a time, based on its relationship to the tonic (or "home") note, and

- **Intervals**, where we recognise pairs of notes, based on the relationship between them.

In this chapter we will introduce our third type of building block: **Chords**, consisting of three or more notes played together.

While it might be tempting to think that our building blocks are becoming more complex as we add more notes (one for Solfa, two for Intervals, three or more for Chords), in fact it's better to think of them as three perspectives, or ways of interpreting the notes we are working with. Developing your ear for Chords is no more complex than for Solfa or Intervals, and (in the spirit of Convergent Learning) you can usefully work on all three together, as they all develop your core sense of Relative Pitch.

With Solfa and Intervals, we focused on a certain moment in time i.e. *"what one (or two) notes are happening right now?"*. With Chords, we can do the same thing, to identify the *type* of Chord being played. For example a "major triad" or a "dominant seventh chord". However, with Chords it is particularly valuable to also consider the flow from one chord to another over time, what we call a "Chord Progression".

In this chapter we will explore both Chords and Chord Progressions, as well as the connections to our other building blocks of Solfa and Intervals. You will see how all three together provide a "360 degree view" of everything pitch-related that's happening in a piece of music.

As with everything in our world of Relative Pitch, we are taking a *descriptive* view of the theory (see *Chapter One: Musicality*) rather than a *prescriptive* one. So we will focus on the building blocks which provide the greatest "bang for our buck", but that doesn't mean that's all that's possible or all that's "allowed". It's purely because if most music tends to use particular elements the most, it makes sense to begin our Ear Training with those, and then introduce the less frequently-used possibilities later.

Overview

We will follow the Learn, Practice, Apply approach of Integrated Ear Training. We'll go through these one by one in this chapter, and you will probably want to read through the chapter in order to begin with—but remember that when it comes to actually doing Ear Training, these are best done as a short loop: learn a little (e.g. by re-reading part of the chapter), practice a little (doing an exercise or two from the chapter), try applying it (doing one or more of the applied activities at the end of the chapter).

Learn

We'll begin by discussing the benefits of training your ear for Chords and Progressions, since the applications vary a lot across musicians. In "What is a Chord?" and "What is a Chord Progression?" we'll lay out the basic definitions and theory, as well as introducing a way of "thinking vertically" which can bring a lot of clarity to your mental model of harmony.

Then in "How Chords and Progressions Work" we will dive deeper into the construction and use of Chords and Progressions, making the links to our other building blocks of Intervals and Solfa.

You'll notice that the "Learn" section is beefier than those for Solfa or Intervals! It's a very Head-heavy chapter.

This is partly because we're tackling both Chords and Progressions, but mostly because if you've read the Solfa and Intervals chapters, or ideally begun working with those building blocks already, we want to really spell out how all these building blocks relate. As you'll discover, this will help you not only intellectually, but in a very practical way with your Ear Training for Chords and Progressions.

Practice

In the "Getting Started" section we'll cover how our Basic Drill (playing examples and trying to identify which building block it was) can be used for Chords and for Progressions, and introduce different ways you can start to distinguish between the different types of Chords and Progressions (Hearing and Heart).

Then, in our "Start With Aiming For..." Section we will focus on just a couple of Chords and the most commonly-used Progressions, to let you reach a highly versatile and practical ability with Chords and

Progressions quickly.

The world of Chords and Progressions is vast! In the "Going Further" section we'll briefly explore several ways you can extend your abilities to handle more varied and complex forms of harmony (Head, Hearing). Depending on your musical interests, activities and background, some of these may be immediately of interest to you to pursue, while others may be irrelevant, or safely left until later.

Apply

Finally, in the "Additional Exercises and Activities" section we show how to use both your singing voice and your instrument (Hands) to develop your ear for Chords and Progressions, as well as how to take your burgeoning skills to practical musical activities such as Playing By Ear, Improvisation and Songwriting.

The Benefits Of Developing Your Ear For Chords

Before we continue, I think it's important to say a few words about why you might want to explore Chords in this way.

Depending on your musical background, this may be obvious to you. For example, if you're a guitarist who's currently dependant on doing a web search or consulting a stack of books to look up the Chords to play any new song you want to, the idea of just being able to "hear it, then play it" probably has you sold already! Or similarly, if your Big Picture Vision depicts you writing wonderful, moving music to bring your poetry to life, knowing how to choose just the right harmonies should have obvious appeal.

But what about if you're a trumpet player? Or a singer? What if you just want to improvise melodies, or perform music more compellingly?

Harmony (meaning how multiple notes work together to create an overall sound) is central to music, and Chords are the building blocks of harmony. Believe it or not, even music which doesn't seem to have harmony (for example, a singer performing unaccompanied) still has an underlying harmonic structure, through the particular melody notes being chosen, and the harmony they imply.

One useful way to think about it is that harmony is about the overall musical flow of a piece. Just like in *Chapter Five: Active Listening* when discussing Form, the progression from one chord to another is what creates the "journey" that the music takes the listener on. This is a big part of why we won't just consider individual Chords in this chapter, but also look at Chord Progressions: how the sequence of Chords work together to create that "musical journey".

Because harmony is so fundamental and prevalent, and because it closely relates to many other aspects of music, learning to hear and understand Chord Progressions can unlock considerable musical understanding for you, whatever your musical life looks like.

Coming back to our two examples above, a trumpet player interested in improvising will find that understanding Chords and Progressions by ear reveals a lot about which notes will be most effective at any given moment in the music. Beyond just "play the notes from the current chord" as some improv methods might preach, you will understand deeply how any note you choose will create an interplay with the underlying harmony and have the musical effect you intend.

An unaccompanied singer, on the other hand, may not be interested in improvising—but understanding the harmony of the full arrangement will both aid memorisation and keeping your place in the music during a performance (through having a clear mental model of the Form). It can also provide a vivid audiated accompaniment, helping with pitching, phrasing, and expression. Even when the harmony isn't heard "out there" in the real world, it can still be alive and influential inside your own musical mind!

Exactly how you make use of your newfound chord skills will be up to you, but there's no doubt that gaining a deep understanding, appreciation, and facility with Chords and Progressions can have a profound and far-reaching positive effect on all your musical activities.

What Are Chords and Progressions?

If you've been learning music for a little while, no doubt you'll be familiar with the concepts of Chords and Progressions. Don't skip ahead! Because different musicians have such different ways of relating to harmony, it's essential that we begin by getting on the same page about what we mean by these terms.

What Is A Chord?

We will use the simple definition that "a chord is three or more notes played at once"[1].

Different combinations of notes will create different chord sounds. As we discussed in *Chapter Eight: Relative Pitch*, it's common for musicians to come from a background of thinking purely in terms of "letter names", which can make it seem like there are an overwhelming number of different possibilities. And yet when we listen to music, we know that harmony often sounds quite simple and natural. This is a clue that (just like with Solfa and Intervals) there are actually patterns and relationships at work which can let things sound "the same" to us across a variety of keys and letter names.

In this chapter we'll look at different types of chord. We'll add a perspective of both Solfa (i.e. which degrees of the key's scale are being used to create the chord) and Intervals (i.e. what are the pitch distances between the notes in the chord), and introduce the shorthand which matches how the ear naturally interprets the sounds created by different combinations.

Just like with Solfa and Intervals, the shorthands and commonly-used patterns of note choices don't limit what can be done with Chords, but they let us rapidly gain a powerful level of ability to recognise and choose chords to suit our musical task. All of the further complexities and possibilities can then be an easy step forwards from there.

Here's an example, to make that concrete: if you are a jazz musician starting from the world of reading notation, you might already be aware of a dizzying array of four-note "seventh" chords. There are several different types of seventh chords, based on any one of our 12 pitch classes, in various inversions... You may have learned to play 50 to 100 different chords! But if you begin with Ear Training for the chord types and progressions introduced in this chapter, you will establish a strong foundation for understanding Chords and Chord Progressions by ear which already lets you start to recognise the underpinnings of all that complex jazz harmony. Extending your ear skills to four-note chords and all of the different possibilities then

---

[1] Some people would consider a harmonic interval (two notes at once) to be a type of chord. It's also possible to analyse the chord implied by a series of notes played one after another (for example, an arpeggio or "broken chord").

For our purposes it will be helpful to keep to this simple definition of "three or more notes played at once", and consider those two to be special cases.

becomes a far easier task.

We'll explore this a bit further in the "Going Further" section below. For now, the main thing to know is that everything we'll cover forms the foundation of Western harmony. Just like mastering Solfa for the pentatonic scale makes it easy to then master the full major scale and start handling accidentals (chromatic) notes too, if you master the material covered in this chapter, you'll be set up to succeed with any more complex harmony you might wish to tackle.

What is a Chord Progression?

A Chord Progression is a sequence of chords played one after another.

Once again, the magic of Relative Pitch means that even though any possible sequence of any possible chords could be used, in practice there are patterns and conventions in music which let us focus on the building blocks which will have the deepest and widest-reaching impact on our Chord Progression skills.

As mentioned above when sharing the two big "epiphanies", there are particular common chord progressions which are used again and again in popular music. This is partly due to the underlying resonances of the notes and chords (i.e. there are meaningful relationships inherent to music itself) and partly because culturally we have learned what sounds "normal" (i.e. the more songwriters and composers used these progressions, the more listeners were trained to expect and appreciate them, influencing the musical choices of the next generation of songwriters and composers).

What's perhaps most exciting for our purposes is that:

A. There is a vast number of so-called "three-chord songs" and "four-chord songs"[2] which use only the chord types and progressions covered in this chapter. This means that a relatively basic ability to recognise Chords and Progressions by ear will take you a very long way.

B. Even music which goes beyond those particular chords and

---

[2] A quick note to avoid any confusion as we continue: these names come from the fact that the songs use just three or four particular chords, rather than referring to the "three chord" (or "iii") or "four chord" ("IV") specifically.

progressions will often still make wide use of some or all of them.

Andrew Says...

I remember my jazz ear training classes at the New England Conservatory, attempting to identify individual chords by ear, complete with all sorts of extensions. (G–7 ♭5 ♭9, anybody?) Yes, there was something to be gained by

learning to reach deep into a mass of notes and pick out enough of the pitches to identify the sound. But when I was done, I wasn't much better at identifying chords in a flowing musical context. And I wasn't able to play along by ear or jam on songs on the piano—I needed someone else's chord sheets for that.

This is what I thought "chord ear training" was, until I came to Musical U and discovered Chord Progressions ear training. Suddenly, I had something I could use. Rather than parsing out each individual chord, I was able to identify a whole progression of them—and it was a breeze compared to picking each chord out, note by note!

Harmony is not static, it flows through time. So focusing on how chords move made much more sense. Accompanying, songwriting, jamming, and improvising with chord progressions were suddenly so much easier than they had been before.

Thinking Vertically

Typically, musicians who are familiar with Chords and Progressions think of each chord as a single unit which occurs as a given moment in time. While this is well-suited to our "building blocks" approach, there is another way of thinking about them which helps to open up the relationships between chords and between the notes they're built from.

In *Chapter Five: Active Listening* we introduced the idea of listening both "horizontally" (how things change over time) and "vertically" (everything that's happening at a given moment):

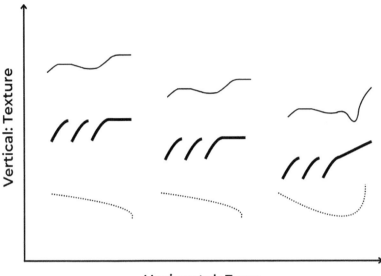

Horizontal: Form

There, we used this idea to set the scene for discussing Texture (the vertical) and Form (the horizontal), but this is also a useful way of thinking about harmony.

In the previous two chapters we used the idea of a Pitch Ladder or Pitch Ruler to analyse how far apart in pitch different Solfa scale degrees or the notes of Intervals are.

Here's the essentials, if you haven't read those chapters or would like a reminder:

- The "Pitch Ruler" shows all 12 of the pitch classes (where, for example, C is one pitch class, C♯ is another, D is another, and so on). The keys of a piano (black and white together) or the frets of a guitar correspond to these *chromatic steps* or *Half Steps*. We usually show one octave on the Pitch Ruler, with a 13th marker bringing us back to the starting pitch class. For example:

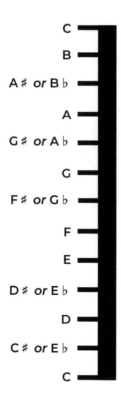

- The "Pitch Ladder" shows just the notes of the scale, and reflects how the notes of a major or minor scale are not evenly-spaced apart. Some are two chromatic steps apart while others are just one chromatic step apart. Here's a Pitch Ladder for the major scale, with the numbers of the scale degrees shown, alongside a Pitch Ruler, to show you the relationship:

Pitch Ladder   Pitch Ruler

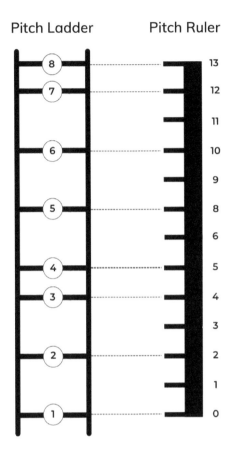

We can now use these same ideas, but introducing a horizontal axis to think about what's happening harmonically over time.

At any given moment, we can imagine a Pitch Ladder or Pitch Ruler, and where the notes of a chord lie on it. We can then see how those notes "move" over time, as the music moves from one chord to the next, for example:

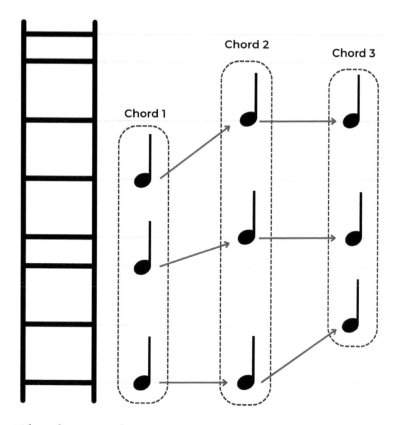

Although it's not the way musicians normally think about Chords and Progressions, imagining music as existing on a "grid" like this can be extremely helpful, especially for making the connections to our building blocks of Solfa and Intervals.

How Chords and Progressions Work

How Chords Work

We defined a chord as "three or more notes played together", and so the simplest chord we could use as a building block will be a 3-note chord, which is called a "triad" chord.

Building Chords

Any combination of 3 notes would be a valid chord, but in practice the most commonly-used chords are created by choosing notes from the key's scale which are each separated by one skipped note.

One way of understanding why we do this is that two adjacent notes from the scale, whether they're a Whole Step or a Half Step apart, will typically sound quite dissonant when played together, so that would be a rare choice, musically. Given that, the most "compact" chord we might construct would be one where we skip one note in between each note of our chord, like this:

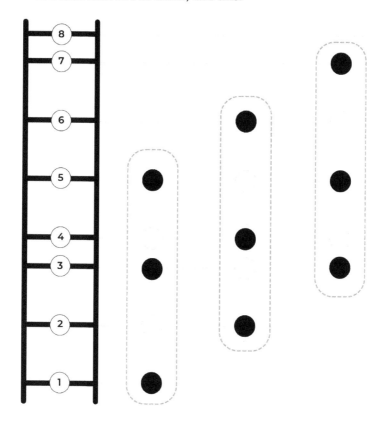

If you're familiar with Solfa or Intervals, let's take a look at what that might look like. If not, don't worry about the details in the diagrams below—the point is just that we're skipping one note of the scale each time to construct the most compact chords.

In terms of the Pitch Ladder and Solfa that might look like this:

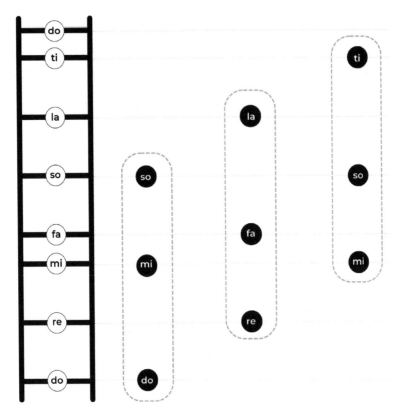

In terms of the Pitch Ruler and Intervals that might look like this:

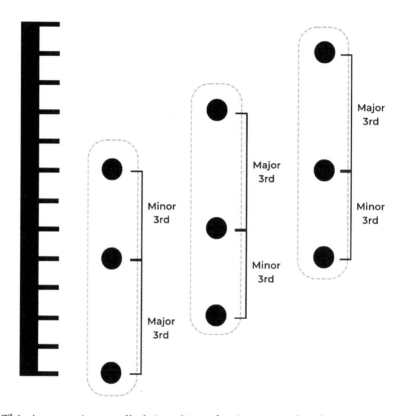

This is sometimes called "stacking thirds" since the chord is built from a Major or Minor Third interval on top of another Major or Minor Third.

If we look at all the 3-note Chords we could construct in this way from the Major Scale, we would get:

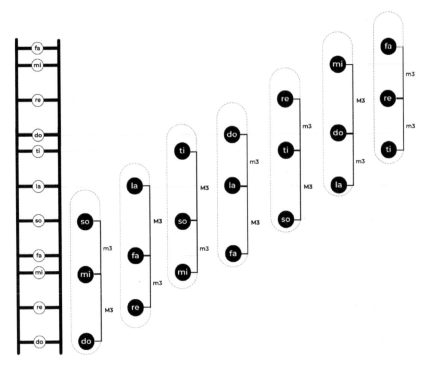

(*Again, if you're not familiar with Solfa or Intervals, you can ignore those details and just focus on how we're skipping a note from the scale each time, and how many chromatic steps apart the notes are as a result.*)

Types of Chord

From *Chapter Eight: Relative Pitch* we know that it's going to be the *relationships* between the notes (i.e. the pitch distances) which define the characteristic musical sound, and so we would expect that those chords which have the same internal pitch distances will sound similar.

Whether we think in terms of Intervals, steps on the Pitch Ladder (i.e. Solfa), or simply the number of chromatic steps apart the notes are, we can see that there are three possibilities emerging:

- Major 3rd + Minor 3rd (4 chromatic steps + 3 chromatic steps)
- Minor 3rd + Major 3rd (3 chromatic steps + 4 chromatic steps)
- Minor 3rd + Minor 3rd (3 chromatic steps + 3 chromatic steps)

And although it doesn't appear in the Major Scale, by deduction we can see there could also be a fourth possible chord type, by stacking two Major Thirds:

- Major 3rd + Major 3rd (4 chromatic steps + 4 chromatic steps)

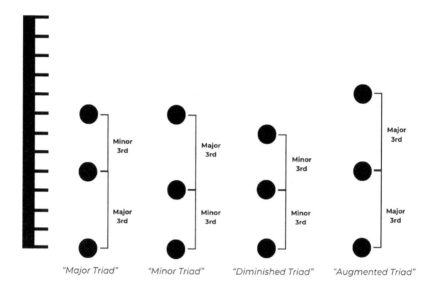

These are the four types of triad chord, and each has a characteristic sound.

This "type" is referred to as the *quality* of the chord: Major, Minor, Diminished or Augmented. The Major and Minor qualities are related to Major and Minor keys and scales in terms of theory, and they have a shared "major-y" sound or "minor-y" sound. There is similarly a characteristic "diminished sound" and "augmented sound". This characteristic sound will be part of what we're listening for when we develop our ear for Chords.

These four types of Triad will be our building blocks for Chords.

In fact, we'll focus on just the Major Triad and Minor Triad since the other two types are relatively rarely used, and can be explored once you're confident with Major vs. Minor. Likewise, there are particular four-note chord types which are commonly used, especially in certain genres (e.g. jazz). We'll explore this a bit in the "Going Further" section below.

The three notes define the chord and we have the shorthand of specifying the root note and the quality (e.g. saying "a C Major" chord rather than needing to spell out "a chord with notes C, E and G"). There's an additional convention that if the quality isn't mentioned, the chord is major. For example you'll hear things like "its a C, F, A minor,

G progression" which indicates the C, F and G chords are all major while the A chord is minor.

Voicing Chords

It's worth noting that a musician is free to choose notes from any octave (register) which match the chord's pitch classes, including repeating one or more of the notes. This is referred to as how the chord is "voiced".

For example, here are several ways of playing a C Major chord on the piano keyboard:

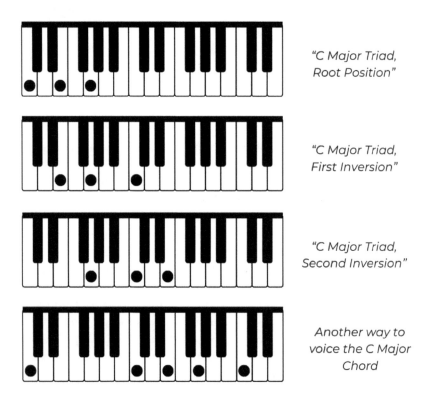

"C Major Triad, Root Position"

"C Major Triad, First Inversion"

"C Major Triad, Second Inversion"

Another way to voice the C Major Chord

Whichever voicing is used, C would still be referred to as the "root" of the chord. The "root" note is the note the chord is built from, whether that is the lowest note in the voicing or not.

This is another case where we will start simple, focusing on just the "root position triad" chord which uses three notes, with the root note at the bottom and the other two in the same order as they appear in the scale. Although different voicings can certainly make our Ear Training tasks more challenging, the distinctive musical sound and role of the chord is common across all of them. This means that once again, if we focus on the simplest, most common building blocks, we will establish a foundation from which it's relatively easy to extend our skills to cover all those other cases too.

A Note To Fretboard Fans

If you play guitar, ukulele, banjo, or another fretboard-based instrument, you will probably be used to thinking about chords in terms of shapes: the position of your fingers across the strings and frets to produce a certain chord.

While it is possible to do Ear Training using only these standard fretboard shapes, and that may seem like the convenient option (since it's what you're used to playing and it's the way you plan to play chords if your goal in Ear Training is to play by ear) we recommend still starting from the basic triad chords introduced below. This provides an easier musical sound for you to get your ears around, particularly if you want to leverage Solfa or Intervals to help you.

Above we discussed how chords can come in various "voicings", and you can consider the standard fretboard shapes as relatively complex voicings. This means that if you go directly to those forms of the chords, you're skipping a few stepping stones which could provide an easier path to developing your ear for Chords and Progressions.

What will generally work best is to first practice with the simplest 3-note versions of the chords, and then extend from there to your "normal" way of playing the same chords. We'll cover this in a bit more detail in the "Going Further" section later in the chapter.

With that being said, the approach presented here encourages you to start trying to play by ear and experimenting with real music tracks early on, and so you can certainly start factoring your normal chord shapes into your Ear Training activities before mastering the simpler Triads. The main thing is to be aware that for focused recognition exercises, Triads will provide you with a simpler task than the regular fretboard shapes, and are a step you probably don't want to skip.

How Chord Progressions Work

We've seen above that there is a "family" of Chords which belong to a given Major Key:

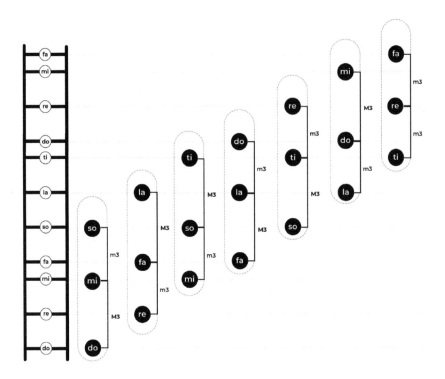

While we could refer to these by the Solfa note they're based on (e.g. "the *do* chord"), the more common approach is to label them with numbers: using either Roman Numerals (I, II, III, IV, V, etc.) which has its roots in Classical music theory, or using regular numbers (1, 2, 3, 4, 5, etc.) which is often called the "Nashville Numbering System" due to its common usage in the songwriting traditions of Nashville, Tennessee.

Just like we prefer to use the Solfa names for scale degrees to provide a clear, dedicated set of labels which aren't used for anything else in music, we will choose to use Roman Numerals to identify the Chords in the family. The convention is to use an uppercase numeral for major chords (e.g. I, IV, V) and a lowercase numeral for minor chords (ii, iii, vi, etc.).

I-IV-V vs. I, IV, V

It can be unclear sometimes whether *"a one-four-five progression"* means a progression featuring the I, IV and V chords, or a progression with the chords in that particular sequence.

We will use a comma to denote a group of chords (e.g. "a I, IV, V progression") and a dash to indicate a particular sequence (e.g. "a I-IV-V-I progression").

Here are the Roman Numerals for the chords in a Major Key:

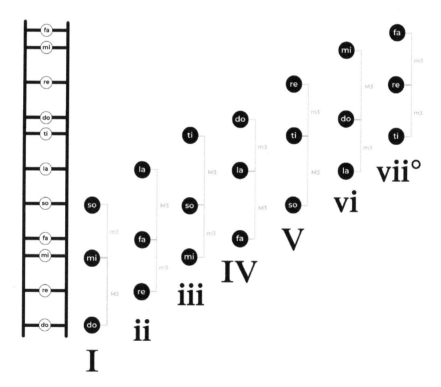

These are our "building blocks" for Chord Progressions: I, ii, iii, IV, V, vi, and vii°. From those, we'll focus on just I, IV and V, and then introduce the vi (in "Going Further"):

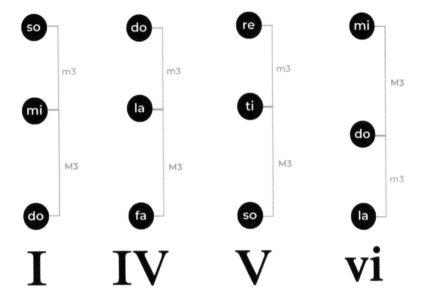

Here's how those four chords would come out in the key of C Major:

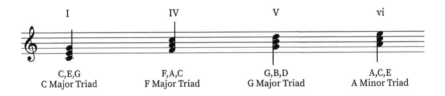

Or the key of A Major:

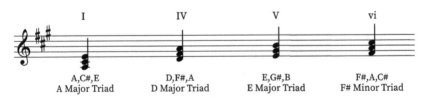

This reflects how frequently the chords are used across a wide range of musical styles and traditions—and as always, starting from a small number of commonly-used building blocks sets us up well to then introduce further possibilities later.

This means we will practice listening for Progressions which feature first just the I, IV and V chords. For example, a piece in C Major might have a progression of:

C Major → F Major → G Major → C Major

And a piece in A Major might have a progression of:

A Major → D Major → E Major → A Major

We will learn to hear that these are both, in fact, I-IV-V-I progressions.

About Functional Harmony

You may hear the term "functional harmony" used when discussing the theory of Chord Progressions.

Very broadly speaking, that is what we're talking about here: thinking in terms of which degree of the key's scale each chord is built on, and using that to understand the musical effect.

However, as the name implies, functional harmony is very focused on the musical "purpose" or "function" of each chord, and tends to very quickly get into intricate theoretical analysis, with multiple schools of thought on how to analyse music and what the "correct" answers might be.

It's a fascinating topic, but one which risks pulling us away from focusing on the sounds of the chords and into a prescriptive view of music theory rather than a descriptive one.

For that reason we won't use that term here, but you might find it helpful to know that very roughly speaking, if musicians refer to the "function" of a chord, or use terms like "subdominant chord" or "dominant chord", they are talking, broadly, about this same approach to understanding harmony.

Connections to Solfa and Intervals

For several years at Musical U, we taught Chord recognition and Chord Progression recognition as distinct skills from Solfa or Intervals. This worked, and you can continue through the rest of this chapter without having studied or done Ear Training for either of those, and successfully start recognising types of Chords and different Progressions.

Then we created a 10-day introductory Ear Training course[3] where we taught the basics of all three in rapid succession. It was the first time we saw clearly the true power of Convergent Learning. By waking up their ears to all three perspectives on Relative Pitch at the same time, students were able to make much faster progress than we'd seen before.

Because it worked so well, we doubled down on this approach when designing the Autumn Season of the *Living Music* program, really immersing students in all three together and making explicit the connections between them. This proved to be the most effective approach yet.

It was remarkable to see how often an apparent issue or sticking point with one skill was actually resolved through doing work on another. For example, when Major Thirds vs. Minor Thirds were proving tricky in the context of Intervals, switching focus to Major vs. Minor Chords suddenly unblocked things. Or when it was difficult to hear a I-IV-V progression, spending some time with *do, fa* and *so* in Solfa quickly tuned the ear in to what it had been trying to hear.

Again and again, that "simmering stew" of Relative Pitch Ear Training coalesced into something much greater than the sum of its parts.

So while you *could* focus solely on Chords and Progressions, and get good results, I would highly encourage you to explore Solfa and Intervals too. It may seem like taking on too much at once, but the beauty of Convergent Learning is that we can trust our musical mind to figure things out "under the hood" and develop the same core sense of Relative Pitch using all three perspectives.

So let's look more closely at how Solfa and Intervals relate to the Chords and Progressions introduced above and how each can reveal more about what's going on, musically.

Solfa and Intervals for Chords

If our main building blocks for Chords are the Major and Minor triad chords, what does that mean in terms of Solfa and Intervals?

Let's look at Intervals first. We've seen above that triad chords can be constructed by "stacking thirds" and there are these four possible combinations:

---

[3] Ear Training For Beginners, 2019.

Bottom interval	Top interval	Type of triad
m3	m3	diminished
m3	M3	minor
M3	m3	major
M3	M3	augmented

Showing the Major and Minor Triads visually, we can see that in both cases, the interval from the bottom note to the top one is a Perfect Fifth:

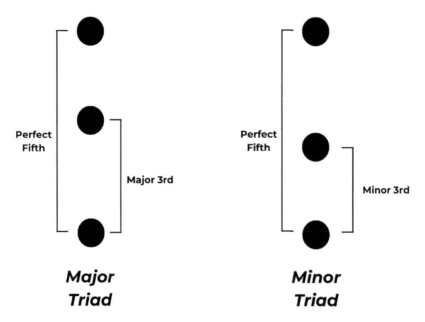

Major Triad   **Minor Triad**

Although it's enlightening to think about "stacking thirds" (particularly when going further, to four-note "seventh" chords—more on that later), in fact from an Ear Training perspective it's more helpful to think about our Major and Minor triads as being "a Perfect Fifth, with either a Major or a Minor Third".

To give a concrete example, a C Major triad has the notes C, E, G, while a C Minor triad has the notes C, E♭, G. Just one note differs between the two. Yet as we'll discover in the listening exercises below, changing that single note by just a Half Step makes a huge difference!

Side Note:

You may remember that in *Chapter Eight: Relative Pitch* we talked about how the terms "major" and "minor" are used for keys, scales and chords, but there isn't a full, universal correspondence between the three.

This is an example where it's helpful to notice that this difference of a Major Third versus a Minor Third can be seen as corresponding to how a Major Scale contains a Major Third between its first and third notes, while a Minor Scale contains a Minor Third between its first and third notes. This gives the same "major-y feel" to a Major Scale and Major Triad, and "minor-y feel" to a Minor Scale and Minor Triad, which is helpful from an Ear Training perspective, getting that sense of tonality.

However, since there are also Minor Triads belonging to a Major Key and found in a Major Scale (just like there are Major intervals found within a Minor Key and Scale), we must remember to let that idea of "tonality" remain a bit broad, and be useful from a perspective of "characteristic sound" rather than trying to fixate on pinning down strict music theory equivalences.

When we listen for chord types and aim to distinguish Major from Minor Triads, this "Major Third vs. Minor Third" difference is what we'll be honing in on. You can probably already see why Convergent Learning works so well! The better we get with our interval recognition skills, the easier it is to hear the differences between chord types, and vice-versa.

So what about Solfa?

Well, there things become a bit more complex, but also more powerful. Remember that with Solfa, we are always thinking about the *context* of the key. With Intervals we are analysing only the relationships between the notes of the chord, and so we can group together all "Major Triads" and all "Minor Triads", since the intervals are identical, regardless of the note chosen to base the chord on.

With Solfa, we're thinking about the relationships of each note to the tonic ("home") note. This means that we actually have various possibilities for our Major and Minor Triads.

Let's look at all the Triad Chords in the Major Scale, in terms of Solfa. Each row of the table below represents one of the Triad Chords.

Choosing each note of the scale in turn as our bottom note, we'll skip a note to find our middle note, and skip a note again to find our top note, then label the type of Triad which results:

Bottom Note	Middle Note	Top Note	Type of Triad
do	mi	so	Major
re	fa	la	Minor
mi	so	ti	Minor
fa	la	do	Major
so	ti	re	Major
la	do	mi	Minor
ti	re	fa	Diminished

So when we take a Solfa view on chord types, we are listening not just for the relationships between the notes, like we do with Intervals—but instead we are taking account of the context of the key by identifying each note with its Solfa identity. This reveals both the type of the chord *and* its role in the chord family of the scale.

For example, we hear *"fa, la and do together"* and know not only that it's a Major Chord, but also that it's the IV chord, specifically.

Hopefully you are starting to see the power of having multiple perspectives on Relative Pitch. Doing Ear Training "purely" for Chord Types is made profoundly more effective and illuminating when we also bring an Intervals perspective and a Solfa perspective.

It does normally take a while to wrap your head around all of the different connections and equivalences. Don't be overwhelmed! Remember that we are taking an Integrated Ear Training approach, so you're not expected to master and memorise all of the "facts" presented here before moving on. As long as you understand the basic concepts of how we can think about Chords in these various ways, that will be enough to continue into the "Practice" and "Apply" material below and start gaining real, practical skills.

Remember also the "Beginners Mind" and "Loose Grip" Mindsets from *Chapter Two: Mindset*. Trust that immersing yourself and taking a playful, curious, exploratory attitude will pay dividends.

Solfa and Intervals for Progressions

How do Solfa and Intervals help us with recognising different types of chord progression?

When it comes to Chord Progressions, the main thing we are wanting to recognise is the degree of the scale that each chord is based on. We will take for granted for now that the chord type will match what we'd expect from the key's family i.e. the "one" chord will be major, the "six" chord will be minor, and so on, as seen in the diagram above of the Major Scale chords.

As we've already seen above, Solfa is a perfect fit for this! If we are trained in recognising scale degrees with Solfa, we need only practice tuning in to which note is the "root" of the chord.

Taking a Solfa view on Chord Progressions means that if, for example, we're listening for the order of I, IV and V chords in a 3-chord song, we are listening out for when the chord is based on *do, fa,* or *so.* There are a couple of ways to do that, which we'll cover in the "Getting Started" section below.

What about Intervals?

Well, with Progressions we also want to hear the *movement* from one chord to the next, and so Intervals can be a valuable aid in comparing the root note of one chord to the root note of the next. Again, we'll need to practice "tuning in" to that root note among the various notes that might be present, but then we can use our interval skills to follow the movement of that root note up and down in pitch over time.

Taking the same example of trying to hear I, IV and V chords, we would be listening for when the root note moved up or down by a Major Second (IV-V or V-IV), a Perfect Fourth (I-IV or IV-I), or a Perfect Fifth (I-V or V-I). We'll look at this in more detail as we continue.

Getting Started

It's time to start bringing the theory to life! Here are some ways to start familiarising yourself with the sounds of Chords and Progressions. Then in later sections below we'll go into more detail on a variety of exercises you can use to develop your chord skills more fully.

How To Use The Basic Drill

Remember that our Basic Drill is simply "listen to some examples of different types of building block, and for each one try to recognise which type it is."

EXERCISE: The Basic Drill For Chords

With Chords, the Basic Drill works in the usual way:

1.   Hear an example chord, from a set of chord types you're working on.

2.   Name the type of chord you think it is.

3.   Find out if you got it right. If not, ideally compare and contrast the sounds of the example and your own answer.

EXERCISE: The Basic Drill For Chord Progressions

With Progressions, it's slightly different, as we need to establish the key first:

1.   Establish the key, by playing the tonic note, the full scale, or perhaps a V7-I Cadence (more on that below).

2.   Hear an example chord progression

3.   Name the chords (by their Roman Numerals)

4.   Find out if you got it right.

As with Solfa and Intervals, this Basic Drill is a good way to assess our abilities, and a good starting point for developing our skills, but should always be done along with other kinds of practice exercises and applied activities, as covered later in the chapter.

With Solfa and Intervals, it is fairly easy to source or produce examples, and to make use of the various ways of recognising the different types we're focused on.

With Chords and Progressions, it can be trickier to source or produce suitable examples, and a little more complex to approach recognising them—mostly due to the way we'll want to leverage Singing, Audiation, Solfa and Intervals.

No need for concern! It just means that as we continue, we're going to spell out the steps for various exercises based on the Basic Drill more than we did with Solfa or Intervals. You'll notice that the simple overall structure of the exercise remains the same though: "listen to some examples of different types of building block, and for each one try to recognise which type it is."

So, how do we make sure that our "answers" are based on recognition skills rather than pure guesswork?

How To Recognise Chords

Let's start familiarising ourselves with the sounds of Major and Minor Triads. If you're keen to, feel free to also include Augmented and Diminished Triads at this stage. You will find that each of the four Triad types has a very distinctive characteristic sound, and while confusion can still arise (for example between Minor and Diminished Triads), most musicians find they can quite quickly learn to recognise each type—at least when played in isolation.

We can use each of the three approaches introduced above: "pure" recognition, using Intervals, and using Solfa. Start with the "pure" exercise below, and then when you're ready, introduce the Intervals and Solfa perspectives to help you advance faster and build the connections between the three.

1. Recognising Directly

Compared to other Ear Training activities, distinguishing the four types of Triad chord is a case where simple familiarisation and direct comparison can work well.

EXERCISE: Recognising Chord Types Directly

As with Solfa and Intervals, you can find pre-made audio tracks for practicing with in the *Additional Resources*, or use interactive quizzes. However, it can be just as effective and a real boost to take matters into your own hands—literally!

1.   Sit with your instrument, choose a starting note, and construct a Triad of one particular type. You can use the information about Solfa and Intervals above, or solely the "Pitch Ruler" view of Half Step measurements to figure out the right notes. Play all three notes together. If you play an instrument which produces a single note at once (e.g. clarinet rather than piano) you can play through the notes in turn, ascending and

descending (an *"arpeggio"*). Play the example a few times, listening carefully.

2.   Change the middle and/or top note by a Half Step to produce one of the other types of Triad. For example, if you started with a Major Triad, bring the middle note down a Half Step to make it a Minor Triad. Again, play it a few times and listen carefully to the overall sound, the character, the emotion, the feel.

3.   When you're ready, move to a different starting note. Bear in mind it may take your musical ear a moment to adjust to a new sense of the key or "tonal centre". This can be frustrating but is a good form of Contextual Interference (see *Chapter Six: Superlearning*) which will produce a more robust and versatile ability for you.

As you do this exercise it's highly valuable to write down any descriptive words that come to mind for each type of chord (e.g. *"Diminished chords really clash!"*), as well as comparisons (e.g. *"Augmented chords sound brighter and lighter than Major chords"*).

TIP:

Remember that when introducing the Basic Drill in *Chapter Eight: Relative Pitch* we suggested using recording as a way to combine instrument practice and recognition practice.

So to make this exercise even more effective, record yourself doing the steps above for a few minutes or more. Then use that recording as a practice track, by listening back to it and trying to identify by ear the choices you were making each time.

If you are playing the examples one note at a time, it will be important to also find some source of examples where the notes are all played together, since this is how you will typically be hearing chords in real music.

Although many musicians find this recognition skill comes relatively quickly for them, it's still worth being thoughtful about your sequencing. If you're going to tackle Augmented and Diminished Triads too, don't dive in with all four types at once! You might like to follow a sequence like this:

- Major vs. Minor

- Major vs. Augmented

- Minor vs. Diminished

- Major vs. Minor vs. Diminished

- Major vs. Minor vs. Augmented

- All Four Types

Aim to achieve something like 80% accuracy with each set before moving on.

2. Using Intervals

To bring your interval recognition skills to the task of recognising chord types, the main thing to practice is learning to hear each note of the chord clearly.

We're restricting ourselves to three-note chords in "root position" for now, so it shouldn't be too overwhelming to "tune in" to each note of the chord. However, it is a skill, and you may be surprised how much concentration is required!

EXERCISE: Recognising Chord Types Using Intervals

Both Singing and Audiation can be a great help:

1. Play the example chord.

2. Take a moment to either sing out loud, or audiate, each note of the chord in turn. You may want to play the example again, to make sure you've matched the pitches correctly.

This exercise alone should be your starting point, until you get some facility with "dissecting" a chord into its component notes.

Next, add a third step:

3.   Now use Singing or Audiation to compare the pairs of notes present, and identify each interval. What type of Third are you hearing between the bottom and middle, and the middle and top notes? Is the interval from bottom to top a Perfect Fifth— or something else?

As we saw above, we can listen for the difference of a Major Third versus a Minor Third to distinguish Major Triads from Minor Triads, so if you are focused on those two types only, you will probably find you can quite quickly tune in to the bottom and middle notes, and distinguish m3 from M3—and hence the type of Triad.

This is a great example of one of the benefits of Singing mentioned in *Chapter Four: Singing*: that it can provide a way to "experiment out loud" and explore the pitches you've heard, giving you time and control to compare and contrast the pitch relationships present. The same goes for Audiation, though you will probably find it easier to "keep a grip on things" when singing.

As you practice, you'll find you can move from doing various comparisons singing out loud, to audiating that same process, and (perhaps quite quickly) being able to just directly hear the three notes present and the intervals between them.

It's worth mentioning that this process may seem like overkill if you work with just Major and Minor Triads, since their overall sound and the difference in tonality is typically enough for most musicians to tell them apart quite reliably. To put that another way, the "pure" recognition approach covered above may well get the job done for you, without needing to dissect the notes and analyse the intervals.

However it's still very valuable to go through this process, because the Intervals approach also works well for Augmented and Diminished Triads, four-note Chords, and all kinds of other harmony you might encounter in future.

3. Using Solfa

When it comes to Solfa for Chord Types, we have two options available to us: practicing with examples in isolation, and practicing with an established key.

EXERCISE: Recognising Chord Types Using Solfa (In Isolation)

The isolated approach involves listening for whether the notes sound like the Solfa corresponding to one type of chord or another. As we saw in the table earlier in the chapter, for Major Triads it should sound like *do mi so* , like *fa la do'* , or like *so ti re'*. For Minor Triads it should sound like *re fa la* , like *mi so ti* , or like *la, do mi*.

1. Play the example chord.

2. Take a moment to either sing out loud, or audiate, each note of the chord in turn. You may want to play the example again, to make sure you've matched the pitches correctly.

3. Now use Singing or Audiation to examine each note and recognise the Solfa identities as either *do mi so* or *la, do mi*. If you're having trouble, try singing up the major scale *do-re-mi-fa-so* from the bottom note of the chord you heard, and see if the third and fifth notes match what you heard in the chord. If not, try singing the *la*-based minor scale: *la,-ti,-do-re-mi* and see if those third and fifth notes match.

This is… okay. But it's a bit like using an electric drill to hammer a nail into the wall. You're missing out on the real power of Solfa.

EXERCISE: Recognising Chord Types Using Solfa (With Context)

As we saw above, the beauty of Solfa for Chords is that it can reveal both the chord's type and the scale degree it's based on, at the same time.

Better is to first establish our key (for example, by playing the scale, or playing through a IV-V-I progression), and then play examples of the actual Major and Minor Chords from the family.

This allows us to hear, for example, not just "it's a Major Chord" but "it's *fa-la-do'* not *do-mi-so*", identifying both the type and the degree in one. This reinforces our Solfa skills and leverages the full power of Solfa.

1. Establish the key, by playing the tonic note, the full scale, or perhaps a V7-I Cadence (more on that below).

2. Hear an example chord.

3. Now use Singing or Audiation to examine each note and recognise the Solfa identities as *do mi so* , *fa la do'* or *so ti re'* (Major Triads) or *re fa la* , *mi so ti* or *la, do mi* (Minor Triads).

As always with Solfa, Singing is going to be your closest ally! In what follows, we'll introduce various ways to sing Solfa to develop your abilities with Chords and Progressions.

How To Recognise Chord Progressions

We'll get started with recognising Chord Progressions a little differently to Chord Types. There are three routes in, and each can usefully leverage any Solfa or Intervals skills you're bringing to the table.

1. Based On Degrees

Just like the "pure" approach for recognising Chord Types, one way to approach Chord Progressions is simply to practice tuning in to the overall sound of each chord in the family. The whole reason we focus on Relative Pitch in our Ear Training is that it matches how our ear naturally hears and makes sense of music, and so it is meaningful to listen directly for *"What does the I chord sound like? How about the IV chord?"* etc.. You can start to get a feel for the musical role, or character, or distinctive sound of each chord in the family.

Note that this is only possible with some sense of the key! For example, a C Major chord would sound like the I chord if our key is C Major—but would be the V chord if our key is F Major, or the IV chord in the key of G Major. So to practice listening for Chord Progressions directly, we must first establish a key. As mentioned in the section above, you can do this by playing through the scale, or playing a quick IV-V-I progression before you start with examples of each chord.

Personally, this is how I learned to recognise Chord Progressions, before I ever went deep with Solfa. Looking back, and now when guiding our members at Musical U, I would absolutely recommend combining it with Solfa for faster, easier progress!

Why? Because recognising Progressions based on degrees is so closely related to Solfa. When we learn to hear the "IV-ness" or the "V-ness" of a chord, we are essentially tuning in to the "*fa*-ness"or "*so*-ness" of it. The same relationship to the tonic is what we're listening for. And so the better you get at distinguishing, say, *do* vs. *fa* vs. *so*, the easier you'll find it to spot the I, IV and V, and vice-versa.

We are essentially trying to tune in to the root note of the chord, with the other notes serving just to reveal its quality (Major/Minor/Augmented/Diminished). And identifying that root note relative to the key's tonic note is exactly what Solfa is all about!

If you've been doing Ear Training for Solfa, then singing Solfa syllables is a great way to explore and test whether you're hearing the right chord degrees. For example if you think a progression goes I-IV-V-IV, sing along with "*do, fa, so, fa*" and see how well the notes gel. It's not foolproof (since, for example, the *so* note is also part of the I chord) but if you're also practicing "dissecting" a chord into its notes as covered above, you can quickly learn to reliably tune in to the root note, and identify it with your Solfa skills.

You can also recognise Chord Progressions based on degrees by using Intervals: simply listen out for the interval between the chord's root and the key's tonic. You are essentially using your interval skills as a proxy for Solfa skills, for example by recognising IV not by recognising *fa* but by recognising a Perfect Fourth above the tonic. This wouldn't be my first choice of approach, but if you're comfortable with Intervals and not yet with Solfa, it'll work just fine.

EXERCISE: Recognising Progressions Based On Degrees

To get started practicing recognising Progressions based on Degrees, you can use the same process as above for Chord Types:

1. Choose a key, and figure out the notes of the triads for I, IV and V.

2. Play through these chords in various orders, saying (or better, singing!) the corresponding degrees (of the chord roots) i.e. "one, four, five, four, five, one" and so on.

3. Listen carefully for the emotion, the feeling, the characteristic

sound of each—as well as what you notice about going from one to another. Write down any observations.

4.   When you're ready, choose a new key and repeat the process.

Again, you can make this even more effective by recording yourself doing it. Either:

A.   With you speaking/singing along, naming the degrees. This can serve as a "practice" or "reinforcement" track to listen to. Or,

B.   Without including the "answers". This can then serve as a "testing" track to practice guessing the answers with. You could also announce each degree only after a second or two rather than simultaneously (i.e. play I, then after a moment say "one", play IV, then after a moment say "four", etc.) which lets you check your answers when listening to the recording after.

Note that although you may be using Solfa skills, you'll still want to label each chord with its numeral rather than the Solfa name for its root note. And although it would be neat to speak in Roman Numerals, the convention is to just use the regular number names! (i.e. "one, four, five, etc.")

TIP:

We are focusing on three-note (triad) Chords in this chapter, but one very helpful stepping-stone to recognising the V chord is to use the V7 instead: for all the exercises, simply play the V7 wherever you would have played the V.

That means adding the fourth degree of the scale, in the octave above. In Solfa: so ti re fa'

Doing this amplifies the "unresolved" feeling of the V chord, making it stand out much more from the IV and I.

Most musicians will find this makes it quite easy to start recognising I, IV, V7 Progressions. This may seem like cheating, both because you've made one chord a four-note chord where the others are triads, and because it stands out so clearly. However, the advantage is that it's genuinely a stepping-stone rather than a diversion, since that same "unresolved" feeling will be present (and now more obvious to you) when you use the simple V triad instead.

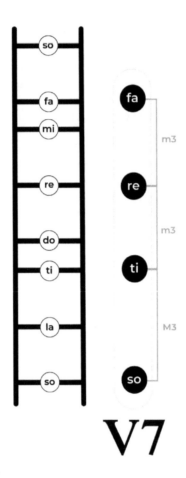

2. Based On Basslines

Another approach to recognising Chord Progressions is to focus on the *bassline* of the progression. In our simple starting case of triad chords in root position, this means honing in on the root note, just like above.

It's worth mentioning in its own right, however, for a couple of reasons:

1. In more complex arrangements, chords can be voiced in a variety of ways, played on multiple instruments, etc. And the bassline may literally be played by a bass guitar or other low-register instrument. This can be easier to tune in to, and even

if it's not literally just playing the root note of each chord in the progression, it's typically very revealing of which chords are being played.

To give a concrete example: you might be listening to a track with a very complex harmonic arrangement, and having a hard time finding the root notes by ear—but (through Active Listening) you tune in to the bass guitar's part, and realise that it is starting each measure by playing the root note of the current chord. This gives you another route in to identifying the Chord Progression by ear.

2.   It helps us to focus more on the *movement* from chord to chord.

It's this second point we'll focus on here, since we'll stick with our simple triads in root position for now.

The "Based on Degrees" approach covered above is based on the harmonic context (i.e. the key and its tonic), but focuses on recognising each chord's degree in its own right.

This "Based on Basslines" approach is about listening for how one chord's degree moves to the next. It's particularly well-suited to taking an Intervals perspective.

The idea is to listen for how one chord's root note moves to the next. With our I, IV, V progressions, the root notes will be moving by intervals of Fourths and Fifths (between I and IV or V) and Major 2nds (between IV and V):

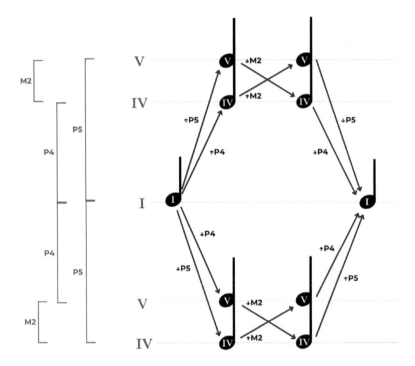

In this diagram we can see all the possibilities for moving between the roots of these three chords. The root note can move upwards or downwards each time, and the possible Intervals are M2, P4 and P5[4].

This means that if you're familiar with recognising Major 2nds, Perfect Fourths and Perfect Fifths, and you wrap your head around the diagram above, you can start to recognise these progressions quite easily.

Here's an example of how the chord roots might move in a I-IV-V-I-IV-V progression, and the corresponding intervals you might hear:

---

[4] Technically we could allow the Chords to "jump" up or down into a different register each time, producing Intervals larger than a P5. However, the same point about such "compound intervals" as covered in *Chapter Ten: Intervals* applies, i.e. it can generally be treated as the smaller interval with a mental note of "plus an octave", rather than requiring a fundamentally different recognition skill.

In any case, we are just getting started here, and needn't worry about such octave leaps —they're part of the whole wider world of voicing and arrangement and how these progressions actually show up in real music. The core skills we're building here will still be a useful and applicable foundation for those tasks.

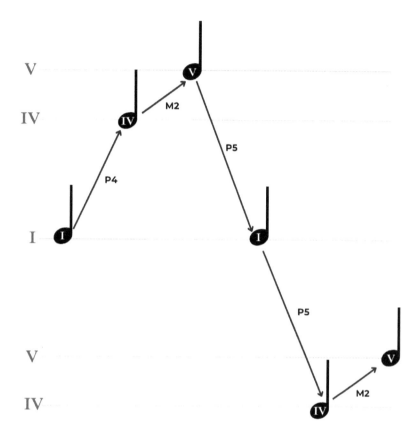

It's true that we've made our task relatively simple by restricting to root-position triads. In real music, things will rarely be so simple. The chords typically won't shift upwards or downwards as a fixed "block" of notes like this. However, the exact same listening skills, of following that chord root upwards and downwards still apply.

So whether you're listening out for the bassline in an arrangement, or honing in on the root note of each chord, learning to listen for that movement in terms of Intervals can be very helpful.

To get started practicing this, you can use exactly the same exercise as above—but pay attention to the movement from one root note to the next, in terms of Intervals.

3. Based On Cadences and Resolution

So far we have been discussing Progressions without specifying how many chords are in the sequence (or how long each is played for). In reality there are conventions for those things.

For example, changing chord more than once or twice per measure would be unusual, and chord progressions often repeat after 4, 8 or 12 measures, and change slightly or entirely when moving to a new section of a piece. These topics are more related to Songwriting (see *Chapter Sixteen: Songwriting*) and to musical Form (see also *Chapter Five: Active Listening*).

For our purposes in Ear Training for Progressions, in a sense it doesn't matter how many chords are in a sequence we're practicing with. We will make some recommendations below about what to aim for.

There is, however, a special case: the shortest possible progression, consisting of just two chords. This is sometimes referred to as a "cadence".[5]

This is interesting for our Ear Training purposes because, just like a melody can be analysed in terms of Intervals by looking at each pair of notes in turn, we can interpret a Chord Progression by analysing each pair of Chords in turn.

If we develop our ability to distinguish, for example, a IV-I cadence versus a V-I, and a I-IV versus a I-V, and a IV-V versus a V-IV, suddenly picking apart a long progression featuring the I, IV and V chords becomes much simpler!

What really makes this interesting though is that it introduces the idea of *resolution*.

In the context of Cadences, this word "resolution" means "coming back home": how does the harmony return us to the tonic chord by the end of the piece?

However, it can also be useful in a broader sense of "resolving musical tension". This is something we'll discuss a lot in *Chapter Sixteen: Songwriting*, because creating and resolving musical tension is at the heart of what makes music interesting, meaningful, and impactful on the listener.

Here, we're interested in how a sequence of chords creates and resolves tension, and how we can start tuning in for how particular chords in the family sound and feel like they "resolve" when followed by particular other chords in the family.

We'll go through this in more detail below, but hopefully you can

---

[5] It's helpful to have this term "cadence" to mean a two-chord progression, but I should mention that the more traditional precise definition specifically refers to the two (or more) chords right at the end of a piece, or section.

already see how this relates to the tip above about using V7 in place of V (V7 has more inherent tension, so that its creation and release is more recognisable) and how it could provide a different route into recognising Progressions than either the Degrees or Basslines approaches outlined above.

Side Note:

If you have read *Chapter Ten: Intervals*, you may remember the discussion there on hearing Intervals in terms of "opening" versus "closing". This is a big part of what made our Winter Season of *Living Music* so impactful for students going through it: the Circle Of Fifths encapsulates this whole idea of "inward vs. outward" or "opening vs. closing", and reveals connections between all the Intervals and Chords contained in the Circle.

Perhaps most notably, it helps greatly with distinguishing Perfect 4ths and Perfect 5ths (remember that "inversion pair" source of confusion mentioned in *Chapter Ten: Intervals*) and the IV and V Chords—which can otherwise be easily mixed up.

That is a whole (wonderful!) rabbithole which we won't be diving into in this book. For now just be aware of this "resolution" perspective on listening to Chord Progressions as we continue, and know that if you want to go on a fascinating music theory exploration in future, wonders await you…!

Start With Aiming For 3-Chord Songs

At this point we've covered a lot! We've unpacked Chord Types and Chord Progressions, and started to explore both their sounds, and the connections to the Solfa and Intervals perspectives on Relative Pitch. If you started to experiment with some of the ideas and exercises above, hopefully you've found that Chords, Progressions, and harmony in general, are coming to life in a new way for you.

Even more than with Solfa or Intervals, the world of Chord Progressions is vast. Why? Because ultimately, as mentioned in the introduction it *can* be a huge mass of notes across multiple instruments, featuring Chord Types beyond the four triads covered here, voicings beyond the simple root position, Progressions featuring the full family and even "borrowed" Chords from outside the family.

But remember the rule of thumb from The Hitchhiker's Guide To The Galaxy:

Don't Panic.

The two-fold good news of Relative Pitch which we keep coming back to is:

1. A huge amount of music uses just a small subset of all those possibilities.

2. If you develop your ear for that small subset, it provides a firm foundation for expanding your skills to everything else— because it isn't just the most commonly-used building blocks we focus on, but those which everything else tends to be built upon.

We've already established that our main building blocks for Chords and Progressions will be the Major and Minor Triad Chords, and Progressions featuring just the I, IV and V Chords. Why? Because that allows us to master so-called "3-Chord Songs"[6].

A 3-chord song as we'll define it is a song which features just three different chords, and specifically the I, IV and V chords. They can appear in any sequence, and there may be a different progression (i.e. sequence) used in different parts of the song.

To make that concrete, a song with the following Chord Progressions:

Verse: I-IV-V-IV
    Chorus: V-I-V-I-V-I

... would be a 3-chord song. However a song with the following Progressions:

Verse: I-V-vi-I

---

[6] In fact, we'll need only our Major Triad building block for 3-chord songs, but the Minor Triad will quickly become useful too, as we introduce the vi chord and move on to 4-chord songs.

It will also prepare us for the ii and iii chords, at which point we are close to having the full Major Key chord family under our belts.

Chorus: vi-V-I-I

... would not, because even though only three different chords are present, they include chords other than the I, IV and V.

Although using just the I, IV and V might seem overly limiting, these "3-Chord Songs" are *everywhere* in music. It's especially true in popular modern genres such as blues, rock, pop, folk and country, but has its roots in classical music and 3-Chord Songs show up frequently in almost every genre.

For example, an analysis of 1300 popular songs by the wonderful website HookTheory showed the following prevalence of chords being used:

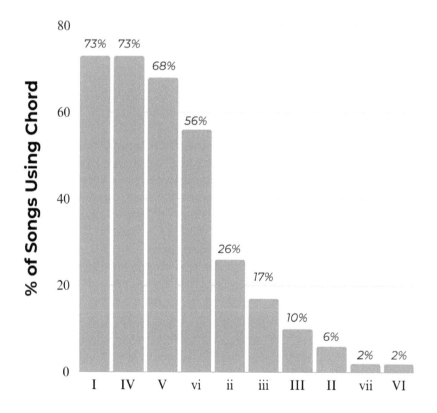

While this doesn't, strictly speaking, show the proportion using *only* I, IV and V, it does powerfully demonstrate the prevalence of the I, IV and V (and the vi). And many songs do, in fact, use only these three (or four) chords. We've included lists in the *Additional Resources* and will discuss how you can use them for your Ear Training later in the chapter.

It's a mind-blowing moment for a lot of musicians the first time they discover that such a huge constraint on the harmony is actually present in such a vast catalog of popular and familiar music!

So if we can reliably recognise just the I, IV and V chord in use, a large repertoire becomes playable by ear, and since these same chords feature frequently even in songs which go beyond these three chords, we've got a huge headstart with an even wider range. Most notably by next adding in the vi chord (covered below), which opens up so-called "4-chord songs" with their I, IV, V, vi progressions.

Of course these ear skills won't just be useful for playing songs by ear. They also empower you to start writing your own 3- and 4-chord songs, improvising more effectively over these progressions, gaining deeper understanding in your Active Listening, and even learning repertoire faster through having a clearer sense of how the harmony is working.

So start with aiming for 3-chord songs.

The Power of Three

As we focus on 3-chord songs, the role of the tonic chord (I) quickly becomes clear. Progressions will often feel like a journey away from the tonic, and back again. It's no coincidence that many songs and pieces of music will both start and end on the tonic chord. So the trick for us is to get good at recognising when we're "home" on that I chord, and when our journey away takes us to the IV versus the V.

Why three? Why not start with 2-chord songs?

Well, for one thing, songs with just two chords tend to sound a bit repetitive and same-y, since there's only ever one possibility for what the next chord will be. Such 2-chord songs do exist, but they're few and far between—contrasting with the huge number of three-chord songs which demonstrate that those three Chords (and the new possibility of having two options for every chord change) certainly can provide enough variety and interest.

It can also be helpful to notice that unless all three of these chords are present, the key can be much more ambiguous. It comes back to that "inversion pairs" issue with Perfect 4ths and Perfect 5ths from *Chapter Ten: Intervals,* and the illustration above of the possible root note movements in terms of intervals.

If we have only the I and IV chords, or only the I and V chords, how do you know which is which? A progression of I-IV in the key of C Major is a C Major chord followed by an F Major chord. A progression of V-I in the key of F Major is... a C Major chord followed by an F Major chord!

Of course we have other clues as to the tonic and key (see the section in *Chapter Eight: Relative Pitch* on "Finding The Key By Ear"), but hopefully you can see how as soon as we introduce the third of our trio of I, IV, V, the tonic and key become unambiguous. If you spent some time in the sections above playing through various example sequences of I, IV and V chords, you will have quickly heard how the I stands out as the most stable, at-home, resting place among the three.

With all that being said, when it comes to *Ear Training*, actually 2-chord "songs" can be very helpful! We touched on this above, introducing the idea of a 2-chord "Cadence". Practicing with just two chords can be an effective starting place for mastering 3-chord songs.

If we have three possible chords to choose from, then we also have three possibilities for chord changes:

1.   Between I and V

2.   Between I and IV

3.   Between IV and V

Rather than jump straight into practicing with progressions featuring all three chords, it will be much more effective to spend some time tuning our ear in to each of these three possibilities. Once you can hear each of these changes, there's still a bit of practice required to handle all possible I, IV, V progressions, but you'll find it much easier to recognise each of the three chords reliably.

The V-I Cadence

If we want to recognise transitions from I to V and vice-versa, it's valuable to focus first on just the V-I Cadence. Similar to how practicing with ascending intervals helps you recognise the corresponding descending interval (even though they are slightly different), tuning your ear in to the characteristic sound of a V-I Cadence will also help you start spotting the I-V Cadence.

In the Classical music world, Cadences are a big deal, and the V-I is so important it gets its own name: an "authentic cadence" (US) or "perfect cadence" (UK).

Let's approach practicing this cadence in three ways, which we have already become familiar with above. You can use the Basic Drill, as laid out in "How To Recognise Chord Progressions" above, adapting it slightly in each case.

1. Listening for the Resolution

As mentioned above in the Tip box above, when we're working on recognising the V chord, using the V7 is a very helpful stepping stone. The V7-I Cadence is even more distinctive than the V-I Cadence. In fact, if you had to pick the shortest possible thing to play, to demonstrate the idea of "resolving to the tonic", the V7-I Cadence might be your best bet.

Play through some examples now (e.g. C7 followed by F, D7 followed by G, E7 followed by A...) and you will probably immediately hear how clearly this sounds like "coming home". With just two chords we have immediately established the tonic of the key and identified the I chord.

You can listen for the same trait with a V-I progression rather than a V7-I. It's not as stark, but once you practice a bit with V7s you should be able to hear the same characteristic "coming home" resolution of the V-I.

2. Listening for the Degree

If you're developing your ear for Solfa too, then it will also be valuable to listen out for the root note of the Chords, and how the V-I Cadence sounds similar to going from *so* to *do* or *so* to *do'* :

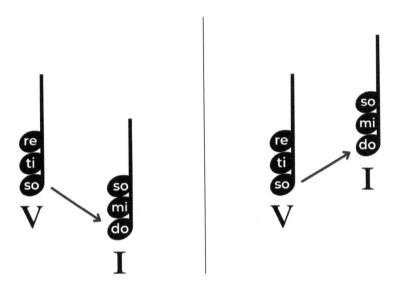

3. Listening for the Bassline

If you're developing your ear for Intervals too, then you can listen out for how the root note of the Chords move either down a Perfect Fifth, or up a Perfect Fourth.

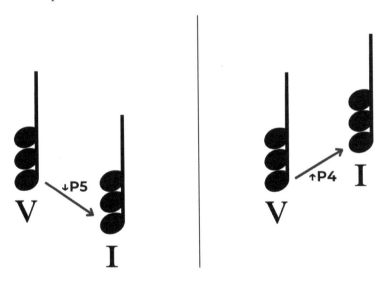

The IV-I Cadence

The second most common Cadence to end a piece of music is probably the IV-I, and again this can provide a great way in to recognising both I-IV and IV-I cadences.

In the Classical music world the IV-I Cadence also gets its own name: the "plagal cadence". Informally it's also often called the "Amen" cadence, because of how many hymns and church music settings end with a final sung *"A-men"* moving from the IV chord on *"Ah"* to the I chord on *"-men"*. If, like me, you've spent a lot of time singing or hearing church music, this can provide a very effective "reference song" for the IV-I Cadence!

Like with the V-I, we can practice this Cadence in each of our three ways, using the Basic Drill:

1. Listening for the Resolution

Since we're "coming home" to the tonic chord, the IV-I Cadence also has a clear sense of resolution, but not nearly as striking as the V-I.

You'll find that the IV chord also sounds relatively "comfortable" or "at rest", so while moving to the I still sounds like "coming home", it can be easy to muddle up the I and IV chords when listening to I, IV, V Progressions.

With the V-I Cadence it was instructive to spend some time tuning in to that resolution. With the IV-I, this aspect only really becomes useful once all three chords are featured. So once you can hear that "it sounds like it's resolving to the I, but not as strikingly as the V-I", that's enough for now.

2. Listening for the Degree

If you're developing your ear for Solfa too, then it will also be valuable to listen out for the root note of the chords, and how the IV-I Cadence sounds similar to going from *fa* to *do* or *fa* to *do'* .

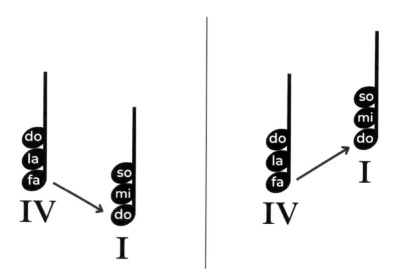

3. Listening for the Bassline

If you're developing your ear for intervals too, then you can listen out for how the root note of the chords move either down a Perfect Fourth, or up a Perfect Fifth.

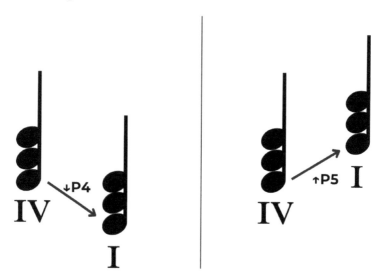

Combining V-I and IV-I Cadences

Before we move on to freely sequencing the I, IV and V chords, let's first compare and contrast these two types of Cadence.

We can do this by playing through Progressions which alternate between the I chord and either the IV or the V chord. So no moving between the IV and V for now.

An example might be: I-IV-I-V-I-V-I-IV-I-V

Listen for the chord changes in each direction (i.e. from the tonic to IV or V, and from IV or V to the tonic) and really pay attention to how the transitions between I and IV sound different to those between I and V.

As always with our Basic Drill:

- You'll want to change key occasionally
- Speak or sing the chord names (as I, IV, V, not letter names) as you play them
- Record yourself practicing, and listen back for further practice. If you omit or delay your spoken/sung "labels", this can provide a great "quiz" for you to test yourself with after.

Full I, IV, V Progressions

Once you have some confidence with distinguishing the two cases above (between the I and IV, and between the I and V), it should be a small step forwards to allow all three to mix freely. Remember our "80% Rule": you don't need to absolutely master each of these steps before moving on to the next, but you want to get to a level of *"I can almost always get it right"*.

In fact, while we stick with root position triads, you should find that the IV-V and V-IV changes are quite easy to spot, because of the much smaller movement in pitch between them, compared with moving from either to the I.

Practice with the Basic Drill, now allowing the progression to move freely between all three:

EXERCISE: Recognising I, IV, V Progressions

1. Choose a key, and a source of example progressions featuring I, IV and V (e.g. a pre-prepared audio track like those in the *Additional Resources*, an interactive app, a recording of your own Progressions practice)

2. Play through each example, and try to name the progression

e.g. *"one, four, five, four, five, five, one"* and so on.

3.   When you're ready, choose a new key and repeat the process.

Now this is where things start to get really fun, because we can start exploring with real music too.

The leap from root position triads to "real music" can seem like a big one at first, and while you can bridge it by introducing different voicings to your practicing first, if you've been tuning your ear in the way we've covered above, you may well be surprised just how much the "I-ness", "IV-ness" and "V-ness" of chords in real music start to jump out at you.

The trick here is to begin practicing with songs where you know the progression.

So don't just jump to real tracks and expect yourself to recognise every chord in the progression. Instead, pick a few 3-chord songs, and start speaking/singing the Chords along as you listen, just like we did with the Basic Drill.

EXERCISE: Naming Progressions In 3-Chord Songs

1.   Select a music track which you know features only the I, IV and V chords (guidance on this below).

2.   Listen to the track, and express the name of each chord as it occurs. You can simply speak its number, but even better is to sing the number on the chord's root note.

You can begin by doing this for tracks where you know the exact progressions used, allowing you to tune your ear (and voice) in to these I, IV, V progressions. Then, when you're ready, try doing it with a track where you know it features only the I, IV and V chords, but you don't know the progressions in advance.

The instructions for this exercise are very simple—but this is an exercise you can fruitfully spend weeks practicing! It is a highly effective complement to all the Basic Drill exercises covered so far, and a great middle stage between those and the Applied Activities you'll find at the end of the chapter.

So where do you find the 3-Chord Songs to do this exercise with?

One of my favourite tracks to start with is "Louie Louie". It's familiar to many people, and the chord progression is absolutely central to its distinctive and memorable sound:

"Louie Louie" Progression

I - IV - V - IV

Louie, Louie   *Oh no*

I - IV - V - IV

We gotta go   *Yeah yeah yeah yeah*

(That's two lines of two measures each, two chords per measure.)

The classic recording of this track by The Kingsmen is particulary helpful because the chords played by the guitar and keyboard follow the simplest root movement we would expect from practicing with root-position Triads i.e. going up a Perfect 4th from the I to the IV, up a Major 2nd to reach the V, back down a Major 2nd to the IV, back down a Perfect 4th to the I. In Solfa terms, the *do fa so fa* movement is very clear.

If all you did for a week was sing the chord names as you listen to this song, it would ingrain that I-IV-V-IV progression so firmly in your ear that you'd take a huge leap forwards in recognising I-IV-V progressions in real music.

Another good "reference song" here is the classic 12-Bar Blues:

The "12-Bar Blues" Progression

I - I - I - I

IV - IV - I - I

V - IV - I - I

(That's three lines of four measures each, one chord per measure.)

This progression is often used exactly as written above, but popular variations include substituting the I7 chord for I at the end of the first and second lines, and moving to the V for the final measure of the progression, creating greater tension before the progression begins again.

This exact same progression has been used across a wealth of blues tracks over the past hundred-plus years. It's a great choice to improvise over, a fun way to explore Songwriting, and an easy progression to find countless varied examples to practice playing by ear or transcribing with. More on these applications in the exercises below and corresponding chapters later in the book. However you choose to use it, the 12-Bar Blues is a reliable way to get a feel for the "journey" that the IV and V chords can take you on.

Those are just two examples. In the *Additional Resources* you'll find a large list of other popular 3-chord songs, and (separately) a list of their progressions. This allows you to use some songs to practice with (knowing the progression in advance) and other songs to test yourself with.

Going Further

Before we move on to Additional Exercises and Applied Activities, let's briefly survey what lies beyond Major and Minor Triads, and the I, IV and V chords. Several of these possibilities have been mentioned already.

For most musicians we recommend first gaining some proficiency with the main building blocks we've been focusing on so far. For that reason, you may wish to skim, or skip over this section entirely for now! Continue working with those building blocks and the "Additional Exercises and Applied Activities" below.

When you are ready to begin introducing other Chord Types or Progressions, you can return to this section. All the same exercises presented throughout this chapter can be used, simply incorporating the new possibilities introduced here.

This allows you to naturally and organically expand your comfort zone and competence with recognising Chords and Progressions, in a way that suits your musical interests and activities.

For example:

- A pianist may wish to move quickly on to exploring different chord voicings, to allow for more variety and creativity in Playing By Ear and Improvising.

- A songwriter may choose to explore Minor Keys sooner rather than later, to suit their songwriting style.

- A guitarist will probably want to adapt their triad skills to the traditional six-string chord shapes before introducing other types of Chords and Progressions.

And so on. In some cases, a musician may know already that they want to introduce some of these possibilities sooner. For example, if you play jazz, you may choose to focus on ii-V-I Progressions even before I, IV, V Progressions.

Whatever route forwards you choose, the information provided in this section should be enough to tailor all the exercises from this chapter to suit.

Chord Voicings

So far we have limited ourselves to root-position Triad chords:

three-note chords consisting of a Third and a Fifth above the root note. There are many other ways to "voice" the same chord. With the same root note (degree) and Chord Type (quality), a musician can choose a variety of notes across different registers to play what is, in terms of overall sound and musical function, the same chord.

For example, in the section "How Chords Work" above, we saw several possibilities for voicing a C Major chord:

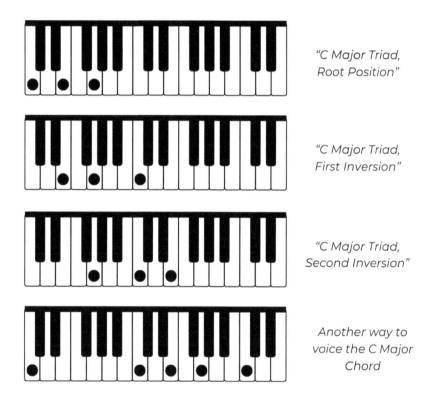

"C Major Triad, Root Position"

"C Major Triad, First Inversion"

"C Major Triad, Second Inversion"

Another way to voice the C Major Chord

Another example is the way a guitarist plays a chord using up to six strings of their instrument, and can choose different chord "shapes" at different positions on the fretboard to play the same chord. Here are three ways to play a C Major chord, for example:

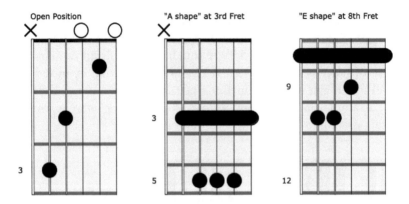

When it comes to Ear Training and voicings, there are two useful skills to develop:

1.   Recognising the chord's identity, regardless of its voicing.

2.   Recognising the voicing being used.

The first skill is important for any musician, because in a real musical context it's rare for the music to use only root-position Triad chords! Fortunately, this is quite an easy skill to develop once you're solid with those root-position Triads, because listening for the degree and quality works the same way, regardless of voicing. Simply broadening the range of example chords you use in practice exercises will allow you to make your recognition skills more versatile and robust. This will also happen naturally as you try the Applied Activities below, using real music tracks.

The second skill is more advanced, and for many musicians won't be a high priority. If you play a keyboard instrument then recognising voicings can be valuable, to let you play them precisely by ear, or to be able to audiate different possibilities for how you might choose to voice the chords you play. If you play guitar then it can be valuable to hear the difference between chords played at different positions on the fretboard, for the same reasons.

If you do want to develop this skill, then one good approach is to adapt the practice exercises in this chapter to feature a variety of voicings, and set yourself the task of identifying the particular voicing being used. On keyboard you'll want to draw on Solfa and Intervals to let you spot the relationships between the notes of the chord.

Guitarists tend to listen more for the distinctive overall sound of each moveable fretboard shape, and the overall highness or lowness of the chord's notes. Compare and contrast, for example, an open-string E chord with the barre-chord version played at the 7th fret, and you should immediately be able to hear a substantial difference between the two. You are still tuning in to the relationships between the notes of the chord, but in a more broad, subconscious way, recognising for example the "A shape" versus the "E shape", and so on.

Four-Note Chords

What about chords with more than three notes? Well, again, we'll tip our hat in acknowledgement to the fundamental truth that a chord *can* use any arbitrary set of notes, but take advantage of common building blocks to help us focus our efforts where they'll produce the greatest payoff.

One possibility is to repeat one of the three notes again. As covered above, we can consider this a different voicing of the same Triad chord, rather than a distinct Chord Type.

If we are adding a different fourth note to a chord, the most common choice is the seventh degree counting up the scale from the chord's root. Just as we skipped a note to go from the root note to the third, and skipped another to get to the fifth, we skip one more to reach the seventh.

Coming back to the idea of seeing this as "stacking thirds", we are stacking one more Major or Minor 3rd above the fifth, which takes us to the seventh.

Since we have four possible Triads and two options for stacking another Third on top, there are actually eight different possibilities. One of these, consisting of all Major 3rds, brings us back to the root note again,[7] so in fact there are seven possibilities.

For the sake of completeness, here they are:

---

[7] Since three Intervals of four Half-Steps each produces a total of 12 Half Steps, which is equivalent to an octave.

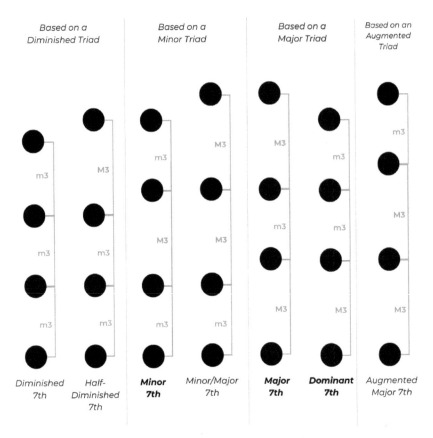

That may well seem overwhelming to you right now! Fortunately there are two valuable simplifications.

Firstly, some of these types of Seventh Chord are used much more often than others. Specifically, the Dominant 7th is probably the most common, followed by the Minor and Major Sevenths (names bolded in diagram). The Minor/Major 7th and the Augmented Major 7th are quite unusual. The Half-Diminished and Diminished Sevenths are somewhere in between.

Secondly (and related), the most common choice of Seventh Chord is to use the type which occurs naturally from a given scale degree. If we choose the type of top 3rd which keeps us within the notes of the key, there is just one Seventh Chord we can build from each degree of the major scale:

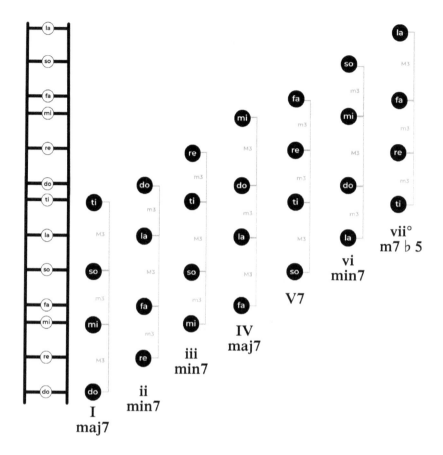

You can see that the three major chords, I, IV and V become Major 7th, Major 7th and Dominant 7th chords, respectively. The three minor chords ii, iii and vi all become Minor 7th chords. And the diminished vii° becomes a Half-Diminished 7th chord (often written "min7♭5", as in the diagram above, because it's the same as a Minor 7th chord but with the fifth lowered a Half Step).

Since the vii° chord is relatively uncommon, you can see that if you want to gain the most payoff from practicing with Seventh Chords, just focusing on the Major 7th, Minor 7th and Dominant 7th types can take you a long way.

A Note For Jazz Musicians

In the jazz world, musicians are often thrown in at the deep end with seventh chords, being encouraged to learn to play all seven types in all 12 keys as soon as possible.

That may or may not be good advice. It certainly can help you gain facility with playing from lead sheets quickly. However, when it comes to Ear Training, the guidance here still applies. You don't want to overwhelm your ears, so introduce the different types gradually, and focus on the most commonly-used to begin with.

Adapting the exercises in this chapter for ii-V-I progressions, first as Triads and then as Seventh Chords (ii, V and I become a Minor 7th, a Dominant 7th and a Major 7th chord respectively) is a great way to start familiarising yourself with the three most common types of Seventh Chords.

We've already featured one of these chords: the V7. As you can see here, that's the only Dominant 7th chord in the major key, and it brings a lot of powerful tension with it! It amplifies the unresolved feeling of the V chord, and even before you tackle Seventh Chords in earnest, it's a great one to start experimenting with, as we saw above and will return to below.

Borrowed, Altered And Suspended Chords

Depending on your musical background and activities you may have come across the terms "borrowed chord", "altered chord" and "suspended chord". We'll provide here a brief description of each, so you can understand how to factor them into your Ear Training.

A *borrowed* chord is simply a chord from outside the "family" of chords which naturally exist in the key. For example, a common choice in Songwriting is to change the quality of a chord in the family from Major to Minor or vice-versa. This can make for a very distinctive progression.

If you "borrow" too many chords from outside the key, it can disorient the listener by making the tonal centre (i.e. which note is the tonic) unclear. This may be the desired effect! But in general, it's more normal to just change one or possibly two chords from the expected family. Aside from changing the quality, it's also of course possible to change the degree, for example moving it up or down by a Half Step[8].

An *altered* chord is a chord in which one or more of its notes have been moved up or down by a Half Step. This moves outside the notes of the key and is typically used momentarily to create a smooth movement from one chord to another.

There are particular norms and expectations in jazz music for how to interpret a chord marked as "alt" which is worth diving into, if relevant for your musical life. In a sense these are a very advanced topic. On the other hand, if your Solfa skills (for example) make it easy for you to spot when one note of the chord is a Half Step higher or lower than you expect it to be, you may find that altered chords are easier to wrap your ears around than all the complicated theory might suggest!

A *suspended* chord is one where the usual 3rd is replaced by either a Major 2nd or a Perfect 4th. So instead of taking the first, third and fifth notes going up from a certain root, you are taking either the first, second and fifth (called a "suspended 2nd" chord, written "sus2") or the first, fourth and fifth (called a "suspended 4th" chord, written "sus4").

In Songwriting these can be used either to replace the regular version completely, or as a flourish by switching between the regular version and one of the suspended versions. On guitar, for example, many simple riffs involve placing and removing one finger, changing back and forth between the 3rd and a 2nd or 4th.

Again, all of these possibilities are relatively advanced topics in Ear Training overall, but depending on your musical background and activities, you may wish to introduce them into your practicing sooner or later.

The various additional Chord Types introduced here (seventh,

---

[8] Note that although we're saying "change a chord", this needn't necessarily replace the chord from the key—it can be an addition rather than replacement. For example, one highly effective technique is to use the "normal" chord from the family in one section of a song or piece, and then change its quality in another, such as featuring the iii chord in verses but the III chord in the chorus.

borrowed, altered, suspended) can all be considered somewhat niche, advanced, or specialist, for the average musician. However, as we move on to additional possibilities in Chord Progressions, we are returning to the mainstream. It will be relevant and useful for any musician to extend their Chords and Progressions Ear Training to what follows.

Introducing vi

If 3-chord songs using I, IV, and V are the most prevalent across the wide world of music, then a close second would be 4-chord songs using I, IV V and vi. It's been said that to write a hit song, all you need is "four chords and the truth". If that's true, then I, IV, V and vi are the chords!

The vi chord is the most commonly-used minor chord in major keys, across a wide range of styles and genres, and 4-chord songs are almost as numerous as 3-chord songs (as suggested by the bar chart of chord use earlier in this chapter). This makes the vi chord an excellent choice for the next one to add to your skillset, once you have a firm grip on I, IV and V.

If you've spent some time working with I, IV and V, then the vi chord will generally stick out clearly, being the only minor chord among them. This goes double if you've diligently spent some time practicing Major vs. Minor Triads too. With that being said, it can be surprising how hard it sometimes is to hear that Major vs. Minor chord quality in a real musical context! So you will want to make use of both listening for the degree and listening for the quality to reliably tune in to the vi chord.

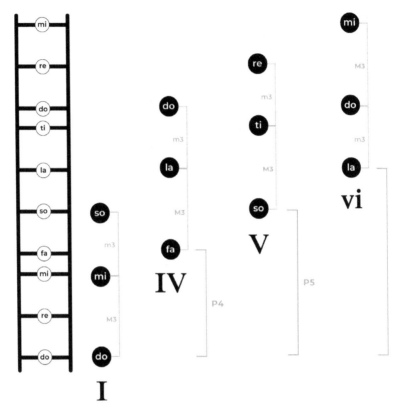

Incorporating the vi chord immediately opens up a whole new emotional world in the harmony. The "musical journey" which the I, IV and V chords can take you on is considerable—but it pales in comparison to a journey featuring the vi (or indeed the ii or iii—but more on those below).

All the exercises mentioned in this chapter, including most notably the three "Instrument Practice" exercises below, can easily be extended to I, IV, V, vi Progressions. You can find a "4-chord songs" list in the *Additional Resources*.

Other chords in the family

There are three more chords in our Major Key "family": the ii, the iii, and the vii°.

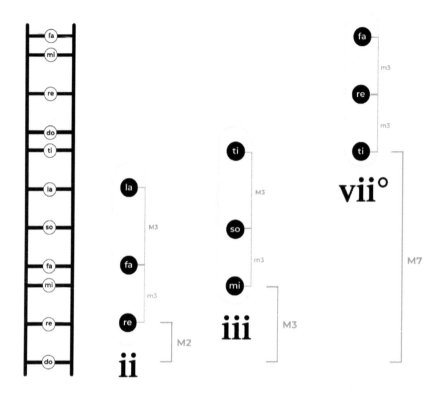

These can be tackled by gradually introducing them as possibilities in your practice exercises, but many musicians will find it more natural to:

1.   Leverage Solfa skills to spot the degree, and Chords skills to recognise the quality.

2.   Get familiar with them as they arise in your real musical activities. For example, if you're using the "Instrument Practice" exercises below, you'll naturally encounter songs or pieces which go beyond the I, IV, V and vi chords, and those provide a perfect opportunity to explore, experiment, and tune your ear in to what those other chords are doing, musically.

ii-V-Is

Just a quick word about the "ii-V-I" ("two five one") progression. If a I, IV, V progression is the most common in rock, pop, electronic, country and many other popular genres, then ii-V-I is the progression which most characterises jazz (and jazz-inspired) music.

In jazz it's more normal to play Seventh Chords than simple Triads, and so in practice this is generally a ii7-V7-I7. As mentioned in the previous aside, this features a Minor 7th, Dominant 7th and Major 7th chord, respectively.

Jazz is known for being perhaps the most harmonically-sophisticated genre, and there's a deep rabbithole you can enjoy exploring when it comes to jazz harmony and how exactly that seemingly-simple ii-V-I actually occurs in pieces. Where I, IV, V Progressions can be seen as a sequence of Chords, the ii-V-I becomes a building block in its own right, featuring those chords in that order, but with twists such as a minor ii-V-I, modulation between keys, and various extended sequences featuring a ii-V-I.

If you are jazz-inclined, then Ear Training for ii-V-I's should be a focus for you. One great habit to form is analysing the chord symbols on lead sheets of jazz standards to spot where a ii-V-I is happening, combined with listening intently as you then play that standard. All the other exercises in this chapter can be adapted for Seventh Chords and for a focus on the ii, V and I chords in place of I, IV and V.

Minor Keys

So far we have only discussed Chords and Progressions based on Major Keys, and while that is the more common tonality across a wide range of music, there is certainly no shortage of music written in a Minor Key!

In a Major Key, the notion of a "family" of Chords which belong is straight-forward. In Minor Keys, things become a bit more complicated, as there are three types of Minor Scale: Natural Minor, Melodic Minor and Harmonic Minor. On top of that, the Melodic Minor features different notes ascending than descending.

This means that to build Chords by choosing particular degrees of the scale (i.e. the first, third and fifth for Triads), actually produces a much larger "family", since we have multiple options for several of the scale degrees.

Here are the Triads which result from each of the three Minor scales, in the key of A Minor, for example. For the sake of space we won't spell out all the Solfa and Intervals and letter names! But you can see at a glance that because the notes of the scales differ, the Triads we build from each scale degree come out differently in each case:

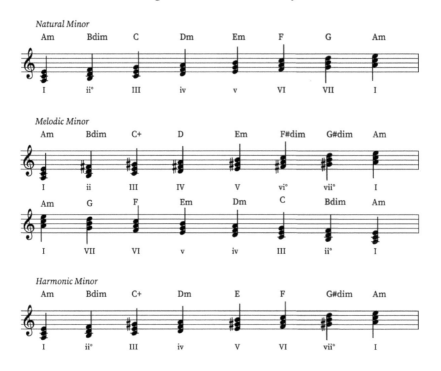

Here is a table showing the possible quality of each chord degree, considering these three types of Minor Key scales:

Scale Degree	Possible Triad Types
1	Minor
2	Minor, Diminished
3	Major, Augmented
4	Minor, Major
5	Minor, Major
6	Major, Diminished
7	Major, Diminished

So you can see, a songwriter or composer has a huge range of options available when writing music in a minor key—and that's even before considering borrowed chords or any of the more sophisticated Chord Types mentioned above!

This can make Ear Training for minor-key Chord Progressions feel somewhat overwhelming. Fortunately the same fundamental approach still applies: listen for the degree, and listen for the quality.

One of the most useful additional exercises you can try is to experiment with varying the quality of certain chords as you play through progressions. As noted above when discussing borrowed chords, switching one chord in the progression from a Major Triad to a Minor Triad or vice-versa will have a significant effect on the musical journey created.

Try using the earlier exercise of creating your own I, IV, V Progressions, but this time choose chords from the table above. Select a certain quality for each chord you'll feature, and spend some time playing through sequences using those chords, getting a feel for the musical impact and role of each. Then "toggle" the quality of one of the chords, and listen for how that changes things. Exploring and experimenting like this is a great way to develop your ears, as well as opening the door to creativity with harmony.

To gain an *"I can handle anything"* level of skill in recognising Chord Progressions is certainly more challenging in Minor Keys than Major— but the skills you develop first in Major Keys will provide a head-start, and from there you can use the exercises in this chapter to continue expanding and refining your ears over time.

Additional Exercises And Activities

So far we've covered two ways to develop your ear for Chords and Progressions:

1. Our Basic Drill: playing through a series of examples of different kinds, paying attention to the sounds and what's distinctive about each. Either labeling them out loud as we go, or using recorded examples and trying to "guess the answer" each time. This can usefully be done with your instrument, trading examples with a friend, using pre-recorded audio tracks, or interactive apps.

2. Using examples from real music, selected to demonstrate the particular Chords and Progressions we are focused on. Again, either speaking/singing the known "answers", or using music

where we don't know the progression to test our skills with.

These are great exercises for getting started with, and can continue to be part of how you do Ear Training for Chords and Progressions—but they're not the only way!

Like we did with Intervals and Solfa, we want to make sure we are not just doing "Practice Exercises" but also "Apply Activities", making sure our Head, Hands, Hearing and Heart are working together, forming connections, and enabling real, practical musical abilities. So in the spirit of Integrated Ear Training, let's look at some other ways you can develop your ear for Chords and Progressions across a range of musical activities.

Singing

At first it might seem wacky to talk about practicing Chords by singing—after all, we can't sing more than one note at once! Additionally, the average singer typically thinks less about Chords and Progressions than instrumentalists do.

If you've read *Chapter Four: Singing* and understand the idea of "singing as a tool" though, you can probably already see the opportunity here…

We've touched on it already, earlier in this chapter: if we want to be able to dissect a chord into its constituent notes, for example to identify the Chord Type or to follow the root note movement in a progression, Singing can be a huge help. As your skills develop you will likely move to audiation or simply hearing what you need to directly, but even musicians with advanced ear skills for harmony can still make good use of singing on occasion.

So the first use of Singing for Chords and Progressions could be described as to "explore" and "check your answers". It's a way for you to grab hold of a note you've heard and give your ears more of a chance to analyse what's going on. That could be singing up the notes of a chord, transforming it into an arpeggio, and giving your Solfa or Intervals skills a chance to help you identify the Chord Type. It could be singing the root notes of the chords in a progression, likewise letting you leverage Solfa or Intervals to identify the progression.

We'll discuss this more in *Chapter Fourteen: Playing By Ear* when we introduce the Listen-Engage-Express approach of the Play-By-Ear Process.

There is a second valuable use of Singing for Chords and

Progressions, which is to actually use your singing voice as your instrument for our Basic Drill. We already mentioned that if you play an instrument which only produces a single note at once (e.g. saxophone rather than ukulele), you can play example chords note-by-note in arpeggio form. This applies to Singing too.

To make that concrete, here are three highly effective Singing exercises, which are each essentially just variants on our Basic Drill, using your singing voice as the instrument:

EXERCISE: Singing Chord Types

This exercise will help you learn to distinguish different types of chord, starting with our main building blocks of Major and Minor Triads:

1. Choose a note which is comfortably in your singing range to serve as the root note, and choose a Chord Type (e.g. Major or Minor Triad)

2. Using one of the following approaches, find the other notes of the chord:

- Solfa: For a Major Triad, treat your root note as *do* and sing *mi* and *so* above it. For a Minor Triad, treat your root note as *la*, and sing *do* and *mi* above it.

- Intervals: For a Major Triad sing up a Major 3rd. For a Minor Triad sing up a Minor 3rd. And in both cases sing up a Perfect 5th from the root to find the top note.

- Without Solfa or Intervals, you can either sing up a major scale or natural minor scale to find the third and fifth notes for Major and Minor Triads respectively. Or simply find the other notes using an instrument and the Pitch Ruler approach, walking up 4 Half Steps for a Major Third or 3 for a Minor Third, and adding the note 7 Half Steps above the root as your top note.

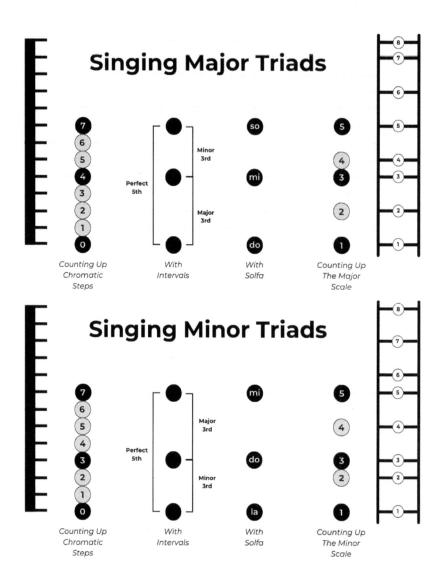

3.   Sing up and down the three notes, and speak the label (e.g. "Major Triad")

This may seem laborious, especially compared to playing examples on an instrument, but the extra effort involved in finding the notes, and then producing the right pitches directly with your own body without relying on an instrument's button-pressing interface, is exactly what makes this exercise so powerful.

EXERCISE: Singing Chord Degrees

This exercise will help you learn to recognise Chord Progressions through identifying the scale degree each chord is based on, starting with our main building blocks of the I, IV and V chords:

1. Choose a note which is comfortably in your singing range to serve as the tonic and the root note of the I chord.

2. Using one of the following approaches, find the root notes of the IV and V chords:

- Solfa: The root of the I chord is *do*, the root of the IV chord is *fa*, the root of the V chord is *so*.

- Intervals: The root of the IV chord is a Perfect 4th above the root, and the root of the V chord is a Major 2nd above that, or a Perfect 5th above the root.

- Without Solfa or Intervals: You can either sing up a major scale from the tonic note to find the fourth and fifth notes of the scale, or use the Pitch Ruler approach to walk up to the notes which are 5 and 7 Half Steps above the tonic to find the roots of the IV and V chord respectively.

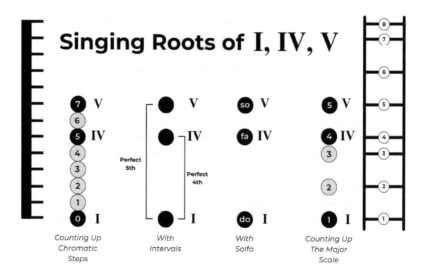

3.   Sing through example progressions featuring the I, IV and V chords, singing the name (i.e. "one", "four", "five") as you sing each chord's root.

This exercise may seem overly-simplified, since we are working with only the root notes and not the full chords, but it can be very effective for helping you tune in to the movement from one chord degree to another.

EXERCISE: Singing Chords In Progressions

This is probably my favourite Singing exercise for practicing Chord Progressions, because you get so much "bang for your buck". We simply combine the two exercises above, singing through example progressions but singing each chord as an arpeggio so that we hear all its notes. It is especially well-suited to a Solfa approach, as you're reinforcing your sense of each Solfa degree at the same time as your familiarity with the Progressions.

1.   Choose a note which is comfortably in your singing range to serve as the tonic and the root note of the I chord.

2.   Find the other notes of the I chord and the IV and V chord

using the same approaches as in the two exercises above. Sing the notes of each chord until you feel you have a good handle on them, before switching to the next chord.

3.   Once you're comfortable finding the notes of the I, IV and V chord, start singing through example progressions.

•   With Triad Chords there is a very natural way to do this with four beats to a measure and one chord per measure, by singing up from the root and then back down to the middle note i.e. root, third, fifth, third.

•   If you're working on 4-note chords you can simply sing up the four notes for each four-beat measure e.g. root third fifth seventh.

•   If you're not using Solfa you can either sing the name of the chord (e.g. "one" for all the notes of I, "four" for all the notes of IV, etc.) or you can sing the scale degree (e.g. "one three five three" for I, "four six one six" for IV, etc.). But really, you're best off using Solfa ;) Just sing the Solfa syllable of each note (e.g. *do mi so mi* for I, *fa la do la* for IV, etc.)

Example in the key of C Major:

> **TIP:**
>
> If you're working on Solfa then just singing examples like the above a handful of times each day would be my #1 recommendation for how to really get a strong feel for I, IV, V progressions quickly.
>
> You leverage your Solfa skills, you get deep inside each chord, you gain an instinctive feeling for how one flows to the next in different combinations, and you continue to level up your Solfa versatility throughout.

Instrument Practice

We've already covered some simple ways to practice Chords and Progressions with various versions of our Basic Drill, where you can use your instrument as a source of examples.

Let's look at some other instrument-based Ear Training exercises you can try.

EXERCISE: Habitual Muttering

One simple but impactful habit you can adopt is to:

1.   Identify the progressions in the music you are learning and playing, and then

2.   Stay conscious of the chord changes any time you play the music.

Depending on your instrument and style of music, step one may be simple—or not!

For example, if you're a guitarist playing from chord charts or from staff notation with chord symbols above, simply take a few minutes to go through and write in the corresponding Roman Numerals beside each letter-name chord symbol. This may be slow-going the first few times, as you learn to identify the key from the key signature or using the "Finding the Key By Ear" process from *Chapter Eight: Relative Pitch*, and the information in this chapter to translate from chord names into Roman Numerals, but once you've done it a handful of times it should become quite quick and easy for you to figure out for a new song.

If you're playing a style of music without obvious chord indications (e.g. Classical music) or you play an instrument which doesn't produce chords, you will first need to either:

A.   Identify the letter-name chord(s) present in each measure, and then translate to Roman Numerals. Or,

B.   Recognise the Chord Progressions directly in Roman Numeral form (using the skills you're developing in this chapter)

For the average instrumentalist, approach A may be quite tricky. You may find it easier (and interesting in its own way) to adopt some repertoire in a style where the sheet music does typically provide the chord names. Or you may relish the challenge of analysing the score, or consulting with a musical friend who can help you determine the chords present.

Once you know the chord progressions, step two of the exercise is very straight-forward: speak, sing, or just audiate yourself saying the name of each chord as it arises.

For a guitarist, this might mean muttering (hence the name of this exercise!) each chord label as you play it. For a trumpeter it might mean hearing *"one….. four….. one….. five….."* in your head as you play the melody or improvise a solo.

The power in this exercise lies not in doing it once or twice, but making it a daily habit. The more you can become aware of the underlying Chords and Progressions in the music you're practicing and playing anyway, the more versatile and instinctive your skills will become.

Building off Exercise 1, once we have the progression of a piece of music in Roman Numeral form, one great activity is to transpose the same progression into another key and try playing it in that key.

EXERCISE: Transposing Progressions

1.   Choose a piece of music which you've done the previous

exercise for, so that you're armed with the chord progression in Roman Numeral form.

2.   Choose a new key (probably one you're comfortable playing in, on your instrument).

3.   Use the information in this chapter, along with your growing familiarity with the chords in each key's family, to determine the chords for the same progression in your new key. You can also make use of the quick reference sheet for I, IV, V and vi chords in each key found in the *Additional Resources*.

4.   Play it in the new key!

As with the previous exercise, for non-chordal instruments this is slightly more challenging, as you'll need to transpose your melody part. Remember Convergent Learning—and don't shy away from the challenge!

If your instrumental focus is playing chords, or you're writing music based on chord progressions, you'll find this activity of transposing the same progression into a variety of keys really helps you to hear the common musical journey across all keys, and helps you to then spot the same kinds of progression in other music too[9].

EXERCISE: The "Axis Of Awesome"

This exercise is named for a viral video from several years ago, by the comedy music act *Axis of Awesome*. The video featured the trio playing through a whole series of 4-chord songs based on the same progression, demonstrating how the exact same progression was actually present across a huge range of hit songs.

---

[9] It's worth mentioning that playalong or backing-track apps can be helpful here, as they can typically directly transpose the same set of chords into a new key at the push of a button. That's handy if you struggle with figuring out the transposition, or if you play a melodic instrument and want a backing part in each new key to play over.

Although you are skipping the legwork of figuring out the transposition, you can still get a lot of benefit by using this convenience in conjunction with the previous exercise (i.e. speak/sing through the same Roman Numeral chord names in each new key you try).

So the exercise here is simple:

1.   Gather a number of 3-chord songs (or 4-chord songs if you're working on those), and practice playing through each in turn, speaking or singing the progression as you go. If you play a chordal instrument, then you can literally play through the chords of each song. If not, you can simply listen to recordings of those songs.

2.   Spend some time jumping from song to song, hearing how the same chord changes are happening, in different keys, styles and arrangements.

You'll find example playlists as well as a link to that original video in the *Additional Resources*.

This isn't just a fun gimmick like the *Axis of Awesome* video might suggest. It is a powerful way to really start hearing the underlying changes.

You'll soon start to notice the same 3-chord and 4-chord progressions jumping out at you in other songs, either because you consciously notice e.g. *"oh, it sounds just like Don't Stop Believing"* or just because you have gained a more general, instinctive grasp of these 3- and 4-chord progressions, and can spot them by their characteristic sounds.

Almut Says...

I am doing this with my music group, but we are singing two or more songs at the same time :-)

There is a musical form that is called "Quodlibet" (a Latin term which translates to "as you like it"), which is really a fun combination of songs that follow the same chord progression and fit together harmonically. Bach was quite fond of them.

It sounds like a round, but with two songs sung in parallel. It always amazes singers if we combine songs and they sound great together—and I continue playing the same chord progressions as accompaniment on the guitar!

Applied Activities

As early as possible, you'll want to start applying your new skills with Chords and Progressions to real, practical musical activities. The Integrated Ear Training approach means developing all four H's (Head, Hands, Hearing, Heart) in each and every practice session. So not just "Learning" (Head) and "Practicing" (Hearing, perhaps Hands) but "Applying" (Head, Hands, Hearing, Heart).

Several of our exercises so far have been quite practical, particularly relating to Playing By Ear. Let's explore how we can further develop our skills with Chords and Progressions through applied musical activities.

Playing By Ear

As you'll learn in *Chapter Fourteen: Playing By Ear*, playing music by ear starts as "figuring it out by ear". This means you can immediately start practicing Playing By Ear, even when just starting out developing your ear for Chords and Progressions.

The process is simple:

EXERCISE: Playing Progressions By Ear

1.   Choose a song or a piece of music. To make things simple to begin with, you might like to choose from the list of 3-chord songs provided in the *Additional Resources*.

2.   Identify the key (see *Chapter Eight: Relative Pitch* for instructions).

3.   Figure out the I, IV and V chords in that key, using the information earlier in this chapter or the quick reference sheet in *Additional Resources*.

4.   Now as you listen to the music, try to figure out which chord is being played in each measure. If you play a chordal instrument, just try out playing each chord and judging with your ear which best matches. If you play a non-chordal instrument you can do the same with the root note of each chord and/or play up the notes of the chord in an arpeggio.

5.   As you figure out the progression(s), jot them down on a piece of paper using Roman Numerals or letter names. If you're able to hear the meter of the music and where each measure begins, you'll probably be writing one or perhaps two chords per measure. If a chord repeats for multiple measures, write its numeral once for each measure.

It will probably take a few listens to get your transcription (yes, you just transcribed the chord progression!) complete and correct. The most important thing is to really pay attention with your ears. If you just guess blindly and rely on your ears to tell you "does this match or not?", that will be of some value—but the real power of this exercise comes when you try to identify each chord before playing anything. Over time your "guesses" will get more and more accurate, until "figuring it out by ear" can become directly "playing it by ear".

If you would like to "check your answers" you can look up the chord chart for the song online. Just search for the name of the song and "chords", and you will typically be able to find a page with the lyrics of the song and the chord symbols written above showing when each change occurs relative to the lyrics. Do keep in mind that these "answers" aren't always perfect, and may include a more detailed or sophisticated interpretation of the harmony. Your own "answer" may be just as valid! Trust your ears and personal taste, and that *"if it sounds good, it is good."*

Note that at first, it may be a challenge to even detect when the chord is changing. This is part of the skill you're developing, so don't worry if at first you miss some changes.

If you have difficulty hearing the meter and when each measure begins, don't worry. The subsequent chapters *Chapter Twelve: The Beat* and *Chapter Thirteen: Rhythm* will help you refine that skill. For now just write things down as best you can, focusing on the changes from one chord to the next.

Once you gain some proficiency working with I, IV, V tracks like this you can continue by:

A. Creating a playlist of 3-chord songs and challenging yourself to tune in and play along as quickly as possible as each song comes up, or

B. Extending to 4-chord songs, and then any songs you choose. You may need to leave some placeholders (just write a question-mark) for unfamiliar chords. Even just listening through and spotting when the tonic chord is appearing can be a valuable exercise!

These simple activities are a great way to bring your burgeoning Chords and Progressions skills into the world of real music, as well as connecting them with your instrument. We'll go into more depth on this in *Chapter Fourteen: Playing By Ear*.

Transcribing

We have already introduced one transcription activity above, as part of capturing the "answer" of figuring a song out by ear. But can you take it a step further, and not use an instrument at all?

Try using the same steps as above, but instead of relying on an instrument to produce notes or chords to compare with what you're hearing in the track, use only your ears. Can you recognise each chord in a I, IV, V progression in the real music track?

You might like to use Singing or Audiation to help you. For example, singing the root notes of I, IV and V to compare, or audiating the tonic to keep a clear sense of the tonal centre as you hear each chord and how it relates.

Once you think you have it, write it down in Roman Numerals. Then identify the key, translate into letter name chords, and check your answer, either by playing through on an instrument and comparing, or by looking up the chords as explained above.

Harmonising By Ear

Did you know that all seven notes of the Major Scale occur in the I, IV and V chords? This is perhaps one reason why 3-chord songs are so prevalent: take any melody using just the notes of the Major Scale, and whatever the current note is, the I, the IV or the V chord features that note.

Naturally we tend not to change chords with every note of a melody! But the principle holds, that you can harmonise (meaning "add harmony to") any major melody comfortably using only the I, IV and V chords.

This allows for a simple but very empowering exercise. As soon as you have some handle on the I, IV and V, take a simple melody, and decide for yourself which chords go best with it.

You might like to use the simple melodies provided in *Chapter Nine: Solfa*. Sing the melody, and use its scale degrees to suggest to you which chord might fit. For example, if the first line of the melody features only the notes *do* and *mi*, the I chord with its *do*, *mi* and *so* notes will fit nicely. If the next line moves on to *mi*, *fa* and *la* then the IV chord with its *fa*, *la* and *do* might work well—or you may well choose to stay on the I and let the *fa* and *la* create some tension!

Try different possibilities, and notice the musical results. It's enlightening to hear the impact of choosing between various "valid" choices, including how often you choose to change the chord.

We've illustrated it in Solfa terms above, but if you're not yet using Solfa, just think in terms of scale degrees and the notes which belong to each chord.

Aside from it being exciting to realise you can harmonise a melody yourself (something many would consider a very advanced skill) this is a really effective way to bridge between melody and harmony skills, and connect the dots between Solfa and Progressions. With practice, you'll be able to instinctively hear which chords would go well with a melody, and when the melody would benefit from the chord changing versus staying the same.

Naturally this is a huge benefit for songwriters and composers, but also valuable if you'd like to improvise full arrangements on keyboard, or accompany yourself singing on guitar, for example. And of course, once you're comfortable with the I, IV and V Chords, the same principle that *"things sound natural when the notes of the chords feature some or all of the notes of the melody"* can be extended to the vi chord and any other chords you're working with.

By Ear—Or By Theory

Another possibility is to harmonise a melody purely based on the theory. If you have the melody written down in staff notation or Solfa, you can come up with your own accompanying progression just by thinking about the notes present and what might fit well. You can write down a harmonisation, and then play it.

Although you're missing out on the experimentation-by-ear when you do it this way, it can still be a good exercise to try in addition to the ear-based one above, particularly if you are still getting comfortable with the connections between scale degrees and the I, IV and V Chords.

Improvising

We've already begun exploring improvised progressions in some of the exercises earlier in this chapter, by simply choosing a key, selecting certain chords (e.g. the I, IV and V) and then spending some time playing through different sequences featuring those chords.

You can take this a step further in a number of ways, such as:

1. Thinking about Form. Pick one chord sequence to represent your "A section" or verse", and then come up with a different sequence to be your "B section" or "chorus", and notice how much richer your improvisation immediately becomes, just by having those two different "journeys" as part of the musical whole.

2. Improvising melody over your chosen progressions. This is well-suited to keyboard instruments where you can play a progression with the left hand and a melody over the top with the right. You can also play the progression on a chordal instrument and improvise the melody with your singing voice. Experiment with letting the harmony inform the melody (e.g.

by choosing notes for the melody based on the notes of the current chord) and vice-versa (e.g. using the "harmonising by ear" principle above). You could also adapt the "Melody-Inspired Improv" exercise from *Chapter Fifteen: Improvisation*, using the same words, rhythm and chords as an existing song you know, but choosing new melody notes to sing the words to, trusting your ear to find notes which fit the harmony.

3.   Exploring different arrangements. How many different ways can you play through the same I, IV V progression, for example? Changing the voicings, using suspended chords, using seventh chords, moving the same progression into another key, etc. If you play a non-chordal instrument how can you switch up the way you play the notes of each chord? For example, playing the notes in different orders, moving one or more notes into a higher or lower octave, mixing up the rhythmic patterns you're playing (not just one note per beat, but all different rhythmic combinations), etc.

Not only is this a fun, creative way to practice with Progressions, it's a great gateway to thinking in a more structured way about your improvised music. If improvisation in the past has felt like "play a random series of notes until it's time to stop", you'll be amazed at the instant effect that thinking in terms of Progressions will have.

More on this in *Chapter Fifteen: Improvisation*.

Songwriting

If you have read through this chapter with Songwriting in mind, hopefully you can already see how Ear Training for Chords and Progressions will develop your instinctive sense of "what chords will work well", and create the connections between harmony, melody, and even lyrics.Whether you're a songwriter who wants to put chords to your lyrics and melody, or you want to sit down with staff paper and write an interesting arrangement that works well harmonically, you'll be empowered to make your own creative choices.

All of the other activities above (Playing By Ear, transcribing, harmonising and Improvisation) will also feed into your ability to compose your own harmony, giving you the ear skills (Hearing) and intellectual understanding (Head) that allow your Heart to express everything you wish to, and building the connection to your instrument (Hands) to be able to freely experiment and express your musical ideas through Chords and Progressions.

We'll discuss this in more detail in *Chapter Sixteen: Songwriting*.

Conclusion

In this chapter you learned all the essential theory relating to Chords and Progressions and began to familiarise yourself with their sounds. You now know a wide range of ways to practice with building blocks for both Chord Types and for Progressions. You can gradually build up your recognition skills, aiming for I, IV, V progressions, and introducing further possibilities for Chord Types and Progressions when you're ready, and to suit your musical life.

We've also covered the connections between Chords and the building blocks of Intervals and Solfa. You can enjoy great success doing Ear Training for all three, either by intentionally using them together, or by working on them separately and trusting in Convergent Learning to provide the multiplicative benefits.

In Part III we'll be focusing on applied skills like Improvisation, Songwriting, and Playing By Ear, and you will see how our building blocks for Chords and Progressions can benefit you in each of those areas.

We have covered a lot! Remember to take small steps forwards, and mix together Learn, Practice and Apply so that you can enjoy the practical payoff of your Ear Training efforts sooner rather than later. You can return to any section of this chapter again later to refresh your memory or expand your focus with Chords and Progressions.

If you could relate to what I said at the outset about *"wandering lost in a sea of chords"*, I hope that as you've read through and started to experiment with the exercises in this chapter, the two big epiphanies I mentioned have become clear and impactful for you too:

1.   Although harmony can mean any possible combination of many notes played at once, in fact there are certain patterns and conventions in music which mean we can greatly simplify to a small number of "building blocks" for Chords and Progressions.

2.   A staggering number of songs and pieces use just a handful of

Chords. By focusing on these particular building blocks in our Ear Training, we can go a long way fast.

Even if you never go beyond the "Start With Aiming For" target of recognising I, IV, V progressions by ear, reaching that stage alone can do wonders for your enjoyment, confidence, creativity and versatility as a musician. So start small and dive in! Soon that "sea of chords" will become a familiar river which you can confidently and joyfully navigate.

CHAPTER TWELVE:
THE BEAT

"Without music to decorate it, time is just a bunch of boring production deadlines or dates by which bills must be paid."

— Frank Zappa

So far in Part II we've focused on the Pitch side of things. As noted in *Chapter Seven: Ear Training*, this is because typically a musician's ear skills are more under-developed for Pitch than for Rhythm. And yet, Rhythm is often the difference-maker—marking out a beginner-sounding performance from one that sounds clearly pro-level, and playing a huge part in how effectively the music connects with the listener.

For the average instrument-learner, it's easy to take Rhythm for granted. As we obey the instructions on the page we tend to worry about "wrong notes" far more than playing notes slightly early or late. As a result, we don't recognise that often it's the rhythms tripping us up at least as much as the note pitches. If you've spent time with the practice techniques of *Chapter Six: Superlearning*, especially exercises involving the metronome, you have probably discovered this becoming painfully clear! And although your expressed rhythms may be "good enough" to be "the right rhythms", the imprecision is not lost on the listener.

With Pitch Ear Training we are primarily interested in recognising note pitches by ear, to enable applied skills like Playing By Ear, Improvisation and Songwriting. With Rhythm Ear Training there is an equivalent (learning to recognise and choose rhythmic patterns by ear) but there is also a profound benefit to be gained for playing music "as written", something we'll explore more in the chapters on Expression and Performance.

So whether you identify most as a Jammer, Creative or Performer, dedicating time to honing your Rhythm skills can have a huge payoff.

You've probably noticed that it's not this chapter but the next one which is titled "Rhythm"—because first we need to lay the foundation.

Even the rare musicians who do intentionally try to improve their sense of rhythm often make the mistake of skipping straight to Rhythm itself. They miss out on laying the firm foundation which makes it all possible: The Beat.

That's why we'll spend this chapter first getting deeply, intimately familiar with The Beat itself.

Here's a way to think about it: as you play a rhythm, your notes and rests may all be the right duration relative to each other, to a decent degree of accuracy...but if they're "floating" in time rather than firmly anchored to a steady underlying pulse. It's unsettling for the audience, and will sound loose and sloppy. Listeners often won't even be consciously aware of this, but it's still greatly affecting their experience and appreciation of the music you play. That's not to say you must strictly adhere to the beat at all times—sometimes "floating" is exactly what we want to do!—but we want that to be an intentional expressive choice, executed precisely.

It's been astonishing at Musical U to observe how so many musicians—even those who've been playing for many years—are fuzzy on what exactly "the beat" is, how it's different to "rhythm", and what more there is to do regarding The Beat than just setting your metronome to the right tempo.

Case in point: many experienced musicians still struggle to clap in time along with a song! And no judgement—I remember being there myself, as a multi-instrumentalist teenager, going to rock shows and feeling sheepish that I had to really pay attention to clap along with the rest of the crowd.

So let me say clearly at the outset: if right now you're fuzzy on Beat vs. Rhythm, or you notice the exercises in this chapter seem much more challenging than you feel they "should" be, just know that it's not unusual and it's not your fault. "Rhythm ear training" wasn't even a phrase being used online until we started to write about it back in 2009!

So before we get into recognising rhythmic patterns by ear or making your own creative choices with Rhythm, let's make sure you are deeply, accurately connected to The Beat.

Overview

In this chapter we'll refine the precision of your sense of The Beat (your "inner metronome") as well as its subdivisions. Once that's in place, all the rhythms you create on top will become more precise, and you'll have a more fine-grained skill with Hearing and Hands to express rhythms, as we'll explore in the next chapter. We will make use of our H4 Model to make sure that we are integrating The Beat into our Head, Hands, Hearing and Heart—in particular, developing a deep physical body-based sense of The Beat.

Andrew Says...

This distinction between "strictly adhering to rhythms" and always being aware of the relationship between rhythms and the beat is profound. I've noticed in myself and others that the most exquisite rubato [intentionally loose rhythmic timing for the sake of expression] derives from this keen awareness.

Inside Next Level we've discovered that this awareness (or lack of it!) extends deeply into the beat divisions. For example, I've coached two quite advanced pianists that painfully discovered that they had very little awareness of the placement of sixteenth notes and triplets. Subsequent rhythm and metronome work has had a profound effect on their flow and presence while playing.

I've joked before that we should change the name of the Next Level program to "Rhythm coaching"! I'm seeing that focus on Beat—in all its levels of divisions and groupings (meter) has brought such a profound transformation in connection, presence, and mindfulness, and has moved clients to the most deeply satisfying musical outcomes.

Back to Basics

It's common to confuse Beat and Rhythm. This isn't helped by the fact that we use the word "beat" to also refer to a certain rhythmic pattern, like *"that track has a great rock beat."*

To really understand the relationship, and start to connect with the underlying beat, separate from any rhythms we might wish to express, we need to go back to basics.

Instead of the *notation-first* approach to Rhythm which is common in instrument learning, we will take a *feeling-first* approach, connecting our Hearing and Hands (body), to the actual pulse of The Beat itself.

Instead of the *linear* approach to Rhythm, where a musician is just thinking about the sequence of note durations, one after another, we will take a *layered* approach. This will let us better understand, appreciate, and express how rhythm exists as a set of layers, from the particular notes played, down through the subdivisions of the beat, and to the beat itself.

Instead of an *instructions-based* approach relying on notation to dictate what notes to play when, we will develop an *instinct-based* approach where you have internalised both a reliable, precise "inner metronome", and a facility with the subdivisions and layers that can be built on top.

So if "the beat" is distinct from "the rhythm", and most musicians have spent little time really studying and connecting with the beat, you might well be waiting to hear:

What is "The Beat"?

The Beat is the *steady, underlying pulse* of the music. There might be any number of rhythms laid on top, playing by various instruments, from long, sustained note pitches to fast flurries of notes. Underneath them all though, is a steady pulse. If it changes, it's either gradual (slowly speeding up or slowing down) or there's an abrupt change, usually marking the start of a new section. For the most part, The Beat is steady and unchanging, no matter what patterns of note durations and silences are being played.

So The Beat is something we *sense* rather than necessarily *play*.

Here's a visual representation of The Beat with two different rhythmic patterns on top:

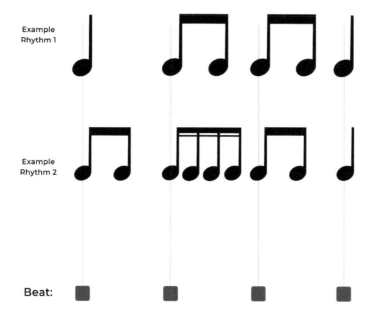

If you're not familiar with these note symbols, here's the same two rhythmic patterns, shown with rectangular blocks indicating the length of each note:

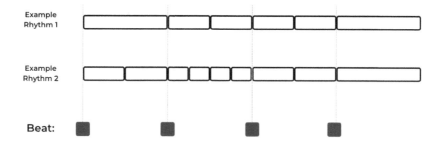

In this diagram we've used a single instantaneous marker, a square, for each beat. Some people also like to draw it as a heart symbol, drawing the analogy to our steady heartbeat.

But beats aren't actually an instant—they're a moment, with duration. This is an important distinction! The overall Beat exists as a series of individual beats, each one an equal-duration segment of time, occurring one after another.[1] If we "clap the Beat", for example, we are marking the *start* of each beat—but each beat actually lasts until the next one begins.

So really, The Beat looks something more like:

For convenience of writing and interpretation, we can leave little gaps between each beat:

We call these short horizontal lines "Beat Blanks" because, as we'll see, they provide a "blank slate" framework of time, to which we can add various annotations to show additional musical information such as rhythms or pitches.

For example, here are the same two example rhythms, shown now on Beat Blanks:

---

[1] If we say "a beat" this can refer either to one of the individual beats which make up the overall pulse (e.g. "on beat two of the measure"), or to a pulse at a certain speed (e.g. "play a fast Beat").

We will use a capital ("Beat") to refer to the concept and to the overall pulse, and lower-case ("beat") to refer to the individual beats within it.

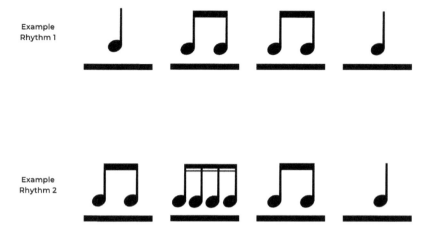

Example Rhythm 1

Example Rhythm 2

Beat Blanks are extraordinarily useful, and we'll come back to them later in the chapter. First, let's get intimately familiar with the Beat, free of any notation at all.

Developing Your Sense of the Beat

To help us get to know the Beat, we're going to borrow the "3 C's" of the Performance Free-Flow framework you'll learn about in *Chapter Eighteen: Performance*: Connection, Creativity and Conversation.

Connection

In the spirit of our *Musical Inside And Out* Pillar Belief, we want to develop both our internal sense of the Beat and our ability to relate to an external Beat we perceive.

Internal Connection

I could wax lyrical about how intrinsic and innately powerful Rhythm is for humans, how the earliest forms of music-making known were for the sake of communal dance, how music could not exist in any meaningful way without Rhythm and its underlying Beat... But instead, let's experience just how innate the concept of a steady pulse is.

EXERCISE: Find Your Heartbeat

1. Place your index and middle fingers on your neck, heart, or wrist—wherever you find it easiest to feel your heartbeat.

2. Take a few seconds to just pay full attention to that steady pulse.

3. Try to tap with your other hand or a foot, in sync with that pulse. Don't be surprised if you find this a bit tricky! The very fact that you can tell when it "clicks" and you're accurately in sync versus being a bit early or late with your taps is exactly what we want to tune in to.

4. Taking your fingers off your pulse, try to continue the steady Beat by clapping. Keep your ears engaged, and listen for how steadily you can keep the pulse going at the same rate.

5. Now jog lightly on the spot, or walk up and down a flight of stairs. Repeat steps 1–4. Can you notice your pulse is a bit faster now? Is it any easier or harder to tap in sync?

Clapping is a powerful tool for expressing Beats and rhythms, really ingraining them into your body physically, without needing to think about note pitches or instrument technique.

It might sound funny to say, but clapping can take practice! Don't start with your hands too far apart from one another, small claps are easier to time accurately. You may find that clapping vertically rather than horizontally, with your dominant hand on top, is easier and more effective.

If you're tapping your foot, some of our members have found that tapping your heel rather than your toes helps internalise the beat more fully.

EXERCISE: Walk The Beat

1. Stand up and clap a steady Beat, at a comfortable speed. A little faster than one beat per second is about right.

2. As you clap, step in place, alternating left foot and right foot.

Just like you're walking in place. Feel free to adjust your clapping speed to make this comfortable for you. What matters is to time each clap and step neatly together, at the same moment in time.

3.   Once that's comfortable, try adjusting your speed up a little, then down a little. Again, just focus on keeping tight synchronisation between your claps and steps.

4.   As you clap and step, start speaking the numbers *"one, two, three, four, one, two, three, four, …"*

Again, don't be surprised or discouraged if you get muddled, or if you find it a challenge to get things as synchronised as you can hear they should be. This is exactly what we need to practice!

The U.K.-based drummer Dave Smith introduced us to a wonderful approach to connecting with The Beat which we call the "Rhythm Dance". The idea is to have a way of moving your body which allows you to express both the Beat and its grouping into measures (a.k.a. "bars"). We'll explore that more in the section on Meter below, but you can try the Rhythm Dance for yourself now:

EXERCISE: Rhythm Dance

1.   Stand up, with feet slightly apart, and clap a steady Beat, as before.

2.   Now, instead of simply stepping "right, left, right, left", we're going to make four distinct movements in turn, in a loop:

•   Left foot steps outwards (to the left) a little.

•   Right foot steps to the left, to meet the left foot.

•   Right foot steps outwards (to the right) a little.

•   Left foot steps to the right, to meet the right foot.

This should leave you where you started. So you are still stepping once on each beat, but now we've got four distinct moves:

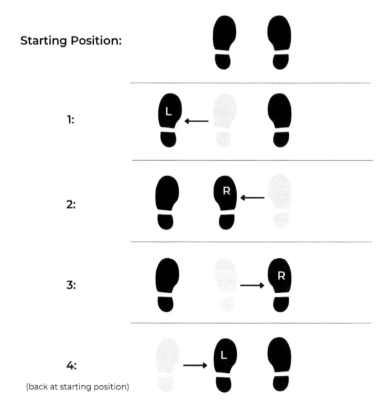

Starting Position:

1:

2:

3:

4:
(back at starting position)

3. Try this for a while, focusing on your synchronisation, until it's comfortable.

4. When you're ready, start speaking the numbers *"one, two, three, four, one, two, three, four ..."* as before, so that you say *"one"* when moving your left foot outwards, and so on.

Practicing just this exercise is a very effective way to get more deeply in touch with the Beat, and it also provides a powerful basis for a range of other Rhythm exercises, as we'll see.

As before, don't worry if you get muddled or find it challenging. Remember Growth Mindset, and acknowledge those difficulties as revealing your learning opportunity. You can adjust the speed as needed, or try just clapping and stepping, or just speaking and stepping, before returning to all three together.

We've seen consistently that musicians who've been taught music in a very Head-and-Hands focused way often haven't learned the fundamental skill of moving our bodies to the Beat. It seems like it should be so simple (especially if the level of our Hands skill on our instruments is high!) it can feel embarrassing when we struggle with it. Practice in private to begin with, and Tak Courag. The results can be truly life-changing.

External Connection

Now that we have a feel for producing a clear, steady Beat, let's start practicing synchronising with some external source of a pulse. You've already had a taste of this, as coordinating your hands, feet and speech may well have felt like you were trying to synchronise two different Beats together!

There are rhythms all around us. This can be anything from the sounds of traffic and the city to the quiet of the woods, to the rushing and cyclical pounding of ocean waves on the shore. Birds, insects, weather… all have rhythm. Learning how to discern different pulses within a greater soundscape will help you learn how to properly clap in time and find the Beat.

EXERCISE: The Pulse of Life

For this exercise, take a few minutes to simply sit still and listen. As you sit:

1. Become aware of all the sounds around you.[2]

2. Try to tune in to different rhythms you hear.

3. See if you can discern any repeating patterns, and if there's an underlying pulse you can notice.

It could be the steady drip, drip, drip of raindrops from your roof, the ticking of a clock, the clattering of trains going past, a gentle pulsing of the human hubbub around you. This is a wonderful Active Listening exercise which you can practice in your day-to-day life, to

---

[2] If your surroundings are truly silent, then:

A. I envy you!

B. Move to another location, or try this exercise next time you're somewhere with a bit of environmental noise.

wake up your ears and become more mindful of the musicality of both
the natural and man-made worlds.

Now let's turn our attention to something which almost always has a
clear, intentional Beat: music!

Funnily enough, the exercise below is often introduced as the first
step in learning to connect with the Beat! But as you've seen, there is
some really important groundwork we can usefully lay, before ever
getting to clapping along with fully-arranged music tracks.

EXERCISE: Clap Along With Music

1.   Select a recording of a song or piece you're familiar with. To
     ease you in, start with something which has a prominent drum
     part (e.g. most rock music, electronic dance music)

2.   Play the track and listen carefully. Try to tune your ear in to
     the Beat of the music. You may find yourself instinctively
     wanting to clap, tap or nod along in a certain way, especially if
     you've spent some time with the previous exercises.

3.   Start to express the Beat you hear, by tapping, clapping,
     stepping, or even using the full Rhythm Dance. You'll know
     you have it right if you *feel* in sync with the music, and you're
     consistently placing your beats at the same moments that
     notes occur in the music. If you don't have it quite right, you'll
     feel like the music is drifting, or jumbled compared to your
     expressed Beat.

> ## TIP:
>
> If you find this tricky, one great stepping-stone is to practice with drum loops. These are short, repeating percussion tracks. The big advantage is that drums will often be playing the pulse itself as part of their rhythm, or it will at least be very clearly implied. You can search online for free examples or see the *Additional Resources*, where you'll find tracks with and without a prominent "click" track to reveal the Beat.
>
> Once you get the hang of finding and clapping along with the Beat in drum loops, you'll find it easier to tune in to the drum part in rock/pop music or other genres with similar drum parts, and then to music where the Beat is less prominent.

We'll explore that sensation of being "in time" (i.e. synchronised with the Beat) and "out of time" more below, so if you found it hard to judge if you were "getting it right", you can return to this exercise again later.

Creativity

As you'll discover in the following chapter on Rhythm, and in *Chapter Fifteen: Improvisation*, simple rhythmic improvisations can be a powerful gateway into improvising your own musical ideas. And the simplest possible rhythm is... the Beat!

Although it may not yet feel like "creating" to you, try creating your own Beats by:

- Using clapping, tapping, stepping or dancing to produce a steady pulse, without reference to anything else. Experiment with starting a pulse which is a moderate speed, then stop, and start again at a new, faster speed. Then slower. Experiment with a wide range of speeds.

- Experiment with emphasising certain beats. For example if

you're speaking the numbers (as in some of the exercises above, including the Rhythm Dance) you can speak the "one" louder than the "two", "three", or "four". How does that change your experience of expressing the Beat? What if you emphasise "two" and "four" instead? What if you ditch the "four" and only speak *"one, two, three, one, two, three, …"* in a loop?

• Extend the Rhythm Dance with your own movements. Start with stepping and counting, as in the earlier exercise. Then try adding finger clicks instead of clapping. Or add arm movements that feel right to you. Do different things on each beat. Follow your instinct!

• This is a great time to introduce any instruments you play. Don't worry about choosing pitches for now, just choose a single note pitch and play that note in place of clapping. Try all the various exercises covered so far, using your instrument to express the Beat.

These may all seem far too simplistic to count as "being creative", but notice how in each case you are conjuring up a steady pulse out of nowhere, relying solely on your own "inner metronome". Notice too how taking on the mindset of "being creative" shifts your experience of the pulse, contrasting with just "following instructions", and how much more deeply these activities invite you into the Beat and connect you with it.

Conversation

In our 3 C's framework, "Conversation" represents the back-and-forth interplay of music. This can be between you and your instrument, you and other musicians, you and the audience, you and the music itself.

Let's try having a "conversation" with the Beat.

We'll invite a friend: the metronome. We cover some metronome basics in *Chapter Six: Superlearning*, but it's enough to know that any physical or software metronome is fine for our purposes here.

EXERCISE: Have a Conversation with the Beat

1. Set your metronome for a moderate tempo, say 60 beats per minute.

2. Begin by expressing the Beat yourself, in sync with the metronome, in whatever way you prefer (clapping, tapping, dancing, etc.). As you do, count *"one, two, three, four, …"* in a loop.

3. Once you're comfortable, start playing around with the Beat: Intentionally place one of your beats a little too early. Then try a little too late. Play a certain-numbered beat the same way each time, e.g. always playing beat "one" a little too early. That way you can try the same thing repeatedly and give yourself a chance to feel the effect, before trying something else.

4. Try a wide variety of combinations of different beats being early or late, a little or a lot. Really pay attention to how you instinctively react to the different options! Does it drive you crazy when *"one"* is a bit too late? Did it make you crack up with laughter the first time you clapped and spoke *"four"* way too early?

The key here is to have fun with it! You might be surprised by how enjoyable, and even humorous this can be, if you treat it like a true musical conversation between you and the metronome. You will probably also realise how much creative freedom you have even when expressing the simplest possible rhythmic pattern—something we'll explore much more in the Expansive Creativity framework of *Chapter Fifteen: Improvisation*, as well as *Chapter Seventeen: Expression*.

Tempo

It's one of the most counter-intuitive truths in all of music, but what my clarinet teacher told me at age 8 turned out to be spot-on: it's actually harder to play slow than fast.

To the 8-year-old me, this sounded like nonsense. There I was, struggling to get my fingers to move fast enough to play that run of

16th notes in the minuet for the concert next week, and she was telling me slower would be… harder?!

Well, it's certainly true that slowing things down gives your brain more time to process what's coming up and your fingers more time to get into the right positions and make the right movements. But when she had me slow it *way* down, although I was now able to hit the right notes in the right sequence, I discovered just how hard it was to *time* each of those notes!

You may have experienced this yourself, in the exercises above or in your own music-making: when we're keeping a Beat at a moderate speed, everything seems comfortable. Go too fast, and it becomes hard to process and move quickly enough. But go too slow, and suddenly you realise how easy it is to get lost in all that time between beats.

A bit later in the chapter we'll look at *subdividing* the Beat, which can go a long way to helping with this challenge. First, let's explore this topic of the speed of the Beat further.

The rate at which beats occur is called the *tempo*. A faster tempo means that there is less time between each beat, while a slower tempo means that there is more time between each beat.

We've already experimented with Beats at a variety of speeds—that is, a range of different tempos.

Typically music is written with an intended tempo in mind. This is generally specified in *beats per minute* (written as "B.P.M.", or sometimes "M.M." which stands for "Maelzel's Metronome", after Johann Maelzel who built the first metronome devices) so that the number 60 implies each beat lasts one second, the number 120 implies each beat lasts half a second, and the number 90 would be halfway in between those two speeds, etc.

The tempo can also be indicated (especially in Western classical music) with Italian terms that are typically placed at the beginning of a piece or a section of music:

Term	Meaning
Prestissimo	Very, Very Fast (> 200 B.P.M.)
Presto	Very Fast (168-200 B.P.M.)
Allegro	Fast (120-168 B.P.M.)
Moderato	Moderately (108-120 B.P.M.)
Andante	Walking Speed (76-108 B.P.M.)
Adagio	Slightly Slow (66-76 B.P.M.)

| *Lento* | Very Slow (40-60 B.P.M.) |
| *Grave* | Slow (20-40 B.P.M.) |

Don't feel you need to memorise these. If they are commonly used in the genres you tend to play, you'll find you get familiar with them over time. We include them here to illustrate the wide range of tempos that are used, even within a single genre of music—from 20 B.P.M. to 200 B.P.M. is a speed difference of 10 times faster!

We have already experienced the effects of changing tempo in our earlier exercises in this chapter. In *Chapter Five: Active Listening* we cover listening for and appreciating the tempo of a piece, in *Chapter Six: Superlearning* we introduce Superlearning techniques which rely on choosing and changing the tempo of the piece you're practicing, and in *Chapter Seventeen: Expression* we'll explore the creative, expressive applications of tempo changes.

As we develop our relationship with the Beat, one of the most important areas to explore is the distinction between how fast the Beat is, and how fast the Rhythm is. If a *grave* section can have a tempo 10 times slower than a *prestissimo* section, does that mean the instruments are playing notes 10 times as quickly? Not necessarily!

Ultimately it is the Rhythm which dictates how frequently notes occur. The Beat is measuring only the perceived underlying pulse. Remember, it's something we *feel* rather than something we necessarily *play*.

It's entirely possible to represent exactly the same musical passage at a range of different tempos. For example, a sequence of quarter notes (which each last one beat)[3] at 120 B.P.M. would sound identical to a sequence of eighth notes (which each last half a beat) at 60 B.P.M.:

---

[3] Technically this will depend on the time signature—see box below. But the relationship described here holds, regardless.

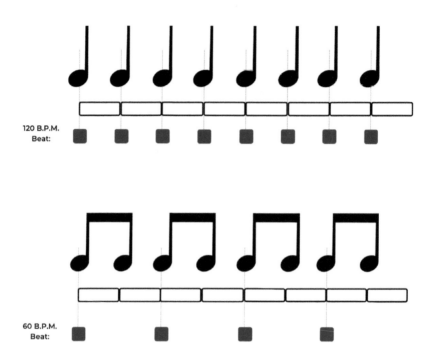

This brings us to our next layer of Rhythm. If the beat is our most basic foundation for musical time, the next layer would be how we *subdivide* each beat into smaller time units. This is what sets up all the rhythmic possibilities which can then be built on top.

Before we dive into subdivisions though, let's zoom out and discuss one more aspect of the Beat which exists at a higher layer of time: how we group beats, known as the *meter*.

Meter

As you may know, or remember from *Chapter Five: Active Listening*, not all beats are created equal! In fact, as music-makers we tend to emphasise some more than others, and do so in a way which groups them together with a set number of beats in each group (most commonly three or four beats to a group) which we then call "a bar" (or "a measure").

This gives music another layer of structure in time, in larger units than beats:

Four beats in a measure:

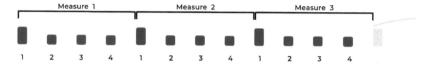

Three beats in a measure:

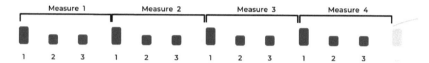

This is convenient when working with written notation, to be able to visually break the music down rather than just having a single endless stream of notes. We use vertical "bar lines" to mark the measures, like this:

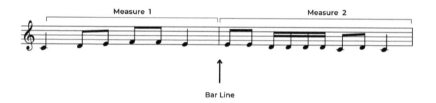

Bar Line

But it's important to know that this is a reflection of the music itself, not just a notation convenience or rule of music theory. Even with no notation involved, we play music in a way that implies this structure to the listener.

As mentioned, we do this by giving more emphasis to the notes which occur on certain beats, most notably the first beat of each measure.

In the exercises above where we spoke *"one, two, three, four"* in a loop, we were communicating the groupings of four beats. You may have also tried the exercise involving speaking certain beat numbers louder than others. If so, did you notice that emphasising the first beat of each group felt particularly familiar and natural?

Dynamics isn't the only way we can emphasise beats or communicate this structure. It can also be reflected in when the chords change, when a new section begins, in which part of the drumkit is played on that beat, and many other ways. How much, and in which ways, the musician (whether composer, songwriter, improviser, or performer) chooses to express the meter is a creative choice.

Having four beats per measure is called *quadruple* meter. Other common meters are *duple* (two beats per measure) and *triple* (three beats per measure).

Earlier in the chapter we introduced the idea of Beat Blanks. Rather than have them go on forever in a single horizontal line as the Beat continues, naturally we can instead write them in a way which also reflects the meter, by having each measure be written as its own line.

Here's what four measures of Beat Blanks would look, with two, with three, and with four beats per measure:

Four Measures of Duple Meter
(2 Beats Per Measure)

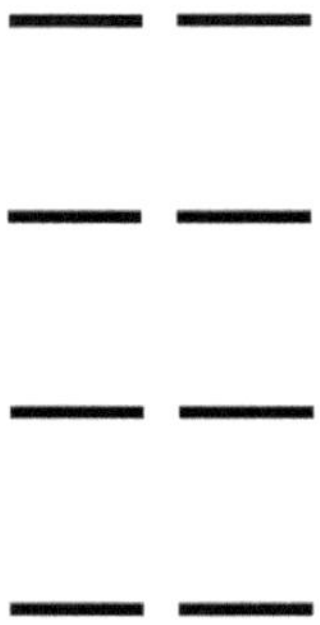

— —

— —

— —

— —

Four Measures of Triple Meter
(3 Beats Per Measure)

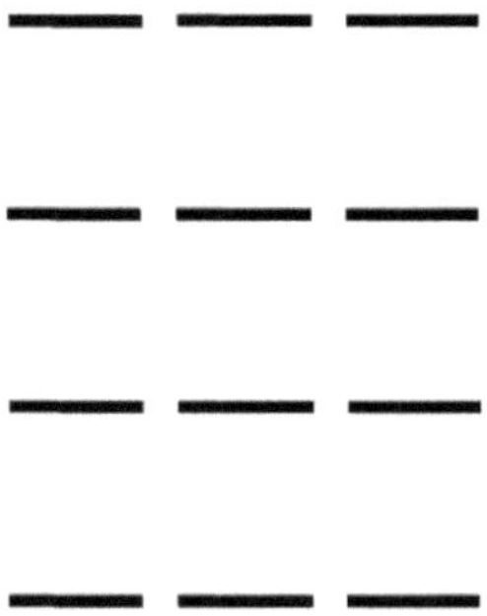

— — —

— — —

— — —

— — —

Four Measures of Quadruple Meter
(4 Beats Per Measure)

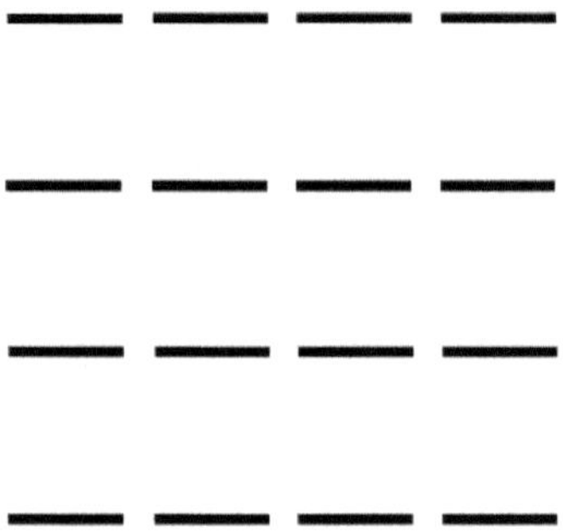

— — — —

— — — —

— — — —

— — — —

So far our Rhythm Dance used quadruple meter, with four movements and counting *"one, two, three, four, one, two, three, four, etc."* You can express a duple meter beat with the Rhythm Dance by simply stepping on the spot *(right, left, right, left, etc.)* and speaking *"one, two, one, two, etc."*.

What about a Rhythm Dance for triple meter?

EXERCISE: Rhythm Dance in Triple Meter

1.   Stand up, with feet slightly apart, and clap a steady Beat, as before.

2.   Imagine a triangle on the floor, with two of its points on your right and left feet (marked "A" and "B" below), and the third behind them and centered (marked "C"):

3.   Now we're going to make six distinct movements in turn, in a loop:

•   Left foot steps back to position C

•   Right foot steps in place on position B

•   Left foot steps forward to position A

•   Right foot steps back to position C

•   Left foot steps in place on position A

•   Right foot steps forward to position B

This should leave you where you started. So you are alternating stepping with your left and right feet, but now we've got six distinct moves, breaking up into two groups of three which each leave you in the starting position.

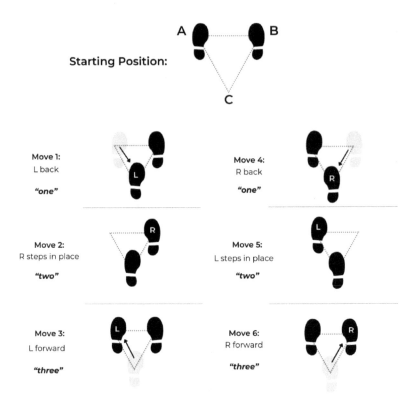

Starting Position:

Move 1:
L back

"one"

Move 2:
R steps in place

"two"

Move 3:
L forward

"three"

Move 4:
R back

"one"

Move 5:
L steps in place

"two"

Move 6:
R forward

"three"

4.   Try this for a while, focusing on your synchronisation, until it's comfortable.

5.   When you're ready, start speaking the numbers *"one, two, three, one, two, three, …"* as before, so that you say *"one"* when moving your left foot back to C, *"two"* when stepping in place with right foot on B, and so on.

Subdivisions

Why is it that slowing down the tempo makes it harder to place each note accurately in time? Our logical brain might tell us that surely it should be easier, with plenty of time to make the decision and execute the movement required to produce the note.

What makes it difficult is that our human brains perceive time as continuous. We experience it as flowing freely from one moment to the next, where each "moment" has no precise duration.

Clearly we do have some kind of "inner metronome" which allows us to judge time in broad terms, and keep a steady Beat, and we are capable of handling a range of tempos. We are able to turn that continuous stream of time into a structured sequence of evenly-spaced moments. But unless we do something further, we don't actually have a precise sense of how time passes during each one of those moments.

The solution? Do the same thing again! Just as we transformed free-flowing time into a series of evenly-spaced beats, we can transform the duration of each one of those beats into its own structured timeline:

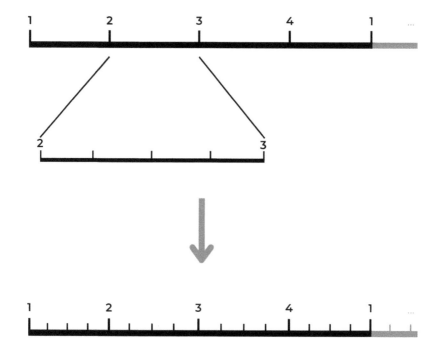

Now our musical mind has something structured to latch on to as each beat occurs.

In music we typically divide each beat into either two or three parts, known as *simple* or *compound* time respectively.

EXERCISE: Simple and Compound Time

1. Select a moderate tempo, such as 60 B.P.M.

2. Begin by clapping, tapping, or stepping the Beat. You can use a metronome as a reference to synchronise with, or trust your own "inner metronome" to produce a comfortable, steady tempo.

3. Once you're in the flow of it, add speaking beat numbers, with four beats to a measure: *"one, two, three, four, one, two, three, four, etc."*

4. Now instead of just speaking one number on each beat, insert the word "and" after each one: *"one and two and three and four and, etc."* Keep the pace of your words steady, so that *"one"* lasts as long as *"and"*, and so on. You are now dividing each beat into two equal parts. This is "simple" time.

5. Next, try adding the words *"and a"* after each number, again giving each word equal duration. The "a" is pronounced like "uh" rather than the letter "A". You are now dividing each beat into three equal parts. This is "compound" time.

You can extend this exercise by stepping a steady Beat (perhaps using the Rhythm Dance) and clapping each of the subdivisions. You will clap twice for each beat for simple time, and three times for compound. Your claps should have their own steady tempo i.e. the claps should be evenly-spaced.

If you've never done this before, don't be surprised if it's a challenge. You may find it easier if you continue speaking the *"one and two and…"* or *"one and a two and a…"* as you add the clapping.

As you do this exercise you'll see clearly how we are using the same ability of our musical mind to produce a steady Beat, but now at two different levels: the underlying "pulse" Beat and another, faster, Beat on top of it and synchronised with it, subdividing each beat of the pulse into equal-duration parts. You'll also see why there isn't a single strict correspondence between the sound of a rhythm and how we might write it down. Are your claps communicating, for example, a 120 B.P.M. pulse? Or are they the simple subdivisions of a 60 B.P.M.

pulse?

These are the two major classifications of subdivisions, but we can of course divide each beat further. For example, if we took things one layer more fine-grained with simple time we could divide each of our two half-beats into two equal parts, each lasting a quarter of a beat.

EXERCISE: Dividing The Beat In Four

- Repeat the exercise above, but speaking the Beat as *"one e and a, two e and a, three e and a, four e and a, etc."* where "e" is pronounced like the letter "E". This can be written more concisely as e.g. *"1 e + a, 2 e + a, etc."*

Side Note: Time Signatures and Meter Names

You may be familiar with the concept of a *time signature*, written at the start of a piece or section. A time signature consists of two numbers, written one above the other, for example:

The bottom number specifies the note symbol used for each beat, so that e.g. "4" indicates quarter notes and "8" indicates eighth notes. Then the top number specifies how many beats are in each measure.

Simple meters have a 2, 3 or 4 on top. So the simple duple meter (*"1 and, 2 and"*) introduced above would be written 2/2 or 2/4. Simple quadruple meter (*"1 and, 2 and, 3 and, 4 and"* or *"1 e + a, 2 e + a, 3 e + a, 4 e + a"*) would be 4/4.

Compound meters have a 6, 9 or 12 on top and almost always an 8 on the bottom. So the compound duple (*"1 and a, 2 and a"*) would be written 6/8, and compound quadruple meter (*"1 and a, 2 and a, 3 and a, 4 and a"*) would be written 12/8.

Zac Says...

I like to encourage people to listen to music in various meters, and allow the music to move them and notice how their body naturally moves to 3/4, 4/4, 6/8, etc.

I find that a balanced practice between two ways of experiencing the beat allows for the most fun and the most progress:

- Practice Experience 1: Allow the beat to move your body, and just noticing how your body moves to different beats.

- Practice Experience 2: Be deliberate about moving to certain beats in certain ways with tools like rhythm walking, rhythm dancing, other types of dancing, body percussion, beat-boxing, clapping, etc.

Stick Notation

Traditional staff notation uses a range of different note symbols to show how long each note lasts. Not only does the musician working from traditional notation need to learn and become adept at quickly deciphering and interpreting these various symbols, they also need to learn to string them all together to produce the corresponding rhythms. Typically a "count chant" method (like the *"one e and a"* approach above) is used to try to distil out, in a very mathematical way, when each note should occur, based on all the note and rest durations coming before it in the measure. While this works, it can be a real challenge to figure out, and is very much based on theory and notation, rather than on the musical sounds themselves. This particularly limits its usefulness for creative purposes like improvising and composing.

In the next chapter we'll introduce an alternative to "count chant", called "rhythm syllables", which is a sound-based approach. There is also an alternative to the traditional staff notation, which makes very clear the relationship between notes and the underlying Beat. This avoids the need to "figure out" when each note occurs in the measure:

you can see it directly.

Not only is this alternative approach much easier to understand and brings the big advantage of keeping us clearly grounded in the underlying pulse, it actually isn't a strict alternative at all. In fact, it becomes easy to transform this notation into the corresponding traditional staff notation, making it a kind of powerful shorthand.

This form of notation comes from the Kodály approach[4] and is called "Stick Notation", because rather than drawing a (sometimes very intricate!) note symbol, we use simple lines, and our simplest building block of a quarter note is one vertical line, looking like a stick:

Stick Notation goes hand-in-hand with Beat Blanks. Here is how we could write a series of four notes, each lasting one beat (i.e. quarter notes) in Stick Notation on Beat Blanks:

If we have more than one note per beat, there are other simple Stick Notation symbols we can use:

---

[4] See *Chapter Nine: Solfa* for background.

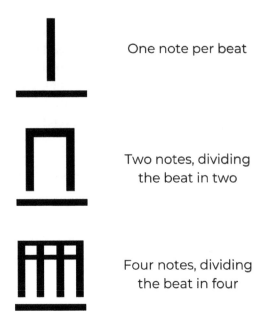

One note per beat

Two notes, dividing
the beat in two

Four notes, dividing
the beat in four

We'll explore these much more in the following chapter on Rhythm! But as an example, here is how we could write the earlier exercise where we spoke e.g. *"one and two and three and four"*, clapping once per word:

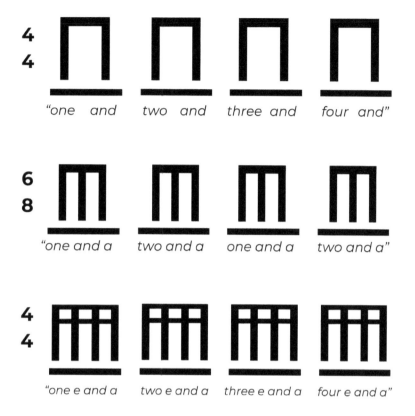

$\frac{4}{4}$ "one   and   two   and   three   and   four   and"

$\frac{6}{8}$ "one and a   two and a   one and a   two and a"

$\frac{4}{4}$ "one e and a   two e and a   three e and a   four e and a"

Conclusion

In this chapter we've gone back to basics on musical Rhythm, to establish a new, deeper relationship with The Beat. Through the exercises you've started to recognise, feel and even create duple and triple meter beats at a variety of tempos and with both simple and compound subdivisions.

What we've covered may seem simple—and conceptually, it is—especially if you've been playing music for years and tackling all kinds of key signatures and written rhythms.

But don't let the conceptual simplicity fool you. The more time you spend focusing on, connecting with, and *feeling* this fundamental Beat in a variety of ways, the easier and faster everything rhythmic will click into place for you, and the more effective and expressive a musician you will become. It can't be over-stated how transformational it is to go from a purely-intellectual understanding of musical time to truly understanding and feeling musical time deep within your body.

Now that we've laid a firm foundation with this framework of time, we are well prepared to explore all the possible rhythms we can build on top of it.

CHAPTER THIRTEEN:
RHYTHM

"Music is the space between the notes."
— Claude Debussy

In the previous chapter we explored the foundation of all things rhythmic: The Beat.

If you skipped over that chapter (perhaps because you're an experienced musician and feel like you know what "the beat" is), I would highly recommend going through it, including trying the exercises, before continuing with this one. Not only does it set the scene for everything we're about to cover, we've found that most musicians' rhythmic challenges actually tend to stem from an under-developed sense of The Beat—meaning it's very easy for the average musician to under-estimate the value of spending time working specifically on their "inner metronome", and then struggle more with Rhythm than they need to.

Once we've truly understood what The Beat is all about, and started to actively develop and refine our relationship with it, we are ready to start exploring the musicality of Rhythm.

Overview

In this chapter we'll introduce a lesser-known *spoken* approach to thinking about, notating, understanding, and creating rhythmic patterns, which is far more aligned with developing your natural musicality than the traditional methods rooted in Western classical music and its corresponding score notation. Although this "Rhythm Syllables" approach is quite different from what you may be used to, it is not a strict alternative—in fact it can beautifully extend and complement anything you do with traditional rhythmic notation and score-reading.

We'll also explain how the Stick Notation introduced in the previous chapter can be combined with Rhythm Syllables to let you translate spoken rhythms to and from the written page. We'll suggest exercises you can use to practice with this approach, and show how to incorporate it into practical activities like Playing By Ear, Improvising and Songwriting.

A Musicality-Based Approach to Rhythm

We first started teaching Rhythm Syllables and Stick Notation in earnest at Musical U with our Kodály-based[1] *Foundations of a Musical Mind* course, which was later integrated into the Spring Season of our *Living Music* program. And that framing of *"Foundations"* is how I'd encourage you to think about what you'll learn in this chapter.

When it comes to learning music and developing yourself as a musician, there are always a vast number of possible options available to you, and so I think it's important to explain that the approach we're recommending here isn't just some arbitrary choice, or doing things differently for the sake of it.

As you'll experience for yourself as you go through this chapter and try the suggested exercises, this approach to Rhythm is very much a foundational way of relating to, understanding, and expressing musical rhythms. Again, it's not intended to fully replace the traditional methods, but rather it can be seen as a simpler, slightly

---

[1] See *Chapter Nine: Solfa* for background on the Kodály approach to music education.

more abstracted way of thinking about Rhythm, which our experience across tens of thousands of musicians has shown is extremely effective for developing an *instinctive* understanding of Rhythm.

Once you put in place this new "mental model" for understanding how Rhythm works, you may find that (like we've heard from so many musicians inside Musical U), it seems a bit crazy that nobody ever showed you this *first*. Just like with our Pitch "building blocks", it can become a hugely versatile, powerful, and liberating asset across everything you do related to musical Rhythm.

So what is this "missing foundation" that needs to be filled in?

It can be explained most clearly by looking at where musicians most commonly struggle with Rhythm.

The traditional approach to Rhythm which I've been referring to is a heavily notation-based approach. Music is represented in score notation, as a series of different symbols for notes and rests, each of which corresponds to a different duration. Vertical bar lines show where each bar (or "measure") begins and ends. Here's an example:

Musicians are taught the durations of each symbol, and how to count through the beats of each bar and figure out where each note begins, relative to the Beat. And therein lies the problem: it is a very analytical, almost mathematical, way of understanding Rhythm, and particularly the relationship between the rhythmic patterns being played, and the underlying Beat.

To understand when to place each note relative to that underlying Beat, this "counting" method requires you to think very analytically about when each note should happen. That certainly works—but it requires a very conscious "figuring out and then executing". It's also easy to get lost or confused within a measure, with the later rhythms dependant on you having got the earlier ones right, or things don't "add up".

To put that another way: it's all Head, with little attention paid to Hearing (the sounds) or Heart (the instinctive feel for rhythm).

When we hear or express rhythms, they exist as a continual stream of moments in time, proceeding moment-to-moment just like the underlying Beat. In other words, music *flows* through time, and so it's valuable to have a way of expressing rhythmic patterns that similarly just flows, from one moment to the next. That goes double if our goal is musical freedom and creativity.

Personally, if you had asked me to improvise a rhythm before I knew about the Rhythm Syllables approach introduced below, then either:

A. My brain would have been envisioning the notation. I would have been carefully trying to think through where the notes lay in relation to the beat, and I would have struggled to do very much fast enough to be useful in improvising. Or,

B. I would have just freely made up a rhythm, and the notes would have been a bit of a jumble, not always relating well to the beat or resulting in very musically-satisfying patterns.

With Rhythm Syllables and Stick Notation, even a complete beginner can write or improvise their own creative, musically-coherent and interesting rhythms. And because "creativity is the vehicle, not the destination", this gives us a wonderful way to develop our rhythmic skills while having creative fun.

On top of that, because it's fully compatible with the traditional approach of counting and score notation, it makes it far easier to decipher rhythms written in that traditional way, or write them yourself.

So this is not a replacement for counting and score notation, but an elegant complement to it. Just like Solfa and Intervals aren't strict alternatives, but each have their own strengths and best uses, counting and Rhythm Syllables do too. We'll focus on Rhythm Syllables in this chapter both because counting is so well covered by traditional music education materials, and because this approach is so intimately tied to the musicality of Rhythm.

As we continue in this chapter, you can see this as both a useful tool in itself, and a previously-missing foundation for everything you've done with Rhythm up until now.

Rhythm Syllables

The auditory processing system of the human brain has considerable overlap between how it processes spoken language and how it processes musical sounds. The big idea with Rhythm Syllables is to leverage our brain's capacity for language, and your lifetime of prior experience subconsciously and automatically recognising rhythmic patterns in speech.

Instead of a notation-first approach where we try to figure out analytically how a series of written symbols should sound, Rhythm Syllables take a sound-first approach, assigning a spoken *syllable* (or combination of syllables) to each building block of rhythmic patterns.

You may have come across the idea of using a spoken word or phrase to help you remember the rhythm corresponding to different note symbols, such as *"ap-ple"* for a pair of eighth notes and *"wa-ter-me-lon"* for a series of four eighth notes together.

Let's try using that simple idea to create our own rhythms:

EXERCISE: Garden Gate

1. Create a Beat. Use clapping, tapping or stepping, as covered in the previous chapter, to express a moderate (e.g. 60 B.P.M. or walking pace) Beat.

2. Now, each time you clap/tap/step, speak either the word *"garden"* or the word *"gate"*. They should each last for the full beat, so that *"gate"* fills the full duration, while "gar-den" splits it into two even parts. Start by just saying *"gate, gate, gate, gate"* then *"gar-den, gar-den, gar-den, gar-den"*, and then start alternating them e.g. *"gate, gate, gar-den, gate"*.

3. Really listen and *feel* the rhythms you are creating.

You have just improvised rhythms using quarter and eighth notes! Simple as it may seem, this has been a breakthrough moment for many members inside Musical U, realising that the intimidating skill of " improvising" could actually feel easy and natural for them. And this is just the beginning...

This simple exercise demonstrates how our spoken language skills can provide a gateway into the musicality of Rhythm. We can see how our Hands, Hearing and Heart can be immersed in rhythmic creativity, with literally zero Head knowledge required!

This informal approach of using random words which naturally have various rhythmic patterns is illustrative—but has limitations.

The Rhythm Syllables approach is similar, in the sense that you can look at written rhythms and speak aloud how they would sound, but there are two important differences from that informal approach:

A. The syllables we use are consistent across each rhythm pattern (just like how with Solfa we use a single, distinctive name for each note of the scale), and

B. The syllables are devoid of any additional meaning which would engage the linguistic part of the brain and distract from the pure rhythms.

There are a few established systems of Rhythm Syllables in use today, including the *Konnakol* approach which is core to Indian music traditions. We've found that the Kodály ones we'll introduce here are a very effective balance of being immediately-usable while still complex enough to allow for sophisticated rhythmic development.

Just like naming notes with Solfa rather than letter names brought us closer to the sounds and to the way the brain naturally interprets Relative Pitch, these Rhythm Syllables reflect the actual musical sounds rather than the mathematical theory of rhythm (e.g. "quarter note plus two eighth notes") or visual symbols in traditional notation (e.g. a quarter-note symbol followed by two eighth-note symbols). This helps us gain an instinctive, physical understanding of rhythm, and connects Head, Hands, Hearing and Heart.

Once you learn and practice Rhythm Syllables, as well as the corresponding Stick Notation, you will be able to use these building blocks to easily create rhythms, interpret written rhythms, and write down rhythms you hear.

Building Blocks of Rhythm

In the previous chapter we introduced Stick Notation as a simplified way of writing rhythmic patterns over a set of Beat Blanks. For example, here's how we would show a steady pulse, clapping or playing once per beat:

As a reminder, this is a simple, fast way to write rhythms, which is essentially the traditional score notation but with staff lines and note heads removed (i.e. stripping away the Pitch dimension entirely). This means you can easily extend Stick Notation to full notation simply by adding the note heads and placing the notes at the right vertical location on the staff:

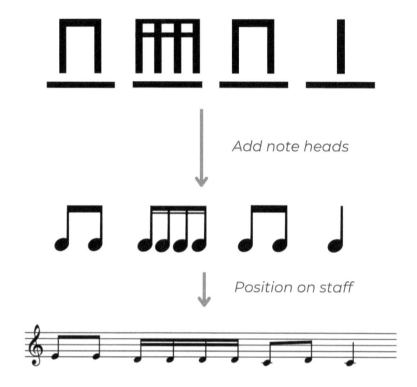

Or even just by annotating below with the Solfa syllable of each note:

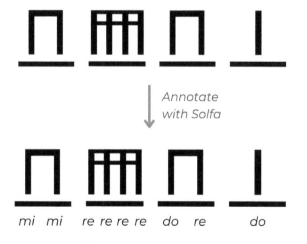

mi   mi   re re re re   do   re   do

Now we'll introduce the Rhythm Syllable building blocks, using Stick Notation to illustrate each one.

Ta

Ta is the rhythm syllable we'll use to represent a note that is one beat long:

Ta	Ta	Ta	Ta

You would speak this as *"Ta Ta Ta Ta"*, with each *"Ta"* synchronised with the Beat. For example, if you were stepping or tapping the beat, you would say *"Ta"* each time you stepped or clapped.

We can show a one-beat rest with the symbol "Z". For example, here's how we could represent clapping on beats 2 and 4 only:

Z		Z	
(Ta)	Ta	(Ta)	Ta

If you were speaking this rhythm you could speak the *"Ta"* of the rest in your head (i.e. audiate it): *"(Ta) Ta (Ta) Ta"*.

Ti-Ti

Our next building block is *"Ti-Ti"* (pronounced *"tee tee"* with a long "e" sound) and represents subdividing the beat into two equal parts:

Ti-Ti	Ti-Ti	Ti-Ti	Ti-Ti

If there's need for a single "Ti" rather than a pair, it's written like this:

𝗋

EXERCISE: Garden Gate With Rhythm Syllables

1. As before, produce a steady Beat with your body.

2. Now on each beat speak one of the rhythm syllables *"Ta"* or *"Ti-Ti"* (just as we did with *"gate"* and *"garden"* in the previous exercise). Start with just *"Ta"*s, then just *"Ti-Ti"*'s, remembering to fill each beat's duration and have the two *"Ti"*'s of *"Ti-Ti"* be of equal duration, subdividing that beat into two even parts. When you're ready, begin mixing the two together.

3. As before, don't let this be a purely intellectual exercise—keep your ears engaged and focus on feeling the rhythms you are creating.

We will introduce some more rhythm syllables below, but you would do well to practice with just these two for at least a few days, if not a week. You can play with this "Garden Gate with Rhythm Syllables" exercise and also make use of the Starter Songs from *Chapter Nine: Solfa* which use only Ta and Ti-Ti. Look out for Ta's and Ti-Ti's in the other music you're working on! Any quarter note can be spoken as a Ta and any eighth note pair as Ti-Ti.

Tika-Tika

Next, to subdivide the beat into four equal parts, we use *"Tika-Tika"*, with a short *"tih"* sound this time (unlike the long *"tee"* of Ti). Here is the stick notation for four beats of sixteenth notes:

Tika-Tika   Tika-Tika   Tika-Tika   Tika-Tika

You might wonder why we write this as "Tika-Tika" rather than "Ti-Ka-Ti-Ka". It both helps distinguish the "ti" of "Ti" from the "ti" in "Tika" and more clearly opens up combinations of eighth and sixteenth notes, which we can express as *"Ti-Tika"* and *"Tika-Ti"*:

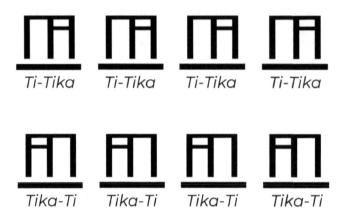

Ti-Tika   Ti-Tika   Ti-Tika   Ti-Tika

Tika-Ti   Tika-Ti   Tika-Ti   Tika-Ti

EXERCISE: Rhythmic Improvisation with Tika-Tika, Ti-Tika, and Tika-Ti

- Repeat the "Garden Gate with Rhythm Syllables" exercise above, this time introducing these new options. You might like to ease in gradually, for example with the following sequence:

1. Using Ta and Tika-Tika only
2. Using Ta, Ti-Ti and Tika-Tika
3. Using Tika-Tika, Ti-Tika and Tika-Ti
4. Using any and all of these syllables.

Notice how sophisticated your rhythmic creations can be already, just with this small number of building blocks! If you look at the Stick Notation of the Starter Songs in *Chapter Nine: Solfa* you'll notice how many of them use only these building blocks.

Getting Started

Just like with our Pitch building blocks, improvising can be a fun and effective way to really familiarise ourselves with these new building blocks for Rhythm, as the simple Garden Gate exercises above demonstrate.

Now let's incorporate some of the movement-based exercises we explored in the previous chapter on The Beat to take our rhythmic creativity even further.

EXERCISE: Rhythm Dance with Rhythm Syllable Improvisation

1. Create a steady Beat at a moderate tempo, using the Rhythm Dance introduced in the previous chapter (reminder: out with left foot on 1, bring right foot to meet it on 2, out with the right foot on 3, bring left foot to meet it on 4).

2. Begin by counting the Beat: *"one, two, three, four"*

3. Now substitute *Ta* for the numbers: *"Ta Ta Ta Ta"*

4. Next move through each of the rhythm syllables introduced so far: *"Ti-Ti, Ti-Ti, Ti-Ti, Ti-Ti"* then *"Tika-Tika, Tika-Tika, Tika-Tika, Tika-Tika"* then *"Ti-Tika, Ti-Tika, Ti-Tika, Ti-Tika"* and finally *"Tika-Ti, Tika-Ti, Tika-Ti, Tika-Ti"*. Pay attention to keeping things synchronised and notice how the feel of the rhythm changes depending on the syllables you use.

5. When you're ready, start mixing it up. You can ease in by just changing the syllable on one of the beats of the measure, for example *"Ta, Ta, Ta, Ti-Ti"*, and expressing the same pattern for the measure several times before changing it again.

6. Explore all different combinations of the rhythm syllables. Have fun with it!

7. If you'd like to, feel free to change from quadruple meter (four beats to a measure) to triple meter (three beats to a measure).

Notice how easy these building blocks make it to create very varied and interesting rhythms! For example *"Ta, Ti-Tika, Tika-Ti, Ti-Tika"* is a rhythm you might have found tricky to sight-read or come up with when improvising before, but using these syllables it's an easy creative choice to make.

If you have difficulty with this exercise, you can use clapping instead of the full Rhythm Dance to begin with. Just clap your steady beat and speak your chosen syllables. Go as slowly as you need to, giving your brain time to make the choice for each beat—just remember to keep the slow beat nice and steady, so that the rhythms exist over a pulse rather than becoming disjointed.

You should naturally find yourself starting to be able to "think ahead" to the rhythms you'd like to express in the next measure. This is a great step forwards in being able to improvise creatively on-the-fly.

Our next step is to use the Rhythm Syllable building blocks without speaking them aloud.

EXERCISE: Rhythm Improvisation

1. Use either simple stepping on the spot, or the full Rhythm Dance if you're comfortable with it, to express a steady Beat at a moderate tempo.

2. Now start to clap on each beat, thinking *Ta* in your head with each one.

3. Next move on to a few measures of clapping *Ti-Ti's*, then *Tika-Tika's*, and so on. Notice how audiating the corresponding rhythm syllables makes it easy to know how your claps should be timed—most likely easier than just thinking *"I need to sub-divide each beat in four"*, for example.

4. When you're ready, start mixing up your rhythm syllable choices, to express your own rhythmic ideas!

5. Once you're comfortable doing this with clapping, select a single note on an instrument you play and repeat the exercise playing that note. Start again with just a single building block at a time, getting the hang of each before starting to mix them up and be creative.

6.   If you'd like, you can try switching to an external source of the Beat, for example a metronome, a music track with a prominent pulse, or a drum loop (as mentioned in the previous chapter).

Remember to focus on *feeling* and *hearing*. The beauty of the Garden Gate exercise (and Rhythm Syllables in general) is that they're so simple, you free up mental capacity and can really focus on the sound and the physical experience of the rhythms.

In Part III we'll discuss creativity and Improvisation much more. For now, just know that any time you feel inspired to go beyond the instructions or "rules" of a creative exercise like this, you are very welcome to! For example, if you're enjoying improvising rhythms using one note and you want to introduce a second note, and a third, feel free. You may find yourself starting to improvise quite interesting and creative music, just with these simple building blocks.

EXERCISE: Rhythmic Scales

1.   Grab your instrument, and express a steady Beat at a moderate tempo using your body. Depending on your instrument, you may be able to step on the spot or use the Rhythm Dance, or just use foot-tapping or head-nodding.

2.   Play up and down a scale on your chosen instrument with one note per beat.

3.   Now go through the same steps as before: use each rhythm syllable in turn and play a note of the scale on each note of the syllable. For example, with a C Major scale and the *Ti-Tika* building block you would play C on the first *Ti*, D on the *Ti-* of *Tika*, then E on the *-ka*, all within the first beat of your pulse. Then the F on the next *Ti*, G on the *Ti-* of the *Tika*, A on the *-ka*, and so on:

C	D	E	F	G	A	B	C	B	A	G	F	E	D
"Ti - Ti	ka	Ti - Ta	ka	Ti - Ti	ka	Ti - Ti	ka	Ti - Ti	k

Remember to audiate the rhythm syllables (hear them in your head).

4.   When you're ready, start mixing up the syllables you use!

If you've read *Chapter Six: Superlearning*, you may recognise this as a form of Contextual Interference. So don't be surprised if you fumble the scale a bit at first! You are challenging your brain in a new way. Not only are you gaining proficiency with these rhythmic building blocks, you are also developing a more resilient and versatile ability to play the scale and its corresponding fingering.

EXERCISE: Rhythmic Improvisation with a Melody

1.   Select a short melody (say, two measures) which you are comfortable playing. It will help to have the notation in front of you.

2.   As before, express a steady Beat at a moderate tempo with your body, in a way that's compatible with your instrument.

3.   Play through the melody with the rhythms as written.

4.   Now "straighten out" the rhythm by replacing every note's duration with *Ta* i.e. playing one note per beat.

5.   Next move on to the other building blocks in turn i.e. playing through the melody pitches on *Ti-Ti's*, then all *Tika-Tika's*, *Ti-Tika's*, etc.

6.   When you're ready, start mixing up the building blocks to improvise your own rhythms for the melody pitches.

Example using Stick Notation:

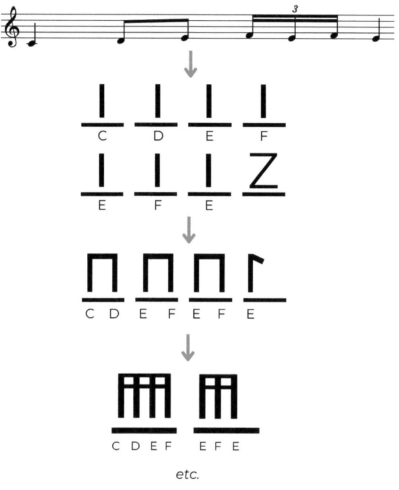

etc.

Example using Staff Notation:

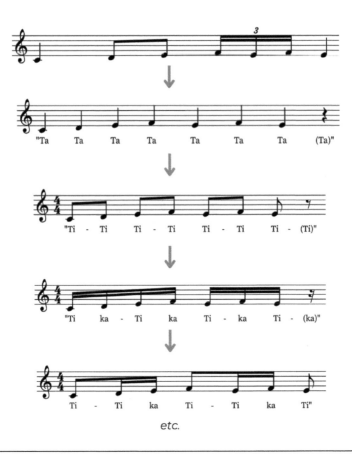

This is an example of the "Constraints and Dimensions" part of the Expansive Creativity framework you'll learn in Chapter Fifteen: Improvisation: we are constraining the Pitch dimension by using the given series of note pitches, allowing us to freely explore the Rhythm dimension in interesting ways.

EXERCISE: Composing Rhythms

1.   Draw a line of four Beat Blanks:

2.   Using the Stick Notation corresponding to our Rhythm
      Syllable building blocks, write a rhythm. You might like to
      also write the rhythm syllables underneath. Example:

3.   Now try performing the rhythm you composed by speaking
      the rhythm syllables!

4.   Repeat this using different combinations of rhythm syllables.

5.   When you're ready, try a Call-And-Response improvisation:
      First perform your measure as written, then improvise one
      measure with rhythm syllables. For example if you wrote *"Ta,
      Ta, Ti-Ti, Ta"* you might follow it up with *"Ta, Ti-Ti, Ti-Ti, Ta"*.
      Write down your response in Stick Notation afterwards.

This is a great way to become more fluent with the correspondence
between Rhythm Syllables and the Stick Notation representation, as
well as bridging the gap between Improvisation and Songwriting.

      You can also make good use of the Starter Songs included in *Chapter
Nine: Solfa* which are shown with Stick Notation and feature all the
rhythm syllables we've covered so far, as well as some from "Going
Further" below. Looking at the Stick Notation, can you figure out the
corresponding Rhythm Syllables and speak them aloud? You can
check yourself against the traditional staff notation also provided, or
the recordings included in the *Additional Resources*.

      Then, when you're ready, try the reverse, going from sound to
symbol:

EXERCISE: Transcribing Rhythms

1.   Listen to a short melody which seems to have a simple rhythm. You can start with recordings of the Starter Songs from *Chapter Nine: Solfa* which all use only the rhythm building blocks introduced so far.

2.   Echo back the rhythm of the melody using a neutral sound like "bah".

3.   Now use your familiarity with Rhythm Syllables to determine which syllables correspond to the pattern of *bah's* you spoke.

4.   Repeat the rhythm in rhythm syllables and then write it down in Stick Notation. Perform it from the transcription you just created, and compare with the original to see if you got it right. If you're using a song from the Starter Songs you can also check back against the Stick Notation provided there.

Going Further

So far we've introduced the Rhythm Syllable building blocks of *Ta, Ti-Ti, Tika-Tika, Ti-Tika and Tika-Ti*. These alone can take you a long way! They cover the most common ways of subdividing a beat in *simple* meter, which as you may recall from *Chapter Twelve: The Beat* means subdividing the beat into two even parts. They correspond to rhythmic patterns featuring quarter, eighth and sixteenth notes.

But what if we wanted an eighth note sandwiched between two sixteenth notes? And what about *compound* meter, subdividing the beat into three even parts?

Let's add some more Rhythm Syllable building blocks to our toolkit. You can practice with these using any of the exercises covered so far, simply by introducing them as new possible choices in your rhythmic patterns.

Too

Nice and simple: a note which lasts for two beats can be expressed with the rhythm syllable "*Too*":

(Stick Notation just uses the traditional staff notation symbol for a half note)

Remember to hold the syllable for the full duration of the two beats!

Syncopation and SynCOpa

In *Chapter Twelve: The Beat* we emphasised the prime importance of the Beat, and how it allows the listener to make sense of musical rhythms and orient themselves in time, anticipating when notes are likely to occur.

As always in music though, there is as much creative power in defying expectations as in meeting them! When we place or emphasise notes at unexpected times, it's referred to as *syncopation.* The use of syncopation varies across genres. For example, it was relatively rare in Western Classical music but very common in jazz, and has become so common in mainstream pop and rock music over the years that to describe it as "unexpected" is now somewhat misleading!

So syncopation isn't about doing something so odd and unusual that the listener is consciously surprised by it—but rather, just a diversion from the strict placement of notes on beats and subdivisions which we've considered so far. If we see that "grid" of beats and measures (with the first beat of each measure being emphasised) as being what the human body and ear "expect" rhythms to align to, then syncopation is when notes are timed or accented differently to that.

We've already experienced a form of syncopation in the previous chapter, in the exercise where you were invited to try clapping early or late, compared with the pulse. You will have experienced how unsettling—but also exciting!—this can feel.

Syncopation can occur on multiple levels. *Beat-level* syncopation is achieved by emphasising the beats that are normally "weak". Remember from *Chapter Twelve: The Beat* that in most genres, beat 1 is usually the strongest. So:

- In duple meter, emphasising beat 2 creates syncopation.

- In quadruple meter, emphasising beats 2 and 4 create

syncopation.

• In triple meter, emphasising beats 2 and 3 create syncopation.
Let's experience this effect:

EXERCISE: Beat-level Syncopation

1. Express a steady Beat at a moderate tempo.

2. Start emphasising beat 1 of each measure. For example, if
counting the beats aloud in quadruple meter, you would say
"ONE, two, three, four, ONE, two, three, four...". If stepping /
clapping / tapping, you would step / clap / tap harder or louder
on beat 1 each time.

3. Now instead of emphasising beat 1, emphasise one or more of
the other beats. In particular try emphasising beats 2 and 4 in
quadruple meter. It may well remind you of styles like reggae
or punk, where that pattern is the norm rather than the
exception!

Division-level syncopation happens when the rhythmic emphasis falls
on a beat subdivision rather than the start of the beat. Again, this can
mean notes are placed "off the beat" or that the notes which are off the
beat are the ones which are emphasised.

EXERCISE: Division-level Syncopation

1. Express a steady Beat at a moderate tempo.

2. Speak the rhythm syllable *Ti-Ti* on each beat, emphasising the
first "*Ti*" of each pair.

3. Now switch to emphasising the second "*Ti*" of each pair
instead, and feel the difference it makes.

4. Do the same with *Tika-Tika*, first emphasising the beginning
"*Ti-*" each time (which lands on the beat) and then switching
to emphasising one of the others (which all land off the beat).
For example, emphasise the final "*-ka*" of each "*Tika-Tika*":

"Tika-TiKA, Tika-TiKA, Tika-TiKA, Tika-TiKA"). It's important to keep expressing the beat with your body—otherwise it's easy for your ear to start interpreting that emphasised subdivision as the start of the beat, and the feeling of syncopation is lost.

5.   Feel free to experiment with other syllables! Notice how much more creativity is opened up for you when you can choose not only the timing of notes (by choosing the syllable) but also the emphasis (by choosing which part of each syllable to express more loudly).

This demonstrates division-level syncopation through emphasising notes. What about by placing the notes at unexpected times?

Probably the most common rhythmic pattern of this kind is a shorter note on the beat, followed by a longer note, so that the longer note is the prominent one but is displaced slightly later than the beat.

The rhythm syllable we can use to represent this is, fittingly, called *"synCOpa"*. It is said with a short *"syn-"*, a longer and emphasised *"-CO-"* and a short *"-pa"*. For example, the pattern just mentioned, of a quarter note sandwiched between two eighth notes can be written like this:

This pattern can be found in "Weevily Wheat" in the Starter Songs in Chapter Nine: Solfa, for example.

Try one of the earlier improvisation-based exercises, including *synCOpa* in your creations! Start simple, for example *"Ta, Ta, synCOpa, Ta, Ta, synCOpa, ..."* and really pay attention to the more interesting, jazzier sound and feeling it creates:

Unlike the rhythm syllables covered so far, *synCOpa* can be used at different levels of granularity. The same spoken pattern can be used to represent an eighth note sandwiched between two sixteenth notes, for example:

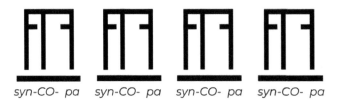

Tri-po-let

Another way to mix things up compared with the strict rhythmic grid is to divide a simple-meter beat into three equal parts instead of the expected two. This is called a *triplet*.

Triplets are often a real challenge for musicians to learn to make sense of and play! Fortunately, this is a great example of the strength of Rhythm Syllables over the traditional approach.

Our building block for triplets is actually the word itself, but pronounced as three syllables: *"Tri-po-let"*. Like *synCOpa*, the Rhythm Syllable *Tri-po-let* can be used at different levels of granularity, for example eighth-note triplets which fill one beat:

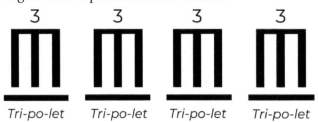

Or sixteenth-note triplets which fill half a beat:

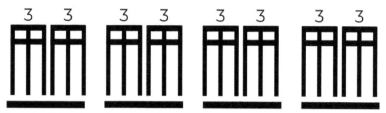

Tri-po-let, Tri-po-let Tri-po-let, Tri-po-let Tri-po-let, Tri-po-let Tri-po-let, Tri-po-let

Or quarter-note triplets which span two beats:

Tri- po- let   Tri- po- let

Notice how even though it might look a little awkward to span two Beat Blanks like this, it actually makes it much clearer how the notes of the triplet are timed, relative to the Beat—something that's often very confusing for musicians with traditional score notation.

Tam-Ti and Tim-Ka

You may be familiar with the idea of "dotted notes". In traditional score notation, one can extend the duration of a note by half its original length again by writing a dot after the note symbol. For example, a dotted quarter note lasts 1½ beats. The remaining time left by that "half" can be filled either with another note or with a rest.

Remember that we can handle rests by audiating the Rhythm Syllables, entirely or in part. And so our building blocks are:

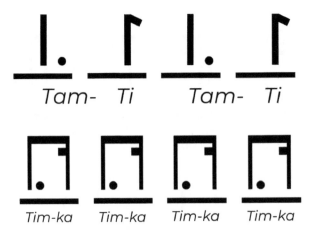

Tam- Ti   Tam- Ti

Tim-ka   Tim-ka   Tim-ka   Tim-ka

The dotted quarter note followed by an eighth note is *Tam-Ti*[2] and the dotted eighth note followed by a sixteenth note is *Tim-ka*. The order can also be swapped, producing *Ti-Tam* and *ka-Tim*:

Ti- Tam   Ti- Tam

ka-Tim   ka-Tim   ka-Tim   ka-Tim

Take some time to play around with these new rhythm syllables. In particular notice how the *Ti-Tam* and *ka-Tim* patterns create a syncopated feel.

Swinging the Beat

If you experimented with a series of *Tim-ka's* you might have noticed it reminded you of something else. Rather than our brain

---

[2] Sometimes *Tai-Ti* or *Tum-Ti* are used instead, but we prefer *Tam-Ti* for consistency of adding the "m" to imply the dotted version.

interpreting it as dotted quarter notes followed by sixteenth notes over a steady beat, you may have started to feel it as expressing a steady *Ti-Ti* rhythm, but with a *swing* feel.

You'll often hear musicians refer to "swung rhythms", "swing rhythms" or "shuffle rhythms". In fact it's not just the Rhythm which is swung in genres like blues, country and jazz—it's the Beat itself.

In duple or quadruple meter, instead of the beat's subdivision in two being two parts of equal duration, they follow a pattern of long and short pairs: *looong, short, loooong, short, loooong, short, loooong.*

EXERCISE: Straight to Swung Beat

1. Select a scale that you can play comfortably.

2. Create a steady beat at a moderate tempo, expressing the subdivision of the beat (e.g. *"one and two and three and four and"*) and play up and down the scale using that beat.

3. Now change the way you express the subdivisions so that the first half of each beat is longer than the second. Here's an illustration:

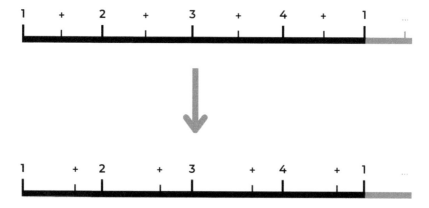

4. Play up and down the scale again using that swung beat. It may help to audiate the rhythm syllables *Tam-Ti* to help produce the long/short pattern. You can also try *Tri-po-let* where the first note lasts over both *Tri* and *po* and the second

note is on *let*. These two options produce different degrees of swing.

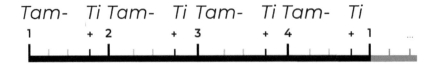

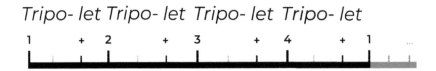

(Light lines show the implied underlying subdivision into four or three, to help explain the relationship with Tam-Ti or Tri-po-let—but note the point here is to create a new, swung subdivision, with the point marked "+" being the only actual subdivision of the beat, just like in the previous diagram.)

5.   Next take a simple song or piece you can play comfortably, which is in duple or quadruple meter. You might like to use one of the Starter Songs from *Chapter Nine: Solfa*. Repeat the same steps: play it first with a regular ("straight") beat, then with a swung beat.

Swing is really something you *feel* more than think through. So although the rhythm syllables suggested above can help ease you into it, don't get caught up trying to "translate" the normal rhythm syllables of a rhythm into swung equivalents! It's a shift in the way you feel the Beat, which you then express the same rhythm on top of. You'll find some examples of turning a straight-Beat melody into a swung version in the *Additional Resources*.

TIP:

One of the easiest ways to feel a swung beat is by thinking about *skipping* rather than *walking*.

We walk down the street with steady left-right-left-right timing, suitable for expressing a straight beat, as we experienced in the previous chapter's exercises.

But if you were to skip along the street instead, the timing would become more like riiiiiiiight-left, leeeeeeft-right, riiiiiiiight-left leeeeeeft-right, etc. It naturally creates a pattern of long/short subdivisions for us, suitable for a swung beat.

So if you're having difficulty understanding, feeling, or expressing a swung beat, or if the final step of the exercise above (where you try playing a piece or song swung) is tricky for you... Skip around the room, and try it again!

Applied Activities

We've introduced a wide range of Rhythm Syllables, as well as ways to create or recognise syncopated rhythms, and swung beats.

Just like our Pitch building blocks, you can make use of these throughout all your musical activities to help you better understand, relate to, and express musical patterns.

Playing By Ear

In *Chapter Fourteen: Playing By Ear* you'll learn the Play-By-Ear Process, a simple approach to methodically figuring out music by ear by using three steps: Listen, Engage, Express.

Rhythm Syllables will be very useful to you in the Engage step. If you haven't read that chapter yet, all you need to know is that the Engage step means bridging from hearing ("Listen") to playing ("Express") by connecting with and analysing what you heard.

In the case of Rhythm, you can use the familiarity you've been building up with Rhythm Syllables to let you interpret rhythmic patterns you hear in terms of these building blocks. For example, rather than relying purely on a fuzzy musical memory for the rhythmic pattern you just heard, or needing to painstakingly count through the beats and try to figure out where each note lands, you'll be able to instinctively recognise *"Oh, that went Ta, Ta, Tika-Tika, Ta"* and so on.

You can begin practicing this in an easy way by recording yourself doing some of the improvisational exercises in this chapter, using clapping or your instrument to express rhythms using the building blocks. Then, when you listen back, try to recognise the rhythm syllables being used. This way, you can begin by focusing just on certain syllables (for example, just with *Ta, Ti-Ti* and *Tika-Tika* to begin with) and you'll know when listening back that all the rhythms you hear will be using just those syllables.

When you're ready, you can take this same approach to any music you're working on playing by ear, either using the Play-By-Ear Process, or just more loosely. Either way, you're now equipped with Rhythm Syllables as a way to interpret the rhythmic patterns you hear, translating them into specific note durations.

Transcribing

Exactly the same process can be used for transcribing music as for playing it by ear. The only difference is that instead of the Express step meaning to sing it or play it on an instrument, we will write it down.

Once Rhythm Syllables have helped you decipher the rhythmic patterns you heard, you can use the corresponding Stick Notation to quickly and easily write it down. From there you can add the pitch information by annotating with Solfa syllables or note names, or convert your Stick Notation into full score notation by adding note heads and placing the notes on the correct positions on the staff.

For most musicians, the main use of transcribing isn't to produce a full, finished score in traditional notation—but rather to capture more concretely what they've been figuring out by ear. Stick Notation provides a very convenient shorthand for representing the rhythmic side of things, and you may find that Stick Notation and Solfa together become your go-to way of jotting things down.

Improvisation

Since most of our exercises in this chapter involved improvising your own rhythmic patterns, you have already had a good taste of how Rhythm Syllables can empower you in Improvisation!

Just like Playing By Ear, using Rhythm Syllables in Improvisation lets you escape from the two very frustrating and limiting approaches to rhythm in Improvisation which I mentioned in the introduction: either "winging it" and hoping it works out, or needing to very carefully think through counting out the rhythms.

By audiating Rhythm Syllables (speaking them in your head) either while you play or before you play a phrase, you're able to conjure up suitable, interesting rhythmic patterns with an elegant balance of " thinking it through" and playing "on instinct". When you craft your improvised phrases using Rhythm Syllables as building blocks, you'll find that your rhythms will be more precise, more structured, and more varied.

Although intentionally audiating the Rhythm Syllables is helpful when getting started, you'll soon find that (like with the Pitch building blocks) you begin to internalise them, and be able to use them subconsciously. Without needing to think through *"I'll play Ta, Ta, Tika-Tika, Ta"* you will be able to assemble your rhythms using those building blocks instinctively.

Songwriting

When it comes to Songwriting and composing, both Rhythm Syllables and Stick Notation can be a huge help. In *Chapter Sixteen: Songwriting* we'll talk more about writing rhythms for your songs and the interplay with lyrics.

You can probably already see though that having the simplified form of notation, along with the building blocks for common rhythmic patterns, drastically simplifies the task of "writing a good rhythm".

You can also combine these building blocks with the Expansive Creativity framework of *Chapter Fifteen: Improvisation* to put certain *Constraints* on the music you write. For example, choosing to limit yourself to using particular Rhythm Syllables, or constraining other *Dimensions* and letting your rhythmic creativity run wild.

Conclusion

In this chapter we built on the deeper relationship with the Beat established as a foundation in the previous chapter, and introduced Rhythm Syllables and the corresponding Stick Notation to equip you with a set of building blocks for Rhythm.

If you've spent some time with the exercises in this chapter, hopefully you've started to experience for yourself how impactful and enlightening having these Rhythm building blocks can be.

Whether your goal is to more easily interpret the rhythms in music you're learning from traditional notation, to play music by ear, to improvise, to write your own music, or any other musical activity, Rhythm Syllables can help you gain a more accurate, versatile and instinctive ability with everything involving Rhythm in music.

Like all the building blocks covered in this part of the book, it will take some time to gain proficiency with all the possibilities and applications. However if you dedicate some time to practicing with the exercises suggested here, and begin to make use of the building blocks throughout everything you do in music, you'll quickly find yourself internalising the patterns and able to use them freely, creatively and instinctively.

Enjoying The Book?

If you are enjoying this book, it would mean the world to me if you could take two minutes to post a short review.

Just visit:

https://musicalitybook.com/review

(it's fine if you've only read part of the book so far!)

This makes a massive difference to helping other musicians discover the book, and start exploring their own musical potential—furthering our mission of creating "a world of natural musicians".

Huge thanks in advance for taking a couple of minutes to do this now!

PART THREE

CHAPTER FOURTEEN:
PLAYING BY EAR

We will begin Part III of the book with one of the most widely-desired and most rewarding applied skills of musicality: Playing By Ear.

If your Big Picture Vision featured you being able to play whatever songs you hear on the radio, being the campfire hero who can strum the chords to any song your friends and family call for, or if your Musical Core seems to lean heavily towards Jammer, then this chapter will be of particular interest.

Learning to play by ear isn't only for those who already know they have their heart set on it though.

If I had to sum up the benefit of Playing By Ear in one word, it would be: "freedom".

This isn't about burning our music books, or swearing off chord charts, sheet music or tab forevermore. As always in musicality training, our goal isn't to take away from any of what traditional music education teaches, but rather to add to it, enhance it, and go beyond it. So this chapter isn't about taking the attitude that reading notation is bad, wrong, or "less than" playing by ear. There's a reason it's included in our list of musicality skills in *Chapter One: Musicality*. And in *Chapter Seventeen: Expression* and *Chapter Eighteen: Performance* we'll dive deep into how much freedom and creativity can be brought to your music-making when playing from notation.

With that being said, anybody who's ever seen the unbridled joy of a pet dog let off its leash in the park, suddenly free to go wherever they dream of, without being led there or restrained by instructions or limits, can appreciate the opportunity in freeing yourself from a dependence on written instructions for your music-making.

What's more, as with many other musicality skills, the value of learning to play by ear has wide-reaching effect, far beyond just the time you may (or may not!) choose to spend in future doing the activity of Playing By Ear. We'll discuss this more in the Conclusion to this chapter. For now, suffice to say that with a H4 approach to developing our musicality, everything we can do to further our Hearing, and connect it with Head, Hands and Heart, is a very good thing indeed.

If you've been through Part II of the book, you will already understand (and have hopefully have even experienced) the benefits of Ear Training, and the way the building blocks presented in those chapters can quickly enable you to play music by ear.

If you haven't yet read Part II, fear not. Ear Training and the building blocks for pitch and rhythm are massive accelerators for learning to play by ear—but the method presented in this chapter is not strictly dependent on them. So you can safely read on and start experimenting and exploring directly. I would encourage you to circle back to Part II and invest some time in dedicated Ear Training in due course though :)

Overview

In this chapter we'll begin by defining "playing by ear", and introducing the idea that it exists as a continuous *spectrum* of abilities. We'll discuss how an approach of "Trial and Improvement" can let you move steadily along that spectrum into greater and greater abilities to play music by ear.

We will introduce the Play-By-Ear Process we've developed at Musical U which can be applied to any piece of music in a step-by-step methodical way. We'll then go through each of its three component parts—Listen, Engage, Express—in turn, explaining and illustrating the process of each.

Finally, we will share a number of ways you can practice Playing By Ear using this process, to gradually improve your skills up to any point you desire.

What is "Playing By Ear"?

Before we go any further, what exactly do we mean by "playing by ear"? Here's a simple definition:

To "play by ear" means to hear some music, and then reproduce it on an instrument.[1]

Note that:

- We didn't say "immediately" nor "perfectly"!

- Nothing was said about the complexity or length of the music. And

- The word "hear" is being used to also include remembering or imagining music, since those can be seen as "hearing it in your head".

This definition may seem vague, particularly if up until now you've thought of Playing By Ear as a single (perhaps magical) skill. However that apparent vagueness actually captures what Playing By Ear truly is...

Side Note:

We've found that there can be some confusion between the terms "playing music *by ear*" and "playing music *off by heart*".

If a musician has been learning a piece from sheet music and then performs it without that visual reference, we would refer to that as playing "off by heart" or "from memory". They aren't necessarily

---

[1] Although we do often include Singing as an instrument in its own right, in this case the skill of Playing By Ear includes the "translation" from knowing how the pitches should sound to being able to find the right letter-name notes or keys to press on an external instrument. To "hear music and then sing it back" is more a skill of Singing than Playing By Ear, and we've explored that already in the corresponding chapter earlier in the book. As we'll see, Singing is still deeply involved in the process though!

using any ability to recognise notes by ear—they are playing notes based on instructions they were previously given by the notation.

We use the term "playing by ear" to indicate that no notation has been used. The musician has relied purely on their inner skills (Head, Hearing and Heart, as we'll explain in this chapter) to determine which notes to play (Hands).

Naturally there can be some overlap, for example if a musician has previously learned a piece from notation and then relies on their ears to fill in a few gaps in their memory—a notable benefit of developing play-by-ear skills, even if your primary focus is on learning from notation!

The Spectrum Of Playing By Ear

One of the biggest misconceptions in the world of music learning is that Playing By Ear is a single skill or ability. Along with the "missing step" discussed below, this is why so few musicians who dream of being able to play by ear ever make that dream a reality.

This is one of those things which I wish I could go back and tell my younger self. A clarification which could have saved me considerable self-doubt, frustration, and wasted energy. As with the other skills we are covering in Part III, there is a cultural assumption that "you've got it or you don't", when in fact there is no mysterious "gift" required, and everything breaks down into simple, learnable skills.

In fact, if you take just one thing away from this chapter, it should be this: Playing By Ear is not a single all-or-nothing ability. It is a skill, with a whole *spectrum* of abilities.

At one end of the spectrum would be *"I can't play anything at all by ear"*, and at the other is *"I can play any music I hear or remember, by ear, immediately, with no mistakes, at full speed."*

If you've gone through the exercises in Part II of this book, you've done some playing by ear already, proving to yourself that you can, fundamentally, do some form of "hearing a note, and then playing back that same note".

And if not, let me ask you: if I clapped a short, simple rhythm, could you clap it back? For most musicians and even the earliest-stage music learners, the answer would be *"sure, yes, I could do that."*

Well, what if instead I played a short musical phrase... but it featured only two different notes and you knew in advance which two notes they were. Could you echo back the short melody I played with those two notes? Again, the answer is probably *"Sure, yes, I could do that."*

So we know you can play by ear to some degree. And although the constraints above might seem like "cheating", they actually just represent a certain spot on that spectrum of Playing By Ear. Which means that now it's just a matter of helping you move along that spectrum, expanding and refining your play-by-ear skills.

Right now, it might seem totally mysterious and even overwhelming to wonder how to get from one end of that spectrum to the other, but I have some great news for you. If you've been going through this book in sequence, you're already equipped with a *lot* of powerful tools to ease and accelerate that journey.

In this chapter we'll reveal the Play-By-Ear Process which transforms playing-by-ear into a simple, learnable skill with clear methodology you can follow. We'll draw on tools from elsewhere in the book, including Mindset, Active Listening, Singing, Audiation, our Ear Training "building blocks", and Improvisation.[2] And we'll provide a range of exercises you can use to start practicing the Play-By-Ear Process.

Before we introduce the process itself, there's one other big idea to discuss. We touched on it in *Chapter Two: Mindset* but it has such vital importance to Playing By Ear, it's worth unpacking now in more detail...

Trial And Improvement

I remember first hearing the phrase "Trial And Improvement" back in my school days, during a maths lesson. We were doing some problem-solving that involved gradually finding the right answer through trial and error. And the teacher made a big point of encouraging us to leave aside the idea of "trial and error", and use the phrase "trial and improvement" instead. Why? Because it more accurately captured how we were gradually moving towards the right

---

[2] If you've been through the earlier chapters which introduce the tools above, that's wonderful: you have a big head start! And if not, just know that you can still dive straight into this chapter, and return to those others in future to help propel your play-by-ear skills forwards.

answer.

That has always stuck in my head, because we're so indoctrinated to think "errors" are bad and something to feel ashamed of. Whereas "improvement" is something to be proud of and aspire to. Just changing that wording somehow really altered the emotional experience of doing those exercises, by clarifying that this wasn't about random guesswork, but rather a process of moving successfully forwards to the answer.

It's going to be the same for you with Playing By Ear.

Above we discussed how the skill of playing by ear isn't all-or-nothing—it's a spectrum of abilities (just like any musical skill).

At one end of the spectrum is someone who's genuinely just guessing notes at random. Maybe they're getting the rhythm right, but really have no hope of magically guessing the right note pitches.

At the other end of the spectrum there's the almost-mythical "gifted" musician who just hears something, however complex, and can immediately play it at full speed with zero mistakes, maybe even throwing in a few embellishments or conjuring up a full arrangement on the fly.

Musicians tend to think they belong right at the "zero" end of the spectrum. And so it's vitally important to understand that the way to learn to play by ear is not to instantly, magically jump to the other end of the spectrum. It's to travel along that spectrum from one end to the other, step by step. Again, just like any musical skill.

So the way you'll learn to play by ear is to start spending time practicing figuring things out by ear.

Through the Play-By-Ear Process, and optionally leveraging our Ear Training "building blocks" from Part II, we're going to equip you with the process and tools which let you move much more quickly and accurately to the target "right answer".

Here's why "Trial And Improvement" is such a vital idea to keep in mind: none of it will work if you get stuck in nervousness or embarrassment over "getting it wrong". Because making mistakes is part of the process. Figuring things out is a process of trying, testing, experimenting. It's "trial and improvement" that will get you to the right answer.

So just like you will experience when exploring Expansive Creativity in *Chapter Fifteen: Improvisation*, it is absolutely vital to put aside the traditional view that "mistakes are the enemy".

We will be working on reducing mistakes, even eliminating them.

But you cannot jump straight to the other end of the spectrum where you play things lightning-fast and ultra-accurate. The only way to get there is being willing to travel along the spectrum, step-by-step. And that means tolerating, even embracing, making mistakes along the way.

As you travel along the spectrum, you are always going to be pushing your comfort zone, and trying to play more and more challenging things by ear. You're always going to need to tolerate mistakes, as part of learning and developing the skills.

But quite soon, you'll find yourself looking back at music you once found incredibly challenging to "figure out by ear"—and realising that now, oh, it's easy to go straight to the "right answer" for that one. And the further you go, the wider the range of music you find you can just instinctively play, straight off, no "mistakes" in sight.

So I encourage you to think not in terms of "making mistakes" or even "trial and error"… but "Trial and Improvement".

Each time you practice with the exercises in this chapter, you are taking a concrete step forwards. And the Play-By-Ear Process and building blocks will accelerate those steps. All you need to do is show up, and keep taking steps forwards, and not let limiting beliefs around mistakes or errors hold you back.

Actually, there is one other thing you need to do. And that's to pay attention.

Or to put it another way, "stay mindful". If you're familiar with the idea of deliberate practice introduced in *Chapter Six: Superlearning*, that can be really helpful here. Remember "Plan, Play, Reflect". You don't want to make the mistake of just doing the "Play" step! Or even just "Plan then Play".

Including that "Reflect" step makes a massive difference to how effective all the "Play"ing is. It's what allows "trial and error" to become "trial and improvement"

Without the "Reflect" step, you're doomed to just "trial and error" with no guaranteed forward progress. But bring mindful attention to the task and reflect as you go, and your "errors" will become "improvement" and you can make steady, reliable forward progress along the spectrum, as far as your heart desires.

The Play-By-Ear Process

Playing By Ear has historically been one of the main reasons a musician will pursue Ear Training, but there was always a big problem. I encountered this myself, very early on in my own Ear Training journey.

I had been elated to discover there was a thing called "ear training" which could finally let me level up my aural skills and have a chance of recognising notes and chords by ear. But after weeks, months, and ultimately a couple of years of diligently doing the exercises from the books and courses I'd bought, I had a painful realisation: I still couldn't actually *do* very much, except pass ear training quizzes.

As we talked about in *Chapter Seven: Ear Training*, this comes down to following an *isolated* Ear Training approach, which in my case was worsened by a focus on Intervals rather than Solfa (as discussed in more in the corresponding chapters).

Shifting to an *integrated* Ear Training approach at Musical U meant introducing an "Apply" step, after "Learn" and "Practice", where the musician actually *did* something musically useful with the core recognition skills they'd been practicing, and Playing By Ear was one of the most interesting, practical and fun activities to include in that Apply step.

It was another couple of years however before we really refined our approach and codified it inside the *Living Music* program as the Play-By-Ear Process. As soon as we did, it was crystal-clear to me looking back at my own journey, that it was kind of crazy that I'd been hoping to start playing music by ear... without having any kind of method or process for doing so! That's what I'm excited to share with you in this chapter.

The Play-By-Ear Process we developed is very simple, but very powerful. It hinges on two insights:

1. Just like Playing By Ear is itself a spectrum of ability levels rather than an all-or-nothing skill, the act of "playing a song or piece by ear" is a *process* of gradually figuring out everything that's happening musically, rather than something you necessarily do in one fell swoop. This is why we refer to it as a *process* rather than a *method* or a single skill.

2. There is a missing middle step in the way most musicians think it must be done, and including this middle step makes all the difference.

Right now that first point might feel like a cop-out to you, like when I said Playing By Ear begins as "figuring things out by ear, step-by-step". But just like that, what begins as a gradual process can, over time, become an instantaneous leap to the "full, correct answer". By treating Playing By Ear as a *process* we allow ourselves the time and space to develop the skills we need to play more and more complex music by ear directly.

The second point probably has you wondering *"Well, what is that missing middle step?"* We know from our definition of Playing By Ear that the first step must be "hear something" and the last step "play that same thing". What comes in between?

If you've read *Chapter Six: Superlearning*, the answer won't come as too much of a shock. There, we discussed how traditional music practice tends to look like an endless cycle of "Plan, Play, Plan, Play, Plan, Play, etc.", and incorporating an extra step of "Reflect" changes everything, by allowing you to refine what you Plan and how you Play.

Here, the missing step is to *engage* with the music you heard. Rather than try to go directly from ear to instrument (from Hearing to Hands), we give ourselves the opportunity to analyse and identify what we heard (Head and Heart).

The core of our Play-By-Ear Process is therefore a sequence of:

Listen: We hear some music, for example a melody, bassline, a full arrangement, etc.

Engage: We connect with the music internally, to make sense of it.

Express: We play the music on an instrument, based on our new understanding of what we heard.

This 3-part process can be applied to each and every part of the music in turn, and may take repeated cycles to fully get to "the answer". It's also not a strict 1-2-3 sequence, you will find yourself naturally moving between the three activities fluidly as you figure things out by ear. However you employ them, these same three steps are all you need to tackle any music you wish to play by ear.

It may help to think of this analogy: when an artist paints a picture, they don't start in the top left corner and paint each square centimetre in turn. They sketch out the most important elements, then gradually fill bits in where they instinctively feel is next. They may well return to earlier areas to refine them further. Eventually they feel like the picture is complete. Similarly, with the Play-By-Ear Process we can use Listen-Engage-Express (which we'll abbreviate as LNX) repeatedly, and focusing on different elements of the music, to gradually fill in the full picture of what we heard.

Listen

In the Listen stage of the LNX process we are absorbing the musical material we wish to play by ear. Note that it is "Listen" and not merely "Hear"! As we saw in *Chapter Five: Active Listening*, there is a big difference between hearing something and truly *listening* to it, and we can make good use of the Active Listening approach of "listening with a question in mind".

The music we are working with may be live music, it may be a recording, or it may be music we remember or imagine in our mind's ear. The same LNX process can be applied in all these scenarios, although when first starting out you will likely find it easier to work with recorded material since that can be easily be played back repeatedly and will be exactly the same each time.

With our 4-D Active Listening framework we analyse and interpret musical sounds across four "dimensions":

- Timbre: the overall tone, "sound colour" or characteristic sound of an instrument or voice.

- Dynamics: the volume (loud vs. quiet) of the sound.

- Pitch: how high or low the sound is.

- Rhythm: the pattern of note durations and silences.

We are listening for the properties of a note or set of notes in each of these dimensions, as well as how they vary over time. We can also consider the bigger-picture Form (what changes and what stays the same from one section of the music to the next) and Texture (at any given time, what are all the layers of musical sounds present).

To help us explore music in these terms, we use the technique of "listening with a question in mind". For more on this, see *Chapter Five: Active Listening*.

Any experience you have with this kind of Active Listening will be hugely helpful to you in Playing By Ear, primarily because it allows you to more clearly and thoroughly hear everything that is happening in a piece of music, and tune your ear and attention in to a certain part.

When it comes to Playing By Ear, our main focus will be on the Pitch dimension. This is because matching the Timbre is quite a different and distinct skill (which we will explore more in *Chapter Seventeen: Expression*), and mimicking Dynamics and Rhythm both tend to come far more easily to musicians without any dedicated practice required. The biggest challenge for musicians in Playing By Ear boils down to "identifying the note pitches being played".

In the Listen stage of LNX therefore we will want to use our overall Active Listening skills to help us focus in on the particular part of the music we want to play by ear (for example, the vocal melody) and then listen intently to each of the note pitches being used.

Engage

In the Engage stage, our goal is to get a firm grip on what we heard, and perform some kind of analysis to help us translate it into a form we can easily Express.

As discussed earlier, the Engage stage of LNX is generally the missing piece in musicians' attempts to play by ear. They try to jump straight from Listening to Expressing (i.e. "hear and play"). While that can work, it's very analogous to the "brute force" approach to Ear Training discussed in *Chapter Seven: Ear Training* i.e. it's far harder and slower than it needs to be, compared with equipping your musical mind with the understanding and building blocks required to make sense of everything.

At first this will be a conscious process, but it can become more and more subconscious/instinctive over time. This will depend on the complexity or sophistication of the music—think back to the simple "clap back" and "two note echo-back" examples given in the introduction: no "Engage" step would be required for you to do either.

There are many different ways we can Engage with the music we heard, including:

- Musical knowledge and music theory.

- Audiation and Singing

- Movement

- Pitch Contour

- Finding the Tonic

- Building Blocks

- Vocabulary

Which of these you use will depend on how familiar and experienced you are with them (or want to be), and you will have the opportunity discover for yourself in the exercises later in this chapter which you find most useful. These are all covered in more detail elsewhere in the book, so here we will just look briefly at each in turn to explain how they can be used in the Engage stage of LNX.

Musical knowledge and music theory.

Your conscious, thinking mind (Head) may well have plenty to tell you about the music you just heard. For example being familiar with common meters, scales and modes, common choices in songwriting and composing, the conventions of the genre, etc. can all inform the way we process and interpret the musical sounds we hear, both consciously and subconsciously.[3]

---

[3] When scientists have used MRI scanners to analyse brain activity during music listening, with trained musicians versus non-musicians, they find that while non-musicians listen with the right-side brain area (associated with more abstract and holistic processing), musicians listen more with the left-brain area (associated with both

Audiation and Singing

The "dynamic duo" of Audiation and Singing are our top recommendation for the Engage stage. Why? Because they allow you to "get a grip" on what you heard, giving you the opportunity to then analyse it to your heart's content.

One of the biggest challenges in Playing By Ear is that music is a time-based artform. Unlike a painting which you can stare at without it changing, music is constantly on the move!

By audiating (hearing back in your mind's ear) or singing/humming the notes you just heard, you not only confirm that you really heard it clearly. You are able to repeat it, again and again, gradually figuring out the exact notes used.

Assuming you've got the hang of the fundamental Singing skills covered in *Chapter Four: Singing,* we've found that a powerful principle to keep in mind is the idea that *"if you can't sing it, you probably haven't really heard it clearly enough yet".*

Movement

If the Rhythm side of things is more complex or challenging, or if you simply want to connect more deeply and instinctively with the music, allowing your body to move with the music as a way to Engage is highly effective.

There's also clapping: can you clap back the rhythm? There's dancing, or more broadly simply "moving to the music". And there's "air playing" in the spirit of "air guitar", where you mime playing the music without your instrument to hand. These are all great ways to engage by really *connecting physically* with the music. They take little or no learning or practice, but deliver vast amounts of musical information to your brain through your body. More on all these techniques in *Chapter Seventeen: Expression.*

Pitch Contour

Having a clear sense of the Pitch Contour (as introduced in *Chapter Eight: Relative Pitch*) is a great first step to identifying the note pitches. After all, if you don't even know when the notes go up, down or stay the same, how can you hope to identify exactly which notes they are?

---

analytical processing and language). For more, see Dr. Molly Gebrian's fascinating paper "The Differences Between Musicians' and Non-musicians' Brains".

Finding the Tonic

In *Chapter Eight: Relative Pitch* we discussed the prime importance of the *tonic* note in music, its relationship with the key and scale being used, and introduced a process you can follow for finding the tonic by ear. This will typically provide a huge clue to all the note pitches being used, and is a valuable thing to focus on early in your Engage activities.

Building Blocks

In Part II we met three types of "building blocks" for understanding and recognising note pitches by ear: Solfa, Intervals and Chords/ Progressions.

Although these aren't required to identify notes by ear, they provide a massive accelerator for you, and your skills with them need not be complete or perfect for them to greatly enhance your success with the Engage stage. In fact, if you've been through the exercises in those chapters, you will have already had a lot of practice with simple forms of Listen-Engage with a small number of notes!

Transcribing what you heard is also a great stepping stone towards playing it, giving you a way to gradually assemble and refine the notes in a concrete way. You can use the Pitch Contour, Solfa, Intervals, Beat Blanks and Stick Notation as fast, easy ways to jot down what you heard, without necessarily going as far as traditional staff notation.

Vocabulary

In those same chapters we discussed the idea of "vocabulary": larger sequences of note pitches which you can recognise as a single unit. For example the common *mi re do* ending of phrases in Solfa, or using arpeggios as a kind of reference song to help with Intervals and Chord Types.

As you Engage with the music you heard, you may well notice familiar "vocab" jumping out at you, as well as having the opportunity to gather more vocab as you practice Playing By Ear over time.

Engage Example

As mentioned, you are free to use any combination of the above to Engage with the music you heard, but here is an example to help illustrate the idea:

- You Listen to a short melody.

- You audiate the melody, hearing it in your head clearly.

- You imagine the Pitch Contour in your mind—it's ascending, then staying around the same level, and then descending to further down than it started.

- You sing the melody out loud to confirm you really have a handle on the sequence of notes.

- As you sing, you use Solfa to recognise one note as *do*, the tonic.

- Based on the accompaniment you heard and how the first note blended so well with the chord, your theory knowledge and Chord Progression skills suggest to you that the first note was a *mi* or a *so*.

- From there you sing short sections of the melody, coming back to that *do* to keep a firm sense of the key, and use Intervals and Solfa to determine the other note pitches. You sing the full melody in Solfa, and then Listen again to check it matches.

Express

Once you have Listened and Engaged, it's time to Express your own rendition of the music. You may have already begun to Express in certain ways—for example singing, clapping, dancing, transcribing—during the Engage stage. Now the final step is to translate what you've Listened to and Engaged with onto your instrument.

This is a combination of translating from Relative Pitch to letter names (as discussed in *Chapter Eight: Relative Pitch* and other Part II chapters) and any technique considerations for your instrument (for example the best register to play it in, or determining left hand vs. right hand note allocation on piano/keyboard).

One useful point here is that you don't necessarily need to play the music in the same key you heard it in. So for example, if you've confidently determined the Solfa identity of each note, you can choose any note to be your tonic, and play the notes on that basis. What you produce won't sound exactly the same as your source music, but like we discussed in *Chapter Eight: Relative Pitch*, it will still be recognisably the same melody. Depending on the musical context and your focus, this may be an acceptable final outcome! Or you may wish to then apply the process for Finding The Key By Ear (from that same chapter) to determine the tonic which will match what you originally heard.

It's also worth noting that you may wish to bring any degree of your own musical creativity into the Express stage. In all the subsequent Part III chapters we'll be exploring different ways to "make the music your own", and although you might think of Playing By Ear as a black-and-white "did I get it right or not" kind of activity, of course it's entirely up to you whether your goal is to play it back exactly as you heard it or not!

This is particuarly helpful to keep in mind if you're working with source material that doesn't directly correspond to the instrument you want to Express on. For example, hearing a full multi-instrument arrangement and wanting to perform a solo rendition on your instrument, or knowing that you want to perform a song in a different style than the original recording. Don't feel like you're only "winning" at Playing By Ear if it's a note-for-note match with the original. It's up to you what you want the "Express" stage to involve.

TIP:

An important point here is that often when a musician struggles with the Express stage, they have not developed a clear enough mental model of the music during the Listen and particularly the Engage stage. If you're having difficulty playing the "right notes", it will probably be more useful to loop back and Listen and Engage some more rather than keep bashing away at note-finding.

You may remember a clear example shared in Chapter Six: Superlearning: team member Anne Mileski once shared the story of a graduation piece she was struggling to play up to tempo without mistakes on French Horn. Her teacher had her pause in her instrumental efforts, and check if she could sing the passage. It turned out she couldn't, which revealed that her mental model of "how it should go" was actually still fuzzy, making it far harder for her hands to do what she expected them to!

By making sure she could first hear the passage clearly in her mind's ear and express it with her singing voice, suddenly she was able to play it easily—something that might have taken far longer to achieve if she'd just kept grinding away on her instrument blaming her fingers and playing technique.

At first the Express stage typically looks like a combination of activities, some circling back to Listen and Engage, and a spirit of "figuring it out" more than simply picking up your instrument and playing it directly.

Over time as you gain experience and develop your skills, you'll move along the spectrum towards just "pick up and play". But note too that it all depends on the complexity of the music! With a simple melody with certain constraints (e.g. our earlier example of using just two melody notes) you may already be able to jump straight to that end goal, while with other music it may for now be more of that "gradual painting things into place".

How To Practice

Now that you're familiar with the Play-By-Ear Process, let's look at a number of activities you can use to practice this process and move yourself along the play-by-ear spectrum.

1. Echo-back singing and playing

A big stumbling block for the aspiring by-ear player is to jump straight to their favourite song and trying to play it by ear. That can be an interesting thing to try (if approached with a Growth Mindset!) but hopefully you can see from our exploration of the Play-By-Ear Process how much of a leap that is, to attempt as a first step!

To give ourselves a chance to gradually develop our play-by-ear skills, we want to be able to work with short, simple, isolated melodies to begin with. From there we can expand to longer, more complex, and more fully-arranged music.

In our training modules at Musical U we provide sample melodies to practice with and you'll find some provided inside the *Additional Resources*.

However, there's actually a source of simple melodies already available to you, which provides ultimate flexibility to match your current abilities and allow gradual progress... you!

EXERCISE: Echo-Back Singing And Playing

The echo-back exercise is very simple:

1.   Choose a small set of notes to use, for example the first few notes of a Scale. If you've been through Part II you can think in terms of certain Solfa notes, or certain Intervals, as well as certain Rhythm building blocks. In Chapter Fifteen: Improvisation we'll refer to these as "Constraints" for our music-making.

2.   Find those notes on your instrument for a key of your choosing, and sing them back.

3.   Make up a short melody and sing it. To begin with you might be using just a few different note pitches, and a melody of four or five notes.

4. Now "echo" it back on your instrument. Since you already know the note correspondence we can skip the effort of "translating".

5. Repeat, making up different melodies.

In this exercise we are merging Listen and Engage, and simplifying the Express stage, but it's a great way to start easing into the Play-By-Ear Process and still developing some essential skills. In *Chapter Fifteen: Improvisation* we'll explore this same idea in more depth, as the "Play-Listen/Listen-Play" feedback loop.

If you like, you can adapt this exercise from "echo back" to call-and-response, by letting what you play back on your instrument be a musical "reply" to the first phrase rather than an exact repetition. This is a great stepping stone to Improvisation!

This exercise may seem like "cheating" in Playing By Ear, since you already know the notes featured, but:

A. It is still very effective for connecting Hearing and Hands, and

B. You can employ the same extension as in our Part II exercises: record yourself doing this exercise, and later return to the recording. Now you will need to find the notes yourself! To make this one notch easier, you might like to speak the name of the tonic note you choose each time.

The exercise can also be a great way to practice that "translation" from a Relative Pitch representation into a certain key, by challenging yourself to echo back the phrase in a series of different keys, rather than only the one you heard.

2. Example Songs

In *Chapter Nine: Solfa* we provide a set of Starter Songs, and you'll find recordings in the *Additional Resources*. These provide a range of simple melodies, with some known constraints (using particular scale degrees and rhythmic building blocks), and so are great ones to practice Playing By Ear with.

Remember that anything you happen to know about these songs already isn't "cheating" but can be more usefully considered a "stepping stone" in your learning journey.

3. Your Music Library

We said above that jumping straight to trying to play your favourite song by ear would likely be too big a leap, but that doesn't mean you can't still make great use of your own music library to practice Playing By Ear.

The two important things to keep in mind are:

1.   Focus on a certain prominent part, for example the vocal melody or the bassline, for just a short section of the song at a time.

2.   Give yourself a lot of grace! Remember "Trial and Improvement", and how much your skills will develop through the process of figuring it out.

4. Combine with Improvisation

If you are developing your Improvisation skills too, you will be producing a rich catalog of musical examples in every practice session! And one big advantage is that you will necessarily be playing a range and complexity of music which is comfortable for you.

Simply record your improv practice, and then return to the recording later, pausing after each phrase you improvised, to try to play it back by ear.

This can become a very powerful combination for you, letting you move both your Improvisation and Playing By Ear skills forwards in tandem, sharing all the Head, Hearing, Hands and Heart abilities and connections across two quite different (but related) activities.

This has the added benefit of giving you the opportunity to do what *Next Level* coach Andy Portas refers to as "mining for diamonds". What did you play during last week's improv practice that really stood out to you now and inspired you to more creativity when you played it again? Taking on this role of the engaged listener gives you a whole new (and likely more appreciative!) perspective on your own creativity.

5. Playing Full Arrangements By Ear

Depending on your instrument, your play-by-ear goal may be to play full arrangements of songs rather than the isolated melodies we've focused on above. In particular, piano and keyboard players who come to us at Musical U typically want to be able to play solo piano renditions, where the listener would tend to expect a full harmonised arrangement played with both hands, rather than an unaccompanied melody alone!

From the chapter so far you will understand that this is a continuation of the same skillset, and that full arrangement can be approached piece by piece.

Your goal may be to replicate the original source arrangement note-for-note, or it may be to replicate the melody and provide some musically-satisfying accompaniment. In both cases you can use a combination of:

1.   The melody-by-ear skills covered so far,

2.   The Chord Progression building blocks covered in Part II,

3.   Active Listening to determine the Texture and Form,

4.   Ideas from the chapters on Improvisation and Songwriting to inform your own creative accompaniment

Remember our analogy of "painting a picture bit by bit" and the helpful Express activity of transcribing, so that you can gradually assemble your own version in a relaxed way.

It's also worth noting that technique and vocabulary, in your Head and Hands, will be invaluable here. For example, familiarising yourself with common left-hand chording patterns and chord voicings on piano can provide a larger kind of "building block" for you to recognise or select, rather than just playing chords as block Triad chords.

As always, it's important to keep your Big Picture Vision in mind. Don't assume that unless you can replicate a complex piano arrangement note-for-note, you "can't play piano by ear". You may find that getting to a decent level with playing melodies by ear and harmonising them with a variety of patterns lets you play the music you love by ear in a way that fully meets your musical goals.

Conclusion

In this chapter we introduced the idea that Playing By Ear is a spectrum, rather than an all-or-nothing ability. You learned about the Play-By-Ear Process, where we use the three steps of Listen-Engage-Express to gradually figure music out by ear. Over time and with practice, these stages can merge and become more instinctive, so that you are able to tackle increasingly sophisticated play-by-ear tasks directly.

If you've tried the exercises in this chapter, you will have discovered something powerful: you can already play by ear! From here, it's just a matter of getting faster and more accurate with your "guesses", through a spirit of "Trial and Improvement".

If you are reading this chapter after having gone through Part II of the book and started practicing Integrated Ear Training with our building blocks for Pitch and Rhythm, you have the benefit of a head-start, and some powerful accelerators for the Engage stage.

You are now equipped with a clear process you can apply to any music you wish to play by ear, as well as some activities you can use to gradually level up your Playing By Ear skills.

These skills will have wide-reaching knock-on effects throughout your musical life, whether the dedicated activity of playing music by ear is a big part of your own Big Picture Vision or not. The LNX approach has been designed with the holistic musicality of the H4 model in mind, meaning your Head, Hands, Hearing and Heart are all improved together, and the connections between them formed naturally. You will see this pay off in activities from Improvisation to Performance, Expression, and Songwriting, as well as further improving your foundational skills like Audiation, Singing, and Active Listening. And of course, as you leverage the building blocks from Part II of this book, you improve your recognition skills too, further feeding the positive feedback loops across your musicality.

Maybe you aspire to be that prototypical Jammer who can grab an instrument and play anything they hear, remember or imagine, jamming along with any group, instinctively recognising the musical accompaniment that would fit perfectly. Maybe you're a dedicated Creative and are excited by how play-by-ear skills can let you deconstruct and more deeply understand the songs and pieces you love and are inspired by, as well as making it easier to bring the music from inside your head out into the real world. Or maybe you're a pure

Performer, who felt like figuring out music by ear wasn't something you were likely to have much need or desire for in your own musical life.

Whatever the case, I hope this chapter has opened your mind to how powerful Playing By Ear can be for connecting Head, Hearing, Hands and Heart—and how rewarding it can be for any musician to spend some time moving themselves further and further along that exciting play-by-ear spectrum. Every step forwards won't just increase your play-by-ear skills, but will contribute significantly to all the other abilities we'll be covering in Part III, as well as your overall musicality.

CHAPTER FIFTEEN:
IMPROVISATION

A quick word before we begin…

This chapter is titled "Improvisation"—and I know that you, as the reader, might be reading through every chapter of the book. You might identify with the "Creative" Core. You might be passionate about improvising or inspired to dive into it for the first time.

But you might also be in the camp who were expecting to skip over this chapter—either because you've been disappointed when trying to learn Improvisation in the past, or it doesn't seem to fit in with your musical life and Big Picture Vision.

If so, thank you for reading at least this much! And please don't skip on just yet…

In this chapter we'll be talking a lot about "improvising", but it's important to make clear at the outset that improvising is simply the one activity we've found most fluid and versatile for developing your musical creativity. In fact, I very nearly named this chapter "Creativity" rather than "Improvisation"!

Whether the activity of "improvising" is part of your own Big Picture

Vision or not, we've found it is the most effective activity for developing your creativity across your musical life, including Songwriting, Expression, Performance, and more.

And whether or not you currently feel "creative" or aspire to be, we've seen again and again that exploring the creative side of music-making has proven, across so many different kinds of musician (including for example, classical musicians focused solely on Performance) to be deeply rewarding, fulfilling, liberating and ultimately indispensable. Once you open the door into creativity, using the approach presented in this chapter, you will never look back.

So if you're willing to entertain the possibility and explore with me—let's dive in.

––––––––––

Of all the applied skills of musicality, Improvisation can seem like the most magical.

The incredible, moving, sophisticated and subtle music we are so passionate about—even non-musicians can wrap their minds around how it might be possible to slave away for days, months, or years, to craft that catchy melody, that beautiful harmony, the groove that gets people dancing, and the track that is remembered through generations.

But to conjure something like that up, out of nowhere, in the moment and on-the-fly?

If I was going to let emoji creep into this book, there would be a head-exploding one here!

Throw in the Talent Myth, the idea of a "muse" or "divine inspiration", and the way people tend to self-categorise as being "a creative person" or not... and it's easy to see why Improvisation can seem particularly magical and mysterious to the average musician.

Interestingly, unlike some aspects of musicality which are rarely taught in mainstream music education, teaching Improvisation actually is quite common, especially in certain styles such as jazz and blues.

The trouble is that the improv methods usually taught can actually make you feel *less* creative. These fall into two main categories:

1. Rule-based or pattern-based approaches. In these you study a lot of music theory to know what's "allowed", and then you choose notes and rhythms according to those rules or patterns.

One example would be the ubiquitous rock guitar improv
methods which teach the minor pentatonic fretboard pattern
and say, basically, "noodle around with that and see what
comes out".

2.   Vocabulary-based approaches. In these you memorise licks,
      riffs and runs, perhaps drawn from famous solos from the
      past, and you reproduce these as your "improvisation".

If you've tried either of these approaches you'll know: they do sort
of work. They enable you to play something that is a little bit
improvised in the moment. But you've probably also experienced how
limiting they are, and how robotic they can leave you feeling.

To put it bluntly: these methods rarely, if ever, deliver the kind of
free, creative, instinctive and inspired improvisations that probably
drew you to want to improvise in the first place.

The reality is we *all* have that creative instinct inside. If you don't
think you do right now, no problem. We'll be unpacking exactly how
you can know this for sure, get in touch with that creative instinct, and
start to bring your own creative musical ideas out into the world.

We'll also explore how "creativity is the vehicle, not the destination".
Meaning that improvising, or more generally "being creative" in music,
is not just an end goal in itself. It's also a highly effective tool we can
use to help us across a wide range of other music-learning activities.

As mentioned in *Chapter One: Musicality*, Improvisation isn't some
far-off, advanced, or mystical ability. It's something which can (and in
our opinion *should*)[1] be done from the very outset in learning music,
and it's never too late to start.

If you've been reading through the chapters of this book in order
and trying the suggested exercises along the way then you'll have
noticed we've already snuck in quite a lot of improvising already!
Inside Musical U this has proven to be a wonderful way to let
musicians slip into Improvisation through the side-door, and many
who hadn't thought they had any real interest in learning to improvise
have discovered just how fun, rewarding, and powerful it can be for
your musicality and musical fulfilment. Now it's time to explain our

---

[1] You won't find us using the word "should" very often at Musical U, but improvising
stands alongside foundational skills like Singing and Audiation which are so beneficial,
we'd be remiss if we didn't at least *strongly encourage* you to take advantage of :)

approach fully, and empower you to really focus on developing your creativity consciously and intentionally.

In this chapter you'll learn the *Expansive Creativity* approach which we created at Musical U to enable any musician to develop the ability to freely express their own creative musical ideas in any situation.

It is a musician-centered approach, meaning that our creativity isn't something bolted-on to existing music, following strict rules and conventions. But rather, in the spirit of our *Musical Inside And Out* Pillar Belief, the goal is to let you create music instinctively inside you, and be empowered to express it outwardly—not just through an instrument, but by Singing, writing, or with any other form of musical expression such as clapping or dancing.

The traditional improv methods referred to above are normally purely Head-based (e.g. letting music theory dictate which notes are "correct") or Hands-based (e.g. relying on muscle memory to reproduce licks, riffs, or other "vocab"). Like everything we do, Expansive Creativity is based on the H4 Model, meaning it draws on your Head, Hands, Hearing and Heart, forging connections between them, and developing your holistic musicality.

If you've been through Part II of this book and started working with the pitch and rhythm building blocks covered there, you'll find these can be a huge help in constructing your improvisations. Any Ear Training you do will increase the ease with which you can bring your musical ideas out into the world, and Integrated Ear Training is naturally a perfect match for Expansive Creativity as they have the same H4 underpinnings.

If you haven't read Part II or begun Ear Training though, that needn't hold you back from diving into this chapter. The approach you'll learn here is intentionally designed to let you get in touch with and channel your creative instinct, even without having developed your ears yet.

Overview

In this chapter we'll begin with "The Improviser's Mindset": four principles for how you can start thinking about music and creativity, which will help to break down limiting beliefs and set you free, creatively.

Then we'll introduce the Expansive Creativity framework, designed to enable a limitless expansion of your natural creative instinct, by equipping you with the concepts and techniques which allow the ideal balance between "staying safe" and exploring freely. Its three components (the Play-Listen/Listen-Play loop, Constraints and Dimensions, and Playgrounds) are what will allow you to start improvising creatively right away, in a way that feels personal, instinctive, and satisfying.

We will also cover how to practice improvising using Expansive Creativity, and connect it with all your other activities, in a spirit of "Improvise to Learn".

The Improviser's Mindset

Before we introduce the Expansive Creativity approach, there are a few important Mindset principles to cover. Without these, any approach or method would be doomed before it began. With them, you're set up for creative success.

1. Improvising Is Natural

One of the most important points I would love to see you take away from this chapter is that improvising is *natural*. If you've struggled learning to improvise before using the methods mentioned earlier, or if you've been too intimidated or overwhelmed by the idea to even try, I realise that "natural" might be far from the word you'd choose for it!

But let's step back from "pressing buttons on an instrument" for a moment, and think about improvising and creativity more broadly.

We are all improvising, all day every day, in our spoken language. In every conversation, we are hearing something, formulating our own thoughts and ideas about it, and conjuring up words and sentences to express those thoughts and ideas out loud by speaking. We don't need to carefully prepare in advance for a conversation, and we aren't reciting lines from a script somebody else gave us beforehand.

As humans we are, inherently, creative beings. The long history of human art demonstrates that clearly—but unfortunately culture has developed so heavily in the direction of hero-worship and idolising the very best artists, it's led to a false dichotomy of the "creative" people versus everyone else.

This is perhaps at its most extreme in the art of music.

Consider other creative arts:

- Painting, and other visual arts,

- The writing of poetry, novels, and plays,

- Modern forms of art like creating online videos,

- More down-to-earth creative pursuits such as cookery or gardening.

In all these cases it's true that we do showcase and admire those who reach the very pinnacle of artistic expression (as measured by career success or critical acclaim). And yet, in all those cases, the amateur or hobbyist is still expected and encouraged to express their own creative ideas, constantly making their own aesthetic judgements and creative choices along the way.

Meanwhile, the amateur or hobbyist *musician*, nine times out of ten, is doing the equivalent of "painting by numbers". They are handed "an artwork" to reproduce themselves.

That's not in itself a bad thing. There's enormous potential artistry in reciting poetry or performing a play, and we'll explore this art of *interpretation* in *Chapter Seventeen: Expression*.

Still, can you imagine the amateur painter being told they didn't have enough "talent" to ever start from a blank canvas? Or the aspiring poet being told that unless they have a "gift" they are wasting their time? Or if those who cooked or did the gardening were taught that only professionals could make decisions about what to add or remove, or which ingredients or seeds were appropriate?

Music is a unique form of art, but hopefully these comparisons help demonstrate both how natural we see creativity as being in other contexts, and frankly how odd it is that we've ended up with a musical culture that sees improvisation as either a matter of "vocab" and "rules", or something restricted to the gifted few.

The good news is that it's never too late, and it does not need to take years or decades of "woodshedding" to start improvising compelling, satisfying music that is in your own unique voice.

When we ran our *Foundations of a Musical Mind* course for the first time, one of my absolute favourite parts was seeing how in Module 1, week 1—literally within a few days of starting—musicians were able to start improvising. You may have met the simple "Garden Gate" rhythmic improvisation exercise they used in *Chapter Thirteen: Rhythm*.

Even though they weren't yet playing mind-blowing solos at lightning speed on their instrument, this simple experience of making their own musically-satisfying creative choices produced a kind of *"Oh my gosh, I'm actually improvising!"* reaction that was an utter joy to see. And from there, not only was adding note pitches just a small additional step, that initial identity shift of *"I can be musically creative"* changed everything for them, forever.

In the next section we'll talk more about adopting that identity of "being creative". In *Chapter Two: Mindset* we introduced the three Musical Cores, and the idea that you may relate strongly to the desire to express your own creative ideas in music—or it may just be one small part of your own Musical Core. Either way, Improvisation is an unmatched skill and activity to develop your creativity, and allow the creative musical ideas you have inside to start flowing out for yourself and others to enjoy.

2. Expanding Your Natural Creativity

Since creativity is a natural part of our humanity, in this chapter our goal is not to "make you creative", but rather to:

A. Show you how to express your musical creativity

B. Empower you to gradually increase how creative you are

That second part is hard to define or measure, but with a view of "creative freedom", we're really talking about how freely you can express your creativity and how free those creative ideas can be. Just like in *Chapter Fourteen: Playing By Ear*, talking about the "play-by-ear spectrum", we can think of creativity as a spectrum. At one end you are only able to express a limited range of creative musical ideas. At the other you feel utterly free to imagine and express anything you dream of.

Earlier we called out the two traditional methods of teaching Improvisation: Rule- or pattern-based approaches, and vocabulary-based approaches. Although these traditions have a lot to answer for in terms of how limited and robotic the aspiring improviser has tended to end up feeling, it is important to make clear that neither is "bad" or to be avoided. If our goal is to improvise freely, creatively, and have it feel like *you*, we do need to go beyond those "handed down from on high" approaches. However, any time and energy you've already invested in either will actually pay off much more when combined with the Expansive Creativity approach you'll learn in this chapter.

Similarly, you don't need the "building blocks" introduced in Part II of the book. If you haven't yet gone through those chapters you can certainly dive straight into this one. However, since the Expansive Creativity approach is very focused on using your own ears to make creative choices, those Ear Training building blocks will enrich your experience and help liberate you creatively much faster.

3. Creative Contexts

Before we dive further into creativity and Improvisation, let's set the scene a little. Part of what limits the traditional approaches to Improvisation is that they are overly-focused on a particular musical context.

For example, rather than teaching the aspiring jazz improviser how to get in touch with their creative instinct and then channel that through their instrument, they are taught the music theory details of a particular jazz standard and the "rules" for which notes are appropriate, or the specific revered solos of the past from which they should memorise licks, riffs and runs.

Since the Expansive Creativity approach is focused primarily on *you* as a musical creator, you'll find that the techniques and exercises in this chapter can actually be applied across a wide range of creative contexts, including:

1. Interpretation of written music, for example in Classical music. Although "improvising" may seem anathema or *verboten* in the Classical world, in fact all the great composers of the past were expected to be accomplished improvisers too, and there is great creative opportunity when playing music "as written"—something we'll explore more specifically in *Chapter Seventeen: Expression.*

2. Song-based improvisation. For example, playing a guitar solo in a rock song, taking a solo in a jazz trio playing a standard, playing along at a local blues jam session, etc.

3. Idiomatic, i.e. matching a certain style or genre. This brings advantages by hinting at what's likely to be appealing to the listener and what creative choices you can make to fit those expectations (or defy them!) but can also be taken too far, as

with the rule- and vocab-based approaches already mentioned.

4.   Non-idiomatic or "free" improvisation. For example sitting down at the end of a long work day with your instrument, and just seeing what flows out.

5.   Improvise-to-learn. This is an activity, habit, or really a wide-reaching mindset, which redefines improvisation from "a thing you learn to do, and then do" to being a *tool* you can use to help you learn whatever musical material or skill you're focused on.

6.   Songwriting and composing. Although often seen as a distinct skill or activity, as you'll discover in this chapter, it's more accurate to see "writing music" as something like "improvising on paper" and "improvising" as "composing music on-the-fly".

All of these different musical contexts bring their own conventions, expectations, and implications, but the same Expansive Creativity approach we'll be learning can set you free to create in any and all of them.

4. Agency and Authority

"There are no wrong notes; some are just more right than others."
                                        — Thelonius Monk

"Do not fear mistakes. There are none."
                                        — Miles Davis

"There's no such thing as a wrong note."
                                        — Art Tatum

Why is it that Improvisation can seem so intimidating and overwhelming to the average musician?

We know that it's partly the Talent Myth at work, making it seem like a magical out-of-reach skill because it's simply not taught in an effective, empowering way.

But it's also something much more fundamental. If all your experience in learning music has been based on playing from notation or step-by-step tutorials, the chances are you have become firmly entrenched in a mindset of "right and wrong notes". Your goal is typically to "avoid mistakes" and "get the notes right when you play".

That is a very good thing, and *Chapter Six: Superlearning* will set you up for greater success in pursuing that goal.

But it comes at a price: it massively inhibits your creativity, to the point where most musicians feel terrified by the idea of choosing the notes themselves. What if you play something and it (shock, horror!) *sounds bad?!*

If we are to have any success in learning to improvise, we need to— at least temporarily—ditch the mindset of "right vs. wrong".

Instead, we need to start focusing on our personal judgement. Our aesthetic preference. Whether we have played something which sounded good and pleased us, or not. For example, starting to consider that "interesting" is better than "right". "Joyful" is more important than "precise". "Adventure" is more desirable than "perfection".

To put it bluntly, when it comes to creativity and Improvisation, there are no mistakes. Only choices.

Easy to say—but if you've spent a lifetime focused on "not getting it wrong", it's not necessarily so easy to make that mindset shift!

The key is for us to restore to you two essential powers: agency and authority.

Agency simply means "you get to choose what to do". This is perhaps what makes the greatest difference, and lets you escape from that feeling of being a musical robot.

If you think about your musical life right now, how much agency would you say you have? No doubt you choose some things, like when to practice and how much to practice. You might (or might not!) be the one who decides what pieces or songs you'll work on. When working on one of those pieces of music, how much decision-making are you doing? If you're like most music-learners, the answer is "not much". You're trying your hardest to "get it right", and so the only decision-making is bundled up in *"how can I make this more right?"*

Contrast that with the musician who can just "pick up and play". Who can improvise something entirely by scratch, or glance at a chord chart or lead sheet and play their own arrangement or interpretation. The musician who clearly has an ownership of the music and seems able to do anything they want to. What they're demonstrating isn't just a set of skills—it's also that agency, that they have given themselves the freedom to choose and make decisions for themselves.

This goes hand-in-hand with the second power: inner authority. Because once you're allowing yourself to make more choices, you immediately hit up against a question of *"how do I know what choices to make?"*

Authority means saying *"That's up to me"*.

Instead of looking to sheet music, or a teacher, or "the way things have always been done" to tell you what's right and what you "should" do, when you take on inner authority you're choosing to believe that what matters most is what *you* like. What *you* think sounds good, or right. What pleases *you*, and perhaps an audience *you* want to perform for.

These two things together—agency, meaning always giving yourself the choice, and inner authority, meaning you decide for yourself which choice is right or best—these two are what will liberate you and give you the opportunity to get in touch with your creative instinct.

Just remember: it's not *"I will develop my creative instinct and then one day I'll feel agency and authority"*. It is a bit chicken-and-egg, and there is a feedback loop. The more you practice creativity, the more agency and authority will become second nature to you, and the more agency and authority you gain, the more creative you will feel and be.

But you need to first open yourself up with an initial willingness to step into agency and authority. And that is simply a choice.

These two together ultimately produce the dramatic mindset shift we're going for: moving away from the idea of "right" and "wrong" notes.

In the sheet music world, your highest potential is to perfectly reproduce what's written on the page, and perhaps add a bit of interpretation or flair to the way you reproduce it. If you play a different note pitch, or don't play a note at exactly the right moment to match the written rhythm—that note is "wrong" and we're taught we should feel bad and guilty because we've made a mistake.

When you step into agency and authority, that whole idea becomes nonsense. There is, absolutely, still a notion of "better or worse", but that is 100% up to your judgement.

This is exciting—because it's what lets you use your own musical taste as a feedback loop to hone your creative instinct.

Almut Says...

I was at a vocal improvisation workshop and I was improvising with notes from the minor pentatonic scale over a drone [a continuously-sustained note].

The facilitator then asked me to start using notes from outside the scale. To slide some note up or down a semitone.

At first, this sounded very strange and irritating. I kept repeating the "wrong" note in this context and it was less irritating each time I sang it, up to the point where it seemed to fit in nicely with my improvisation.

It can feel scary to be creative and to explore—but don't all new things feel strange at first yet can quickly become a normal part of your life?

One final remark before we move on to the Expansive Creativity framework itself: your musical taste is just as good and important as anybody else's. Arguably much more so. And the most exciting thing about taking an Expansive Creativity approach is that your taste is all you need! The whole framework simply helps you level up your ability to express what your taste tells you is "good" music.

Expansive Creativity

When you read above that all the choices were up to you, did you feel a slight twinge of overwhelm, or that intimidation factor kicking in? I wouldn't be surprised if so.

The Expansive Creativity approach was designed to help you overcome the #1 biggest challenge in Improvisation, which is feeling caught between either:

- Overly-constrained (with rules/patterns/vocab), robotic playing, or

- Terrifying, anything-goes overwhelm.

The one compelling advantage of the traditional improv methods is that for a complete beginner they keep you "safe" by limiting your choices to what's likely to sound fitting, musically. Without that, it's easy to feel instantly overwhelmed. If every note is possible, that's an awful lot to try to choose from! And not just once, but again and again, moment by moment. For a pianist with 88 keys and ten fingers, surely some kind of rules or patterns are required—or some mysterious talent for knowing which notes to play?

Expansive Creativity is designed to connect you with your creative instinct and help you develop increasingly free, sophisticated and satisfying improvisations which are truly you, while keeping you feeling "safe", helping you create satisfying music from day one, and still letting you become increasingly free over time.

 It's named *Expansive* Creativity because it's not an A-Z sequence of particular lessons. It's an approach which allows an infinite journey of gradually *expanding* your creativity (and through that your overall musicality).

It provides you with an ability to express your own creative ideas which you can then channel not only into Improvisation but also Songwriting and composing, Expression and Performance, and across all of your music-making, in any musical context. Like I mentioned in the introduction to this chapter, Improvisation is simply the most effective activity we've found for developing your creative instinct and the ability to express your creative musical ideas.

So how do we achieve that delicate balance between providing "guard rails" that prevent overwhelm, and still allowing you to feel freely creative?

There are three components to Expansive Creativity:

A. The Play-Listen/Listen-Play loop

B. Constraints and Dimensions

C. Playgrounds

These aren't strictly sequential. Each component can be used alone, but they work best all together. We'll go through each in turn, and show you how they inter-relate and combine.

TIP:

In everything that follows, we recommend recording your practice, and listening back. As noted in the "Agency and Authority" section above, the Expansive Creativity approach is very much about allowing you to become your own best teacher.

Listening in-the-moment as you play is vital—but recording and listening back can provide a valuable additional opportunity to learn from what you created.

On top of that, when you routinely record your improvisation practice, you can return to the recordings later—not just later in the same practice session, but days, weeks or months later—and have the chance to recognise and appreciate the progress you've made. It's often hard to see any improvement when we're in the thick of it, but comparing your improvised creations from a few weeks or months ago with what you're able to do today can become a significant source of increased confidence and momentum.

It also brings a major side benefit, something which Next Level coach Andy Portas describes as "mining for diamonds".

As you listen back to a recording of something you improvised, don't just critique what you played. Be on the lookout for anything that makes you go "oh, that was interesting" or "I actually quite liked that bit!" It may look more like a lump of coal with a slight twinkle to it right now, but if you grab onto it and play around with it some more, you might discover there was a true diamond hiding inside. You can collect these "diamonds" as part of your own personal vocabulary and sense of your musical taste, as well as drawing further encouragement from them about your own creative potential. We'll explore this idea more in Chapter Sixteen: Songwriting.

A. Play-Listen/Listen-Play

The renowned producer of the long-running radio show *This*

American Life, Ira Glass, once gave an interview in which he discussed the creative process, and he said something that has stuck with me ever since, and which I've often shared with members at Musical U:

"Nobody tells people who are beginners—and I really wish somebody had told this to me—all of us who do creative work, we get into it because we have good taste. But it's like there's a gap, that for the first couple years that you're making stuff, what you're making isn't so good, OK? It's not that great. It's really not that great. It's trying to be good, it has ambition to be good, but it's not quite that good. But your taste—the thing that got you into the game—your taste is still killer, and your taste is good enough that you can tell that what you're making is kind of a disappointment to you.

A lot of people never get past that phase. A lot of people at that point, they quit. And the thing I would just like say to you with all my heart is that most everybody I know who does interesting creative work, they went through a phase of years where they had really good taste and they could tell what they were making wasn't as good as they wanted it to be—they knew it fell short, it didn't have the special thing that we wanted it to have.

And the thing I would say to you is everybody goes through that. And for you to go through it, if you're going through it right now, if you're just getting out of that phase, you gotta know it's totally normal.

And the most important possible thing you can do is do a lot of work—do a huge volume of work. [...] Because it's only by actually going through a volume of work that you are actually going to catch up and close that gap. And the work you're making will be as good as your ambitions. It takes a while, it's gonna take you a while—it's normal to take a while. And you just have to fight your way through that, okay?"

Fortunately with musical Improvisation, it needn't take years to start playing things which sound good! And the key is to have a way to let your taste be your guide.

The Play-Listen/Listen-Play technique fixes a common problem with Improvisation (and creativity in general): the tendency to be "all output", with no feedback loop in place to assess, analyse, and learn from what you created. In other words, we tend to be "all Play, no Listen".

The idea is simply to intentionally create a feedback loop:

- Play, and Listen to what you are playing.

- Listen to the music, and Play something in response.

With Play-Listen, your source of inspiration is the music you just played, whether something learned, random, inspired, intentional, or anything else.

With Listen-Play, you can be responding to a music recording, another musician, or what you yourself just played.

These two form a loop, creating a conversation (input *plus* output) between you and the musical context you are in.

Play-Listen/Listen-Play lets you leverage your ear skills (both Active Listening and Ear Training) and forms connections between Hands, Hearing, Head and Heart. It is what lets you shift from a mentality of *"did I get it right?"* to *"how did that sound?"*

Just like adding the "Reflect" step in Superlearning (see *Chapter Six: Superlearning*), this allows you to become your own best teacher, and nurtures the agency and authority we talked about earlier. Your own creativity (your personal "taste", to use Glass' word) starts to come through.

Depending on where you're applying the Play-Listen/Listen-Play technique, you may be relying on (and therefore developing) your musical memory. For example, if you were improvising call-and-response phrases with another musician, where your improvised phrase formed an "answer" to their musical "question", you would need to absorb what you heard fully and retain it long enough in the "Listen" step to then be able to "Play". It's helpful to be aware of this, to make sure you're not over-taxing your musical memory and struggling as a result of that, rather than the improvising itself.

As always, the foundational skills of Audiation and Singing can be a huge accelerator and amplifier for you. Audiation can be used both to create the musical stimulus (i.e. you "Listen" to something that's purely in your mind) or to re-create it after you heard it, so that you can Listen again before responding. Singing can be used both to echo back what you heard before responding, and as a stepping stone to "Play" by letting you express your improvised musical idea without the added burden of translating it onto an instrument.

If you've read *Chapter Fourteen: Playing By Ear*, you'll see clear parallels with the Listen-Engage-Express process. The major difference is the idea of making this a continual back-and-forth loop, so that whether your musical stimulus is something external, something imagined, or what you yourself just played, you are continually feeding back from Listening to Playing and vice-versa. This is what lets your creative instinct start to emerge.

Let's try this out, with something our Head Educator Andrew Bishko named the "Babbling Baby" exercise, inspired by the way young children find their way into spoken language by babbling nonsense to begin with. Hearing both their own babbled nonsense and what, to them, is the nonsense babbled by adults around them, they start to gradually mimic and repeat back particular sounds and patterns, until comprehensible speech emerges.[2]

EXERCISE: The Babbling Baby

1. PLAY: Grab your instrument, and play something. Forget about repertoire, don't think ahead, plan in advance, or let your inner critic worry about how it will sound. Be a "babbling baby" and spend just 5 seconds or so making some musical sounds.

2. LISTEN: As you play, pay attention. Listen to the musical sounds you made. Now, *after* playing, allow yourself to critique what you heard. What sounded good? What didn't you like? Was there anything cool or interesting?

3. Now repeat Step 1, informed and inspired by what you observed in Step 2. You might like to repeat something you liked, or refine something you didn't—or start from scratch!

4. Continue this Play, Listen, Play, Listen loop, exploring and experimenting.

---

[2] One can take analogies between spoken language and music too far, and we're not suggesting a direct neurological correspondence between this exercise and how babies learn to speak. It's simply a helpful and inspiring analogy to inspire you in this initial exercise.

If you do this for a few minutes, it's more than likely you'll discover a musical idea or two that you think actually sounds pretty good! Take a moment to recognise yourself as a musical creator and enjoy how purely through experimentation and your own judgement you were able to come up with something you liked the sound of.

As we continue with the other two techniques we'll put more structure around this Improvisation practice, but the spirit of this exercise—to create something musical and let our own ears and taste be our guide—is at the heart of the Expansive Creativity approach.

Here's a variant exercise you can try which bridges between Improvisation and Playing By Ear, using Audiation and/or Singing:

EXERCISE: Babbling Baby With Singing/Audiation

1. Repeat the Babbling Baby exercise, but this time use Audiation or Singing to come up with a musical idea, still with the "babbling" mentality of "making some musical sounds".

2. Now use your instrument to either try replicating what you heard in your mind or from your singing voice, or responding to it with some more musical sounds.

Now that you've had your first taste of the Play-Listen/Listen-Play technique and started adopting the Improviser's Mindset, let's move on to the next technique: Constraints and Dimensions.

B. Constraints and Dimensions

We've discussed how limiting it can be to rely on strict rules, patterns, or memorised "vocabulary", if our goal is free, creative, personal improvisation—but also how overwhelming it can be when "anything goes"!

The core principle behind the "Constraints and Dimensions" technique is that there can be freedom through constraints. With the right approach, we can both eliminate overwhelm and allow real creative freedom.

I must give credit for this way of thinking about Improvisation to our long-standing Resident Pro for bass guitar, Steve Lawson. Steve is perhaps the most admired solo bassist in the world today, and his approach is highly improvisational. I was fortunate to take one-to-one bass lessons with Steve a number of years ago and it happened to be around the time we were designing the Expansive Creativity framework for our earliest training on Improvisation at Musical U.

He shared a perspective of thinking in terms of the *dimensions* available to us when making musical choices. It's not just *"which note should I play next?"* but a whole set of choices we are making moment-to-moment when improvising—of which the note pitch is just one. There are also things like volume, playing technique, the timing, and so on. To my mathematically-inclined brain, this made sense immediately! And it immediately reveals that whichever dimension we are focused on, we are (either intentionally, or implicitly) making decisions about the others i.e. we are constraining them in some way.

This developed into the idea of Constraints and Dimensions: a clear way of thinking about the fact that by adding certain intentional *constraints* to our music-making, we free ourselves up to choose more easily in other *dimensions*. Over time, as we codified our 4-Dimensional Active Listening framework (see *Chapter Five: Active Listening*) this became even clearer, with the four Dimensions of Timbre, Dynamics, Pitch and Rhythm.

Dimensions Recap

We cover the four Dimensions in detail in Chapter Five: Active Listening and Chapter Seventeen: Expression but here's a brief overview if you haven't read those chapters yet or want to refresh your memory:

A "note" simply means "a sound used to make music". A note has four dimensions:

- *Pitch*
- *Rhythm*
- *Timbre*
- *Dynamics*

Pitch is the perceived highness or lowness of a sound. "Where on the whole continuum of high sounds to low sounds does this particular pitch in the music fall?". Not all notes have a single well-defined pitch, but almost all musical sounds can be described in terms of where they exist on this dimension of pitch.

Musical notes also exist for a certain length of time. The musical term Rhythm describes the pattern of the longness and shortness of notes and the silences in between.

Sounds carry varying degrees of energy. When it's a small amount of energy, the sound is what we call a "soft" or "quiet" sound. Sounds with a large amount of energy are called "loud". We refer to this as softness, loudness, or "volume". Changes in volume over time in music are called Dynamics.

Timbre is a word borrowed from the French and pronounced like the first part of the word "tambourine". An English term with similar meaning is "tone colour". It refers to the properties of a sound that can make one note sound different than another, even if they're playing the same pitch.

For example if you listen to a flute playing middle C and you listen to a piano playing that same pitch, at the same volume and for the same duration, you can still immediately tell the difference between the piano and the flute by their timbres.

Here's a simple example to illustrate. If we come back to that earlier scenario of a pianist sitting at the keyboard feeling overwhelmed by being free to play several notes using 88 keys at any given moment, we can reduce that overwhelm by applying certain Constraints. For example, we might decide on a particular rhythmic pattern to play repeatedly, in a certain range for each hand on the keyboard, and perhaps even a particular key and scale. There is still a huge range of creative choices available in Pitch, as well as Dynamics and the subtleties of Rhythm and Timbre—but suddenly the musician feels far less overwhelmed.

The point is that we constrain *some* Dimensions in *some* ways, to let you more easily and expansively explore what's still possible.

This idea alone is often a game-changer for musicians! You can apply as many or as few Constraints as you like, and they can be as broad or specific as is helpful. In the exercises below you'll have the chance to experiment with a wide range of Constraints and explore the varying freedom across Dimensions they produce.

Just like with Active Listening, we can also think bigger-picture in terms of Form i.e. what changes and stays the same over time. One of the easiest ways to start adding clear musical structure to your improvisations is simply to apply certain Constraints for a time, and then change the Constraints to begin a new section.

With this view on things, it's easy to see that the traditional approaches we've been contrasting Expansive Creativity with are limiting because they essentially apply Constraints which are too strict and too set-in-stone, which naturally produces same-y sounding improvisations and the musician feeling more robotic than creative. You can also see why we say those approaches aren't bad or to be avoided, necessarily—they're just too small a subset of what's really possible and helpful.

Let's start exploring what improvising using Constraints and Dimensions is like. There are several exercises below. You might like to go through them in turn, and then come back to those you enjoy most. Each of the exercises has the same format: set a particular Constraint (or multiple) and then try improvising accordingly, exploring the creative choices still available to you.

In all cases, use the Play-Listen/Listen-Play technique to learn from your own creations and continue to refine your creative instinct. And if you find yourself noticing something you like, you have full permission (and encouragement!) to explore it further and have fun experimenting creatively. Remember that the whole Expansive Creativity framework is designed to set you free creatively, so we are never setting strict "rules". Even our Constraints should be considered guidelines or guard-rails. They can and should be ignored any time your creative instinct knows better!

EXERCISE: One-Note Improv

Constraint: Use just a single note pitch.

1.   Choose a note on your instrument. For example, Middle C. You can also use your singing voice if you prefer. This is the only note pitch you'll use—but all other Dimensions are completely free.

2.   Play a short musical phrase, using just that note. Listen as you play.

3.   Now do it again, and create something different. You can just play and see what comes out, or think more intentionally about exploring Rhythm, Dynamics and Timbre.

4.   See how different-sounding you can make your improvisation each time. Any of the detailed coverage of the four Dimensions in *Chapter Five: Active Listening* or *Chapter Seventeen: Expression* can help inspire your explorations.

We've found that musicians often find it a bit mind-blowing to discover how much musical freedom is possible with the One-Note Improv! If you've started from a place of thinking that improvising means "picking which notes to play", it can be exciting to discover how much is possible even with just a single note pitch.

When you're ready you can expand this exercise into...

EXERCISE: Two- and Three-Note Improv

Constraint: Use just two (and then three) note pitches.

1.   Repeat the One-Note Improv exercise, but this time choose two notes to work with. This could be, for example, the first two notes of a major scale, but it could also be two random notes, two notes far apart in pitch, or two notes of a chord. Notice how even choosing your Constraints can involve considerably creative choice and express your taste!

2.   When you're ready, choose a different pair of notes to use, or
       expand to using three different note pitches.

What was your experience? Did you get bored with such tight
Constraints on Pitch? If so, imagine what else you can do with
Rhythm, Dynamics and Timbre. Look for more ways to creatively
exercise your choices. It can be tempting to just flip back and forth
between the notes, but what happens if you hold one of them back for
a time, making use of all the one-note improv skills you've developed,
and then bring in a new note, presenting it like a jewel?

The big opportunity here is to notice how liberating it can feel to
introduce a second note pitch after some time spent on One-Note
Improv. And then introducing a third note can feel very exciting
indeed! We can start to notice how much musicality is glossed over
when improv is approached from a starting point of a whole scale, or
focused on playing "as many notes as possible, as fast as possible". We
also begin to appreciate the huge musical significance of each note
pitch we choose to include in our improvising.

If you're studying Solfa or Intervals, this is a great opportunity to
get more deeply familiar with those building blocks through the Play-
Listen/Listen-Play loop and the musical impact of the choices you
make. For example, practicing Two-Note Improv with the *do re* toneset
feels very different than with *do mi* or *la, do*—and improvising
melodies using the two notes of a Major Third has a very different
character to using a Minor Third or a Perfect Fourth.

If you're focused on the Pentatonic Scale (as recommended in
Chapter Nine: Solfa) or the Pentascale (as recommended in *Chapter Ten:
Intervals*), using those scales as a Constraint on Pitch is a perfect way to
dovetail your Improvisation practice with your Ear Training.

Andy Says...

I like to think of the pentatonic as the "scale that keeps on giving"! I'm regularly discovering new and exciting ways to use it, whether that's within a composition, a production, or in improvisation (free or jazz).

The major and minor pentatonic scales are very user-friendly, due to there being no Half Step movement, and therefore no (troublesome) Tri-Tone interval. So it creates a very consonant sound against its relative harmony. Who hasn't noodled away with a C Major pentatonic over a C chord for many minutes (or hours!) at a time? :)

While this is great fun to experience and experiment with, we can start to miss the tensions created by pitches outside of that pentatonic scale...

Fortunately, one simple means of adding more tension is to simply play a pentatonic scale rooted on the 5th of our chord.

So if our backing is a C Major chord we can play a G Major pentatonic against it, which introduces a little tension in the form of the note B against the C chord. Swapping between the two scales (rooted on the tonic vs. rooted on the fifth) can deliver enough tension and resolution to create a more interesting sound that feels a little more above the harmony.

If you're feeling adventurous, try playing a pentatonic from the second scale degree e.g. a D Major pentatonic over a C chord. That will give you a rather jazzy sounding major 7th, 9th and #11th!

e.g. Over a C Chord:
C Major pentatonic: C D E G A
G Major pentatonic: G A B D E
D Major pentatonic: D E F# A B
Give it a try!

Next, let's try applying a very different kind of Constraint. We've said that we can constrain any of our four Dimensions—but that's not the only kind of Constraint that can be useful...

EXERCISE: 10-Second Improv

Constraint: Improvise a melody for ten seconds.

1. Set a timer for ten seconds.

2. Start the timer and begin improvising. When the timer stops, stop.

You may find it easier to include additional Constraints to prevent overwhelm. For example, you can use the One-, Two- or Three-Note Constraints here too. The purpose of the exercise however is to notice the effect it has to constrain your creation to a fixed time period.

How does it affect the musical choices you make? Do you have to think differently about Rhythm? What about Pitch?

Your musical taste will naturally make you want to bring your improvised melody to some kind of satisfying completion by the time the alarm goes off. What can you discover through experimentation about how to make that happen?

This exercise is a great illustration of constraints that go beyond the four Dimensions. Can you think of others that would be interesting to try?

EXERCISE: Melody-Inspired Improv

Constraint: Use either the Pitch or Rhythm of a given melody to create your own.

1. Select a short melody you're familiar with. You can use something from your own repertoire, or the example Starter Songs in *Chapter Nine: Solfa*. You can even use a technical exercise like a scale.

2. Use the note pitches from that source melody, but make up your own rhythm. Try this a few times.

3. When you're ready, switch to using the rhythm from that source melody but choosing the note pitches yourself. You can make this easier at first by constraining yourself to a few pitches like in the One/Two/Three-Note Improv exercises above, or you can use the same pitches featured in the source melody (but deciding for yourself which to play when).

Something valuable which will emerge as you practice this exercise is the power of "same vs. different" in music, and the impact it can have to keep some things the same while varying others. Let's explore that further...

Musicians often wonder how to make their improvisations or compositions more interesting or effective, musically. A core part of what makes music interesting or effective is how it plays with the listener's expectations, by creating some form of *tension* and then *releasing* it. There are many ways to do this, but one simple way is to do something repetitive until the listener is almost itching for a change... and then play something different.

EXERCISE: Tension and Release

Constraint: Do the same thing for a while... Then switch it up.

- Using any form of improvisation you're comfortable with (for example, any of the exercises above), play the same thing three times. Then make a change.

For example you might play the exact same phrase three times... and then play a slight variation in Pitch or Rhythm on the fourth time. You might play a series of long, quiet phrases... and then a short, loud one. You might play a series of phrases using just a single note pitch... and then finally introduce a second.

Really pay attention (i.e. Listen, don't just Play) to how the repetition creates a form of tension for the listener which is then released, by setting their expectations about what's likely to come next... and then defying them.

Let's try one more exercise with another Constraint on Form. One very common structure in musical Form is some kind of "call and response": a musical phrase is played, and then the following phrase (which might be played by the same musician or another musician) seems to "answer" it.

EXERCISE: Call And Response Improv

Constraint: Play a response which "answers" the musical "question" of a given phrase.

1.   Listen to a musical phrase. You can play or sing something yourself (improvised or from existing music) or you can play just one phrase from a recording. This will be our "call".

2.   Play your own musical phrase which aims to respond or reply to what you heard: the "response".

3.   Do this multiple times for the same call. Then choose a different phrase to be your call, and repeat.

As you get started with this, you might find it helpful to use the idea from the Melody-Inspired Improv exercise above, i.e. mimic either the rhythm of the "call" phrase or its pitches, while making the other Dimension your own. If you've read *Chapter Eight: Relative Pitch* or you're otherwise familiar with the idea of a *tonic* note, you might also like to make use of the fact that ending a phrase on that tonic note tends to feel like "coming home".

These exercises are all great ways to start practicing improvising, but more than that, they provide an introduction to thinking in terms of Constraints and Dimensions. You will start to notice the implicit or assumed Constraints in use across all the music you listen to and play. You'll also gain an increased awareness of the possibilities across all Dimensions, as well as the Form and other aspects of the music.

As you tried these exercises, you've almost certainly had moments of being surprised, both by your own creativity, and by the huge impact that choosing different Constraints can have on the resulting improvisations. Now it's time to build on Play-Listen/Listen-Play and Constraints and Dimensions, to provide you with an easy, flexible and fun way to continue practicing Improvisation: Playgrounds.

C. Playgrounds

The two techniques we've covered so far (Play-Listen/Listen-Play and Constraints and Dimensions) are highly effective in themselves. But they can still leave you prone to feeling overly-limited or overwhelmed, especially when just starting. Either you try to come up with Constraints yourself, and it can be hard to know which to use—or if you just stick to those spelled out in the exercises above, that's limiting in the same way as the traditional rule- and pattern-based approaches to improvising.

Let's fix that, by helping you to establish your own sets of Constraints that you enjoy and find useful, and a way to think about them which can let them become a continual source of creative activities for you.

When we were designing the Expansive Creativity framework, my two daughters were both under five years old. We were living in Valencia, Spain, which is blessed with an abundance of children's playgrounds. They're dotted all around residential areas, not just limited to parks like in most cities.

As I watched them playing one day, I was suddenly struck by how elegant a concept the playground is. We want our children to explore freely, and push the boundaries to learn what they're capable of. But of course, as parents what we want most of all is for them to be safe and avoid any serious injury.

As I saw my girls run and jump and climb and dangle themselves from all of the rides and structures and equipment, protected from the surrounding roads by a certain fenced-off area and cushioned by the rubbery flooring, I realised how beautifully playgrounds achieve both goals together: the children get to feel (and be) free and adventurous, but everything is designed to still keep them safe.

This is why we call the third component of the Expansive Creativity framework "Playgrounds". They allow you to explore safely, in a way that's well-matched to your current abilities, while keeping you "safe" by helping you play things that will be musically satisfying to you (and others).

 A "Playground" is simply a particular set of Constraints, and optionally a specific activity you'll do using those Constraints.

Here are some examples of creating Playgrounds:

- Any of the exercises in the previous section can be considered a Playground! The Constraint(s) are stated at the top, and the steps constitute the "activity' to do with those Constraints.

- Dimensional Exploration: Choose one or more Constraints for one of the four Dimensions (Pitch, Rhythm, Timbre and Dynamics). For example, using only the notes of the C Major Pentatonic Scale (Pitch). Now improvise, focusing on each of the other three Dimensions in turn, pushing the boundaries of what's still possible. Finally, combine what you liked along the way to create a final improvisation more intentionally.

- Backing Track Constraints: Put on a backing track (you can find many free ones online or in the *Additional Resources*) and improvise from start to finish. The first time through, try to respect the Constraints on Pitch and Rhythm suggested by the track (e.g. its key will suggest certain Pitch choices, its meter will suggest certain Rhythm choices). Then repeat, but intentionally *defy* those implicit Constraints! Then go through a third time using a mix of both approaches, according to your own musical taste and what you've discovered.

- Repertoire-Based Improv: Select a song or piece you've learned, and choose a particular section (e.g. the chorus of the song, or the B section of a piece) to replace with something improvised. You can use the Key and meter to influence your Pitch and Rhythm choices, and might even like to use the "Melody-Inspired Improv" exercise from earlier to modify that section of music rather than replacing it from scratch.

- Interpretation Improv: Select a song or piece you've learned and play the notes as written... But see how creative you can still be! Play it slow, play it fast, play it cheerfully or gloomily, play it carefully or loosely. This is a glimpse of what we'll explore much more in *Chapter Seventeen: Expression*.

- Building Blocks Improv: For any of the Pitch and Rhythm building blocks you're practicing with (see Part II), select from those building blocks as your constraints. You may have already tried this in some of the improv-based exercises in those chapters!

- Challenge-Based Improv: Play a challenge-yourself game. Take any other Playground but set yourself particular creative challenges. For example: *"How many different ideas can I come up with in 5 minutes?"*, *"How different can I make each time through?"*, *"What if I only change one thing each time through?"*, *"How can I make my improvisation sound like classical/rock/jazz/ blues/dance music—or like my favourite band/artist?"*, *"What if I tried improvising on an instrument I haven't yet learned to play?"*

- Form-Based Improv: Create musical Form by moving through a series of Playgrounds: Choose a set of Constraints to begin with, then change them slightly (or entirely!) for each section.

- External Inspiration: Choose a song or piece you love, or a piece of poetry, or a life experience. Identify any Constraints implied (for example, the Rhythm of the poetry, the mood of the life experience) and then improvise accordingly.

As you can see, Playgrounds can be hugely varied, but each one helps guide your creative choices to both eliminate overwhelm and allow satisfying musical choices. Some are suited to particular musical contexts (for example the "Backing Track Constraints" Playground) while others can be used very widely.

There are three important guidelines to keep in mind:

1. Don't limit yourself to the examples above! They are intended to illustrate what Playgrounds can be, and to get you started with this approach.

2. Choose and extend them to match your own abilities, Musical Core, and Big Picture Vision. For example, you can tailor them to perfectly match your current focus in Ear Training or Active Listening, or integrate them into practicing Playing By Ear or Songwriting. Choose Constraints which provide you with that "sweet spot" where you feel safe (i.e. you can easily play things which sound good to you) and you still feel creative freedom.

3.   Create your own! Jot down the Constraints and activities you find most fruitful, and incorporate those favourite, personalised Playgrounds into your regular practice. More on this below.

If you follow these three guidelines you'll find that Playgrounds truly live up to the name, allowing you to develop your Improvisation skills gradually, enjoyably, and quickly.

Andy Says...

Another way the pentatonic is the "scale that keeps on giving" is through diving into its modes. Just as the major scale creates seven modes by treating each of its notes as the tonic, the pentatonic scale creates five.

If we take a C Major pentatonic (C D E G A) and start a new scale, or mode, from each of its steps we get four more scales each with a different character or flavour:

#1 - C D E G A
#2 - D E G A C
#3 - E G A C D
#4 - G A C D E
#5 - A C D E G (= the minor pentatonic)

To get curious with these you could record a drone note to play over, or if you have a keyboard you could play a drone with your left hand. A drone can be a single sustained pitch, or a rhythmic pattern on one pitch.

Let's try the second mode. Play a low D drone and play the second mode of the C Major pentatonic (so D E G A C) over that. Take note of how each degree of the mode sounds and feels against the drone. Does it create any tension, or does it feel resolved?

Take each of the modes through the same process and have fun with it. You may find some of these sound quite filmic in nature!

As an extension to this, if you have a keyboard, you could also reverse the roles of the low drone and higher melody by playing an ostinato (repeat) pattern in the right hand, for example: D E G A. Then play the pentatonic scale with the left hand in the lower register. This sounds particularly dramatic if you play octaves in the left hand.

How to Practice

I've always liked the saying that "creativity is a muscle", and I have definitely found it to be true that the more you practice creativity, the more creative you become. As we ran through the Expansive Creativity framework, I hope you could see how much it's geared towards practicing creativity as an activity in its own right, as well as encouraging a mindset of creative choices throughout your music-making.

You can incorporate Play-Listen/Listen-Play into everything you do musically. It goes hand-in-hand with Plan-Play-Reflect from Superlearning and Listen-Engage-Express from Playing By Ear, and you'll find it feeds into the approaches we'll cover for Songwriting, playing with Expression, and Performance too. Just like with Active Listening, you can get into the habit of making sure your ears are really "switched on" each time you play, and allow that to feed back into your own creativity.

Constraints and Dimensions, and the Playgrounds which are built with them, are a great practice activity in themselves. Practicing Improvisation can be as simple as setting aside time during your music practice to have fun in a Playground or two—or being on the lookout for opportunities which arise during your other practice activities to take things in a creative direction, applying whatever Constraints make sense.

So everything we've covered so far has set you up well to practice Improvisation, and continually develop, refine and extend your skills. However, there's one additional idea which can have a profound impact on your Improvisation, creativity, and musicality.

Improvise To Learn

Up to this point we've been discussing "learning to improvise", and that's probably what made you want to read this chapter: a desire to learn the skill of Improvisation (or more broadly, creativity in music). All well and good.

But along the way at Musical U, as we developed the H4 model and the methodology to match, and especially when we created materials for Integrated Ear Training and incorporated more "Apply" activities close together with the corresponding "Learn" material and "Practice" exercises, something became very clear. The more we included *creative* activities, often specifically Improvisation, the faster progress our students had—and the more ease and joy they experienced along the way.

What emerged was a principle of *Improvise To Learn*.

Remember at the start of this chapter when I said that "creativity is the vehicle, not the destination"? This is how to make that happen.

Rather than thinking of Improvisation as a distinct, separate skill from everything else you do, and instead of seeing it as an aspirational goal you're working towards, we flip both of those on their head. We treat Improvisation as a *method through which we can learn whatever we want to.*

For example:

- If we're working on Ear Training for Solfa, we don't try to master Solfa in isolation, so that one day we can hopefully use it to improvise. Instead, we use creative improvisational exercises from the very beginning of our Solfa journey (just as we did in *Chapter Nine: Solfa*).

- If we want to improve our sense of Rhythm, we use creative rhythmic exercises (just like in *Chapter Thirteen: Rhythm*), not just pre-written patterns.

- If we want to truly maximise our learning speed with new pieces, songs, or technique, then even if our goal is to play everything "as written", we explore the creative opportunities and our own creative ideas along the way (as per the Creative Superlearning idea introduced in *Chapter Six: Superlearning*).

- If we're practicing Active Listening then even this seemingly "all input" activity can become a creative one, through the Creative Listening ideas introduced in *Chapter Five: Active Listening*.

- If we're focused on Songwriting, composing or arranging, we don't purely work with "writing" activities, seeing Improvisation as something we might do in a live performance or some separate musical activity. Instead we use improvising to inspire and explore new musical ideas which we can then refine and develop through our writing.

Here's what's really exciting about *Improvise To Learn:* Not only does it level up your Improvisation abilities along the way and bring out your creative instinct, it actually turns out to be one of the fastest and most enjoyable ways to learn! When we bring a playful spirit to our practice, we tend to perform at our best. When we engage the right-side creative brain, our attention is more fully engaged. When we explore and experiment, we find new possibilities and keep interest and motivation high. And when we feel like we're truly bringing our own creativity to our music-making, everything we play comes to life in a more exciting and rewarding way.

If all that sounds a bit too good to be true, you don't need to take my word for it. You may have already experienced it a bit for yourself going through previous chapters, or you can start experimenting with it now. It all comes back to the point I mentioned when talking about our *Enjoying the Journey* Pillar Belief in *Chapter Two: Mindset*: *"Fun is not the opposite of learning"*.

I know this can be hard to embrace for many adult music learners, after a lifetime of being told "learning is serious". Anything fun, playful, or creative can seem like a distraction from "the real thing we're trying to do". So like I said, don't take my word for it. As the spiritual teacher Lester Levenson was fond of saying, *"Don't believe me —but take it for checking."*

I encourage you to find out for yourself how rewarding, enjoyable, and *effective* the Improvise To Learn approach can be. Let yourself take a week, or two, or three, with the intention of "improv everywhere, improv everything". Discover for yourself exactly where and how Improvisation fits in best to your musical life and your journey towards your Big Picture Vision.

Conclusion

In this chapter we introduced the Expansive Creativity framework, for getting in touch with your musical instinct, and learning to express your own musical ideas in a way that feels good and sounds good.

We discussed the significant mindset shift required, to set aside strict "right and wrong notes" thinking in favour of a greater respect for your own musical taste and focus on learning to let that taste be your guide and teacher.

With Play-Listen/Listen-Play, Constraints and Dimensions and Playgrounds, you are equipped to gradually develop the sophistication and freedom of your own creative improvising. And with an attitude of creativity as the vehicle, not the destination, and the practice of Improvise To Learn, you can start to incorporate creative activities throughout your musical life.

This is also something you can apply through all other chapters of the book. Though we're covering it in Part III, it is arguably a foundational skill which would fit well in Part I! So you might like to go back and revisit some exercises from previous chapters (especially those in Part II), now that you have this Expansive Creativity framework (and particularly the awareness of Constraints and Dimensions) to approach them with.

Ultimately our goal here wasn't to make you a master improviser so that you could bust out brain-melting solos in a particular musical context. It was to unleash the creativity that you already had inside, which you can then channel into Improvisation, yes—but also Songwriting and composing, playing with Expression, enabling spellbinding Performance, and feeding into every aspect of your music-making in future.

Whatever your Musical Core and Big Picture Vision look like, I hope this has helped make sure that creativity is in there somewhere, by getting you in touch with your personal taste and natural creative instinct, and helping you to feel and be empowered to express your own wonderful musical ideas throughout everything you do.

CHAPTER SIXTEEN: SONGWRITING

Note: This chapter is entitled "Songwriting" and we'll be discussing "writing a song" rather than "composing a piece" only because songs have the additional element of lyrics. What you'll learn in this chapter will serve you equally well if you want to compose instrumental music (whether that's classical symphonies or electronic dance music), and the word "song" can mean "anything with lyrics"—not just mainstream pop/rock/folk music but any other genre, a capella music, operas and more. So as we continue, please take mentions of "songs" to generally mean "pieces" too, and "songwriting" to encompass the whole art of writing music.

————

"Without John Williams, bikes don't really fly, nor do brooms in
Quidditch matches, nor do men in red capes. There is no Force,
dinosaurs do not walk the Earth. We do not wonder, we do not
weep, we do not believe. [John] breathes belief into every film we

have made."

— Steven Spielberg

I can still remember the first song I ever wrote. A folks-y guitar ballad entitled "The Land of Milk and Honey". Like most teenage compositions, the memory of it makes me cringe a little now. But at the time I was really proud to listen back to my demo recording on my minidisc player on the way to school, and even to nervously share what I'd created with a friend. The fact that I can still remember the melody and lyrics 25 years later speaks to the deep, personal impact that writing music can have on us.

I went on to write other songs, including a 3-track EP of love songs for my then-girlfriend, now wife, Natalina, and do extensive electronic music creation using Digital Audio Workstation (DAW) software over the years, purely for my own enjoyment and creative expression. And although my own Creative Core swings more towards improvisation than writing music, every minute of the time and drop of the energy I've spent in creating my own music compositions has proven to be a wonderful investment in my musicality.

I've seen this repeatedly over the years inside Musical U. So many of our members came in never having aspired to write songs, or compose or arrange their own music. Then, through the way these activities featured in our other material, they discovered just how valuable and rewarding writing music can be.

For those who do already have a clear interest in writing music, it may be interesting to know that many of the blockers, obstacles and frustrations aspiring songwriters and composers face—for example writer's block, struggling to finish their works, feeling like writing something truly unique and your own is a deeply mysterious task— are all deeply related to one, perhaps surprising, fact:

Just like musicians in general, there are actually very few songwriters and composers who have actively, intentionally, spent time on musicality training.

If you look at songwriting books, courses and tutorials, they are typically either extremely heavy on the intellectual side (step-by-step processes, rules, formulas, and music theory), or very heavy on the mysterious-inspiration (*"write when you're inspired!"*, *"the melody will just come to you out of nowhere!"*, *"nobody can explain 'the muse'!"*, etc.). There's normally a real lack of tools, frameworks, or building blocks for music-making itself.

The result is similar to the extreme focus on Hands in the context of instrument learning: the musician is taught to "go through the motions" and can have some success... But they are often left feeling like they're fumbling in the dark and leaving a lot to luck—rather than basing everything on a firm, integrated, holistic musicality which allows them to be *Musical Inside and Out.*

In this chapter we'll approach Songwriting from the perspective that it's simply one of the many natural ways for a musician to express their own musicality. Yes, there are certainly specific things to learn, norms to be aware of, processes that can help, and so on. But for a musician with great musicality to write their own music is ultimately a simple thing.

The generations of renowned songwriters and composers who produced great works without having formally studied "songwriting" or "composing" attests to that. The Beatles example, already shared in *Chapter One: Musicality.* Bob Dylan, who made it to the Songwriters Hall of Fame without ever learning to read sheet music, or Dolly Parton, who to this day has never learned how to. Irving Berlin, who for most of his songwriting career only composed in the key of $F\sharp$—because he was only comfortable playing the black keys of the piano keyboard! And even global phenomenon Taylor Swift, who has said she couldn't have majored in music because *"when music becomes technical for me, I don't like that part of it."*

To put that another way: this chapter isn't designed to replace the considerable amount of excellent "how to write songs" material that's out there, but rather to:

A.   Provide an easy, rewarding route in for musicians who are actively developing their musicality, and

B.   Fill in the "musicality" side of things, which will complement and enhance all the more technical and theory-based material that's out there.

If you have jumped straight to this chapter first, then the approach that's shared will certainly be usable and useful to you, but please note that it's designed to be part of a holistic approach to musicality, drawing particularly on the building blocks for Pitch and Rhythm in Part II, and the Expansive Creativity framework from *Chapter Fifteen: Improvisation.* If you've been through those chapters and spent some time developing your musicality in those areas, you will find that the approach presented here allows you to easily, confidently and freely start writing songs which are musically satisfying and meaningful to you.

> ### Mark Says...
>
> *It's probably something I've underappreciated in my own journey: I started writing songs (first lyrics to band-mates' music, and then my own harmony, melody, and lyrics) quite early in my musical journey.*
>
> *I never thought about how that would influence my overall musicality, and sometimes I felt almost guilty for "just fooling around" with songwriting instead of "woodshedding" on the guitar—but just couldn't help it!*

Overview

In this chapter we'll give an overview of the Songwriting approach we recommend, and introduce several key mindsets which can free you up creatively and help you avoid common pitfalls.

We'll then tackle five elements of a song in turn: Form, Ideas and Emotion, Lyrics, Melody, and Harmonisation/Arrangement. We'll explain how to approach writing each, and how they are inter-related and can be combined.

We will draw on the building blocks for Pitch and Rhythm from Part II and the Expansive Creativity framework from *Chapter Fifteen: Improvisation,* but you needn't necessarily have explored those yet to have success with this chapter.

Finally, we'll finish with some guidance on how to practice Songwriting using the approach presented here.

How To Write A Song

In our Songwriting material inside Musical U we teach a couple of different step-by-step approaches to writing a song. Here, we'll leave the exact 1-2-3 sequence fuzzy. Some musicians will want to start with an idea, emotions, and lyrics—and set their lyrics to music after, figuring out the form as they go. Others may prefer to start with the form and a musical idea, and see how the music inspires emotion and lyrics. And many experienced and successful songwriters and composers would tell you that their own sequencing of tackling each element varies from song to song.

So you can think of what's presented in this chapter as a set of techniques and ways to approach each element of writing a song, and use your own inspiration and preference to draw on each at the best time, and in the order which seems best to you. To put it another way: there's no wrong way to write a song!

As always, our approach will be informed by the H4 Model of Complete Musicality:

- Head: understanding the relevant theory, thinking up ideas for lyrics, planning your next songwriting session, etc.

- Hearing: using Audiation and Singing, leveraging Ear Training and its building blocks, etc.

- Hands: experimenting with ideas, arranging using instruments, expressing demo versions of a work-in-progress or recording the finished version, etc.

- Heart: connecting with emotion, intuition, inspiration, creative choices, aesthetic judgement, etc.

We encourage a Singing-based approach, because it's the most direct way to express your musical ideas, and helps to distinguish the idea itself from the particular way it's expressed on a specific instrument. You don't need any ability more advanced than what's covered in *Chapter Four: Singing* to make full use of singing in your Songwriting.

We will make use of the Expansive Creativity framework (*Chapter Fifteen: Improvisation*), especially the techniques of Constraints and Dimensions, and Playgrounds. These provide an ideal way to gradually develop your Songwriting chops while eliminating "writer's block" or the need to "wait for inspiration to strike". You can make use of this chapter without having read that one, but it's well worth being aware of the whole framework and activities covered there.

We will use Improvisation for easy idea generation, experimentation, and exploration. Again, that dedicated chapter isn't a strict prerequisite, we'll explain as we go—but the more you practice Improvisation in its own right, the more useful it will be to you in Songwriting.

Any experience and ability you have with the building blocks of Part II will be hugely useful for you. Even just the intellectual understanding from reading through those chapters will give you a much clearer perspective on how to tackle Pitch and Rhythm in your writing. And if you are actively working on Ear Training to develop the ability to recognise and express those building blocks instinctively, it will be transformative for your writing.

Arguably there's no better way to learn how to write songs than by studying songs you love and admire. So the "listen with a question in mind" approach in *Chapter Five: Active Listening* will be a great asset to you. When Benny Romalis of *How To Write Songs* presented a masterclass for us at Musical U he described this as taking a "car mechanic's" approach: by dissecting and analysing popular songs or those we personally prefer (i.e. taking songs apart, like a mechanic takes apart an engine), we can discover the best elements and techniques to construct our own songs from. We'll learn as much about Songwriting in this chapter by listening as we will by writing!

The Songwriter's Mindset

As we touched on in the introduction to this chapter, Songwriting is a deeply personal thing. Not only is your own taste and aesthetic judgement crucial, at its best Songwriting means expressing the emotions and ideas that are most significant and personal to you as an individual.

This means that it is particularly important to be mindful of the Heart: all the emotional and psychological aspects of taking on this task, both the positive and the challenging.

Remember the Pillar Belief of *Enjoying the Journey* (*Chapter Two: Mindset*) and the principle that "creativity is the vehicle, not the destination". Even if your Big Picture Vision has you writing incredible songs that blow people away and stand the test of time as classics, you will have the most success if you focus primarily on enjoying the experience of expressing your own creativity. Try to see the final songs which emerge as a happy byproduct of time spent delighting purely in the experience of creating.

> **Andy Says...**
>
> *Many of my songwriting students have found it helpful to focus on "process" rather than "outcome".*
>
> *Your songwriting process is within your control, and something you can improve over time. By focusing on the process, it takes the pressure off. Not only is it more enjoyable —in my experience, it tends to produce better outcomes, too!*

Put Your Inner Critic On Hold

One of the biggest tips I can give you is to very intentionally fire your "Inner Critic". That voice in your head that tells you *"it's no good"*, *"that sounds rubbish"*, *"you never come up with anything worth listening to"*, or whatever other negative, judgemental, or discouraging thoughts pop into your head.

The trick is to not try to argue with it, or even to suppress those thoughts by brute force. Instead, we acknowledge that this voice exists and that it has things to say—and we invite it to wait its turn.

During the act of creating, we want to turn off that "inner editor" entirely. Self-critique has its place, but just like a literary writer must write before an editor can edit, we must allow ourselves the free creative space to come up with ideas and capture them, quite separate from any critique, editing, or judgement.

Our members have found this a really helpful mindset principle: to not fight against that Inner Critic, but to simply put it aside "for now", making a promise to listen to it later on. And that's a promise you have my full permission to break ;)

We'll discuss this more in *Chapter Eighteen: Performance.*

Make It A Habit

A common piece of advice is to make writing a habit, and that's very good advice indeed. Like anything related to musicality, you do need to "put in the reps" to improve. Not mindlessly, and not allowing it to become a dreaded burden. But forming a habit of writing something every day, for example, will do wonders for how creative you are in your writing and how easy you find it to write music you're happy with.

If you take the approach presented here, you'll find there's always something interesting to do next with your Songwriting, and (just like with Ear Training) "a little and often" tends to work best.

Share Your Creations

One of the most challenging Heart aspects of Songwriting is sharing your music with others. We'll talk about this more in *Chapter Eighteen: Performance,* but just know that it's perfectly normal to be shy and nervous to share what you've written. But the strong emotion there also points to the enormous power in learning to do so!

One of the most impactful books I read in my 20s was "Feel The Fear And Do It Anyway" by Susan Jeffers. The big takeaway was that fear isn't an indicator to avoid something—it's most often a good indicator that that's the direction we need to move in, if we're to grow and improve—and that rather than try to eliminate fear, we simply need to practice being okay with doing something *through* the fear.

So if Songwriting is new to you, or you haven't been comfortable sharing what you wrote in the past, try to start being more willing to share your creations with others.

It is important to be thoughtful about who you choose to share with. One of the parts of Musical U that I'm most proud of is how friendly and supportive the community is, and whether it's there, or with trusted friends, or some other group of people you can rely on to encourage rather than tear down what you share, make it a priority to find a way to share what you write.

Not only can this be huge for motivation and provide objective feedback on what you've created, ultimately music is a social artform and if we're not sharing our music, we're missing out. Although it may seem like this would flip your Inner Critic into overdrive, with the right person it can actually help you to "get out of your head" and move forwards.

Stewart Says...

Having been in bands and collaborated with folks for many years now, I have found some that I really connect with in terms of writing and sharing things.

I tend to have a musical picture in my head which I am trying to paint with the guitar and more. If I feel like I am in a "satisfied" state with it, I will share it—even if it is part of a work in progress.

When I find folks I really have chemistry with, I tend to stick with them. The back-and-forth you have as you put music together can be an amazing experience.

You may even consider collaborating with other musicians. This can be enormously rewarding, not just for motivation and to reduce musical loneliness, but also to make writing easier for you. If some of the elements we cover in this chapter feel "easy" for you while others are intimidating or challenging, you may turn out to be the mirror image of another musician you know, who would love to partner up. In the immortal words of Captain Planet, *"Let your powers combine!"*

Andy Says...

One easy and light way to collaborate is by trying some of the exercises in this chapter at the same time as a friend, and comparing results.

You could do this in person or remotely (online).

It's a particularly great fit for the time-restricted exercises ("write a song in 10 minutes!") which lend themselves to being treated as a fun game or challenge.

Document The Process

With Songwriting we generally have in mind the end product we're aiming for, i.e. a song, or other piece of "finished" music. But our desire to have that end product be the best it can be often actually sabotages us, by making us resistant or unwilling to document things that feel far from "good enough" yet.

However there's no doubt that the more you document the process, the easier it will be to get to a final result you're happy with. That means jotting down lyric ideas, making notes on what you worked on each day, recording little sung melody fragments, or even recording very rough takes of very early, half-finished songs.

Try to be organised. For example, if you're keeping notes digitally, come up with a naming convention for files and/or a structure of folders to use consistently. This makes it much easier to return to earlier ideas and keep track of what stage different projects are at.

This point ties in with sharing and collaborating (don't be afraid to share early drafts and ideas) and with making it a habit (because with a stash of notes, recordings and ideas, there will always be something to work on next).

Zac Says...

If you're unsure where to start with songwriting, establishing a system for capturing ideas can be a powerful first step.

Then you just live your life and every time you come up with ideas, capture them immediately. I call this my "C minor" approach, or "CMIN" which means: Capture Musical Ideas Now.

Any time a bell goes off in my head, and an idea excites me, I capture the idea immediately.

As a default I will use the date and location I came up with the idea in the name. for example, "Verse idea March 25th sitting by the lake"

Don't Put Songwriting In A Box

Like we said at the outset, what's presented here is an approach to Songwriting which is designed to be part of your overall holistic musical development i.e. your musicality.

So don't treat Songwriting as an activity separate from other things you might be working on. You can "mine for diamonds" in your Improvisation practice, you can find inspiration and greater understanding through your Active Listening, you can let Creative Superlearning spawn new musical creations out of pieces you're working on, and so on.

The more you allow Songwriting activities to flow into and out of your other music-making, the faster you'll improve and the richer your creativity will become.

Adopt The Identity

In the Introduction to this book, we said that anybody who makes music is "a musician". In the same way, I would encourage you right now, whatever your past experience might be, to start considering yourself "a songwriter" (or if you prefer, "a composer").

You may not have written anything yet. You may not yet think you know the first thing about writing music. Or you may think you're just not any good at it yet.

Adopting the identity today allows you to start seeing it as a journey, and start respecting and appreciating each step forwards you take towards becoming the songwriter or composer you wish to be.

So that begs the question then: how do you take those steps forwards? How do we learn to write songs we can be proud of?

We're going to go through each of five elements of a song (Form, Ideas and Emotion, Lyrics, Melody, and Harmonisation and Arrangement), providing ways for you to create each, and then discuss how to bring it all together and practice writing songs.

TIP:

Adopting the identity of "songwriter" is powerful—but there's an important caveat: You are not your songs!

Andy Says...

We have to be aware that our songs/creations are not us. A rubbish song does not equate to being a rubbish person. This can be rather difficult for some... Being more unattached and childlike about it can help.

Andrew Says...

Identification of the musical product with the producer is a core problem, and one of the reasons so many are terrified of sharing their music and "being judged". It's corroborated by the common way of speaking about musicians as "good"or "bad", e.g. "He's really good", "so-and-so is better than her" etc. As if our musical production was an outgrowth of our morality!

Almut Says...

Keep in mind that not everything can be great. We learn. We improve. And even great composers often had others to bounce ideas off and to collaborate on songs. It is a process and hardly ever finished. I went to a Bob Dylan concert a few years ago and he played one of his earlier songs in a completely new version—everything but the lyrics had changed! While as a listener I would have loved to hear this familiar old version, I understand that songs do change and that this is fine.

So as you adopt the identity of being a songwriter or composer, remember not to attach your own self-worth to your musical output. The approach presented here will help you to instead focus on the joyful process of creating.

1. Form

We call the overall structure of a piece of music its "Form". We'll start here because it's the big-picture view which the other elements exist within, but remember: that doesn't necessarily mean you must decide the Form before tackling any of the other elements.

You can think of Form as the blueprint or skeleton of a song or piece. We'll give an overview here with some specifics for songs, but you may also want to refer to *Chapter Five: Active Listening*.

Form consists of a series of sections. Each section is defined by some noticeable change. This could be in the lyrics, the melody, the arrangement, or any other aspect, and often some combination. In written music notation, sections are often clearly marked, but if you're identifying sections purely by listening (or when creating them yourself) it can be open to interpretation exactly what the sections are.

Form also exists at different levels of scale. For example a song might have a clear sequence of verses and choruses, but within each verse you could also analyse the form of the lyrics in terms of their rhyme scheme. Larger orchestral works might have a series of "movements", each with its own main sections lasting for a few minutes each, and within those sections the pattern of phrases might reveal its own structure.

So Form is a very versatile term, simply meaning "the structure or patterns in music".

Our main focus here will be on the top-level organising structure, for example how a song breaks down into verses and choruses, or a jazz standard has an "A section" and a "B section".

We put particular labels on the different sections, which help us to see the commonalities and differences, and how everything fits together. For the examples just given, we would expect that the "verse" sections had a very similar melody to each other but different words, while the "chorus" sections had the same melody each time (probably a catchy, memorable one!) and the same words each time. Similarly all the instances of the "A section" of a jazz standard would be almost identical, while any section we label "B" would be noticeably different to the "A" section and similar to each other.

There are many conventional words used as labels, like "verse", "chorus", "movement" already mentioned. The principle that *"a rose by any other name would smell as sweet"* applies (i.e. it doesn't fundamentally matter what labels you use). But like with the Ear Training building blocks from Part II, using standard shared terminology helps keep things clear and consistent, and helps us to communicate with other musicians.

Common Song Forms

The particular types of song section used, and the labels put on them, vary across different styles and genres. Let's look at some of the most common, so that you can start listening for them and using them yourself. Do keep in mind that although often the sections and their types are clear, these terms can also overlap and be debatable!

The most commonly-used and well-known types of section in Song Form are:

- **Chorus**: A section which is repeated multiple times in the song. The melody and lyrics will be the same each time, or have only small variations. This is often the most defining or memorable part of the song, typically used to communicate the main message and emotion of the song. Also commonly known as the "refrain", though that term can also be used to mean a shorter melodic phrase, such as a particular line of the chorus.

- **Verse**: A section which has the same melody but different lyrics each time. Typically used to tell the "story", with each verse playing a different part in that story-telling.

- **Bridge**: A section which is noticeably different from both the chorus and the melody, often appearing just once. The bridge is typically used to add interest amid a pattern of alternating verses and choruses. A "middle eight" is a particular kind of bridge consisting of eight measures, close to the middle of the song's overall form.

Then there are several other common types of section, including:

- **Intro**: The introduction to the song. This can be of very varied lengths, from no introduction at all through to multiple minutes. It is often instrumental, leading up to the first verse or chorus where a vocal part enters.

- **Outro**: The ending of the song. Again this can be non-existent, with the song ending with some other type of section (e.g. the final verse, or a final solo), or of any length. It's common for a song to "fade out", with another section continuing but gradually reducing in volume, so that the "outro" is a variant of a prior section rather than being something musically unique.

- **Solo**: A section where a different instrument takes the prominent lead part. Typically this is an instrument taking the place of vocals, but it could also be a vocal solo (e.g. jazz scatting). This usually has its own distinct melody which isn't repeated elsewhere, though can also build off a riff or hook from elsewhere in the song.

- **Pre-chorus**: A section occurring before the chorus, typically shorter, and used to increase the musical effect of the chorus. Can often be labelled a "bridge" instead, as it "bridges" from a verse to a chorus, for example.

- **Post-chorus**: A section occurring after the chorus, typically similar musically to the chorus but distinct. If a chorus seems to have two distinct parts to it, often the second part can be seen as a post-chorus instead.

- **Hook**: The term "hook" refers to a catchy phrase which "hooks" the listener. Although it can be a section in its own right, distinct from the chorus, it can also just be an element (often melodic) such as a prominent guitar riff or a vocal phrase which appears as part of another section.

You can think of these all as "ingredients" for creating your song's form. None are better or worse than the others. They all serve a particular purpose, and your own taste can guide if and how you choose to use them.

How To Recognise Form

The best way to start understanding and appreciating Form is by analysing existing music.

EXERCISE: Labelling Sections

1. Select a song or short piece of music that you're familiar with

2. Listen through, noting the prominent changes in each section. Use the principle from *Chapter Five: Active Listening* of listening for when some aspect of the music (Pitch, Rhythm, Dynamics, Timbre, Texture, lyrics) changes significantly. You might like to jot down the time at which each occurs, and a few words

describing the change.

3. Write down a series of letter labels to show which sections seem to be the same type and which are different. For example if you hear one type of section, then a different type, then it returns to the first type you would write "A B A". If a third type of section appeared you would label it "C", and so on. Listen through as many times as you need to, to feel like you've captured it well.

4. Once you have your letter-name form written down, consider which of the terms above best suits each—if any!

For example, you might first write down the start time of each section you heard, and label them as:

A B C B C C D

You might then decide that A = "Intro", D = "Outro", and based on the lyrics being the same or different, B = "Verse" and C = "Chorus". You could then write the form as:

Intro, Verse, Chorus, Verse, Chorus, Chorus, Outro

Repeat this with a few familiar songs in different styles.

Since Form is the overall structure, it's not particularly interesting or meaningful to create or write Form in isolation. Instead, as you continue through all the other song elements which follow, you can try incorporating Form into what you write. For example, in the lyric exercises below, you could aim to write a chorus and three verses.

We mentioned above that Form also exists within sections. Let's explore this through the same kind of analysis.

EXERCISE: Labelling Form Within A Section

1. Select a song you're familiar with (i.e. something with lyrics)

2. Write down the overall Form using the previous exercise.

3. Pick one section which features lyrics, and listen through to just that section. Write down the structure using letter names,

based on the same "repetition vs. change" principle. For example, a verse may feature different lyrics for every line but the same melody three times before a variation for the fourth line. You could write this as "A A A B". Or a chorus may consist of the same lyrics repeated four times, but with two different melodies alternating. You could write this as "A B A B". Rhyme can be a big factor here, something we'll discuss more below in the section on lyrics. If there is a slight variation rather than something completely different you can use an apostrophe after the same letter name e.g. A' for a small variation on the A phrase.

Again, this is a concept you can take with you as you try creating the other elements which follow. For example with the melody exercises, you can begin by deciding to write an AAAB melody for a chorus, which repeats the same 2-measure phrase three times before wrapping up with a new 2-measure phrase.

Andrew Says...

In my experience teaching songwriting, Form is hands-down the most powerful lever.

Oftentimes, beginning songwriters might have one or two musical ideas and then they get stuck. Form gives you a path to build the rest of the song from that initial inspiration.

(Side note: I like the idea of "building" a song rather than "writing" a song because it highlights the importance of structure and Form.)

The most awesome thing about Form, and which blows away beginning songwriters, is that, e.g. you don't have to write the whole song from beginning to end—you can write ONE chorus, ONE verse, both of which are usually quite short sections—and then it's much easier to plug everything else in.

2. Ideas/Emotion

No-one could doubt that the underlying ideas and emotions of a song or piece are crucial to how musically-compelling and effective it is. And yet these things are often discussed only in passing, as part of learning to write music or lyrics.

With the greater attention to Heart which we aim for with the H4 Model, we want to make sure we're actively paying attention specifically to these elements in our music-making.

So rather than sitting down to write some lyrics and hoping some interesting ideas will emerge, or working on a melody and wondering how to make it more emotionally impactful, we can instead explore the ideas and emotions of our writing as an element in their own right. When we do this, we have a much clearer intention when working on the other elements and can create music and lyrics which are true to that intent.

Again, that's not to say you ought to do this first, necessarily, nor that it needs to be a strict sequential step done before or after the other elements. Just that it's an element which runs through everything else, and we can intentionally develop our skills with creativity on this element specifically. It's interesting to start noticing how the same idea or same emotion can be expressed in so many ways in music.

The idea is to find a seed of inspiration. This could be from any of your senses (sight, sound, touch, taste, smell), an experience you have, an emotion you feel, or anything else from your life. Anything which catches your attention can serve as a starting point for writing.

Be on the lookout for potential "diamonds". These could be words or phrases you hear or speak, something visual you find remarkable, fragments of music which resonate with you (other people's or from your own Improvisation, Active Listening, or Expression practice, for example). They may currently be unpolished gems, still a bit buried in coal—but you see a spark that catches your attention. These diamonds can be incorporated directly, or used as a "seed" for exploration.

Remember to document what you find! You may not be working on a song or piece where a given seed or diamond fits right now, but if you capture it in some way, you may well find the perfect use for it later on. And simply by setting your brain the task to be on the lookout for interesting ideas and emotions, you'll open up your creative imagination significantly.

Zac Says...

I believe there are no bad musical ideas, you just have to find a fitting context.

For my song "Party Life" that I released last year, I needed another verse. I went through my old ideas and found a verse I had mostly written about 15 years ago.

I was able to tweak a few words and the verse fit perfectly in my song! I was so grateful to myself for saving all my ideas.

Almut Says...

I keep a note file on my phone and add interesting words, impressions, combinations of words or descriptions of feelings to come back to.

It is often when I am travelling that I see a sign with an interesting word, or I overhear a conversation I can derive an idea from. Reading is another great source of inspiration.

I find it easier to find my way back to those feelings or ideas that I have written down than to generate them on the spot when I am looking for inspiration.

How to Write With Clear Ideas and Emotions

We will explore coming up with ideas more when discussing lyrics below, and expressing emotion much more in *Chapter Seventeen: Expression*. For now, let's start becoming more aware of the ideas and emotions at play in music.

EXERCISE: Analyse Ideas and Emotions

1. Select a song that you're familiar with.

2. Listen through, and write down the "big ideas" which come across in the lyrics. This could be, for example, *"teen romance, heartbreak, destiny vs. random chance, finding solace in family"*, or *"it's time for a revolution, everyone's against us, we fight even though we may not win"*.

3.   Listen again, this time writing down the main emotions you hear in the lyrics and music. For example *"love, hope, disappointment, sorrow"*, or *"anger, frustration, determination."*

4.   You can take this a step further by combining with Form analysis, and writing down the main ideas and emotions in each section. This is a great way to start becoming more aware of the musical purpose each section serves in the song.

5.   Repeat with another song. You might like to choose another song from the same artist or genre, and then one which seems very different. What do you notice about similarities and differences in the ideas and emotions?

EXERCISE: Start Documenting

•   Begin writing down or recording the day-to-day life experiences which catch your attention or seem to spark some creative inspiration in you. Start paying attention to the things which resonate with you most. This will help you tune in to your own taste, and the ideas and emotions you might want to bring into your own Songwriting.

Like with Form, ideas and emotions run through all the other song elements, so bring this perspective with you as you continue through the following sections and exercises below.

3. Lyrics

Debates have raged through the ages over what matters more in a song: the words or the music? It even inspired a Hugh Grant movie![1] With some songs we tend to remember the tune but may struggle to remember the words, while in other cases the lyrics can stand alone as

---

[1] Music and Lyrics (2007)

great works of poetry, regardless of the melody they are set to.

One thing is for sure: the combined effect of words and music together is unlike anything else in the world of art, and I would argue has the power to move us as humans more than any other artform.

Music itself operates in the world of emotion, something we'll explore more in *Chapter Seventeen: Expression*. Words can certainly also elicit emotions, but also bring intellectual ideas into play. That can be story-telling, it can be reasoning and argument, it can be jokes, or sharing life lessons learned.

It's easy to see how the combination of evoking emotions and ideas has such power, when so much of our inner experience as humans boils down to thoughts and emotions. We'll explore the musical side in the following sections, and of course there is (or generally should be) great interplay between the music and words, but for now let's set our focus on the words alone, which in the context of a song we call *lyrics*.

There's a great deal we can learn here from poetry—about word choice, rhyme schemes, Form, story-telling, and more. At the same time, we don't want to fall into the trap which many aspiring writers do, of writing endless words like a poet, and then eventually getting around to "setting them to music" (or not). As a musician interested in developing their musicality, you will find it far easier and more rewarding to explore the two together.

Andrew Says...

Compared with our musical development, we are all stunning virtuosos with language, having practiced it from soon after birth.

As we'll explore in Chapter Seventeen: Expression, language shares so many qualities with music—including rhythm, timbre, pitch, emotion, improvisation, and more.

When we take on combining lyrics with melody, we are leveraging this virtuosity to come up with musical ideas that may go way beyond our current capacity to conceive in musical terms.

How to Write Lyrics

We all write words every day, even if it's just a text message or email to a friend. So why does "writing lyrics" feel so intimidating to most musicians and aspiring songwriters?

I would suggest it's two things:

1. There is a difference between writing prose and writing poetry, and lyrics are typically much more like poetry. Prose is written in a simple, straight-forward manner, primarily for the sake of clearly communicating ideas. Poetry typically employs rhyme, rhythm, line breaks and paragraph breaks, as well as much more imaginative, evocative, richly descriptive wording. And if producing an emotional response isn't the primary purpose, it's at least right up there alongside communicating ideas.

2. Lyrics are a creative artform, more akin to writing fiction than writing an email, and we place a much greater importance on how elegant, refined, and beautiful the end product is, compared to day-to-day writing. This creates a perceived pressure to make it "good enough"—which most of us don't experience when dashing off a quick message to a friend!

If we want writing lyrics to feel as easy and natural as the more mundane writing abilities we all take for granted, we need to address these two points: writing more poetically, and overcoming perfectionism.

Let's tackle perfectionism first, since it can otherwise be like trying to drive with one foot on the gas and the other on the brakes.

Overcoming Perfectionism

If writing lyrics feels big, scary or hard to you, or if you've been too nervous to even try, or if you've written some lyrics before and felt disappointed and discouraged, the chances are high that some form of perfectionism is holding you back. That doesn't mean that you're consciously thinking *"this needs to be perfect or it's not worth trying"*—but rather that *subconsciously* your thoughts and emotions are sending you that signal.

We've already discussed putting your Inner Critic "on hold", and that's a big part of avoiding perfectionism and letting you move forwards more smoothly with creative activities.

But there's another huge mindset shift which can liberate you, which is to remove all expectations about how the thing you're creating will turn out.

There's a traditional name for this idea among writers, which for the sake of propriety I'll paraphrase! They call it writing "a rubbish first draft".

I can't tell you the number of creative projects I've procrastinated on, until I finally faced up to the fact that it was perfectionism holding me back, making me feel intimidated and overwhelmed about even starting. To then take a step forwards with a mindset of *"it's gonna be rubbish to begin with, and I probably won't even finish a draft, but let's bash something out"* is an astonishingly reliable way to get into momentum. Often you find that what you come up with is better than you thought it would be, you get further than you expected to, and (most importantly) you now have something to work with, which is always easier than sitting down with a blank sheet.

Some related ideas which may resonate with you and help eliminate perfectionism are:

- *"Done is better than perfect."*
- *"You have to go through a lot of bad ideas to get to the good ones."*
- *"Nobody's going to see this but me, and I know I'm just practicing right now."*
- *"All the greatest songwriters have stacks of notebooks filled with lyrics that never made it into songs, but led to the ones which did."*

Zac Says...

I've had Next Level clients have a lot of fun and unlock more progress by writing a bad, or dumb, song on purpose. I like to even have dumb song competitions.

Writing bad songs on purpose always makes people laugh, and it's surprising how often something exciting and usable comes out of it. For example, the lyrics may have been really stupid but actually the melody was really cool.

There's also one specific technique which has proven invaluable to songwriters through the ages, as well as being my own #1 go-to tool for being productively creative.

Some people call it "stream of consciousness" writing. I learned it as "free-writing",[2] which has a slightly more defined process, so that's what we'll call it here.

It's incredibly simple. It does take some practice. But if you've never tried it before, you'll be amazed by how effective it is for unleashing creative ideas, right from the outset. I've had many people tell me after I shared it with them that it was life-changing—either for curing their "writer's block", or actually for their emotional well-being, when applied to more therapeutic or introspective purposes.

EXERCISE: Free-Writing

1. Select a topic or writing task. This could be anything from *"let's braindump all the chores and errands which are clogging up my brain"* to *"let's try to discover why I have such resistance to writing songs"*, using a random word or random topic generator online, or any of the lyric-writing exercises below. Write this down as a one-sentence "prompt" to focus on.

2. Set a timer for a certain number of minutes. If you're just starting out, try 3 minutes. I've found that 5+ minutes, ideally more like 10-15, is what really allows the unexpected thoughts and ideas to emerge.

3. Start the timer and start writing. There's just one rule: you can't stop writing until the timer goes off! That means you don't write a sentence and then pause to think about it before writing the next one, and you don't go back to improve wording or correct typos. You must. Just. Keep. Writing.

4. When the timer goes off, you can stop writing. If you're on a roll, you're welcome to continue though.

You'll quickly discover three things!

Firstly, that you end up typing a lot of babble and gibberish along the way. With the *"why do I have resistance to writing songs?"* example prompt above, it might look something like:

---

[2] I learned this from the book *Accidental Genius* by Mark Levy, which I would highly recommend.

"Okay, so why am I resisting writing lyrics well Iknow that it's a bit big and scary and I want my songs to be really good but what else what else well I think when I listen to songs and love the lyrics I wonder how did they ever do that like Bob Dylanor Joni Mitchel it's like how couldI ever be so creative but I know that's a limiting belief and maybe if I could overcome that then it would help but I don't' really know how and what else what is it what could I do about that well I could..."

No doubt you can see why some describe this as "stream of consciousness" writing!

The second thing you'll notice is that by not allowing any pauses, your Inner Critic doesn't have a chance to butt in. This is one thing which gives free-writing its power: it's a highly effective way to prevent yourself from wanting to "edit" or judge what you're writing, and so silence that Inner Critic.

The third thing is that, depending on how long you've set the timer for, you may quickly run out of things to write. *Don't stop!* This is the other part of the power of free-writing: it forces you to go beyond the obvious, and uncover ideas and thoughts from your subconscious mind or creative instinct, which you'd never have reached if you stopped too soon.

This can be uncomfortable at first, so let me just share that I've had countless free-writing sessions where multiple minutes of gibberish and tangents had to pass before I tapped into something unexpected. Then suddenly a whole new world of ideas and possibilities opened up. So be strict with yourself about writing until that timer goes off!

Only after the timer goes off are you allowed to read back over what you wrote. The wonderful thing is that because there's likely a lot of gibberish and filler in there, you can't possibly be too judgemental about what you wrote! But you *can* look for the (unpolished) diamonds. What emerged that's worth coming back to, exploring more, or refining further?

Try this now, using anything you've felt stuck on. And then I would encourage you to give it a try with any of the writing exercises below.

From Prose to Poetry

We know we can "write words", but that "writing lyrics" is going to take something more. Let's extend our existing ability to string words together in a more poetic direction.

We've already identified a few ways that poetry or lyrics are different from everyday writing or prose. Let's go through them and see how we can start to make our writing more poetic. We'll go through them one-by-one, but naturally in practice they all work together.

Remember to bring your Heart and Hearing into play as you go through the exercises, paying attention to your own taste and what you hear, not just intellectually following the steps and thinking in terms of "right" and "wrong" (Head).

Internal Form

In writing prose, we structure our words into sentences, sentences into paragraphs, and perhaps paragraphs into headed sections. We are strict about the rules of punctuation and grammar. In poetry we structure our words into lines, lines into *stanzas*, and we are much more relaxed and flexible about grammar, bending rules where it suits our creative intentions.

With lyrics, we can think of each stanza as corresponding to a section of the Form, and so "Internal Form" means the structure or pattern of lines within a stanza of the lyrics. For example, you could annotate the two stanzas of "Chatter with the Angels" from the Starter Songs in *Chapter Nine: Solfa* like this:

(A) *Chatter with the angels,*
(B) *Soon in the morning.*
(A) *Chatter with the angels,*
(C) *in that land.*

(A) *Chatter with the angels,*
(B) *Soon in the morning.*
(A) *Chatter with the angels,*
(D) *join that band!*

The choice of where each line starts and ends is part of our creative expression, informed by rhythm, rhyme, and the phrasing of the melody it will be set to.

For example, the Starter Song "Frosty Weather" has four measures, but the intended phrasing of the lyrics means we would write it as two short lines and one longer line, like this:

Frosty Weather,
Snowy Weather,
When the wind blows we all go together.

Let's repeat the earlier exercise "Labelling Form Within A Section" but pay closer attention to the structure of the lyrics.

EXERCISE: Analysing Internal Form

1. Select a section of a song you're familiar with (i.e. something with lyrics)

2. Listen through just that section. Write down the lyrics.

3. Now annotate the structure of the lyrics using letter names, based on the "repetition vs. change" principle. For example, a verse may feature different lyrics for every line but the same melody three times before a variation for the fourth line. You could write this as "A A A B". Or a chorus may consist of the same lyrics repeated four times, but with two different melodies alternating. You could write this as "A B A B". If there is a slight variation rather than something completely different you can use an apostrophe after the same letter name e.g. A' for a small variation on the A phrase.

4. What do you notice about the way you naturally wrote down the lyrics, and the structure you've identified? Did you automatically put the lyrics of each phrase on their own line? Can you see any other ways to write the lyrics which would make sense (e.g. splitting the lines in two, or joining some together)?

One thing you may quickly notice is that although there are many similarities between song lyrics and poetry, lyric writers tend to be far more flexible with line lengths! While poems typically have a consistent pattern of matching line lengths in their internal form, song lyrics often vary far more. The underlying music provides a different kind of regular structure which allows for this freedom, without the listener feeling things are jumbled or disjointed, the way they might with poetry whose lines varied so much. Keep this in mind as we continue and look in more detail at the rhythmic patterns of the words in lyics.

Rhythm

When we read prose, we decide for ourselves the pacing of words, and what pauses to add between words, sentences and paragraphs. With poetry there is normally much less leeway: it is written with the intention of being read in a certain rhythmic pattern. With lyrics, this leeway is reduced even further, and while a musician might well choose to bend that[3], the lyrics are written to correspond to the melody with quite clearly-defined timing of each syllable of each word.

In poetry there's a tradition of analysing the rhythm as a pattern of long and short syllables. For example the *iambic pentameter* favoured by Shakespeare has each line as a pattern of five Short-Long syllable pairs: "dah-DUM, dah-DUM, dah-DUM, dah-DUM, dah-DUM", so that *"Two households, both alike in dignity"* was written to naturally have the rhythm *"two HOUSE-holds BOTH a-LIKE in DIG-ni-TY"*.[4]

In lyrics, you can take that same approach. But if you've been through the Part II chapters on The Beat and Rhythm, you'll be equipped with a much more versatile tool: our Rhythm Syllable building blocks! For example, the example above could be expressed as *ka-Tim ka-Tim ka-Tim ka-Tim ka-Tim*.

Let's start to explore the Rhythm of lyrics.

EXERCISE: Hearing the Rhythm in Lyrics

1.   Select a stanza of lyrics (e.g. the verse or chorus to your favourite song) and write them out.

2.   Speak them aloud, as if you'd never heard the song and were handed the lyrics as a poem.

3.   Mark the syllables you naturally emphasised, whether by duration (short versus long) or which you would naturally stress (e.g. one would naturally say "TEApot" rather than

---

[3] See *Chapter Seventeen: Expression*, on the expressive possibilities even when performing rhythms "as written".

[4] Note the actor may or may not recite the line like this! This is an example of poetry allowing more leeway than lyrics. If one performed Shakespeare strictly according to the underlying rhythmic patterns it would feel more like a poetry recital than a dramatic performance! Nevertheless, the words were written with that clear, consistent rhythmic pattern, which is part of what gives them their elegance.

"teaPOT"). Also mark where you naturally paused between phrases or lines. It may take multiple repeats of lines or the whole stanza to figure this out!

4.   Write out a fresh copy of the lyrics.

5.   Now either sing the lyrics, or audiate the song and speak the lyrics with their sung rhythm.

6.   Mark the emphasis and pauses which occurred this time.

7.   Compare the two. What do you notice about how the natural spoken rhythms correspond—or don't—to the sung rhythms?

8.   If you're familiar with rhythm syllables, you might like to try transcribing the rhythm of the sung lyrics using Rhythm Syllables and/or Stick Notation.

Once you've tried this kind of analysis once or twice, let's experiment creatively:

EXERCISE: Writing Lyrics for a Rhythm

1.   Compose a short rhythmic pattern. This can simply be a sequence of "short vs. long" or "stressed vs. unstressed" like the traditional approach in poetry, or if you're familiar with Rhythm Syllables, write a pattern of your choosing in syllables and/or Stick Notation.

2.   Now come up with words which fit that pattern—as nonsensical as you like![5]

3.   Optional: Try to write something which makes some sense as a line of lyrics, or extend to a full stanza of multiple lines following the same rhythmic pattern.

---

[5] The Beatles were fond of putting nonsensical lyrics into their songs as placeholders during the writing process. Anything which fit the rhythm was fair game! "Yesterday", one of the most famous songs of all time, began with dummy lyrics *"Scrambled eggs... Oh my baby, how I love your legs."*
Perhaps that will remove a bit of the intimidation factor of lyric-writing for you! :)

Exploring the rhythm of lyrics like this is valuable both for how cohesive and elegant it can help our lyrics to be, and as a bridge towards setting the lyrics to a melody. As we saw in the first exercise above, the words alone can indicate a suitable rhythm, which you can then use as-is, or as the basis for composing your melody's rhythm. Or vice-versa, if you've got a melodic idea with its own rhythm, you now have a way to help you better find words which fit.

Rhyme

Sticking with our Shakespearean theme, we might well ponder: *"To rhyme, or not to rhyme? That is the question."*

In poetry there are great works which rhyme, great works which don't, and even some which mix the two. In lyrics, it's very rare to make no use of rhyme at all, and in most genres there's a convention that each stanza will have a structure of how its lines rhyme (called a *rhyme scheme*).

This gives a satisfying hint to the listener about the internal form, rather than it sounding like a series of unrelated lines. It makes the song feel more cohesive, and also contributes a form of tension and release, where we as listeners are anticipating the rhyming word to close the "open loop" that's been set up.

The most common and basic is that each pair of lines will rhyme, for example in the hymn "Be thou my vision":

> *Be thou my vision, O Lord of my heart,*
>
> *be all else but naught to me, save that thou art;*
>
> *be thou my best thought in the day and the night,*
>
> *both waking and sleeping, thy presence my light.*

Another very common four-line scheme is ABCB, for example in The Mountain Goats' "This Year":

> *I broke free on a Saturday morning.*
>
> *I put the pedal to the floor.*
>
> *Headed north on Mills Avenue,*

and listened to the engine roar.

More complex rhyme schemes are also possible, for example in Lewis Carroll's poem "Jabberwocky", after four stanzas with ABAB rhyme scheme (i.e. lines one and three rhyme, lines two and four rhyme), we find:

> *One, two! One, two! And through and through*
>
> *The vorpal blade went snicker-snack!*
>
> *He left it dead, and with its head*
>
> *He went galumphing back.*

We can see the second and fourth lines rhyme (*"snack"* and *"back"*) but the first and third don't—an ABCB rhyme scheme. But there is also internal rhyme in the first line (*"two"*, *"two"*, and *"through"*).

Rhyme is certainly a matter of taste, and as always in music, bending or breaking the "rules" produces an unexpected twist which keeps listener's attention and helps make the music compelling.

There's also a middle ground: the *near-rhyme* or *slant-rhyme*, where the words have a similar sound but don't technically rhyme.

Typically this means having the same vowel sound but a different final consonant, for example *"This little piggy stayed home"* being paired with *"This little piggy had none"*.

It can also be a similar vowel and the same or similar final consonant, for example Taylor Swift's *"'Cause baby now we got bad blood. / You know it used to be mad love."* This can satisfy the listener's ear and demonstrate the internal form in the same way a true rhyme can, while allowing more creative freedom for the writer to choose just the right word.

To start tuning our Head and Hearing in to the world of rhyme, let's keep it simple and just look for possible rhymes without worrying yet about writing a whole line or whether the meaning of the word is relevant.

EXERCISE: Find Rhyming Words

Constraint: find many possible rhymes for one particular word.

1.   Select a word. This could be the final word of a line from your
     favourite song or a line you've written, or you could pick a
     word completely at random from a page of prose (like this
     one!). Example: "twist", from the section above.

2.   Brainstorm as many words as you can which rhyme with that
     word. You might like to set a timer and try a free-writing
     approach. It will probably be easy to think of some one-
     syllable words, but look for some longer words which still
     rhyme too. You can also explore near-rhymes. Example with
     "twist" as prompt: *list, gist, mist, grist... sexist, facist, nihilist...*
     furthest, blessed, bird's nest.

3.   Select another word and repeat!

Now let's try a more practical application of our rhyming imagination,
by writing our own second line for a *rhyming couplet*: two lines whose
final words rhyme with each other.

EXERCISE: Write Your Own Rhyming Couplet
Responses

1.   Select a line to be the first line of your couplet. This can be
     from a song you like, something you've written yourself, or
     one of the Starter Songs from Chapter Nine: Solfa. Example:
     "Mary had a little lamb"

2.   Write a line which rhymes and makes some sense following
     the first. Aim to have it be the same length, as measured in
     number of syllables or (jumping ahead a little to the Melody
     section below) the same number of beats. Examples:

          "This sheep was from Amsterdam."
          "Lamb was happy as a clam."
          "It got her out of many a jam."[6]

---

[6] Some creative use of rhythm required for this one, landing "got" on the first beat and
conjoining "many-a"!

> **TIP:**
>
> These often-silly rhyme exercises are great ones
> to treat as a game and play with a friend, as
> mentioned earlier in the chapter!

Emotion

The best music elicits an emotional response in the listener. Not just emotions like "happy" or "sad", but including humour (think Weird Al Yankovic, Adam Sandler, or They Might Be Giants) or the uplifting urge to dance (think electronic dance music at a rave). This can be driven by the music alone, but with a song there is also great power in the lyrics to convey and provoke emotions.

As a songwriter you can either first get clear on the emotion you want to capture, express, and evoke, or you can simply stay mindful of the emotions which arise as you explore writing lyrics. Either way, as noted in the previous section on Emotion and Ideas, having a clear, intentional, cohesive concept of the emotional content of your song will make a huge difference to the effectiveness of your songs.

In particular, we want to pay attention to emotion because it's a huge part of how we can take the listener on a journey through the course of a song. The song's Form and musical content can do this too, as is the case with purely-instrumental music—but again, songs have the added power of lyrics to shape and guide the listener's inner experience as they listen.

In the earlier exercise "Analyse Ideas and Emotions" we wrote down a description of the emotions evoked in a song, and optionally for each section of the song. Now let's take that a step further.

EXERCISE: Emotion Map

1.   Select a song, and write down (or look up) its lyrics.

2.   Thinking just about the lyrics, write down the emotions conveyed in each section.

3.   Now sketch out the emotional journey of the song. You might

like to draw something like a Pitch Contour (see Chapter Eight: Relative Pitch) showing emotions rising and falling, or a "mindmap" type diagram of how one emotion develops into another from section to section. If you can, try to write a short description of the emotional journey, for example *"The first verse begins in a state of heartbroken despair, which is then amplified in the chorus. The second verse looks back to happier times with cheerfulness and a sense of nostalgia, which then contrasts with the chorus returning to heartbreak and sorrow. The final verse hints at acceptance and a new seed of hopefulness for the future."*

As always, be on the lookout for potential diamonds! After doing this exercise a few times, choose the "emotion map" you liked best, and use it as a creative prompt:

EXERCISE: Write Lyrics for an Emotion Map

Constraint: Use a given emotion map and write your own lyrics to match.

- Using one of the emotion maps you've come up with, or the example above, try writing your own lyrics which convey that same emotional journey.

If this seems like too much of a "blank sheet" to you right now you can:

- Use the free-writing technique introduced earlier (i.e. set a timer and just braindump whatever comes out, as a first draft —or use free-writing to brainstorm the ideas which will be ingredients, such as characters, scenes, experiences).

- Add further Constraints, for example follow a particular rhyme scheme, using as few words as possible, or even using only one-syllable words! Remember our goal isn't to produce Grammy-worthy lyrics, but to exercise our lyric-writing muscles.

Almut Says...

This illustrates how you don't need to have the emotion you are writing about, to be able to write about it. You can write in any mood and don't have to wait for a particular emotion to be present in yourself.

Instead, you can set an intention and then see yourself as a spectator of this emotion, expressing it as clearly as you can.

Sometimes it is even better to not be in a difficult emotional state when writing, but to be able to reflect about the feelings. We draw on our experiences with emotions. This way, we can even imagine emotions others might have (e.g. characters in a song) and write about them without having been in the exact same situation.

Writing does not have to be autobiographical; the important thing is conveying the emotion of the experience.

Imagery

One thing which sets poetry apart from prose is its use of imagery. This can be using more romantic, evocative vocabulary, it can be literally describing visuals, it can be using analogy or metaphor instead of literal statements. The degree to which songwriters use these techniques varies. Some prefer simple, straight-forward language, and others far more abstract lyrics which only hint at the underlying story.

Whatever your personal style might turn out to be, we want to stimulate the listener into creating a "mind movie" as they listen. That might mean imagining the characters and events of your song, or recalling their own experiences which are brought to mind by your words and the emotions evoked.

You can probably think of songs which have that kind of clear visual scene associated in your memory. It's amazing how vivid those mental movies can be, inspired by a purely non-visual artform!

EXERCISE: Increase the Imagery

1.   Select a short piece of prose, for example a news article, diary

entry, or part of a work of fiction (like a short story or a novel).

2. Distil out the story as a short bullet-point list of the events which occurred. One example bullet point could be *"He bought a book."*

3. Try writing your own version, making use of one or more of the following techniques:

- Sensory writing: think about sight, smell, taste, hearing, and touch, and include lines which conjure up the experience for one or more of those senses. Our example above might become: *"He could smell the years in the pages."*

- Romantic writing: replace literal, factual words and phrases with more imaginative, evocative, poetic alternatives. Example: *"Finally he found his saviour, bound in black and white."*

- Analogy and Metaphor: Instead of saying what literally happened, use an analogy (e.g. *"Its pages shone like a lighthouse in the darkest night."*) or metaphor (*"From the Everest of irrelevance he drew his prize."*).

- Big theme: Identify and communicate the central theme of the story. This is often a good fit for the chorus, but can also be woven throughout. Think in terms of "ideas and emotions", as covered earlier (e.g. *"He held relief and salvation in his hands."*)

- Zoom In/Out: Instead of simply telling the story as a sequence of events, you can "zoom in" (going into greater detail on one moment or experience) or "zoom out" (communicating the bigger-picture story these events were part of).

- Point of View: Prose is typically written from a single, consistent point of view. For example, an external narrator, the protagonist or hero, or an observer who's also part of the story. With more poetic lyric-writing we have the opportunity to change the point of view, even verse-by-verse. Is there part of the story that would be well served by switching from first person (*"I did ..."*) to third person (*"They did..."*) or from one person's perspective to another's?

4. Once you've explored the possibilities of each of the

techniques above, try writing a version of the lyrics which uses whichever you feel fit best, according to your own taste.

Bringing It All Together

We've covered several ways you can extend your existing prose-writing skills to more poetic writing, better suited to writing lyrics. Now let's have fun bringing it all together.

EXERCISE: Write New Lyrics For An Existing Melody

Constraint: Use a given form and internal form. Optionally also use the same rhyme/rhythms and emotions/ideas.

1.   Select a song you know well.

2.   Using all the techniques covered so far, write your own lyrics for the same melody. Keep the same form, and the same inner form (line length in syllables or beats, and number of lines). You may find it easier (or harder!) to also keep the same rhyme scheme and rhythm, and/or the same ideas and emotions. To help avoid perfectionism, you may like to set a timer, and see how far you can get in, say, 10 minutes.

Now let's remove those Constraints and try writing a set of lyrics from scratch.

Starting with a blank sheet of paper can be scary! The sequence below should be helpful for you, but remember also that you need not share what you write with anybody just yet, and that setting a timer can help you accept that it's not going to be finished or perfect.

EXERCISE: Write Lyrics For A Song

1.   Select ideas and emotions for your lyrics.

2.   Use the free-writing technique to brainstorm possibilities based on those ideas and emotions. You may find words,

phrases or full lines emerging, as well as a sense of the overall story and emotional journey you wish to capture and convey.

3. Decide on the form to use (knowing that you are free to change it along the way)

4. Use the free-writing technique to draft some lyrics

5. Pin down a rhyme scheme (if any) and the rhythm (which can be just the line length in number of syllables or beats, or a specific pattern of short/long or weak/stressed syllables). Refine your lyrics to match. Free write again if needed.

6. Speak (or even sing) your lyrics. Pay attention to your Hearing and Heart response, and refine further.

7. If you feel stuck or blocked at any point, turn your attention to another section or aspect of the lyrics, or use free-writing or additional Constraints to help get your creativity flowing.

After going through this process, you might well produce something you're pleasantly surprised by! It may not feel "finished" or "good enough" yet, and that's fine. You can return to it later, or treat it as purely practice. Are there any potential diamonds you can spot— words, phrases, lines, ideas which stand out as worth hanging onto for future writing? Could you see your creativity and skills increasing with the practice?

If you've read *Chapter Six: Superlearning*, also keep in mind the "Power of Not Finishing": often if we move on, our brain will continue churning away in the background. So rather than strain away trying to "solve" the problem, release your grip. Later on, perhaps in the shower or while washing the dishes, suddenly things may well click into place.

4. Melody

The melody of a song is a series of notes which represent the main or most prominent musical part. It's "the notes of the tune of the song".

Each section type typically has its own distinct melody (e.g. the verse melody will be different to the chorus melody) but may also have none (e.g. an instrumental intro which has harmony but no clear melody).

Melody and lyrics go hand-in-hand. When it comes to writing, you can write lyrics first and then compose the melody (sometimes called "setting the words to music"). You can also start from a melody and allow it to inspire lyrics which fit. In practice you will probably go back-and-forth, adjusting the lyrics to fit the emerging melody or tweaking the melody to match the lyrics as they shape up.

We know from *Chapter Five: Active Listening* that notes have four dimensions: Pitch, Rhythm, Dynamics and Timbre. Although Dynamics and Timbre are important, they belong more to the particular performance or expression of the music, whereas Pitch and Rhythm are what define the melody itself. We'll cover these two dimensions separately below, for the sake of explanation and because tackling just one at a time can make things easier at first. In practice, and as your skills develop, you will most likely tackle the two simultaneously.

How To Write A Melody

Writing a "good" melody is often one of the most mysterious parts of Songwriting for the aspiring writer, especially for those who find that lyrics come easily but who haven't studied music very much. What's more, what constitutes "good" to one writer may not to another —or to a listener! Does "good" mean it's catchy? Easy to sing? Fits the genre conventions? Distinctive?

As a musicality-focused songwriter, you'll find that there are actually a range of building blocks and techniques you can draw on to demystify the process of composing a melody, and with our musician-centric Expansive Creativity approach, you can trust your own aesthetic taste and judgement to guide you to something you're pleased with.

Rhythm

The Rhythm of a melody is its pattern of note durations and silences. In *Chapter Thirteen: Rhythm, Chapter Fifteen: Improvisation,* and *Chapter Seventeen: Expression* we explore the power of rhythm for expressiveness and creativity. Although it's easy to get fixated on note pitches when writing a melody, the impact of its rhythm is not to be under-estimated!

In Songwriting, the melody's rhythm is very closely related to the lyrics—but, as we saw above, it is not necessarily the same as the rhythm you might naturally use when speaking the lyrics.

The major difference is that you may not assign one syllable per note. A single syllable may span multiple notes (for example, singing one syllable across the Solfa notes *mi re do*). Or a note of the melody may be held across multiple syllables. For example, "the verse melody" could have a single sustained note at the end of a line, but then have some verses placing a single syllable on that note and other verses having multiple syllables there. So we want to allow some flexibility in the correspondence between lyrics and melody, and allow the melody to exist in its own right.

When we discussed lyrics earlier, we highlighted how poetry typically allows much more leeway in rhythm than song lyrics. This comes down to the relationship between Beat and Rhythm, as covered in those Part II chapters, which boils down to: musical rhythms exist as a layer on top of an established beat. You can think of this as being a "grid" which determines the most likely placement of notes. If you paid no attention to that Beat grid when defining the rhythm of your lyrics, it would sound more like a spoken-word performance than a song. Clearly, that's a valid artistic choice! But for the most part, songwriters will compose the rhythm of their melody primarily based on the Beat and the musical rhythms which fit it.

Here are a couple of exercises which can help you tune in to the Rhythm dimension of a melody, and start exploring your own creative ideas.

EXERCISE: Clap the Rhythm of a Melody

1. Select a single line from the sung melody of a song you know well.

2. Listen to (or ideally sing) the line.

3. Clap the rhythm, by clapping once on each syllable. Then repeat, clapping once on each note. Was there a difference between the two?

An interesting example would be the B Section of "Weevily Wheat" from the Starter Songs in *Chapter Nine: Solfa*. Even though each line has similar lyrical content, the exact words produce three different rhythmic patterns.

EXERCISE: From Spoken Lyrics To Melody Rhythm

1.   Select a single line of lyrics from a song you know well.

2.   Try clapping the rhythm in each of these ways:

•   The rhythm of the line as it's sung in the song.

•   Speak the words as if reciting poetry.

•   Experiment with different ways you might naturally speak the line, and clap each back.

This exercise will help you become aware of how a melody rhythm may or may not correspond to how the lyrics would naturally be recited or spoken, and how your natural abilities with spoken language can prompt rhythmic creativity when writing a melody.

TIP:

As you experiment with these exercises, don't forget that rhythm is the pattern of notes *and silences.*

Giving a melody "room to breathe" (and your singer a chance to take a literal breath!) is a key part of writing an effective rhythm.

Sitting down to "compose a rhythm" can seem highly complex to a musician immersed in traditional notation and music theory, or one to whom notation is a mystery. We've already seen how our spoken language skills, optionally enhanced by familiarity with Rhythm Syllables, can provide a gateway into rhythmic creativity.

Let's explore that further in two ways. Firstly, by leveraging our years—or likely decades—of experience hearing music in different styles. And then by more intentionally using the building blocks from Part II.

When we invited vocal expert Jeremy Ryan-Mossman to present a masterclass at Musical U, he included a surprisingly powerful exercise for exploring and expanding your singing voice's potential. He had our members sing a few lines from a song they know well. Then he invited them to "switch off" their voice, and mime it instead. And then to do the same thing, but imagining the song in a variety of styles, one after another. For example, starting with a folk song, but then imagining (and miming) how an opera singer would perform it. What would it sound like as a country song? What about a heavy metal song? After miming each style, try singing it.

The "mime" step naturally allowed for more effusive and (dare I say) flamboyant performances! And then with voice "switched on" again, it was surprisingly easy to sing in those other styles. The whole process resulted in much freer, more expressive singing when returning to the original style, or something which had emerged as a new style that better fit your own taste.

What does all that have to do with rhythmic creativity?

Well, you've spent a lifetime absorbing musical material in a wide range of styles. Your subconscious mind has access to vast amounts of information about what different styles do rhythmically. The following exercise, based loosely on Jeremy's, will let you tap into that instinctive understanding of musical styles, and free up your own rhythmic creativity.

The exercise is best done recording yourself and listening back, but you can also just listen in-the-moment if you prefer.

EXERCISE: Exploring Stylistic Rhythm

Constraint: Sing a given melody, with the same words and note pitches.

Activity: Vary your rhythmic choices, instinctively, according to different styles.

1. Select a short segment (e.g. just one verse or chorus) of a song you know well, which you can comfortably sing.

2. Sing through the segment "as normal" i.e. in the style you're familiar with.

3.   Now, with voice "turned off", try miming singing it in a very different style. Take it from rock to opera, or from classical to funk—whatever seems a little bit crazy to you! Really exaggerate your facial expressions, mouth movements, body movements.

4.   Now with voice "on", sing it in that same style.

5.   What do you notice about the *rhythm* specifically? Most likely you sang more or less the same note pitches in your new style. How did you adjust the note durations, the spaces between notes, the accents/emphasis, the overall tempo (speed) to express the new style?

6.   Repeat with another style. After you've explored a range of styles, repeat with a segment of another song, ideally in a different original style.

With this exercise we aren't necessarily trying to learn specific lessons or "rules" about different styles—merely to become aware of how deeply-ingrained our instinct for rhythm is, and how easy it can be to be rhythmically creative, when freed up from the world of visual symbols and mathematical music theory. Still, as always, you can be on the lookout for "diamonds": what ideas or effects did you notice which you might like to deploy in your own songwriting?

Now let's explore a more precise and conscious approach to writing rhythms, based on the Rhythm Syllable building blocks from *Chapter Thirteen: Rhythm*. If you haven't been through that chapter, you can feel free to skip this exercise for now.

EXERCISE: Compose with Rhythm Syllables

1.   Select a short section of any lyrics you've been developing as you go through this chapter. For example, one stanza of draft lyrics which you think could become the verse of a song.

2.   Write out a set of Beat Blanks with four beats per measure, and one measure for each line of your lyrics. For example, if your draft lyrics have four lines, write four lines of four beats:

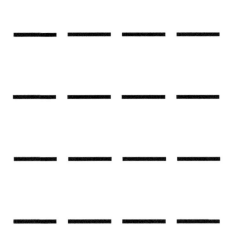

3. Go through your lyrics line by line. Count the number of syllables in the line, and then use Rhythm Syllables and Stick Notation to compose a rhythmic pattern with the same number of notes. For example, if your first line was *"Every day I wake up early"* you would count 8 syllables and write Rhythm Syllables with 8 notes. This could be *Ti-Ti Ti-Ti Ti-Ti Ti-Ti* or it could be *Ti-Ti Ta Tri-po-let Ti-Ti*, etc.

4. Try speaking the line with the rhythm you've written. Adjust according to taste! And continue with the other lines, until you've written a rhythm you like for the whole section.

This exercise should prove enlightening for you! You will quickly notice where the emphasis is coming out oddly. For example if your first line was instead *"I wake up early every morning"* we would naturally emphasise *"wake"* rather than *"I"* at the beginning, and you might decide that the *"I"* needs to be placed just before the first beat of the measure, a common feature in setting lyrics to music which is called *anacrusis*. Or perhaps your first line was *"Everywhere I look, I see new signs of new beginnings."* Counting 14 syllables and realising that's hard to cram into four beats, you might decide to split the line into two measures: *"Everywhere I look, I see / new signs of new beginnings."*

Combining the cut-and-dried notation of Rhythm Syllables with your natural instinct for spoken words and musical style in this way can provide you with a wonderful and liberating way to be creative with rhythm.

Pitch

The Pitch dimension of a melody means the particular note pitches used. In *Chapter Eight: Relative Pitch* we discussed how what matters in music is actually the pitch *relationships* between those notes, and especially relating to the tonic or "home" note, rather than the specific letter-name notes.

There are particular conventions relating to Pitch, most notably that songs will mostly (or exclusively) use the notes from a particular key, and that ending a phrase or section on the tonic note will tend to sound like "coming home" and bring a sense of resolution or completion for the listener. These ideas are explored more in Part II.

There are also common patterns relating to form. For example the sequence of notes *"mi re do"* is a common way to bring a phrase "home" to the tonic. There are also common patterns for the Pitch Contour's directions and trends, and the overall pitch of a section (for example having the chorus be at a notably higher or lower pitch overall to the verses, to create contrast).

The more time you've spent with the building blocks of Pitch covered in Part II, the easier you will find it to intentionally choose suitable notes for your melodies, but our Expansive Creativity approach also allows you to have success without necessarily using those. The exercises below cover both scenarios.

In both *Chapter Five: Active Listening* and *Chapter Eight: Relative Pitch*, we introduced the idea of a Pitch Contour: drawing the overall shape of a series of pitches as a line which goes up and down. This can be drawn on paper or indicated by moving your hand up and down. It is often unknown to songwriters and skipped in the process of writing a melody—but it can be a wonderfully helpful starting point, both for understanding melodies in existing songs, and shaping the melodies you write yourself.

EXERCISE: Draw the Pitch Contour

1.   Select a section of a song you know well, for example the chorus.

2.   Listen, and sketch out what you hear as the Pitch Contour for each line in turn. You're aiming to capture the overall up-and-down journey. Ideally also aim to reflect when movements in pitch are small versus larger leaps, and whether the phrase ends higher or lower than it started. You may need to listen a few times! You can start by just listening, then try showing the contour with hand movement up and down while you listen, then try writing it down (in pencil rather than pen!)

3.   Repeat this for another section. Then repeat with some other songs.

4.   Once you've done this for a few melodies, use what you've observed to sketch your own Pitch Contour for a melody. You can have in mind a song you're working on (for example, a set of lyrics you wrote in the earlier exercises) or see it as starting something new.

If you've gone through *Chapter Fifteen: Improvisation* then try the following next:

EXERCISE: Writing the Pitch of a Melody with Expansive Creativity

1.   Select any of the exercises from *Chapter Fifteen: Improvisation* which involve improvising with pitches. For example, "Melody-Inspired Improv" or "Call and Response Improv".

2.   Go through the exercise, using your singing voice as your instrument. If you're not yet comfortable singing then you can use an instrument you play instead.

3.   Once you encounter a potential "diamond" you like, capture it by either transcribing (writing down, for example with Solfa

and optionally Stick Notation for the Rhythm too, or traditional notation if you prefer) or simply recording yourself singing/playing it.

4.   Now repeat the same exercise, but with a set of lyrics in mind. You can use lyrics from a song you know well, or some that you've written yourself. How does your improvising change, to suit the lyrics?

Note that with the variety of Playgrounds that are possible, you could use this exercise alone as your entire melody-writing method going forwards!

TIP:

You may find it valuable to record *all* your Songwriting experimentation. Often the musical ideas we express in the moment prove elusive when we try to capture them afterwards... and there's nothing more frustrating than losing a diamond you just caught a glimpse of!

Just like we recommended in *Chapter Fifteen: Improvisation*, recording yourself as a habit can provide endless material to use in practicing Playing By Ear or transcribing, further Improvisation, inspiration for Songwriting, and so on—as well as helping you see clearly the progress you've made over time.

One defining trait of a melody is how its pitches move in either *steps* or *skips*. A "step" is when one note pitch is followed by a neighbouring pitch from the scale, i.e. the note directly above or below. A "skip" is when a note pitch is followed by a pitch which is not directly adjacent (named so because it "skips" over one or more notes in the scale to reach the next one).

EXERCISE: Writing the Pitch of a Melody with Steps and Skips

1. Select a section of a song you know well, for example the chorus.

2. Listen to the melody and try to hear where it moves in steps versus skips. If you've already drawn the Pitch Contour you can use that as a clue and/or annotate it to mark the steps and skips. If you'd like to find the scale by ear and use that as a reference to figure out the steps and skips, you can, but just using your best guess is also fine.

3. Repeat for other sections and other songs.

4. Once you've done this for a few melodies, choose a scale and try writing a melody with steps and skips in mind. You could try the Constraints of "only steps" or "only skips" or "all steps with one big skip", for example. This can be usefully combined with the previous exercise ("Writing the Pitch of a Melody with Expansive Creativity") but you can also just explore and experiment within the scale.

As you do this exercise, really pay attention to the musical effect of steps and skips, and of different-sized skips. This adds a layer of granularity to our Pitch Contour model of the melody, even before getting as far as specific note pitches. And just like the Pitch Contour it can be a helpful step forwards in defining our melody and understanding those we hear in music we love.

Like with the Rhythm side, we'll wrap up with an exercise leveraging any experience you have with the building blocks of Part II. So if you are working on either Solfa, Intervals, or both, now is a perfect time to start putting them to use in your Songwriting!

EXERCISE: Writing the Pitch of a Melody with Building Blocks

1. Choose either Solfa or Intervals, and a subset of those building

blocks to work with. For example, just the Pentatonic Scale in Solfa (*do re mi so la do'*) or just Major and Minor 2nds and 3rds in Intervals.

2. Compose a melody using those building blocks. You might like to first sketch your intended Pitch Contour and think about steps and skips.

3. Once you've done that a few times, repeat with a set of lyrics in mind. This can be either from an existing song (composing your own melody for the same words) or poem, or a set of lyrics you're working on.

Bringing It All Together

Now let's draw on all these techniques (Pitch Contour, Steps and Skips, Expansive Creativity, Building Blocks) to write a melody.

We said in *Chapter Fifteen: Improvisation* that improvising can be considered "composing on-the-fly" and writing music as being something like "improvising on paper". The following two exercises will help bridge between these two activities.

EXERCISE: From Improvisation to Composition

1. Lay the groundwork by drawing a Pitch Contour.

2. Improvise to find a melody that fits that contour. If you're familiar with Expansive Creativity, you can apply certain Constraints or a whole Playground to help you. If you're practicing Ear Training with our Pitch building blocks, you can leverage those skills to help you choose notes. If neither, you can still sit with an instrument and use the Pitch Contour and steps-and-skips ideas to explore within a particular scale you choose (e.g. C Major, using just the white notes of a piano keyboard).

3. Experiment and explore freely, refining your ideas until you have composed a melody you're happy with. Capture it by transcribing or recording.

Zac Says...

I highly recommend recording these free explorations. I like to press record and really focus on the feeling and the expression in the moment.

Then I'll listen back to the recording, usually at least a day later, and listen for what excites me. I find that I gain more clarity on what ideas I want to develop further from listening to recordings.

While I'm recording I focus on playing things that "feel" good in the body. When I listen back I am listening for things that excite and delight me.

I am a lot more free in my explorations when I don't have to think about creating something I'll want to use, or being sure to pay attention so that I can capture the ideas after.

I feel much freer, I generate more creative ideas, and I am more excited and satisfied with what I come up with when I default to recording all of my explorations.

Over time it's training my brain to be better and better at flowing in the moment while I'm recording, and better and better at active listening to my own recordings and finding ideas that excite me.

Improvisation is not the only way to compose melodies. Let's try composing a melody by writing first.

EXERCISE: Composing on Paper

1. Again, begin by sketching a Pitch Contour.

2. Write down the pitches of a melody, in whatever form is comfortable for you e.g. Solfa note names, letter note names, traditional staff notation. If you're familiar with Expansive Creativity and/or building blocks, feel free to use either or both to inform your note choices. Otherwise choose a scale to select pitches from, like in the previous exercise.

4. Sing or play the melody. Use your Hearing and Heart to

evaluate what you wrote, and then refine it. In this way we can avoid overly-theoretical composing (i.e. Head-only choices).

I encourage you to try both of these approaches. Some musicians will find they prefer freely improvising and distilling out the "diamonds", while others will prefer having the concrete written representation to work with and refine. Both have their advantages, and you may like to use a mix of the two as your melody develops.

The important thing is to make sure you're using Head, Hands, Hearing and Heart together, and taking an exploratory approach to discover what pleases you most.

4. Arrangement

If you wrote a song with just the elements covered so far, you could produce a lovely, singable melody with lyrics, in a neat, effective structure. And you could perform it, singing *a cappella* (unaccompanied) or playing the melody on an instrument. Arguably, this is the most important goal to achieve in writing a song!

Still, you might already be concerned that an unaccompanied melody feels a bit barebones and overly simple, since the vast majority of music is written and performed with instrumental accompaniment.

So how do we go from the "pure" melody of a song, to that fully-fledged musical arrangement we're used to hearing and perhaps playing?

We can see this arrangement as the combination of *harmonisation* (in simple terms: adding chords) and *instrumentation* (assigning particular instruments to play each musical part, also called *orchestration*). There may also be various embellishments and additional musical parts to write, to create the full Timbre and Texture (see *Chapter Five: Active Listening* and *Chapter Seventeen: Expression*).

How To Arrange A Song

Although there are things we could say about the overall harmony and instrumentation of a song, the details of both will vary from section to section within a song.

The harmony should match/support the melody and vice-versa—so if the melody is different across two sections then the harmony probably will be too.

Instrumentation is one powerful way to convey a clear change from section to section. For example adding or removing percussion, adding backing vocals, introducing a mariachi horn part, etc.

So it's important to think about the role, purpose or function of each section, and design the harmony and instrumentation for each to help build and release tension, increase interest, or help you convey the emotions you're aiming for.

Instrumentation

The instruments you choose to use in a song can make an enormous difference to its musical impact. Imagine a love ballad played by a four-piece rock band, complete with heavily-distorted lead guitar... compared with the same music played by a classical string quartet (*a la* Metallica-tribute band Apocalyptica!) The underlying music composition might be almost identical, but the instrumentation makes all the difference.

This can be a vast topic, taking into account not just which instruments suit the style you're going for, but also the particular strengths, limitations and peculiarities of particular instruments, to make sure the musical part you write for them fits.

For our purposes the most valuable way to start exploring is to work with instruments we can play (or have a friend who plays), and focus on the choices we can make for musical effect.

Supposing, for example, that you play guitar and a friend plays saxophone. How could you make use of those two instruments in a song you're writing? If the guitar is to provide the harmony, will it be through regular chords, power chords, broken (arpeggiated) chords or something else? Will the saxophone have a counter-melody to the vocal part, or contribute a riff or lick that acts like a hook? Will both be present throughout the song, or only in particular sections?

If you're working with a Digital Audio Workstation (DAW) then you may have unlimited realistic-sounding synthetic instruments at your fingertips. This opens up a world of possibilities. Exploring freely and being ambitious can both be rewarding. As always, you're encouraged to find your own best Songwriting process, but based on experience with our members I would suggest letting the instrumentation serve the song, rather than getting lost in all the instruments you want to include and then trying to figure out what to write for each of them without having the core elements of the song (form, Melody, Harmony, etc.) defined—at least, to begin with.

EXERCISE: Analysing Instrumentation

1. Select a song you're familiar with.

2. Listen through, and write down all the instruments you hear in each section. If you can't identify it specifically, just identify the instrument family (e.g. "strings" rather than "viola"). Feel free to pause, or listen multiple times to capture it in full.

3. Repeat, but this time pay attention to the differences / changes from section to section, and jot down your observations on the role you think these changes serve. For example, *"Drums drop out completely during the chorus, making the whole texture lighter and giving a dreamier, floating feel to the vocals."*

This is an Active Listening exercise, and the more you practice it, the more you'll start to automatically notice the instrumentation in music you listen to, which can help you get in touch with your own taste and preferences, and inform the choices you make for your own songs.

EXERCISE: Brainstorming Instrumentation

1. Select some musical material you've been working on in this chapter so far.

2. Based on what you discovered in the previous exercise, or just thinking about the music you listen to day-to-day or the genres you prefer, brainstorm a variety of instrumentations you could use for your musical material. Don't limit yourself to what you think "would be best" or "is normal"—really explore a wide range of possibilities. You can use Audiation to imagine what those different instrumentations might sound like—and you might discover some surprising "diamonds" along the way!

Harmonisation

Harmony refers to the collection of notes present at any given moment in the music, which with our building blocks from Part II in mind we can simplify as "the chords which accompany the melody".

Chords and Progressions are covered in detail in *Chapter Eleven: Chords and Progressions*, including guidance on harmonising a melody by ear.

We won't repeat those explanations and exercises here, but now would be a good time to check out that chapter if you haven't already, and to try applying the ideas there to some of the musical material you've been working on here.

Additional Elements

Often a song will have various musical elements which aren't the melody or the chords. Percussion would be one prominent example, but this also includes embellishments from other instruments, such as riffs and hooks, instrumental solos, basslines, etc.

Riffs, hooks and solos can all be considered to be kinds of secondary melodies, and the same writing techniques from the Melody section above can be used. Basslines fall somewhere between "mini melody" and harmony, since they can be as sophisticated as a melody in their own right, but are typically core to how the harmony is perceived too (because the lowest note of a harmony has a particularly strong effect on what chord we interpret it as).

You might like to repeat the "Analysing Instrumentation" exercise above, this time noting where instruments are contributing to the Melody, the Harmony, or providing embellishments of one kind or another. Again, this can inform your own creative choices when arranging songs of your own.

How to Practice Writing Songs

If you've been following along with the exercises throughout this chapter, at this stage you will have a number of musical creations in progress! You are also now familiar with a number of techniques for tackling each element of a song: Form, Ideas/Emotion, Lyrics, Melody, Harmony, Arrangement and Instrumentation.

As we said at the outset, we're not dictating a 1-2-3 process for you to follow in this chapter. Creativity is unpredictable! And with practice, you'll find your own preferences.

Armed with the understanding and techniques that can allow creative Songwriting, the important thing now is to continue practicing regularly. All of the exercises so far can be useful, just as they are. More likely, you may wish to adapt and combine them into activities you find enjoyable and fruitful.

Document everything along the way, and make it a habit to work on some kind of Songwriting—ideally daily—and you'll find songs shape up faster than you might expect.

Some musicians like to focus on one element of a song at a time, others to move them all forwards together. Some will want to "work on a song" for multiple sessions, getting it finished (or close) before moving on to another. Most find that having a number of songs underway helps keep things interesting and progressing.

Whichever approach you prefer, keeping your tasks focused and simple during a session can help prevent perfectionism and overwhelm. Applying Constraints can also greatly help—for example setting a specific amount of time aside to work on a song, or deciding to only work on the lyrics today.

Don't neglect the Heart side of things! Stay focused on the process more than the outcome, and be mindful of what helps or hinders your creativity. Beyond the step-by-step methods presented here, and your overall process for bringing a song to completion, there are other factors and types of context which can be important. For example, you may prefer certain ways of jotting down notes (e.g. pencil vs. pen vs. electronic) or certain writing locations (e.g. quiet room vs. noisy café vs. out in nature). Many of the things which we think "shouldn't" matter really can.

Remember the encouragement to share what you're working on. Not only will the encouragement and objective feedback you get from others spur you on, it can be motivating and exciting to know that the music you're writing won't just languish in a drawer or in a file, but will be heard and enjoyed by others.

Conclusion

We've covered a lot in this chapter! The task of "writing a great song" may still feel like a big one—but hopefully the sub-tasks of tackling each element, and taking an exploratory approach which leverages your other musicality skills make that task feel not just manageable, but exciting.

My final piece of guidance is a simple one: Start today.

If nothing else, start documenting the potential "diamonds" which you spot throughout your other musicality training and music practice. Dabble with the exercises in this chapter in a playful way, and focus on enjoying the creative experimentation. Maybe an amazing song emerges, maybe it doesn't. Let yourself off the hook for the final outcome, and focus on enjoying the journey. As you adopt the identity of the songwriter, everything you experience becomes potential inspiration for a song.

If you're working on Ear Training, you can leverage the building blocks of Part II to great effect in your Songwriting, as well as incorporating Songwriting activities into your practice with those building blocks. For example, composing your own melodies to help you internalise certain intervals or solfa notes.

If you're practicing Active Listening or Playing By Ear, you'll find that both can be a tremendous source of inspiration and greater understanding which can feed into your own writing. Naturally the Expansive Creativity approach to Improvisation can be an endless source of new musical ideas to write lyrics for and refine into songs. And as you explore the approaches to Expression and Performance presented in the following chapters, you'll find new levels of emotional expression available to you, to enhance your songs.

Remember above all that we are all naturally creative, and that the more you create, the more creative you'll become. Ultimately it all comes down to your own musical taste, and finding better, faster, easier, and more enjoyable ways to express your own musical creativity in ways you enjoy and can be excited and proud to share with others.

I'll finish by repeating what I said at the start: whether or not "Songwriting" features in your Big Picture Vision, I cannot overstate the impact that writing your own music will have on your musicality, and your musical fulfilment. And if it turns out that actually, writing songs delights you and becomes a big part of your musical identity— all the better!

CHAPTER SEVENTEEN:
EXPRESSION

"Even when I'm singing on record there's a lot of times when I'll fight for a bit of imperfection. I might not have quite hit the note to the perfect pitch, but there was a soul in there and feeling that, to me, delivers the emotion of that moment."

— Alicia Keys

"To play a wrong note is insignificant; to play without passion is inexcusable."

— Ludwig van Beethoven

Think back to what first inspired you to pick up an instrument or open your mouth to sing. I'm guessing it wasn't a desire for dry, robotic "getting the notes right"!

More likely it was the *emotion* of music, and a deep desire to express your own emotions through music that you love.

Sadly, many of us wind up sat with our instrument in hand, pressing the buttons, and even if the "right" notes come out... where is that feeling?

We watch and listen to our musical heroes, we see and hear how they embody the music, reach into our hearts, and touch us deeply. Perhaps you have had moments where you felt the music moving like that through you, and wondered *"Where did that come from? And how can I do it again?!"*

You might have been told by a teacher or well-meaning friend to "play with more expression". Or perhaps you've commented yourself on how a musician plays "so expressively".

We know what "playing expressively" means in terms of its effect and impact on the audience. And we know instinctively when we hear (or play) music with great expression versus a dry, lifeless performance.

In *Chapter One: Musicality* several of the featured descriptions highlighted how central this is to musicality itself. For example *"It's the way the performer makes a piece of music uniquely his/her own"*, *"Musicality means being able to express your thoughts/feelings through music"*, *"Musicality to me would be when you have a little more freedom to make the best piece you can of any piece of music."*

But what is it that actually constitutes "playing with expression"— and is it something you can learn to do?

If you've read this far, you'll appreciate by now that at Musical U we're never satisfied with answers like "it just happens", "nobody really knows" or "it's just a gift" when it comes to music! There is always an explanation, if we have the courage and the determination to seek it out. And fortunately musical expression is no exception.

In our H4 Model of Complete Musicality, this represents a large part of the Heart component, as well as being deeply tied to our *Musical Inside And Out* Pillar Belief. How do you go from "operating an instrument" to feeling like the music is flowing out from inside you, through your instrument?

In the next chapter, we'll cover one big part of it: how to *connect* more deeply with your instrument, the music, other musicians and your audience.

Here, we'll introduce a way of thinking about "playing expressively" which transforms it from a mysterious abstract "you've got it or you don't" phenomenon into something clear, concrete and practical. You'll learn to expand your musicality through playing each and every note with intentional musical expression, and do so in a way which lets you intuitively infuse your music with the emotions you feel inside.

Overview

In this chapter we'll begin by introducing "The Musical Language of Emotion" as a way to think about playing expressively, using analogies between spoken language and music to gain greater insight into what it means to "play with expression". We'll discuss phrasing and its importance for expressing emotions through music, and then give some general pointers for finding success with the exercises in this chapter.

Then we will go through the four Dimensions of music, as you may have encountered already in *Chapter Five: Active Listening* and elsewhere in the book: Timbre, Dynamics, Pitch and Rhythm. For each one, we'll unpack the various ways you can make creative choices to express emotions, and practice exploring and experimenting—first with a single note, and then across a musical phrase. Then we'll bring your experiences with all four together, to practice shaping a note and then a phrase using everything you've learned so far.

Then, in the second half of the chapter, we'll look at four musical activities and how you can practice expressing emotions with each: Active Listening, Movement, Audiation and Singing, and Creativity. This will help you to bring your new ability to "speak the language of emotion" into every area of your music-making.

The Musical Language Of Emotion

Our gateway into playing expressively will be the idea that there is a musical language of emotion. This language can be learned quickly, and you can "speak" it with your instrument or singing voice immediately, to provide a clear and reliable way for your feelings to be expressed through music. Merely speaking these musical "words" of emotion will automatically create more feeling and connection in both yourself and your listener, something we'll then explore more in *Chapter Eighteen: Performance*.

As with any language, it will take practice to achieve skill and fluency in the musical language of emotion. While we will suggest dedicated exercises in this chapter, your progress will increase dramatically if you aim to be expressive in everything you play or sing. That goes from the most "boring" scale or technical exercise through to the most challenging pieces of music you play.

What do we mean by "emotion"? Just like when learning a language, we want to go beyond the most basic vocabulary and have a rich range of expressive possibilities. It is often hard for us as humans to capture emotions accurately with words, and our goal is not to try to conclusively "define" each emotion word with corresponding musical techniques, but for the sake of sketching out an emotional landscape we might want to explore, here are some emotion words you might like to have in mind as we continue:

- Happiness, Joy, Pride, Relief, Cheerfulness, Hope

- Fear, Anxiety, Nervousness, Horror, Panic

- Anger, Irritation, Rage

- Sadness, Exhaustion, Boredom

- Embarrassment, Shame, Disappointment

- Love, Caring, Contentment, Satisfaction

- Excitement, Surprise, Shock, Amazement, Wonder

In the process of learning this language of emotion, you'll be placing a lot of attention on details. Not just which notes you're playing, but on the beginning, middle, and end of each and every note.

This attention to shaping everything you play with expression will keep you very busy at first. You may even feel that it is the exact opposite of that free, flowing feeling of just "being" the music which is our goal! However, it is just this intense engagement with the details of musical expression that will unlock an abundant world of musical possibilities for you.

In various contexts throughout this book we discuss the importance of music being a conversation, featuring both "input" and "output". For example, the Play-Listen/Listen-Play of Expansive Creativity (*Chapter Fifteen: Improvisation*), the Listen-Engage-Express of the Play-By-Ear Process (*Chapter Fourteen: Playing By Ear*), the Plan-Play-Reflect of Deliberate Practice (*Chapter Six: Superlearning*), and the 3 C's of Performance Free-Flow (*Chapter Eighteen: Performance*). And if there is a musical language of emotion, we must learn to both understand and speak it!

As we learn this language, we will experience both how the sounds of this musical language of emotion make us feel, which we'll refer to as "Outside → In". Then, equipped with this "vocabulary", we will access our own creativity to start expressing our own emotions musically, which we'll refer to as "Inside → Out".

A word of warning: The exercises below involve some wide-ranging exploring and experimenting. More than likely, this will make you uncomfortably aware of how restricted and limited your expressive choices have been until now! Remember Growth Mindset (*Chapter Two: Mindset*): this isn't a failing, but rather a wonderful new opportunity for you to have discovered. And as you spend time exploring and experimenting in these ways, you will find your playing automatically starts to become more expressive, as you internalise the musical language of emotion.

Learning The Language

We will start learning the musical language of emotion by familiarising ourselves with how the four *dimensions* of a musical sound can each be used to shape a musical phrase expressively: Pitch, Rhythm, Timbre and Dynamics.

If you've read *Chapter Five: Active Listening* or *Chapter Fifteen: Improvisation*, these four dimensions should be familiar! As you read through the explanation of each dimension below, you can use your Active Listening skills to start listening for it in all the music you hear and play each day. What do you notice about the variety of each dimension, the choices being made, and what the possibilities are? As always, it will reward you to keep notes on your observations, and reflect on what you're learning.

For each dimension we will first explore the possibilities present in a single note, and then how we can use our choices in that dimension to shape a musical *phrase*. Finally, we'll practice using all the dimensions together to play the music we love with greater expression.

Phrasing and Expressive Choices

Notes and motifs join together to form musical *phrases*—larger meaningful groups, analogous to sentences in spoken language. Our musical language of emotion can powerfully shape these phrases, transforming them from a simple series of seemingly-unrelated notes into a cohesive, musically-compelling expression.

In spoken language, we enhance sentences with the sounds of our voices, shaping the words and groups of words with loudness and softness, enunciating more or letting words run together, speeding up or slowing down... and so many other sonic and visual enhancements, including our facial expressions and body language.

So we can see that in verbal communication, the actual words are only a part of the picture. All these things and more work together to express very precise shades of meaning and emotion. In the same way, in music the "dots on the page" are only part of the picture. The four dimensions of a musical sound which we'll be exploring can all be used together to infuse meaning and emotion into each musical phrase.

As we explore, you will notice that certain choices seem to go together naturally. For example, have you noticed a tendency to play louder when you play faster, or slow down when you play more quietly? When playing scales, do you tend to grow louder as the notes go up? Maybe softer as they descend?

Challenging ourselves to create new and sometimes unexpected combinations can result in some really special musical moments. Slow does not always have to equal quiet, and fast does not always have to equal loud. Sometimes mixing and matching the energies that it takes to play with these different qualities of music can result in a new way to express ourselves in a way that we haven't quite been able to before.

Finding (or Choosing) the Phrasing in Music

When listening to music, we naturally recognise the phrasing i.e. which notes group together, especially in the melody. Through years of experience, as well as our inbuilt biological capacity for understanding spoken language, we instinctively interpret all the variations in Pitch, Rhythm, Dynamics and Timbre to recognise when one musical "sentence" has ended and the next one is beginning.

When reading music notation, that process is not always so easy. Our written music divides into regular groups of notes, shown with vertical bar lines in staff notation, but these do not necessarily line up with the phrasing at all! For example, looking at this score, it may be difficult to tell at first glance where the phrases begin and end and how many there are:

When we add the lyrics to this score, we can now easily see how the musical phrases line up with the phrases and sentences of the lyrics, where each starts and ends, and when it would be appropriate to pause, take a breath, articulate differently, or do something else to express each phrase:

With instrumental music notation, we do not have the luxury of lyrics to guide us in our phrasing, so often the first task to playing expressively is to decide for ourselves where the phrases lie. Looking for longer notes, resolutions and rests can all be clues, but sometimes the phrasing is really open to interpretation.

We can discover through exploration how we wish to shape our phrases with all our expressive musical language. In the exercises which follow you'll have the chance to try this with each of the four dimensions individually, as well as all together.

Explore and Experiment

The spirit of all of the exercises which follow is to *explore* and *experiment*.

Our goal is not to "find the answer", but rather to "explore the possibilities". Some things may sound terrible to you, while others make you think *"gosh, I should always play it like that!"* This is a great opportunity to start acknowledging and valuing your own aesthetic judgements. There are no "right" and "wrong" answers here. Playing expressively is all about your own musical taste and intention.

It's also important to keep in mind that the note-by-note microscopic attention and experimentation is not something you will necessarily carry out for every piece you play in future! As you learn the language of emotion, these choices will become more and more instinctive for you.

TIP:

As you go through this chapter, the expressiveness of your playing will naturally increase. You might like to create a before-and-after comparison, to help you see how far you've come by the end:

1. Choose a piece you can play comfortably. Before you continue through this chapter, record yourself performing the piece.

2. Then, after trying the various exercises in this chapter, perform and record the piece again, aiming to make use of some of the techniques and ideas you've learned and practiced.

3. Compare the two recordings to see how the expressiveness of your playing has increased!

The exercises are designed to help you experience both "Outside →
In" (hearing and appreciating the emotions created by certain musical choices) and "Inside → Out" (expressing emotions yourself, through your own musical choices).

To avoid repeating the same guidance and suggestions each time, here are some pointers to help you get the best results with the exercises:

General Guidance

• As you do each exercise, try to stay as present and mindful as you can, both of the physical movements you're making, and the sounds you're hearing. Leverage all four H's: as you read through the sections below, you'll be equipped with information and knowledge about what's possible (Head). You will be given instructions in the exercises about what to try (Hands). And you will have the opportunity to bring your attention to the sounds created (Hearing) and emotions evoked (Heart).

- If you play multiple instruments, try each exercise with each instrument, and see what commonalities and differences emerge. Repeat the exercises with your singing voice too. You may find it much easier to express the emotions! Pay attention to the choices you're making, both instinctively and consciously. Then repeat the exercise on an instrument and see what you can "translate" across from what your singing voice has revealed.

- Record yourself doing the exercises with an audio recorder or (even better) a video camera, and listen or watch back. It can be hard to realise in the moment everything we're doing and every aspect of the sounds created. When we watch or listen back we can learn even more.

- Make notes of your discoveries. These may be certain aesthetic choices (e.g. *"I love how this song comes out when I play with a broad timbre and legato articulation"*) or rules of thumb you're noticing are helpful for you (e.g. *"For playing quieter, it really helps to loosen my grip a little"*, or *"I tend to make the notes more disjointed in fast passages than I mean to—remember to play through from one note to the next."*)

Single-Note Exercises

For exercises which invite you to choose a single note to work with:

- Don't overlook or rush through these! Although we typically think about "playing with expression" as it applies to whole phrases or pieces, it all boils down to our note-by-note choices. Until today, if somebody asked you to "play a C", you would likely have played a C, and thought that if you played the correct pitch, you'd done the job. As you explore the expressive possibilities of all four dimensions, possibly using various instruments and your singing voice, you'll discover that there is a *vast* universe of what "playing a C" can sound like, and the musical effect created.

- Repeat the exercise, choosing a different note each time. Notice how the options available to you and the playing technique required to produce them may vary across your instrument's range.

Phrase-Based Exercises

For exercises which invite you to choose a musical phrase to work with:

- Choose phrases which are well within your currently abilities, so that your full focus can be on the expressive explorations, rather than needing to devote some attention purely to "playing the right notes". Remember that it's better to play a very simple phrase with great expression than a fast, complex phrase robotically!

- Choose phrases of one or two measures. That typically means roughly 4-8 seconds in duration.

- Once you feel like you've explored a given phrase enough, repeat the exercise with another one. This can be from the same piece or a different piece.

- Try to select phrases from songs or pieces which you think are expected to convey a wide range of emotions. It can be enlightening, for example, to try a phrase from a fast, heavy rock song and then one from a soulful love ballad. This will help you to explore more widely and experiment more freely, helping you become fluent in the full musical language of emotion more quickly and easily.

We are now ready to start learning the musical language of emotion, by exploring the expressive possibilities of each of the four dimensions in turn.

1. Timbre

Each of us has a distinctive speaking and singing voice, perhaps as unique as our faces and fingerprints. We have the capacity to recognise the speaking voice of hundreds of people we know.

In our spoken language, words consist of syllables in which longer vowel sounds are sandwiched between shorter consonant sounds. The specific ways that each of our bodies produces these vowels and consonants creates the individual sounds of our voices.

In music, this quality of sound is referred to as *timbre* (pronounced "*tam*-ber"), or *tone colour*. It's sometimes referred to simply as "the sound", or "the tone". It's partly determined by the instrument being used (both the type of instrument and the specific model) and partly by how that instrument is played.

Timbre comes through both in the musical "consonants" (the beginnings and endings of our musical notes) commonly known as "articulation", as well as in the "vowels" (the longer sound which forms the middle of each note). In fact, if the only thing you did to increase the expressiveness of your playing was to start really paying attention to how each note starts, continues, and ends, it would go a very long way!

In spoken language we can express a great variety of emotions through our voices. Quite apart from the words we choose, we can convey anger, happiness, sadness, hope and more just with the *sound* of our voice. Similarly in music: beyond paying attention to which notes we're playing, we can do a lot to bring out emotion by working with the timbre.

Timbre and Emotion

The mere sound of a musical instrument or voice can evoke emotion, even before our ears begin to piece the music together. For example, some people feel a sense of relaxation when listening to a harp, excitement with the distorted tone of an electric guitar, melancholy with the sound of a cello, or joy with the sound of an accordion.

While there are common responses like these, in fact our emotional responses to timbres are not universal, and may well reflect our upbringing, culture, and personal associations. To one person, the Scottish bagpipes may be the sweetest sound in the world, while to another it's hard to even appreciate the music being played when they hear that distinctive sound!

What are your own favourite (or least favourite!) musical sounds?

What feelings do they stimulate in you?

Articulation

Spoken syllables begin and end with a variety of consonant sounds, which help mark the boundary between one word and another. The musical language of emotion also has its "consonants", referred to as *articulation*.

There are numerous ways that we can initiate a sound, as well as connect sounds together, and these vary widely according to the instrument, style, and technique.

Traditional "staff" music notation differentiates many of these with additional markings in the score. Some common ones include:

Symbol	Term	Meaning
	staccatissimo	Play extremely short and separated
	staccato	Play short and separated
	legato	Play smoothly, no breaks between notes
	portato / *mezzo-staccato*	Play smoothly but with a slight emphasis on each note

In reality the possibilities for articulation are endless, and go far beyond what may normally be notated in a score.

Also, while most of the discussion about articulation focuses on the *beginnings* of notes, it's worth giving attention to the *ends* of notes. Do they end suddenly, with a clear, distinct finish? Do they tail off more gradually? Do any other aspects of the sound vary right at the end?

So we can see that varying the start and end of each note with articulation is a powerful way to bring the music to life. But what about that middle part?

The Body Of The Note

Depending on your instrument, you may have thought very little about what goes on between the beginning and end of the note... or you might have spent hours practicing it!

A pianist, for example, has no way to change the timbre of the body of the note after it is played, only the start when they press the key, and the end. On the other hand, wind and brass players are taught a lot about "developing your tone", and so-called "long notes practice" is traditionally a key part of the practice routine. By changing the embouchure (mouth position) and flow of air through the instrument, a wide range of timbres can be created, independent of how the note starts or ends.

So what's interesting to note is that, as we'll explore below, there is both "the timbre of the note" as a whole, which all instruments can control, and also "how the timbre changes during the note". Every instrument allows expressive choices about timbre by how the start and end of the note is played, and some can also vary timbre during the note's sustained middle.

Exploring the Timbre of a Note

How exactly we explore timbre varies greatly with the structure and mechanisms of our instruments. Bowed string players adjust the details of their bow arm and finger pressure on the fingerboard. Acoustic guitar players focus on their left hand finger pressure and placement and on the variety of picking and plucking sounds available to them. Electric guitarists, synthesizer players, and DAW producers have a vast arsenal of timbres available to them at the stomp of a pedal, the flick of a button, or the click of a mouse.

If the options seem limited to you at first when thinking about your primary instrument, try thinking about your singing voice instead. Just as we naturally, intuitively know how to express different emotions when speaking, the singing voice is arguably unparalleled in its expressive possibilities, and the exercise below will be very revealing if you try it with your singing voice as well as any instruments you play.

Each timbre possibility we discover and connect with becomes part of our emotional vocabulary in expressing our music.

Unfortunately, sometimes we focus too much on attaining that one "perfect tone" on our instrument. Then as beautiful as that sound may be, we sacrifice the wide potential of emotional vocabulary available to us in changing timbres.

"Emotion" can be thought of as "Energy in Motion". Indeed, if there is one thing that's always the same about emotion, it's that it's always changing! This is powerful to keep in mind as you explore the possibilities in this chapter.

Timbral changes may be noticed between different pieces of music, different instruments, different styles, as well as within a given piece, or even across a short series of notes.

Let's start exploring the possibilities with timbre.

EXERCISE: Exploring The Timbre Of A Note

1. Select a note on your instrument.

2. **Outside → In:** Spend a few minutes playing this one note repeatedly, with no particular rhythm or tempo, just allowing each note as much time as you need, to explore. Focus first on the start of the note, then on the middle, and then on the end. For each, explore as widely as you can the options available to you. Draw on all the different techniques you may know of on your instrument, as well as pure physical experimentation (for example, shifting your hands or mouth in a certain direction or into a different shape). As you listen, notice what emotional effect different choices have. For example, do certain timbres sound more calm or soothing than others?

3. **Inside → Out:** Once you've explored the space of possibilities, start thinking about emotions. For example, happy, sad, angry, restless, calm, or any others from the list earlier in the chapter... Without trying to "figure out" how to express the emotion, just conjure up the emotion inside, and then see how you instinctively play the note. It may be helpful to imagine that someone is listening and you want them to guess which emotion you chose.

Using Timbre to Shape a Phrase

Now that we've explored the timbre possibilities of an individual note, let's see what we can do with a whole phrase. Naturally this includes everything we can do with each individual note, but now we can think too about how things change over the course of the phrase.

EXERCISE: Using Timbre to Shape a Phrase

1.   Select a short phrase from a piece you can play (or if you prefer, improvise a phrase to then work with).

2.   **Outside → In:** As before, take a few minutes to play it repeatedly, exploring all the possible ways you can play the notes' starts, middles and ends. Try going to extremes, both for the phrase as a whole, and transitioning from one extreme to another over the course of the phrase. Notice the emotions different choices seem to suggest.

3.   **Inside → Out:** Now let's try using these newly-discovered possibilities to intentionally express emotions. Again, think of any emotion, and see how you could make timbre choices to convey that emotion with the phrase. You may then wish to try shifting from one emotion to another over the course of the phrase.

---

2. Dynamics

One of my favourite interviews for the Musicality Now podcast was with Dr. Melody Payne, a piano teacher and widely-respected expert in piano pedagogy, who shared the following story relating to helping students start playing more expressively.

She had found that her young beginner students were so absorbed in "getting the notes right" that their playing would often come out boring and mechanical. She knew how much they loved music, and how expressive the children were in their daily lives as they talked and played. But when it came to playing piano, they would sit with furrowed brows in deep concentration, plunking out one note at a time without an ounce of musicality.

She was looking for some way to bring out expression in their playing, and finally hit on one simple instruction: as they approached the end of their piece, she asked them to slow down and play more softly.

This instruction was easy for them to follow, and the effects were immediate. Suddenly, the students were engaged with the new expressiveness of their music. At the recital, their parents were so moved by the performances that many were wiping away tears. Even the very youngest beginner had connected with the audience through their command of musical expression.

This is a testament to the "Outside → In" power of the musical language of emotions. When we apply expressive actions, like slowing down and getting softer, we give our feelings someplace to go, and suddenly both performer and listener feel a deeper emotional connection with the music.

Changes in the volume of music, the softness and loudness, are referred to as *dynamics*. The word implies *change* in its very definition, as "force producing motion".

The Western music notation system has devised a number of symbols and terms to describe volume:

Symbol	Term	Meaning
fff	*fortississimo*	Very, very loud
ff	*fortissimo*	Very loud
f	*forte*	Loud
mf	*mezzo forte*	A little loud
mp	*mezzo piano*	A little soft
p	*piano*	Soft
pp	*pianissimo*	Very soft
ppp	*pianississimo*	Very, very soft

And then another set of symbols and terms that describe *changes* in volume:

Symbol	Term	Meaning
<img crescendo symbol>	*crescendo*	Gradually getting louder

	decrescendo or *diminuendo*	Gradually getting quieter
sfz	*sforzando*	A sudden emphasis (loud then quiet)

Dynamics in Different Styles

Classical music and instrumental movie scores are well-known for expressive dynamic shifts. Ravel's *Bolero* combines changes in timbre with one massive 15-minute long crescendo on the same repeated melody to great expressive effect. Usually though, the dynamic changes come quicker.

Much of today's popular music has been shaped by the need to stand out on the radio, with the overall volume *compressed* to stay at a relatively constant level throughout the song.

Popular music producers however can still give the illusion of volume changes by changing timbres and instrumentation from section to section. For example, we tend to associate more busy or distorted timbres as "louder" and clear or acoustic timbres as "softer". They also make great use of audio mixing, letting different instruments be heard as louder and softer in the overall sound.

Exploring The Dynamics Of A Note

The above examples illustrate the dynamics created with a large number of musical sources, either in an orchestra or in the recording studio, but the impact of dynamics can be felt in a single instrument expressing a melody—or even a single note.

The type of dynamic indications listed above, like we might find in a classical music score, are but broad guidelines in comparison with the infinite and detailed dynamic possibilities. Indeed, every single note of a melody can be shaped with dynamics, both relative to the notes around it and through the duration of that note. We can call that constant, detailed, expressive use of dynamics "microdynamics".

One clear example of the impact such microdynamics can have is in establishing the Meter of a piece, as covered in *Chapter Five: Active Listening* and *Chapter Twelve: The Beat*. If you were to play an even, steady pulse on a snare drum, with every drum hit at the exact same volume, a listener would have no sense of the meter or how beats were grouped. But if you instead emphasised certain notes by playing them louder (e.g. LOUD quiet quiet quiet, LOUD quiet quiet quiet) suddenly the meter becomes clear and the music is perceived as grouped into measures.

Let's explore the dynamics of a single note.

EXERCISE: Exploring The Dynamics Of A Note

Select a note on your instrument.

Outside → In:

1. Spend 30 seconds or so playing the note at a range of volumes. You can start as quiet as possible, then gradually build up to as loud as possible, then work your way back down.

    You may find it helpful to think of the dynamic terms in the table above (piano, forte, etc.) as markers or set volume levels, and try to target each one. This can help you go beyond just "quiet, medium, and loud" as options—but do keep in mind that there is an entire spectrum of possible volumes, not just a handful of "settings"!

    Do you notice any correlation between different volumes and different emotions—or intensity of emotion?

2. Next, if your instrument allows it, spend some time varying the volume across the note. for example starting quiet and getting louder by the end, vice-versa, or "swelling" from quiet to loud to quiet again. Again, notice what internal, emotional effect these different possibilites have on you. There may not be a specific emotion word you'd associate with them, but do you feel the energetic impact of each differently?

Inside → Out:

Based on what you've discovered, what different emotions, feelings, or energies can you now create intentionally, through your dynamic choices?

Using Dynamics to Shape a Phrase

Now that we've calibrated our volume control a bit, let's try exploring the dynamic possibilities across a phrase.

EXERCISE: Using Dynamics to Shape a Phrase

Select a phrase from a piece you play (or if you prefer, improvise a phrase to work with).

Outside → In:

1.   Spend a minute or two playing the phrase a number of times. Explore the different volumes available to you. As before, you can vary from quietest to loudest and back again, and then try targeting different levels (e.g. using the dynamic terms such as *pianissimo, mezzo forte*, etc.)

2.   Next experiment with varying the volume across the phrase. You can begin with a simple *crescendo* or *diminuendo* (as introduced above) across the whole phrase. Then try including both. You may even wish to sketch out on paper a shape of volume changes you wish to play, similar to the idea of a Pitch Contour from *Chapter Eight: Relative Pitch*, but for Dynamics rather than Pitch. This could feature multiple increases and decreases in volume, over various parts of the phrase.

Inside → Out:

Based on what you've discovered, try to express different emotions, or simply different levels of energy by your choice of Dynamics.

As you do this exercise, really pay attention to the interplay between Pitch, Rhythm, and Dynamics. While the Pitch and Rhythm are remaining constant with each play-through, what impact do your dynamic choices have? How does the emotion of the phrase seem to be affected by your use of Dynamics?

3. Pitch

In our explorations so far, we have been working with a particular note or phrase, and varying the Timbre and/or Dynamics to see what effect it has on the musical expression, and emotions suggested. If we were to change the note pitches or durations, we would be playing different music each time rather than just changing the expression of that music… right?

In fact, things are not so clear-cut! In the second part of this chapter we'll see how there's actually more of a spectrum between *interpreting* a given piece of music and *improvising* (or writing) your own musical creation, and we'll begin to explore that now, as we see how in fact Pitch and Rhythm both allow for endless expressive choices, even while playing the notes "correctly, as written".

As with timbre, the expressive possibilities for Pitch vary across instruments. Some instruments allow for smooth gradual variations in pitch, for example singing, slide guitar or pedal steel guitar, wind instruments through embouchure, electronic keyboards through a pitch wheel, fretless bass or non-fretted string instruments such as violin or cello. Others, such as piano, can only move in fixed intervals, typically half steps, but can still achieve similar effects.

Here are some examples of how a musician might bring their own expression to the music they play through Pitch changes, even while playing the same notes each time[1]. Note that the terminology overlaps somewhat (e.g. slides vs. bends) and can also sometimes be seen as a form of articulation (e.g. ornaments as a way to change the start or end of notes).

- **Vibrato**: Varying a note's pitch up and down repeatedly, typically in a steady fluctuating way. This is a key characteristic of the operatic singing style, but is used by singers in many genres, as well as guitarists, wind and brass players. It can be done prominently on certain notes for effect, or consistently across all notes as part of the overall style (which could be considered part of the Timbre).

- **Slides**: Playing a pitch above or below the target note either before or after it and smoothly gliding to or from the target note's pitch. There is also the *glissando*, where you move through individual notes rather than smoothly varying the

---

[1] If you've read *Chapter Eight: Relative Pitch*, we're talking about playing the given Pitch Classes while varying the exact pitches.

pitch.

- **Bends**: Similar to slides but typically just a half step or two, and often used to describe moving from one note in the phrase to the next by a smooth slide rather than playing each target pitch directly.

- **Ornaments**: Playing a distinct note or two before, during or after the target note. These include *trills* (alternating back-and-forth with another note, usually a half or whole step away), *mordents* (a single visit to another note, usually a half or whole step away), and *turns* (alternating to a note above, back to the target note, then a note below, and back to the target note—or vice-versa, going below then above).

- **Detuning**: Playing or singing certain notes (or even the whole piece) slightly "off key", where all target pitches are above or below the "correct" pitches. In most contexts this would be seen and heard as a "mistake" which detracted from the musical experience for the listener, but used judiciously on certain notes it can be highly effective by creating tension or contrast. Particular styles (e.g. early punk rock vocals, Spanish/Latin *champeta* music) also use it throughout, to create a very distinctive overall sound.

Typically certain styles and genres will have conventions about which alterations to Pitch are expected or considered appropriate to the style. For example blues music is often heavy on slides and bends, while these would be out of place in most Western classical music (unless marked explicitly as a *glissando*). Vibrato, as mentioned, is a requirement for operatic singing, and an expected part of classical violin. Singing "out of tune" or "off key" was a defining part of the punk rock sound but would generally be unacceptable in modern orchestral cinematic music. Some genres even have their own whole set of embellishments, such as the Klezmer tradition where particular Pitch bends and flourishes are used to make melodies sound more emotive and more evocatively mimic the human singing voice with instruments such as clarinet.

As we'll explore more in *Chapter Sixteen: Songwriting*, music is a dance of setting and then defying expectations, and so while it's valuable to know what's "normal" or "acceptable" in a particular style, ultimately it's up to your aesthetic judgement as a musician to decide, from all the options available to you, which will convey the emotion and create the musical effect you desire.

To put that another way, if your Head knows a range of options, and your Hands are able to produce them, then your Hearing and Heart can let you make the expressive choices you wish to, in any musical situation.

Exploring the Pitch of a Note

Using your primary instrument, and then any other instruments you have access to, as well as your singing voice, try exploring the Pitch possibilities of a single note.

EXERCISE: Exploring the Pitch of a Note

1. Select a note on your instrument.

2. **Outside → In:** Experiment with each of the Pitch techniques listed above, as far as your instrument allows. How far can you push things, while still having it sound like you're playing the target note? What emotions or feelings do the different possibilities stir up?

3. **Inside → Out:** If you had to play just a single note, to convey a particular emotion to a listener, what Pitch choices would you make? Try a range of emotions, from subtle to strong, and from positive to negative.

If you're unsure which of the techniques can be done on your instrument, or how to produce them, you may wish to consult a teacher or perform an online search (e.g. search for "trumpet vibrato", or "harmonica bends")

Using Pitch to Shape a Phrase

Now that you've familiarised yourself with the expressive Pitch possibilities of a single note, let's see what it opens up for us when playing a whole phrase.

EXERCISE: Using Pitch to Shape a Phrase

1. Select a phrase from a piece you play (or if you prefer, improvise a phrase to work with).

2. **Outside → In:** Spend a minute or two playing the phrase a number of times. Experiment with all the Pitch techniques available to you. At first, try applying the technique just to one or two notes (often the first, last, or any longer sustained notes are good candidates). Next experiment with varying the techniques you use across the phrase. For the sake of experimentation you can just choose intellectually or at random.

3. **Inside → Out:** Now try to use your Hearing and Heart to find your way to the Pitch alterations which best suit the phrase and your musical intent. It may be that a single technique on a single note pleases you most—or you may find that certain techniques delight you, or applying a mix creates a version of the phrase which feels just right to you.

If you've been going through the exercises in order, you may well find yourself instinctively starting to make Timbre and Dynamics choices to shape the phrase too. We'll work on this explicitly in "Bringing It All Together" below, but feel free to follow your Hearing and Heart and include variations in those dimensions which you feel complement the Pitch choices you are experimenting with.

4. Rhythm

In *Chapter Twelve: The Beat* and *Chapter Thirteen: Rhythm* we defined the *beat* as the steady underlying pulse of the music, which changes only gradually or at major transitions (e.g. between sections of a classical symphony), and *rhythm* as the pattern of notes played on top of that steady beat, featuring notes of different durations and occurring at specific times relative to the beat.

As with Pitch, this may make it seem like there isn't much choice left to us, if we are to play a piece of music "correctly, as written". After all, the sheet music or recording we're learning to piece from will indicate the specific rhythms to use. But, as with Pitch, even without moving from *interpreting* a piece to *improvising* or writing our own music, in fact there is a whole world of expressive possibilities available to us.

Whenever we speak to express ourselves in words, we speed up or slow down according to the emotions we wish to communicate. When we begin to feel excited or cheerful, our speech may be faster, or when we want to get a serious point across, we may slow down and become very deliberate.

The natural cadence of our speech may be quite flexible, speeding up or slowing down expressively within the same sentence. And the exact timing of each word can significantly affect the impact it has, and therefore the emotion or even the entire meaning of the sentence.

For example, imagine the sentence *"I knocked over the cup, because of the cat"* spoken with the first phrase slowly, and then the second phrase very quickly, and how this would emphasise the broken cup, with the cause as a by-the-way addition. And now imagine it with the first phrase fast, the second much slower, and a clear moment's pause before the word "cat". Suddenly the whole point of the sentence appears to be to blame the poor cat!

Similarly in music, the overall speed as well as the exact timing of each note can have a dramatic effect. The two major ways we can add our own expression to a given rhythm are:

1. To alter the underlying beat. We can do this either through our choice of overall speed, or by varying that speed over time.

2. To adjust the exact timing of the notes, while still staying within the range that produces recognisably the rhythm as written.

Let's look at each of these in more detail.

Tempo

The overall speed of our music is referred to as *tempo*. In traditional "staff" music notation, there is a range of Italian terms to indicate the expected tempo. These typically come at the beginning of a piece or a section of music:

Term	Meaning

Prestissimo	Very, Very Fast (> 200 B.P.M.)
Presto	Very Fast (168-200 B.P.M.)
Allegro	Fast (120-168 B.P.M.)
Moderato	Moderately (108-120 B.P.M.)
Andante	Walking Speed (76-108 B.P.M.)
Adagio	Slightly Slow (66-76 B.P.M.)
Lento	Very Slow (40-60 B.P.M.)
Grave	Slow (20-40 B.P.M.)

Some of these tempos even have their origins in emotion words. For example *grave* meant "serious", and *allegro* originally meant "happy" —though in Classical music there are plenty of intense minor-key allegros that are less than cheerful!

Often a section of a piece may even be named after its tempo marking. For example, if you were practicing the second movement of a Handel sonata with a friend, you might say *"Let's start again at the Allegro."*

Italian tempo markings leave room for subjectivity and interpretation, including variation in your day-to-day performance. For example you can play an "Andante" at a wide range of speeds, and still be within an acceptable tempo range.

When musicians want to indicate tempo more specifically, we can choose a number measured in B.P.M. (Beats Per Minute), also shown in staff notation as "M.M." ("Maelzel's Metronome", after Johann Maelzel who built the first metronome devices). Both indicate the number of beats per minute, so that the number 60 indicates one beat per second. The numeric tempo ranges corresponding to the shorthand terms are included in the table above.

In Western Classical Music and some other genres, tempo can be used as a highly expressive tool. Remember the beginner piano students who slowed down at the end of their performance? Composers, teachers, or music editors will indicate tempo changes in the music, again traditionally using a set of Italian terms:

Term	**Meaning**
Accelerando	Gradually getting faster
A tempo	Return to the prior speed
Ritardando	Getting a little slower
Rallentando	Getting slower

| *Allargando* | Getting much slower |
| *Rubato* | Adjusting tempo freely for the sake of expression |

As with the other tempo terms, these are also open to interpretation —especially *rubato*. The literal Italian translation is "stolen", as if the time itself was stolen from the rest of the performance. *Rubato* indicates a very free and speech-like expressive use of tempo, which brings us more into the second way of altering Rhythm for expressive purposes.

True to its origins in social dance music (where sudden tempo changes would be dangerous!) contemporary popular music typically keeps the same tempo throughout a song. However, the tempo of one part of certain instruments or voices can change (usually by an even factor, for example slowing down by half or doubling in speed) even when the layers stay in the same tempo. Even when a song is recorded all the way through to a steady click track, these illusions of tempo changes can be quite expressive.

Exploring the Rhythm of a Note

Even with a fixed tempo (i.e. a steady, unchanging beat), we have expressive choices available in how exactly we time each note we play.

For example, a musician might play or sing "behind" or "on top of" or "ahead of" the beat. This can have a huge effect on the energy and emotion of the music: if just one member of the band lags behind the beat, the music can start to feel like it's dragging ponderously forwards (for better or worse!) while even a single member playing ahead of the beat can make things seem like they're hurtling forwards, slightly out of control. When these choices are intentional, and especially when applied only at particular moments, they can have a powerful impact. For example if a lead guitar riff pushes ahead of the beat in the pre-chorus section it can build anticipation for the emotional payoff of the chorus arriving. Or if the singer chooses to lag slightly behind the beat as the song draws to a close, it can produce a similar satisfying winding-down as a *rallentando*, even while the perceived beat remained perfectly steady.

In addition, a musician can make very flexible and expressive rhythmic choices moment-to-moment and note-to-note. This can be seen as a microcosm of the same "playing ahead of or behind the beat" idea, since ultimately you are choosing whether to play each note before, exactly on, or after its expected time.

These expressive rhythmic choices all depend on their relationship to the beat rather than the suspension of a steady beat (as happens in the case of *rubato*), and so they can also be combined with overall tempo changes. You often hear in the outro of a rock track, for example, a heavy *rallentando*, where one or more lead instruments also places each of its final notes later and later compared with the anticipated time, giving the impression that it is reluctantly agreeing to bring the song to a close.

It's important to note that all these rhythmic possibilities do not excuse sloppy rhythm! On the contrary, they require an even greater command of rhythmic precision, knowing and feeling *precisely* where each note "belongs", to be able to place it slightly before or after, as intended.

This is analogous to the principle, popularly attributed to Pablo Picasso, that one should *"Learn the rules like a pro... so you can break them like an artist."* If you cannot play the rhythms precisely without adding your own expressive flourishes, there's a great risk that the music will sound rough or unstable to the listener, rather than having the expressive effect you intend.

So be sure to make good use of the practice techniques in *Chapter Six: Superlearning* as well as *Chapter Twelve: The Beat* and *Chapter Thirteen: Rhythm*, to dial in your "inner metronome" and rhythmic precision, and you'll be well prepared to make use of all the rhythmic choices available to you.

EXERCISE: Exploring the Rhythm of a Note

"The rhythm of a note" may seem like a nonsense phrase, since we typically think of rhythms as being created by the relative durations and timings of a series of notes! However, as discussed above, the placement of each and every note has expressive possibilities, and we can use the steady pulse of a metronome (or backing track) to provide us with a reference "grid" that gives musical meaning to even the playing of a single note.

Set your metronome or select a backing track with a certain moderate tempo and a fixed meter. For example 60 B.P.M. in 4/4 time.

Outside → In:

1. Begin by playing a single note on each beat, lasting for the duration of that beat. Give yourself a few measures to settle in to doing just this, placing the start and end of each note as precisely as you can.

2. Now start to experiment with moving the start of each note a little ahead of, and then a little behind the beat. Can you feel the "rushing" or "dragging" feeling it creates? Try not to change the timing so much that it feels like a different rhythm… and then see how far you can push it before it does —for example, your quarter notes starting to sound more like eighth notes.

3. Next, see what happens if you vary the timing of just one note per measure. Does it matter if it's the first note or one of the others? Again, really focus deeply on how you feel the timing and any emotions which arise in you from certain choices. You may well be surprised at how amusing, alarming, unsettling or even irritating you find some of the possibilities!

Inside → Out:

Using everything you've discovered about the emotional impact of different choices, try intentionally creating certain emotional effects through your rhythmic choices. If you wanted to irritate the listener (or your band-mates!) what would you do? If you wanted to bring down the energy a bit and create a lazy feeling, what would you do? If you wanted to created a sense of chaotic anxiety, what would you do?

You can repeat this exercise with a different tempo. Keep in mind that faster tempos will make it increasingly challenging to place notes as precisely as required, to avoid changing the perceived rhythm completely, while much slower tempos, counter-intuitively, can have exactly the same effect! This is one reason for the truism that "it can be harder to play music well at slower tempos rather than easier": when the space is really opened up for each note to be placed, one needs a great deal of precision to place it effectively! To simply play ahead of or behind the beat is indeed easier at slower tempos, but to achieve the desired expression can actually be surprisingly tricky.

Using Rhythm to Shape a Phrase

Now that you've experimented with placing each note in a steady, unchanging rhythm, it's time to use that same idea but with a musical phrase which actually has a rhythmic pattern of its own.

EXERCISE: Using Rhythm to Shape a Phrase

Choose a phrase from a piece you play (or if you prefer, improvise one to work with). Pick one which has an interesting rhythm, but which is not challenging for you to play at your normal practice tempo.

Outside → In:

1. Set a metronome for an appropriate tempo, and play the phrase a few times at that tempo, aiming to play the rhythm as precisely as possible. Now change the tempo and repeat. Pay attention to how merely changing the tempo has some impact on the musical effect of the phrase. Push beyond what seems like a "sensible" tempo range, and explore excessively slow speeds, as well as the fastest tempos at which you can still comfortably play the phrase.

2. Next, turn off the metronome, play the rhythm again at a moderate tempo. Start to explore how gradual changes of tempo can affect the phrase, speeding up or slowing down the beat over the course of the phrase. What seems to suit the phrase best, or please your ear the most?

3. Now, with metronome back on, play with changing the timing of particular notes. Start with playing everything a little ahead of the beat... then a little behind... and finally select certain notes to play a little early or late.

Inside → Out:

Based on what you've discovered, how could you produce

different emotional effects with this phrase, through your rhythmic choices?

Once you feel you've explored a wide range of possibilities, decide for yourself which of the options (if any!) you think enhance the musical effect of the phrase.

Bringing It All Together

Now it's time to really have some fun! Let's try using all four dimensions together to shape a single note, and to shape a phrase.

EXERCISE: The Expressive Possibilities Of A Note

1. Select a note on your instrument.

2. Play the note a number of times, now exploring all of the expressive possibilities available to you. You might like to think through the four dimensions, go back to the techniques which most resonated with you, aim to play all the most extreme and different versions of the note you can come up with… or simply follow your Heart and see what comes out.

If you've been through *Chapter Fifteen: Improvisation* then this "One-Note Improv" exercise will be familiar to you! Have new possibilities now opened up?

Next, do the same with a musical phrase:

EXERCISE: The Expressive Possibilities Of A Phrase

1. Select a phrase from a piece you play (or if you prefer, improvise a phrase to work with).

2. Play through the phrase repeatedly, each time exploring different combinations of techniques from the four dimensions. You can do this for the phrase as a whole, or for particular notes in the phrase. Again, you can work through

all the techniques methodically, you can revisit the ones you enjoyed exploring the most, you can try creating the most varied and different-sounding versions of the phrase possible... or you can "switch off" your Head, follow your Heart, and see what your instinct for expression is now able to produce.

By this stage you should start to feel empowered by the new "language of emotion" you have been learning, and be able to feel and hear a real difference in the expressiveness of your playing.

This activity, of applying all the expressive techniques of all four dimensions thoughtfully to a musical phrase (or whole piece) is a great one to incorporate into your practice going forwards. But that's just one way to ingrain the musical language of emotion and help it become intuitive and instinctive for you...

Expression Practice

In the first part of this chapter we explored the expressive musical language of emotion. As we learned about Timbre, Dynamics, Pitch, and Rhythm, and how they can be varied for individual notes and across phrases, we experienced how just by learning to "speak" this emotional language, our music-playing becomes more expressive.

Now we will explore some other ways to connect with what lies within us and bring it out to where we can express it, so that our music is not just "more expressive", but is expressive of what we have inside.

We'll look at four further forms of musical Expression, and how the language we've been learning can be practiced and applied: Active Listening, Movement, Audiation and Singing, and Creativity.

1. Active Listening

In this introduction to this chapter we talked about how even if we don't yet understand how to play music expressively and convey the emotions we intend, we all innately appreciate expressive, emotional playing when we listen to music.

Now that we understand the musical language of emotion, we can start to not only experience the emotion when listening, but also take real steps to the expression of our own feelings through music.

As covered in *Chapter Five: Active Listening*, "listening with a question in mind" can let us go beyond casual listening, using a specific question to focus our attention on the particular musical aspects that we wish to explore. To learn more about our own expressive possibilities, let's listen with questions of emotion and expression in mind.

EXERCISE: Active Listening for Expression

1. Select a music recording that you know well, and listen to a particular section. For example, just the first verse, or the solo you love, or the first minute or so of a longer work.

2. Listen through once, purely for enjoyment's sake.

3. Now listen again multiple times, each time focusing your attention on one of the questions below each time. Feel free to also choose questions of your own, based on your Active Listening experience, but tailored to our current interest in expression, and the musical language of emotion. You can focus on a single instrument (most likely the lead/melody instrument to begin with) or the arrangement as a whole.

4. Once you feel like you've explored quite fully, repeat with another section of the same piece or another piece.

   Example Questions:
   - What emotions come through most clearly? (You may like to reference the emotion list at the beginning of this chapter)
   - Do the emotions expressed vary during the section? When and how?
   - How is emotion being expressed through changes to Timbre? Which emotions and how?
   - How is emotion being expressed through changes to Dynamics? Which emotions and how?
   - How is emotion being expressed through changes to Pitch? Which emotions and how?

- How is emotion being expressed through changes to Rhythm? Which emotions and how?

- As a whole, which techniques in which dimensions are being used to make the music more than a dry, robotic performance?

You may wish to look back over each dimension's section above to remind yourself what techniques may be being used. Keep in mind that the expressive possibilities in each of the four dimensions vary by instrument and by genre. This means you may well not be able to discern *any* ways a particular dimension is being used for expressive purposes! This is part of what we are listening for, as the last question in the list above indicates. But don't give up too easily... For example, even if there aren't prominent pitch bends and slides, that doesn't mean there aren't subtle nuances to the pitching of notes which enhance their expressive effect.

It would be valuable to jot down notes as you go through this exercise. For example you might write something like *"The lead vocal uses clear Pitch embellishments throughout, including heavy vibrato and slides into sustained notes. This gives it a heavier, somber feeling, especially at the end of each phrase. In the last line of the lyrics there is some rubato, as the notes seem to float freely above the beat rather than being strictly in time, and this adds a sense of weightlessness and freedom."*

Now that we've woken up our ears to the way emotion is expressed in music played by others, there is a simple gateway to bringing that same expressive palette to our own playing.

We can do this by actively listening *while we are playing*. Listening not just to ourselves, but also any other music going on around us, for example our fellow musicians or recorded accompaniment like a backing track.

An inner "Listening Voice" can keep us engaged in the music and in actively making musically-expressive choices—considering what has come before, responding to the moment, and projecting into the future. Note that this Listening Voice is the friend of expressive playing, whereas the (probably all-too-familiar!) judgemental Inner Critic is often the enemy of our free-flowing musical expression. We'll discuss this more in *Chapter Eighteen: Performance*.

EXERCISE: Active Listening for Your Own Expression

1.   Select a section of a recording of a piece which you can play yourself.

2.   If you haven't already, carry out the exercise above to discover the expressive techniques being used, and the emotional results.

3.   Now play the piece yourself, recording the performance, and aiming to mimic the expressive techniques you heard, to convey the same emotions. Remember to "keep your ears turned on" and listen carefully as you play.

4.   Listen back to your own recording. How did you do? Remember to suspend your Inner Critic and listen as objectively and constructively as you can.

5.   If you'd like to, you can repeat the process based on what you heard in your own expression.

6.   Now play the piece one more time, but use your own aesthetic judgement and the emotions you feel, to create your own expressive performance. Record it, listen back, and repeat if you would like.

By mimicking a recording in this way we can "bootstrap" our own awareness of the expressive possibilities for a piece, which can help free us up to express our own personal rendition based on the emotions we feel or wish to convey.

The second part of this exercise, recording your own rendition and then actively listening to the recording to assess the effectiveness of your own expressive playing, is something you may well wish to add as part of your standard practice habits. Even if you don't do so, from now on you can make use of Active Listening every time you play, to make sure you are bringing Heart into your playing with each and every note.

2. Movement

"Got this feeling in my body"
— from "Can't Stop the Feeling", by Timberlake, Martin, and
Shellback

"If you don't stand like that, it ain't gonna sound like that."
— Carlos Santana

Philosopher and educator Rudolph Steiner believed that we feel music as the *urge to move*. Sometimes we physically move with the music, other times we choose to feel the movement within our bodies.

Remember the idea that "Emotion is Energy in Motion". Music stimulates us to feel energy movement within our bodies, and invites us to respond with our own physical action. When we desire to express our musical feelings from the inside out, this urge must be translated in part into bodily movements that produce sound.

Depending on the physical characteristics of our instrument or voices, even big emotions may actually need to be translated into quite delicate nuances of movement in order to produce the sounds we desire. When that movement isn't enough to encompass the emotion we feel, we can hold it inside, or we may move, sway, or position our bodies to more fully express what we're feeling.

Discovering the way to move which both produces the sound we desire and satisfies our innate urge to move with the music can open new doors of expression in our music. Earlier in this chapter we explored the physical movements on our instruments required to express the musical language of emotion through Timbre, Dynamics, Pitch and Rhythm. Now let's fuse these movements with the more primal movements that originate inside us.

The following exercises will help us unleash the emotion in our bodies.

TIPS:

1. With all of the exercises in this lesson, it can be very helpful to close your eyes. When we remove the visual sense, which is so dominant in much of our human experience, we heighten our focus on our senses of movement and hearing, which are more directly involved in music making.

2. The movement and "air play" exercises may seem awkward or silly. Try to suspend any self-consciousness or Inner Critic. Remember that feeling awkward or silly is a feeling, meaning you're touching some deep emotion!

It may be not be comfortable, but don't let that Inner Critic cheat you of the profound musical possibilities that happen when you connect with music and emotion on such a deep level. If you have difficulty with this, it may be helpful to intentionally try an "as silly as possible" version of the exercise, where you make feeling silly the goal rather than something to be embarrassed about or suppress.

EXERCISE: Dance Party!

First, let's loosen up by moving our bodies without the complication of playing your instrument. You can do this standing, or seated if you prefer.

1. Select a track with some groove to it. Anything which has previously made you feel the urge to dance, or even just tap your foot or nod your head along with the beat.

2. Listen, and let any movement you feel the urge for flow naturally. Don't worry about whether it looks good or what anyone else might think, just follow your instinct and be

aware of any emotions that arise.

If you've read *Chapter Twelve: The Beat*, you might like to experiment with the Rhythm Dance, letting your feet follow the meter and the rest of your body express any other urges, with swaying, clapping, bopping your head, wild arm movements, or whatever you feel moved to do, to express the energy you feel inside.

EXERCISE: Air Play

We've all heard of "Air Guitar"—but we can play any instrument in the air. And while some consider "air guitar" to be a joke, it's actually an excellent way to visualise and feel expressive instrument playing without the usual technical restrictions or mental load of "getting the notes right". It can help you to actually release and move beyond restrictions, bridging the gap between freely moving to the music and moving emotion into your instrument.

- Imagine you are holding your instrument. Put on a recording of music that you love to play, or wish you could play, and pantomime playing your instrument along with the music. If it feels a bit silly, go with it! Humour can relax our bodies and let everything flow more freely.

EXERCISE: Moving into Your Expression

1. Pick a piece you can play comfortably. You may like to choose one you've used previously in this chapter.

2. Play through the music and record yourself. It's likely by this point that you're already playing more expressively, but don't worry if you're not.

3. Listen back to your recording. As you do so, move freely to the music.

4. Listen again, and this time "air play" your instrument.

5. Now take your instrument and play the piece again, allowing your body to move with the music. Record your new performance.

6. Compare the new recording with the one you made at the beginning of the exercise. What did you notice when comparing the two recordings? Why do you think that is?

Depending on the musical context, moving freely as you play may be desirable or a real *faux-pas*. For example, I remember vividly how irritated my high school orchestra conductor would be if he noticed anyone tapping their foot during practice or a performance. I learned to tap my toes inside my shoe instead! At the same time, the lead violinist, standing for their big solo part, would be admired for how they swayed evocatively as they played. And nobody who's ever been to a live rock gig needs to be told that the way a band moves energetically on stage is a huge part of the audience's experience of the music. This visual aspect of an audience's experience is something we'll explore more in *Chapter Eighteen: Performance*.

The important thing here is that when we constrain our physical movement during practice, we are actually suppressing some of the emotional energy that could come out through our playing. When we learn to better recognise, appreciate, and channel that emotional energy, through allowing it to express freely through any movement you feel the urge for, we become able to express it more freely and fully through our instrument.

So for now, it's fine to ignore any constraints there may be for your expected performance situations. Our goal is to get more deeply in touch with that instinct to move, and the way we can connect with the "energy in motion" emotions inside of us and start bringing them out through our playing—whether or not our wild, uninhibited practice-room movements are something we ever share an audience!

3. Audiation and Singing

As we explore musical emotion through Active Listening and Movement, we're getting closer to how we feel inside about music, and how we can bring those feelings out into our playing. There is something else that we all do which we can harness to help express our music from the inside out.

Audiation, as covered in *Chapter Three: Audiation,* is the practice of hearing music in your head. It's quite common for us all to audiate on a casual basis, as we create imaginary soundtracks for our lives or simply get a song stuck in our head. As musicians, we can go beyond that and develop our Audiation skills to do quite a lot of "work" for us, even without touching our instruments.

Just as we have the (sometimes unwelcome!) ability to conjure up thoughts in our own heads that lead to strong emotions, we can do the same with "thinking music" or *audiating.* And just as a feeling may in turn produce a thought, we can begin with an emotion and transform it into music before it ever makes its way into the actual physical vibrations produced by our instrument.

A simple example of this in practice is when we have a feeling or we're in a certain mood, and a song pops into our head which reflects that emotion. Through Audiation we can explore similar possibilities within a piece of music, conjuring up the sounds which would best express the emotions we feel.

EXERCISE: Audiate Your Expression

1. Choose any of the exercises from the first part of this chapter, exploring a single dimension or the "Bringing It All Together" exercises at the end.

2. Perform the exercise… without your instrument. Imagine yourself going through the steps and try to hear as clearly as possible in your mind's ear the sounds it would produce.

3. Now pick up your instrument and try to recreate the performance you audiated.

You can even do step 2 with techniques not normally possible on your instrument (e.g. what if your piano could bend pitches? What if you could produce a deep operatic vibrato with your singing voice?)

As is so often the case with Audiation, this pairs beautifully with Singing. We mentioned above how uniquely expressive the human singing voice can be. This provides us with a wonderful way to explore expressive possibilities even before touching our instrument, and can provide a stepping stone to "translate" what we intend and imagine (with Audiation) through our singing voice, and then have a clearer sense of what we're aiming for with our instrument

---

EXERCISE: Intend, Imagine, Sing, Play

1. Select a short melodic section from any piece you can play comfortably.

2. Take a moment to think about how you would like to play it expressively. What emotions would you want to convey, what expressive techniques could you make use of?

3. Now audiate your ideal performance, as vividly as you can.

4. Next, try singing the performance you just audiated. Really focus on listening to the emotion you're expressing, just like in the Active Listening exercises above.

5. Finally, pick up your instrument and try to recreate the same expressive performance.

What did you notice about each of the renditions? As always, recording can be your friend. Were you able to audiate a performance which expressed the emotions you'd intended? How closely did your sung performance match what you'd audiated? Were you able to translate that onto your instrument?

Did adding the stepping stone of Singing make it easier to produce the instrumental performance you intended, compared with the previous Audiation-only exercise?

It might feel cumbersome to go through all these steps if you're used to simply grabbing your instrument and playing a piece. But as with all the exercises in this chapter, by taking the time to explore and experiment step-by-step, we are internalising the language of emotion and making it instinctive, levelling up the expressiveness of our playing even if we do just "grab our instrument and play".

4. Creativity

Musical creation happens in many ways. Through our upbringing and musical lives we tend to accumulate stereotyped images like:

- the obsessed composer, locked up in a drafty room, scratching away at a score with a feather quill and Indian ink,

- the jazz saxophonist, improvising exquisite embellishments on a slow ballad,

- the classical violinist, striving to express every nuance of the score,

- the rock band, creating original songs together with energetic camaraderie,

- the heavy-metal lead guitarist, viciously shredding up and down the neck,

- the "bar band", who can play covers of just about *anything* at the drop of a hat...

Which of these, if any, do you relate to?

We tend to divide musicians into *creators*—those who improvise or compose new music—and *performers*—those who only play and perform music that other people wrote.

But perhaps these two worlds aren't quite as far apart as they may seem...

As humans, we love to create. So why is it that we take so much pleasure in playing *other people's music?* Why is it that we will listen to the same recording, over and over again, and still want to go hear the same band play the same songs? Why do we learn a piece of music and then play it again and again?

We all have music that we love, which each time we listen to, play or sing it, makes us feel deeply connected with our inner emotions. Often, as we do so, we find ourselves making new discoveries about songs that we thought we knew inside and out.

If the emotions and how we experience and express them is shifting or deepening each time we hear or play the music... is it *really* the same music each time?

The emotions we feel can be different in different contexts. And as musicians—even if we're playing the same music—we have the potential to play it a little differently, to *feel* it a little differently each time.

In other words, we can bring our own creativity to music even when playing it "as written". The pioneering music educator Forrest Kinney classed this act of "interpretation" as a musical art, right alongside improvising, arranging and composing.

Let's explore these two forms of creativity in Expression: Improvisation[2] and Interpretation.

Improvisation and Interpretation

When we create music spontaneously, we term this the musical art of "improvisation". This is generally taken to mean that we are choosing all the notes and rhythms ourselves, on-the-fly in the moment. As with all music, Improvisation can include varying levels and means of emotional expressivity.

In music that we are *interpreting*, we may not have as much choice over the actual notes but (as we learned in the first part of this chapter) we do still have plenty of choices in Timbre, Dynamics, Pitch, and Rhythm. For each note, across each phrase, and even for the piece as a whole.

In essence, we can "compose" the emotional dimension of our expressive performance, and even *improvise* in the moment, through our musical language of emotion. This means that interpretation is also a creative musical art, which is why we as naturally creative humans take such pleasure in it.

If you love interpretation, then it can be very helpful to shift your mindset into being a "co-creator" with the composer. For example, next time you play your favorite Beethoven Sonata, or you cover The Clash's "London Calling", consider that when you access and express your own inner feelings through this music, you are—in a very real sense!—entering into a profound collaboration with Beethoven or The Clash.

When you shift your mindset in this way, you're more likely to recognise and honour the importance of your own musical expression and your own creativity.

Mars Gelfo, creator of the popular Modacity practice app, once told

---

[2] Just a reminder that we use improvising as a lightweight and versatile way to develop our creativity, even if our end goal is writing or composing music.

me about his "emotions practice". He would first choose pieces from his repertoire. Then, like an actor, he would conjure up emotional states inside himself and play that particular piece of music while feeling that emotion. He was careful to introduce both positive and negative emotions, ranging from joy to shame, and thus build great resilience as a performer on a very challenging and exacting instrument, the symphonic horn.

Improvisation adds to this the opportunity to fully change the note pitches and rhythms creatively and expressively. And, depending on the genre, style, or the musician's choices, there are plenty of areas in which interpretation can be even more improvisational.

In the following exercises we'll experiment with making expressive choices in both interpretation and improvisation.

EXERCISE: Creative, Expressive Interpretation

1. Choose a short section of music you can comfortably play.

2. Jot down several positive and negative emotional states to express. You might like to refer to the list of emotion words at the beginning of this chapter, or any of your notes from the exercises in part one of the chapter.

3. Using your musical language of emotion, as well as Active Listening, Movement, Audiation (and perhaps Singing), record yourself playing this piece several times over with each of the different emotions.

4. Listen back to your recordings and see what you can discover.

EXERCISE: Creative, Expressive Improvisation

• Repeat Exercise 1, but this time give yourself more freedom to improvise new notes and rhythms. You can choose your select piece of music as a jumping-off point, or start a new improvisation from scratch based on your musical experience and interests.

EXERCISE: Pushing The Limits

1. Choose a short piece of music that you would like to play more expressively.

2. Play through it and record your performance.

3. Now interpret it several times over, each time intentionally cultivating more intense emotions and creatively stretching your expressive use of Timbre, Dynamics, Pitch, Rhythm, and phrasing.

4. If you like, take your interpretation further by creatively improvising new notes and rhythms.

5. Record yourself once you have intentionally taken it as far "out" as you can go.

6. Now return to playing it more naturally and record this too.

7. Compare the three recordings. Which one did you like the best? Why? How did the last recording differ from the first, after having gone through the step of "taking it all the way out"?

Conclusion

Often, as musicians hungry to learn and improve, we get swept away in the task of learning this or that skill, and forget what brought us to music in the first place. Even when we are focused on musicality skills like Playing By Ear, Improvisation, or leveling up our practice with Superlearning, we can lose sight of the most basic truth about our musical experience:

Music has the power to evoke emotion in us like no other form of human expression on the planet.

Sound and emotion weave together inextricably as we listen to and play music.

Imagine if our language had no emotion to it, and that we were unable to change the tone of our voice, its speed, pitch, or volume to express what we were feeling! It sounds crazy, but that's what it's like to play music when you don't know what to do on your instrument or voice to express emotion.

In this chapter we've explored and experimented, using an "Outside → In" perspective to become more aware of the language of emotion in music, and how Timbre, Dynamics, Pitch, and Rhythm all provide choices we can make throughout the music, to bring out the emotions we intend. Then, equipped with this new awareness and the corresponding connections between Head, Hearing, Hands and Heart, we began to intentionally express emotions through sound. And through Active Listening, Movement, Audiation and Singing, and Creativity (both in interpretation and improvisation) we discovered new opportunities to use this language of emotion to express ourselves musically.

If nothing else, this chapter should have given you a lot of new things to pay attention to when playing music! The more we can guide this attention, the more connected, expressive and "at one" we will feel with our music.

Perhaps along the way you have felt yourself becoming less judgemental and more engaged in your music. When we feel this way, sharing our music with others becomes easier and more enjoyable, both with other musicians and with the audience in Performance situations.

Of course the journey is far from over! I almost included this chapter in Part I as one of our "foundational skills", because it can be applied everywhere, throughout your music-making, to level up the experience and enjoyment of music, both for yourself and for your listeners. In fact, I would invite you to cast your eye down the Table of Contents at the start of this book, and take a moment to think about how you could incorporate Expression practice into each and every one of the topics covered.

Just by going through the exercises in this chapter, you should find you have opened up a whole new world of expressive possibilities, which you are starting to instinctively draw on to more easily express emotion through every note and piece you play. The more you continue to bring conscious attention and effort to increasing your fluency in this "language of emotion", the more effective, fulfilling and beautiful your music-making will become.

CHAPTER EIGHTEEN: PERFORMANCE

"You keep using that word. I do not think it means what you think it means."

— Inigo Montoya, *The Princess Bride*

Two of my most memorable performances went... badly.

When I was about six or seven, I'd been taking trampolining classes for several months, and having a great time with it. The big day had finally arrived: our first public performance. My sisters, parents and grandparents were all in the audience. And as I got a couple of moves into my prepared routine... my mind went blank. I froze, embarrassed to my core, and had to slink off the trampoline in shame and misery.

About ten years later, I was finally given a lead in a high school musical, after years of only ever being part of the chorus. As the title part in Gilbert and Sullivan's *The Mikado*, I had a few solo numbers, and I was so excited and so proud to have my moment in the spotlight.

The first performance went great! The second one, with my parents in attendance... did not. Midway through one of my solo numbers, during an instrumental interlude between verses, I somehow got distracted in my thoughts. Suddenly it was my cue, and my mind was blank for the lyrics to the next verse.

I managed to recover it better than in my trampolining days, coming in on time for the second line of the verse. It made for a slightly confusing moment to the audience, but at least I recovered.

Of course, in both cases, I beat myself up for the mistake afterwards and wondered what I could have done better or differently. Blaming myself... feeling inadequate as a musician... and feeling like a failure for not delivering the perfect performance when my big moment came.

Maybe you can relate?

The mind going blank like this is just one of many problems that plague musicians, when it comes to performance. There's also nervousness, stage fright, and performance anxiety which can strike before and/or during a performance. There's making mistakes and playing the notes wrong, getting lost in your music, playing badly because your fingers aren't co-operating... The list goes on. If you've been a musician for a while, no doubt you have a few painful, embarrassing memories of your own.

The traditional advice is to keep doing more performances, and you'll get better over time. Or that you need to practice more, before the show. Or that you should learn some tips and techniques for helping with stage fright.

All of these "solutions" miss the point.

We have fundamentally misunderstood what a performance can and should be—and turned it into a kind of "final exam" to prepare for.

We've all been taught that *"you practice, and then you perform."* Actually, it's more like *"you practice, and then when you're finally good enough you perform."* Performing is set up as "the test" of what you've practiced.

Well, that immediately sounds scary, right? *Of course* you're going to feel pressure to prove yourself. And *of course* that threat to our self-esteem and personal identity hits hard.

On top of that, by setting up performing as the "test" of what you've practiced—the "reward" you only deserve when you've perfected your playing—there's automatically an expectation that "learning to play perfectly during practice" is how you get ready to perform.

So you slave away, desperately trying to nail every last inch of the song or piece you want to perform. Ironing out every kink. Until finally, you feel like you've got it.

And then the deck gets stacked against you. Because as we all know, abilities tend to break down significantly during testing. Being thrust into some new, alien environment—whether that's in a driving test, a university exam hall, or a concert stage—is going to instantly throw a spanner in the works.

Everything you've carefully prepared and perfected in the practice room suddenly feels awkward and unfamiliar. Your fingers don't function, they freeze or fumble. Your performance begins to collapse. The audience starts to shift, feeling restless and uneasy. They're mirroring back your own discomfort. With every second, your self-esteem crumbles away.

And it gets worse. If it was only about that "alien environment", you'd be fine. You would just need to get used to performing on stage, give it a few tries, acclimatise yourself, maybe do a run-through at the venue before the performance, right?

That might well get you over the hump, so that you can step out on stage and not fall apart completely. But even then, you know you'll never sound good or enjoy it if you're nervous and timid. So all that time and hard work during practice was a waste.

No matter how good you sounded at home, you can never seem to replicate it when it comes to "the real thing". It's painfully ironic, but it seems like the better a player you become, the harder it is to perform well.

And so naturally you start looking for solutions to "stage fright", to "performance anxiety", to "overcoming nerves". You study up on "peak performance" and learn how to engineer yourself to better handle that performance pressure.

Which is all well and good.

But it's a bit like putting a band-aid on a gunshot wound. You're not addressing the problem at its root. Because the real problem isn't "playing better" or "removing performance anxiety". The real problem is that we've disastrously misunderstood what it truly means to "perform music".

"You probably know me, if you know me at all, as someone who [performs on cello]. And I've done it for 60 years, so I should be

getting it right by now.

However, is that what I'm trying to do? Am I trying to get it right? Or am I trying to find something?

At one point, I had the audacity to think I could play a perfect concert. I came to the concert and I started playing. I was in the middle of the concert, and I realized everything was going perfectly well. And I was bored out of my mind.

I still remember it, during the concert, saying, you know, I could actually just stop, and walk off the stage, and not feel a thing, because I had separated the act of doing something from the act of being present.

That was the moment that I made a fateful decision that I was actually going to devote my life to human expression versus human perfection."

— Yo Yo Ma

Overview

In this chapter we'll begin by re-evaluating and defining anew what we mean by "Performance". We'll introduce the *Performance Free-Flow* framework and its 3 C's: Conversation, Creativity and Connection, and look at the difference these can make to your experience of performing.

Before going further into the framework, we'll lay out an approach to *practicing performance* and a flexible blueprint for creating a "performance pathway" for yourself. This will let you gradually take steps forwards into a wider range of performance situations: from being alone in your practice room by yourself, through to any live stage you might wish to step onto one day. Even before adopting the Performance Free-Flow approach, these principles of Performance Practice and having a clear Pathway can help transform "performing" from a scary, intimidating, seemingly-dangerous thing—into something that feels as easy, fun and natural as any music-making you currently do.

Then we'll dive into the framework itself, by examining each of the 4 H's of our H4 Model (Head, Hands, Hearing and Heart), how the 3 C's of "Conversation", "Creativity", and "Connection" relate, and how you can improve and enhance your performance with each one.

Together, Performance Practice and Performance Free-Flow can provide the solution to all the common performance woes mentioned above, and allow you to bring your full musicality into every note you play.

So whether you're already a seasoned performer, or you could relate all-too-well to everything I described above (or perhaps both!) this chapter can help you to become a performance powerhouse.

Let's begin by asking the fundamental question:

What Is Performance?

I had mixed feelings about letting this be the last chapter in the book. On one hand, performing is ultimately what music is all about, and so it makes sense as the culmination of all the other musicality topics we've covered in earlier chapters. On the other hand, as you'll soon see in this chapter, we are big proponents of two somewhat unusual perspectives on "Performance":

1. Performance isn't just about the "big show"

"Performing" doesn't just mean standing up on stage in front of an audience of strangers and delivering a carefully-prepared rendition of certain repertoire. It is an all-encompassing term, covering every type of musical performance. Any time you are expressing yourself musically for someone[1] else to enjoy, that counts as performing. So "Performance" really boils down to *sharing your music-making*.

2. Performance is about much more than "getting the notes right"—and our preparation must reflect that.

When we misunderstand what Performance is all about, it naturally leads to also misunderstanding "how to get good at performing". In particular the big misconception that *"if I get good enough at my instrument, THEN I can put on amazing performances"*.

This misses the point entirely. In terms of our H4 Model of Complete Musicality, it's a "Hands-only" approach, neglecting the Head, Hearing and, most crucially, the Heart.

Deep down we know there must be more to a great performance

---

[1] That "someone else" could even be you, reviewing a recording of a performance you did alone in a room by yourself!

than just getting all the notes right, at the target tempo. Otherwise by now all concerts would be performed by robots, playing from digital sheet music. We know instinctively that getting every note right is really only table stakes for a great performance.

> *"Of course, it's not the technique that makes the music; it's the sensitivity of the musician and his ability to be able to fuse his life with the rhythm of the times. This is the essence of music."*
> — Herbie Hancock

We're taught from a young age that the greatest performances of all time came from "talent". If you've been reading through this book's chapters in order, by now you understand well how every aspect of apparent "talent" actually breaks down into simple, learnable skills. Performance is no exception.

So how do we acquire those skills?

The traditional idea of "practicing and practicing until you're ready, and then finally performing" is a broken model. By blurring the line between "practicing" and "performing" we can not only remove the intimidation factor of "giving a performance", but learn to actually develop the skills needed to perform well. And we can do this in the practice room, right alongside all the rest of our musicality training.

The *Performance Free-Flow* framework consists of three parts: Creativity, Conversation, and Connection. It is designed to transform "performing" from a high-pressure event into a sheer delight, by returning us to the true roots of music's power to move us. Instead of being constantly fixated on "getting the notes right", you're able to take for granted that the right notes will come out—and put your energy and focus into what will turn that "technically correct" performance into one that your audience will never forget.

What's more, you'll discover along the way that the ideal performance can even allow for a "wrong" note or two—something which should come as no surprise if you've read *Chapter Seventeen: Expression!*

Before we dive into Performance Free-Flow itself, we need to first set you up with an environment and mindset which will allow for you to make that transformation.

We'll do this by establishing a new relationship with "performing", including how it relates to "practice", and what "practicing performance" could look like.

Practicing Performance

"One gig is worth 20 rehearsals."
– Andrew Bishko (Mariachi Flor de Missouri)

We said above that "practicing" is traditionally seen as distinct from "performing", and that the old model of "practicing endlessly until finally proving yourself with a performance" is fundamentally broken. So what do we mean by "practice" and "performance", and what would a better relationship between the two be?

Music practice is an activity where we work out all the details of our musical tasks. We take our music apart, work on small bits, and put it back together again. Naturally, that's not what we want to do on stage or in front of an audience!

Musical performance is when we share our music with others. This could be live or via a recording, but in both cases we are playing through the music start to finish, for the sake of creating a fulfilling and moving musical experience for ourselves and for the listener.

Right now these may seem like two very different activities—but they don't have to be. In fact, we can bridge the apparent gap, by bringing performance activities into the practice room. This idea is at the heart of the Performance Free-Flow approach: to make "performing" such a regular, everyday part of our music practice, that stepping into a new environment to deliver a performance doesn't feel like a big, intimidating and fundamentally different activity. Instead, it's a natural continuation of what we've been doing in all our preparation.

Through a variety of practice-room activities you'll be able to gradually "raise the stakes", and build up the mental, emotional, and physical skills required of the performer, developing your Head, Hands, Hearing and Heart together.

Environmental Impact

What does it mean to "raise the stakes"? At the extreme, a musician might sit alone in their practice room, practicing long and hard until they know their music inside-out and can play through it flawlessly. Then, it comes time to perform it for someone… and whether that's a big, formal recital, an audition, or just finally allowing a family member to hear you play, suddenly everything feels very risky and possibly scary. It's a one-shot deal. What if you screw it up? The stakes have been raised, all in one go.

On top of that, typically the environment or *context* also changes significantly, all in one go. You might be playing on a stage or just a different room, you now have an audience in front of you, you might be playing a different instrument, wearing a different outfit, there might be different acoustics or environmental noise. We like to think these things shouldn't matter—but they absolutely do. You may well have experienced this with some of the Contextual Interference exercises in *Chapter Six: Superlearning*!

Research has shown that if you take a group of students who have prepared for a test, and have half the group take the test in their usual, familiar classroom while the other half take it in a new, unfamiliar room, the second group performs measurably worse. The simple change in context which "shouldn't" matter actually has a significant impact.

So when it comes to musical performance, not only are we trying to "pass the big exam", we've introduced all of these additional challenges that the practice room hasn't prepared us for at all. Given that, is it really reasonable to expect our best rendition of the music to come out?

Performance requires its own group of mindsets and skills. Being able to play the music correctly, alone in the practice room is only the starting point.

The good news is that all these skills and mindsets are learnable, and can be acquired through simply practicing performing itself. Regular "performance practice" can also be combined with a *pathway* of performance tasks and situations which let you gradually expand your comfort zone, develop your performance skills, and build resilience.

When Gerald Klickstein (author of the classic book on practice and performance, *The Musician's Way*) gave a masterclass at Musical U, he really highlighted this core idea of *gradually* raising the stakes. Many of the problems and issues which we feel prevent our practicing from producing a great performance can actually be tackled simply by giving ourselves a clear pathway, which gradually raises the stakes and lets us build up our skills, experience and confidence as we practice performing.

Performance Pathway

How would you feel if I invited you to walk across a wooden plank between two skyscrapers? Scary prospect, right? In fact, right now even walking across a plank that was four feet in the air, like a gymnastic balance beam, might be nerve-wracking.

But now supposing we placed that wooden plank on the floor. Not scary at all, right? Then we raise it an inch above the floor—still not scary…

Now, what if every day you practiced walking across the beam, raising its height just a little each day. As your balance improves and your experience grows, those small increases in height don't throw you off. Soon the balance beam feels easy. Perhaps one day even that skyscraper situation just feels like the "same old" experience to you.

This is what we're aiming for with a "Performance Pathway". How can we take small steps into performing, gradually raising the stakes, so that no one step feels too scary, or introduces too many new factors for us to tackle.

Here is a suggested pathway, to paint a picture of what that could look like. The ideas and sequencing below can be applied flexibly, to fit your own musical life and Performance development. It can also be combined with gradually tackling more challenging repertoire. For example, you might already feel comfortable playing a scale in front of a family member—but that doesn't mean you're ready to put on a whole show for them!

Keep in mind that taking the next step will almost always feel slightly uncomfortable, unfamiliar, and intimidating. The key word there is "slightly"! Pushing the boundaries of our comfort zone is exactly the purpose here (remember Growth Mindset)—but make sure you choose a comfortable amount of discomfort :)

> *"If you feel safe in the area you're working in, you're not working in the right area. Always go a little further into the water than you feel you're capable of being in. Go a little bit out of your depth. And when you don't feel that your feet are quite touching the bottom, you're just about in the right place to do something exciting."*
>
> — David Bowie

Phase 1: Solo practice room performances

The first phase involves blurring that traditional line between "practice room" and "performance", without yet inviting an audience.

Step 1: Turn play-throughs into performances

As noted above, our typical practice activities involve taking pieces apart, and working on particular sections or details. We might "put it together again"—or we might not! And even if we do, are we really playing through with the intention of it being "a performance"?

When we only practice a piece bit-by-bit, it can produce a mental representation of the piece which is incomplete or even inaccurate, resulting in friction and mistakes when we try to perform it in full.

To quote the King of Hearts from *Alice in Wonderland*, a "play-through" means:

> *"Begin at the beginning, and go on till you come to the end: then stop."*

So no freezing up if something goes awry. No circling back to try a section again. No wandering off mid-piece to practice that tricky measure which just tripped you up. A "play-through" means you play it all the way through.

If you aren't already including true play-throughs in your practice, this alone can go a long way! But unless we treat the play-through as "a performance", we aren't giving ourselves the opportunity to develop any performance skills beyond just "getting the notes right".

That's why if we're aiming to improve our performance skills as well as our playing technique, we must also allocate time to playing the piece from start to finish, as if it's a real performance for an audience.

Step 2: Self-recording

Most of us carry around with us every day devices which have the ability to record portions of our practice sessions with reasonable quality. Self-recording gives you the opportunity to listen to your work with more accuracy, and obtain better insights to adjust and focus your practice.

Recording your practice performances provides a powerful way to "be your own audience", hear the piece as listeners would hear it, and gently give yourself feedback to continually improve your performance.

TIP:

Record multiple takes in a row, and start by evaluating the strengths of each. It is important to listen back to the recordings in different moments and environments. While some practice apps automatically play the recording back to you immediately after, it is also advisable to listen to the recording outside of the practice room and away from your instrument. This makes it easier to listen objectively, and your ear is more likely to identify both the strengths and the areas for improvement.

Step 3: Practice performing

You do not need an auditorium or stage to practice performing in different contexts. Look for other spaces around the house, or rearrange your practice space to recreate a new context which is a more performance-like situation. Your initial audience can be your recording device—or perhaps your pet! Do your regular warmup routine, and then perform your musical piece from start to finish.

Some musicians find it useful to face a mirror during this. Others perform looking at a picture of someone they respect, like their teacher. Pictures of crowds or artists that you would like to collaborate with can also work

However you choose to do it, the goal here is to make your private solo performance feel another step more like a "real" performance.

Phase 2: Sharing recordings

If the goal of performing is to share music with other people, then sharing recordings can be a great way to ease into that, including the opportunity to receive constructive feedback.

Step 1: Share with your musical community

In the initial stages it is important to share your recordings only within a supportive and friendly environment, and ideally with others who can relate to the vulnerability of sharing your music.

If you're a member of Musical U, then our community is an excellent place to share your music with like-minded individuals who understand the challenges of putting our creative work out into the world, and will offer only positive support and constructive feedback. Otherwise, share with any musical friends you know and who you trust to listen with this same attitude.

Simply share your recording—and invite people to take a listen!

TIP:

It's a good idea to let people know whether you are looking for feedback and critique, or simply want to share it with them. It's fine to let them know you're nervous about sharing it!

If you do want feedback it can be helpful to request specific kinds of feedback. For example if there's a certain section you're unsure about, or you want to know how to improve a particular aspect of your expressive playing, let people know! You might be surprised what somebody else's ears and experience can reveal about your performance.

Step 2: Share with close friends and family

When you're ready, share your performance recordings with other groups or communities you're part of, such as close friends and family, or via social media or messaging systems. You might like to sign up to an online audio- or video-sharing platform where you can easily create a profile page and add your tracks. There are also platforms which enable easy collaboration which can be a great help when you're ready for that step.

Start by creating private links to share with friends, family and other people that may be excited to learn more about your music. Do not be surprised if these recordings encourage you to move on to public sharing!

TIP:

When sharing with friends and family it's highly advisable to let them know this makes you nervous, or that you're sharing for the first time! Otherwise they may not realise how scary it can be for you, and how much courage it's taking for you to share. This will help them to understand how to communicate their feedback and show their support.

Phase 3: Live informal performance for friends and family

One considerable benefit of sharing via recordings is that you have the chance to listen back and evaluate which tracks you are comfortable sharing. If your Big Picture Vision includes playing live though, you will want to take steps into giving live performances when you feel ready.

Step 1: Invite a guest

If you are confident performing a piece in private in your practice room, one easy step forwards is to simply invite somebody into that same environment with you. A pet, a child, a spouse or other family member, a friend, a fellow musician. Start with someone you feel confident will understand and have empathy if your performance doesn't go to plan, and then gradually raise the stakes with who you invite in.

Step 2: Play somewhere else

It is never too early to start moving your performances out of your regular practice environment. Arrange to play somewhere other than the practice room and invite friends or family members to share a musical moment with you. Again, you can be intentional about who you invite, to gradually raise the (perceived) stakes for you.

Step 3: Attend or organise events

Your regular life probably includes a variety of events where giving a short performance would feel natural and be appreciated. It doesn't have to feel like a formal performance. Play your instrument for house guests, maybe invite friends to sing along as you play. Holiday events, barbecues at the neighbours' house or campfires are usually good moments to share the joy of music-making with other people. Keep in mind that you can organise something with the intention of sharing your music, without that being the official purpose, or anybody even knowing that's your motivation!

Events for a cause, such as fundraisers, usually create friendly environments that are ideal for this phase of your musical growth. By making your performance about something bigger than yourself you can also fuel your motivation and take some pressure off your shoulders. After all, the audience isn't there to critique you, they're there to support the cause.

Step 4: Livestream your music online

Performing during a videocall, even if there is no one on the other side, can help you become more familiar with being in a performance situation. After a few tries alone, you can start inviting close friends. Gradually you can extend the invitation to multiple people in your circle, and eventually you can post the invitation on social media for the general public.

Stewart Says...

Don't forget about recording yourself—even once you get to playing shows for audiences!

When my wife Jacci is able to attend my shows, she'll record parts of songs for me, especially solo sections, as I wanted to hear what I was doing—to make sure what I was playing worked, and sounded right, even though it may not be a note-for-note solo cover.

I also liked to watch the video to see how I looked: if I looked like I was having fun, or if I looked in pain! I also found that over time it helped me get rid of bad habits, such as staring at the floor while playing.

Phase 4: Open mics and jam sessions

Throwing in a musical performance as part of a regular event takes the pressure off you, since the audience are there for other reasons. To raise the stakes you can move on to events where the official purpose is musical performance.

Step 1: Where do local musicians hang out?

Look for local venues that offer performance opportunities for musicians. Find open mic sessions and jams in your area. You can attend without playing to begin with, to get familiar with the session and environment.

While it's true that some of these events can feel like competitive scenarios, most open mics and jams are welcoming spaces for anyone who loves sharing live music with others.

If it feels intimidating at first, spend some time visualising yourself at the open mic. Signing up to perform on a future date can create a positive sense of commitment and accountability to help you take the next step. You can also look for online open mics and showcase events.

Step 2: Busking

If you've ever looked at a busker and heard an inner voice saying *"I would like to do that someday"*, maybe now is the right time to give it a try! Busking is not only an excellent opportunity to try your music-making abilities in a new context, it's also a great way to socialise with other musicians and learn new tips from their experiences.

Phase 5: Multi-song set

Performing a series of pieces or songs can introduce its own challenges compared with playing just one—and so intentionally practicing this is another important step forwards.

Step 1: Design a setlist, practice performing it

Make a list of the songs or pieces you are planning to perform. Try different options to structure the order of your performance. Try to find contrasting pieces in your repertoire and put them together in some type of curve that builds up towards a climax. Compelling performances need to catch and keep the audience's attention, so playing five tunes in the same key, tempo, and style may well have your audience losing concentration and checking their phones, even if each one is performed well!

You can gradually build up your setlist. Starting with even just two or three songs or pieces will be a big step forwards. Spend some time working on planning your set, and practice performing it from beginning to end. This is something you can even start doing as early as Phase 1!

Step 2: Share your set

Once you're comfortable playing through your set in private, use the previous Phases to move towards performing your set for other people.

Phase 6: Find or create more formal performance opportunities

When you're ready, look for or organise opportunities to give a more official "performance". This needn't necessarily be very polished, professional or formal. The point is simply for it to be a performance where an audience, ideally including people you don't know, is attending specifically to hear you perform.

Here are a few ideas:

1. Ask friends, family, mentors and fellow musicians

Spread the word in your networks that you're looking for chances to perform. Although they may not immediately know of an opportunity, the chances are that someone in your network of friends, family, teachers, musicians etc. will have a suggestion or two.

Be patient. You never know what opportunities will arise, once you've let people know you're on the lookout! More than one of our *Next Level* members who were eager to start performing but felt like there just weren't any local opportunities were surprised how many possibilities emerged, as soon as they started spreading the word that they would be available and interested.

2. Volunteer to perform for organisations

Charities, care facilities, nursing homes and hospitals are excellent alternative performance sites. Not only will you find an enthusiastic audience, you will likely find that it makes your performances even more meaningful for you.

3. Seek out other performance opportunities

Join mailing lists that regularly publicise local events and concert series. Visit those venues and make a list of the ones where you would love to perform. Leverage relationships from the open mics, livestreams, and any other circles that may help you establish contact with concert programmers or local bookers. Identify what type of events are more likely to catch their attention.

If your goal is to play big venues and stages, you can stair-step your way there, building up your experience gradually and gaining assets like your performance recordings or online artist profile which help you land bigger and bigger opportunities. There are a wealth of experts and resources available out there to help you with this more career-oriented aspect of performing, but the phases and steps above will help make sure you're ready and able for each step along the way.

Plan Your Pathway

Whatever your current experience with performing might be, hopefully reading through the suggestions above sparked a few new ideas for how you could take steps towards your dream performances. Take a few minutes now to jot down any thoughts you have about what your own Performance Pathway could look like. This can serve as a valuable map for you, and be a living plan which evolves as you move forwards. There may be times when it's helpful to set target dates to aim for, but the most important thing is to keep gradually expanding your comfort zone and gaining performance experience.

Keep in mind that (as a wise hobbit once put it) *"The road goes ever on and on."* Practicing performing is something which continues even once you're out there "doing real performances". In fact, coming back to Andrew's quote which opened this section (*"One gig is worth 20 rehearsals."*), your performance abilities will start to grow exponentially as you continue along the journey.

Performance Free-Flow

Now that we've laid out what the pathway from practice room to dream stages might look like, let's explore the *Performance Free-Flow* framework which can transform "a play-through" into a truly special musical performance.

Performance Free-Flow consists of three parts: Conversation, Creativity and Connection. These are each aspects of performing which are often overlooked—but are always present in the most compelling, impactful, memorable musical performances.

You can think of them as the missing ingredients which explain why a performance might fall flat, even though you "got the notes right". Or, contrariwise, as the ingredients you can start to include in your own Performance Practice and performances, to produce the experiences you've dreamed of, for yourself and for your audiences.

Conversation

Most musicians treat performing as a "recital". It's purely about "output": doing the physical actions which will produce the sounds they intend the audience to hear.

In truth, the best performances are a *conversation*. Between you, your instrument, your music, and your audience. Input and output, playing and listening, back and forth.

Until you make your performance a Conversation, it will always just feel like you're trying to hit "play" on a recording, and have it played out for the audience without any glitches.

But when you transform "performing" into "communicating", activate your musical ears, and allow that powerful back-and-forth conversation—that's when magic begins to happen. Like when you can tweak the melody just *here* in instinctive response to how you just saw the man in the front row lean forwards slightly a moment ago... or hold that crucial note juuuuuust a moment longer, to make sure the crowd is with you before you barrel through the next section... or adjust your volume *just so*, making sure nobody's mind starts to wander for an instant and their full attention remains firmly and intently on you and your music.

To have a real conversation like that, you can't just be blindly following instructions. You need to have some choice about exactly what you play when. You need to be able to respond to what you hear, and observe, and experience.

Which means you also need...

Creativity

Although only a small fraction of musicians feel like they "are creative", it's possible for any musician to re-discover the vast creative freedom you have to express yourself through music. And that holds true even if you're strictly playing music "as written", as we explored fully in the previous chapter on Expression.

Creativity is what distinguishes a beautiful, powerful, nuanced rendition of a piece from an auto-generated "MIDI file" computer synthesis which will never move a human listener.

The truth is, until you internalise Creativity and learn to express your ideas through what you play, you will always feel like some kind of emotionless robot. But when you put Creativity in place, you'll find a new freedom and delight in performing even the simplest music.

Then, when you're able to creatively express yourself in musical conversation, the final step is to develop your...

Connection

You may never have thought of music in terms of "connection" before, but if you stop and think about it, you'll see how the desire to *connect*—with music, with your instrument, with a listener (both loved ones and strangers alike)—is at the heart of what inspired you to pick up and play in the first place.

Without Connection, even the most technically-proficient performance will feel dull, lifeless, perhaps even pointless.

But when you're prepared to make a true connection, and you develop your intuitive ability to connect, then every single note you play becomes an opportunity to feel more fully and deeply connected to everything around you that you love.

Then you never need to wonder whether you'll get applause or compliments after the show—you've already felt the deep appreciation and admiration of your listeners, every step of the way. And with each and every performance your love of music and love of playing grows even more.

Performance Free-Flow

With these three parts in place, you're able to tap into a whole new kind of musical performing, a state we call "Performance Free-Flow".

In Performance Free-Flow:

- Confidence is no longer something you need to work on. In fact, the idea of "working on your confidence" becomes almost like nonsense to you. You don't need to "get confident" about having brown hair or speaking your native language, do you? Performing music is just part of who you are—so naturally confidence isn't even an issue to begin with.

- Everything just flows. Part of the method relates to the "flow states" you might have heard of world-class athletes and performers of all kinds tapping into. Getting into "the zone", where peak performance becomes almost effortless. Performance Free-Flow shows you how to engineer those flow states on demand.

- It's easy to find that "click". You'll find that listening in a conversational way is the secret to getting in the groove with other musicians around you, and creating those moments where everything "clicks". Even most pros don't fully understand how to make that "click" happen—they think it's mostly luck. But we will see exactly where it comes from, and how to make it your "new normal".

- You always feel expressive, and have charisma on stage. With the 3 C's unlocking your ability to express yourself fully, you'll be amazed to find how naturally charismatic you are on stage and how easy it is to interact with an audience before, during and after a performance. All that was holding you back were the limitations and anxiety that the old model of "performing" had shackled you with.

- Finally the Inner Critic is banished for good. As you learn a healthier and more effective way to "self critique" and start experiencing for yourself the near-magical performance states previously reserved for the "gifted" pros, you'll find all that "head trash" naturally starts slipping away. Your inner "gremlin" voice quietens down, never to return. And you'll stop all the unconscious self-sabotage you may never have realised was constantly happening.

- Failure is no longer possible. Conversation, creating and connecting are all natural parts of being a human. We create ideas and sentences and communicate them with other people all day long to connect with them. Once you learn how to approach performance as simply a chance to connect with other people and with music, through a creative conversation —how could you fail at that?

When you master this method, "performing" is no longer a special skill to struggle with, or a big event to aspire to and feel intimidated by. To you, it's now just "letting the music flow".

With its 3 C's of Connection, Creativity and Conversation, the Performance Free-Flow framework will reveal to you how even playing relatively simple music can produce a spellbinding performance, and why your level of instrument technique is *not* the limiting factor in how great your performances can be. Of course, when you *do* want to up the complexity or sophistication level of the music you perform, you've got *Chapter Six: Superlearning* to help you master tricky sections, eliminate mistakes, memorise easily, and perform up to speed reliably and comfortably.

As we cover the 3 C's of Performance Free-Flow, you'll start to understand and experience how to change "performance" from a big, scary final exam, into a musical activity that feels natural, enjoyable, and even easy for you—all while upgrading the experience your audience enjoys when you play.

We'll do this through the lens of the H4 Model: Head, Hands, Hearing and Heart.

1. Head

"You will never feel ready.

There's always going to be something that you wish you had two more weeks to work on."

– Hannah Dobra (Opera Singer)

Hand a drum to a three-year-old child, and what happens?

I'll give you a moment to imagine it ;)

When children are introduced to music-making, they naturally and automatically come to it with a spirit of joy, exploration, and creativity.

Fast-forward through several years of formal lessons, method books and grade exams... and that once-carefree toddler is now wracked with anxiety before their end-of-term recital.

Adult musicians have often either been through that same transformation, or they begin learning music as an adult but bring into it all their academic baggage, jumping straight to that "final test" mentality around performance.

We know in our hearts that music is a social artform. It's about sharing, it's about connecting, it's about expressing. And not to take away from the joy one can have, playing music by yourself, alone in a room—but even someone who feels great resistance (and even fear) around performing knows deep down that if they *could* bring themselves to "put on a show", it would take their musical fulfilment to a whole new level.

So how can we get back to that deep-rooted spirit of music-making as centred on sharing the music we love with others?

We need to re-examine the "Head" aspect of Performance: all the ways we think about and approach performing.

One key difference between that toddler with a drum and the nervous, trained musician is that the toddler is fully focused on the activity and the experience of music-making. Yes, they're also blessed with a complete disregard for the judgement of those around them! But they see music-making as a process or an activity, rather than a series of lessons to later be tested on. This can transform our relationship with performing—and it's never too late.

We can do this both through Performance Practice (as already discussed) so that performing becomes a natural part of our day-to-day musical activities, and by shifting our mindset from aiming for the "perfect" performance to aiming for the *"ideal"* performance.

This isn't about lowering our standards, or limiting our aspirations. Remember the "Shoot for the moon" principle from *Chapter Two: Mindset*: we do want to aim high. But if our goal is to bring out our best possible performance, then that should be what we're aiming for. Not the black-and-white "don't make any mistakes" robotic perspective on what makes a "good" performance, but a much broader, all-encompassing perspective which recognises that the best performances of all time, and the ones which truly move the listener, are about much *more* than just "getting the notes right".

When we shift our perspective in this way we can begin to see that there are actually things more important than "not making mistakes". In fact, our *ideal* performance on any given day could, in technical terms, actually include a mistake or two.

If that's hard for you to swallow right now, let me share something I found fascinating, and which I often think of in this context of "the ideal performance".

When I studied for my Masters degree, my final research project was on automatic transcription of vocal melodies. Feed in an MP3 of a song, and my program would spit out a MIDI transcription of the melody being sung. This involved first separating out the vocalist's part of the overall mix, and then analysing the pitches.

What blew my mind was that one of the easiest ways to identify the vocal part was that its pitch was all over the place! Generally, the other instruments like piano or guitar would hit their notes pretty much dead-on and stay on that pitch for each note. The vocal part, on the other hand, would swoop up and down to each note. It would wobble throughout the note. Often it would actually be a bit sharp or flat compared to the notional target pitch. And these weren't amateur singers—these were world-renowned artists on classic tracks!

It made a massive impact on me to see so clearly that the "ideal" vocal performance was, in technical terms, always full of "mistakes".

Having been raised to think purely in terms of "right and wrong notes", it opened my mind to the reality that music is an extremely fuzzy art—and that often the beauty and power of music lies in its deviations from the notional music theory definition of "right and wrong".

This can free you up to focus on what truly matters: Creativity, Connection and Conversation.

Creativity

Depending on your personal balance of Performer and Creative Cores, the idea of Creativity being key to great musical performances might seem quite odd, even alien.

Here's a wonderful metaphor which our Head Educator Andrew introduced in our course on performing, which many members found liberating:

"Imagine driving at night. All you see are the lines on the road and the signs that guide you from one location to another. As long as you follow all the instructions, you will arrive at your destination. But if you miss a turn, it might be some time before you realise it and can get back on track.

Often, we play music as we would drive at night. We pay exclusive attention to the signs that tell us where to go, and we congratulate ourselves if we've made it to the end without getting lost. But making music can be so much more than that!

Now imagine that you're driving the same route during the day. You see not just the road, but the trees and the buildings. You pass a street and know that your hairdresser's shop is just around the corner. You pass a building and remember the wonderful lunch you had with your spouse on the top floor.

You know not just your own route, but everything around you. No matter how many times you drive it, there is always something different—the clouds, the seasons, new construction, different memories.

And if you run into a detour, or decide to make a quick stop to visit a friend, you know a myriad of possible ways to get back on track.

Our musical experiences can be just as rich and varied. Even if we're playing the same piece over and over, we can rejoice in all the choices and possibilities that surround us."

Improvisation vs. Interpretation

When we play "other people's music" (whether from a written score or by ear) there seems to be a clearly-defined "right" and "wrong" way to do it. We want to get the rhythms right, the notes right, the expression right, the chords right. All these "rights" are pre-determined by the composer's choices.

We tend to see playing everything "right" as the main (or only) goal of our performance. Not playing the right notes means that we've made a "mistake", and it can derail our whole performance if we let it.

When we improvise, we choose the notes ourselves. Some notes may sound better to us than others, but we can always choose the next one to bring the music closer to what we want to create. We are not judging ourselves against the right and wrong of a pre-composed piece, but purely on what sounds good to us and where we want to take the music.

Improvisation can help us recapture that childhood love of creating and sharing music, spontaneously and naturally.

At the same time, playing "other people's music" can also be deeply inspiring and satisfying. When we learn music that we enjoy, we tend to play it again and again, maybe even for the rest of our lives.

So how can we harness the power of Creativity that inspires us to want to share our music, even when playing pre-composed music?

The key is in our choices, and the art of making choices when playing pre-composed music is what we call *interpretation*.

In an episode of our *Coaches Corner* video series, *Next Level* coach Zac Bailey shared a huge breakthrough one of his clients had. She realised that they had been treating the sheet music as the boss—and yet without her, the player, the sheet music was just dots on a page. She was then able to reclaim her musical authority by realising that *she* was the boss—and the sheet music was simply there to serve her in her music-making.

So our first creative choice is the simple act of bringing the music to life by choosing to play the piece!

From there, even though we do not necessarily choose the notes, there are so many other places for us to exercise our creative choices.

We explore this art of interpretation in detail in *Chapter Seventeen: Expression*, unpacking all of the possibilities available to us in Pitch,

Rhythm, Dynamics and Timbre, with each and every note. We become a co-creator with the original composer of the music, conjuring up our own unique rendition of the music each time we play.

Expression can be worked out in advance, but can also occur as spontaneous musical choices in the moment. In this way even a performance of pre-composed music can tap into the energy and power of Improvisation.

The more we can engage ourselves in creative choices before and during our performance experience, the more connected we feel, and the more excitement we feel about sharing the music with others. Rather than seeing our experience as "following the signs and staying inside the lines", we are surrounded by a rich context of possibilities, and we reach new levels of confidence that if there's a bump in the road, we have the resources and experience to get back on track.

The "perfect" performance leaves nothing to the imagination. There are no creative choices to make. The music is frozen in time, like a robot replaying a recording.

The "ideal" performance can be new and exciting each time, through the infinite creative choices we can make to respond to each moment and bring out our own unique musical expressiveness.

Stewart Says...

I have learned quite a bit on this topic over the last decade, playing cover songs in tribute bands. The term "make it your own" has become a real thing.

When I first got into playing tribute shows, the first goal was getting that music down the best I could for the show. Given there were zero band rehearsals, it meant playing the music "correctly" was HUGE.

But once I got to a comfortable point with learning the music, that is when "make it your own" could start happening.

I knew the parts of the songs that needed to be played, but they started becoming less a copy/cover and became more "my own", including having my own interpretations of a guitar solo, adding an extra lick, or I may even take a transition a different way, to build a dynamic that may not have been on the original recording.

"Making it my own" has become a really enjoyable and satisfying part of what I'm doing.

Conversation

"These are people who could very easily have stayed home. But they got up, got cleaned up, and put on their coolest clothes. They picked a place they liked, got their crew together and drove to the venue. No-one goes to that much trouble to have a bad time. They want you to be great. Nobody wants the band to be good more than the audience does. So as an artist, put yourself in the mindset that you are in a place of support and encouragement, surrounded by people who are on your side."

— Matt Middleton, drummer

Like Creativity, "Conversation" may not seem like an obvious part of what a great musical performance is all about! As we noted in the introduction, musicians tend to be "all output" when it comes to performing music, fully focused on their own playing and making sure they "get it right".

But if music is a social artform and all about sharing musical experiences with others, we can immediately see the problem there.

Imagine trying to have a conversation with somebody where they had their eyes closed, their fingers in their ears, and any time you tried to speak they said *"la la la, I can't hear you!"*. You wouldn't put up with that shared social experience for long.

Spoken conversations involve a back-and-forth interaction, with each person responding in the moment to the other. Not just the words, but the way they speak them, their facial expressions, their gestures, their body language. In a true conversation, even the most complex and challenging topics can be productively, creatively, and successfully tackled.

Music can be no less complex, meaningful, emotional and personal than a spoken conversation—but that will never happen if it's "all output".

So how can we bring the safe vulnerability, the creative communication, and the exhilaration we feel in spoken conversation with friends and loved ones into the way we perform music?

Contexts for Conversation

The type of Conversation available to us in a live performance varies widely according to the genre.

In many popular genres, it's common to have literal verbal conversations with audience members in between songs, and to engage with audience members directly while singing or playing an instrument. The audience may be invited to participate directly in the performance through singing, clapping, dancing, etc. Intimate performances (meaning small spaces and/or small audiences) in any genre can also include less ritual formality and more interaction, at least in between songs or pieces. There may also be the opportunity to mingle with the audience afterwards—when, notably, you are still playing the role of "performer"!

In some genres, it's customary for there to be a separation between the performers and the audience: what's known in the theatre world as "the fourth wall". For example, at a classical symphony concert there is a ritualised beginning where the conductor acknowledges the applauding audience. The audience will then sit in complete silence during the performance, only to respond with applause—or perhaps "pre-approved" words like *"bravo!"* or *"brava!"* at the end.

Yet even where there is this fourth wall, the wall is transparent. And even if the performance space is dark, the audience is felt.

Even with some of the forms of interaction mentioned above, we might still consider the audience to be the "listener" and the performer to be the "speaker". But in a true conversation, every participant expresses, and every participant listens.

Conversation with the Audience

It's common for musicians to play mind games and use other techniques to pretend the audience isn't there, or to make them seem less intimidating. Closing your eyes, focusing on one audience member, maybe even imagining them in their underwear, as the classic advice goes! These techniques can help alleviate nerves, but they're all ways to avoid fully feeling the audience's presence and tend to block the true conversation we could be having.

Andrew Says...

One of the things I tell all my Next Level clients is that performing with an audience is not and never will be the same as playing by oneself in a practice room.

No matter what you do to minimize and block out the audience, they will always be there, and we will always feel them.

So what if we leaned *into* that energy—what Musical U team member and professional opera singer Hannah Dobra calls *"the frizzle"*?

What if, as well as expressing our musical message, we also listened to the roar of the silent audience? What would they be saying?

The reason we find audiences intimidating is that we are projecting our own idea of what they are thinking and feeling—and typically the voice we "hear" from them is in fact our own Inner Critic. More on that in a moment.

But have you ever stopped to think about what you think and feel yourself, when you go to a live musical performance?

As audience members ourselves, we don't show up looking for mistakes and imperfections, and thinking about all the ways the show is lacking. Our inner voice tends to sound a lot more like *"I'm so excited! I love this band! This is going to be amazing!"*

So while we may not have the opportunity to literally hear those supportive thoughts out loud like with a spoken conversation, it's helpful to remember that when we are with our audience, we are among people that want to love and support us.

When we open ourselves up to listen to the true message of the "frizzle", we can elevate our "recital" into becoming a deep and uplifting conversation.

Conversation with Other Musicians

Another level of Conversation takes place between us and our fellow musicians. Whether we're walking with them into a rehearsal or onto the stage, this conversation can bring a greater level of comfort, ease, and a constructive place for any jitters to flow into.

Audiences love to witness the relationships that musicians have with each other. They love to see the band members interacting, whether it's the subtle swaying of a string quartet or the wild stage antics of a metal band.

Our audience may or may not be familiar with all the intricacies of music-making, but our fellow musicians share that deeper knowledge. This can be a source of comfort—or a cause of terror, since we may feel like they can really see inside us and judge our skills.

I'm not going to pretend there isn't sometimes elitism, snobbery and judgemental behaviour on full display in certain musical communities! But even if you're faced with those kinds of attitudes, the conversation which happens during the music-making itself is one that every musician is eager to engage in.

When we embrace that shared goal of interacting musically with one another, we open ourselves up to the rich and unique context of each live performance. Rather than just focusing in on our own separate parts, we can engage in Conversation by listening to the other musicians, reaching out to them visually, through the way we play, or even just in our minds, feeling how our parts interact with theirs as we move with the music.

Conversation with the Music

Music itself is saturated with Conversation. Each note is in relationship with the notes before and after. Each phrase responds in some way to the last, and calls out for the next. Pitch converses with rhythm, melody converses with harmony, instruments converse one with another. Our right hands converse with our left hands, and with every other part of our body to bring out the sounds we desire through our instruments. And our instruments respond to our movements in another kind of musical conversation.

Through listening, we can become more aware of and engaged in the conversations embedded in our music, more engaged in our expression and our flow, and more able to connect with our fellow musicians and our audiences. We'll explore these ideas about listening more in the Hearing section below.

Connection

When we open up to Conversation, we have the opportunity for deeper Connection with our audience and fellow musicians. When we tap into our Creativity, we find Connection through owning our choices in our musical expression.

Some describe this deep connection as being "in the zone". In the scientific world, researchers like Mihaly Csikszentmihalyi have come to call this the "Flow state".

Some describe "being in the zone" as some kind of out-of-body place. They may describe it as being "lost in the music", where the awareness and performance rise to such a high level that it's difficult to describe or even remember the experience.

While there's no question that these heightened states exist, we can also make it into the Flow state while keeping our conscious awareness. While it may seem like we have to find some magical switch to turn on, our access to Flow is built bit-by-bit as we root out resistance and learn to become more engaged, present, and connected with the moment-by-moment process of our musical performance.

There are precise scientific definitions of that Flow state, but it's also valuable to us in the more informal sense. Music *flows* from moment to moment, and our ideal performance can too.

We can start to nurture our ability to find flow through paying attention to Creativity and Conversation in our performances. Later in the chapter we'll look at how you can plan for, practice, and develop your own approach to finding Flow. But all of it is for naught if we don't also learn to reduce our *resistance* to flow, and there's one major barrier in particular which can easily prevent us from ever getting "in the zone" during a performance.

The Inner Critic

Perhaps you've heard the performance advice before that you need to *"Get out of your head!"* Easy to say... Not so easy to do!

Thinking during a performance isn't itself necessarily a problem. That advice to "get out of your head" is referring more to that critical, overly-analytical voice. You know the one. It yammers on and on, picking apart everything you do, highlighting all the mistakes and imperfections. Sometimes it grows quieter as we get more connected with our music—but make one little mistake, and all the criticism comes flooding back in.

We can try to reason with our "Inner Critic". We can try asking it to be nicer, or to quiet down. But the Inner Critic is a master of logic and finds every possible opportunity to speak up. It's extremely hard to simply "fire" your Inner Critic.

We've found that one of the most effective ways to deal with that critical voice is to not fire it—but to give it a new job.

The Inner Critic's job qualifications include careful observation, precise analysis, attention to detail, and tenacity. Flow state researchers have shown over and over that rather than being the enemy, these very same qualities can actually help us to access our Flow.

Remember that the "ideal" performance does not exclude the possibility of mistakes—of learning, growing, and improving. Every performance provides us with direction of what we can improve on next, to level up our performing skills.

So rather than trying to shut down this inner observer which has been so effective in its Critic role, let's leverage its strengths but reassign it to the role of "Inner Listener":

- The Listener is responsible for simply *observing* the details of our musical performance.

- The Listener remembers the past, responds to the present, and helps us make choices for the future as we unfold the flow of our music in time.

- If we go off course, the Listener notes that, without judgment, and (with rapid-fire analysis) helps us make course-correcting choices.

- The Listener keeps a list of details that we may want to address in our practicing as we prepare for the next performance.

- The Listener encourages and supports us, by noticing

everything that's going *right* in our performance too.

While the Critic's job is to prove that you are unworthy, the Listener's job is to keep you always on course to grow and improve.

Reassigning our inner observer to the "Listener" role helps us to shift from "right or wrong" to "better or worse", and from black-and-white judgement to a more constructive *spectrum* of evaluation.

There's plenty of work to keep it busy! And if it slips sometimes into Critic mode, we can gently and compassionately redirect it into Listener mode—because we've experienced how counter-productive the Critic is, and how beneficial the Listener can be.

Just as we will learn to open up the flow of love and support from our audience, we will learn to engage the inner observer's skills as a flow of love and support from within us. Our trusted Listener becomes one with our Creativity, transforming our inner Conversation.

2. Hands

With our Head now suitably prepared, let's turn to the mechanics of how we produce musical sounds with our bodies and instruments. A reminder that in our H4 Model, we refer to all the physical aspects of music-making as "Hands".

As we have seen, preparing and performing can include much more than just whether or not we can technically play the music "correctly" —but of course there is no denying that we do feel more confident and deliver a better performance when our Hands know what they're doing!

In *Chapter Six: Superlearning* we go deep on the topic of practicing and introduce a range of Superlearning techniques which can help you to learn pieces and technique faster, break through apparent sticking-points and plateaus, and memorise and retain music efficiently and reliably. All of these can greatly accelerate your progress in preparing music for performance.

Let's look at how three of the main principles and techniques of Superlearning can be incorporated into our Performance Practice through Creativity, Conversation and Connection, to make sure that our Hands do as well during a live performance as they did in the practice room. These are: Deliberate Practice, Contextual Interference, and Retrieval Practice.

A. Deliberate Performance Practice

With Deliberate Practice, we use a three-part cycle of "Plan, Play, Reflect" to make sure our practicing is always focused on the highest-impact areas, and using our practice time most effectively. We Plan what we're going to try next, we Play it, and we Reflect on the result, feeding into the next Plan, and so on.

We can see Deliberate Practice as the overarching approach to all our practicing, guiding us to make more productive choices for what we're going to do next. We are able to identify the cause of mistakes and correct them at their source, and to become intimately familiar with every aspect of our music, preparing us for the kind of heightened levels of engagement that characterise the Flow state.

In *Chapter Six: Superlearning* we were primarily focused on using Deliberate Practice for traditional practice activities: the "take the music apart and work on small sections" process discussed earlier. What about the Performance Practice we've been discussing, where we play through the whole piece start to finish, intentionally treating it more like a "performance" than a "play-through"?

We need to draw a clear boundary for ourselves between these two modes: focusing on details and fixing things vs. playing through a piece from beginning to end as a performance. This way we learn how to keep going during a performance, no matter what—rather than being in the habit of always stopping to fix mistakes.

The overarching principle of Deliberate Practice can still be applied. We are now simply applying the Plan-Play-Reflect cycle to the performance as a whole.

Perhaps when you practiced performing, there was one particular section where you fumbled a few notes. You might choose to switch mode, and use Deliberate Practice on a smaller scale to address the root cause of that fumbling. Or perhaps there wasn't a particular section which your Inner Listener picked up on as needing attention, but when you Reflect after the performance, you feel like it lacked a certain emotional oomph. You can use Deliberate Practice to experiment with the techniques of *Chapter Seventeen: Expression* to dial it up—or simply practice the performance again, now with the Plan of playing more expressively.

In this way, Deliberate Practice becomes not just a tool for "fixing mistakes" and "getting up to speed", but a highly versatile way to continually improve your musical performances.

So although it's typically seen as a method for nitty-gritty technical refinement, we can see that Deliberate Practice can also be a powerful route into Performance Free-Flow:

- Deliberate Practice can be a very enjoyable and creative experience, particularly if you leverage the Creative Superlearning techniques of *Chapter Six: Superlearning*. As we expand our Creativity to help us reach greater depth and skill with our music, we prepare ourselves to keep a creative mindset during performance.

- Deliberate Practice can reveal the Conversations within the music, helping us to practice the back-and-forth input/output flow of musical awareness and decision-making.

- Deliberate Practice helps us forge deeper and more resilient Connection with our music both on a granular level and as a whole, leading to a more flowing experience when performing.

As well as this overarching approach to practicing, we can also make use of the "powertool" of Superlearning: Contextual Interference.

B. Contextual Interference For Performance Practice

Remember the research finding that a group of students will perform worse on a test if they take it in an unfamiliar environment? If you've read about Contextual Interference in *Chapter Six: Superlearning*, this result shouldn't have surprised you! The same effect happens in music: our performance stage and our practice room are very different contexts, even when we're playing the same music. Yet we somehow expect that we can prepare for performance out there in the wide world by practicing in the safety and comfort of our own homes.

The good news is that Contextual Interference works its magic just as reliably for tackling this type of context change, allowing us to become more resilient performers, able to perform our music reliably, no matter where we are.

The goal of Contextual Interference is to produce Desirable Difficulty: a level of novelty and challenge which keeps our brains active, engaged, and learning.

In our "practice mode" that might mean troubleshooting a difficult passage by playing it with different rhythms, different articulations, in a different key, or maybe even backwards. When we return to playing it normally, we find our abilities have improved.

So what does Contextual Interference look like for our "performance mode"?

We can begin our journey to the stage right in the practice room by altering our immediate surroundings.

Simply turn your chair around, face a different wall or window or mirror, stand up if you've been sitting or vice-versa (if your instrument allows), or play in a different room. All these changes in context will build your ability to focus on the music itself, as well as strengthening your brain's representation of what a "good" performance looks and feels like.

The various phases and steps of the Performance Pathway introduced earlier, including recording yourself, can also all be seen as forms of Contextual Interference. Not only are you pushing your comfort zone emotionally, you are developing a more resilient ability to perform in a variety of contexts.

Close your eyes

As humans, we are very visually-oriented, especially in this age of ubiquitous screens and visual interfaces. But while we all love to watch our favorite singer or symphony orchestra, the greatest power of music is in the *sound*.

When we close our eyes, we enter a new world, where sounds come to life in a whole new way. And when we close our eyes while playing our instruments, we immediately gain more focus on the details of that experience, discovering sensations we overlooked when our attention was caught up with visual stimuli.

Try simply closing your eyes while you practice. Focus on the sounds, emotions, and the physical sensations of playing your instrument.

One *Next Level* client referred to this as *"choosing to live in a world of sound"* and found that committing to more eyes-closed practicing utterly transformed the expressiveness of his performances, as well as his confidence.

You might not believe that this is possible. How can you play without looking at the sheet music? Or watching your fretboard? And what if you don't have the music memorised yet?

While it's true that you may not be ready to play your whole piece right now with eyes closed, you may be surprised by how much you actually can do. More surprising still will be what the experience of playing music feels and sounds like when you do.

Contextual Interference and Performance Free-Flow

As well as building our resilience in performance, Contextual Interference brings other benefits. The idea of Desirable Difficulty can help us overcome emotional resistance to pushing beyond our comfort zone, as well as helping us shift from the black-and-white "no mistakes" mentality, to a Growth Mindset which recognises issues as the opportunities they really are.

Contextual Interference can also really loosen us up, providing more "scenery" for "driving during the day", to return to our earlier analogy. Imagining new ways to "mess up" your music can bring fun and humour into your practicing, helping to shift our Inner Critic into its new Inner Listener role.

And on top of all that, Contextual Interference will do its primary job of stimulating deeper learning. What used to be a tedious process of fixing mistakes and struggling through difficult passages can become a creative process of musical exploration, and discovery of deeper connections with your music.

C. Retrieval Practice and Performance Practice

In the practice room we have the luxury of starting right away, warming up, and then playing a song repeatedly until we "get it right". When it comes to a live performance... Well, let's just say the audience might raise an eyebrow if you tried the same thing! There may be some waiting around before your moment to perform arrives, you may not have the opportunity to warm up, and you probably want to avoid starting the piece all over again if you flub a note or two.

So how do we prepare for that?

In *Chapter Six: Superlearning* we introduced the distinction between *Encoding* and *Retrieval,* and highlighted how the traditional practice methods tend to involve large amounts of attempting to encode the music, but very little practice of retrieving it from memory.

Retrieval practice is the ideal fit for preparing for those live performance situations. By its nature, the goal is to just "pull out" a piece at a moment's notice, possibly in a new context, and perhaps without having played it recently. We play it through once, without stopping to correct mistakes or trying it a second time, and that's that.

If you simply treat this retrieval as a performance rather than a play-through, you can effectively combine Retrieval Practice and Performance Practice.

Note this doesn't mean that your Inner Listener isn't still on the job! With our principle of Deliberate Practice, we can still Reflect, even if we won't "Play" again immediately, so that we can Plan for improving our next performance.

We can also use the approach presented in *Chapter Six: Superlearning* for getting "off book" i.e. learning to play without reliance on the visual cues of sheet music or notation. Whether you expect to perform with or without the notation in front of you, practicing playing without it will again build your resilience for a variety of performance contexts which might arise, and lead you to a deeper connection with the music.

3. Hearing

As you may have noticed, one major recurring theme throughout this book is the vital importance of *listening:* keeping your ears "turned on" when engaged in music-making. In *Chapter Five: Active Listening* we learned a powerful way to do this through Active Listening. In *Chapter Fourteen: Playing By Ear* we introduced the Listen-Engage-Express process, and in *Chapter Fifteen: Improvisation* the Play-Listen/Listen-Play loop. And earlier in this chapter we discussed how listening can transform our "all output" recital into a musical Conversation.

Nobody would doubt that a musical performance will be far better if the musician is alert to the sounds being made—and yet it's all too easy for us to be so wrapped up in Head and Hands that our Hearing shuts off almost entirely!

In the previous section on Head we began to open up our awareness during a performance. Now let's look in more detail at the specific ways we can engage our Hearing. We'll use that term here to mean both literal listening with our ears, and the broader mindful awareness which can include everything we see, feel, and experience in the moment.

Intentionally cultivating our Hearing during performance not only enables Conversation, it enhances our Creativity and brings us a deeper Connection: between our Head, Hands and Heart, to the music itself, to our instrument, to other musicians and to our audience.

Hearing The Music

Music is broadcast into every corner of modern life. A musical soundtrack accompanies our shopping, our driving, our socialising, our internet surfing, our movies, our worship, our dancing, our sleeping, our waking, our exercise…

Personally, I wouldn't have it any other way! But it does make it all too easy for music to be relegated to the background, training us to mostly tune it out and be aware only of the surface level (if that).

As music-makers, rather than just music consumers, we need to take music out of the background and into the foreground. We learn to do this through Active Listening, as covered in detail in *Chapter Five: Active Listening.*

You can make use of the same technique of "listening with a question in mind" in your Performance Practice and in your real performances, asking questions like:

- *"What's my musical role in this part of the song?"*

- *"What difference does it make if I add a slight crescendo here?"*

- *"Is my switch from strumming to palm-muted picking here sounding smooth enough?"*

- *"Which other member of the band do I most need to blend and synchronise with?"*

- *"What Expression techniques can I use to amplify the emotion in the bridge?*

We can also make good use of Audiation to enable Performance Practice even when away from our instrument. Often deficiencies, limitations, and weak points in our real performances will show up even in our imagined performances, and can be practiced and improved surprisingly effectively there too, through Mental Play (see *Chapter Three: Audiation* for details).

Every aspect of our performance can be examined and experimented with through Active Listening and Audiation. Using Deliberate Practice (Plan, Play, Reflect) we can identify what to focus on and how.

Active Listening brings creative choices into the listening process, and through experimenting in Audiation, we can develop our

Creativity with the performance itself. When we engage our Hearing we are able to participate in a lively Conversation with the music itself as we play, resulting in a deeper and broader Connection with the music we hear and the music we play.

Hearing the Form

One particularly valuable aspect to consider is the Form. With a strict "play through with no mistakes" mentality, it's very easy for musicians to get lost during a performance. This often becomes one of the biggest causes of anxiety, whether playing with the visual cue of sheet music or without.

By increasing our awareness and understanding of the Form, and keeping our Hearing engaged, we can gain a firm sense of where we are in the music at any given moment—and if you do happen to lose your place momentarily, your grasp of the Form can provide the "signposts" to get you back on track fast.

We cover Form in *Chapter Five: Active Listening* and *Chapter Sixteen: Songwriting*, including guidance on how to identify the top-level structure of the music (its sections such as verse, chorus, bridge, or A and B sections) and more fine-grained structure (such as individual phrases and the layers of Texture). If you're playing from notation these may be marked—but don't let that cheat you out of gaining the inner mental representation of the structure and the ear-based recognition of what happens when.

When we engage our Hearing during Performance Practice we can gain a very detailed and clear mental representation and aural image of "how the music goes" in our head, letting us connect more deeply and always know where we are during performance.

Hearing Other Musicians

We've already mentioned the added pressure that can be felt when other musicians are in your audience, and that goes double when you're actually playing together with them!

When we play in a group, we tend to focus so intently on staying in our lane and playing our part correctly that it's easy to let our ears "turn off". As long as everyone starts at the same time and plays their part correctly, it should all work out, right?

In fact, this is another clear example of where stellar performances go far beyond just "getting the notes right". When we're in the audience for an amazing performance by a band, we love the way the musicians interact on stage. Whether they dance and sway in their chairs like a string quartet, sing harmony while staring into each other's eyes, or leap and headbang in unison, we can see that there's nothing like the joy of making music together, and there's something special going on.

We can see and hear the Conversation that's occurring, we can witness the raw Creativity, we can feel the deep Connection.

So how do we go from "carefully staying in our lane, with ears off" to that kind of free, connected, alive musical performance?

Again, the solution isn't to develop our Hands to be so incredible that we finally, hopefully, one day feel that freedom. The solution is to make full use of our Hearing.

Active Listening can be your gateway here too, and if you've been practicing finding Creativity, Connection and Conversation between yourself and the music, finding it with other musicians will feel like a natural next step.

This doesn't need to be a "one day, maybe". The sooner in our musical journey that we begin to "reach out" to other musicians with our ears, the more enjoyment and Connection we feel, and the deeper we will understand the musical context in which we're playing. In turn, our experience listening to the other musicians will accelerate our mastery of our own parts in the music.

What exactly does it mean to "Hear Other Musicians"? Let's have a look at just a few ways we can start to truly hear our fellow musicians as we perform together:

- **Musical Form:** As well as helping us keep our place in the music, musical Form is also the glue that holds a group of musicians together. Pay attention to the structures and sections of the music. What changes and what stays the same when moving from one section to another? What is your musical role in defining the Form? What are the other musicians doing in these transitions?

- **Cues:** We can rely on musical cues at strategic moments to help us keep our place in the music and coordinate with the other musicians. For example, ensemble players with long periods of silence can easily lose their place while counting many measures of rest. But if we know the music, we'll remember how it goes and be able to cue ourselves from the

other musicians to know where to come in. We can then sit
back and enjoy the music and come in at just the right time
(which also happens to be much more fun than counting
measures!)

- **Groove:** How does your part fit in rhythmically with the other
  musicians' rhythms? From classical to funk, there is a special
  feeling when the parts "lock" together. Listen for and cultivate
  that feeling when playing with others.

- **Musical Roles:** Depending on the musical genre, certain
  instruments tend to take on certain roles. Western music
  commonly divides into melody, chords/rhythm, and bass,
  though many other layers can be added. Appreciating the role
  of each musician goes a long way to blending and balancing
  well with them.

- **Foreground/Background:** Relating to musical roles, also listen
  specifically for which instruments or voices belong in the
  foreground, and which in the background. When everyone is
  listening carefully to each other, we can make sure the
  audience are most aware of the right parts at the right times.

- **Dynamics:** Acoustics and amplification in live performance
  are a whole topic in themselves, but no matter the
  performance context, musicians still have to listen carefully to
  one another to know how loudly to play at any given moment.
  It will take practice to be able to judge how loud your
  instrument sounds to you when it's at the right level in the
  overall blend of instruments, but the most important thing is
  to stay mindful of it and respond (Conversation) as needed,
  moment to moment.

Playing with other musicians can rapidly develop our Creativity as
we become more fully engaged in the musical Conversations within
the group and forge deeper Connection with them, as well as with the
music itself.

Hearing The Audience

If we're hearing the music, and hearing the other musicians around us, engaged in a creative, connected conversation... then it's up to the audience to be hearing that, right?

As we touched on in the Head section earlier, some musicians do believe this, even making use of intentional techniques to block out and ignore the audience as much as possible.

But you've probably experienced the result yourself, as an audience member. Can you think of a concert you went to where a performer came on stage without even glancing at the audience, performed their music, and then walked off? It happens regularly at children's music recitals, but I've also seen world-class professional musicians do the same thing. The aural experience of hearing the musical performance might be good—but it leaves you feeling a little cold. Again, music is a social artform, and when a performer behaves like that, we naturally feel a bit neglected and excluded.

Contrast that with any concert, gig or performance you can remember where the musician *truly* connected with the audience. Maybe they were looking out and smiling before and after playing, maybe they took a bow, maybe there was banter between songs, maybe they even encouraged you in the audience to clap, sing, or dance along. Think about how much more vibrant and memorable that made the entire experience for you.

And now, with those two extreme examples in mind... Would you prefer to attend an audience-oblivious performance with not a single wrong note—or a vibrant, audience-inclusive performance where there was a musical flub or two?

Naturally, there are conventions and expectations that differ across genres and performance contexts. A string quartet at a funeral probably shouldn't be inviting the audience to dance and clap along. But hopefully the point is clear: the audience is there to enjoy a meaningful musical experience, and that is so much harder for a musician to accomplish if they're pretending the audience aren't there at all.

Again, this shouldn't be seen as a "one day, maybe" which you might feel ready for after years of honing your craft. Personally, I'd rather see and hear an engaging and enthusiastic rendition of "Twinkle, Twinkle, Little Star" than a dry, rigid, robotic Beethoven Sonata! With that being said, the more comfortable and confident you are with the playing itself, the more attention and awareness is freed up to engage with the audience.

There are specific things you can practice, to help engage with the audience, such as:

- Planning your stage routine: how will you enter, exit, move between pieces.

- Preparing and practicing any on-stage speaking or banter you'll include (you might be surprised to know just how much of what seems ad hoc and improvised to you as an audience member has actually been thoughtfully planned, and even scripted!)

- Considering if and when it would make sense to involve audience participation.

- Choosing the thoughts you project onto the audience, remembering they are there to enjoy and support, not to criticise and judge. You'll almost inevitably project some assumptions about the audience's experience, whether you mean to or not—so why not choose to make them positive and uplifting?

- Being thoughtful about how you hold yourself and move onstage, as well as your facial expressions. Remember we humans are highly visually-oriented creatures, including those in your audience! They may have come to listen, but they'll be watching in every moment too.

- Focusing on one audience member at a time, making eye contact where appropriate.

- Feeling that "frizzle" of energy from the audience, and interpreting it in a positive way.

Any subset or combination of these will greatly help your audience feel included and involved, but remember that our goal is to turn the performance into a Conversation. Adding more forms of "output" is only going to be effective if you are "Hearing" the audience too.

Making eye contact, feeling the frizzle, facial expressions, anything you've planned to do on stage—all of these can be planned for and practiced, but must ultimately be handled with Creativity in the moment, adapting to the audience, if it's to feel like a true Connection and Conversation.

"I can't help but treat it like it's this tangible ball of energy that we can explore back and forth together. I want [the audience] to be with me on this journey and I'm really trying to get them over the finish line, so to speak. That's on me to try to get people to feel what's really going on. I get caught up in it and I just kind of lose myself. It helps when everyone else gets on it too because you can see it, it's real. It becomes this thing and then we realize that we're on it together and at the end it's like this massive applause and an expression of gratitude that, "Yeah, we did this. We made it. It was awesome. I hope you had a good time."

— Tim DeLaughter, The Polyphonic Spree

4. Heart

So far we've discussed quite concrete, tangible aspects of Performance through the lenses of Head, Hands and Hearing. But when we created our dedicated course for Performance, on which this chapter is based, we named it *Supernatural Performance*[2]—to capture the seemingly-mystical, almost-magical nature of the very best musical performances.

Whether as the musician or part of the audience, I think we can all relate to the transcendental experience of a musical performance which has that special something, taking us beyond the mundane day-to-day physical world.

If you followed all the advice and carried out all the practices suggested in this chapter so far, your musical performances would certainly reach new heights. But until we address the Heart, those most profound experiences will happen only occasionally, seemingly at random, and feel more like luck than anything you can intentionally produce on demand.

We use "Heart" in the H4 Model to encompass everything that's going on emotionally and psychologically in the process of learning and playing music. When it comes to Performance, there's one particular concept which encapsulates what happens when our Heart

---

[2] In the logo for the course, we colour "Super" differently to "natural", as a gentle acknowledgement that really we're not talking about something mystical and inexplicable—but rather something which at its best is truly and deeply *natural*.

is opened, aligned, and integrated into our musical whole: Flow.

Flow

> "[It's] the music inside the music. John Coltrane called it A Love
> Supreme. I call it the Universal Tone, and with it ego disappears
> and energy takes over. You realize that you are not one alone; you
> are connected to everyone. Everybody's born with a way to
> receive the Universal Tone, but very few allow it to give birth to
> itself. [...] The Universal Tone is outside of me, and it's through
> me. I don't create it. I just make sure I don't get in its way."
> — Carlos Santana, The Universal Tone

Earlier we introduced the idea of Flow, or "being in the zone", and highlighted how music itself is a flowing thing. Our inner experience is too, with one moment flowing into the next and one emotion into another.

Just as blood flows steadily through our physical heart, we can feel the flow of energy within us and how it's affected moment-to-moment as we listen to and play music. Even without going as far as Eastern spiritual ideas around chakras and energy,[3] we can all relate to the idea of our heart being our emotional centre, and what it feels like when your heart is open and the energy is flowing—versus having your heart tense and closed-off, and the energy blocked.

If we imagine our ideal musical performance, it is surely one in which we are experiencing that open-hearted flow of energy, without a clutter of negative emotions, disruptive thoughts or inner tension holding us back.

Flow is a fascinating topic because these loose, instinctive ideas about a "flowing" musical performance experience are complemented by some very down-to-earth scientific research into what's going on when an athlete, musician or other performance-based expert finds themselves "in the zone". We're able to join the dots between that magical, mystical, memorable performance we all aspire to, and the specific, practical things we can do to attain the state which makes it possible.

Perhaps the most important thing to know is that achieving Flow

---

[3] If you *are* intrigued in this direction, I can't recommend the work of Michael Singer highly enough. His book *The Untethered Soul* is a great place to start.

state does not involve shutting off the mind entirely and getting "lost in the music". It's true that it can feel like a loosening of your conscious, thinking mind, and your sense of time can shift in a way that could be described as getting lost for minutes or hours at a time. What produces and maintains Flow though is actually a beautiful balance between immersing in the Flow, and staying entirely mindful and present.

Andrew once described it with this lovely metaphor:

"Imagine standing on the banks of a river, experiencing the musical waters flowing by. Look upstream and see where the water comes from. Look downstream and see where the water is going.

Step into the water and your perspective changes. You feel the current more strongly, and as you lift your feet, you float down the river, carried by the current. The scenery flashes by, without knowing what will happen around the next bend.

As thinkers and observers, we may relate more to standing in a state of stillness on the banks of the river. From this perspective, we have more clarity on where we came from, where we are, and where we are going to. Yet as music lovers, we long to be immersed in the flow and carried along on the currents.

When we achieve flow state – "flow" being "a smooth uninterrupted movement or progress" and "state" from the Latin "to stand" – we can be present in both the motion of the music and the perspective of the observer at the same time."

In his book on Flow, pioneering researcher Mihaly Csikszentmihalyi, describes it like this:

"The best moments in our lives are not the passive, receptive, relaxing times. The best moments usually occur if a person's body or mind is stretched to its limits in a voluntary effort to accomplish something difficult and worthwhile. "

And in his popular TED Talk said:

"There's this focus that, once it becomes intense, leads to a sense of ecstasy, a sense of clarity: you know exactly what you want to do from one moment to the other; you get immediate feedback."

So how do we achieve this balance between being immersed in the flow of the music and still being present?

As you read Csikszentmihalyi's comments above about "effort", "focus" and "feedback" you might have started to suspect that in fact, we've already encountered all of the ingredients we need to draw on.

The Inner Critic Prevents Flow—The Inner Listener Enables It

When we reassigned our Inner Critic to a new role of Inner Listener, we gained the ability to get continual, immediate feedback on our performance. Through experience with the Plan-Play-Reflect cycle of Deliberate Practice, we're able to do what needs to be done creatively in each moment, without needing to stop and start, or throw on the brakes when something doesn't go to plan. As you combine your role as musician with the role of Inner Listener, the music itself becomes both the task and the reward.

Unlike the Critic, the Listener is not out to prove anything—merely to observe, enjoy, and offer guidance and direction. The Listener's observations roll right along with the flow of the music, allowing us to immerse fully, without losing ourselves. The Listener's observations tend to be less word-y and more instinctive, and with the noisy verbal thoughts of the Inner Critic quietened down, we can respond more freely to increase and maintain our Flow.

Many who experience the Flow state report that time seems to slow down. They feel like they have ample time to make what were previously split-second decisions about their musical expression. With the Inner Listener we can draw on the power and speed of our subconscious mind, and remove resistance that would otherwise prevent or limit our Flow.

Finding Your Flow

The "zone" appears to be a supernatural place, beyond what we've come to accept as our natural experience. So we assume that all of our "normal" practicing won't quite get us there, and most of the time, we're right.

But there are tangible, understandable, and accessible steps that we can take in our "normal" reality to change the way we practice and perform music. These are the steps that bring us into our Flow.

So far, we've looked at a variety of ways to enhance our musical performance through the 3 C's of *Performance Free-Flow*:

- Creativity: bringing more of ourselves and our own personal creative choices into all of our music-making.

- Conversation: deeply engaging in the back-and-forth between ourselves and our listeners, ourselves and other musicians, the relationships between parts of ourselves, and the conversations throughout music itself.

- Connection: the feeling of all of our inner resources working together with the music, other musicians, and the audience, to create a powerful musical experience.

Through Head, Hands, Hearing, and now Heart, you've examined the dimensions of your musical experience in great detail—perhaps more than ever before.

All that effort may seem to be just the opposite of what you previously thought "flow" was. After all, when we are "in the zone", it's meant to feel effortless, right?

The surprising conclusion from the scientific research is that this deep attention to detail is exactly how we can access Flow. Which means it should come as no surprise that the three C's provide us with a reliable path into Flow. The more we can channel our Creativity, engage in Conversation, and build Connection in our music-making, the more we are taken away from down-to-earth "get the notes right" mechanical playing, and able to access our highest levels of instinctive ability.

Although the scientific literature helps by defining characteristics of the Flow state and behaviours which tend to produce it, we've found the work of Diane Allen (author of *Flow: Unlock Your Genius, Love What You Do*) adds a very helpful clarification. In her masterclass at Musical U, Diane shared the idea of Flow being a highly *personal* thing. Becoming able to reliably find your Flow involves figuring out for yourself, through experimentation and reflection, what most produces that special state for *you*.

This is a great fit for the approach we've described above. Practicing the 3 C's of Performance Free-Flow with Deliberate Performance Practice can let you understand more and more what your own route into Flow looks, sounds and feels like.

As we practice with the intention of finding Flow, it will become a more and more frequent occurrence. We are able to identify, in greater and greater detail, all the steps and practices that build our own clearest, most reliable path into "the zone".

Staying In Flow

One of the myths about "being in the zone" is that it's all or nothing. You're either there or you're not. But as you practice developing your own path into Flow, you'll realise that (yet again!) what once seemed black-and-white actually exists on a spectrum.

This means we needn't treat it as some mysterious state and fear falling out of it once we finally get there. Just as we can learn to cultivate the Flow state at will, we can practice recovering if something threatens our Flow in the midst of a performance.

Let's look at the two biggest apparent threats to our Flow: mistakes, and nerves.

1. Flowing through mistakes

When you're writing, typing or drawing, mistakes are easy to go back and correct. When you're speaking, you can pause, and re-state what you meant, correctly this time.

Music is different. It flows in time like speech, but during a performance, the audience expects it to flow only forwards. If a mistake occurs, you don't have a way to go back in time and fix it.

That doesn't, however, mean that a musical mistake needs to end a performance—or even interrupt our Flow.

In other parts of this book we've discussed re-imagining what a "mistake" is, and questioned whether "getting it wrong" is a meaningful concept in music. If you've developed your Authority and Agency (as per *Chapter Fifteen: Improvisation*) and nurtured your Creativity (as per *Chapter Fifteen: Improvisation* and *Chapter Sixteen: Songwriting*, as well as earlier in this current chapter), then you will recognise how playing a "wrong" note, or having something else unintended or unexpected occur genuinely doesn't need to detract from the beauty of the musical performance or the experience of the audience.

Every apparent "mistake" is simply a new, possibly even exciting, opportunity. Mistakes tend to instantly increase our focus, and if we've prepared ourselves with ways to handle it happening, that surge of emotion which feels like fear or panic can actually be channeled into something constructive and creative.

2. Learn to enjoy the rollercoaster

Did you know that the human body's physiology of fear and excitement are almost identical?

Imagine two young children in the front seat of a rollercoaster car, as it climbs slowly up the first peak. They are both gripping the safety bar white-knuckle tight, their eyes are wide, their hearts are racing.

One child is muttering *"oh no, oh no, oh no..."*

The other exclaims *"here we go, here we go, here we go!"*

The *physical* experience of the two children is the same. What differs is their subconscious choice of whether to interpret all the heightened awareness and adrenaline as fear, or as excitement.

This choice doesn't have to be subconscious and automatic.

What if the next time you fumbled a note during a performance, and the world suddenly snapped into sharper focus, and that burst of energy coursed through your body... you found it *thrilling?* What if rather than *breaking you out of* your Flow state, it immersed you more deeply *into* it?

This same principle can be an enormous help with nerves, jitters, stage fright, performance anxiety. Whatever you choose to call it, and however you experience it physically, through Performance Practice you can develop the ability to re-interpret the symptoms in a positive way, and channel that "extra" energy constructively.

Resilient Flow

As we aim for our "ideal" performance, arguably the best way to make it happen is to learn to stay "in the zone" when we perform.

You can appease your Inner Critic in advance, with the reminder that the audience didn't come to hear a robot perform, and that the unexpected can make for a more engaging and memorable experience for them. Often what seems like a disaster in the moment becomes something you look back on and laugh—or even hear a recording of after and realise was barely noticeable to anybody but yourself.

You can allow your Inner Listener to be effective by preparing yourself with ways to react to unexpected moments. Will you simply play on? Will you draw on Improvisation skills to bridge back into the intended music? If a band-mate doesn't show up, or an audience member heckles, what techniques or strategies can you have in mind, ready to deploy?

Through Performance Practice and Deliberate Performance Practice, we can gain great resilience to any kind of "mistake", and use Contextual Interference to prepare ourselves for handling whatever situations may arise.

If you continually design your own Performance Pathway, to

gradually raise the stakes rather than attempting great leaps, you can give yourself the opportunity to build your experience, your confidence, and your ability to "expect the unexpected"—and handle it with grace.

All these ideas and techniques can help you stay in Flow, but remember that ultimately it's Creativity, Conversation, and Connection which fuel the Flow to begin with. The more you can focus on those, the more easily you'll be able to recover your Flow any time it wavers.

Flow With The Audience

As audience members, we love being swept up in the moment with our favourite musicians. We gleefully follow them on a fantastic voyage through sounds and emotions. Our only responsibility is to show up and enjoy the show.

As performers, we ourselves take responsibility for leading the experience. Our goal is not only to achieve Flow state ourselves, but to bring the audience along for the ride.

The 3 C's hold the key to creating a performance the audience will love, as well as the key to finding our Flow. So as long as we are engaging with the audience through Creativity, Conversation and Connection, we will find that the abundance of energy and well-being which comes from being in Flow ourselves becomes magnified by the Flow of the audience. This energy of "being in the zone" together is what makes for the most unforgettable musical experiences, for the musicians and audience alike.

Conclusion

It's no coincidence that the word "Flow" is in the name of our framework for Performance, *Performance Free-Flow*.

If you take the purely-scientific view of Flow state, there's a lot to be learned, and we've only scratched the surface in this chapter. But as we said at the start of the Heart section, the concept of Flow is useful to us also in the looser, broader sense, as a way to encapsulate what it feels like to play that "ideal" performance. The music just flows out of you, you're immersed in the moment, your senses are heightened, it all feels easy and natural, and everything just "clicks".

Flow can also be helpful to us as a way to think about and approach the bigger picture of our musical journey. All the same emotions—fear, excitement, wonder, anxiety, discouragement, confusion, joy—are present on a timescale of days, weeks, months and years as well as the second-by-second and minute-by-minute flow of a musical performance. We face many of the same challenges: things not going to plan, interactions with other people throwing us off (whether our fellow musicians or the audience), doubting ourselves or our potential, and wondering if it's all going to work out in the end.

Everything we've been learning about Creativity, Conversation and Connection, all the ideas and techniques around mistakes, other musicians, comfort zones and inner experience—it can all help us not just in Performance Practice and during a performance, but as we navigate towards our Big Picture Vision.

Just as we seek to get "in the zone" and find Flow during a performance, we can aspire to experience that same smooth, easy, joyful forwards momentum in our musical lives.

Shifting into a Growth Mindset. The reflection and creative problem-solving of Deliberate Practice. The Authority and Agency of our Creativity. The Pillar Belief of *Enjoying the Journey*. The development and integration of our Head, Hands, Hearing and Heart. All these things work together to transform a frustrating journey of stumbling, stopping and starting, wandering lost, and struggling for every inch of progress—into something that can look and feel a lot like being "in the zone" throughout.

If that sounds far-fetched and fanciful to you, just know that we see it every day inside Musical U. It's probably the most rewarding part of the work we do, supporting musicians in their musicality training: seeing how their musical journey takes on a whole new, far more rewarding, relaxed, and enjoyable nature.

If you've read through this chapter and not yet had a chance to put some of these new ideas to use, it may still be hard to imagine yourself putting on a "supernatural" performance, or even an "ideal" one. But going forwards, every moment you spend in Performance Practice, leveraging the 3 C's of Creativity, Conversation and Connection, and increasing your ability to access and maintain Flow, will increase not only the impact and experience of your performances—but the overall enjoyment and progress of your musical journey as a whole.

One of the first things that comes to mind when musicians think about performance is a fourth "C" which we haven't even mentioned so far: Confidence.

"If only I was confident enough to perform."

"I've lost my confidence since I screwed up at that gig."

"I just don't have the confidence to ever get out there and play in front of people."

The reality is that confidence isn't something you need to have before you perform, or something you need to be "good enough" to have. It's something that will develop automatically and continually as you take steps on your own Performance Pathway and prove to yourself that there is every reason to have confidence in your own musicality.

Everything else covered in the rest of this book—Improvisation and "Improvise to Learn", the principles and techniques of Superlearning, the habit of recording yourself, learning to play with Expression, waking up your ears with Active Listening, and everything else—it all serves to increase your natural musicality and expand what you're capable of as a musician.

Start including Performance Practice in your daily music activities, and draw on the ideas shared here for developing Creativity, Conversation and Connection with your Head, Hands, Hearing and Heart—and I can promise your confidence and your musicality will start to blossom like never before.

CONCLUSION

Congratulations!

That may seem like an odd thing to say, in the conclusion to a book. *"Well"*, you might think, *"all I did was read!"*

And while I certainly hope that this was a very active read-through for you, trying out at least some of the exercises and techniques along the way, clearly this book was written as something to come back to again and again, as your musical journey continues. And the very fact that you picked up a book on musicality and read some or all of its chapters, both puts you way ahead of the pack in terms of achieving your own highest musical potential—and contributes in a significant way to our mission of bringing about a world of natural musicians.

So well done—and thank you.

At the beginning of this book I invited you to think about your own Musical Core, made up of some combined balance of Jammer, Creative and Performer, and contemplate what becoming the "Complete Musician" would mean to you. I encouraged you to define your own Big Picture Vision, to gain crystal clarity on what "success" would look like in your musical life, so that it can serve as a personal "North Star" guiding you steadily forwards.

Through all the subsequent chapters we had the chance to explore every topic and skill which we've found can help musicians of any kind to actually achieve that Big Picture Vision. Which of them you tackle first, which you choose to go deep on, which ones turn out to be the most rewarding for you—these questions are all highly personal to you. But I hope that you have found these chapters both inspire you as to what's possible, and lay out a clear path for you to start pursuing that Big Picture Vision in earnest.

You're now equipped with everything you need to learn music like a "gifted prodigy", to unlock your musical instinct, and to unleash your inner "natural".

If you'd like more assistance along the way, we would be honoured and delighted to help you, personally, inside Musical U. All of the frameworks and methods presented in this book originated there, where we have a wealth of step-by-step training modules to make it easy to follow through on learning any topic or skill you've encountered in these pages. It's also the most friendly and supportive community of musicians around, with unlimited personal help on hand, from our devoted team of experts.

However you decide to go forwards in your musical journey, I invite and encourage you to share it. Share your journey with like-minded friends, share your music with other people, and please share your successes with us as you go. I would welcome hearing from you any time, at christopher@musical-u.com.

Again, thank you for being part of this mission with us. Together we can achieve the vision of a world of natural musicians. It all starts with you.

To your musical success,

Christopher Sutton

Get Additional Resources, Free!

We've prepared an extensive set of Additional Resources for you, to support the material inside this book.

This includes extra explanations and tutorials, quick reference sheets, reading lists and references, as well as audio and video materials to help you succeed.

Get access to the full set of Additional Resources for free:

https://musicalitybook.com/resources

An Invitation To Join Us

If you've enjoyed this book, then you belong with us at Musical U.

We would be delighted to welcome you into our community of passionate, supportive musicians, and help you step-by-step to achieve your musical dreams.

Learn more and join today:

https://musicalitybook.com/join

Members say...

*"I am absolutely loving it.
I feel like I've snuck in the back door of the most supportive conservatoire in the world."*

— Dave A.

"I play music every day, but Musical U is the first place I realized that I could be a 'musician'!"

— Meredith F.

"It's not easy to find such a great music course for adults. Here in Musical U, I don't need to feel embarrassed any more by being challenged "you are too old for that!" Thank you Musical U team! I am so happy to find and join this community."

— Min F.

"It wouldn't be an exaggeration to say that in a few months I have learned more than through many years of classical studies in my conservatory. I would really like to take this opportunity and thank you for the abundance of knowledge you provide through your website."

— Athina R.

"I was skeptical for a long time. I finally took the plunge, and in just three months I'm thinking about and playing music in ways I couldn't imagine. This place is magical!"

— Mitchell W.

"[Musical U] has boosted my confidence as a music maker, shaping my identity in profound ways. It has such hidden gems that even seasoned people I know find wonderful learnings, aha moments, and more."

— Ted B.

"The difference it's made for me, I can sum up in two words: Joy and Confidence.

I went from a shy bedroom musician to a person who regularly frequents all sorts of jam sessions and feels comfortable in musical situations with other musicians."

— Lloyd N.

Music Educators say...

"I can highly recommend the resources on Musical U for musicians at all stages."

— Katie Wardrobe, Midnight Music

"Fantastic ideas and inspiring insights into learning, playing and teaching music!"

— Glory St. Germaine, Ultimate Music Theory

"Kudos, Christopher and the team at Musical U. They are doing incredible work with expanding the repertoire of teaching that goes on around the world to beyond the notes and to all those skills that people need to really immerse themselves in music and become more musical beings. And that's what we want for our musician and students."

— Tim Topham, TopMusic Co.

"What makes Musical U a great place to learn music is their atmosphere of caring about their students and really sharing the joy of music. It's a refreshing and welcome resource for all music lovers."

— David Reed, Improvise For Real

"The guidance and content found at Musical U is outstanding for those seeking to find their musical voice as well as those who've found it and need support to further their skills and creativity."

— Leila J. Viss, 88 Piano Keys

"Musical U is one of the best, most devoted resources on the internet for musicians who are serious about growing their musical skills. I am constantly amazed at the depth of insight and the quality of resources that are available."

— Natalie Weber, Music Matters

———————

Learn more and join today:

<u>https://musicalitybook.com/join</u>

Ready For Next Level?

If you're ready to go "all in" on your musical development, then our *Next Level* coaching program might be just what you're looking for.

Inside *Next Level* you get to work personally, one-to-one, with a world-class expert on all the topics covered in this book, and who cares deeply about getting <u>you</u> results.

Suitable for all levels, from beginner through to pro, this fully-bespoke program is designed to make it easy, fast and joyful for you to reach your own personal "next level" in music.

Places are limited and by application only.[1]

Learn more and apply today:

https://musicalitybook.com/nextlevel

---

[1] There's no audition, and we're not here to judge you—but we do need to ensure that everybody who comes into the program is set up for maximum success with it.

Have You Enjoyed The Book?

If you've enjoyed this book and found it useful, it would mean the world to me if you could take two minutes to post a short review.

Just visit:

https://musicalitybook.com/review

(it's fine if you've only read part of the book so far!)

This makes a massive difference to helping other musicians discover the book, and start exploring their own musical potential—furthering our mission of creating "a world of natural musicians".

Huge thanks in advance for taking a couple of minutes to do this now!

About The Author

Christopher Sutton is the founder and Director of Musical U, the home of musicality training online. He is a graduate of Cambridge University and the Centre for Digital Music, Queen Mary, University of London.

A lifelong music-learner and devoted musician, he has benefitted beyond measure from a wide range of music teachers over the years. From his early instruction in the excellent music department of Dulwich College, London, through years spent studying with phenomenal instrument teachers, and more recently through having the opportunity to learn from his colleagues in the team at Musical U, and its numerous collaborators across the world of music education.

Christopher never intended to start a company, and never expected to write a book. But here we are.

He considers Musical U to be less a company or career than a calling, and feels honoured and blessed to have the opportunity to pursue its vital mission: to put musicality back at the heart of music-learning.

Christopher lives in London with his wife Natalina, daughters Alice and Laura—and far too many instruments.

About The Team

As mentioned in the Acknowledgements and Introduction, this book is not the work of any one individual. The Musical U team has featured many outstanding educators over the years, each with their own unique background, experience and insights.

You can learn more about each member of the current team at:

https://www.musical-u.com/about

Christopher Sutton   Andrew Bishko   Stewart Hilton   Zac Bailey

Andy Portas   Camilo Suárez   Almut Spaeth   Mark Hanna

Nicholas Price   Mohammed Wael   Charm Cajurao